REA's Test Prep B̶̶̶̶̶̶̶̶̶̶̶t!

(a sample of the <u>hundreds of</u> ̶̶̶̶̶̶̶̶̶̶̶̶̶̶̶ each year)

" I used [*The Best Test Preparation for the NYSTCE*] to study for the LAST and ATS-W tests — and passed them both with *perfect* scores. This book provided excellent preparation.... "

Student, New York, NY

" My students report your chapters of review as the most valuable single resource they used for review and preparation. "

Teacher, American Fork, UT

" Your book was such a better value and was so much more complete than anything your competition has produced (and I have them all!) "

Teacher, Virginia Beach, VA

" Compared to the other books that my fellow students had, your book was the most useful in helping me get a great score. "

Student, North Hollywood, CA

" Your book was responsible for my success on the exam, which helped me get into the college of my choice... I will look for REA the next time I need help. "

Student, Chesterfield, MO

" Just a short note to say thanks for the great support your book gave me in helping me pass the test... I'm on my way to a B.S. degree because of you! "

Student, Orlando, FL

(more on next page)

" I just wanted to thank you for helping me get a great score
on the AP U.S. History exam... Thank you for making great test preps! "
Student, Los Angeles, CA

" Your Fundamentals of Engineering Exam book was the absolute best
preparation I could have had for the exam, and it is one of the major
reasons I did so well and passed the FE on my first try. "
Student, Sweetwater, TN

" I used your book to prepare for the test and found that the advice and the
sample tests were highly relevant... Without using any other material, I earned
very high scores and will be going to the graduate school of my choice. "
Student, New Orleans, LA

" What I found in your book was a wealth of information sufficient to shore up
my basic skills in math and verbal... The section on analytical analysis was
excellent. The practice tests were challenging and the answer explanations most
helpful. It certainly is the Best Test Prep for the GRE! "
Student, Pullman, WA

" I really appreciate the help from your excellent book. Please keep up
the great work. "
Student, Albuquerque, NM

" I am writing to thank you for your test preparation... your book helped me
immeasurably and I have nothing but praise for your GRE preparation."
Student, Benton Harbor, MI

(more on back page)

The Best Test Preparation for the

NYSTCE

New York State Teacher Certification Examinations

Staff of Research & Education Association
Dr. Max Fogiel, Director

Research & Education Association
61 Ethel Road West
Piscataway, New Jersey 08854

The Best Test Preparation for the
NEW YORK STATE TEACHER
CERTIFICATION EXAMINATIONS (NYSTCE)

Printed in the United States of America

Library of Congress Catalog Card Number 99-70427

International Standard Book Number 0-87891-866-3

Research & Education Association
61 Ethel Road West
Piscataway, New Jersey 08854

CONTENTS

SIX PRACTICE TESTS

About Research & Education Association

Research & Education Association (REA) is an organization of educators, scientists, and engineers specializing in various academic fields. Founded in 1959 with the purpose of disseminating the most recently developed scientific information to groups in industry, government, high schools, and universities, REA has since become a successful and highly respected publisher of study aids, test preps, handbooks, and reference works.

REA's Test Preparation series includes study guides for all academic levels in almost all disciplines. Research & Education Association publishes test preps for students who have not yet completed high school, as well as high school students preparing to enter college. Students from countries around the world seeking to attend college in the United States will find the assistance they need in REA's publications. For college students seeking advanced degrees, REA publishes test preps for many major graduate school admission examinations in a wide variety of disciplines, including engineering, law, and medicine. Students at every level, in every field, with every ambition can find what they are looking for among REA's publications.

Unlike most test preparation books—which present only a few practice tests that bear little resemblance to the actual exams—REA's series presents tests that accurately depict the official exams in both degree of difficulty and types of questions. REA's practice tests are always based upon the most recently administered exams, and include every type of question that can be expected on the actual exams.

REA's publications and educational materials are highly regarded and continually receive an unprecedented amount of praise from professionals, instructors, librarians, parents, and students. Our authors are as diverse as the subjects and fields represented in the books we publish. They are well-known in their respective fields and serve on the faculties of prestigious high schools, colleges, and universities throughout the United States and Canada.

Acknowledgments

We would like to thank Dr. Max Fogiel, President, for his overall guidance, which brought this publication to completion; John Paul Cording, Manager of Software Development, for coordinating the development of the book; Larry B. Kling, Quality Control Manager of Books in Print, for his editorial direction of revisions; Jacquelin Kovacs of the Cincinnatus Central School, Cincinnatus, New York, for sharing her knowledge and experience as well as her writing and editorial skills; and Craig Yetsko, Elizabeth Powell, and Margaret Vezza for their editorial contributions.

NYSTCE

New York State Teacher Certification Examinations

Passing the NYSTCE

Chapter 1

Passing the NYSTCE

ABOUT THIS BOOK

This text provides a complete and accurate representation of the New York State Teacher Certification Examinations (NYSTCE), one of the most broad-based teacher certification exams used in the United States today. We include comprehensive topical reviews correlating to each of the test sections on all three NYSTCE exams, along with six practice tests, which are based on the current format of the NYSTCE. Our practice tests contain every type of question you can expect to encounter on the actual exam; as with the NYSTCE, you are allowed four hours to complete each of them. Detailed explanations of each answer — as well as sample essays — are included with the practice exams to help you better absorb the test material.

ABOUT THE TEST

Who Takes the Test and What Is It Used for?

The NYSTCE is taken by individuals seeking certification to teach in New York state. Candidates may be beginning their teaching career, or may be seeking additional certification.

Who Administers the Test?

The NYSTCE is administered by National Evaluation Systems (NES) in conjunction with the New York State Education Department. A comprehensive test development process was designed and implemented specifically to ensure that the content and difficulty level of the exam are appropriate.

When and Where Is the Test Given?

The NYSTCE is usually administered three times a year at several locations throughout the state of New York, generally on either a Saturday or

Sunday. Selective administrations are offered in Puerto Rico as well. To receive information on upcoming test dates and locations, you may wish to contact either of the following:

New York State Education Department
Office of Teaching
Albany, NY 12234
Website: *http://www.nysed.gov/tcert/homepage.htm*

NYSTCE
National Evaluation Systems, Inc.
P.O. Box 660
30 Gatehouse Road
Amherst, MA 01004-9008
Phone: (413) 256-2882
TTY for Deaf: (413) 256-8032

Registration information, as well as test dates and locations, is provided in the registration bulletin. Information regarding testing accommodations for candidates with special needs is also included in this bulletin.

Is There a Registration Fee?

You must pay a registration fee in order to take the NYSTCE. A complete outline of registration fees is provided in your registration bulletin.

HOW TO USE THIS BOOK

When Should I Start Studying?

An eight-week study schedule is provided in this text to assist you in preparing for the exam. Fortunately, this study schedule allows for a great deal of flexibility. If your test date is only four weeks away, you may halve the time allotted to each section — keep in mind, however, that this is not the most effective way to study. If you have several months before your test date, you may want to extend the time allotted to each section. Remember, the more time you spend studying, the better your chances of achieving a passing score.

FORMAT OF THE NYSTCE

The NYSTCE is really a group of three tests: the Liberal Arts and Sciences Test (LAST), the Assessment of Teaching Skills–Written (ATS-W), and the Assessment of Teaching Skills–Performance (ATS-P).

This group of tests is designed to assess your knowledge of subject matter, as well as your ability to convey that knowledge to a student.

The Liberal Arts and Sciences Test is composed of roughly 80 multiple-choice questions and one essay, divided into five subject areas. You will have four hours to complete the exam. The subject areas are as follows:

> Scientific and Mathematical Processes
> Historical and Social Scientific Awareness
> Artistic Expression and the Humanities
> Communication Skills
> Written Analysis and Expression

The exact number of questions in each area *will* vary, as will the total number of questions on the exam. The test administrators often include a number of test questions that do not count toward your score, but are used to prepare future exams.

Like the LAST, the Assessment of Teaching Skills–Written is composed of roughly 80 multiple-choice questions and one essay. As with the LAST, the number of questions may vary. The breakdown of the ATS–W subject matter is as follows:

> Knowledge of the Learner
> Instructional Planning, Assessment, and Delivery
> The Professional Environment

This book includes the best test preparation materials based on the information available from test administrators. The number and distribution of questions can vary from test to test. Accordingly, prospective examinees should pay strict attention to their strengths and weaknesses on the LAST and ATS–W and not depend on specific proportions of any areas appearing on the actual exam.

Unlike the LAST and the ATS–W, the Assessment of Teaching Skills–Performance is not a so-called paper-and-pencil test. The ATS–P requires the candidate to videotape him or herself in the classroom environment. Our ATS–P review outlines the requirements of the videotaped lesson and some suggestions on how to make your video the best it can be.

ABOUT THE REVIEW SECTIONS

By using our review material in conjunction with our practice tests, you should be well prepared for the actual NYSTCE. At some point in your educational experience, you have probably studied all the material that makes up the test. For most candidates, however, this was most likely some time ago.

The reviews will serve to refresh your memory of these topics, and the practice tests will help you gauge which areas you need to work on. Please note that both the LAST and the ATS–W test sections contain an essay. Therefore, the Writing Skills review included in the LAST section will be helpful for both test areas.

SCORING THE NYSTCE

How Do I Score My Practice Test?

The NYSTCE has a score range of 100–300 points. You must achieve a minimum of 220 to pass the exam. Your total score will derive from a combination of the number of multiple-choice questions that you answer correctly and your essay scores; however, the multiple-choice sections account for a larger percentage of your overall score than your essays do.

In order to achieve a passing score on the exam, you should answer at least 60% of the multiple-choice questions correctly, and your essay grades should fall no lower than the middle of the NYSTCE scoring range, as set forth in our Detailed Explanations of Answers. It may be helpful to have a friend or colleague score your essays, since you will benefit from his or her ability to be more objective in judging the clarity and organization of your written responses.

If you do not achieve a passing score on your first practice test, don't worry. Review those sections with which you have had the most difficulty, and try the second practice test. With each practice test, you will sharpen the skills you need to pass the actual exam.

When Will I Receive My Score Report?

Your score report should arrive about six weeks after you take the test. No scoring information will be given over the telephone. Remember, the data on your score report will reflect your *scaled* score, *not* the number of questions you have answered correctly.

Even if you do not pass every *section* of the NYSTCE you will still pass the exam so long as your individual scores are above the minimum and your *overall* score is above 220.

STUDYING FOR THE NYSTCE

There is no one correct way to study for the NYSTCE. You must find the method that works best for you. Some candidates prefer to set aside a few hours every morning to study, while others prefer to study at night before going to sleep. Only you can determine when and where your study time will be most effective, but it is helpful to be consistent. You may retain more information if you study every day at roughly the same time. A study schedule appears at the end of this chapter to help you budget your time.

When taking the practice tests you should try to duplicate the actual testing conditions as closely as possible. A quiet, well-lit room, free from such distractions as the television or radio, is preferable. As you complete each practice test, score your test and thoroughly review the explanations. Information that is wrong for one item may be correct for another, so it will be helpful for you to absorb as much data as possible. Keep track of your scores so you can gauge your progress accurately, and develop a clear sense of where you need improvement.

NYSTCE TEST-TAKING TIPS

Although you may have taken standardized tests like the NYSTCE before, it is crucial that you become familiar with the format and content of each section of this exam. This will help to alleviate any anxiety about your performance. Listed below are several ways to help you become accustomed to the test.

➤ *Become comfortable with the format of the test.* The NYSTCE covers a great deal of information, and the more comfortable you are with the format, the more confidence you will have when you take the actual exam. If you familiarize yourself with the requirements of each section individually, the whole test will be much less intimidating.

➤ *Read all of the possible answers.* Even if you believe you have found the correct answer, read all four options. Often answers that look right at first prove to be "magnet responses" meant to distract you from the correct choice.

➤ *Eliminate obviously incorrect answers immediately.* In this way, even if you do not know the correct answer, you can make an educated guess. Do not leave anything blank; it is always better to guess than to not answer at all. Even if you have absolutely no clue what the correct answer might be, you have a 25% chance of being correct. If you do not mark any answer, you have a 100% chance of being wrong.

➤ *Work quickly and steadily.* Remember, the final question on both the Liberal Arts and Sciences Test and the Assessment of Teaching Skills–Written is in essay form. You need more time to compose a clear, concise, well-constructed essay than you need to answer a multiple-choice question, so don't spend too much time on any one item. Try to pace yourself. If you feel that you are spending too much time on any one question, mark the answer choice that you think is most likely the correct one, circle the item number in your test booklet, and return to it if time allows. Timing yourself while you take the practice tests will help you learn to use your time wisely.

➤ *Be sure that the circle you are marking corresponds to the number of the question in the test booklet.* Multiple-choice tests like the NYSTCE are graded by a computer, which has no sympathy for clerical errors. One incorrectly placed response can upset your entire score.

THE DAY OF THE TEST

Try to get a good night's rest, and wake up early on the day of the test. You should have a good breakfast so you will not be distracted by hunger. Dress in layers that can be removed or applied as the conditions of the testing center require. There is no guarantee that the temperature in the testing center will be comfortable for you. Plan to arrive early. This will allow you to become familiar with your surroundings in the testing center, and minimize the possibility of distraction during the test.

Before you leave for the testing center, make sure you have any admissions material you may need, as well as photo identification. None of the mathematics items covered on the test requires scientific functions, so a calculator is neither necessary nor permitted. Calculators, however, will be provided for any Content Specialty Tests for which they are required. No eating, drinking, or smoking will be permitted during the test, so be sure to get these things out of the way before the test.

During the test, follow the proctor's instructions carefully. Fill out all paperwork very carefully — the information you give will be used to process your score reports, which you can expect to receive in about six weeks.

NYSTCE INDEPENDENT STUDY SCHEDULE

This study schedule allows for thorough preparation for the New York State Teacher Certification Examinations. It applies equally well whether you're taking the LAST, the ATS-W, or both. Although designed for eight weeks, it can be condensed into a four-week course by collapsing each two-week block into a one-week period. If you are not enrolled in a structured course, be sure to set aside enough time — at least two or three hours each day — to study. But no matter which study schedule works best for you, the more time you spend studying, the more prepared and relaxed you will feel on the day of the exam.

Week	Activity
1	Take your first exam (either the LAST or ATS-W) as a diagnostic test. Your score will be an indication of your strengths and weaknesses. Carefully review the explanations for the items you answered incorrectly.
2	Study REA's NYSTCE review material and answer the drill questions provided. Highlight key terms and information. Take notes on the important theories and key concepts, since writing will aid in the retention of information.
3 and 4	Review your references and sources. Use any supplementary material that your education instructors recommend.
5	Condense your notes and findings. You should have a structured outline with specific facts. You may want to use index cards to help you memorize important facts and concepts.
6	Test yourself using the index cards. You may want to have a friend or colleague quiz you on key facts and items. Take your second exam (either the LAST or ATS-W). Review the explanations for the items you answered incorrectly.
7	Study any areas you consider to be your weaknesses by using your study materials, references, and notes.
8	Take your third exam (either the LAST or ATS-W). Review the explanations for the items you answered incorrectly.

NYSTCE

New York State Teacher Certification Examinations

LAST and
ATS Reviews

Chapter 2

Science and Mathematics Review

The Science and Mathematics section of the LAST focuses on the understanding of mathematical concepts necessary for teachers, as well as the ability to relate these concepts to others. The emphasis is on the candidate's ability to use logic and reason when solving problems.

The following Mathematics Review concisely summarizes the information you will need to do well on the mathematics portion of the LAST. There is probably nothing in this section that you have not studied before, so most of the topics should be familiar to you. The review will serve to refresh your memory on some of the more difficult topics, and the practice tests will show which areas need more work. Remember, the LAST focuses primarily on the *processes* involved in mathematics. Therefore, factual recall is less important than a general understanding of the material when taking the LAST.

KEY STRATEGIES FOR ANSWERING THE MATHEMATICS QUESTIONS

1. **Make effective use of your time.** If you find yourself taking longer than one minute on a given question, mark the answer you think is most likely correct, circle the number of the item in the test booklet, and come back to it later if time allows.

2. **Answer all questions on this section of the test.** There is no penalty for guessing on the LAST, so do not leave any question unanswered. If you are not sure of the correct answer, narrow the choices to the two or three

most likely, and choose one. Eliminate answers that could not possibly be correct before you choose.

3.   **Read each question carefully.** Be sure you understand what the question is actually asking, not what a casual reading of the question might suggest. Be sure you have separated all the relevant information from the irrelevant information in the question.

4.   **Devise a plan for answering the question.** This plan will be especially useful on the word problems and geometry items.

5.   **Work the problem backwards to check your answer.** If time allows, check your work by substituting the answer into the original problem. Be certain that the answer meets all the conditions in the original question.

6.   **Draw a diagram, sketch, or table to organize your work or to explain the question.** Not all questions that you need an illustration to understand will include an illustration, so make one yourself.

7.   **Write in the test booklet.** Mark up diagrams as needed. Write in the margins and other blank spaces. Write information directly into the statement of the problem, especially if you are having trouble setting up a solution.

8.   **Look for similar questions.** Similar items may have appeared elsewhere on the test. You also may recall similar questions from classes you have taken previously. Apply suitable strategies from related work to the problem at hand.

PART I: ARITHMETIC

INTEGERS

Natural or counting numbers are 1, 2, 3, …

Whole numbers are 0, 1, 2, 3, …

Integers are …, −2, −1, 0, 1, 2, …

As shown below, a number line is often used to represent integers.

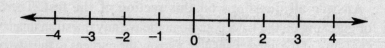

The following are properties of integers:

Commutative property: $a + b = b + a$

Example

$2 + 3 = 3 + 2$

Associative property: $(a + b) + c = a + (b + c)$

Example

$(2 + 3) + 4 = 2 + (3 + 4)$

Distributive property: $a(b + c) = ab + ac$

Example

$2(3 + 4) = (2 \times 3) + (2 \times 4)$

$2 \times 7 = 6 + 8$

$14 = 14$

Additive identity: $a + 0 = a$

Example

$2 + 0 = 2$

Multiplicative identity: $a \times 1 = a$

Example

$2 \times 1 = 2$

PRIME AND COMPOSITE NUMBERS

When two whole numbers are multiplied, they yield a product. These two whole numbers can be called *factors* or *divisors* of the product. (An exception to this is 0. Zero can be a factor, but not a divisor, since division by 0 is undefined.)

Example

$2 \times 3 = 6$. 2 and 3 are factors or divisors of the product 6.

Example

$0 \times 3 = 0$. 3 is a factor and divisor of the product 0, but 0 is only a factor of the product 0, since $0 \div 0$ is undefined.

A *prime number* is a whole number, greater than 1, that has only two different whole number factors, 1 and the number itself.

Example

5 is a prime number, because it has only two different factors, 1 and 5.

A *composite number* is a whole number that has three or more whole number factors.

Example

6 is a composite number, because it has four different factors, 1, 2, 3, and 6.

EVEN AND ODD NUMBERS

Even numbers are whole numbers that have 2 as a factor.

Example

6 is an even number, since $2 \times 3 = 6$.

Odd numbers are whole numbers that do not have 2 as a factor.

Example

5 is an odd number, since 2 is not a factor of 5.

PLACE VALUE

Our numeration system uses the *Hindu-Arabic numerals* (0, 1, 2, 3, 4, 5, 6, 7, 8, 9) to represent numbers.

Our numeration system follows a *base 10 place-value scheme*. As we move to the left in any number, each place value is ten times the place value to the right. Similarly, as we move to the right, each place value is one-tenth the place value to the left.

Example

In the number 543.12, the place value of the 5 (100's) is ten times the place value of the 4 (10's). The place value of the $1\left(\frac{1}{10}\text{'s}\right)$ is one-tenth the place value of the $2\left(\frac{1}{100}\text{'s}\right)$.

The concept of place value will be discussed in the Arithmetic Operations and Decimal Fractions sections.

POWERS AND ROOTS OF WHOLE NUMBERS

Exponents and Bases

In the expression 5^3, 5 is called the *base* and 3 is called the *exponent*. The expression $5^3 = 5 \times 5 \times 5$. The base (5) gives the factor used in the expression and the exponent (3) gives the number of times the base is to be used as a factor.

Example

$$4^2 = 4 \times 4$$

$$3^5 = 3 \times 3 \times 3 \times 3 \times 3$$

When the base has an exponent of 2, the base is said to be *squared*. When the base has an exponent of 3, the base is said to be *cubed*.

The Basic Laws of Exponents are

1) $b^m \times b^n = b^{m+n}$

   Example

   $$2^5 \times 2^3 = 2^{5+3} = 2^8$$

2) $b^m \div b^n = b^{m-n}$

   Example

   $$2^5 \div 2^3 = 2^{5-3} = 2^2$$

3) $(b^m)^n = b^{m \times n}$

   Example

   $$(2^5)^3 = 2^{5 \times 3} = 2^{15}$$

Roots

Consider again the expression 5^3. If we carry out the implied multiplication, we get $5^3 = 5 \times 5 \times 5 = 125$. 5 is called the cube root of 125, since $5^3 = 125$. In general, when a base is raised to a power to produce a given result, the base is called the *root* of the given result.

If the power for the base is 2, the base is called the *square root.* If the power for the base is 3, the base is called the *cube root.* In general, if $b^n = p$, then b is the nth root of p.

Examples

Since $4^2 = 16$, 4 is the square root of 16.

Since $2^3 = 8$, 2 is the cube root of 8.

Since $3^5 = 243$, 3 is the 5th root of 243.

ARITHMETIC OPERATIONS AND INTEGERS

Integers are *signed numbers* preceded by either a "+" or a "−" sign. If no sign is given for the integer, one should infer that the integer is positive (e.g., 3 means +3). On a number line, integers to the *left of zero are negative* and integers to the *right of zero are positive*.

The *absolute value* of an integer is the measure of the distance of the integer from zero. Since the measure of distance is always positive, absolute value is always positive. The absolute value of the real number a is denoted by $|a|$ (e.g., $|-3| = 3$, $|3| = 3$).

Addition

When two integers are added, the two integers are called *addends,* and the result is called the sum, as illustrated in the following:

$$5 \quad + \quad 3 \quad = \quad 8$$

(addend)   (addend)   (sum)

or

$$\begin{array}{ll} 5 & \text{(addend)} \\ \underline{+\ 3} & \text{(addend)} \\ 8 & \text{(sum)} \end{array}$$

When adding two integers, one of the following two situations might occur:

Situation 1: Both integers have the same sign. In this case, add the absolute values of the two addends and give the sum the same sign as the addends.

Examples

2 + 3 = 5, and

−2 + (−3) = −5

Situation 2: The two integers have different signs. In this case, subtract the addend with the smaller absolute value from the addend with the larger absolute value. The sum gets the sign of the addend with the larger absolute value.

Examples

−2 + 5 = 3, but

2 + (−5) = −3

Subtraction

In a subtraction sentence, the top or first number in the subtraction is the *minuend,* the bottom or second number is the *subtrahend,* and the result is the *remainder or difference.* These quantities are demonstrated in the following figure:

$$5 \quad - \quad 3 \quad = \quad 2$$

(minuend) (subtrahend) (remainder)

or

> 5   (minuend)
> −3   (subtrahend)
> ———
> 2   (remainder)

When subtracting a negative integer, change the sign of the subtrahend and add the resulting two integers, following the procedures given above.

Examples

5 − 3 = 2, but

5 − (−3) = 5 + (+3) = 5 + 3 = 8

Multiplication

When multiplying two integers, the two integers are called *factors,* and the result is called the *product,* as illustrated in the following:

$$5 \quad \times \quad 3 \quad = \quad 15$$

(factor)   (factor) (product)

or

5	(factor)
× 3	(factor)
15	(product)

When multiplying two integers, multiply the absolute values of the factors. If the factors have the *same sign,* the product is *positive;* if the factors have *different signs,* the product is *negative.* If either factor is zero, the product is zero.

Example

$3 \times 5 = 15$ and $(-3) \times (-5) = 15$, but

$(-3) \times 5 = -15$ and $3 \times (-5) = -15$.

Division

When dividing two integers, the number being divided is the *dividend,* the number being divided into another integer is the *divisor,* and the result is the *quotient,* as illustrated in the following:

10	÷	2	=	5
(dividend)		(divisor)		(quotient)

When dividing two integers, divide the absolute values of the dividend and divisor. The sign of the quotient can be obtained by following the same procedures given above in the multiplication section.

Examples

$10 \div 2 = 5$ and $(-10) \div (-2) = 5$, but

$(-10) \div 2 = (-5)$ and $10 \div (-2) = (-5)$.

ARITHMETIC OPERATIONS AND COMMON FRACTIONS

A common fraction is a number that can be written in the form $\frac{a}{b}$ where a and b are whole numbers. In the expression $\frac{a}{b}$, the dividend a is called the *numerator* and the divisor b is called the *denominator.*

Example

In the expression $\frac{3}{4}$, 3 is the numerator and 4 is the denominator.

A common fraction may not have 0 as a denominator, since *division by 0 is undefined.*

A fraction is in *lowest terms* if the numerator and denominator have no common factors.

Examples

$\frac{1}{2}$, $\frac{3}{4}$, and $\frac{5}{6}$ are in lowest terms, since the numerator and denominator of each have no common factors.

$\frac{2}{4}$, $\frac{9}{21}$, and $\frac{20}{24}$ are *not* in lowest terms, since the numerator and denominator of each have common factors.

Fractions are *equivalent* if they represent the same number.

Example

$\frac{8}{16}$, $\frac{4}{8}$, $\frac{2}{4}$, and $\frac{5}{10}$ are equivalent fractions, since each represents $\frac{1}{2}$.

A *mixed numeral* is a number that consists of an integer and a common fraction.

Example

$5\frac{3}{4}$ is a mixed numeral since it consists of the integer 5 and the common fraction $\frac{3}{4}$.

An *improper fraction* is a common fraction whose numerator is larger than its denominator. A mixed numeral can be expressed as an improper fraction by multiplying the denominator of the common fraction part times the integer part and adding that product to the numerator of the common fraction part. The result is the numerator of the improper fraction. The denominator of the improper fraction is the same as the denominator in the mixed numeral.

Example

$5\dfrac{3}{4} = \dfrac{23}{4}$ since $(4 \times 5) + 3 = 23$, and 4 was the denominator of the common fraction part, $\dfrac{23}{4}$ is an improper fraction, since the numerator 23 is larger than the denominator 4.

Addition

In order to *add* two fractions, the denominators of the fractions must be the same; when they are, they are called *common denominators*. The equivalent fractions with the smallest common denominator are said to have the *lowest common denominator*.

Examples

$$\dfrac{3}{8} + \dfrac{2}{8} = \dfrac{5}{8} \quad \text{but} \quad \dfrac{3}{8} + \dfrac{1}{4} = \dfrac{3}{8} + \dfrac{2}{8} = \dfrac{5}{8}$$

Note that while 16, 24, 32, and so forth, could have been used as common denominators to obtain equivalent fractions, the lowest common denominator, 8, was used to generate like denominators.

The procedures regarding the addition of signed numbers given in the addition section also apply for the addition of common fractions.

Subtraction

The procedures given for the addition of common fractions together with the procedures for subtraction of signed numbers form the basis for the subtraction of common fractions.

Examples

$$\dfrac{3}{8} - \dfrac{2}{8} = \dfrac{1}{8}, \quad \text{but} \quad \dfrac{3}{8} - \dfrac{1}{4} = \dfrac{3}{8} - \dfrac{2}{8} = \dfrac{1}{8}$$

As also suggested:

$$\dfrac{3}{8} - \left(-\dfrac{2}{8}\right) = \dfrac{3}{8} + \dfrac{2}{8} = \dfrac{5}{8} \quad \text{and}$$

$$\frac{3}{8} - \left(-\frac{1}{4}\right) = \frac{3}{8} + \frac{1}{4} = \frac{3}{8} + \frac{2}{8} = \frac{5}{8}.$$

Multiplication

To *multiply* two common fractions, simply find the product of the two numerators and divide it by the product of the two denominators. Reduce the resultant fraction to lowest terms.

Example

$$\frac{2}{3} \times \frac{9}{11} = \frac{18}{33} = \frac{6}{11}$$

In addition, the procedures regarding the multiplication of integers given in the multiplication of integers section, apply to the multiplication of common fractions.

Division

To find the *reciprocal* of a common fraction, exchange the numerator and the denominator.

Examples

The reciprocal of $\frac{2}{3}$ is $\frac{3}{2}$.

The reciprocal of $\frac{21}{4}$ is $\frac{4}{21}$.

To *divide* two common fractions, multiply the fraction which is the dividend by the reciprocal of the fraction which is the divisor. Reduce the result to lowest terms.

Examples

$$\frac{4}{9} \div \frac{2}{3} = \frac{4}{9} \times \frac{3}{2} = \frac{12}{18} = \frac{2}{3}$$

$$\frac{7}{8} \div \frac{21}{4} = \frac{7}{8} \times \frac{4}{21} = \frac{28}{168} = \frac{1}{6}$$

In addition, the procedures regarding the division of integers given above apply for the division of common fractions.

ARITHMETIC OPERATIONS AND DECIMAL FRACTIONS

As discussed above, our numeration system follows a base 10 place value scheme. Another way to represent a fractional number is to write the number to include integer powers of ten. This allows us to represent *decimal fractions* as follows:

$$\frac{1}{10} = 10^{-1} = 0.1 \text{ (said "one-tenth")}$$

$$\frac{1}{100} = 10^{-2} = 0.01 \text{ (said "one-hundredth")}$$

$$\frac{1}{1,000} = 10^{-3} = 0.001 \text{ (said "one-thousandth"), and so forth.}$$

Examples

3.14 is said "three and fourteen hundredths."

528.5 is said "five hundred twenty-eight and five-tenths."

Addition

To *add decimal fractions,* simply line up the decimal points for each decimal numeral to be added, and follow the procedures for the addition of integers. Place the decimal point in the sum directly underneath the decimal point in the addends.

Examples

$$
\begin{array}{r}
89.8 \\
152.9 \\
+\quad 7.21 \\
\hline
249.91
\end{array}
\qquad
\begin{array}{r}
32.456 \\
6,561.22 \\
+\quad 2.14 \\
\hline
6,595.816
\end{array}
$$

Subtraction

To *subtract decimal fractions,* place zeros as needed so that both the minuend and the subtrahend have a digit in each column.

Examples

$$
\begin{array}{r}
152.9 \\
-\quad 7.21 \\
\end{array}
\qquad \rightarrow \qquad
\begin{array}{r}
152.90 \\
-\quad 7.21 \\
\hline
145.69
\end{array}
$$

$$
\begin{array}{r}
32.456 \\
-\ \ 2.14 \\
\hline
\end{array}
\quad \rightarrow \quad
\begin{array}{r}
32.456 \\
-\ \ 2.140 \\
\hline
30.316
\end{array}
$$

Multiplication

To *multiply decimal fractions,* follow the procedures given in the multiplying integers section and then place the decimal point so that *the total number of decimal places in the product is equal to the sum of the decimal places in each factor.*

Examples

$(3.14)(0.5) = 1.570$, and

$(89.8)(152.9) = 13,730.42$

Division

To *divide decimal fractions,*

1) move the decimal point in the divisor to the right, until there are no decimal places in the divisor,

2) move the decimal point in the dividend the same number of decimal places to the right, and

3) divide the transformed dividend and divisor as given above.

4) The number of decimal places in the quotient should be the same as the number of decimal places in the transformed dividend.

Examples

$15.5 + 0.5 \rightarrow 155 \div 5 = 31$, and

$32.436 + 0.06 \rightarrow 3,243.6 \div 6 = 540.6$

PERCENT

Percent is another way of expressing a fractional number. Percent always expresses a fractional number in terms of $\dfrac{1}{100}$'s or 0.01's. Percents use the "%" symbol.

Examples

$$100\% = \frac{100}{100} = 1.00, \text{ and}$$

$$25\% = \frac{25}{100} = 0.25$$

[handwritten: 28% $\frac{28}{100} = 0.28$]

As shown in these examples, a percent is easily converted to a common fraction or a decimal fraction. To convert a decimal to a common fraction, place the percent in the numerator and use 100 as the denominator (reduce as necessary). To convert a percent to a decimal fraction, divide the percent by 100, or move the decimal point two places to the left.

Examples

$$25\% = \frac{25}{100} = \frac{1}{4} \text{ and}$$

$$25\% = 0.25$$

$$\text{Similarly, } 125\% = \frac{125}{100} = 1\frac{25}{100} = 1\frac{1}{4} \text{ and}$$

$$125\% = 1.25$$

To convert a *common fraction to a percent*, carry a division of the numerator by the denominator of the fraction out to three decimal places. Round the result to two places. To convert a *decimal fraction to a percent*, move the decimal point two places to the right (adding 0's as place holders, if needed) and round as necessary.

Examples

$$\frac{1}{4} = 1 \div 4 = 0.25 = 25\%, \text{ and}$$

$$\frac{2}{7} = 2 \div 7 = 0.28 = 28\%$$

[handwritten computations: 0.25, 68, 17.00, ×4, 68, ×0.25, 340, 360]

If one wishes to find the *percentage* of a known quantity, change the percent to a common fraction or a decimal fraction, and multiply the fraction times the quantity. The percentage is expressed in the same units as the known quantity.

Example

To find 25% of 360 books, change 25% to 0.25 and multiply times 360, as follows: $0.25 \times 360 = 90$. The result is 90 books.

(Note: The known quantity is the *base,* the percent is the *rate,* and the result is the *percentage.)*

ELEMENTARY STATISTICS

Mean

The average, or *mean,* of a set of numbers can be found by adding the set of numbers and dividing by the total number of elements in the set.

Example

The mean of 15, 10, 25, 5, 40 is

$$\frac{15+10+25+5+40}{5} = \frac{95}{5} = 19$$

Median

If a given set of numbers is ordered from smallest to largest, the *median* is the "middle" number; that is, half of the numbers in the set of numbers is below the median and half of the numbers in the set is above the median.

Example

To find the median of the set of whole numbers 15, 10, 25, 5, 40, first order the set of numbers to get 5, 10, 15, 25, 40. Since 15 is the middle number (half of the numbers are below 15, half are above 15), 15 is called the median of this set of whole numbers. If there is an even number of numbers in the set, the median is the mean of the middle two numbers.

Mode

The *mode* of a set of numbers is the number that appears most frequently in the set. There may be no mode or more than one mode for a set of numbers.

Example

In the set 15, 10, 25, 10, 5, 40, 10, 15, the number 10 appears most frequently (three times); therefore, 10 is the mode of the given set of numbers.

Range

The *range* of a set of numbers is obtained by subtracting the smallest number in the set from the largest number in the set.

Example

To find the range of 15, 10, 25, 5, 40, find the difference between the largest and the smallest elements of the set. This gives $40 - 5 = 35$. The range of the given set is 35.

PART II: ALGEBRA

ALGEBRAIC EXPRESSIONS

An *algebraic expression* is an expression using letters, numbers, symbols, and arithmetic operations to represent a number or relationship among numbers.

A *variable,* or unknown, is a letter that stands for a number in an algebraic expression. *Coefficients* are the numbers that precede the variable to give the quantity of the variable in the expression.

Algebraic expressions are comprised of *terms,* or groupings of variables and numbers.

An algebraic expression with one term is called a *monomial;* with two terms, a *binomial;* with three terms, a *trinomial;* with more than one term, a *polynomial.*

Examples

$2ab - cd$ is a binomial algebraic expression with variables a, b, c, and d, and terms $2ab$ and $(-cd)$. 2 is the coefficient of ab and -1 is the coefficient of cd.

$x^2 + 3y - 1$ is a trinomial algebraic expression using the variables x and y, and terms x^2, $3y$, and (-1);

$z(x - 1) + uv - wy - 2$ is a polynomial with variables z, x, u, v, w, and y, and terms $z(x - 1)$, uv, $(-wy)$, and (-2).

As stated above, algebraic expressions can be used to represent the relationship among numbers. For example, if we know there are ten times as many students in a school as teachers, if S represents the number of students in the school and T represents the number of teachers, the total number of students and teachers in the school is $S + T$.

If we wished to form an algebraic sentence equating the number of students and teachers in the school, the sentence would be $S = 10T$. (Note that if either the number of students or the number of teachers were known, the other quantity could be found.)

SIMPLIFYING ALGEBRAIC EXPRESSIONS

Like terms are terms in an algebraic expression that are exactly the same; that is, they contain the same variables and the same powers.

Examples

The following are pairs of like terms:

x^2 and $(-3x^2)$, abc and $4abc$, $(x - 1)$ and $(x - 1)^2$.

The following are not pairs of like terms:

x and $(-3x^2)$, abc and $4a^2bc$, $(x - 1)$ and $(x^2 - 1)$.

To simplify an algebraic expression, combine like terms in the following order:

1) simplify all expressions within symbols of inclusion (e.g., ( ), [ ], { }) using steps 2–4 below;

2) carry out all exponentiation;

3) carry out all multiplication and division from left to right in the order in which they occur;

4) carry out all addition and subtraction from left to right in the order in which they occur.

FACTORING ALGEBRAIC EXPRESSIONS

When two numbers are multiplied together, the numbers are called factors and their result is called the product. Similarly, algebraic expressions may be the product of other algebraic expressions.

In factoring algebraic expressions, first remove any monomial factors, then remove any binomial, trinomial, or other polynomial factors. Often one may find other polynomial factors by inspecting for the sum and difference of two squares; that is, $x^2 - y^2 = (x + y)(x - y)$.

Examples

$2a + 2b = 2(a + b)$

$4x^2y - 2xy^2 + 16x^2y^2 = 2xy(2x - y + 8xy)$

$x^2 - 4 = (x + 2)(x - 2)$

$4a^2 - 16b^2 = 4(a^2 - 4b^2) = 4(a + 2b)(a - 2b)$

In factoring polynomials, one often uses what is called the *"FOIL"* method *(First, Outside, Inside, Last)*.

Examples

$x^2 + 3x - 10 = (x - 2)(x + 5)$

$6y^2 - y - 2 = (2y + 1)(3y - 2)$

$ab^2 - 3ab - 10a = a(b^2 - 3b - 10) = a(b + 2)(b - 5)$

SOLVING LINEAR EQUATIONS

To solve a linear equation, use the following procedures:

1) isolate the variable; that is, group all the terms with the variable on one side of the equation (commonly the left side) and group all the constants on the other side of the equation (commonly the right side);

2) combine like terms on each side of the equation;

3) divide by the coefficient of the variable;

4) check the result in the original equation.

Problem

Solve $3x + 2 = 5$ for x.

Solution

$3x + 2 = 5$ (add –2 to both sides)

$3x = 3$ (multiply by $\frac{1}{3}$)

$x = 1$

Problem

Solve $a + 3a = 3a + 1$ for a.

Solution

$$a + 3a = 3a + 1 \qquad \text{(add } -3a \text{ to both sides)}$$
$$a = 1$$

Problem

Solve $3(y-2) + 5 = 3 + 5y$ for y.

Solution

$$3(y-2) + 5 = 3 + 5y \qquad \text{(simplify)}$$
$$3y - 6 + 5 = 3 + 5y \qquad \text{(combine like terms)}$$
$$3y - 1 = 3 + 5y \qquad \text{(add 1 to both sides)}$$
$$3y = 4 + 5y \qquad \text{(add } -5y \text{ to both sides)}$$
$$-2y = 4 \qquad \text{(multiply by } -\frac{1}{2}\text{)}$$
$$y = -2$$

SOLVING INEQUALITIES

The equivalence properties of integers given in the integers section and the procedures for solving linear equations given in the section solving linear equations are used *to solve inequalities*. In addition, the following properties of inequalities should be noted:

If $x < y$ and $z > 0$, then $zx < zy$.

If $x > y$ and $z > 0$, then $zx > zy$.

If $x < y$ and $z < 0$, then $zx > zy$.

If $x > y$ and $z < 0$, then $zx < zy$.

In other words, if both sides of an inequality are *multiplied by a positive number, the sense of the inequality remains the same*. If both sides of an inequality are *multiplied by a negative number, the sense of the inequality is reversed*.

Examples

Since $3 < 5$ and 2 is positive,

(2) (3) < (2) (5) or 6 < 10.

But since $3 < 5$ and -2 is negative,

(–2) (3) > (–2) (5) or $-6 > -10$.

The above properties are also demonstrated in the following problems:

Problem

Find the values of y for which $2y > y - 3$.

Solution

$2y > y - 3$ (add $-y$ to both sides)

$y > -3$

Problem

Find the values of x for which $x > 4x + 1$.

Solution

$x > 4x + 1$ (add $-4x$ to both sides)

$-3x > 1$ (multiply by $-\dfrac{1}{3}$)

$x < -\dfrac{1}{3}$

EVALUATING FORMULAS

Formulas are algebraic sentences that are frequently used in mathematics, science, or other fields. Examples of common formulas are $A = l \times w$, $d = r \times t$, and $C = \left(\dfrac{5}{9}\right)(F - 32°)$. *To evaluate a formula,* replace each variable with the given values of the variables and solve for the unknown variable.

Example

Since $A = l \times w$, if $l = 2$ ft. and $w = 3$ ft.,

then $A = 2$ ft. $\times 3$ ft. $= 6$ sq. ft.

Example

Since $d = r \times t$, if $r = 32$ m/sec² and $t = 5$ sec,

then $d = (32 \text{ m/sec}) \times 5 \text{ sec} = 160$ m.

Example

Since $C = \left(\dfrac{5}{9}\right)(F - 32)$, if $F = 212°$,

then $C = \left(\dfrac{5}{9}\right)(212° - 32°) = 100°$.

ELEMENTARY PROBABILITY

The likelihood or chance that an event will take place is called the *probability* of the event. The probability of an event is determined by dividing the number of ways the event could occur by the number of possible events in the given sample. In other words, if a sample space S has n possible outcomes, and an event E has m ways of occurring, then the probability of the event, denoted by $P(E)$, is given by

$$P(E) = \frac{m}{n}$$

It should be noted that $0 \le P(E) \le 1$.

Problem

What is the probability of getting "heads" on the toss of a coin?

Solution

Since the number of possible outcomes in the toss of a coin is 2 and the number of ways of getting "heads" on a coin toss is 1, $P(\text{heads}) = \dfrac{1}{2}$.

Problem

What is the probability of drawing an ace from a standard deck of playing cards?

Solution

Since the number of aces in a standard deck is 4 and the number of cards in a standard deck is 52, $P(\text{ace}) = \dfrac{4}{52} = \dfrac{1}{13}$.

ALGEBRA WORD PROBLEMS

A general procedure for solving problems was suggested by Polya. His procedure can be summarized as follows:

1) Understand the problem.

2) Devise a plan for solving the problem.

3) Carry out the plan.

4) Look back on the solution to the problem.

When taking the mathematics section of the LAST, you can use this procedure by translating the word problem into an algebraic sentence, then follow the procedures for solving an algebraic sentence. Find a variable to represent the unknown in the problem. Look for key synonyms such as "is, are, were" for "=", "more, more than" for "+" "less, less than, fewer" for "–", and "of" for "x."

Problem

The sum of the ages of Bill and Paul is 32 years. Bill is 6 years older than Paul. Find the age of each.

Solution

If p = Paul's age, then Bill's age is $p + 6$. So that $p + (p + 6) = 32$. Applying the methods from above, we get $p = 13$. Therefore, Paul is 13 and Bill is 19.

Problem

Jose weighs twice as much as his brother Carlos. If together they weigh 225 pounds, how much does each weigh?

Solution

If c = Carlos' weight, then Jose's weight is $2c$. So $c + 2c = 225$ pounds. Applying the methods above, we get $c = 75$. Therefore, Carlos weighs 75 pounds and Jose weighs 150 pounds.

Problem

Julia drove from her home to her aunt's house in 3 hours and 30 minutes. If the distance between the houses is 175 miles, what was the car's average speed?

Solution

As noted above, distance = rate × time. Since we know $d = 175$ mph and $t = 3\frac{1}{2}$ hr., then 175 mph = $r \times 3\frac{1}{2}$ hr. Solving for the rate (r), we get $r = 50$ mph.

(It is strongly suggested that individuals who feel they need additional practice in solving word problems using the above procedures seek out additional practice problems in a standard high school first-year algebra textbook.)

PART III: MEASUREMENT AND GEOMETRY

PERIMETER AND AREA OF RECTANGLES, SQUARES, AND TRIANGLES

Perimeter refers to the measure of the distance around a figure. Perimeter is measured in linear units (e.g., inches, feet, meters). *Area* refers to the measure of the interior of a figure. Area is measured in square units (e.g., square inches, square feet, square meters).

PERIMETER OF RECTANGLES, SQUARES, AND TRIANGLES

The *perimeter of a rectangle* is found by adding twice the length of the rectangle to twice the width of the rectangle. This relationship is commonly given by the formula $P = 2l + 2w$, where l is the measure of the length and w is the measure of the width.

Example

If a rectangle has $l = 10$ m and $w = 5$ m, then the perimeter of the rectangle is given by $P = 2(10\ m) + 2(5\ m) = 30$ m.

The *perimeter of a square* is found by multiplying four times the measure of a side of the square. This relationship is commonly given by the formula, $P = 4s$, where s is the measure of a side of the square.

Example

If a square has $s = 5$ feet, then the perimeter of the square is given by $P = 4(5 \text{ feet}) = 20$ feet.

The *perimeter of a triangle* is found by adding the measures of the three sides of the triangle. This relationship can be represented by $P = s_1 + s_2 + s_3$, where s_1, s_2, and s_3 are the measures of the sides of the triangle.

Example

If a triangle has three sides measuring 3 inches, 4 inches, and 5 inches, then the perimeter of the triangle is given by $P = 3$ inches + 4 inches + 5 inches = 12 inches.

AREA OF RECTANGLES, SQUARES, AND TRIANGLES

The *area of a rectangle* is found by multiplying the measure of the length of the rectangle by the measure of the width of the rectangle. This relationship is commonly given by $A = l \times w$, where l is the measure of the length and w is the measure of the width.

Example

If a rectangle has $l = 10$ m and $w = 5$ m, then the area of the rectangle is given by $A = 10 \text{ m} \times 5 \text{ m} = 50 \text{ m}^2$

The *area of a square* is found by squaring the measure of the side of the square. This relationship is commonly given by $A = s^2$, where s is the measure of a side.

Example

If a square has $s = 5$ ft., then the area of the square is given by $A = (5 \text{ ft})^2 = 25 \text{ ft}^2$.

The *area of a right triangle* is found by multiplying $\frac{1}{2}$ times the product of the base and the height of the triangle. This relationship is commonly given by $A = \frac{1}{2}bh$, where b is the base and h is the height.

Example

If a triangle has a base of 3 in. and a height of 4 in., then the area of the triangle is given by

$$A = \frac{1}{2}(3 \text{ in.} \times 4 \text{ in.}) = \frac{1}{2}(12 \text{ in}^2) = 6 \text{ in}^2$$

CIRCUMFERENCE AND AREA OF CIRCLES

The *radius of a circle* is the distance from the center of the circle to the edge of the circle. The *diameter of a circle* is a line segment that passes through the center of the circle, the end points of which lie on the circle. The *measure of the diameter of a circle* is twice the measure of the radius.

The number π (approximately 3.14) is often used in computations involving circles.

The *circumference of a circle* is found by multiplying π times the diameter (or twice the radius). This relationship is commonly given by $C = \pi \times d$, or $C = 2 \times \pi \times r$.

The *area of a circle* is found by multiplying it by the square of the radius of the circle. This relationship is commonly given by $A = \pi \times r^2$.

Example

If a circle has a radius of 5 cm, then

$C = \pi \times 10 \text{ cm} = 3.14 \times 10 \text{ cm} \approx 31.4 \text{ cm}$, and

$A = \pi \times (5 \text{ cm})^2 \approx 3.14 \times (5 \text{ cm})^2 = 78.50 \text{ cm}^2$

VOLUME OF CUBES AND RECTANGULAR SOLIDS

Volume refers to the measure of the interior of a three-dimensional figure.

A *rectangular solid* is a rectilinear (right-angled) figure that has length, width, and height. The volume of a rectangular solid is found by computing the product of the length, width, and height of the figure. This relationship is commonly expressed by $V = l \times w \times h$.

Example

The volume of a rectangular solid with $l = 5$ cm, $w = 4$ cm, and $h = 3$ cm is given by

$$V = 5 \text{ cm} \times 4 \text{ cm} \times 3 \text{ cm} = 60 \text{ cm}^3.$$

A *cube* is a rectangular solid, the length, width, and height of which have the same measure. This measure is called the *edge of the cube*. The volume of a cube is found by cubing the measure of the edge. This relationship is commonly expressed by $V = e^3$.

Example

The volume of a cube with $e = 5$ cm is given by $V = (5 \text{ cm})^3 = 125 \text{ cm}^3$.

ANGLE MEASURE

An *angle* consists of all the points in two noncollinear rays that have the same vertex. An angle is commonly thought of as two "arrows" joined at their bases.

Two angles are *adjacent* if they share a common vertex, share only one side, and one angle does not lie in the interior of the other.

Angles are usually measured in *degrees*. A circle has a measure of 360°, a half circle 180°, a quarter circle 90°, and so forth. If the measures of two angles are the same, then the angles are said to be *congruent*.

An angle with a measure of 90° is called a *right angle*. Angles with measures less than 90° are called *acute*. Angles with measures more than 90° are called *obtuse*.

If the sum of the measures of two angles is 90°, the two angles are said to be *complementary*. If the sum of the measures of the two angles is 180°, the two angles are said to be *supplementary*.

If two lines intersect, they form two pairs of *vertical angles*. The measures of vertical angles are equivalent; that is, vertical angles are congruent.

PROPERTIES OF TRIANGLES

Triangles are three-sided polygons.

If the measures of two sides of a triangle are equal, then the triangle is called an *isosceles triangle*. If the measures of all sides of the triangle are equal, then the triangle is called an *equilateral triangle*. If no measures of the sides of a triangle are equal, then the triangle is called a *scalene triangle*.

The sum of the measures of the angles of a triangle is 180°.

The sum of the measures of any two sides of a triangle is greater than the measure of the third side.

If the measure of one angle of a triangle is greater than the measure of another angle of a triangle, then the measure of the side opposite the larger angle is greater than the side opposite the smaller angle. (A similar relationship holds for the measures of angles opposite larger sides.)

Related to the discussion of angles, if all of the angles of a triangle are acute, then the triangle is called an *acute triangle*. If one of the angles of a triangle is obtuse, then the triangle is called an *obtuse triangle*. If one of the angles of a triangle is a right angle, then the triangle is called a *right triangle*.

Two triangles are *congruent* if the measures of all corresponding sides and angles are equal. Two triangles are *similar* if the measures of all corresponding angles are equal.

Problem

Find the measures of the angles of a right triangle, if one of the angles measures 30°.

Solution

Since the triangle is a right triangle, a second angle of the triangle measures 90°. We know the sum of the measures of a triangle is 180°, so that, $90° + 30° + x° = 180°$. Solving for $x°$, we get $x° = 60°$. The measures of the angles of the triangle are 90°, 60°, and 30°.

THE PYTHAGOREAN THEOREM

In a right triangle, the side opposite the 90° angle is called the *hypotenuse* and the other two sides are called the *legs*. If the hypotenuse has measure c and the legs have measures a and b, the relationship among the measures, known as the *Pythagorean Theorem,* is given by

$$c^2 = a^2 + b^2$$

Problem

Find the length of the hypotenuse of a right triangle if the measure of one leg is 3 cm and the other leg is 4 cm.

Solution

By the Pythagorean Theorem, $c^2 = (3 \text{ cm})^2 + (4 \text{ cm})^2$ so that $c^2 = 9 \text{ cm}^2 + 16 \text{ cm}^2$, $c^2 = 25 \ cm^2$. Taking the square root of both sides, we get $c = 5$ cm.

PROPERTIES OF PARALLEL AND PERPENDICULAR LINES

If lines have a point or points in common, they are said to *intersect.*

Lines are *parallel* if they do not intersect.

Lines are *perpendicular* if they contain the sides of a right angle.

If a third line intersects two other lines, the intersecting line is called a *transversal.*

Two lines crossed by a transversal form eight angles. The four angles that lie between the two lines are called *interior angles.* The four angles that lie outside the two lines are called *exterior angles.*

The interior angles that lie on the same side of the transversal are called *consecutive interior angles.* The interior angles that lie on opposite sides of the transversal are called *alternate interior angles.* Similarly, exterior angles that lie on the same side of the transversal are called *consecutive exterior angles,* and those that lie on opposite sides of the transversal are called *alternate exterior angles.*

An interior angle and an exterior angle that have different vertices and have sides that are on the same side of the transversal are called *corresponding angles.*

PROPERTIES OF PARALLEL LINES

The following are true for parallel lines:

Alternate interior angles are congruent. Conversely, if alternate interior angles are congruent, then the lines are parallel.

Interior angles on the same side of the transversal are supplementary. Conversely, if interior angles on the same side of the transversal are supplementary, then the lines are parallel.

Corresponding angles are congruent. Conversely, if corresponding angles are congruent, then the lines are parallel.

PROPERTIES OF PERPENDICULAR LINES

If two lines are perpendicular, the four angles they form are all right angles.

If two lines are perpendicular to a third line, the lines are parallel.

If one of two parallel lines is perpendicular to a third line, so is the other line.

COORDINATE GEOMETRY

The rectangular coordinate system is used as a basis for coordinate geometry. In this system, two perpendicular lines form a plane. The perpendicular lines are called the *x-axis* and the *y-axis*. The coordinate system assigns an *ordered pair of numbers* (x, y) to each point in the plane. The point of intersection of the two axes is called the origin, O, and has coordinates (0, 0).

As shown in the figure below, the x-axis has positive integers to the right and negative integers to the left of the origin. Similarly, the y-axis has positive integers above and negative integers below the origin.

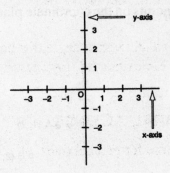

The distance between any two points in the coordinate plane can be found by using the *distance formula*. According to the distance formula, if P_1 and P_2 are two points with coordinates (x_1, y_1) and (x_2, y_2) respectively, then the distance between P_1 and P_2 is given by

$$P_1 P_2 = \sqrt{(x_2 - x_1)^2 + (y_2 - y_1)^2}$$

Problem

Compute the distance between the points *A* and *B* with coordinates (1, 1) and (4, 5) respectively.

Solution

Using the distance formula,

$$AB = \sqrt{(4-1)^2 + (5-1)^2}$$
$$= \sqrt{3^2 + 4^2}$$
$$= \sqrt{9 + 16}$$
$$= 5$$

GRAPHS

To *plot a point* on a graph, first plot the *x*-coordinate, then plot the *y*-coordinate from the given ordered pair.

Problem

Plot the following points on the coordinate plane: *A* (1, 2), *B* (2, 1), *C* (–2, –1).

Solution

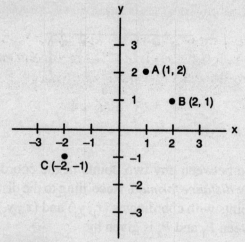

THE METRIC SYSTEM

The *metric system of measurement* is closely related to the base 10 place value scheme. The prefixes commonly used in the metric system are:

Prefix	Meaning
kilo–	thousand (1,000)
deci–	tenth (0.1)
centi–	hundredth (0.01)
milli–	thousandth (0.001)

The basic unit of linear measure in the metric system is the *meter,* represented by m. The relationship among the commonly used linear units of measurement in the metric system is as follows:

1 kilometer (km)	=	1,000 m
1 meter (m)	=	1.0 m
1 decimeter (dm)	=	0.1 m
1 centimeter (cm)	=	0.01 m
1 millimeter (mm)	=	0.001 m

The basic unit of measurement for mass (or weight) in the metric system is the *gram,* represented by g. The relationship among the commonly used units of measurement for mass in the metric system is as follows:

1 kilogram (kg)	=	1,000 g
1 gram(g)	=	1.0 g
1 milligram (mg)	=	0.001 g

The basic unit of measurement for capacity (or volume) in the metric system is the liter, represented by L or l. The most commonly used relationship between two metric units of capacity is

1 liter (l)	=	1,000 ml.

SCIENCE REVIEW

This review contains a concise summary of the areas you can expect to be covered in the Science section of the LAST. Remember, the LAST focuses primarily on the *processes* involved in the sciences. Therefore, factual recall is less important than a general understanding of the material when taking the LAST.

GENERAL SCIENCE

General Science, as its name implies, is a broad survey of the most important concepts from the three basic fields of science: life science, physical science, and Earth science. This review is not meant to be a textbook or comprehensive study of any given topic; rather, its purpose is to remind readers of topics and concepts that are normally taught in science courses in high school science classes.

Each of the basic science fields contains major specializations, viz.:

Life science—biology, ecology, human health

Physical science—measurement, chemistry, physics

Earth science—astronomy, geology, meteorology, oceanography

LIFE SCIENCE

BIOLOGY

Biology is the study of living things. Living things are differentiated from nonliving things by the ability to perform a particular group of life activities at some point in a normal life span. These activities are summarized in the table that follows.

Life Activity	Function
food getting	procurement of food through eating, absorption, or photosynthesis
respiration	exchange of gases
excretion	elimination of wastes
growth and repair	increase in size over part or all of a life span, repair of damaged tissue
movement	willful movement of a portion of a living thing's body, or direction of growth in a particular direction
response	reaction to events or things in the environment
secretion	production and distribution of chemicals that aid digestion, growth, metabolism, etc.
reproduction	the making of new living things similar to the parent organism(s)

It is important to note that living things *must*, during a typical life span, be able to perform all these activities. It is quite common for nonliving things to perform one or more of these activities (for example: robots—movement, response, repair; crystals—growth).

Cells

Cells are the basic structure unit of living things. A cell is the smallest portion of a living thing that can, by itself, be considered living. Plant cells and animal cells, though generally similar, are distinctly different because of the unique plant structures, cell walls, and chloroplasts.

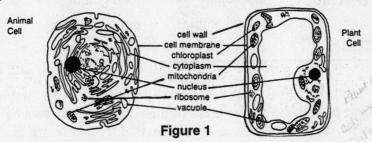

Figure 1

Cells are made of several smaller structures, called organelles, which are surrounded by cell fluid, or cytoplasm. The function of several cell structures, including organelles, is listed on the following page.

Cell Structure	Function
cell membrane	controls movement of materials into and out of cells
cell wall	gives rigid structure to plant cells
chloroplast	contains chlorophyll, which enables green plants to make their own food
cytoplasm	jellylike substance inside a cell; comprises the cytosol and organelles but not the nucleus
mitochondria	liberate energy from glucose in cells for use in cellular activities
nucleus	directs cell activities; holds DNA (genetic material)
ribosome	makes proteins from amino acids
vacuole	stores materials in a cell

There are several processes cells perform to maintain essential life activities. Several of these processes, related to cell metabolism, are described below. Metabolism is the sum of chemical processes in living things.

Process	Organelle	Life Activity
diffusion	cell membrane	food getting, respiration, excretion
osmosis	cell membrane	food getting, excretion
phagocytosis	cell membrane	food getting
photosynthesis	chloroplasts	food getting
respiration (aerobic)	mitochondria	provides energy
fermentation	mitochondria	provides energy

Cells need to move materials into their structures to get energy and to grow. The cell membrane allows certain small molecules to flow freely across it. This flow of chemicals from areas of high concentration to areas of low concentration is called diffusion. Osmosis is diffusion of water across a semipermeable membrane. Particles too large to be passed through the cell membrane may be engulfed by the cell membrane and stored in vacuoles until they can be digested. This engulfing process is called phagocytosis.

All cells need energy to survive. Sunlight energy can be made biologically available by converting to chemical energy during photosynthesis. Photosynthesis is carried out in the chloroplasts of green cells. Chlorophyll, the pigment found in chloroplasts, catalyzes (causes or accelerates) the photosynthesis reaction that turns carbon dioxide and water into glucose (sugar) and oxygen.

$$6CO_2 + 6H_2O \xrightarrow[\text{chlorophyll}]{\text{sunlight}} C_6H_{12}O_6 + 6O_2$$

(handwritten annotations: carbon dioxide, water, glucose, oxygen)

Sunlight and chlorophyll are needed for the reaction to occur. Chlorophyll, because it is a catalyst, is not consumed in the reaction and may be used repeatedly.

The term "respiration" has two distinct meanings in the field of biology. Respiration, the life activity, is the exchange of gases in living things. Respiration, the metabolic process, is the release of energy from sugars for use in life activities. Respiration, the metabolic process, occurs on the cellular level only. Respiration, the life activity, may occur at the cell, tissue, organ, or system level, depending on the complexity of the organism involved.

All living things get their energy from the digestion (respiration) of glucose (sugar). Respiration may occur with oxygen (aerobic respiration) or without oxygen (anaerobic respiration or fermentation). When respiration is referred to, it generally means aerobic respiration.

aerobic respiration: $C_6H_{12}O_6 + 6O_2 \rightarrow 6CO_2 + 6H_2O + \text{energy}$

(handwritten annotation: anaerobic respiration)

fermentation: $C_6H_{12}O_6 \rightarrow CO_2 + \text{alcohol} + \text{energy}$

Aerobic respiration occurs in most plant and animal cells. Fermentation occurs in yeast cells and other cells in the absence of oxygen. Fermentation by yeast produces the alcohol in alcoholic beverages and the gases that make yeast-raised breads light and fluffy.

Classification

All known living things are grouped in categories according to shared physical traits. The process of grouping organisms is called classification. Carl Linné, also known as Linnaeus, devised the classification system used in biology today. In the Linnaeus system, all organisms are given a two-word name (binomial). The name given consists of a genus (ex. Canis) and a species (ex. lupus) designation. Genus designations are always capitalized and occur first in the binomial. Species designations usually start with a lowercase letter and occur second. Binomials are usually underlined or italicized, ex. *Genus species,* or *Homo sapiens,* or *Canis lupus.*

There exists just one binomial for each organism throughout the scientific community. Similar genera of organisms are grouped into families. Families are grouped into orders, orders are grouped into classes, classes are grouped into phyla, and phyla are grouped into kingdoms. The seven basic levels of classification, listed from the largest groupings to the smallest, are: kingdom, phylum, class, order, family, genus, species.

Most biologists recognize five biological kingdoms today, the Animals, Plants, Fungi, Protists, and Monerans. Most living things are classified as plants or animals.

Monerans (ex. bacteria, blue-green algae) are the simplest life forms known. They consist of single-celled organisms without a membrane-bound cell nucleus. Blue-green algae make their own food by photosynthesis; bacteria are consumers or parasites.

Protists (ex. protozoa, single-celled algae) are single-celled organisms having cell nuclei. Protozoa (ex. amoeba, paramecia) are predators or decomposers. Algae (ex. Euglena, diatoms) are producers and utilize photo-synthesis.

Fungi (ex. molds, mushrooms, yeast) are many-celled decomposers that reproduce through spores. Yeast constitute an exception to the multicellular makeup of most fungi, in that they are single-celled and reproduce through budding.

Plants

Plants are multicellular organisms that make their own food through photosynthesis. Plants are divided into two phyla, the Bryophyta and Tracheophyta. Bryophytes are nonvascular plants. They lack true roots and woody tissues. Bryophyta (ex. moss, liverworts, and multicellular algae) live in water or in damp areas and reproduce by spores. Bryophytes do not grow very tall because they lack the structural support of vascular tissue.

Tracheophytes are vascular plants. They have woody tissues and roots. The woody tissues in vascular plants enable them to grow quite large. The roots of vascular plants enable them to find water even in soils that are dry at the surface.

Tracheophytes are divided into three classes, Filicinae, Gymnospermae, and Angiospermae. Filicinae are ferns. They reproduce by spores. Gymno-sperms (ex. spruce, pines) are plants whose seeds form in cones. The seeds are unprotected. Angiosperms (ex. apple trees, grass) are plants whose seeds are protected by fruits or other structures. Angiosperms are further divided into monocots or dicots, based on seed structure. Cotyledons are food storage structures in seed embryos. Monocots (ex. grasses, bananas) have one cotyledon per seed. Dicots (ex. oak trees, pumpkins) have two cotyledons per seed.

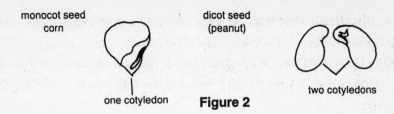

monocot seed
corn

dicot seed
(peanut)

one cotyledon

two cotyledons

Figure 2

Animals

Animals are multicellular organisms that cannot make their own food but can move themselves about. The animal kingdom is divided into 26 phyla. Some of the phyla most important to humans are listed below.

Phyla	Examples	Traits
Porifera	sponges	no organs, pores in body let water flow through, bringing food and taking away wastes
Coelenterata (Cridaria)	jellyfish, corals, hydra	no organs, body sac-like, stinging cells to capture prey
Platyhelminthes	flatworms, flukes, tapeworms	single opening to body, true organs, often parasitic to humans
Aschelminthes (Nematoda)	roundworms	two openings to body, may be parasitic
Mollusca	snails, octopus, clams	gills, open circulatory system, produce shells (internal or external)
Annelida	earthworms, leeches	closed circulatory system
Arthropoda	spiders, insects, crabs	jointed exoskeletons, jointed legs
Echinodermata	starfish, sea urchins	plate-like internal skeleton, tube feet, spiny or knobby surface
Chordata	fish, birds, mammals, reptiles	some form of spine (bone or cartilage, hollow dorsal nerve cord

The arthropod and chordata phyla deserve special note. The arthropods include ten classes, three of which are very important to humans: the arachnidae, insecta, and crustaceae. Arachnids include spiders and ticks.

These animals have two body regions and eight legs. Insects have three body regions and six legs. They include an incredible variety of animals, including grasshoppers, flies, beetles, and butterflies. Crustaceans have two body regions and ten legs and live mostly in water. Crabs, crayfish, and lobsters are all crustaceans.

The chordate phylum has three subphyla, one of which is the vertebrata, or vertebrates. Vertebrates have an internal skeleton which includes a spine made up of vertebrae. The spine protects the dorsal nerve cord (spinal cord). Animals without spines (ex. all phyla except Chordata) are called invertebrates.

Vertebrates

Eight classes of vertebrates exist, though four are often spoken of collectively as "fish."

	Class	Traits	Examples
F	Agnatha	jawless fish, no scales, cartilaginous skeleton	lampreys, hagfish
I	Placodermi	hinged jaws	extinct
S	Chondrichthyes	cartilaginous skeleton, no scales, jaws	sharks, skates, rays
H	Osteichthyes	bony skeleton, scales, jaws	bass, trout, goldfish
	Amphibia	aquatic eggs and larvae, terrestrial adults	frogs, toads, salamanders
	Reptilia	terrestrial eggs and adults, cold-blooded	turtles, snakes, lizards
	Aves	feathers, warm-blooded, external egg development	eagles, ducks, pigeons
	Mammalia	fur, milk-producing, internal egg development, warm-blooded	rats, horses, humans

Most vertebrates are cold-blooded. Their bodies do not generate heat, so their body temperature is determined by their environment. Fish are cold-blooded animals with gills for respiration and fins for limbs. Reptiles are cold-blooded animals with lungs for respiration and legs for limbs (except for snakes). Amphibians are cold-blooded animals that start life with gills and fins, but then change. The change in form that amphibians undergo as they mature is called metamorphosis. Adult amphibians have lungs and legs.

Birds (Aves) and mammals are warm-blooded. Their bodies generate heat. Birds and mammals can also sweat to lower body temperature. Birds are covered with feathers and have eggs that develop outside the mother's body. Mammals are covered with fur and have eggs that develop within the mother's body.

Mammals are divided into seventeen orders, based on body structure. Some of the more familiar orders are listed below.

Order	Examples	Traits
Marsupials	kangaroos, opossums	pouches in mothers for carrying young
Rodents	mice, rats, beavers, squirrels	gnawing teeth
Carnivores	dogs, bears, cats, skunks	meat eaters
Cetaceans	whales, dolphins, porpoises	aquatic, flippers for limbs
Primates	monkeys, apes, humans	opposable thumbs, erect posture, highly developed brains
Ungulates (2 orders)	horses, camels, buffaloes	grass chewers

Viruses

Viruses are organic particles that are capable of causing diseases in living things, such as smallpox, rabies, and influenza. Viruses are sometimes classified as living things because they contain genetic material and create offspring similar to themselves. Viruses are often not classified as living things because they have no ability to synthesize or process food, and cannot reproduce without the help of other organisms. Viruses are parasitic. Their basic structure is a protein shell surrounding a nucleic acid core.

ECOLOGY

Ecology is the study of the relationship between living things and their environment. An environment is all the living and nonliving things surrounding an organism.

POPULATIONS AND COMMUNITIES

A population is a group of similar organisms, like a herd of deer. A community is a group of populations that interact with one another. A pond community, for example, is made up of all the plants and animals in the pond. An ecosystem is a group of populations which share a common pool of resources and a common physical/geographical area. A beech-oak-hickory forest ecosystem, for example, is made up of populations in the forest canopy, on the forest floor, and in the forest soil.

Each population lives in a particular area and serves a special role in the community. This combination of defined role and living areas is the concept of niche. The niche of a pond snail, for example, is to decompose materials in ponds. The niche of a field mouse is to eat seeds in fields. When two populations try to fill the same niche, competition occurs. If one population replaces another in a niche, succession occurs. Succession is the orderly and predictable change of communities as a result of population replacement in niches.

A climax community is a community in which succession no longer occurs. Climax communities are stable until catastrophic changes, such as forest fires, hurricanes, or human clearing of land occurs. Each ecosystem type is defined by its climax communities—for example, beech-oak-hickory forests in the American Northeast or prairies in the American Midwest.

Food and Energy

Energy enters ecosystems through sunlight. Green plants turn this energy into food in the process of photosynthesis. Organisms that make their own food are called producers. Some animals get their food from eating plants or other animals. Animals that get their food energy from other living things are called consumers. Consumers that eat plants are herbivores; those that eat animals are carnivores; those that eat plants and animals are called omnivores. Animals that eat other organisms are called predators; the organisms that get eaten are called prey. Organisms that get their food energy from dead plants or animals are called decomposers.

As energy moves from one organism to another, it creates a pattern of energy transfer known as a food web.

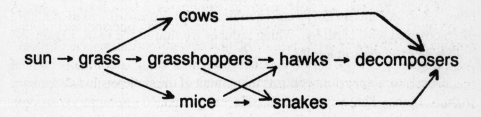

Figure 3

Arrows represent energy transfer in a food web. At each energy transfer (arrow) some energy is lost. Energy is lost because organisms use energy to grow, move, and live.

Many nutrients, such as nitrogen and phosphorous, are routinely cycled through the bodies of living things. These nutrient cycles are disrupted when humans remove parts of the ecosystem or add excess materials to an ecosystem.

Pollution is any material added to an ecosystem that disrupts its normal functioning. Typical pollutants are excess fertilizers and industrial emissions. Conservation is the practice of using natural areas without disrupting their ecosystems. Conservationists try to limit the amounts of pollution entering ecosystems.

HUMAN HEALTH

The Human Body

A human is a very complex organism. This complexity requires individual cells to become specialized at certain tasks. Groups of specialized cells form tissues, such as muscles, skin, or blood. Tissues are specialized to perform specific tasks. Groups of tissues form organs, such as the heart, kidney, or brain. Systems are groups of organs working together to perform the basic activities of life, such as excretion or reproduction. The human body is made up of several systems.

The skeleton supports the body and gives it shape. The skeletal system is composed of bones, cartilage, and ligaments. The human body contains 206 bones. The areas where two or more bones touch one another are called joints. Five types of joints exist in the human body; fixed joints (skull bones), hinge joints (elbow or knee), pivot joints (neck bones), sliding joints (wrist bones), and ball and socket joints (shoulder or hip). Bone surfaces in joints are often covered with cartilage, which reduces friction in the joint. Ligaments hold bones together in a joint.

The muscular system controls movement of the skeleton and movement within organs. Three types of muscle exist: striated (voluntary), smooth (involuntary), and cardiac. Cardiac muscle is found only in the heart and is involuntary. Smooth muscle is found in organs and cannot be consciously controlled. Striated muscle is attached to a skeleton and its actions can be controlled at will, or voluntarily. Tendons attach muscles to bone. Muscles perform work by contracting. Skeletal muscles work in pairs. The alternate contraction of muscles within a pair causes movement in joints.

The digestive system receives and processes food. The digestive system includes the mouth, stomach, large intestine, and small intestine. Food is physically broken down by mastication, or chewing. Food is chemically broken down in the stomach, where digestive enzymes further break the food down into simple chemicals. The small intestine absorbs nutrients from food. The large intestine absorbs water from solid food waste.

The excretory system eliminates wastes from the body. Excretory organs include the lungs, kidneys, bladder, large intestine, rectum, and the skin. The lungs excrete gaseous waste. The kidneys filter blood and excrete wastes, mostly in the form of urea. The bladder holds liquid wastes until they can be eliminated via the urethra. The large intestine absorbs water from solid food waste, and the rectum stores solid waste until it can be eliminated. The skin excretes waste through perspiration.

The circulatory system is responsible for internal transport in the body. It is composed of the heart, blood vessels, lymph vessels, blood, and lymph. The heart is a muscular four-chambered pump. The upper chambers are called atria and the lower chambers are called ventricles. Blood flows from the body to the (1) right atrium, to the (2) right ventricle, to the lungs, then to the (3) left atrium, to the (4) left ventricle, and back to the body.

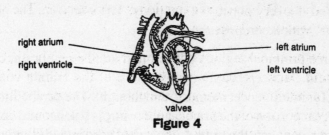

right atrium
right ventricle

left atrium
left ventricle

valves

Figure 4

The heart chambers contract to expel the blood they contain. Blood flows in one direction through the heart because of valves within the heart and blood vessels. The closing of valves during heart contractions creates an audible heartbeat. An adult human heart normally contracts 60–80 times per minute.

There are three types of blood vessels: arteries, veins, and capillaries. Arteries have thick, muscular walls and carry oxygenated blood away from the heart. Veins have thin walls and carry de-oxygenated blood to the heart. Capillaries have extremely thin walls and connect arteries to veins.

Blood is always under pressure in the arteries. Blood pressure increases when the heart is contracting. Blood pressure during heart contractions is systolic pressure. Blood pressure during heart relaxation is diastolic pressure. Human blood pressure is always reported as a ratio of systolic pressure/ diastolic pressure. Typical blood pressure for adults is 140 mm Hg/90 mm Hg. Pressures ranging far above or below these values indicate illness.

The fluid portion of blood is called plasma. The solid material in blood includes red blood cells, white blood cells, and platelets. Red blood cells carry oxygen to cells and carry carbon dioxide away from cells. White blood cells fight infections and produce antibodies. Platelets cause the formation of clots.

The lymphatic system drains fluid from tissues. Lymph nodes filter impurities in the lymph fluid, and often become swollen during infections.

The respiratory system exchanges oxygen for carbon dioxide. The respiratory system is composed of the nose, trachea, bronchi, lungs, and diaphragm. Air travels from the nose through the trachea and bronchi into the lungs. The air is drawn in by the contraction of the diaphragm, a muscle running across the body below the lungs. Gas exchange occurs in the lungs across air sacks called alveoli. Air is then pushed back toward the nose by relaxation of the diaphragm.

The nervous system controls the actions and processes of the body. The nervous system includes the brain, spinal cord, and nerves. Electrical impulses carry messages to and from the brain across the spinal cord and nerves.

Nerves extend to every portion of the body. The spinal cord is protected by the vertebrae, which compose the spine.

The three principal regions of the brain are the cerebrum, cerebellum, and brain stem. The cerebrum occupies 80% of the brain's volume and is responsible for intelligence, memory, and thought. The cerebellum is located at the lower rear portion of the brain, and it controls balance and coordination. The brain stem connects the brain to the spinal cord and is found at the lower central portion of the brain. The brain stem controls autonomic (involuntary) body functions and regulates hormones.

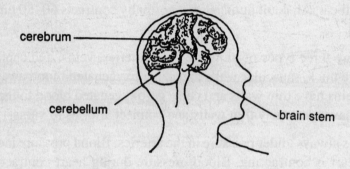

Figure 5

The endocrine system controls activities in the body through chemical agents called hormones. Hormones are produced in glands throughout the body and are excreted into the bloodstream. The brain controls production and release of hormones.

Listed below are several major endocrine glands and the most important hormones they produce.

Gland	Hormone	Action
hypothalamus	oxytocin	stimulates labor in childbirth and production of milk in females
pituitary	growth hormone	stimulates growth
thyroid	thyroxin	controls rate of cellular respiration
parathyroid	parathormone	controls amount of calcium in the blood
thymus	thymosin	helps to fight infections
adrenals	adrenalin	helps during stress and shock, activates flight-or-fight response

Gland	Hormone	Action
pancreas	insulin	regulates blood sugar
ovaries (female)	estrogen, progesterone	controls female maturing process, maintains pregnancy
testes (male)	testosterone	controls male maturing process

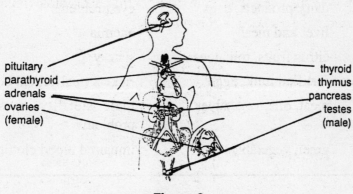

pituitary
parathyroid
adrenals
ovaries
(female)

thyroid
thymus
pancreas
testes
(male)

Figure 6

The reproductive system produces eggs and sperm which can combine to create an embryo. The female reproductive system includes the ovaries, fallopian tubes, uterus, and vagina. Each month, one egg is released from the ovaries and then travels down the fallopian tubes. If it is fertilized, it becomes implanted in the lining of the uterus, where a baby begins to form. When sufficiently grown, the baby leaves the uterus and its mother's body through the vagina, or birth canal.

The male reproductive system consists of the testicles, vas deferens, urethra, and penis. Sperm are produced in the testicles. They move through the vas deferens from the testicles to the urethra. During intercourse, sperm pass through the penis (via the urethra) and into a woman's body. In a woman's body, sperm pass through the cervix into the uterus and up the fallopian tubes, where fertilization of an egg may take place.

Nutrition

Nutrition is the study of how living things utilize food substances. Food provides energy and raw materials for growth, repair, and metabolism. Energy (calories) is derived chiefly from carbohydrates, but also from fats and proteins. Raw materials for life processes come chiefly from protein, but also from carbohydrates (starches and sugars), fats, minerals, and vitamins. Fiber in the diet helps in elimination of wastes.

Listed below are several vitamins important to human health.

Vitamin	Principal Source	Deficiency Symptom(s)
A	green and yellow vegetables	night blindness, dry, brittle skin
B_1	cereals, yeast	beriberi (muscular atrophy and paralysis)
B_2	dairy products, eggs	eye problems
B_{12}	liver and meat	anemia
C	citrus fruits, tomatoes	scurvy
D	fortified milk, eggs	rickets (malformed bones)
E	meat, oils, vegetables	male sterility, muscular problems
K	green vegetables	impaired blood clotting

Foods can be placed in one of four basic food groups. These groups are listed below, in order of their need by the body.

Food Group	Importance	Examples
Grains and Cereals	starch (for energy), protein, fiber	bread, pasta
Fruits and Vegetables	fiber, minerals, vitamins	apples, carrots
Dairy	fats, calcium, protein	milk, cheese
Meat, Fish, and Eggs	protein	steak, trout

Human Genetics

Each of the cells in a living thing has a specific structure and role in the organism. The structure of a cell and its function are determined, to a large degree, by the genes within a cell. Genes are code units of chromosomes within the nucleus of a cell. Genes give information about the structure and function of a cell.

Cells age and die. Organisms continue to live despite the death of individual cells because cells reproduce. Mitosis is the process of cell reproduction through cell division; one cell divides to become two new cells. During mitosis, the genetic material (genes) in the parent cell is copied so each of the offspring gets the same instructions (genes). The passing of genetic material from one generation to the next is called inheritance. The study of genetic material and inheritance is called genetics.

Most cells in the human body have 46 chromosomes. Some special cells, called eggs and sperm, have only 23 chromosomes. Egg and sperm cells get 23 chromosomes through meiosis, a process of cell division that reduces the number of chromosomes in a cell. Most cells in the human body reproduce quite often. Egg and sperm cells (sex cells) cannot reproduce until they join with another sex cell. The process of an egg and sperm cell joining is called fertilization.

A fertilized human sex cell has 46 chromosomes, 23 from the mother and 23 from the father. This fertilized sex cell will multiply to form a new organism. The genes of the new organism are a mixture of genes from both parents, so the new organism will be unique from each parent. The process of combining genetic materials from two parent organisms to form a unique offspring is called sexual reproduction.

During sexual reproduction an organism receives two genes for each trait, one from each parent. Sometimes one trait will mask another, as is the case with eye color. If a person has one gene for brown eyes and one gene for blue eyes, the person will always have brown eyes. A genetic trait that masks another, like the gene for brown eyes, is called a dominant trait. A gene that can be masked, like the gene for blue eyes, is called a recessive trait.

Understanding dominance helps us to figure out the genetic configuration of an individual. An individual with blue eyes must have two genes for blue eyes, since it is a recessive trait. Recessive traits are shown by lowercase letters, so the genetic symbol for blue eyes is "bb." An individual with brown eyes must have at least one gene for brown eyes, which is dominant. Dominant genes are shown by uppercase letters, so the genetic symbol for brown eyes could be "Bb" or "BB."

An individual with two different genes (ex. Bb) for a trait is called heterozygous for that trait. An individual with two similar genes (ex. BB or bb) for a trait is called homozygous for that trait.

When the genetic type of parents is known, the probability of the offspring showing particular traits can be predicted using the Punnett Square. A Punnett Square is a large square divided into four small boxes. The genetic symbol of each parent for a particular trait is written alongside the square, one parent along the top and one parent along the left side.

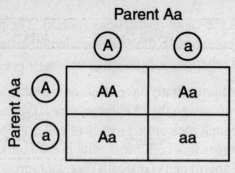

Figure 7

Each gene symbol is written in both boxes below or to the right of it. This results in each box having two gene symbols in it. The genetic symbols in the boxes are all the possible genetic combinations for a particular trait of the offspring of these parents. Each box has a 25% probability of being the actual genetic representation for a given child.

The genetic symbol "AA" in the example has a 25% probability of occurring. If a genetic symbol occurs in more than one box, the genetic probabilities are added. The genetic code "Aa" in the example has a 50% probability of occurring because it is shown in two boxes of the Punnett Square.

The Punnett Square shows how two parents can have a child with traits different from either parent. Two parents heterozygous for brown eyes (Aa), have a 25% probability of producing a child homozygous for blue eyes (aa), as shown in the example.

Human sex type is determined by genetic material in sperm. The genetic sex code for human females is XX. The genetic sex code for human males is XY. Eggs carry only X genes. Sperm carry X or Y genes. The probability of a fertilized human egg being male, or XY, is 50%.

PHYSICAL SCIENCE

MEASUREMENT

The physical characteristics of an object are determined by measurements. Measured characteristics include mass, volume, length, temperature, time, and area. There are two common measurement systems, English and metric.

Characteristic	English System	Metric System
mass/weight	pound (weight)	kilogram (mass)
volume	quart	liter
length	foot	meter
temperature	°Fahrenheit	°Celsius

The English system, used most often in the United States, does not have a consistent system of conversion factors between units.

Example

1 yard = 3 feet, 1 foot = 12 inches, 1 yard = 36 inches

The metric system, used most often in science, has conversion factors between units based on multiples of 10.

Example

1 kilometer = 1000 meters,
1 meter = 100 centimeters = 1000 millimeters

Prefixes in the metric system indicate the number of multiples of the base units, so it is simple to determine the conversion factors between units.

Prefix	Multiplication Factor	Unit Symbols
kilo	× 1000	km, kg, kl
no prefix (base unit)	× 1	m, g, l
deci	× 0.1	dm, dg, dl
centi	× 0.01	cm, cg, cl
milli	× 0.001	mm, mg, ml

A third measurement system, the Systeme International d' Unités, or SI, is based on the metric system. This system differs from the metric system by using the Kelvin temperature scale. The size of a degree in the Celsius and Kelvin scale are the same, but "0°" is different. 0 Kelvin = – 273°Celsius. 0 Kelvin, also known as absolute zero, is the temperature at which, theoretically, all molecular movement ceases.

To convert from °Celsius to °Fahrenheit, use the following equation:

$$°C = \frac{5}{9}(°F - 32).$$

To convert from °Celsius to Kelvin, use the following equation:

$$°C + 273 = K.$$

CHEMISTRY

MATTER

Matter is everything that has volume and mass. Water is matter because it takes up space; light is not matter because it does not take up space.

States of Matter

Matter exists in three states, as follows:

State	Properties	Example
solid	definite volume, definite shape	ice
liquid	definite volume, no definite shape	water
gas	no definite volume, no definite shape	water vapor or steam

Thermal energy causes molecules or atoms to vibrate. As vibration of particles increases, a material may change to a different state; it may melt or boil. Decreasing energy in a material may cause condensation or freezing. Another name for thermal energy is heat. Temperature is a measure of the average kinetic energy, or vibration, of the particles of a material. For most materials, the boiling point and freezing point are important. The boiling point of water is 100°C, and its freezing point is 0°C.

State Change	Process Name	Heat Change
solid → liquid	melting	heat added
liquid → gas	evaporation or boiling	heat added
gas → liquid	condensation	heat removed
liquid → solid	freezing	heat removed

Structure of Matter

Atoms are the basic building blocks of matter. Atoms are made of three types of subatomic particles, which have mass and charge. Protons and neutrons are found in the nucleus, or solid center of an atom. Electrons are found in the outer portion of an atom. This outer portion is mostly made of empty space. Under most conditions, atoms are indivisible. Atoms may be split or combined to form new atoms during atomic reactions. Atomic reactions occur deep inside the sun, in nuclear power reactors and nuclear bombs, and in radioactive decay.

Subatomic Particle	Mass	Charge	Location
proton	1 amu	+1	nucleus
neutron	1 amu	0	nucleus
electron	0 amu	−1	outside nucleus

Most atoms have equal numbers of protons and electrons, and therefore no net charge. Atoms with unequal numbers of protons and electrons have net positive or negative charges. Charged atoms are called ions. Atomic mass is determined by the number of protons and neutrons in an atom. Atomic mass is expressed in atomic mass units (amu).

A material made of just one type of atom is called an element. Atoms of an element are represented by symbols of one or two letters, such as C or Na. Two or more atoms may combine to form molecules.

Atoms of the same element have the same number of protons in their nucleus. An atom is the smallest particle of an element that retains the characteristics of that element. Each element is assigned an atomic number, which is equal to the number of protons in an atom of that element. The Periodic Table is a chart listing all the elements in order according to their atomic number. The elements are grouped vertically in the Periodic Table according to their chemical properties. The Periodic Table is a reference tool used to summarize the atomic structure, mass, and reactive tendencies of elements.

Molecules are clusters of atoms. Molecules form, decompose, or recombine during chemical reactions. Materials made of one type of molecule are called compounds. Compounds may be represented by formulae using atomic symbols and numbers. The numbers show how many atoms of each type are in the molecules. For example, the symbol for water, H_2O, shows that a molecule of water contains two hydrogen atoms and one oxygen atom. Atomic symbols without subscript numbers represent just one atom in a molecule.

Chemical compounds containing carbon are called organic, because these materials are often made by living things. The chemistry of organic compounds is complex and distinct from that of other compounds. Therefore, organic chemistry is a large and distinct discipline. Compounds without carbon are called inorganic.

Mixtures are materials made of two or more compounds or elements. They can be separated by physical means, such as sifting or evaporation. Liquid or gas mixtures are called suspensions, colloids, or solutions. Suspensions have particles that settle out unless the mixture is stirred. Dust in air is a suspension. Colloids have particles large enough to scatter light, but small enough to remain suspended without stirring. Milk is a colloid; it is opaque because its particles scatter light. Solutions have particles so small, they do not scatter light. They are transparent to light and their particles do not settle out.

A substance that dissolves another to form a solution is called the solvent. Chemicals that are dissolved in solutions are called solutes. In a salt water solution, water is the solvent. Not all chemicals can function as solvents. Some solvents (like gasoline) are able to dissolve only certain solids. Water is sometimes called the "universal solvent" because it is able to dissolve so many chemicals.

Concentration is a measure of how much solute is in a solution. A given amount of solvent is able to dissolve only a limited amount of solute. This amount may be increased if the solution is heated or pressure on the solution is increased. Dilute solutions have relatively little solute in solution. Concentrated solutions have a lot of solute in solution.

Solutions that are able to dissolve more solute are called unsaturated. Solutions that cannot dissolve more solute are called saturated. Solutions that are saturated at high temperature or high pressure may become supersaturated at lower temperatures or pressures. Supersaturated solutions contain more dissolved solute than normally is present in a saturated solution. These solutions are unstable, and solute may crystallize out of the solution easily.

CHEMICAL REACTIONS

Matter may undergo chemical and physical changes. A physical change affects the size, form, or appearance of a material. These changes can include melting, bending, or cracking. Physical changes do not alter the molecular structure of a material. Chemical changes do alter the molecular structure of matter. Examples of chemical changes are burning, rusting, and digestion.

Under the right conditions, compounds may break apart, combine, or recombine to form new compounds. This process is called a chemical reaction. Chemical reactions are described by chemical equations, such as $NaOH + HCl \rightarrow NaCl + H_2O$. In a chemical equation, materials to the left of the arrow are called reactants and materials to the right of the arrow are called products. In a balanced chemical equation, the number of each type of atom is the same on both sides of the arrow.

unbalanced: $H_2 + O_2 \rightarrow H_2O$

balanced: $2H_2 + O_2 \rightarrow 2H_2O$

There are four basic types of chemical reactions: synthesis, decomposition, single replacement, and double replacement. A synthesis reaction is one in which two or more chemicals combine to form a new chemical.

Example

$A + B \rightarrow AB$, or $2H_2 + O_2 \rightarrow 2H_2O$

A decomposition reaction is one in which one chemical breaks down to release two or more chemicals.

Example

$AB \rightarrow A + B$, or $2H_2O \rightarrow 2H_2 + O_2$

A single replacement reaction involves a compound decomposing and one of its constituent chemicals joining another chemical to make a new compound.

Example

$AB + C \rightarrow A + BC$, or $Fe + CuCl_2 \rightarrow FeCl_2 + Cu$

A double replacement reaction is one in which two compounds decompose and their constituents recombine to form two new compounds.

Example

$AB + CD \rightarrow AC + BD$, or $NaOH + HCl \rightarrow NaCl + H_2O$

ACIDS AND BASES

Acid and base are terms used to describe solutions of differing pH. The concentration of hydrogen ions in a solution determines its pH, which is based on a logarithmic scale.

Solutions having pH 0–7 are called acids and have hydrogen ions (H+) present. Common acids include lemon juice, vinegar, and battery acid. Acids are corrosive and taste sour. Solutions pH 7–14 are called bases (or alkaline), and have hydroxide ions (OH⁻) present. Bases are caustic and feel slippery in solution. Common bases include baking soda and lye. Solutions of pH 7 are called neutral and have both ions present in equal but small amounts.

The reaction created when an acid and base combine is a double replacement reaction known as a neutralization reaction. In a neutralization reaction, acid + base → water + salt.

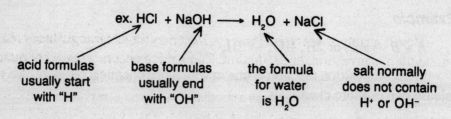

ex. HCl + $NaOH$ ⟶ H_2O + $NaCl$

| acid formulas usually start with "H" | base formulas usually end with "OH" | the formula for water is H_2O | salt normally does not contain H⁺ or OH⁻ |

Figure 8

PHYSICS

MOTION

Moving objects can be measured for speed or momentum. Speed is the distance an object travels per unit of time. Cars measure speed in miles per hour (mph).

$$Speed = \frac{distance}{time}$$

If a car travels 3.5 km in 7 minutes, it has a speed of 3.5 km/7 min, or 0.5 km/min.

Momentum is the tendency of an object to continue in its direction of motion.

Momentum = mass × speed

The heavier a moving object is, or the faster it is moving, the harder it is to stop the object or change its direction.

ENERGY

Energy is the ability to do work. Energy comes in many different forms, ex. heat, light, and sound. All energy can be described as potential or kinetic. Potential energy is stored through chemical structure, position, or physical configuration. Kinetic energy is energy of motion. Light, sound, and heat are kinetic energy, as is the energy possessed by a moving object.

Energy can be transformed from one type to another, but it never is created or destroyed. The potential chemical energy in a peanut butter sandwich is transformed through digestion and metabolism into the kinetic energy of heat and motion. The potential energy of a book sitting on a shelf is turned into the kinetic energy of motion, sound, and heat as the book falls and hits the floor.

Heat is an important type of energy. Heat may travel through three paths: conduction, convection, and radiation. Conduction occurs when a hot material comes in contact with a cold one. Heat moves from a hot material into a cold material until the temperature of both is equal. An example of conduction is the heating of a metal spoon when it is used to stir a cup of hot tea.

Convection is based on a density change caused by heating. As materials, especially gases and liquids, are heated, they become less dense. Warm air, which is less dense, rises, while cold air, which is more dense, sinks. In a room or other enclosed space, this rising and falling of materials of different density creates a current of air (or other heated material). As heat is added to the space, from a source like a stove or sunny window, the current carries the heat through the space.

Radiation is heat that spreads out from a very hot source into the surrounding material. Radiant heat energy is carried by electromagnetic waves, just like the light given off by a hot light bulb filament. Radiant heat energy travels in straight lines in all directions from its source. Sources of radiant heat include wood stoves and light bulbs in homes.

Insulators are materials that slow down or prevent the movement of heat. Air is a good insulator. Most commercial insulation consists of a material with many pockets of air. Conductors are materials which transmit heat well. Metals are excellent heat conductors.

WORK

Work occurs when a force (push or pull) is applied to an object, resulting in movement.

Work = force × distance

The greater the force applied, or the longer the distance traveled, the greater the work done. Work is measured in newton-meters or foot-pounds. One newton-meter equals one joule.

Mass is a measure of the amount of matter in an object. Weight is the gravitational force on an object. Mass is a constant; it never changes with location. Weight varies with the pull of gravity. Objects weigh less on the moon than on Earth. In space, where there is no gravity, objects are weightless (but they still have mass).

Power is work done per unit time.

$$\text{Power} = \frac{\text{work done}}{\text{time interval}}$$

If someone moves an object weighing 5 newtons over a distance of 10 meters in 30 seconds, they use the power of 1.7 watts.

$$\frac{5n \times 10m}{30 \text{ sec}} = 1.7 \text{ n-m/sec, or } 1.7 \text{ watts}$$

1 watt = 1n-m/sec

Machines change the direction or strength of a force. Simple machines are used throughout our lives.

Simple Machine	Examples
inclined plane	ramp, wedge, chisel
screw	threads on bolts, cork screws, jar lids
lever	seesaw, crowbar
wheel and axle	doorknob, bicycle
pulley	fan belt, elevator

In designing machines, 100% efficiency is the goal.

$$\% \text{ efficiency } = \frac{\text{work done}}{\text{energy used}} \times 100$$

100% efficiency can never be achieved, because some energy is always lost through friction or heat production.

WAVE PHENOMENA

Sound and light are wave phenomena. Waves are characterized by wavelength, speed, and frequency. Wavelength is the distance between crests or troughs of waves.

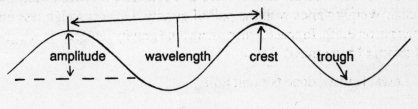

Figure 9

Speed is how fast a wave crest or trough moves. If a wave moves 4 meters in 2 seconds, its

$$\text{speed} = \frac{\text{distance}}{\text{time}} = \frac{4m}{2 \text{ sec}} = 2m/sec.$$

Frequency is the number of crests or troughs that move past a point per second. Frequency is measured in Hertz. One wave moving past a point per second equals one Hertz.

$$\text{Frequency} = \frac{\text{speed}}{\text{wavelength}}$$

Sound is caused by the vibration of objects. This vibration creates waves of disturbance that can travel through air and most other materials. If these sound waves hit your eardrum, you perceive sound.

Sound is characterized by its pitch, loudness, intensity, and speed. Pitch is related to frequency. High pitches (ex. high music notes) have high frequencies. Loudness is related to wave amplitude. Loud sounds have big amplitudes. Sound intensity is measured in decibels. Intensity is related to amplitude and frequency of sound waves. Loud, high-pitched music has a much greater intensity than quiet, low-pitched music.

The speed of sound waves is related to their medium. Sound travels more quickly through more dense materials (solids, liquids) than less dense materials (gases). Sound does not travel through a vacuum.

Light is a type of electromagnetic wave. The chief types of electromagnetic waves, listed according to their relative frequency and wavelength, are shown below.

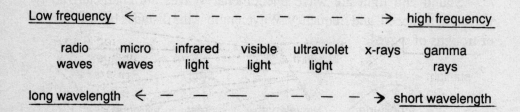

Low frequency $\leftarrow$ – – – – – – – – – – $\rightarrow$ high frequency

| radio waves | micro waves | infrared light | visible light | ultraviolet light | x-rays | gamma rays |

long wavelength $\leftarrow$ – – — — – – — — $\rightarrow$ short wavelength

Figure 10

Light travels much more quickly (300,000 km/sec) than sound does (330 m/sec). It can pass through a vacuum. As light passes through a material, it travels in a straight path. When light moves from one material to another, it may be transmitted, absorbed, reflected, or refracted.

Transparent materials (ex. water, glass) allow light to pass directly through them. This passing through is called transmission. Opaque objects (ex. wood) absorb light. No light comes out of them. Mirrors reflect light. They re-emit light into the medium it came from. Light rays going into a mirror are called incident rays. Light rays going out of a mirror are called reflected rays.

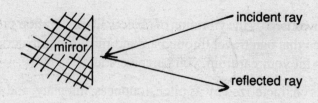

Figure 11

Refraction is the bending of light. Light may be refracted when it moves from one material to another (ex. air → water). Mirages are formed when light refracts while moving from cool air to warm air.

Sometimes, during refraction, sunlight is broken into the colors that form it, causing a spectrum. The colors in a spectrum are red, orange, yellow, green, blue, indigo, and violet. A rainbow is a spectrum caused when light passes from dry air into very humid air.

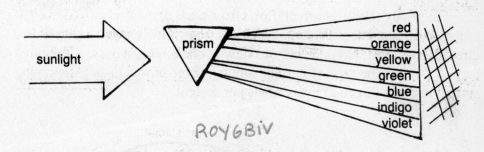

ROYGBIV

Figure 12

Lenses are transparent materials used to refract light. The shape of a lens determines how light passing through it will be bent.

BASIC ELECTRICITY

All matter is made of atoms. All atoms contain positively charged particles, called protons, and negatively charged particles, called electrons. Protons are tightly bound to atoms and cannot move much. Electrons are loosely attached to atoms, and may leave one atom to join another.

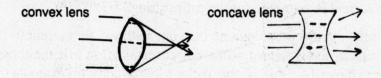

Figure 13

Atoms may carry electrical charges. A neutral atom has equal numbers of protons and electrons in it. The charges of the protons and electrons cancel each other, so the atom has no net charge. If an atom has more electrons than protons, the extra electrons give the atom a negative charge. If an atom has less electrons than protons, the missing electrons leave the atom with a positive charge.

Electrons may not be destroyed. If two objects are rubbed together, however, electrons may move from one object to another, leaving both charged. Electrons may also flow through certain materials. The flow of electrons produces an electric current. Conductors are materials that let electrons flow freely (ex. metals, water). Insulators are materials that do not let electrons flow freely (ex. glass, rubber, air).

Electricity (electric current) flows from areas of many electrons to areas of few electrons. The path along which electrons flow is called a circuit. In a direct current (DC) circuit, electrons flow in one direction only. Alternating current (AC) is the type of current supplied over power lines. Alternating current changes direction many times per second.

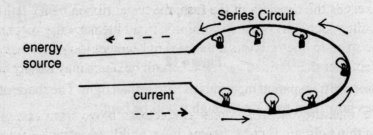

Figure 14

Circuits may be described as being in series or in parallel. Series circuits are made of a single pathway, through which all current must flow. If any part of a series circuit breaks, the circuit is "opened," and the flow of the current must stop. Some sets of Christmas tree lights are designed in series. If one bulb in the string of lights burns out, none of the lights in the string will work, because current is disrupted for the entire string.

Parallel circuits provide more than one pathway for current to flow. If one of the pathways is opened, so that current cannot flow in it, the current will continue to move through the other paths. Most circuits, for example those in our homes, are wired in parallel, so that burned out light bulbs and turned off television sets do not disrupt electricity used in other parts of our homes.

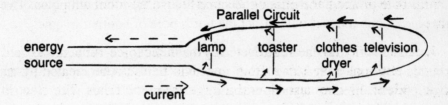

Figure 15

Fuses and circuit breakers are safety devices that limit the current flow in a circuit. Wires (lines) are limited in the amount of current they can safely carry. If too much current passes through them, they may heat up and melt or cause a fire. Current passing through lines increases with each appliance added to the circuit.

Fuses work by passing current through a thin metal ribbon. When the current exceeds the capacity of the fuse, the metal ribbon melts, leaving an open circuit, which cannot carry current. Circuit breakers use magnets and bimetallic strips to open circuits if the current becomes too great. Fuses must be replaced after they "blow," or melt. Circuit breakers may simply be reset to be used again.

Volts measure the work done as electrons move from one point to another within a circuit. Battery "strength," or ability to do work, is measured by volts. Amperes measure the current, or flow of charge through a circuit. Ohms measure the resistance to the flow of electrons.

Volts = amperes × ohms

Watts measure electrical power consumption. Electrical appliances and light bulbs are rated by their wattages so consumers can compare power consumption before purchasing these products. One watt equals one joule per second of power (one newton-meter per second). One watt of energy can lift an object weighing one newton over one meter in one second. A kilowatt-hour is the amount of energy used in one hour by one kilowatt of power.

Power = current × voltage, or 1 watt = 1 ampere × 1 volt

MAGNETISM

Magnets are solids that attract iron. Naturally occurring magnets are called lodestones. Magnetic forces make magnets attract or repel each other. Magnetic forces are created by regions in magnets called magnetic poles. All magnets have a north and a south pole. The north pole of one magnet will repel the north pole of another magnet; the same holds true for south poles. The south pole of one magnet will attract the north pole of another magnet.

A magnetic field is the area affected by magnetic force. A magnetic field surrounds both poles of a magnet. A magnetic field can be created by an electric current. Electromagnets create large magnetic fields with electric current. Similarly, if a wire is moved through a magnetic field, a current is produced. Electric generators make electricity by passing wires through a magnetic field.

The Earth has a magnetic field. Compasses are magnets that align themselves with Earth's magnetic field.

EARTH SCIENCE

Earth science is the study of the Earth and its parts. Earth science has many subgroups, including, but not limited to, astronomy, geology, meteorology, and oceanography.

ASTRONOMY

Astronomy is the study of celestial bodies and their movements.

The Earth is one of nine planets in our solar system. A solar system is composed of a star and the objects that move about it. The largest objects moving about a star are called planets. The planets in our solar system, beginning at the sun and moving away from it, are Mercury, Venus, Earth, Mars, Jupiter, Saturn, Uranus, Neptune, and Pluto.

Many objects smaller than planets exist in our solar system. If one of these smaller objects collides with Earth, it is called a meteor or "shooting star." The glow of a meteor is caused by its burning as it passes through our atmosphere. Meteors that reach the Earth's surface are called meteorites.

Earth's path around the sun is called its orbit. Earth's orbit around the sun, called a revolution, is completed in $364\frac{1}{4}$ days. An axis is an imaginary line passing through the poles of the Earth. The Earth spins on its axis, and each spin is called a rotation. One rotation takes 24 hours. Rotation causes the alternation of day and night on Earth.

The Earth revolves about the sun. Its axis is tilted $23\frac{1}{2}°$ from perpendicular to the plane of Earth's orbit. This tilt results in differing proportions of day and night on Earth throughout the year, and also causes the seasons. Day and night are of equal length only twice each year, at the autumnal equinox and vernal equinox (the first day of autumn and the first day of spring).

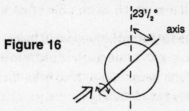

Figure 16

The moon is a satellite of Earth. It moves in orbit about Earth, and one revolution takes $27\frac{1}{3}$ days. The moon reflects sunlight, which causes it to glow. When the Earth blocks sunlight from reaching the moon, it creates a shadow on the moon's surface, known as a lunar eclipse. If the moon blocks sunlight from hitting the Earth, a solar eclipse is created. The moon has a gravitational pull on the Earth which causes tides, or periodic changes in depth of the ocean.

GEOLOGY

Geology is the study of the structure and composition of the Earth.

The Earth is composed of three layers, the crust, mantle, and core. The core is the center of the Earth, and is made of solid iron and nickel. It is about 7,000 km in diameter. The mantle is the semi-molten layer between crust and core, and is about 3,000 km thick. The crust is the solid outermost layer of the Earth, ranging from 5–40 km thick. It is composed of bedrock overlaid with mineral and/or organic sediment (soil).

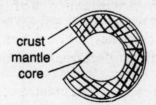

Figure 17

Large sections of Earth's crust, called plates, move at times, creating earthquakes, volcanoes, faults, and mountains. The study of these movements is called plate tectonics. Faults are cracks in the crust formed when plates move. Faults gape open when plates move apart and are closed when plates slide past one another. Earthquakes occur when plates slide past one another quickly. Earthquakes may also be caused by volcanoes. Earthquakes are measured by a seismograph on the Richter scale.

Volcanoes form where plates move away from one another to let magma reach the crust's surface. Magma is molten rock beneath the Earth's crust.

Lava is molten rock on the Earth's surface. Mountains are formed by volcanic activity or the collision of plates, which causes the crust to buckle upward.

Rocks are naturally occurring solids found on or below the surface of the Earth. Rocks are made of one or more minerals. Minerals are pure substances made of just one element or chemical compound. Rocks are divided into three groups, based on the way they are formed.

1. **Igneous**—rocks formed by cooling of magma or lava (ex. granite, obsidian).

2. **Sedimentary**—rock formed from silt or deposited rock fragments by compaction at high pressures and/or cementation (ex. shale, limestone).

3. **Metamorphic**—rocks formed from igneous or sedimentary rock after exposure to high heat and pressure (ex. marble, slate).

Weathering is the breaking down of rock into small pieces. Rock is weathered by acid rain, freezing, wind abrasion, glacier scouring, and running water. Erosion is the transportation of rock or sediment to new areas. Agents of erosion include wind, running water, and glaciers.

METEOROLOGY

Meteorology is the study of the atmosphere and its changes.

The atmosphere is a layer of air surrounding the Earth. Air is a mixture of gases, the most common being nitrogen and oxygen. The atmosphere is studied because 1) it protects (insulates) the Earth from extreme temperature changes, 2) it protects the Earth's surface from meteors, and 3) it is the origin of weather.

The atmosphere can be divided into several layers. The troposphere is the layer closest to Earth. Almost all life and most weather is found there. The stratosphere is the chief thermally insulating layer of the atmosphere. It contains the ozone layer and jet stream. The stratosphere is the region where ozone is produced. The thermosphere causes meteors to burn up by friction as they pass through. This layer reflects radio waves. The exosphere is the outer layer of the atmosphere. It eventually blends into the vast region we call "space."

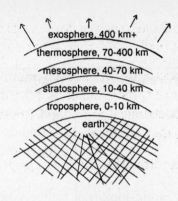

exosphere, 400 km+
thermosphere, 70-400 km
mesosphere, 40-70 km
stratosphere, 10-40 km
troposphere, 0-10 km
earth

Figure 18

Weather is the local, short-term condition of the atmosphere. The two factors that affect weather most are the amounts of energy and water present. Most of the energy that affects weather comes from the sun. As solar (sun) energy hits the Earth, most of it is scattered or reflected by the atmosphere. The solar energy that gets through the atmosphere warms the Earth's crust, which in turn warms the atmosphere. The Earth does not absorb solar energy uniformly; the equator absorbs more than the poles do. This difference in energy (heat) absorption causes, in part, winds.

Water covers about 70% of the Earth's surface. As that water slowly evaporates, some of the vapor is held in the atmosphere. It is the water vapor in our atmosphere that causes humidity, fog, clouds, and precipitation.

An air mass is a huge area of air that has nearly uniform conditions of temperature and moisture. When two air masses meet, the boundary between them is called a front. Fronts are the location of most stormy weather.

Warm air is less dense than cold air. This means that a given volume of warm air weighs less than an equal volume of cold air. Air masses push down on the earth below them, causing air pressure. Warm air masses, because they are less dense, push down less and cause low pressure areas. Cold air masses, which are more dense, cause high air pressure. Air moves from high pressure to low pressure areas, causing wind.

Clouds can be used to predict the weather.

Cloud Type	Appearance	Weather
stratus	flat, broad	light colored—stable weather conditions dark colored—rain expected soon
cumulus	fluffy, solid-looking	light colored—good weather dark colored—heavy rains, perhaps thunderstorms
cirrus	thin, wispy	changes in weather

Climate is the general atmospheric condition of a region over a long period of time.

OCEANOGRAPHY

Oceanography is the study of the ocean.

Sea water differs from fresh water in its salinity, or saltiness. Fresh water, the water we drink, has relatively few dissolved solids in it and has low salinity. Ocean water has a lot of dissolved material in it and therefore has a high salinity. Many materials are dissolved in sea water, but the most abundant dissolved material is common salt, sodium chloride.

Ocean waters move through tides, waves, and currents. Tides are periodic changes in ocean depth. They are caused by the gravitational pull of the moon on Earth. Most waves are caused by winds. Some ocean currents are caused by density differences in sea water. Currents are like rivers within the ocean. The swift-moving water in currents can transport material over large distances very quickly.

DRILL: MATHEMATICS

1. $\sqrt{100} =$
   (A) 10   (C) 200
   (B) 50   (D) 500

2. $(2^2)^4 =$
   (A) $\sqrt{2}$ (C) 2^7
   (B) 2^6 (D) 2^8

3. $\dfrac{3}{4} \times \dfrac{8}{9} =$

   (A) $\dfrac{24}{9}$ (C) $\dfrac{2}{3}$

   (B) $\dfrac{32}{3}$ (D) $\dfrac{11}{13}$

4. Solve $2x + 5 = 9$ for x.
   (A) -5 (C) 2
   (B) -2 (D) 7

5. $5mn^2 \times 4mn^2 =$
   (A) $20m^2n^2$ (C) $9mn^2$
   (B) $20m^2n^4$ (D) mn^2

6. Solve for the value of y:
   $$3x + 2y = 12$$
   $$2x - 2y = 8$$
   (A) 0   (C) 3
   (B) 2   (D) 4

7. Change the fraction $\dfrac{7}{8}$ to a decimal.

   (A) .666   (C) .777
   (B) .75   (D) .875

8. $7.04 \times 2.5 =$
   (A) 17.6   (C) 9.25
   (B) 176   (D) 1.76

9. Forty-eight percent of the 1,200 students at Central High are males. How many male students are there at Central High?

    (A) 57

    (B) 576

    (C) 580

    (D) 600

10. $4x - 2 = 10$: Solve for x.

    (A) −1

    (B) 2

    (C) 3

    (D) 4

11. Quadrilateral $ATUV$ is a square. If the perimeter of the square is 44 cm, find the length of AT.

    (A) 4 cm

    (B) 11 cm

    (C) 22 cm

    (D) 30 cm

12. John bought a $250 radio. The salesman gave him a 10% discount. How much did he pay for the radio?

    (A) $25

    (B) $125

    (C) $175

    (D) $225

13. Which of the following figures has exactly two lines of symmetry?

    (A) A trapezoid which is not a parallelogram

    (B) A parallelogram which is not a rectangle

    (C) A rectangle which is not a square

    (D) A square

14. Laura went cruising in her motor boat. She cruised for 2 hours and 20 minutes and found she had traveled 21 nautical miles. What was her speed to the nearest knot? (One knot = one nautical mile in one hour.)

    (A) 7 knots

    (B) 2   knots

    (C) 21 knots

    (D) 9 knots

15. When a number is multiplied by 6 and that product is subtracted from 70 the difference is 4. What is the number?

    (A) −11.

    (B) 10

    (C) 11

    (D) 12

DRILL: SCIENCE

1. Which of the following organisms contain chlorophyll?
    - (A) Viruses
    - (B) Fungi
    - (C) Bacteria
    - (D) Blue-green algae

2. Kangaroos are best classified as
    - (A) carnivores.
    - (B) primates.
    - (C) marsupials.
    - (D) ungulates.

3. Bryophytes
    - (A) make seeds.
    - (B) are nonvascular.
    - (C) produce wood.
    - (D) have roots.

4. The large intestine is part of the _____ system.
    - (A) digestive
    - (B) respiratory
    - (C) endocrine
    - (D) circulatory

5. Which of the following do not provide calories in your diet?
    - (A) Protein
    - (B) Carbohydrates
    - (C) Fiber
    - (D) Fats

6. The normal number of chromosomes in a human cell is
    - (A) 52.
    - (B) 108.
    - (C) 30.
    - (D) 46.

7. In an ecosystem, an example of a producer is a
    - (A) fungus.
    - (B) maple tree.
    - (C) wolf.
    - (D) rock.

8. Animal cells do not contain
    - (A) cell membranes.
    - (B) ribosomes.
    - (C) chloroplasts.
    - (D) mitochondria.

9. Light waves have a longer wavelength than
    - (A) microwaves.
    - (B) radio waves.
    - (C) radar.
    - (D) x-rays.

10. Sound waves of a loud sound have a greater _____ than those of quiet sounds.
    - (A) speed
    - (B) frequency
    - (C) amplitude
    - (D) intensity

11. Organic compounds are compounds containing
    (A) oxygen.   (C) carbon.
    (B) hydrogen.   (D) water.

12. A material with definite volume but no definite shape is called a
    (A) plasma.   (C) liquid.
    (B) gas.   (D) solid.

13. An acidic solution will have a pH of
    (A) 20.   (C) 7.
    (B) 10.   (D) 5.

14. The intensity of an earthquake is measured by a(n)
    (A) thermograph.   (C) telegraph.
    (B) seismograph.   (D) oscilloscope.

15. Air pressure is measured with a
    (A) thermometer.   (C) hygrometer.
    (B) barometer.   (D) anemometer.

ANSWERS TO DRILL QUESTIONS: MATHEMATICS

1.	(A)	6.	(A)	11.	(B)
2.	(D)	7.	(D)	12.	(D)
3.	(C)	8.	(A)	13.	(C)
4.	(C)	9.	(B)	14.	(D)
5.	(B)	10.	(C)	15.	(C)

ANSWERS TO DRILL QUESTIONS: SCIENCE

1.	(D)	6.	(D)	11.	(C)
2.	(C)	7.	(B)	12.	(C)
3.	(B)	8.	(C)	13.	(D)
4.	(A)	9.	(D)	14.	(B)
5.	(C)	10.	(C)	15.	(B)

Chapter 3

Historical and Social Scientific Awareness Review

The purpose of the Historical and Social Scientific Awareness section of the Liberal Arts and Sciences Test is to assess knowledge in five subareas. The first of these areas is an understanding of the relationships that exist among historical, geographical, cultural, economic, political, and social issues and factors. The second looks for an understanding of the principles and concepts underlying modern political and social concepts, arguments, and interpretations. The third area looks for an understanding of different values and priorities, and how they shape contemporary society. The fourth subarea asks the candidate to apply inquiry and problem-solving skills in the subjects of history and the social sciences. The final subarea calls for an understanding of visual interpretations of historical and social scientific information. The following review provides a comprehensive historical context for all of these skills, and concisely summarizes the information you will need to do well on this section of the exam.

WORLD HISTORY: THE ANCIENT AND MEDIEVAL WORLDS

THE APPEARANCE OF CIVILIZATION

Between 6000 and 3000 B.C., humans invented the plow, utilized the wheel, harnessed the wind, discovered how to smelt copper ores, and began to develop accurate solar calendars. Small villages gradually grew into populous cities. The invention of writing in 3500 B.C. in Mesopotamia marks the beginning of civilization, and divides prehistoric from historic times.

MESOPOTAMIA

Sumer (4000 to 2000 B.C.) included the city of Ur. The *Gilgamesh* is an epic Sumerian poem. The Sumerians constructed dikes and reservoirs and established a loose confederation of city-states. They probably invented writing (called cuneiform because of its wedge-shaped letters). The Amorites, or Old Babylonians (2000 to 1550 B.C.), established a new capital at Babylon, known for its famous Hanging Gardens. King Hammurabi (reigned 1792–1750 B.C.) promulgated a legal code that called for retributive punishment ("an eye for an eye") and provided that one's social class determined punishment for a crime.

The Assyrians (1100–612 B.C.) conquered Syria, Palestine, and much of Mesopotamia. They controlled a brutal, militaristic empire. The Chaldeans, or New Babylonians (612–538 B.C.), conquered the Assyrian territory, including Jerusalem. In 538 B.C., Cyrus, king of the southern Persians, defeated the Chaldeans. The Persians created a huge empire and built a road network. Their religion, Zoroastrianism, promoted the worship of a supreme being, Ahura Mazda, in the context of a cosmic battle with the forces of evil. After 538 B.C., the peoples of Mesopotamia, whose natural boundaries were insufficient to thwart invaders, were absorbed into other empires and dynasties.

EGYPT

During the end of the Archaic Period (5000–2685 B.C.), Menes, or Narmer, probably unified Upper and Lower Egypt around 3200 B.C. During the Old Kingdom (2685–2180 B.C.), the pharaohs came to be considered living gods. The capital moved to Memphis during the Third Dynasty (ca. 2650 B.C.). The pyramids were built during the Fourth Dynasty (ca. 2613–2494 B.C.).

After the Hykos invasion (1785–1560 B.C.), the New Kingdom (1560–1085 B.C.) expanded into Nubia and invaded Palestine and Syria, enslaving the Jews. King Amenhotep IV or Akhenaton (reigned c. 1372–1362 B.C.) promulgated the idea of a single god, Aton, and closed other temples. His successor, Tutankhamen, returned to pantheism.

After 1085 B.C., in what is known as the Post-Empire Period, Egypt came under the successive control of the Assyrians, the Persians, Alexander the Great, and finally, in 30 B.C., the Roman Empire. The Egyptians developed papyrus and made many medical advances. Other peoples would elaborate their ideas of monotheism and the notion of an afterlife.

PALESTINE AND THE HEBREWS

Phoenicians settled along the present-day Lebanon coast (Sidon, Tyre, Beirut, Byblos) and established colonies at Carthage and in Spain. They spread Mesopotamian culture through their trade networks.

The Hebrews probably moved to Egypt around 1700 B.C. and were enslaved about 1500 B.C. The Hebrews fled Egypt under Moses and around 1200 B.C. returned to Palestine. Under King David (reigned ca. 1012–972 B.C.), the Philistines were defeated and a capital established at Jerusalem. Ultimately Palestine divided into Israel (10 tribes) and Judah (two tribes). The 10 tribes of Israel (Lost Tribes) disappeared after Assyria conquered Israel in 722 B.C.

The poor and less attractive state of Judah continued until 586 B.C., when the Chaldeans transported the Jews to Chalden as advisors and slaves (Babylonian captivity). When the Persians conquered Babylon in 539 B.C., the Jews were allowed to return to Palestine. Alexander the Great conquered Palestine in 325 B.C. During the Hellenistic period (323–63 B.C.), the Jews were allowed to govern themselves. The Romans restricted Jewish autonomy. The Jews revolted in 70 A.D. The Romans quashed the revolt and ordered the dispersion of the Jews. The Jews also revolted in 132-135 A.D. These uprisings ultimately led to the loss of their holy land. The Jews contributed the ideas of monotheism and humankind's convenant with God to lead ethical lives, along with a strong reliance on law in connection with religious observance.

GREECE

Homer's epic poems the *Iliad* and the *Odyssey* dramatized ideas like personal excellence (*arete*), courage, honor, and heroism for ancient Greek civilization. Hesiod's *Works and Days* summarized everyday life. His *Theogony* recounted Greek myths. Greek religion was based on their writings.

In the Archaic Period (800–500 B.C.) Greek life was organized around the polis (city-state). Oligarchs controlled most of the polis until near the end of the sixth century, when individuals holding absolute power (tyrants) replaced them. By the end of the sixth century, democratic governments in turn replaced many tyrants.

Sparta, however, developed into an armed camp. Sparta seized control of neighboring Messenia around 750 B.C. To prevent rebellions, every Spartan entered lifetime military service (as hoplites) at age seven. Around 640 B.C., Lycurgus promulgated a constitution. Around 540 B.C., Sparta organized the Peloponnesian League.

Athens was the principal city of Attica. Draco (ca. 621 B.C.) first codified Athenian law. His Draconian Code was known for its harshness.

Solon (ca. 630–560 B.C.) reformed the laws in 594 B.C. He enfranchised the lower classes and gave the state responsibility for administering justice. Growing indebtedness of small farmers and insufficient land strengthened the nobles. Peisistratus (ca. 605–527 B.C.) seized control and governed as a tyrant. In 527 B.C., Cleisthenes led a reform movement that established the basis of Athens's democratic government, including an annual assembly to identify and exile those considered dangerous to the state.

THE FIFTH CENTURY (CLASSICAL AGE)

The fifth century was the high point of Greek civilization. It opened with the Persian Wars (490; 480–479 B.C.) after which Athens organized the Delian League. Pericles (ca. 495–429 B.C.) used League money to rebuild Athens, including construction of the Parthenon and other Acropolis buildings. Athens's dominance spurred war with Sparta.

The Peloponnesian War between Athens and Sparta (431–404 B.C.) ended with Athens's defeat, but weakened Sparta as well. Sparta fell victim to Thebes, and the other city-states warred amongst themselves until Alexander the Great's conquest.

A revolution in philosophy occurred in classical Athens. The Sophists emphasized the individual and his attainment of excellence through rhetoric, grammar, music, and mathematics. Socrates (ca. 470–399 B.C.) criticized the Sophists' emphasis on rhetoric and emphasized a process of questioning, or dialogues, with his students. Like Socrates, Plato (ca. 428–348 B.C.) emphasized ethics. His *Theory of Ideas* or *Forms* said that what we see is but a dim shadow of the eternal Forms or Ideas. Philosophy should seek to penetrate to the real nature of things. Plato's *Republic* described an ideal state ruled by a philosopher king.

Aristotle (ca. 384–322 B.C.) was Plato's pupil. He criticized Plato, arguing that ideas or forms did not exist outside of things. He contended that it was necessary to examine four factors in treating any object: its matter, its form, its cause of origin, and its end or purpose.

Greek art emphasized the individual. In architecture, the Greeks developed the Doric and Ionian forms. Euripides (484–406 B.C.) is often considered the most modern tragedian because he was so psychologically minded. In comedy, Aristophanes (ca. 450–388 B.C.) was a pioneer who used political themes. The New Comedy, exemplified by Menander (ca. 342–292 B.C.), concentrated on domestic and individual themes.

The Greeks were the first to develop the study of history. They were skeptical critics, who banished myth from their works. Herodotus (ca. 484–424 B.C.), called the "father of history," wrote *History of the Persian War*. Thucydides (ca. 460–400 B.C.) wrote *History of the Peloponnesian War*.

THE HELLENISTIC AGE AND MACEDONIA

The Macedonians were a Greek people who were considered semi-barbaric by their southern Greek relatives. They never developed a city-state system and had more territory and people than any of the polis.

In 359 B.C. Philip II (382–336 B.C.) became king. To finance his state and secure a seaport, he conquered several city-states. In 338 B.C., Athens fell. In 336 B.C., Philip was assassinated.

Philip's son, Alexander the Great (356–323 B.C.) killed or exiled rival claimants to his father's throne. He established an empire that included Syria and Persia and extended to the Indus River Valley. At the time of his death, Alexander had established 70 cities and created a vast trading network.

With no succession plan, Alexander's realm was divided among three of his generals. By 30 B.C., all of the successor states had fallen to Rome.

ROME

The traditional founding date for Rome is 753 B.C. Between 800 and 500 B.C., Greek tribes colonized southern Italy, bringing their alphabet and religious practices to Roman tribes. In the sixth and seventh centuries, the Etruscans expanded southward and conquered Rome.

Late in the sixth century (the traditional date is 509 B.C.), the Romans expelled the Etruscans and established an aristocratically based republic in place of the monarchy.

In the early Republic, power was in the hands of the patricians (wealthy landowners). A Senate composed of patricians governed. The Senate elected two consuls to serve one-year terms. Roman executives had great power (the imperium). They were assisted by two quaestors, who managed economic affairs.

Rome's expansion and contact with Greek culture disrupted the traditional agrarian basis of life. Tiberius Gracchus (163–133 B.C.) and Gaius Gracchus (153–121 B.C.) led the People's party (or *Populares*). They called for land reform and lower grain prices to help small farmers. They were opposed by the *Optimates* (best men). Tiberius was assassinated. Gaius continued his work, assisted by the *Equestrians*. After several years of struggle, Gaius committed suicide.

Power passed into the hands of military leaders for the next 80 years. During the 70s and 60s, Pompey (106–48 B.C.) and Julius Caesar (100–44 B.C.) emerged as the most powerful men. In 73 B.C., Spartacus led a slave rebellion, which General Crassus suppressed.

In 60 B.C., Caesar convinced Pompey and Crassus (ca. 115–53 B.C.) to form the First Triumvirate. When Crassus died, Caesar and Pompey fought for leadership. In 49 B.C., Caesar crossed the Rubicon, the stream separating his province from Italy, and a civil war followed. In 47 B.C., the Senate proclaimed Caesar as dictator, and later named him consul for life. Brutus and Cassius believed that Caesar had destroyed the Republic. They formed a conspiracy, and on March 15, 44 B.C. (the Ides of March), Caesar was assassinated in the Roman Forum. His 18-year-old nephew and adopted son, Octavian, succeeded him.

Caesar reformed the tax code and eased burdens on debtors. He instituted the Julian calendar, which remained in use in Catholic Europe until 1582. The Assembly under Caesar had little power.

In literature and philosophy, Plautus (254–184 B.C.) wrote Greek-style comedy. Terence, a slave (ca. 186–159 B.C.), wrote comedies in the tradition of Menander. Catullus (87–54 B.C.) was the most famous lyric poet. Lucretius's (ca. 94–54 B.C.) *Nature of Things* described Epicurean atomic metaphysics, while arguing against the immortality of the soul. Cicero (106–43 B.C.), the great orator and stylist, defended the Stoic concept of natural law. His *Orations* described Roman life. Roman religion was family centered and more civic-minded than Greek religion.

THE ROMAN EMPIRE

After a period of struggle, Octavian (63 B.C.–14 A.D.), named as Caesar's heir, gained absolute control while maintaining the appearance of a republic. When he offered to relinquish his power in 27 B.C., the Senate gave him a vote of confidence and a new title, "Augustus." Augustus ruled for 44 years (31 B.C.–14 A.D.) He introduced many reforms, including new coinage, new tax collection, fire and police protection, and land for settlers in the provinces.

Between 27 B.C. and 180 A.D., Rome's greatest cultural achievements occurred under the Pax Romana. The period between 27 B.C. and 14 A.D. is called the **Augustan Age**. Vergil (70–19 B.C.) wrote the *Aeneid,* an account of Rome's rise. Horace (65–8 B.C.) wrote the lyric *Odes.* Ovid (43 B.C.–18 A.D.) published the *Ars Amatoria,* a guide to seduction, and the *Metamorpho-*

ses, about Greek mythology. Livy (57 B.C.–17 A.D.) wrote a narrative history of Rome based on earlier accounts.

The Silver Age lasted from 14–180 A.D. Writings in this period were less optimistic. Seneca (5 B.C. to 65 A.D.) espoused Stoicism in his tragedies and satires. Juvenal (50–127 A.D.) wrote satire, Plutarch's (46–120 A.D.) *Parallel Lives* portrayed Greek and Roman leaders, and Tacitus (55–120 A.D.) criticized the follies of his era in his histories.

Stoicism was the dominant philosophy of the era. Epictetus (ca. 60–120 A.D.), a slave, and Emperor Marcus Aurelius were its chief exponents. In law, Rome made a lasting contribution. It distinguished three orders of law: civil law (*jus civile*), which applied to Rome's citizens, law of the people (*jus gentium*), which merged Roman law with the laws of other peoples of the Empire, and natural law (*jus naturale*), governed by reason.

After the Pax Romana, the third century was a period of great tumult for Rome. Civil war was nearly endemic in the third century. Between 235 and 284 A.D., 26 "barracks emperors" governed, taxing the population heavily to pay for the Empire's defense.

Rome's frontiers were under constant attack. Emperors Diocletian (reigned 285–305 A.D.) and Constantine (reigned 306–337 A.D.) tried to stem Rome's decline. Diocletian divided the Empire into four parts and moved the capital to Nicomedia in Asia Minor. Constantine moved the capital to Constantinople.

Some historians argue that the rise of Christianity was an important factor in Rome's decline. Jesus was born around 4 B.C., and began preaching and ministering to the poor and sick at the age of 30. The Gospels provide the fullest account of his life and teachings. Saul of Tarsus, or Paul (10–67 A.D.), transformed Christianity from a small sect of Jews who believed Jesus was the Messiah into a world religion. Paul won followers through his missionary work. He also shifted the focus from the early followers' belief in Jesus's imminent return to concentrate on personal salvation. His *Epistles* (letters to Christian communities) laid the basis for the religion's organization and sacraments.

The Pax Romana allowed Christians to move freely through the Empire. In the Age of Anxiety, many Romans felt confused and alienated, and thus drawn to the new religion. And unlike other mystery religions, Christianity included women. By the first century, the new religion had spread throughout the Empire.

Around 312 A.D., Emperor Constantine converted to Christianity and ordered toleration in the Edict of Milan (ca. 313 A.D.). In 391 A.D., Emperor Theodosius I (reigned 371–395 A.D.) proclaimed Christianity as the Empire's official religion.

By the second century, the church hierarchy had developed. Eventually, the Bishop of Rome came to have preeminence, based on the interpretation that Jesus had chosen Peter as his successor.

THE BYZANTINE EMPIRE

Emperor Theodosius II (reigned 408–450 A.D.) divided his empire between his sons, one ruling the East, the other the West. After the Vandals sacked Rome in 455 A.D., Constantinople was the undisputed leading city of the Empire.

In 527 A.D., Justinian I (483–565 A.D.) became emperor in the East and reigned with his controversial wife Theodora until 565 A.D. The Nika revolt broke out in 532 A.D. and demolished the city. It was crushed by General Belisarius in 537 A.D., after 30,000 had died in the uprising.

The Crusaders further weakened the state. In 1204 A.D., Venice contracted to transport the Crusaders to the Near East in return for the Crusaders capturing and looting Constantinople. The Byzantines were defeated in 1204 A.D. Though they drove out the Crusaders in 1261 A.D., the empire never regained its former power. In 1453 A.D., Constantinople fell to the Ottoman Turks.

ISLAMIC CIVILIZATION IN THE MIDDLE AGES

Mohammed was born about 570 A.D. and received a revelation from the Angel Gabriel around 610 A.D. In 630 A.D., Mohammed marched into Mecca. The Sharia (code of law and theology) outlines five pillars of faith for Muslims to observe. The first pillar is the belief that there is one God and that Mohammed is his prophet. Second, the faithful must pray five times a day. Third, they must perform charitable acts. Fourth, they are required to fast from sunrise to sunset during the holy month of Ramadan. Finally, they must make a haj, or pilgrimage, to Mecca. The Koran, which consists of 114 suras (verses), contains Mohammed's teachings. Mullahs (teachers) occupy positions of authority, but Islam did not develop a hierarchical system comparable to that of Christianity.

A leadership struggle developed after Mohammed's death. His father-in-law, Abu Bakr (573–634 A.D.), succeeded as caliph (successor to the prophet) and governed for two years, until his death in 634 A.D. Omar succeeded him. Between 634 and 642 A.D., Omar established the Islamic Empire.

The Omayyad caliphs, based in Damascus, governed from 661–750 A.D. They called themselves Shiites and believed they were Mohammed's true successors. (Most Muslims were Sunnites, from "sunna," oral traditions about the prophet.) They conquered Spain by 730 A.D. and advanced into France until they were stopped by Charles Martel (ca. 688–741 A.D.) in 732 A.D. at Poitiers and Tours. Muslim armies penetrated India and China. They transformed Damascus into a cultural center and were exposed to Hellenistic culture from the nearby Byzantine Empire.

The Abbasid caliphs ruled from 750–1258 A.D. They moved the capital to Baghdad and treated Arab and non-Arab Muslims as equals. Islam assumed a more Persian character under their reign. In the late tenth century, the empire began to disintegrate. In 1055 A.D., the Seljuk Turks captured Baghdad, allowing the Abbasids to rule as figureheads. Genghis Khan (ca. 1162–1227 A.D.) and his army invaded the Abbasids. In 1258 A.D., they seized Baghdad and murdered the last caliph.

FEUDALISM IN JAPAN

Feudalism in Japan began with the arrival of mounted nomadic warriors from throughout Asia during the Kofun Era (300–710). Some members of these nomadic groups formed an elite class and became part of the court aristocracy in the capital city of Kyoto, in western Japan. During the Heian Era (794–1185), a hereditary military aristocracy arose in the Japanese provinces, and by the late Heian Era, many of these formerly nomadic warriors had established themselves as independent landowners, or as managers of landed estates *(shoen)* owned by Kyoto aristocrats. These aristocrats depended on these warriors to defend their *shoen,* and in response to this need, the warriors organized into small groups called *bushidan.*

As the years passed, these warrior clans grew larger, and alliances formed among them, led by imperial descendants who moved from the capital to the provinces. After victory in the Taira-Minamoto War (1180–1105), Minamoto no Yorimoto forced the emperor to award him the title of *shogun,* which is short for "barbarian subduing generalissimo." He used this power to found the Kamakura Shogunate which survived for 148 years. Under the Kamakura Shogunate, many vassals were appointed to the position of *jitro* or land steward, or the position of provincial governors *(shugo)* to act as liaisons between the Kamakura government and local vassals.

By the fourteenth century, the *shugo* had augmented their power enough to become a threat to the Kamakura, and in 1333 lead a rebellion that overthrew the shogunate. Under the Ashikaga Shogunate, the office of *shogu* was made hereditary, and its powers were greatly extended. These new *shogu* turned their vassals into aggressive local warriors called *kokujin,* or *jizamurai.* Following this move, the Ashikaga shoguns lost a great deal of their power to political fragmentation, which eventually lead to the Warring States Era (1467–1568).

By the middle of the sixteenth century, the feudal system had evolved considerably. At the center of this highly evolved system was the *daimyo,* a local feudal lord who ruled over one of the many autonomous domains.

Far reaching alliances of *daimyo* were forged under the Tokugawa Shogunate, the final and most unified of the three shogunates. Under the Tokugawa, the *daimyo* were considered direct vassals of the shoguns, and were kept under strict control. The warriors were gradually transformed into scholars and bureaucrats under the *bushido,* or code of chivalry, and the principles of Neo-Confucianism. A merchant class, or *chonin,* gained wealth as the samurai class began to lose power, and the feudal system effectively ended when power was returned to the emperor under the Meji Restoration of 1868, when all special privileges of the samurai class were abolished.

CHINESE AND INDIAN EMPIRES

The Harappan or Indus civilization, which was confined to the Indus basin, was the early Indian civilization built around 1500 B.C., during the so-called Vedic Age, India came to be ruled by the Indo-Aryans, a mainly pastoral people with a speech closely related to the major languages of Europe.

The religion of the Harappan peoples revolved around the god Siva, the belief in reincarnation, in a condition of "liberation" beyond the cycle of birth and death, and in the technique of mental concentration which later came to be called *yoga.* The religion of the Indo-Aryans was based on a pantheon of gods of a rather worldly type, and sacrifices were offered to them. The traditional hymns that accompanied them were the Vedas, which form the basic scriptures for the religion of Hinduism. Indian society also came to be based on a *caste* system.

In the third century B.C., the Indian kingdoms fell under the Mauryan Empire. The grandson of the founder of this empire, named Asoka, opened a new era in the cultural history of India by believing in the Buddhist religion. Buddha had disregarded the Vedic gods and the institutions of caste and had preached a relatively simple ethical religion which had two levels of aspiration—a monastic life of renunciation of the world and a high, but not too difficult, morality for the layman. The two religions of Hinduism and Buddhism flourished together for centuries in a tolerant rivalry, and in the end Buddhism virtually disappeared from India by the thirteenth century A.D.

Chinese civilization originated in the Yellow River Valley only gradually extending to the southern regions. Three dynasties ruled early China: the Xia or Hsia, the Shang (c. 1500 to 1122 B.C.), and the Zhou (c. 1122 to 211 B.C.). After the Zhou's fell, China welcomed the teachings of Confucius as warfare between states and philosophical speculation created circumstances ripe for such teachings. Confucius made the good order of society depend on an ethical ruler, who should be advised by scholar-moralists like Confucius himself.

In contrast to the Confucians, the Taoists professed a kind of anarchism; the best kind of government was none at all. The wise man did not concern himself with political affairs, but with mystical contemplation which identified himself with the forces of nature.

SUB-SAHARAN KINGDOMS AND CULTURES

The Nok were a people that lived in the area now known as Nigeria. Artifacts indicate that they were peaceful farmers who built small communities consisting of houses of wattle and daub.

The people referred to as the Ghana lived about 500 miles from what we now call Ghana. The Ghana peoples traded with Berber merchants. The Ghana offered these traders gold from deposits found in the south of their territory. In the 1200s the Mali kingdom conquered Ghana and the civilization mysteriously disappeared.

The people known as the Mali lived in a huge kingdom that lay mostly on the savanna bordering the Sahara Desert. The city of Timbuktu, built in the thirteenth century, was a thriving city of culture where traders visited stone houses, shops, libraries, and mosques.

The Songhai lived near the Niger River and gained their independence from the Mali in the early 1400s. The major growth of the empire came after 1464 A.D. under the leadership of Sunni Ali, who devoted his reign to warfare and expansion of the empire.

The Bantu peoples, numbering about 100,000,000 lived across large sections of Africa. Bantu societies lived in tiny chiefdoms, starting in the third millennium B.C., and each group developed its own version of the original Bantu language.

CIVILIZATIONS OF THE AMERICAS

The great civilizations of early America were agricultural, and foremost of these was the Mayan, in Yucatan, Guatemala, and eastern Honduras.

Mayan history is divided into three parts, the Old Empire, Middle Period, and the New Empire. By the time the Spanish conquerors arrived, most of the Mayan religious centers had been abandoned and their civilization had deteriorated seriously, perhaps due to the wide gulf between the majority of the people, who were peasants, and the priests and nobles.

Farther north in Mexico there arose a series of advanced cultures that derived much of their substance from the Maya. Such peoples as the Zapotecs, Totonacs, Almecs, and Toltecs evolved into a high level of civilization. By 500 B.C. agricultural peoples had begun to use a ceremonial calendar and had built stone pyramids on which they performed religious observances.

The Aztecs then took over Mexican culture, and a major feature of their culture was human sacrifice in repeated propitiation of their chief god. Aztec government was centralized, with an elective king and a large army. Like their predecessors, they were skilled builders and engineers, accomplished astronomers and mathematicians.

Andean civilization was characterized by the evolution of beautifully made pottery, intricate fabrics, and flat-topped mounds called *huacas*.

The Incas, a tribe from the interior of South America who termed themselves "Children of the Sun," controlled an area stretching from Ecuador to central Chile. Sun worshippers, they believed themselves to be the vice-regents on earth of the sun god; the Inca were all powerful; every person's place in society was fixed and immutable; the state and the army were supreme. They were at the apex of their power just before the Spanish conquest.

In North America two major groups of mound builders are known as the Woodland and Mississippian peoples.

In the present-day southwestern United States and northern Mexico, two varieties of ancient culture can be identified. The Anasazi developed adobe architecture, worked the land extensively, had a highly developed system of irrigation, and made cloth and baskets. The Hohokam built separate stone and timber houses around a central plaza.

EUROPE IN ANTIQUITY

Between 486 and 1050 A.D., Europe underwent changes that led to increasing ethnic diversity. In antiquity, much of Europe was occupied by Germanic tribes.

Nomadic tribes from the central Asian steppes invaded Europe and pushed Germanic tribes into conflict with the Roman Empire. Ultimately, in 410 A.D., the Visigoths sacked Rome, followed by the Vandals in 455 A.D. In 476 A.D., the Ostrogoth king forced the boy emperor Romulus Augustulus to abdicate, ending the empire in the West.

The Frankish Kingdom was the most important medieval Germanic state. Under Clovis I (reigned 481–511 A.D.), the Franks finished conquering France and the Gauls in 486 A.D. Clovis converted to Christianity and founded the Merovingian dynasty.

Charles the Great, or Charlemagne (reigned 768–814 A.D.), founded the Carolingian dynasty. In 800 A.D., Pope Leo III named Charlemagne Emperor of the Holy Roman Empire. In the Treaty of Aix-la-Chapelle (812 A.D.), the Byzantine emperor recognized Charles's authority in the West.

The Holy Roman Empire was intended to reestablish the Roman Empire in the West. Charles vested authority in 200 counts, who were each in charge of a county. Charles's son, Louis the Pious (reigned 814–840 A.D.), succeeded him. On Louis's death, his three sons vied for control of the Empire. The three eventually signed the Treaty of Verdun in 843 A.D. This gave Charles the Western Kingdom (France), Louis the Eastern Kingdom (Germany), and Lothair the Middle Kingdom, a narrow strip of land running from the North Sea to the Mediterranean.

In the ninth and tenth centuries, Europe was threatened by attacks from the Vikings in the north, the Muslims in the south, and the Magyars in the east. In the eleventh century, under the leadership of William the Conqueror (reigned 1066–1087), the Normans conquered England in 1066 A.D. (Battle of Hastings).

Rome's collapse had ushered in the decline of cities, a reversion to a barter economy from a money economy, and a fall in agricultural productivity with a shift to subsistence agriculture.

Manorialism and feudalism developed in this period. Manorialism refers to the economic system in which large estates, granted by the king to nobles, strove for self-sufficiency. Large manors might incorporate several villages. The lands surrounding the villages were usually divided into long strips, with common land in-between. Ownership was divided among the lord and his serfs (also called villeins).

Feudalism describes the decentralized political system of personal ties and obligations that bound vassals to their lords. Serfs were peasants who were bound to the land. They worked on the demesne, or lord's property, three or four days a week in return for the right to work their own land. In difficult times, the nobles were supposed to provide for the serfs.

The church was the only institution to survive the Germanic invasions intact. The power of the popes grew in this period. Gregory I (reigned 590–604 A.D.) was the first member of a monastic order to rise to the papacy. He advanced the ideas of penance and purgatory. He centralized church administration and was the first pope to rule as the secular head of Rome.

Monasteries preserved the few remnants of antiquity that survived the decline.

THE HIGH MIDDLE AGES (1050–1300)

1050 A.D. marked the beginning of the High Middle Ages. Europe was poised to emerge from five centuries of decline. Between 1000 and 1350 A.D., the population grew from 38 million to 75 million. Agricultural productivity grew, aided by new technologies, such as heavy plows, and a slight temperature rise which produced a longer growing season. Horses were introduced into agriculture in this period, and the three-field system replaced the two-field system.

Enfranchisement, or freeing of serfs, grew in this period, and many other serfs simply fled their manors for the new lands.

THE HOLY ROMAN EMPIRE

Charlemagne's grandson, Louis the German, became Holy Roman Emperor under the Treaty of Verdun. Under the weak leadership of his descendants, the dukes in Saxony, Franconia, Swabia, Bavaria, and the Lorraine eroded Carolingian power. The last Carolingian died in 911 A.D. The German dukes elected the leader of Franconia to lead the German lands. He was replaced in 919 A.D. by the Saxon dynasty, which ruled until 1024 A.D. Otto became Holy Roman Emperor in 962 A.D. His descendants governed the Empire until 1024 A.D., when the Franconian dynasty assumed power, reigning until 1125 A.D.

When the Franconian line died out in 1125 A.D., the Hohenstaufen family (Conrad III, reigned 1138–1152 A.D.) won power over a contending family. The Hapsburg line gained control of the Empire in 1273 A.D.

The Romans abandoned their last outpost in England in the fourth century. Alfred the Great (ca. 849–899 A.D.) defeated the Danes who had begun invading during the previous century in 878 A.D. In 959 A.D., Edgar the Peaceable (reigned 959–975 A.D.) became the first king of all England.

William (reigned 1066–1087 A.D.) stripped the Anglo-Saxon nobility of its privileges and instituted feudalism. He ordered a survey of all property of the realm, which was recorded in the Domesday Book (1086 A.D.).

In 1215 A.D., the English barons forced John I to sign the Magna Carta Libertatum, acknowledging their "ancient" privileges. The Magna Carta established the principle of a limited English monarchy. Henry III reigned from 1216–1272 A.D. In 1272 A.D., Edward I became king. His need for revenue led him to convene a parliament of English nobles, which would act as a check upon royal power.

In 710 A.D., the Muslims conquered Spain from the Visigoths. Under the Muslims, Spain enjoyed a stable, prosperous government. The caliphate of Córdoba became a center of scientific and intellectual activity. Internal dissent caused the collapse of Córdoba and the division of Spain into more than 20 Muslim states in 1031 A.D.

The Reconquista (1085–1340 A.D.), wrested control from the Muslims. Rodrigo Diaz de Bivar, known as El Cid (ca. 1043–1099 A.D.), was the most famous of its knights. The fall of Córdoba in 1234 A.D. completed the Reconquista, except for the small state of Granada.

Most of Eastern Europe and Russia was never under Rome's control, and it was cut off from Western influence by the Germanic invasions. Poland converted to Christianity in the tenth century, and after 1025 A.D. was dependent on the Holy Roman Empire. In the twelfth and thirteenth centuries, powerful nobles divided control of the country. After 1226 A.D., the Teutonic Knights controlled most of Poland.

In Russia, Vladimir I converted to Orthodox Christianity in 988 A.D. He established the basis of Kievian Russia. After 1054 A.D., Russia broke into competing principalities. The Mongols (Tatars) invaded in 1221 A.D.,

Caliphate = title of the head of Islam

completing their conquest in 1245 A.D., and cutting Russia's contact with the West for almost a century.

The Crusades attempted to liberate the Holy Land from infidels. There were seven major crusades between 1096 and 1300 A.D. Urban II called Christians to the **First Crusade** (1096–1099 A.D.) with the promise of a plenary indulgence (exemption from punishment in purgatory). Younger sons who would not inherit their fathers' lands were also attracted.

The Crusades helped to renew interest in the ancient world. But thousands of Jews and Muslims were massacred as a result of the Crusades, and relations between Europe and the Byzantine Empire collapsed.

Charlemagne mandated that bishops open schools at each cathedral, and founded a school in his palace for his court. The expansion of trade and the need for clerks and officials who could read and write spurred an 1179 A.D. requirement that each cathedral set aside enough money to support one teacher.

Scholasticism was an effort to reconcile reason and faith and to instruct Christians on how to make sense of the pagan tradition.

Peter Abelard (ca. 1079–1144 A.D.) was a controversial proponent of Scholasticism. In *Sic et Non* (Yes and No), Abelard collected statements in the Bible and by church leaders that contradicted each other. Abelard believed that reason could resolve the apparent contradictions between the two authorities, but the church judged his views as heretical.

Thomas Aquinas (ca. 1225–1274 A.D.) believed that there were two orders of truth. The lower, reason, could demonstrate propositions such as the existence of God, but on a higher level, some of God's mysteries such as the nature of the Trinity must be accepted on faith. Aquinas viewed the universe as a great chain of being, with humans midway on the chain, between the material and the spiritual.

Latin was the language used in universities. But the most vibrant works were in the vernacular. The *chansons de geste* were long epic poems composed between 1050 and 1150 A.D. Among the most famous are the *Song of Roland,* the *Song of the Nibelungs,* the Icelandic *Eddas,* and *El Cid.*

The fabliaux were short stories, many of which ridiculed the clergy. Boccaccio (1313–1375 A.D.) and Chaucer (ca. 1342–1400 A.D.) belonged to this tradition. The work of Dante (1265–1321 A.D.), the greatest medieval poet, synthesized the pagan and Christian traditions.

In this period, polyphonic (more than one melody at a time) music was introduced. In architecture, Romanesque architecture (rounded arches, thick stone walls, tiny windows) flourished between 1000 and 1150 A.D. After 1150 A.D., Gothic architecture, which emphasized the use of light, came into vogue.

DRILL: THE ANCIENT AND MEDIEVAL WORLDS

1. The nomadic warriors who would later become the lords of feudal Japan arrived in the:

    (A) Kofun Era.   (D) Warring States Era.

    (B) Heian Era.   (E) Kamakura Era.

    (C) Sengoku Era.

2. The conversion of Asoka to which of the following religions facilitated its passage into Indian society:

    (A) Taoism.   (D) Jainism.

    (B) Hinduism.   (E) Shintoism

    (C) Buddhism.

3. Which of the following Meso-American civilizations first established the concept of zero?

    (A) Toltec.   (D) Inca.

    (B) Maya.   (E) Zapotecs.

    (C) Aztec.

4. Which of the following is NOT one of the five pillars of the Islamic faith?

    (A) Confession of faith.

    (B) Payment of alms.

    (C) Fasting from sunrise to sunset during Ramadhan.

(D) The jihad.

(E) Pilgrimage to Mecca

5. Which of the following Sub-Saharan peoples created life-sized figures of humans and animals in terra cotta?

(A) The Nok.   (D) The Bantu.

(B) The Songhai.   (E) Mali.

(C) The Ghana.

THE LATE MIDDLE AGES AND THE RENAISSANCE (1300–1648)

THE LATE MIDDLE AGES

The Middle Ages fell chronologically between the classical world of Greece and Rome and the modern world. The papacy and monarchs, after exercising much power and influence in the high Middle Ages, were in eclipse after 1300. During the late Middle Ages (1300–1500), all of Europe suffered from the Black Death. While England and France engaged in destructive warfare in northern Europe, in Italy the Renaissance had begun.

Toward the end of the period, monarchs began to assert their power and control. The major struggle, between England and France, was the Hundred Years' War (1337–1453).

The war was fought in France, though the Scots (with French encouragement) invaded northern England. A few major battles occurred—Crécy (1346), Poitiers (1356), Agincourt (1415)—although the fighting consisted largely of sieges and raids. Eventually, the war became one of attrition; the French slowly wore down the English. Technological changes during the war included the use of English longbows and the increasingly expensive plate armor of knights.

Joan of Arc (1412–1431), an illiterate peasant girl who said she heard voices of saints, rallied the French army for several victories. But she was captured by the Burgundians, allies of England, and sold to the English who tried her for heresy (witchcraft). She was burned at the stake at Rouen.

England lost all of its Continental possessions, except Calais. French farmland was devastated, with England and France both expending great sums of money. Population, especially in France, declined.

Both countries suffered internal disruption as soldiers plundered and local officials were left to fight the war. Trade everywhere was disrupted and England's wool trade with the Low Countries slumped badly. To cover these financial burdens, heavy taxation was inflicted on the peasants.

In both countries, the war, fed by propaganda, led to the growth of nationalism.

Literature also came to express nationalism, as it was written in the language of the people instead of in Latin. Geoffrey Chaucer, the first of the great English poets, was inspired by Italian authors, particularly Boccaccio; his best known work is the unfinished *Canterbury Tales*. Meanwhile, François Villon (1431–1463), in his *Grand Testament*, emphasized the ordinary life of the French with humor and emotion.

THE NEW MONARCHS

The defeat of the English in the Hundred Years' War and of the duchy of Burgundy in 1477 removed major military threats. Trade was expanded, fostered by the merchant Jacques Coeur (1395–1456). Louis XI (1461–1483) demonstrated ruthlessness in dealing with his nobility as individuals and collectively in the Estates General.

The marriage of Isabella of Castile (reigned 1474–1504) and Ferdinand of Aragon (reigned 1474–1516) created a united Spain. The Moslems were defeated at Granada in 1492. Navarre was conquered in 1512.

THE BLACK DEATH AND SOCIAL PROBLEMS

The bubonic plague ("Black Death") is a disease affecting the lymph glands. It causes death quickly. Conditions in Europe encouraged the quick spread of disease. There was no urban sanitation, and streets were filled with refuse, excrement, and dead animals. Living conditions were overcrowded, with families often sleeping in one room or one bed. Poor nutrition was rampant. There was also little personal cleanliness.

Carried by fleas on rats, the plague was brought from Asia by merchants, and arrived in Europe in 1347. The plague affected all of Europe by 1350 and killed perhaps 25 to 40 percent of the population, with cities suffering more than the countryside.

THE RENAISSANCE (1300–1600)

The Renaissance emphasized new learning, including the rediscovery of much classical material, and new art styles.

Italian city-states, such as Venice, Milan, Padua, Pisa, and especially Florence, were the home to many Renaissance developments, which were limited to the rich elite.

LITERATURE, ART, AND SCHOLARSHIP

Humanists, as both orators and poets, were inspired by and imitated works of the classical past. The literature was more secular and wide-ranging than that of the Middle Ages.

Dante (1265–1321) was a Florentine writer whose *Divine Comedy*, describing a journey through hell, purgatory, and heaven, shows that reason can only take people so far and that God's grace and revelation must be used.

Petrarch (1304–1374) encouraged the study of ancient Rome, collected and preserved work of ancient writers, and produced much work in the classical literary style.

Boccaccio (1313–1375) wrote *The Decameron*, a collection of short stories in Italian, which were meant to amuse, not edify, the reader.

Artists also broke with the medieval past, in both technique and content. Renaissance art sometimes used religious topics, but often dealt with secular themes or portraits of individuals. Oil paints, chiaroscuro, and linear perspectives produced works of energy in three dimensions.

Leonardo da Vinci (1452–1519) produced numerous works, including *The Last Supper* and *Mona Lisa*. Raphael (1483–1520), a master of Renaissance grace and style, theory and technique, represented these skills in *The School of Athens*. Michelangelo (1475–1564) produced masterpieces in architecture, sculpture (*David*), and painting (the Sistine Chapel ceiling). His work was a bridge to a new, non-Renaissance style called Mannerism.

Renaissance scholars were more practical and secular than medieval ones. Manuscript collections enabled scholars to study the primary sources and to reject all traditions which had been built up since classical times. Also, scholars participated in the lives of their cities as active politicians.

Leonardo Bruni (1370–1444), a civic humanist, served as chancellor of Florence, where he used his rhetorical skills to rouse the citizens against external enemies.

Machiavelli (1469–1527) wrote *The Prince*, which analyzed politics from the standpoint of expedience rising above morality in the name of maintaining political power.

THE REFORMATION

The Reformation destroyed Western Europe's religious unity and introduced new ideas about the relationships between God, the individual, and society. Its course was greatly influenced by politics and led, in most areas, to the subjection of the church to the political rulers.

MARTIN LUTHER (1483–1546)

Martin Luther, to his personal distress, could not reconcile the sinfulness of humans with the justice of God. How could a sinful person attain the righteousness necessary to obtain salvation? he wondered. During his studies of the Bible, especially of Romans 1:17, Luther came to believe that personal efforts—good works such as a Christian life and attention to the sacraments of the church—could not "earn" the sinner salvation, but that belief and faith were the only way to obtain grace. By 1515 Luther believed that "justification by faith alone" was the road to salvation.

On October 31, 1517, Luther nailed 95 theses, or statements, about indulgences, the cancellation of a sin in return for money, to the door of the Wittenberg church and challenged the practice of selling them. At this time he was seeking to reform the church, not divide it.

In 1519 Luther presented various criticisms of the church and was driven to say that only the Bible, not religious traditions or papal statements, could determine correct religious practices and beliefs. In 1521 Pope Leo X excommunicated Luther for his beliefs.

In 1521 Luther appeared in the city of Worms before a meeting (Diet) of the important figures of the Holy Roman Empire, including the Emperor, Charles V. He was again condemned. At the Diet of Worms Luther made his famous statement about his writings and the basis for them: "Here I stand. I can do no other." After this, Luther could not go back; the break with the pope was permanent.

Frederick III of Saxony, the ruler of the territory in which Luther resided, protected Luther in Wartburg Castle for a year. Frederick never accepted

Luther's beliefs but protected him because Luther was his subject. The weak political control of the Holy Roman Emperor contributed to Luther's success in avoiding the pope's and the Emperor's penalties.

OTHER REFORMERS

Anabaptist (derived from a Greek word meaning to baptize again) is a name applied to people who rejected the validity of child baptism and believed that such children had to be rebaptized when they became adults. A prominent leader was Menno Simons (1496-1561).

Anabaptists sought to return to the practices of the early Christian church, which was a voluntary association of believers with no connection to the state. Anabaptists adopted pacifism and avoided involvement with the state whenever possible.

In 1536 John Calvin (1509–1564), a Frenchman, arrived in Geneva, a Swiss city-state which had adopted an anti-Catholic position. He left after his first efforts at reform failed. Upon his return in 1540, Geneva became the center of the Reformation. Calvin's *Institutes of the Christian Religion* (1536), a strictly logical analysis of Christianity, had a universal appeal.

Calvin emphasized the doctrine of predestination (God knew who would obtain salvation before those people were born) and believed that church and state should be united.

Calvinism triumphed as the majority religion in Scotland, under the leadership of John Knox (ca. 1514–1572), and in the United Provinces of the Netherlands. Puritans in England and New England also accepted Calvinism.

REFORM IN ENGLAND

England underwent reforms in a pattern different from the rest of Europe. Personal and political decisions by the rulers determined much of the course of the Reformation there, when in 1533 Henry VIII defied the pope and turned to Archbishop Thomas Cranmer to dissolve his marriage to Catherine of Aragon.

Protestant beliefs and practices made little headway during Henry's reign, as he accepted transubstantiation, enforced celibacy among the clergy, and otherwise made the English church conform to most Catholic practices.

Under Henry VIII's son, Edward VI (1547–1553), who succeeded to the throne at age 10, the English church adopted Calvinism. Clergy were allowed to marry, communion by the laity expanded, and images were removed from churches. Doctrine included justification by faith, the denial of transubstantiation, and only two sacraments.

Some reformers wanted to purify (hence "Puritans") the church of its remaining Catholic aspects. The resulting church, Protestant in doctrine and practice but retaining most of the physical possessions, such as buildings, and many of the powers, such as church courts, of the medieval church, was called Anglican.

THE COUNTER REFORMATION

The Counter Reformation brought changes to the portion of the Western church which retained its allegiance to the pope.

Ignatius of Loyola (1491–1556), a former soldier, founded the Society of Jesus in 1540 to lead the attack on Protestantism. Jesuits became the leaders of the Counter Reformation.

The Sack of Rome in 1527, when soldiers of the Holy Roman Emperor captured and looted Rome, was seen by many as a judgment of God against the lives of the Renaissance popes. In 1534 Paul III became pope and attacked abuses while reasserting papal leadership.

THE WARS OF RELIGION (1560–1648)

The period from approximately 1560 to 1648 witnessed continuing warfare, primarily between Protestants and Catholics. In the latter half of the sixteenth century, the fighting was along the Atlantic seaboard between Calvinists and Catholics; after 1600 the warfare spread to Germany, where Calvinists, Lutherans, and Catholics fought.

THE CATHOLIC CRUSADE

The territories of Charles V, the Holy Roman Emperor, were divided in 1556 between Ferdinand, Charles's brother, and Philip II (1556–1598), Charles's son. Ferdinand received Austria, Hungary, Bohemia, and the title of Holy Roman Emperor. Philip received Spain, Milan, Naples, the Netherlands, and the New World. It was Philip, not the pope, who led the Catholic attack on Protestants.

Spain dominated the Mediterranean following a series of wars led by Philip's half-brother, Don John, against Moslem (largely Turkish) forces.

Don John secured the Mediterranean for Christian merchants with a naval victory over the Turks at Lepanto off the coast of Greece in 1571.

Portugal was annexed by Spain in 1580 following the death of the king without a clear successor. This gave Philip the only other large navy of the day as well as Portuguese territories around the globe.

ENGLAND AND SPAIN

England was ruled by two queens, Mary I (reigned 1553–1558), who married Philip II, and then Elizabeth I (reigned 1558–1603), while three successive kings of France from 1559 to 1589 were influenced by their mother, Catherine de' Medici (1519–1589).

Mary I sought to make England Catholic. She executed many Protestants, earning the name "Bloody Mary" from opponents.

Mary married Philip II, king of Spain, and organized her foreign policy around Spanish interests. They had no children.

Elizabeth I, a Protestant, achieved a religious settlement between 1559 and 1563 which left England with a church governed by bishops and practicing Catholic rituals, but maintaining a Calvinist doctrine.

Catholics participated in several rebellions and plots. Mary, Queen of Scots, had fled to England from Scotland in 1568, after alienating the nobles there. In Catholic eyes, she was the legitimate queen of England. Several plots and rebellions to put Mary on the throne led to her execution in 1587. Elizabeth was formally excommunicated by the pope in 1570.

In 1588, as part of his crusade and to stop England from supporting the rebels in the Netherlands, Philip II sent the Armada, a fleet of more than 125 ships, to convey troops from the Netherlands to England as part of a plan to make England Catholic. The Armada was defeated by a combination of superior English naval tactics and a wind which made it impossible for the Spanish to accomplish their goal.

A peace treaty between Spain and England was signed in 1604, but England remained an opponent of Spain.

THE THIRTY YEARS' WAR

Calvinism was spreading throughout Germany. The Peace of Augsburg (1555), which settled the disputes between Lutherans and Catholics, had no provision for Calvinists. Lutherans gained more territories through conversions and often took control of previous church-states—a violation of the Peace of Augsburg. A Protestant alliance under the leadership of the Calvinist ruler of the Palatinate opposed a Catholic League led by the ruler of Bavaria. Religious wars were common.

The Thirty Years' War brought great destruction to Germany, leading to a decline in population of perhaps one-third, or more, in some areas. Germany remained divided and without a strong government until the nineteenth century.

After 1648, warfare, though often containing religious elements, would not be executed primarily for religious goals.

The Catholic crusade to reunite Europe failed, largely due to the efforts of the Calvinists. The religious distribution of Europe has not changed significantly since 1648.

Nobles, resisting the increasing power of the state, usually dominated the struggle. France, then Germany, fell apart due to the wars. France was reunited in the seventeenth century.

Spain began a decline which ended its role as a great power of Europe.

THE GROWTH OF THE STATE AND THE AGE OF EXPLORATION

In the seventeenth century the political systems of the countries of Europe began dividing into two types, absolutist and constitutionalist. England, the United Provinces, and Sweden moved towards constitutionalism, while France was adopting absolutist ideas.

Overseas exploration, begun in the fifteenth century, expanded. Governments supported such activity in order to gain wealth and to preempt other countries.

ENGLAND

The English church was a compromise of Catholic practices and Protestant beliefs and was criticized by both groups. The monarchs, after 1620, gave leadership of the church to men with Arminian beliefs, a modified Calvinist creed that deemphasized predestination.

Opponents to this shift in belief were called Puritans, a term that covered a wide range of beliefs and people. To escape the church in England, many Puritans began moving to the New World, especially Massachusetts.

In financial matters, inflation and Elizabeth's wars left the government short of money. Contemporaries blamed the shortage on the extravagance of the courts of James I and Charles I. The monarchs lacked any substantial source of income and had to obtain the consent of a parliament to levy a tax.

Parliament met only when the monarch summoned it. Though parliaments had existed since the Middle Ages, there were long periods of time between parliamentary meetings. Parliaments consisted of nobles and gentry, and a few merchants and lawyers. The men in a parliament usually wanted the government to remedy grievances as part of the agreement to a tax.

Charles I inherited both the English and Scottish thrones at the death of his father, James I. He claimed a "divine right" theory of absolute authority for himself as king and sought to rule without Parliament. That rule also meant control of the Church of England.

Charles stumbled into wars with both Spain and France during the late 1620s. A series of efforts to raise money for the wars led to confrontations with his opponents in Parliament. A "forced loan" was collected from taxpayers with the promise it would be repaid when a tax was voted by parliament. Soldiers were billeted in subjects' houses during the wars. In 1628 Parliament passed the Petition of Right, which declared royal actions involving loans and billeting illegal.

Charles ruled without calling a parliament during the 1630s.

In August 1642 Charles abandoned all hope of negotiating with his opponents and instead declared war against them. Charles's supporters were called Royalists or Cavaliers. His opponents were called Parliamentarians or Roundheads, due to many who wore their hair cut short. This struggle is called the Puritan Revolution, the English Civil War, or the Great Rebellion.

Charles was defeated. His opponents had allied with the Scots who still had an army in England. Additionally, the New Model Army, with its General Oliver Cromwell (1599–1658), was superior to Charles's army.

FRANCE

The regions of France had long had a large measure of independence, and local parliaments could refuse to enforce royal laws. The centralization of all government proceeded by replacing local authorities with intendants, civil servants who reported to the king.

Henry IV relied on the Duke of Sully (1560–1641), the first of a series of strong ministers in the seventeenth century. Sully and Henry increased the involvement of the state in the economy, acting on a theory known as mercantilism.

Louis XIII reigned from 1610 to 1643, but Cardinal Richelieu became the real power in France. The unique status of the Huguenots was reduced through warfare and the Peace of Alais (1629), when their separate armed cities were eliminated. The nobility was reduced in power through constant attention to the laws and the imprisonment of offenders.

Cardinal Mazarin governed while Louis XIV (reigned 1643–1715) was a minor. During the Fronde, from 1649 to 1652, the nobility controlled Paris, drove Louis XIV and Mazarin from the city, and attempted to run the government. Noble ineffectiveness, the memories of the chaos of the wars of religion, and the overall anarchy convinced most people that a strong king was preferable to a warring nobility.

Louis XIV saw the need to increase royal power and his own glory and dedicated his life to these goals. He steadily pursued a policy of "one king, one law, one faith."

EXPLORATIONS AND CONQUESTS

Portugal. Prince Henry the Navigator (1394–1460) supported exploration of the African coastline, largely in order to seek gold. Bartholomew Dias (1450–1500) rounded the southern tip of Africa in 1487. Vasco de Gama (1460–1524) reached India in 1498 and, after some fighting, soon established trading ports at Goa and Calicut. Albuquerque (1453–1515) helped establish an empire in the Spice Islands after 1510.

Spain. Christopher Columbus (1451–1506), seeking a new route to the (East) Indies, "discovered" the Americas in 1492. Ferdinand Magellan (1480–1521) circumnavigated the globe in 1521–1522. Conquests of the Aztecs by Hernando Cortes (1485–1547), and the Incas by Francisco Pizarro (ca. 1476–1541), enabled the Spanish to send much gold and silver back to Spain.

Other Countries. In the 1490s the Cabots, John (1450–1498) and Sebastian (ca. 1483–1557), explored North America, and after 1570, various Englishmen, including Francis Drake (ca. 1540–1596), fought the Spanish around the world. Jacques Cartier (1491–1557) explored parts of North America for France in 1534.

Samuel de Champlain (1567–1635) and the French explored the St. Lawrence River, seeking furs to trade. The Dutch established settlements at

New Amsterdam and in the Hudson River Valley. The Dutch founded trading centers in the East Indies, the West Indies, and southern Africa. Swedes settled on the Delaware River in 1638.

DRILL: THE LATE MIDDLE AGES AND THE RENAISSANCE

1. Italian Renaissance art can be most appropriately described as

   (A) neoclassicism, in which the traditional characteristics of harmony and symmetry were valued.

   (B) a revolt against the classical style and the advancement of a new artistic standard based on humanism.

   (C) characterized by the spectacular and the deliberately nonsymmetrical.

   (D) romantic idealism predicated upon notions of secular fantasy.

   (E) the triumph of symbolism.

2. All of the following are characteristics of Renaissance humanism EXCEPT

   (A) sanctity of the Latin texts of scriptures.

   (B) belief that ancient Latin and Greek writers were inferior to later authors.

   (C) rejection of Christian principles.

   (D) that it functioned as a primary cause of the Reformation.

   (E) that it resulted in scholarship in ancient languages.

3. Luther supported all of the following EXCEPT

   (A) the doctrine of consubstantiation.

   (B) publication of the Scriptures in the vernacular.

   (C) elimination of the indulgence system.

(D) the significance of predestination.

(E) revision of sacramental theology.

4. The Thirty Years' War became primarily a political conflict during the

(A) Danish phase.   (D) Swedish-French phase.

(B) Swedish phase.   (E) Italian phase.

(C) Bohemian phase.

5. The Society of Jesus (Jesuits) was founded by

(A) Pope Paul III.   (D) Michael Servetus.

(B) Francis Xavier.   (E) John Knox.

(C) Ignatius Loyola.

BOURBON, BAROQUE, AND THE ENLIGHTENMENT

Through the Treaty of Paris (1763), France lost all possessions in North America to Britain. (In 1762 France had ceded to Spain all French claims west of the Mississippi River and New Orleans.)

France entered the French-American Alliance of 1778 in an effort to regain lost prestige in Europe and to weaken her British adversary. In 1779 Spain joined France in the war, hoping to recover Gibraltar and the Floridas.

With the Treaty of Paris (1783), Britain recognized the independence of the United States of America and retroceded the Floridas to Spain. Britain left France no territorial gains by signing a separate and territorially generous treaty with the United States.

ECONOMIC DEVELOPMENTS

There were several basic assumptions of mercantilism: 1) Wealth is measured in terms of commodities, especially gold and silver, rather than in terms of productivity and income-producing investments; 2) Economic activities should increase the power of the national government in the direction of state controls; 3) Since a favorable balance of trade was important, a nation should purchase as little as possible from nations regarded as enemies. The concept of the mutual advantage of trade was not widely accepted; 4) Colonies existed for the benefit of the mother country, not for any mutual benefit that would be gained by economic development.

Absentee landlords and commercial farms replaced feudal manors, especially in England. Urbanization, increased population, and improvements in trade stimulated the demand for agricultural products.

The steam engine, developed by James Watt between 1765 and 1769, became one of the most significant inventions in human history. It was no longer necessary to locate factories on mountain streams where water wheels were used to supply power. Its portability meant that both steamboats and railroad engines could be built to transport goods across continents. Ocean-going vessels were no longer dependent on winds to power them. At the same time, textile machines revolutionized that industry.

BOURBON FRANCE

Louis XIV (reigned 1643–1715) believed in absolute, unquestioned authority. Louis XIV deliberately chose his chief ministers from the middle class in order to keep the aristocracy out of government.

Council orders were transmitted to the provinces by intendants, who supervised all phases of local administration (especially courts, police, and the collection of taxes).

Louis XIV never called the Estates General. His intendants arrested the members of the three provincial estates who criticized royal policy, and the parlements were too intimidated by the lack of success of the *Frondes* to offer further resistance.

Control of the peasants, who comprised 95 percent of the French population, was accomplished by numerous means. Some peasants kept as little as 20 percent of their cash crops after paying the landlord, the government, and the Church. Peasants also were subject to the *corvée*, a month's forced labor on the roads. People not at work on the farm were conscripted into the French army or put into workhouses. Finally, rebels were hanged or forced to work as galley slaves.

Under Louis XV (reigned 1715–1774) French people of all classes desired greater popular participation in government and resented the special privileges of the aristocracy. All nobles were exempt from certain taxes. Many were subsidized with regular pensions from the government. The highest offices of government were reserved for aristocrats. Promotions were based on political connections rather than merit.

There was no uniform code of laws and little justice. The king had arbitrary powers of imprisonment. Government bureaucrats were often petty tyrants, many of them merely serving their own interests. The bureaucracy became virtually a closed class. Vestiges of the feudal and manorial systems taxed peasants excessively compared to other segments of society. A group of intellectuals known as the *philosophes* gave expression to these grievances and discontent grew.

Louis XVI (reigned 1774–1792) married Marie Antoinette (1770), daughter of the Austrian Empress Maria Theresa. Louis XVI was honest, conscientious, and sought genuine reforms, but he was indecisive and lacking in determination. One of his first acts was to restore judicial powers to the French parlements. When he sought to impose new taxes on the undertaxed aristocracy, the parlements refused to register the royal decrees. In 1787 he granted toleration and civil rights to French Huguenots (Protestants).

In 1787 the king summoned the Assembly of the Notables, a group of 144 representatives of the nobility and higher clergy. Louis XVI asked them to tax all lands, without regard to privilege of family; to establish provincial assemblies; to allow free trade in grain; and to abolish forced labor on the roads. The Notables refused to accept these reforms and demanded the replacement of certain of the king's ministers.

The climax of the crisis came in 1788 when the king was no longer able to achieve either fiscal reform or new loans. He could not even pay the salaries of government officials. By this time one-half of government revenues went to pay interest on the national debt.

For the first time in 175 years, the king called for a meeting of the Estates General (1789). The Estates General formed itself into the National Assembly, and the French Revolution was under way.

ENGLAND, SCOTLAND, AND IRELAND

One of the underlying issues in this conflict was the constitutional issue of the relationship between the king and Parliament. In short, the question was whether England was to have a limited constitutional monarchy, or an absolute monarchy as in France and Prussia.

The theological issue focused on the form of church government England was to have. The episcopal form meant that the king, the Archbishop of Canterbury, and the bishops of the church would determine policy, theology, and the form of worship and service in the presbyterian form. Each congregation would have a voice in the life of the church, and a regional group of ministers, or "presbytery," would attempt to ensure "doctrinal purity."

The political implications for representative democracy were present in both issues. That is why most Presbyterians, Puritans, and Congregationalists sided with Parliament and most Anglicans and Catholics sided with the king.

The Parliament in effect bribed the king by granting him a tax grant in exchange for his agreement to the Petition of Right in 1628. It stipulated that no one should pay any tax, gift, loan, or contribution except as provided by an act of Parliament; no one should be imprisoned or detained without due process of law; all were to have the right to the writ of *habeas corpus;* there should be no forced billeting of soldiers in the homes of private citizens; and martial law was not to be declared in England.

In 1629 Charles I dissolved Parliament—for 11 years. Puritan leaders and leaders of the opposition in the House of Commons were imprisoned by the king, some for several years.

The established Church of England was the only legal church under Charles I, a Catholic. Archbishop of Canterbury William Laud (1573–1645) sought to enforce the king's policies vigorously. Arminian clergymen were to be tolerated, but Puritan clergymen silenced. Criticism was brutally suppressed. Several dissenters were executed.

The king , however, had no money, no army, and no popular support. He summoned the Parliament to meet in November 1640. With mobs in the street and rumors of an army enroute to London to dissolve Parliament, a bare majority of an underattended House of Commons passed a bill of attainder to execute the Earl of Strafford, one of the king's principal ministers. Fearing mob violence as well as Parliament itself, the king signed the bill and Strafford was executed in 1641. Archbishop William Laud was also arrested and eventually tried and executed in 1645.

The House of Commons passed a series of laws to strengthen its position and protect civil and religious rights. The Triennial Act (1641) provided that no more than three years should pass between Parliaments. Another act provided that the current Parliament should not be dissolved without its own consent. Various hated laws, taxes, and institutions were abolished: the Star Chamber, the High Commission, and power of the Privy Council to deal with property rights.

Men began identifying themselves as Cavaliers if they supported the king, or Roundheads if they supported Parliament.

The king withdrew to Hampton Court and sent the queen to France for safety. In March 1642 Charles II went to York, and the English Civil War began.

Charles put together a sizeable force with a strong cavalry and moved on London, winning several skirmishes.

Oliver Cromwell (1599–1658) led the parliamentary troops to victory, first with his cavalry, which eventually numbered 1,100, and then as lieutenant general in command of the well-disciplined and well-trained New Model Army. He eventually forced the king to flee.

During the Civil War, under the authority of Parliament, the Westminster Assembly convened to write a statement of faith for the Church of England that was Reformed or Presbyterian in content. Ministers and laymen from both England and Scotland participated for six years and wrote the *Westminster Confession of Faith*, still a vital part of Presbyterian theology.

The army tried Charles Stuart, formerly king of England, and sentenced him to death for treason.

After the execution of the king, Parliament abolished the office of king and the House of Lords. The new form of government was to be a Commonwealth, or Free State, governed by the representatives of the people in Parliament. This commonwealth lasted four years, between 1649 and 1653.

Royalists and Presbyterians both opposed Parliament for its lack of broad representation and for regicide. The army was greatly dissatisfied that elections were not held, as one of the promises of the Civil War was popular representation.

Surrounded by foreign enemies, the Commonwealth became a military state with a standing army of 44,000. The North American and West Indian colonies were forced to accept the government of the Commonwealth.

When it became clear that Parliament intended to stay in office permanently, Cromwell agreed to serve as Lord Protector from 1653–1659, with a Council of State and a Parliament. The new government permitted religious liberty, except for Catholics and Anglicans.

The new Parliament restored the monarchy from 1660–1688, but the Puritan Revolution clearly showed that the English constitutional system required a limited monarchy. Parliament in 1660 was in a far stronger position in its relationship to the king than it ever had been before.

Two events in 1688 goaded Parliament to action. In May, James reissued the Declaration of Indulgence with the command that it be read on two successive Sundays in every parish church. On June 10, 1688, a son was born to the king and his queen, Mary of Modena. As long as James was childless by his second wife, the throne would go to one of his Protestant daughters, Mary or Anne. The birth of a son, who would be raised Roman Catholic, changed the picture completely.

A group of Whig and Tory leaders, speaking for both houses of Parliament, invited William and Mary to assume the throne of England.

On November 5, 1688, William and his army landed at Torbay in Devon. King James offered many concessions, but it was too late. He finally fled to France. William assumed temporary control of the government and summoned a free Parliament. In February 1689 William and Mary were declared joint sovereigns, with the administration given to William.

The English Declaration of Rights (1689) declared the following:

1) The king could not be a Roman Catholic.

2) A standing army in time of peace was illegal without parliamentary approval.

3) Taxation was illegal without parliamentary consent.

4) Excessive bail and cruel and unusual punishments were prohibited.

5) Right to trial by jury was guaranteed.

6) Free elections to parliament would be held.

The Toleration Act (1689) granted the right of public worship to Protestant Nonconformists, but did not permit them to hold office. The Act did not extend liberty to Catholics or Unitarians, but normally they were left alone. The Trials for Treason Act (1696) stated that a person accused of treason should be shown the accusations against him and should have the advice of counsel. They also could not be convicted except upon the testimony of two independent witnesses. Freedom of the press was permitted, but with very strict libel laws.

Control of finances was to be in the hands of the Commons, including military appropriations. There would no longer be uncontrolled grants to the king.

Judges were made independent of the Crown. Thus, England declared itself a limited monarchy and a Protestant nation.

RUSSIA UNDER THE TSARS

In 1480, Ivan III (1440–1505), "Ivan the Great," put an end to Mongol domination over Russia. Ivan took the title of Caesar (Tsar) as heir of the Eastern Roman Empire (Byzantine Empire). He encouraged the Eastern Orthodox Church and called Moscow the "Third Rome."

Ivan IV (1530–1584), "Ivan the Terrible," grandson of Ivan III, began westernizing Russia. A contemporary of Queen Elizabeth, he welcomed both the English and Dutch and opened new trade routes to Moscow and the Caspian Sea. English merchant adventurers opened Archangel on the White Sea and provided a link with the outer world free from Polish domination.

After a "Time of Troubles" following Ivan's death in 1584, stability returned to Russia in 1613 when the Zemsky Sobor (Estates General representing the Russian Orthodox Church, landed gentry, townspeople, and a few peasants) elected Michael Romanov, who ruled as tsar from 1613 to 1645.

Under Michael Romanov, Russia extended its empire to the Pacific. Romanov continued westernization. By the end of the seventeenth century, 20,000 Europeans lived in Russia, developing trade and manufacturing, practicing medicine, and smoking tobacco, while Russians began trimming their beards and wearing Western clothing.

In 1649 three monks were appointed to translate the Bible for the first time into Russian. The Raskolniki (Old Believers) refused to accept any Western innovations or liturgy in the Russian Orthodox Church and were severely persecuted as a result.

Peter I (reigned 1682–1725) was one of the most extraordinary people in Russian history. The driving ambitions of Peter the Great's life were to modernize Russia and to compete with the great powers of Europe on equal terms. By the end of Peter's reign, Russia was producing more iron than England.

Peter built up the army through conscription and a 25-year term of enlistment. He gave flintlocks and bayonets to his troops instead of the old muskets and pikes. Artillery was improved and discipline enforced. By the end of his reign, Russia had a standing army of 210,000, despite a population of only 13 million.

The tsar ruled by decree (*ukase*). Government officials and nobles acted under government authority, but there was no representative body.

All landowners owed lifetime service to the state, either in the army, the civil service, or at court. In return for government service, they received land and serfs to work their fields.

Conscription required each village to send recruits for the Russian army. By 1709 Russia manufactured most of its own weapons and had an effective artillery.

After a series of largely ineffective rulers, Catherine II, "the Great," (reigned 1762–1796) continued the westernization process begun by Peter the Great. The three partitions of Poland, in 1772, 1793, and 1795, respectively, occurred under Catherine II's rule. Russia also annexed the Crimea and warred with Turkey during her reign.

ITALY AND THE PAPACY

Italy in the seventeenth and eighteenth centuries remained merely a geographic expression divided into small kingdoms, most of which were under foreign domination. Unification of Italy into a national state did not occur until the mid-nineteenth century.

THE SCIENTIFIC REVOLUTION AND SCIENTIFIC SOCIETIES

Science and religion were not in conflict in the seventeenth and eighteenth centuries. Scientists universally believed they were studying and analyzing God's creation, not an autonomous phenomenon known as "Nature." There was no attempt, as in the nineteenth and twentieth centuries, to secularize science.

For the first time in human history, the eighteenth century saw the appearance of a secular worldview. This became known as the age of the Enlightenment. In the past, some kind of a religious perspective had always been central to Western civilization. The philosophical starting point for the Enlightenment was the belief in the autonomy of man's intellect apart from God. The most basic assumption was faith in reason rather than faith in revelation.

The Enlightenment believed in the existence of God as a rational explanation of the universe and its form; "God" was a deistic Creator who made the universe and then was no longer involved in its mechanistic operation. That mechanistic operation was governed by "natural law."

Rationalists stressed deductive reasoning or mathematical logic as the basis for their epistemology (source of knowledge). They started with "self-evident truths," or postulates, from which they constructed a coherent and logical system of thought.

René Descartes (1596–1650) sought a basis for logic and thought he found it in man's ability to think. "I think; therefore, I am" was his most famous statement.

Benedict de Spinoza (1632–1677) developed a rational pantheism in which he equated God and nature. He denied all free will and ended up with an impersonal, mechanical universe.

Gottfried Wilhelm Leibniz (1646–1716) worked on symbolic logic and calculus, and invented a calculating machine. He, too, had a mechanistic world- and life- view and thought of God as a hypothetical abstraction rather than a persona.

Empiricists stressed inductive observation—the "scientific method"—as the basis for their epistemology.

John Locke (1632–1704) pioneered in the empiricist approach to knowledge and stressed the importance of environment in human development. He classified knowledge as 1) according to reason, 2) contrary to reason, or 3) above reason. Locke thought reason and revelation were both complementary and from God.

David Hume (1711–1776) was a Scottish historian and philosopher who began by emphasizing the limitations of human reasoning and later became a dogmatic skeptic.

The Enlightenment believed in a closed system of the universe in which the supernatural was not involved in human life, in contrast to the traditional view of an open system in which God, angels, and devils were very much a part of human life on earth.

The "Counter-Enlightenment" is a comprehensive term encompassing diverse and disparate groups who disagreed with the fundamental assumptions of the Enlightenment and pointed out its weaknesses.

Roman Catholic Jansenism in France argued against the idea of an uninvolved or impersonal God. Hasidism in Eastern European Jewish communities, especially in the 1730s, stressed a joyous religious fervor in direct communion with God.

CULTURE OF THE BAROQUE AND ROCOCO

The Baroque emphasized grandeur, spaciousness, unity, and emotional impact. The splendor of Versailles typifies the baroque in architecture; gigantic frescoes unified around the emotional impact of a single theme is Baroque art; the glory of Bach's *Christmas Oratorio* expresses the baroque in music. Although the Baroque began in Catholic Counter-Reformation countries to teach in a concrete, emotional way, it soon spread to Protestant nations as well, and some of the greatest Baroque artists and composers were Protestant (e.g., Johann Sebastian Bach and George Frideric Handel).

Characteristics of the Rococo can be found in the compositions of both Franz Josef Haydn (1732–1809) and Wolfgang Amadeus Mozart (1756–1791).

DRILL: BOURBON, BAROQUE AND THE ENLIGHTENMENT

1. Among the non-French intellectuals who participated in the Enlighten-ment were all of the following EXCEPT

    (A) Edward Gibbon.   (D) Leopold von Ranke.

    (B) David Hume.   (E) John Locke.

    (C) Benjamin Franklin.

2. Which of the following characteristics best describe the values of the Baroque period?

    (A) Symmetry, harmony, order

    (B) Gigantism, spectacular, lack of symmetry

    (C) Flatness, otherworldliness, spirituality

    (D) Introspective, psychoanalytical, independence

    (E) Materialistic, order, harmony

3. The Enlightenment philosopher who believed that civilization has been corrupting influence in history was

    (A) Jean-Jacques Rousseau.

    (B) Denis Diderot.

    (C) Baron Charles de Montesquieu.

    (D) Voltaire.

    (E) Marquis Marie Jean de Condorcet.

4.   The Enlightenment philosopher Voltaire sought to accomplish all of the following EXCEPT

    (A) religious toleration.

    (B) ridicule the English political system.

    (C) win sympathy for the Calas family.

    (D) win acceptance of Enlightened Despotism.

    (E) decrease the power of the French nobility.

5.   The Royal Society of London is most logically associated with

    (A) the Scientific Revolution.

    (B) James II Stuart of England.

    (C) efforts to bring the Christian faith to the natives of Africa.

    (D) financing the establishment of colonial settlements in British North America.

    (E) supporting commercial activities in the Far East.

REVOLUTION AND THE NEW WORLD ORDER (1789–1848)

THE FRENCH REVOLUTION I (1789–1799)

Radical ideas about society and government were developed during the eighteenth century in response to the success of the "scientific" and "intellectual" revolutions of the preceding two centuries. Armed with new scientific knowledge of the physical universe, as well as new views of the human capacity to detect "truth," social critics assailed existing modes of thought governing political, social, religious, and economic life. Ten years of up-heaval in France (1789–1799) further shaped modern ideas and practices.

Napoleon Bonaparte spread some of the revolutionary ideas about the administration of government as he conquered much of Europe. The modern world that came of age in the eighteenth century was characterized by rapid, revolutionary changes that paved the way for economic modernization and political centralization throughout Europe.

INFLUENCE OF THE ENLIGHTENMENT (C. 1700–1800)

While they came from virtually every country in Europe, most of the famous social activists were French, and France was the center of this intellectual revolution. Voltaire, Denis Diderot, Baron de Montesquieu, and Jean Jacques Rousseau were among the more famous philosophers.

The major assumptions of the Enlightenment were as follows:

Human progress was possible through changes in one's environment, i.e., better people, better societies, better standard of living.

Humans were free to use reason to reform the evils of society.

Material improvement would lead to moral improvement.

Natural science and human reason would discover the meaning of life.

Laws governing human society would be discovered through application of the scientific method of inquiry.

Inhuman practices and institutions would be removed from society in a spirit of humanitarianism.

Human liberty would ensue if individuals became free to choose what reason dictated was good.

The Enlightenment's Effect on Society:

Religion. Deism or "natural religion" rejected traditional Christianity by promoting an impersonal God who did not interfere in the daily lives of the people. The continued discussion of the role of God led to a general skepticism associated with Pierre Bayle (1647–1706), a type of religious skepticism pronounced by David Hume (1711–1776), and a theory of atheism or materialism advocated by Baron d'Holbach (1723–1789).

Political Theory. John Locke (1632–1704) and Jean Jacques Rousseau (1712–1778) believed that people were capable of governing themselves, either through a political (Locke) or social (Rousseau) contract forming the basis of society. However, most philosophes opposed democracy, preferring a limited monarchy that shared power with the nobility.

Economic Theory. The assault on mercantilist economic theory was begun by the physiocrats in France, who proposed a "laissez-faire" (nongovernmental interference) attitude toward land usage, and culminated in the theory of economic capitalism associated with Adam Smith (1723–1790) and his slogans of free trade, free enterprise, and the law of supply and demand.

Attempting to break away from the strict control of education by the church and state, Jean Jacques Rousseau advanced the idea of progressive education, where children learn by doing and where self-expression is encouraged. This idea was carried forward by Johann Pestalozzi, Johann Basedow, and Friedrich Fröbel, and influenced a new view of childhood.

Psychological Theory. In the *Essay Concerning Human Understanding* (1690), John Locke offered the theory that all human knowledge was the result of sensory experience, without any preconceived notions.

CAUSES OF THE FRENCH REVOLUTION

The rising expectations of "enlightened" society were demonstrated by the increased criticism directed toward government inefficiency and corruption, and toward the privileged classes. The clergy (First Estate) and nobility (Second Estate), representing only two percent of the total population of 24 million, were the privileged classes and were essentially tax exempt. The remainder of the population (Third Estate) consisted of the middle class, urban workers, and the mass of peasants, who bore the entire burden of taxation and the imposition of feudal obligations. As economic conditions worsened in the eighteenth century, the French state became poorer, and totally dependent on the poorest and most depressed sections of the economy for support at the very time this tax base had become saturated.

Designed to represent the three estates of France, the Estates General had only met twice, once at its creation in 1302 and again in 1614. When the French parlements insisted that any new taxes must be approved by this body, King Louis XVI reluctantly ordered it to assemble at Versailles by May 1789.

Election fever swept over France for the very first time. The election campaign took place in the midst of the worst subsistence crisis in eighteenth-century France, with widespread grain shortages, poor harvests, and inflated bread prices. Finally, on May 5, 1789, the Estates General met and argued over whether to vote by estate or individually. Each estate was ordered to meet separately and vote as a unit. The Third Estate refused and insisted that the entire assembly stay together.

PHASES OF THE REVOLUTION

The National Assembly (1789–1791): After a six-week deadlock over voting methods, representatives of the Third Estate declared themselves the true National Assembly of France (June 17). Defections from the First and Second Estates then caused the king to recognize the National Assembly (June 27) after dissolving the Estates General. At the same time, Louis XVI ordered troops to surround Versailles.

The "Parisian" revolution began at this point. Angry because of food shortages, unemployment, high prices, and fear of military repression, the workers and tradespeople began to arm themselves.

The Legislative Assembly (1791–1792): While the National Assembly had been rather homogeneous in its composition, the new government began to fragment into competing political factions. The most important political clubs were republican groups such as the Jacobins (radical urban) and Girondins (moderate rural), while the Sans-culottes (working class, extremely radical) were a separate faction with an economic agenda.

The National Convention (1792–1795): Meeting for the first time in September 1792, the Convention abolished monarchy and installed republicanism. Louis XVI was charged with treason, found guilty, and executed on January 21, 1793. Later the same year, the queen, Marie Antoinette, met the same fate.

The most notorious event of the French Revolution was the famous "Reign of Terror" (1793–1794), the government's campaign against its internal enemies and counterrevolutionaries.

The Directory (1795–1799): The Constitution of 1795 restricted voting and office holding to property owners. The middle class was in control. It wanted peace in order to gain more wealth and to establish a society in which money and property would become the only requirements for prestige and power. Despite rising inflation and mass public dissatisfaction, the Directory government ignored a growing shift in public opinion. When elections in April 1797 produced a triumph for the royalist right, the results were annulled, and the Directory shed its last pretense of legitimacy.

But the weak and corrupt Directory government managed to hang on for two more years because of great military success. French armies annexed the Austrian Netherlands, the left bank of the Rhine, Nice, and Savoy. The Dutch republic was made a satellite state of France. The greatest military victories were won by Napoleon Bonaparte, who drove the Austrians out of northern Italy and forced them to sign the Treaty of Campo Formio (October 1797), in return for which the Directory government agreed to Bonaparte's scheme to conquer Egypt and threaten English interests in the East.

THE FRENCH REVOLUTION II: THE ERA OF NAPOLEON (1799–1815)

Consulate Period, 1799–1804 (Enlightened Reform): The new government was installed on December 25, 1799, with a constitution which concentrated supreme power in the hands of Napoleon. His aim was to govern France by demanding obedience, rewarding ability, and organizing everything in orderly hierarchical fashion. Napoleon's domestic reforms and policies affected every aspect of society.

Empire Period, 1804–1814 (War and Defeat): After being made Consul for Life (1801), Napoleon felt that only through an empire could France retain its strong position in Europe. On December 2, 1804, Napoleon crowned himself emperor of France in Notre Dame Cathedral.

Militarism and Empire Building: Beginning in 1805 Napoleon engaged in constant warfare that placed French troops in enemy capitals from Lisbon and Madrid to Berlin and Moscow, and temporarily gave Napoleon the largest empire since Roman times. Napoleon's Grand Empire consisted of an enlarged France, satellite kingdoms, and coerced allies.

French-ruled peoples viewed Napoleon as a tyrant who repressed and exploited them for France's glory and advantage. Enlightened reformers believed Napoleon had betrayed the ideals of the Revolution. The downfall of Napoleon resulted from his inability to conquer England, economic distress caused by the Continental System (boycott of British goods), the Peninsular War with Spain, the German War of Liberation, and the invasion of Russia. The actual defeat of Napoleon was the result of the Fourth Coalition and the Battle of Leipzig ("Battle of Nations"). Napoleon was exiled to the island of Elba as a sovereign with an income from France.

After learning of allied disharmony at the Vienna peace talks, Napoleon left Elba and began the Hundred Days by seizing power from the restored French king, Louis XVIII. Napoleon's gamble ended at Waterloo in June

1815. He was exiled as a prisoner of war to the South Atlantic island of St. Helena, where he died in 1821.

THE POST-WAR SETTLEMENT: THE CONGRESS OF VIENNA (1814–1815)

The Congress of Vienna met in 1814 and 1815 to redraw the map of Europe after the Napoleonic era, and to provide some way of preserving the future peace of Europe. Europe was spared a general war throughout the remainder of the nineteenth century. But the failure of the statesmen who shaped the future in 1814–1815 to recognize the forces, such as nationalism and liberalism, unleashed by the French Revolution, only postponed the ultimate confrontation between two views of the world—change and accommodation, or maintaining the status quo.

The Vienna settlement was the work of the representatives of the four nations that had done the most to defeat Napoleon: England (Lord Castlereagh), Austria (Prince Klemens Von Metternich), Russia (Tsar Alexander I), and Prussia (Karl Von Hardenberg).

Arrangements to guarantee the enforcement of the status quo as defined by the Vienna settlement included two provisions: The "Holy Alliance" of Tsar Alexander I of Russia, an idealistic and unpractical plan, existed only on paper. No one except Alexander took it seriously. But the "Quadruple Alliance" of Russia, Prussia, Austria, and England provided for concerted action to arrest any threat to the peace or balance of power.

From 1815 to 1822, European international relations were controlled by the series of meetings held by the great powers to monitor and defend the status quo: the Congress of Aix-la-Chapelle (1818), the Congress of Troppau (1820), the Congress of Laibach (1821), and the Congress of Verona (1822).

THE INDUSTRIAL REVOLUTION

Twentieth-century English historian Arnold Toynbee began to refer to the period since 1750 as "the Industrial Revolution." The term was intended to describe a time of transition when machines began to significantly displace human and animal power in methods of producing and distributing goods, and an agricultural and commercial society converted into an industrial one.

These changes began slowly, almost imperceptibly, gaining momentum with each decade, so that by the middle of the nineteenth century, industrialism had swept across Europe west to east, from England to Eastern Europe. Few countries purposely avoided industrialization, because of its promised material improvement and national wealth. The economic changes that constitute the Industrial Revolution have done more than any other movement in Western civilization to change Western life.

Roots of the Industrial Revolution could be found in the following: 1) the Commercial Revolution (1500–1700), which spurred the great economic growth of Europe and brought about the Age of Discovery and Exploration, which in turn helped to solidify the economic doctrines of mercantilism; 2) the effect of the Scientific Revolution, which produced the first wave of mechanical inventions and technological advances; 3) the increase in population in Europe from 140 million people in 1750 to 266 million people by the mid-part of the nineteenth century (more producers, more consumers); and 4) the political and social revolutions of the nineteenth century, which began the rise to power of the "middle class," and provided leadership for the economic revolution.

The revolution occurred first in the cotton and metallurgical industries, because those industries lent themselves to mechanization. A series of mechanical inventions (1733–1793) would enable the cotton industry to mass-produce quality goods. The need to replace wood as an energy source led to the use of coal, which increased coal mining, and resulted ultimately in the invention of the steam engine and the locomotive. The development of steam power allowed the cotton industry to expand and transformed the iron industry. The factory system, which had been created in response to the new energy sources and machinery, was perfected to increase manufactured goods.

A transportation revolution ensued in order to distribute the productivity of machinery and deliver raw materials to the eager factories. This led to the growth of canal systems, the construction of hard-surfaced "macadam" roads, the commercial use of the steamboat (demonstrated by Robert Fulton, 1765–1815), and the railway locomotive (made commercially successful by George Stephenson, 1781–1848).

A subsequent revolution in agriculture made it possible for fewer people to feed the population, thus freeing people to work in factories, or in the new fields of communications, distribution of goods, or services like teaching, medicine, and entertainment.

The Industrial Revolution created a unique new category of people who were dependent on their job alone for income, a job from which they might be dismissed without cause. Until 1850 workers as a whole did not share in the general wealth produced by the Industrial Revolution. Conditions would improve as the century wore on, as union action combined with general prosperity and a developing social conscience to improve the working conditions, wages, and hours first of skilled labor, and later of unskilled labor.

The most important sociological result of industrialism was urbanization. The new factories acted as magnets, pulling people away from their rural roots and beginning the most massive population transfer in history. Cities made the working class a powerful force by raising consciousness and enabling people to unite for political action and to remedy economic dissatisfaction.

IMPACT OF THOUGHT SYSTEMS ("ISMS") ON THE EUROPEAN WORLD

Romanticism was a reaction against the rigid classicism, rationalism, and deism of the eighteenth century. Strongest between 1800 and 1850, the romantic movement differed from country to country and from romanticist to romanticist. Because it emphasized change, it was considered revolutionary in all aspects of life.

English literary Romantics like Wordsworth and Coleridge epitomized the romantic movement. Other romantics included Goethe of Germany, Hugo of France, and Pushkin of Russia. Romanticism also affected music and the visual arts.

Romantic philosophy stimulated an interest in Idealism, the belief that reality consists of ideas, as opposed to materialism. This school of thought (Philosophical Idealism), founded by Plato, was developed through the writings of Immanuel Kant, Johann Gottlieb Fichte, and Georg Wilhelm Hegel, the greatest exponent of this school of thought. Hegel believed that an impersonal God rules the universe and guides humans along a progressive evolutionary course by means of a process called dialecticism; this is a historical process by which one thing is constantly reacting with its opposite (the thesis and antithesis), producing a result (synthesis) that automatically meets another opposite and continues the series of reactions.

Conservatism arose in reaction to liberalism and became a popular alternative for those who were frightened by the violence, terror, and social disorder unleashed by the French Revolution. Early conservatism was allied to the restored monarchical governments of Austria, Russia, France, and England. Support for conservatism came from the traditional ruling classes as well as the peasants who still formed the majority of the population. In essence, conservatives believed in order, society, and the state, as well as faith and tradition.

The theory of liberalism was the first major theory in the history of Western thought to teach that the individual is a self-sufficient being whose freedom and well-being are the sole reasons for the existence of society. Liberalism was more closely connected to the spirit and outlook of the Enlightenment than to any of the other "isms" of the early nineteenth century. Liberalism was reformist and political rather than revolutionary in character.

Liberals also advocated economic individualism (i.e., laissez-faire capitalism), heralded by Adam Smith (1723–1790) in his 1776 economic masterpiece, *Wealth of Nations*.

The regenerative force of liberal thought in early nineteenth-century Europe was dramatically revealed in the explosive force of the power of nationalism. Raising the level of consciousness of people having a common language, soil, traditions, history, culture, and experience to seek political unity around an identity of what or who constitutes the nation, nationalism was aroused and made militant during the turbulent French Revolutionary era.

Nationalistic thinkers and writers examined the language, literature, and folkways of their people, thereby stimulating nationalist feelings. Emphasizing the history and culture of the various European peoples reinforced and glorified national sentiment.

SOCIALISM

The Utopian Socialists (from *Utopia*, Saint Thomas More's (1478–1535) book on a fictional ideal society) were the earliest writers to propose an equitable solution to improve the distribution of society's wealth. While they endorsed the productive capacity of industrialism, they denounced its mismanagement. Human society was to be organized as a community rather than a mixture of competing, selfish individuals. All the goods a person needed could be produced in one community.

The Anarchists rejected industrialism and the dominance of government.

"Scientific" Socialism, or Marxism, was the creation of Karl Marx (1818–1883), a German scholar who, with the help of Friedrich Engels (1820–1895), intended to replace utopian hopes and dreams with a militant blueprint for socialist working-class success. The principal works of this revolutionary school of socialism were *The Communist Manifesto* and *Das Kapital*.

The theory of dialectical materialism enabled Marx to explain the history of the world. By borrowing Hegel's dialectic, substituting materialism and realism in place of Hegel's idealism, and inverting the methodological process, Marx was able to justify his theoretical conclusions. Marxism consisted of a number of key propositions: 1) An economic interpretation of history, i.e., all human history has been determined by economic factors (mainly who controls the means of production and distribution); 2) Class struggle, i.e., since the beginning of time there has been a class struggle between the rich and the poor or the exploiters and the exploited; 3) Theory of surplus value, i.e., the true value of a product was labor, and since the worker received a small portion of his just labor price, the difference was surplus value, "stolen" from him by the capitalist; and 4) Socialism was inevitable, i.e., capitalism contained the seeds of its own destruction (overproduction, unemployment, etc.); the rich would grow richer and the poor would grow poorer until the gap between each class (proletariat and bourgeoisie) is so great that the working classes would rise up in revolution and overthrow the elite bourgeoisie to install a "dictatorship of the proletariat." As modern capitalism was dismantled, the creation of a classless society guided by the principle "from each according to his abilities, to each according to his needs" would take place.

THE REVOLUTIONARY TRADITION

The year 1848 is considered the watershed of the nineteenth century. The revolutionary disturbances of the first half of the nineteenth century reached a climax in a new wave of revolutions that extended from Scandinavia to southern Italy, and from France to central Europe. Only England and Russia avoided violent upheaval.

The issues were substantially the same as they had been in 1789. What was new in 1848 was that these demands were far more widespread and irrepressible than ever. Whole classes and nations demanded to be fully included in society. Aggravated by rapid population growth and the social disruption caused by industrialism and urbanization, a massive tide of discontent swept across the Western world.

Generally speaking, the 1848 upheavals shared the strong influences of romanticism, nationalism, and liberalism, as well as a new factor of economic dislocation and instability.

Specifically, a number of similar conditions existed in several countries: 1) Severe food shortages caused by poor harvests of grain and potatoes (e.g., Irish potato famine); 2) Financial crises caused by a downturn in the commercial and industrial economy; 3) Business failures; 4) Widespread unemployment; 5) A sense of frustration and discontent among urban artisan and working classes as wages diminished; 6) A system of poor relief which became overburdened; 7) Living conditions, which deteriorated in the cities; 8) The power of nationalism in the Germanys, Italys, and in Eastern Europe to inspire the overthrow of existing governments. Middle-class predominance within the unregulated economy continued to drive liberals to push for more government reform and civil liberty. They enlisted the help of the working classes to put more pressure on the government to change.

In France, working-class discontent and liberals' unhappiness with the corrupt regime of King Louis Philippe (reigned 1830–1848)—especially his minister Guizot (1787–1874)—erupted in street riots in Paris on February 22–23, 1848. With the workers in control of Paris, King Louis Philippe abdicated on February 24, and a provisional government proclaimed the Second French Republic.

The "June Days" revolt was provoked when the government closed the national workshop. This new revolution (June 23–26) was unlike previous uprisings in France. It marked the inauguration of genuine class warfare; it was a revolt against poverty and a cry for the redistribution of property. It foreshadowed the great social revolutions of the twentieth century. The revolt was extinguished after General Cavaignac was given dictatorial powers by the government. The June Days confirmed the political predominance of conservative property holders in French life.

The new Constitution of the Second French Republic provided for a unicameral legislature and executive power vested in a popularly elected president of the Republic. When the election returns were counted, the government's candidate was defeated by a "dark horse" candidate, Prince Louis Napoleon Bonaparte (1808–1873), a nephew of the great emperor. On December 20, 1848, Louis Napoleon was installed as president of the Republic.

In December 1852 Louis Napoleon became Emperor Napoleon III (reigned 1852–1870), and France retreated from republicanism again.

Italian nationalists and liberals wanted to end Hapsburg (Austrian), Bourbon (Naples and Sicily), and papal domination and unite these disparate Italian regions into a unified liberal nation. A revolt by liberals in Sicily in January 1848 was followed by the granting of liberal constitutions in Naples, Tuscany, Piedmont, and the Papal States. Milan and Venice expelled their Austrian rulers. In March 1848 upon hearing the news of the revolution in

Vienna, a fresh outburst of revolution against Austrian rule occurred in Lombardy and Venetia, with Sardinia-Piedmont declaring war on Austria. Simultaneously, Italian patriots attacked the Papal States, forcing the pope, Pius IX (1792–1878), to flee to Naples for refuge.

The temporary nature of these initial successes was illustrated by the speed with which the conservative forces regained control. In the north Austrian Field Marshal Radetzky (1766–1858) swept aside all opposition, regaining Lombardy and Venetia and crushing Sardinia-Piedmont. In the Papal States the establishment of the Roman Republic (February 1849) under the leadership of Giuseppe Mazzini and the protection of Giuseppe Garibaldi (1807–1882) would fail when French troops took Rome in July 1849 after a heroic defense by Garibaldi. Pope Pius IX returned to Rome cured of his liberal leanings. In the south and in Sicily the revolts were suppressed by the former rulers.

The immediate effect of the 1848 Revolution in France was a series of liberal and nationalistic demonstrations in the German states (March 1848), with the rulers promising liberal concessions. The liberals' demand for constitutional government was coupled with another demand—some kind of union or federation of the German states.

GREAT BRITAIN AND THE VICTORIAN COMPROMISE

The Victorian Age (1837–1901) is associated with the long reign of Queen Victoria, who succeeded her uncle King William IV at the age of 18, and married her cousin, Prince Albert. The early years of her reign coincided with the continuation of liberal reform of the British government, accomplished through an arrangement known as the "Victorian Compromise." The Compromise was a political alliance of the middle class and aristocracy to exclude the working class from political power. The middle class gained control of the House of Commons, the aristocracy controlled the government, the army, and the Church of England. This process of accommodation worked successfully.

Parliamentary reforms continued after passage of the 1832 Reform Bill. Laws were enacted abolishing slavery throughout the Empire (1833). The Factory Act (1831) forbade the employment of children under the age of nine. The New Poor Law (1834) required the needy who were able and unemployed to live in workhouses. The Municipal Reform Law (1835) gave control of the cities to the middle class. The last remnants of the mercantilistic age fell with the abolition of the Corn Laws (1846) and repeal of the old navigation acts (1849).

The revolutions of 1848 began with much promise, but all ended in defeat for a number of reasons. They were spontaneous movements which lost their popular support as people lost their enthusiasm. Initial successes by the revolutionaries were due less to their strength than to the hesitancy of governments to use their superior force. Once this hesitancy was overcome, the revolutions were smashed. They were essentially urban movements, and the conservative landowners and peasants tended, in time, to nullify the spontaneous actions of the urban classes. The middle class, who led the revolutions, came to fear the radicalism of their working-class allies. Divisions among national groups, and the willingness of one nationality to deny rights to other nationalities, helped to destroy the revolutionary movements in Central Europe.

However, the results of 1848–1849 were not entirely negative. Universal male suffrage was introduced in France; serfdom remained abolished in Austria and the German states; parliaments were established in Prussia and other German states, though dominated by princes and aristocrats; and Prussia and Sardinia-Piedmont emerged with new determination to succeed in their respective unification schemes.

A new age followed the revolutions of 1848–1849, as Otto von Bismarck (1815–1898), one of the dominant political figures of the second half of the nineteenth century, was quick to realize. If the mistake of these years was to believe that great decisions could be brought about by speeches and parliamentary majorities, the sequel showed that in an industrial era new techniques involving ruthless force were all too readily available. The period of *Realpolitik*—of realistic, iron-fisted politics and diplomacy—followed.

DRILL: REVOLUTION AND THE NEW WORLD ORDER

1. During the "Liberal Regime" of Louis Philippe, radical economic and social plans were advanced by all of the following EXCEPT

    (A) Saint-Simon.

    (B) Charles Fourier.

    (C) Louis Blanc.

    (D) Auguste Blanqui.

    (E) Pierre Joseph Proudhon.

2. The French Revolution of 1830 was primarily caused by

    (A) the desire for a dynastic change.

    (B) fierce French nationalism.

    (C) the need for a liberal government.

    (D) the collapse of the French economy.

    (E) the failure of French foreign policy.

3. The "Reign of Terror" was

    (A) a reaction by monarchists to crush the revolutionary movement in the countryside.

    (B) the persecution of Huguenots by Catholics.

    (C) the invasion by Austria to re-establish the monarchy.

    (D) the famine and shortages in Paris caused by the French Revolution.

    (E) the Revolutionary government's campaign against internal enemies and counter-revolutionaries.

4. The main goals of the Directory government, dominated by the middle class, included

    (A) establishing a society where money and property were the only requirements for prestige and power.

    (B) re-establishing the monarchy in France.

    (C) redistributing property to the peasants.

    (D) eliminating the Catholic Church.

    (E) eliminating all taxes.

5. How many times prior to 1787 had the Estates-General met?

    (A) It met every year since its creation in 1302.

    (B) It had met twice since its creation in 1302.

    (C) It had only met at its creation in 1302.

(D) It had met every five years since its creation in 1302.

(E) It had met twelve times since its creation in 1302.

REALISM AND MATERIALISM (1848–1914)

REALPOLITIK AND THE TRIUMPH OF NATIONALISM

After the collapse of the revolutionary movements of 1848, the leadership of Italian nationalism was transferred to Sardinian leaders Victor Emmanuel II (1820–1878), Camillo de Cavour (1810–1861), and Giuseppe Garibaldi (1807–1882). The new leaders did not entertain romantic illusions about the process of transforming Sardinia into a new Italian kingdom; they were practitioners of the politics of realism, *Realpolitik*.

In 1855, under Cavour's direction, Sardinia joined Britain and France in the Crimean War against Russia. At the Paris Peace Conference (1856), Cavour addressed the delegates on the need to eliminate the foreign (Austrian) presence in the Italian peninsula and attracted the attention and sympathy of the French Emperor, Napoleon III.

After being provoked, the Austrians declared war on Sardinia in 1859. French forces intervened, and the Austrians were defeated in the battles of Magenta (June 4) and Solferino (June 24).

Napoleon III, without consulting Cavour, signed a secret peace treaty (The Truce of Villafranca) on July 11, 1859. Sardinia received Lombardy but not Venetia; the other terms indicated that Sardinian influence would be restricted and that Austria would remain a power in Italian politics. The terms of Villafranca were clarified and finalized with the Treaty of Zurich (1859).

In 1860, Cavour arranged the annexation of Parma, Modena, Romagna, and Tuscany into Sardinia. These actions were recognized by the Treaty of Turin between Napoleon III and Victor Emmanuel II; Nice and Savoy were transferred to France.

Giuseppe Garibaldi and his Red Shirts landed in Sicily in May 1860 and extended the nationalist activity to the south. Within three months, Sicily was taken and by September 7, Garibaldi was in Naples and the Kingdom of the Two Sicilys had fallen under Sardinian influence. Cavour distrusted Garibaldi, but Victor Emmanuel II encouraged him.

In February 1861, in Turin, Victor Emmanuel was declared King of Italy and presided over an Italian Parliament which represented the entire Italian peninsula with the exception of Venetia and the Patrimony of St. Peter (Rome). Cavour died in June 1861.

Venetia was incorporated into the Italian Kingdom in 1866 as a result of an alliance between Bismarck's Prussia and the Kingdom of Italy which preceded the Austro-Prussian War between Austria and Prussia. In return for opening a southern front against Austria, Prussia, upon its victory, arranged for Venetia to be transferred to Italy.

Bismarck was again instrumental in the acquisition of Rome into the Italian Kingdom in 1870. In 1870, the Franco-Prussian War broke out and the French garrison, which had been in Rome providing protection for the Pope, was withdrawn to serve on the front against Prussia. Italian troops seized Rome, and in 1871, as a result of a plebiscite, Rome became the capital of the Kingdom of Italy.

BISMARCK AND THE UNIFICATION OF GERMANY

In the period after 1815, Prussia emerged as an alternative to a Hapsburg-based Germany.

Otto von Bismarck (1810–1898) entered the diplomatic service of Wilhelm I as the Revolutions of 1848 were being suppressed. By the early 1860s, Bismarck had emerged as the principal adviser and minister to the king. Bismarck was an advocate of a Prussian-based (Hohenzollern) Germany.

In 1863, the Schleswig-Holstein crisis broke. These provinces, which were occupied by Germans, were under the personal rule of Christian IX (1818–1906) of Denmark. The Danish government advanced a new constitution which specified that Schleswig and Holstein would be annexed into Denmark. German reaction was predictable, and Bismarck arranged for joint Austro-Prussian military action. Denmark was defeated and agreed (Treaty of Vienna, 1864) to give up the provinces, and Schleswig and Holstein were to be jointly administered by Austria and Prussia.

In 1870, deteriorating relations between France and Germany collapsed over the Ems Dispatch. Wilhelm I was approached by representatives of the French government who requested a Prussian pledge not to interfere on the issue of the vacant Spanish throne. Wilhelm I refused to give such a pledge and informed Bismarck of these developments through a telegram from Ems.

Bismarck exploited the situation by initiating a propaganda campaign against the French. Subsequently, France declared war and the Franco-Prussian War (1870–1871) commenced. Prussian victories at Sedan and Metz proved decisive; Napoleon III and his leading general, Marshal MacMahon, were captured. Paris continued to resist but fell to the Prussians in January 1871. The Treaty of Frankfurt (May 1871) concluded the war and resulted in France ceding Alsace-Lorraine to Germany and a German occupation until an indemnity was paid.

The German Empire was proclaimed on January 18, 1871 with Wilhelm I becoming the Emperor of Germany. Bismarck became the Imperial Chancellor. Bavaria, Baden, Württemberg, and Saxony were incorporated into the new Germany.

THE CRIMEAN WAR

The Crimean War originated in the dispute between two differing groups of Christians and their protectors over privileges in the Holy Land. During the nineteenth century, Palestine was part of the Ottoman Turkish Empire. In 1852, the Turks negotiated an agreement with the French to provide enclaves in the Holy Land to Roman Catholic religious orders; this arrangement appeared to jeopardize already existing agreements which provided access to Greek Orthodox religious orders. Czar Nicholas I (reigned 1825–1855), unaware of the impact of his action, ordered Russian troops to occupy several Danubian principalities; his strategy was to withdraw from these areas once the Turks agreed to clarify and guarantee the rights of the Greek Orthodox orders. In October 1853, the Turks demanded that the Russians withdraw from the occupied principalities. The Russians failed to respond, and the Turks declared war. In February 1854, Nicholas advanced a draft for a settlement of the Russo-Turkish War; it was rejected and Great Britain and France joined the Ottoman Turks and declared war on Russia.

With the exception of some naval encounters in the Gulf of Finland off the Aaland Islands, the war was conducted on the Crimean Peninsula in the Black Sea. In September 1854, more than 50,000 British and French troops landed in the Crimea, determined to take the Russian port city of Sebastopol. In December 1854, Austria reluctantly became a co-signatory of the Four Points of Vienna, a statement of British and French war aims. In 1855, Piedmont joined Britain and France in the war. In March 1855, Czar Nicholas I died and was succeeded by Alexander II (reigned 1855–1881), who was opposed to continuing the war. In December 1855, the Austrians, under excessive pressure from the British, French, and Piedmontese, sent an ultimatum to Russia in which they threatened to renounce their neutrality. In response, Alexander II indicated that he would accept the Four Points.

The resulting Peace of Paris had the following major provisions: Russia had to acknowledge international commissions to regulate maritime traffic on the Danube, recognize Turkish control of the mouth of the Danube, renounce all claims to the Danubian Principalities of Moldavia and Wallachia (which later led to the establishment of Rumania), agree not to fortify the Aaland Islands, renounce its previously espoused position of protector of the Greek Orthodox residents of the Ottoman Empire, and return all occupied territories to the Ottoman Empire. The Straits Convention of 1841 was revised by neutralizing the Black Sea. The Declaration of Paris specified rules to regulate commerce during periods of war. Lastly, the independence and integrity of the Ottoman Empire were recognized and guaranteed by the signatories.

THE EASTERN QUESTION AND THE CONGRESS OF BERLIN

In 1876, Turkish forces under the leadership of Osman Pasha soundly defeated Serbian armies. In March 1878, the Russians and the Turks signed the Peace of San Stephano; implementation of its provisions would have resulted in Russian hegemony in the Balkans and dramatically altered the balance of power in the eastern Mediterranean.

Britain, under the leadership of Prime Minister Benjamin Disraeli (1804–1881), denounced the San Stephano Accord, dispatched a naval squadron to Turkish waters, and demanded that the San Stephano agreement be scrapped. The German Chancellor, Otto von Bismarck, intervened and offered his services as mediator.

The delegates of the major powers convened in June and July 1878 to negotiate a settlement. Prior to the meeting, Disraeli had concluded a series of secret arrangements with Austria, Russia, and Turkey. The combined impact of these accommodations was to restrict Russian expansion in the region, reaffirm the independence of Turkey, and maintain British control of the Mediterranean.

The Russians, who had won the war against Turkey and had imposed the harsh terms of the San Stephano Treaty, found that they left the conference with very little (Kars, Batum, etc.) for their effort. Although Disraeli was the primary agent of this anti-Russian settlement, the Russians blamed Bismarck for their dismal results. Their hostility toward Germany led Bismarck (1879) to embark upon a new system of alliances which transformed European diplomacy and rendered any additional efforts of the Concert of Europe futile.

CAPITALISM AND THE EMERGENCE OF THE NEW LEFT (1848–1914)

During the nineteenth century, Europe experienced the full impact of the Industrial Revolution. The Industrial Revolution resulted in improving aspects of the physical lives of a greater number of Europeans; at the same time, it led to a factory system with undesirable working and living conditions and the abuses of child labor.

As the century progressed, the inequities of the system became increasingly evident. Trade-unionism and socialist political parties emerged which attempted to address these problems and improve the lives of the working class.

During the period from 1815 to 1848, Utopian Socialists such as Robert Owen (1771–1858), Saint Simon, and Charles Fourier advocated the establishment of a political-economic system which was based on romantic concepts of the ideal society. The failure of the Revolutions of 1848 and 1849 discredited the Utopian Socialists, and the new "Scientific Socialism" advanced by Karl Marx (1818–1883) became the primary ideology of protest and revolution. Marx stated that the history of humanity was the history of class struggle and that the process of the struggle (the dialectic) would continue until a classless society was realized. The Marxian dialectic was driven by the dynamics of materialism. The proletariat, or the industrial working class, needed to be educated and led towards a violent revolution which would destroy the institutions which perpetuated the struggle and the suppression of the majority. After the revolution, the people would experience the dictatorship of the proletariat, during which the Communist party would provide leadership. Marx advanced these concepts in a series of tracts and books, including *The Communist Manifesto* (1848), *Critique of Political Economy* (1859), and *Das Kapital*.

BRITAIN

In 1865, Palmerston died, and during the next two decades significant domestic developments occurred which expanded democracy in Great Britain. The dominant leaders of this period were William Gladstone (1809–1898) and Benjamin Disraeli (1804–1881). As the leader of the Liberal party (until 1895), Gladstone supported Irish Home Rule, fiscal responsibility, free trade, and the extension of democratic principles. He was opposed to imperialism, the involvement of Britain in European affairs, and the further centralization of the British government. Disraeli argued for an aggressive foreign policy, the expansion of the British Empire, and, after opposing democratic reforms, the extension of the franchise.

THE SECOND FRENCH REPUBLIC AND THE SECOND EMPIRE

Louis Napoleon became the president of the Second French Republic in December 1848. During the three-year life of the Second Republic, Louis Napoleon demonstrated his skills as a gifted politician through the manipulation of the various factions in French politics. His deployment of troops in Italy to rescue and restore Pope Pius IX was condemned by the republicans, but strongly supported by the monarchists and moderates.

Louis Napoleon minimized the importance of the Legislative Assembly, capitalized on the developing Napoleonic Legend, and courted the support of the army, the Catholic Church, and a range of conservative political groups. The Falloux Law returned control of education to the church. Further, Louis Napoleon was confronted with Article 45 of the constitution, which stipulated that the president was limited to one four-year term; he had no intention of relinquishing power. With the assistance of a core of dedicated supporters, Louis Napoleon arranged for a coup d'état on the night of December 1–2, 1851. The Second Republic fell and was soon replaced by the Second French Empire.

Louis Napoleon drafted a new constitution which resulted in a highly centralized government. On December 2, 1852, he announced that he was Napoleon III, Emperor of the French.

The Second Empire collapsed after the capture of Napoleon III during the Franco-Prussian War (1870–1871). After a regrettable Parisian experience with a communist type of government, the Third French Republic was established; it would survive until 1940.

IMPERIAL RUSSIA

The autocracy of Nicholas I's (reigned 1825–1855) regime was not threatened by the revolutionary movements of 1848. In 1848 and 1849, Russian troops suppressed disorganized Polish attempts to reassert Polish nationalism.

Russian involvement in the Crimean War met with defeat. Russian ambitions in the eastern Mediterranean had been thwarted by a coalition of Western European states. In 1855 Nicholas I died and was succeeded by Alexander II (reigned 1855–1881).

Fearing the transformation of Russian society from below, Alexander II instituted a series of reforms which altered the nature of the social contract in Russia. In 1861, Alexander II declared that serfdom was abolished. Further, he issued the following reforms: 1) The serf (peasant) would no longer be dependent upon the lord; 2) all people were to have freedom of movement and were free to change their means of livelihood; and 3) the serf could enter into contracts and could own property.

The last years of the reign of Alexander II witnessed increased political opposition, manifested in demands for reforms from an ever more hostile group of intellectuals, the emergence of a Russian populist movement, and attempts to assassinate the czar. As the regime matured, greater importance was placed on traditional values. This attitude developed at the same time that nihilism, which rejected romantic illusions of the past in favor of a rugged realism, was being advanced by such writers as Ivan Turgenev in his *Fathers and Sons*.

The notion of the inevitability and desirability of a social and economic revolution was promoted through the Russian populist movement. Originally, the populists were interested in an agrarian utopian order. The populists had no national support. Government persecution of the populists resulted in the radicalization of the movement. In the late 1870s and early 1880s, leaders such as Andrei Zheleabov and Sophie Perovsky became obsessed with the need to assassinate Alexander II. In March 1881, the czar was killed in St. Petersburg when his carriage was bombed. He was succeeded by Alexander III (reigned 1881–1894), who advocated a national policy based on "Orthodoxy, Autocracy, and Nationalism." Alexander III died in 1894 and was succeeded by the last of the Romanovs to hold power, Nicholas II (reigned 1894–1917). Nicholas II displayed a lack of intelligence, wit, political acumen, and the absence of a firm will throughout his reign. From his ministers to his wife, Alexandra, to Rasputin (1872–1916), Nicholas was influenced by stronger personalities.

The opposition to the Czarist government became more focused and thus, more threatening, with the emergence of the Russian Social Democrats and the Russian Social Revolutionaries. Both groups were Marxist. Vladimir Ilyich Ulyanov, also known as Lenin, became the leader of the Bolsheviks, a splinter group of the Social Democrats. By winter (1904–1905), the accumulated consequences of inept management of the economy and the prosecution of the Russo-Japanese War reached a critical stage. A group under the leadership of the radical priest Gapon marched on the Winter Palace in St. Petersburg (January 9, 1905) to submit a list of grievances to the czar. Troops fired on the demonstrators and many casualties resulted on this "Bloody Sunday." In June 1905, naval personnel on the battleship Potemkin mutinied while the ship was in Odessa. In October 1905, Nicholas II issued the October Manifesto calling for the convocation of a Duma, or assembly of state, which would serve as an advisory body to the czar, extending civil liberties to include freedom of speech, assembly, and press, and announcing that Nicholas II would reorganize his government.

The leading revolutionary forces differed in their responses to the manifesto. The Octobrists indicated that they were satisfied with the arrangements; the Constitutional Democrats, also known as the Kadets, demanded a more liberal representative system. The Duma convened in 1906 and, from its outset to the outbreak of the First World War, was paralyzed by factionalism which was exploited by the czar's ministers. By 1907, Nicholas II's ministers had recovered the real power of government. Russia experienced a general though fragile economic recovery by 1909, which lasted until the war.

ORIGINS, MOTIVES, AND IMPLICATIONS OF THE NEW IMPERIALISM (1870–1914)

By the 1870s, the European industrial economies required external markets to distribute products which could not be absorbed within their domestic economies. Further, excess capital was available and foreign investment, while risky, appeared to offer high returns. Finally, the need for additional sources of raw materials served as a rationale and stimulant for imperialism. Politicians were also influenced by the numerous missionary societies which sought government protection, in extending Christianity throughout the world. European statesmen, were also interested in asserting their national power overseas through the acquisition of strategic (and many not so strategic) colonies.

The focus of most of the European imperial activities during the late nineteenth century was Africa. Initially, European interest in these activities was romantic. With John Hanning Speke's discovery of Lake Victoria (1858), Livingstone's surveying of the Zambezi, and Stanley's work on the Congo River, Europeans became enraptured with the greatness and novelty of Africa south of the Sahara.

Disraeli was involved in the intrigue which would result in the British acquisition of the Suez Canal (1875), and during the 1870s and 1880s Britain was involved in a Zulu War and announced the annexation of the Transvaal, which the Boers regained after their great victory of Majuba Hill (1881).

At about the same time, Belgium established its interest in the Congo; France, in addition to seizing Tunisia, extended its influence into French Equatorial Africa; and Italy established small colonies in East Africa. During the 1880s Germany acquired several African colonies including German East Africa, the Cameroons, Togoland, and German South West Africa. The Berlin Conference (1884–1885) resulted in an agreement which specified the following: 1) The Congo would be under the control of Belgium through an International Association; 2) More liberal use of the Niger and Congo rivers; 3) European powers could acquire African territory through first occupation and second notifying the other European states of their occupation and claim.

British movement north of the Cape of Good Hope involved Europeans fighting one another rather than a native African force. The Boers had lived in South Africa since the beginning of the nineteenth century. With the discovery of gold (1882) in the Transvaal, many English Cape settlers moved into the region. The Boers, under the leadership of Paul Kruger, restricted the political and economic rights of the British settlers and developed alternative railroads through Mozambique which would lessen the Boer dependency on the Cape colony. The crisis mounted and, in 1899, the Boer War began. Until 1902, the British and Boers fought a war which was costly to both sides. Britain prevailed and by 1909, the Transvaal, Orange Free State, Natal, and the Cape of Good Hope were united into the Union of South Africa.

Another area of increased imperialist activity was the Pacific. In 1890, the American naval Captain Alfred Mahan published *The Influence of Sea Power Upon History*; in this book he argued that history demonstrated that nations which controlled the seas prevailed. During the 1880s and 1890s naval ships required coaling stations. While Britain, the Netherlands, and France demonstrated that they were interested in Pacific islands, the most active states in this region during the last 20 years of the nineteenth century were Germany and the United States. The United States acquired the Philippines in 1898. Germany gained part of New Guinea, and the Marshall, Caroline, and Mariana island chains. The European powers were also interested in the Asian mainland. Most powers agreed with the American Open Door Policy which recognized the independence and integrity of China and provided economic access for all the powers. Rivalry over China (Manchuria) was a principal cause for the outbreak of the Russo-Japanese War in 1904.

THE AGE OF BISMARCK (1871–1890)

During the period from the establishment of the German Empire in January 1871 to his dismissal as chancellor of Germany in March 1890, Otto von Bismarck dominated European diplomacy and established an integrated political and economic structure for the new German state. Bismarck established a statist system which was reactionary in political philosophy and based upon industrialism, militarism, and innovative social legislation.

During the 1870s and 1880s, Bismarck's domestic policies were directed at the establishment of a strong united German state which would be capable of defending itself from a French war of revenge designed to restore Alsace-Lorraine to France. Laws were enacted which unified the monetary system, established an Imperial Bank and strengthened existing banks, developed universal German civil and criminal codes, and required compulsory military service. All of these measures contributed to the integration of the German state.

In order to develop public support for the government and to minimize the threat from the left, Bismarck instituted a protective tariff, to maintain domestic production, and introduced many social and economic laws to provide social security, regulate child labor, and improve working conditions for all Germans.

Bismarck's foreign policy was centered on maintaining the diplomatic isolation of France. In the crisis stemming from the Russo-Turkish War (1877–1878), Bismarck tried to serve as the "Honest Broker" at the Congress of Berlin. Russia did not succeed at the conference and incorrectly blamed Bismarck for its failure. Early in the next year, a cholera epidemic affected Russian cattle herds, and Germany placed an embargo on the importation of Russian beef. The Russians were outraged by the German action and launched an anti-German propaganda campaign in the Russian press. Bismarck, desiring to maintain the peace and a predictable diplomatic environment, concluded a secret defensive treaty with Austria-Hungary in 1879. The Dual Alliance was very significant because it was the first "hard" diplomatic alliance of the era. A "hard" alliance involved the specific commitment of military support; traditional or "soft" alliances involved pledges of neutrality or to hold military conversations in the event of a war. The Dual Alliance, which had a five-year term and was renewable, directed that one signatory would assist the other in the event that one power was attacked by two or more states.

In 1882, another agreement, the Triple Alliance, was signed between Germany, Austria-Hungary, and Italy. In the 1880s, relations between Austria-Hungary and Russia became estranged over Balkan issues. Bismarck, fearing a war, intervened and by 1887, had negotiated the secret Reinsurance

Treaty with Russia. This was a "hard" defensive alliance with a three-year term that was renewable.

In 1888, Wilhelm I died and was succeeded by his son Friedrich III, who also died within a few months. Friedrich's son, Wilhelm II (reigned 1888–1918), came to power and soon found himself in conflict with Bismarck. Early in 1890, two issues developed which led ultimately to Bismarck's dismissal. First, Bismarck had evolved a scheme for a fabricated attempted coup by the Social Democratic party; his intent was to use this situation to create a national hysteria through which he could restrict the SPD through legal action. Second, Bismarck intended to renew the Reinsurance Treaty with Russia to maintain his policy of French diplomatic isolation. Wilhelm II opposed both of these plans; in March 1890, Bismarck, who had used the threat of resignation so skillfully in the past, suggested that he would resign if Wilhelm II would not approve of these actions. Wilhelm II accepted his resignation; in fact, Bismarck was dismissed.

THE MOVEMENT TOWARD DEMOCRACY IN WESTERN EUROPE TO 1914

Even after the reform measures of 1867 and 1884 to 1885, the movement toward democratic reforms in Great Britain continued unabated.

The most significant political reform of this long-lived Liberal government was the Parliament Act of 1911, which eliminated the powers of the House of Lords and resulted in the House of Commons becoming the unquestioned center of national power.

The most recurring and serious problem which Great Britain experienced during the period from 1890 to 1914 was the "Irish Question." The Irish situation became more complicated when the Protestant counties of the north started to enjoy remarkable economic growth from the mid-1890s; they were adamant in their rejection of all measures of Irish Home Rule. In 1914, an Irish Home Rule Act was passed by both the Commons and the Lords, but the Protestants refused to accept it. Implementation was deferred until after the war.

THE THIRD FRENCH REPUBLIC

In the fall of 1870, Napoleon III's Second Empire collapsed when it was defeated by the Prussian armies. Napoleon III and his principal aides were captured; later, he abdicated and fled to England. A National Assembly (1871–1875) was created and Adolphe Thiers was recognized as its chief executive. At the same time, a more radical political entity, the Paris Commune (1870–1871), came into existence and exercised extraordinary power during the siege of Paris. After the siege and the peace agreement with Prussia, the Commune refused to recognize the authority of the National Assembly. Led by radical Marxists, anarchists, and republicans, the Paris Commune repudiated the conservative and monarchist leadership of the National Assembly. From March to May 1871, the Commune fought a bloody struggle with the troops of the National Assembly. France began a program of recovery which led to the formulation of the Third French Republic in 1875. The National Assembly sought to 1) put the French political house in order; 2) establish a new constitutional government; 3) pay off an imposed indemnity and, in doing so, remove German troops from French territory; and 4) restore the honor and glory of France. In 1875 a constitution was adopted which provided for a republican government, consisting of a president (with little power), a Senate, and a Chamber of Deputies, which was the center of political power.

During the early years of the Republic, Leon Gambetta (1838–1882) led the republicans.

The most serious threat to the Republic came through the Dreyfus Affair. In 1894, Captain Alfred Dreyfus (1859–1935) was assigned to the French General Staff. A scandal broke when it was revealed that classified information had been provided to German spies. Dreyfus, a Jew, was charged, tried, and convicted. Later, it was determined that the actual spy was Commandant Marie Charles Esterhazy (1847–1923), who was acquitted in order to save the pride and reputation of the army. In 1906, the case was closed when Dreyfus was declared innocent and returned to the ranks. Rather than lead to the collapse of the Republic, the Dreyfus Affair demonstrated the intensity of anti-Semitism in French society, the level of corruption in the French army, and the willingness of the Catholic Church and the monarchists to join in a conspiracy against an innocent man.

From 1905 to 1914 the socialists under Jean Jaurès gained seats in the Chamber of Deputies. The Third French Republic endured the crises which confronted it and, in 1914, enjoyed the support of the vast majority of French citizens.

INTERNATIONAL POLITICS AND THE COMING OF THE WAR (1890–1914)

During the late nineteenth century, the economically motivated "New Imperialism" resulted in further aggravating the relations among the European powers. The Fashoda Crisis (1898–1899), the Moroccan Crisis (1905–1906), the Balkan Crisis (1908), and the Agadir Crisis (1911) demonstrated the impact of imperialism in heightening tensions among European states and in creating an environment in which conflict became more acceptable.

In 1908, the decadent Ottoman Empire was experiencing domestic discord which attracted the attention of both the Austrians and the Russians. These two powers agreed that Austria would annex Bosnia and Herzegovina, and Russia would be granted access to the Straits and thus the Mediterranean. Great Britain intervened and demanded that there be no change in the status quo in the Straits. Russia backed down from a confrontation, but Austria proceeded to annex Bosnia and Herzegovina.

On June 28, 1914, Archduke Franz Ferdinand (1863–1914), heir to the Austro-Hungarian throne, and his wife were assassinated while on a state visit to Sarajevo, the capital of Bosnia. The assassination resulted in a crisis between Austria-Hungary and Serbia, and would be the trigger for a series of events that in just two months' time would envelop Europe in war.

German Chancellor Bethmann-Hollweg and British Foreign Secretary Sir Edward Grey attempted to mediate the conflict. It was too late. On July 28, Austria declared war on Serbia and by August 4, Britain, France, and Russia (The Allies) were at war with Germany and Austria-Hungary (The Central Powers); later, other nations would join one of the two camps.

The initial military actions did not proceed as planned. The German Schlieffen Plan failed to succeed in the West as a result of German tactical adjustments and the French and British resistance in the First Battle of the Marne (September 1914). In the East, the Germans scored significant victories over the numerically superior Russians at the battles of Tannenberg and Masurian Lakes (August–September 1914).

DRILL: REALISM AND MATERIALISM

1. Venetia was annexed by Italy

    (A) through the Peace of Villafranca.

(B) immediately after Garibaldi's expedition.

(C) after the German Civil War.

(D) after the Franco-Prussian War.

(E) when Pius IX recognized the new Italian kingdom.

2. Bismarck was involved in negotiating all of the following diplomatic arrangements EXCEPT the

(A) Dual Alliance.   (D) Dual Entente.

(B) Triple Alliance.   (E) Congress of Berlin.

(C) Reinsurance Treaty.

3. The Third French Republic was endangered by which of the following internal crises?

I.   Panama Scandal   IV.   Paris Commune

II.   Boulanger Crisis   V.   The Dreyfus Affair

III. War in Sight Crisis

(A) I and II only.   (D) I, II, and V only.

(B) I, II, and III only.   (E) I, II, III, IV, and V.

(C) I, II, IV, and V only.

4. Which one of the following countries was LEAST active in acquiring a colonial empire during the period from 1870 to 1914?

(A) Britain   (D) Germany

(B) France   (E) Spain

(C) Belgium

5. All of the following became independent nations during the 19th century EXCEPT

(A) Bulgaria.

(D) Greece.

(B) Poland.

(E) Belgium.

(C) Italy.

WORLD WAR I AND EUROPE IN CRISIS (1914–1935)

THE ORIGINS OF WORLD WAR I

The long-range roots of the origins of World War I can be traced to numerous factors, beginning with the creation of modern Germany in 1871. Achieved through a series of wars, the emergence of this new German state completely destroyed Europe's traditional balance of power, and forced its diplomatic and military planners back to their drawing boards to rethink their collective strategies.

From 1871 to 1890, balance of power was maintained through the network of alliances created by the German Chancellor, Otto von Bismarck, and centered around his *Dreikaiserbund* (League of the Three Emperors) that isolated France, and the Dual (Germany, Austria) and Triple (Germany, Austria, Italy) Alliances. Bismarck's fall in 1890 resulted in new policies that saw Germany move closer to Austria, while England and France (Entente Cordiale, 1904), and later Russia (Triple Entente, 1907), drew closer.

Germany's dramatic defeat of France in 1870–1871 coupled with Kaiser William II's decision in 1890 to build up a navy comparable to that of Great Britain created a reactive arms race. This, blended with European efforts to carve out colonial empires in Africa and Asia—plus a new spirit of nationalism and the growing romanticization of war—helped create an unstable international environment in the years before the outbreak of World War I.

IMMEDIATE CAUSE OF WORLD WAR I

The Balkans, the area of Europe that now comprises Yugoslavia, Albania, Greece, Bulgaria, and Rumania, was Europe's most unstable area. Part of the rapidly decaying Ottoman (Turkish) Empire, it was torn by ethnic nationalism among the various small groups that lived there and competition between Austria-Hungary and Russia over spheres of influence in the region. In 1912, with Russian encouragement, a Balkan League which included

Serbia, Montenegro, Greece, and Bulgaria went to war with Turkey. Serbia, which wanted a spot on the Adriatic, was rebuffed when Austria created Albania in an attempt to deter Serbia. This intensified bitterness between both countries and prompted Russia to take a more protective attitude toward its southern Slavic cousins.

THE OUTBREAK OF THE WORLD WAR

On June 28, 1914, the Archduke Franz Ferdinand (1863–1914), heir to the Austrian throne, was assassinated by Gavrilo Princip, a young Serbian nationalist. Austria consulted with the German government on July 6 and received a "blank check" to take whatever steps necessary to punish Serbia. On July 23 1914, the Austrian government presented Serbia with a 10-point ultimatum that compelled Serbia – with the help of Austrian officials – to supress and punish all forms of Anti-Austrian sentiment within its borders. On July 25, 1914, three hours after mobilizing its army, Serbia accepted most of Austria's terms; it asked only that Austria's unprecedented demand to participate in judicial proceedings against anti-Austrian agitators be adjudicated by the International Tribunal at the The Hague.

Austria immediately broke official relations with Serbia and mobilized its army. On July 28, 1914, Austria went to war against Serbia, and began to bombard Belgrade the following day. At the same time, Russia gradually prepared for war against Austria and Germany, declaring full mobilization on July 30.

German military strategy, based in part on the plan of the Chief of the General Staff Count Alfred von Schlieffen, viewed Russian mobilization as an act of war. The Schlieffen Plan was based on a two-front war with Russia and France. It was predicated on a swift, decisive blow against France while maintaining a defensive position against slowly mobilizing Russia, which would be dealt with after France.

Germany demanded that Russia demobilize in 12 hours and appealed to the Russian ambassador in Berlin. Russia's offer to negotiate the matter was rejected, and Germany declared war on Russia on August 1, 1914. On August 3, Germany declared war on France. Berlin asked Belgium for permission to send its troops through its territory to attack France, which Belgium refused. On August 4, England, which agreed in 1839 to protect Belgian neutrality, declared war on Germany; Belgium followed suit. Between 1914 and 1915, the alliance of the Central Powers (Germany, Austria-Hungary, Bulgaria, and Turkey) faced the Allied Powers of England, France, Russia, Japan, and in 1917, the United States. A number of smaller countries were also part of the Allied coalition.

THE WAR IN 1914

The Western Front: After entering Belgium, the Germans attacked France on five fronts in an effort to encircle Paris rapidly. However, the unexpected Russian attack in East Prussia and Galicia from August 17 to 20 forced Germany to transfer important forces eastward to halt the Russian drive.

To halt a further German advance, the French army, aided by Belgian and English forces, counterattacked. In the Battle of the Marne (September 5–9), they stopped the German drive and forced small retreats. Mutual outflanking maneuvers by France and Germany created a battlefront that would determine the demarcation of the Western Front for the next four years. It ran, in uneven fashion, from the North Sea to Belgium and from northern France to Switzerland.

The Eastern Front: The Germans retreated after their assault against Warsaw in late September. Hindenburg's attack on Lodz, 10 days after he was appointed Commander-in-Chief of the Eastern Front (November 1), was a more successful venture; by the end of 1914 this important textile center was in German hands.

THE WAR IN 1915

The Western Front: Wooed by both sides, Italy joined the Allies and declared war on the Central Powers on May 23 after signing the secret Treaty of London (April 26). This treaty gave Italy Austrian provinces in the north and some Turkish territory.

The Eastern Front: On January 23, 1915, Austro-German forces began a coordinated offensive in East Russia and in the Carpathians. The two-pronged German assault in the north was stopped on February 27, while Austrian efforts to relieve their besieged defensive network at Przemysl failed when it fell into Russian hands on March 22.

German forces, strengthened by troops from the Western Front under August von Mackensen, began a move on May 2 to strike at the heart of the Russian Front. By August 1915, much of Russian Poland was in German hands.

In an effort to provide direct access to the Turks defending Gallipoli, Germany and Austria invaded Serbia in the early fall, aided by their new ally, Bulgaria. On October 7, the defeated Serbian army retreated to Corfu.

THE EASTERN MEDITERRANEAN

Turkey entered the war on the Central Power side on October 28, 1914, which prevented the shipment of Anglo-French aid to Russians through the Straits.

THE WAR IN 1916

The Western Front: The Battle for Verdun lasted from February 21 to December 18, 1916. From February until June, German forces, aided by closely coordinated heavy artillery barrages, assaulted the forts around Verdun. The Germans suffered 281,000 casualties while the French, under Marshal Henri Pétain (1856–1951), lost 315,000 while successfully defending their position.

To take pressure off the French, an Anglo-French force mounted three attacks on the Germans to the left of Verdun in July, September, and November. After the Battle of the Somme (July 1–November 18), German pressure was reduced, but at great loss. Anglo-French casualties totaled 600,000.

The Eastern Front: Orchestrated by Aleksei Brusilov (1853–1926), The Brusilov Offensive (June 4–September 20) envisioned a series of unexpected attacks along a lengthy front to confuse the enemy. By late August, he had advanced into Galicia and the Carpathians.

Rumania entered the war on the Allied side as a result of Russian successes and the secret Treaty of Bucharest (August 17). The ensuing Rumanian thrust into Translyvania was pushed back, and on December 6, a German-Bulgarian army occupied Bucharest as well as the bulk of Rumania.

The death of Austrian Emperor Franz Joseph (reigned 1848–1916) on November 21 prompted his successor, Charles I (1887–1922), to discuss the prospect of peace terms with his allies. On December 12, the four Central Powers, strengthened by the fall of Bucharest, offered four separate peace proposals based on their recent military achievements. The Allies rejected them on December 30 because they felt them to be insincere.

By the end of 1914, Allied fleets had gained control of the high seas, which caused Germany to lose control of its colonial empire. Germany's failure in 1914 to weaken British naval strength prompted German naval leaders to begin using the submarine as an offensive weapon to weaken the British. On February 4, Germany announced a war zone around the British Isles, and advised neutral powers to sail there at their own risk. On May 7,

1915 a German submarine sank the *Lusitania*, a British passenger vessel because it was secretly carrying arms.

NEW MILITARY TECHNOLOGY

Germany, Russia, and Great Britain all had submarines, but the German U-boats were the most effective. Designed principally for coastal protection, they increasingly used them to reduce British naval superiority through tactical and psychological means.

By the spring of 1915, British war planners finally awoke to the fact that the machine gun had become the mistress of defensive trench warfare. In a search for a weapon to counter trench defenses, the British developed tanks as an armored "land ship," and first used them on September 15, 1916, in the battle of the Somme.

Airplanes were initially used for observation purposes in the early months of the war. As their numbers grew, mid-air struggles using pistols and rifles took place, until the Germans devised a synchronized propeller and machine gun on its Fokker aircraft in May 1915. The Allies responded with similar equipment and new squadron tactics during the early days of the Verdun campaign in February 1916, and briefly gained control of the skies. They also began to use their aircraft for bombing raids against Zeppelin bases in Germany. Air supremacy shifted to the Germans in 1917.

During the first year of the war, the Germans began to use Zeppelin airships to bomb civilian targets in England. Though their significance was neutralized with the development of the explosive shell in 1916, Zeppelins played an important role as a psychological weapon in the first two years of the war.

In the constant search for methods to counter trench warfare, the Germans and the Allied forces experimented with various forms of internationally outlawed gas. On October 27, 1914, the Germans tried a nose/eye irritant gas at Neuve-Chapelle, and by the spring of 1915 had developed an asphyxiating lachrymatory chlorine gas at the Battle of Ypres. The British countered with a similar chemical at the battles of Champagne and Loos that fall.

THE RUSSIAN REVOLUTIONS OF 1917

The government's handling of the war prompted a new wave of civilian unrest. Estimates are that 1,140 riots and strikes swept Russia in January and

February, 1917. Military and police units ordered to move against the mobs either remained at their posts or joined them.

Though ordered by the czar not to meet until April, Duma leaders demanded dramatic solutions to the country's problems. Though dissolved on March 11, the Duma met in special session on March 13 and created a Provisional Committee of Elders to deal with the civil war. After two days of discussions, it decided that the czar must give up his throne, and on March 15, 1917, President Michael Rodzianko and Aleksandr Ivanovich Guchkov, leader of the Octobrist party, convinced the czar to abdicate.

THE BOLSHEVIK OCTOBER REVOLUTION

On October 23–24, 1917 Lenin returned from Finland to meet with the party's Central Committee to plan a coup. Though he met with strong resistance, the Committee agreed to create a Political Bureau (Politburo) to oversee the revolution.

Leon Trotsky, head of the Petrograd Soviet and its Military Revolutionary Committee, convinced troops in Petrograd to support Bolshevik moves. While Trotsky gained control of important strategic points around the city, Aleksandar Kerensky, well-informed of Lenin's plans, finally decided on November 6 to move against the plotters.

In response, Lenin and Trotsky ordered their supporters to seize the city's transportation and communication centers. The Winter Palace was captured later that evening, along with most of Kerensky's government.

The Second Congress opened at 11 p.m. on November 7, with Lev Kamenev (1883–1936), a member of Lenin's Politburo, as its head. Soon after it opened, many of the moderate socialists walked out in opposition to Lenin's coup, leaving the Bolsheviks and the Left Socialist Revolutionaries in control of the gathering.

At the Congress, it was announced that the government's new Cabinet, officially called the Council of People's Commissars (Sovnarkom), and responsible to a Central Executive Committee, would include Lenin as Chairman or head of government, Trotsky as Foreign Commissar, and Josef Stalin as Commissar of Nationalities. The Second Congress issued two decrees on peace and land. The first called for immediate peace without any consideration of indemnities or annexations, while the second adopted the Socialist Revolutionary land program that abolished private ownership of land and decreed that a peasant could only have as much land as he could farm. Village councils would oversee distribution.

THE CONSTITUENT ASSEMBLY

The Constituent Assembly, long promised by the Provisional Government as the country's first legally elected legislature, presented serious problems for Lenin, since he knew the Bolsheviks could not win a majority of seats in it. Regardless, Lenin allowed elections for it to be held on November 25 under universal suffrage. When the assembly convened on January 18 in the Tauride Palace, it voted down Bolshevik proposals and elected Victor Chernov, a Socialist Revolutionary, as president, and declared the country a democratic federal republic. The Bolsheviks walked out. The next day, troops dissolved the Assembly.

WORLD WAR I: THE FINAL PHASE (1917–1918)

As order collapsed among Russian units along the Eastern Front, the Soviet government began to explore cease fire talks with the Central Powers. Leon Trotsky, the Commissar of Foreign Affairs, offered general negotiations to all sides, and signed an initial armistice as a prelude to peace discussions with Germany at Brest-Litovsk on December 5, 1917.

The Soviets accepted terms that were integrated into the Treaty of Brest-Litovsk of March 3, 1918. According to its terms, in return for peace, Soviet Russia lost its Baltic provinces, the Ukraine, Finland, Byelorussia, and part of Transcaucasia. The area lost totaled 1,300,000 square miles and included 62 million people.

THE AMERICAN PRESENCE: NAVAL AND ECONOMIC SUPPORT

The United States, which had originally hoped that it could simply supply the Allies with naval and economic support, made its naval presence known immediately and helped Great Britain mount an extremely effective blockade of Germany and, through a convoy system, strengthened the shipment of goods across the Atlantic.

An initial token group, the American Expeditionary Force under General John J. Pershing (1860–1948), arrived in France on June 25, 1917, while by the end of April 1918, 300,000 Americans a month were placed as complete divisions alongside British and French units.

Stirred by the successes on the Marne, the Allies began their offensive against the Germans at Amiens on August 8, 1918. By September 3, the Germans retreated to the Hindenburg Line. On September 26, Foch began his final offensive, and took the Hindenburg Line the following day. Two days later, General Erich Ludendorff advised his government to seek a peace settlement. Over the next month, the French took St. Quetin (October 1), while the British occupied Cambrai, Le Cateau, and Ostend.

On September 14, Allied forces attacked in the Salonika area of Macedonia and forced Bulgaria to sue for peace on September 29. On September 19, General Allenby began an attack on Turkish forces at Megiddo in Palestine and quickly defeated them. In a rapid collapse of Turkish resistance, the British took Damascus, Aleppo, and finally forced Turkey from the war at the end of October. On October 24, the Italians began an assault against Austria-Hungary at Vitto Veneto and forced Vienna to sign armistice terms on November 3. Kaiser William II, pressured to abdicate, fled the country on November 9, and a republic was declared. On November 11, at 11 a.m., the war ended, with Germany accepting a harsh armistice.

THE PARIS PEACE CONFERENCE OF 1919–1920

The sudden, unexpected end of the war, combined with the growing threat of communist revolution throughout Europe created an unsettling atmosphere at the conference. The "Big Four" of Wilson (U.S.), Clemenceau (France), Lloyd-George (England), and Orlando (Italy) took over the peace discussions. The delays caused by uncertainty over direction at the beginning of the conference, Wilson's insistence that the League of Nations be included in the settlement, and fear of European-wide revolution resulted in a hastily prepared, dictated peace settlement.

THE TREATY OF VERSAILLES

The treaty's war guilt statements were the justification for its harsh penalties. The former German emperor, William II, was accused of crimes against "international morality and the sanctity of treaties," while Germany took responsibility for itself and for its allies for all losses suffered by the Allied Powers and their supporters as a result of German and Central Power aggression.

Germany had to return Alsace and Lorraine to France and Eupen-Malmedy to Belgium. France got Germany's Saar coal mines as reparations, while the Saar Basin was to be occupied by the major powers for 15 years, after which a plebiscite would decide its ultimate fate. Poland got a number of German provinces and Danzig, now a free city, as its outlet to the sea. Additionally, Germany lost all of its colonies in Asia and Africa.

The German Army was limited to 100,000 men and officers with 12-year enlistments for the former and 25 for the latter. The General Staff was also abolished. The Navy lost its submarines and most offensive naval forces, and was limited to 15,000 men and officers with the same enlistment periods as the army. Aircraft and blimps were outlawed. A Reparations Commission was created to determine Germany's war debt to the Allies, which it figured in 1921 to be $32.4 billion, to be paid over an extended period of time. In the meantime, Germany was to begin immediate payments in goods and raw materials.

The Allies presented the treaty to the Germans on May 7, 1919, but the Germans stated that its terms were too much for the German people, and that it violated the spirit of Wilson's Fourteen Points. After some minor changes were made, the Germans were told to sign the document or face an Allied advance into Germany. The treaty was signed on June 28, 1919, at Versailles.

TREATIES WITH GERMANY'S ALLIES

The Allied treaty with Austria legitimized the breakup of the Austrian Empire in the latter days of the war and saw Austrian territory ceded to Italy and the new states of Czechoslovakia, Poland, and Yugoslavia. The agreement included military restrictions and debt payments.

WEIMAR GERMANY (1918–1929)

The dramatic collapse of the German war effort in the second half of 1918 ultimately created a political crisis that forced the abdication of the kaiser and the creation of a German Republic on November 9.

From the outset, the Provisional Government, formed by a coalition of Majority and Independent Social Democrats Socialists, was beset by divisions from within and threats of revolution throughout Germany.

Elections for the new National Constituent Assembly, which was to be based on proportional representation, gave no party a clear majority. A coalition of the Majority Socialists, the Catholic Center party, and the German Democratic party (DDP) dominated the new assembly. On February 11, 1919, the assembly met in the historic town of Weimar and selected Friedrich Ebert as President of Germany. Two days later, Phillip Scheidemann (1865–1939) formed the first Weimar Cabinet and became Germany's first Chancellor.

On August 11, 1919, a new constitution was promulgated, which provided for a bicameral legislature.

POLITICS AND PROBLEMS OF THE WEIMAR REPUBLIC (1919–1923)

The territorial, manpower, and economic losses suffered during and after the war, coupled with a $32.4 billion reparations debt, had a severe impact on the German economy and society, and severely handicapped the new government's efforts to establish a stable governing environment.

In an effort of good faith based on hopes of future reparation payment reductions, Germany borrowed heavily and made payments in kind to fulfill its early debt obligations. The result was a spiral of inflation. After the Allied Reparations Commission declared Germany in default on its debt, the French and the Belgians occupied the Ruhr on January 11, 1923.

Chancellor Wilhelm Cuno (1876–1933) encouraged the Ruhr's Germans passively to resist the occupation, and printed worthless marks. The occupation ended on September 26, and helped prompt stronger Allied sympathy to Germany's payment difficulties, though the inflationary spiral had severe economic, social, and political consequences.

Weimar Politics (1919–1923): Germany's economic and social difficulties deeply affected its infant democracy. From February 1919 to August 1923, the country had six chancellors.

Growing right-wing discontent with the Weimar Government resulted in the assassination of the gifted head of the Catholic Center Party, Matthias Erzberger (1875–1921), on August 29, 1921, and the murder of Foreign Minister Walter Rathenau (1867–1922) on June 24, 1922. These were two of the most serious of over 350 political murders in Germany since the end of the war.

Following the death of President Ebert on February 28, 1925, two ballots were held for a new president, since none of the candidates won a majority on the first vote. On the second ballot on April 26, the Reichsblock, a coalition of Conservative parties, was able to get its candidate elected. War hero Paul von Hindenburg was narrowly elected.

The elections of May 20, 1928, saw the Social Democrats get almost one-third of the popular vote which, blended with other moderate groups, created a stable, moderate majority in the Reichstag, which chose Hermann Müller (1876–1931) as chancellor.

ITALY

Benito Mussolini, capitalizing on the sympathy of unfulfilled war veterans, disaffected nationalists, and those fearful of communism, formed the Fascio Italiano di Combattimento (Union of Combat) in Milan on March 23, 1919. Initially, Mussolini's movement had few followers, and it did badly in the November 1919 elections. However, Socialist strikes and unrest enabled him to convince Italians that he alone could bring stability and prosperity to their troubled country.

The resignation of the Bonomi Cabinet on February 9, 1922, underlined the government's inability to maintain stability. In the meantime, the Fascists seized control of Bologna in May, and Milan in August. In response, Socialist leaders called for a nationwide strike on August 1, 1922; it was stopped by Fascist street violence within 24 hours. On October 24, 1922, Mussolini told followers that if he was not given power, he would "March on Rome." Three days later, Fascists began to seize control of other cities, while 26,000 began to move towards the capital. On October 29, the king, Victor Emmanuel III (1869–1947), asked Mussolini to form a new government as Premier of Italy.

Beginning in 1925, Mussolini arrested opponents, closed newspapers, and eliminated civil liberties in a new reign of terror. On December 24, 1925, the legislature's powers were greatly limited, while those of Mussolini were increased as the new Head of State. Throughout 1926, Mussolini intensified his control over the country with legislation that outlawed strikes and created the syndicalist corporate system. A failed assassination attempt prompted the "Law for the Defense of the State" of November 25, 1926, that created a Special Court to deal with political crimes and introduced the death penalty for threats against the king, his family, or the Head of State.

ITALIAN FOREIGN POLICY

The nation's wish for post-war peace and stability saw Italy participate in all of the international developments in the 1920s aimed at securing normalcy in relations with its neighbors. Because Italy did not receive its desired portions of Dalmatia at the Paris Peace Conference, Italian nationalist Gabriele D'Annunzio seized Fiume on the Adriatic in the fall of 1919. D'Annunzio's daring gesture as well as his deep sense of Italian national pride deeply affected Mussolini. However, in the atmosphere of detente prevalent in Europe at the time, he agreed to settle the dispute with Yugoslavia in a treaty on January 27, 1924, which ceded most of the port to Italy, and the surrounding area to Yugoslavia.

In the fall of 1923, Mussolini used the assassination of Italian officials, who were working to resolve a Greek-Albanian border dispute, to seize the island of Corfu. Within a month, however, the British and the French convinced him to return the island for an indemnity.

SOVIET RUSSIA

The Civil War and "War Communism" had brought economic disaster and social upheaval throughout the country. On March 1, 1921, as the Soviet leadership met to decide on policies to guide the country in peace, a naval rebellion broke out at the Kronstadt naval base. The Soviet leadership sent Trotsky to put down the rebellion, which he did brutally by March 18.

Vladimir Ilyich Lenin, the founder of the Soviet State, suffered a serious stroke on May 26, 1922 and a second in December of that year. Lenin died on January 21, 1924.

Iosef Vissarionovich Dzugashvili (Joseph Stalin, 1879–1953) took over numerous, and in some cases, seemingly unimportant party organizations after the Revolution and transformed them into important bases of power. Among them were the Politburo (Political Bureau), which ran the country; the Orgburo (Organizational Bureau), which Stalin headed, and which appointed people to positions in groups that implemented Politiburo decisions; the Inspectorate (Rabkrin, Commissariat of the Workers' and Peasants' Inspectorate), which tried to eliminate party corruption; and the Secretariat, which worked with all party organs and set the Politburo's agenda. Stalin served as the party's General Secretary after 1921.

Lev Davidovich Bronstein (Trotsky, 1879–1940) was Chairman of the Petrograd Soviet, headed the early Brest-Litovsk negotiating team, served as Foreign Commissar, and was father of the Red Army. A brilliant organizer and theorist, Trotsky was also brusque and, some felt, overbearing.

In China the Soviets helped found a young Chinese Communist party (CCP) in 1921. When it became apparent that Sun Yat-sen's (1866–1925) revolutionary Kuomintang (KMT) was more mature than the infant CCP, the Soviets encouraged an alliance between its party and this movement. Sun's successor, Chiang Kai-shek (1887–1975), was deeply suspicious of the Communists and made their destruction part of his effort to militarily unite China.

Founded in 1919, the Soviet-controlled Comintern (Third International or Communist International) sought to coordinate the revolutionary activities of Communist parties abroad, though it often conflicted with Soviet diplomatic interests. It became an effectively organized body by 1924, and was completely Stalinized by 1928.

EUROPE IN CRISIS: DEPRESSION AND DICTATORSHIP (1929–1935)

In Great Britain in 1929, Ramsay MacDonald formed a minority Labour government that would last until 1931. The most serious problem facing the country was the Depression, which caused unemployment to reach 1,700,000 by 1930 and over 3 million, or 25 percent of the labor force, by 1932. To meet growing budget deficits caused by heavy subsidies to the unemployed, a special government commission recommended budget cuts and tax increases. Cabinet and labor union opposition helped reduce the total for the cuts but this could not help restore confidence in the government, which fell on August 24, 1931.

THE "NATIONAL GOVERNMENT" (1931–1935)

King George VI (1895–1952) helped convince MacDonald to return to office as head of a National Coalition cabinet made up of four Conservatives, four Labourites, and two Liberals. MacDonald's coalition swept the November 1931 general elections winning 554 of 615 seats.

The British government abandoned the gold standard on September 21, 1931, and adopted a series of high tariffs on imports. Unemployment peaked at 3 million in 1932 and dropped to 2 million two years later.

MacDonald resigned his position in June 1935 because of ill health and was succeeded by Stanley Baldwin, whose conservative coalition won 428 seats in new elections in November.

FRANCE: RETURN OF THE CARTEL DES GAUCHES (1932–1934)

France remained plagued by differences over economic reform between the Radicals and the Socialists. The latter advocated nationalization of major factories, expanded social reforms and public works programs for the unemployed, while the Radicals sought a reduction in government spending. This instability was also reflected in the fact that there were six Cabinets between June 1932 and February 1934. The government's inability to deal with the country's economic and political problems saw the emergence of a number of radical groups from across the political spectrum.

GERMANY: THE DEPRESSION

The Depression had a dramatic effect on the German economy and politics. The country's national income dropped 20 percent between 1928 and 1932, while unemployment rose from 1,320,000 in 1929 to 6 million by January 1932. This meant that 43 percent of the German work force were without jobs (compared to one-quarter of the work force in the U.S.).

In 1919, Adolf Hitler joined the German Workers party (DAP), which he soon took over and renamed the National Socialist German Workers party (NAZI). In 1920, the party adopted a 25-point program that included treaty revision, anti-Semitism, and economic and other social changes. They also created a defense cadre of the *Sturm-abteilung* (SA), "Storm Troopers," or "brown shirts," which was to help the party seize power.

The Beer Hall Putsch (1923): In the midst of the country's severe economic crisis in 1923, the party, which now had 55,000 members, tried to seize power, first by a march on Berlin, and then, when this seemed impossible, on Munich. The march was stopped by police, and Hitler and his supporters were arrested. Though sentenced to five years imprisonment, he was released after eight months. While incarcerated, he dictated *Mein Kampf* to Rudolf Hess.

Hitler's failed coup and imprisonment convinced him to seek power through legitimate political channels, which would require transforming the Nazi party. To do this, he reasserted singular control over the movement from 1924 to 1926. Party districts were set up throughout Germany, overseen by *gauleiters* personally appointed by Hitler.

Hindenburg's seven-year presidential term expired in 1932, and he was convinced to run for reelection to stop Hitler from becoming president in the first ballot of March 13. Hitler got only 30 percent of the vote (11.3 million) to Hindenburg's 49.45 percent (18.6 million).

On June 1, Chancellor Bruenig was replaced by Franz von Papen (1879–1969), who formed a government made up of aristocratic conservatives and others that he and Hindenburg hoped would keep Hitler from power.

Later in the year, von Papen convinced Hindenburg to appoint Hitler as chancellor and head of a new coalition cabinet with three seats for the Nazis. Hitler dissolved the Reichstag and called for new elections on March 5. Using presidential decree powers, he initiated a violent anti-Communist campaign that included the lifting of certain press and civil freedoms. On February 27, the Reichstag burned, which enabled Hitler to get Hindenburg to issue the

"Ordinances for the Protection of the German State and Nation," that removed all civil and press liberties as part of a "revolution" against communism. In the Reichstag elections of March 5, the Nazis only got 43.9 percent of the vote and 288 Reichstag seats but, through an alliance with the Nationalists, got majority control of the legislature.

Once Hitler had full legislative power, he began a policy of *Gleichschaltung* (coordination) to bring all independent organizations and agencies throughout Germany under his control. All political parties were outlawed or forced to dissolve, and on July 14, 1933, the Nazi party became the only legal party in Germany. In addition, non-Aryans and Nazi opponents were removed from the civil service, the court system, and higher education. On May 2, 1933, the government declared strikes illegal, abolished labor unions, and later forced all workers to join the German Labor Front (DAF) under Robert Ley. In 1934 the Reichsrat was abolished and a special People's Court was created to handle cases of treason. Finally, the secret police or Gestapo (*Geheime Staatspolizei*) was created on April 24, 1933 under Hermann Göring to deal with opponents and operate concentration camps. The party had its own security branch, the SD (*Sicherheitsdienst*) under Reinhard Heydrich.

From the inception of the Nazi state in 1933, anti-Semitism was a constant theme and practice in all *Gleichschaltung* and nazification efforts. Illegal intimidation and harassment of Jews was coupled with rigid enforcement of civil service regulations that forbade employment of non-Aryans. This first wave of anti-Semitic activity culminated with the passage of the Nuremburg Laws on September 15, 1935, that deprived Jews of German citizenship and outlawed sexual or marital relations between Jews and other Germans, thus effectively isolating them from the mainstream of German society.

Hitler's international policies were closely linked to his rebuilding efforts to give him a strong economic and military base for an active, aggressive, independent foreign policy. The Reich simultaneously quit the League of Nations. On January 26, 1934, Germany signed a non-aggression pact with Poland, which ended Germany's traditional anti-Polish foreign policy and broke France's encirclement of Germany via the Little Entente. This was followed by the Saarland's overwhelming decision to return to Germany. The culmination of Hitler's foreign policy moves, though, came with his March 15, 1935, announcement that Germany would no longer be bound by the military restrictions of the Treaty of Versailles, that it had already created an air force (Luftwaffe), and that the Reich would institute a draft to create an army of 500,000 men.

ITALY

Until Mussolini's accession to power, the pope had considered himself a prisoner in the Vatican. In 1926, Mussolini's government began talks to resolve this issue, which resulted in the Lateran Accords of February 11, 1929. Italy recognized the Vatican as an independent state, with the pope as its head, while the papacy recognized Italian independence. Catholicism was made the official state religion of Italy, and religious teaching was required in all secondary schools.

In an effort to counter the significance of France's Little Entente with Czechoslovakia, Yugoslavia, and Rumania, Mussolini concluded the Rome Protocols with Austria and Hungary which created a protective bond of friendship between the three countries.

In response to Hitler's announcement of German rearmament in violation of the Treaty of Versailles on March 16, 1935, France, England, and Italy met at Stresa in northern Italy on April 11–14, and concluded agreements that pledged joint military collaboration if Germany moved against Austria or along the Rhine.

Ethiopia (Abyssinia) became an area of strong Italian interest in the 1880s. The coastal region was slowly brought under Italian control until the Italian defeat at Ethiopian hands at Adowa in 1894. In 1906, the country's autonomy was recognized and in 1923 it joined the League of Nations. Mussolini, who had been preparing for war with Ethiopia since 1932, established a military base at Wal Wal in Ethiopian territory. Beginning in December 1934, a series of minor conflicts took place between the two countries, which gave Mussolini an excuse to plan for the full takeover of the country in the near future.

On October 2, 1935, Italy invaded Ethiopia, while the League of Nations, which had received four appeals from Ethiopia since January about Italian territorial transgressions, finally voted to adopt economic sanctions against Mussolini. Unfortunately, the League failed to stop shipments of oil to Italy and continued to allow it to use the Suez Canal. On May 9, 1936, Italy formally annexed the country and joined it to Somalia and Eritrea, which now became known as Italian East Africa.

SOVIET RUSSIA

The Second Five Year Plan (1933–1937) was adopted by the Seventeenth Party Congress in early 1934. Its economic and production targets were less severe than the First Plan, and thus more was achieved. By the end of the Second Plan, Soviet Russia had emerged as a leading world industrial power, though at great costs. It gave up quality for quantity, and created tremendous social and economic discord.

In the spring of 1935, the recently renamed and organized secret police, the NKVD, oversaw the beginnings of a new, violent Purge that eradicated 70 percent of the 1934 Central Committee and a large percentage of the upper military ranks. Stalin sent between 8 and 9 million to camps and prisons, and caused untold deaths before the Purges ended in 1938.

The period from 1929 to 1933 saw the U.S.S.R. retreat inward as the bulk of its energies were put into domestic economic growth. Regardless, Stalin remained sensitive to growing aggression and ideological threats abroad such as the Japanese invasion of Manchuria in 1931 and Hitler's appointment as Chancellor in 1933. As a result, Russia left its cocoon in 1934, joined the League of Nations, and became an advocate of "collective security" while the Comintern adopted Popular Front tactics, allying with other parties against fascism, to strengthen the U.S.S.R.'s international posture. Diplomatically, in addition to League membership, the Soviet Union completed a military pact with France.

INTERNATIONAL DEVELOPMENTS (1918–1935)

Efforts to create an international body to arbitrate international conflicts gained credence with the creation of a Permanent Court of International Justice to handle such matters at the First Hague Conference (1899). But no major efforts towards this goal were initiated until 1915, when pro-League of Nations organizations arose in the United States and Great Britain. Support for such a body grew as the war lengthened, and creation of such an organization became the cornerstone of President Woodrow Wilson's postwar policy, enunciated in his "Fourteen Points" speech before Congress on January 8, 1918.

The Preamble of the League's Covenant defined the League's purposes, which were to work for international friendship, peace, and security. To attain this, its members agreed to avoid war, maintain peaceful relations with other countries, and honor international law and accords.

Headquartered in Geneva, the League came into existence as the result of an Allied resolution on January 25, 1919, and the signing of the Treaty of Versailles on June 28, 1919. The League had the right, according to Article 8 of the League Covenant, to seek ways to reduce arms strength, while Articles 10 through 17 gave it the authority to search for means to stop war. It could recommend ways to stop aggression, and could suggest economic sanctions and other tactics to enforce its decisions, though its military ability to enforce its decisions was vague.

THE LOCARNO PACT (1925)

Signed on October 16, 1925, by England, France, Italy, Germany, and Belgium, the Locarno Pact guaranteed Germany's western boundaries and accepted the Versailles settlement's demilitarized zones. Italy and Great Britain agreed militarily to defend these lines if flagrantly violated.

In the same spirit, Germany signed arbitration dispute accords that mirrored the Geneva Protocol with France, Belgium, Poland, and Czechoslovakia, and required acceptance of League-determined settlements.

Since Germany would only agree to arbitration and not finalize its eastern border, France separately signed guarantees with Poland and Czechoslovakia to defend their frontiers.

The Locarno Pact went into force when Germany joined the League on September 10, 1926, acquiring, after some dispute, the U.S.'s permanent seat on the Council. France and Belgium began to withdraw from the Rhineland, though they left a token force there until 1930.

THE PACT OF PARIS (KELLOGG-BRIAND PACT)

The Locarno Pact heralded a new period in European relations known as the "Era of Locarno" that marked the end of post-war conflict and the beginning of a more normal period of diplomatic friendship and cooperation. It reached its peak, with the Franco-American effort in 1928 to seek an international statement to outlaw war. On August 27, 1928, 15 countries, including the U.S., Germany, France, Italy, and Japan, signed this accord with some minor limitations, which renounced war as a means of solving differences and as a tool of national policy. Within five years, 50 other countries signed the agreement.

LEAGUE AND ALLIED RESPONSE TO AGGRESSION

On September 19, 1931, the Japanese Kwantung Army, acting independently of the government in Tokyo, began the gradual conquest of Manchuria after fabricating an incident at Mukden to justify their actions. Ultimately, they created a puppet state, Manchukuo, under the last Chinese emperor, Henry P'u-i. China's League protest resulted in the creation of an investigatory commission under the Earl of Lytton that criticized Japan's actions and recommended a negotiated settlement that would have allowed Japan to retain most of its conquest. Japan responded by resigning from the League on January 24, 1933.

Hitler's announcement on March 15, 1935, of Germany's decisions to rearm and to introduce conscription in violation of the Treaty of Versailles prompted the leaders of England, France, and Italy to meet in Stresa, Italy (April 11–14). They condemned Germany's actions, underlined their commitment to the Locarno Pact, and re-affirmed the support they collectively gave for Austria's independence in early 1934. Great Britain's decision, however, to separately protect its naval strength vis-à-vis a German buildup in the Anglo-German Naval Treaty of June 18, 1935, effectively compromised the significance of the Stresa Front.

DRILL: WORLD WAR I AND EUROPE IN CRISIS

1. Which of the following would a historian be LEAST likely to accept as a cause of World War I?

    (A) The public and open nature of Great Power diplomacy in Europe

    (B) Loss of civilian control over the military establishments of European nations

    (C) A continuing arms race among the Great Powers of Europe

    (D) Rivalry over expanding colonial empires

    (E) Rivalry between the governments of Austria-Hungary and Russia over control of the Balkans

2. All of the following countries fell victim to military intervention or invasion by Fascist armies during the 1930s EXCEPT

    (A) Poland.   (D) Austria.

    (B) Spain.   (E) Yugoslavia.

    (C) Albania.

3.   The "Triple Entente" was an agreement between

   (A) Britain, Germany, and France.

   (B) Russia, Germany, and Spain.

   (C) Britain, Japan, and France.

   (D) Germany, Austria, and Turkey.

   (E) Britain, France, and Russia.

4.   The first two countries to declare war on each other at the start of World War I were

   (A) Germany and Russia.   (D) France and Austria.

   (B) Prussia and Austria.   (E) England and Germany.

   (C) Austria and Serbia.

5.   Which of the following best characterizes the Russian Provisional Government of March-November 1917?

   (A) A group of radical intellectuals committed to world revolution.

   (B) Military commanders who wanted to install a dictatorship.

   (C) Monarchists who supported the czar.

   (D) Radical workers led by the Communists.

   (E) Middle-class and intellectual leaders who had little sympathy for workers and peasants.

FROM WORLD WAR II TO THE DEMISE OF COMMUNISM (1935–1991)

THE COURSE OF EVENTS

Using a Franco-Soviet agreement of the preceding year as an excuse, Hitler, on March 7, 1936, repudiated the Locarno agreements and reoccupied the Rhineland (an area demilitarized by the Versailles Treaty). Neither France (which possessed military superiority at the time) nor Britain was willing to oppose these moves.

The Spanish Civil War (1936–1939) is usually seen as a rehearsal for World War II because of outside intervention. The government of the Spanish Republic (established in 1931) caused resentment among conservatives by its programs, including land reform and anti-clerical legislation aimed at the Catholic church. Following an election victory by a popular front of republican and radical parties, right-wing generals in July began a military insurrection. Francisco Franco, stationed at the time in Spanish Morocco, emerged as the leader of this revolt, which became a devastating civil war lasting nearly three years.

The democracies, including the United States, followed a course of neutrality. Nazi Germany, Italy, and the U.S.S.R. did intervene despite non-intervention agreements negotiated by Britain and France. Spain became a battlefield for fascist and anti-fascist forces with Franco winning by 1939 in what was seen as a serious defeat for anti-fascist forces everywhere.

The Spanish Civil War was a factor in bringing together Mussolini and Hitler in a Rome-Berlin Axis. Already Germany and Japan had signed the Anti-Comintern Pact in 1936. Ostensibly directed against international communism, this was the basis for a diplomatic alliance between those countries, and Italy soon adhered to this agreement, becoming Germany's ally in World War II.

In 1938 Hitler pressured the Austrian chancellor to make concessions and when this did not work, German troops annexed Austria (the *Anschluss*). Again Britain and France took no effective action, and about six million Austrians were added to Germany.

Hitler turned next to Czechoslovakia. Three million persons of German origin lived in the Sudetenland, a borderland between Germany and Czechoslovakia given to Czechoslovakia in order to provide it with a more defensible boundary. In 1938, after a series of demands from Hitler, a four-power conference was held in Munich with Hitler, Mussolini, Chamberlain, and Daladier in attendance, at which Hitler's terms were accepted. Britain (Chamberlain) and France (Daladier), despite the French alliance with Czechoslovakia, put pressure on the Czech government to force it to comply with German demands. Hitler signed a treaty agreeing to this settlement as the limit of his ambitions. At the same time the Poles seized control of Teschen, and Hungary (with the support of Italy and Germany and over the protests of the British and French) seized 7,500 square miles of Slovakia. By the concessions forced on her at Munich, Czechoslovakia lost its frontier defenses and was totally unprotected against any further German encroachments.

In March 1939, Hitler annexed most of the Czech state while Hungary conquered Ruthenia. At almost the same time Germany annexed Memel from Lithuania. In April, Mussolini, taking advantage of distractions created by Germany, landed an army in Albania and seized that Balkan state in a campaign lasting about one week.

Disillusioned by these continued aggressions, Britain and France made military preparations. Guarantees were given to Poland, Rumania, and Greece. The two democracies also opened negotiations with the U.S.S.R. for an arrangement to obtain that country's aid against further German aggression. Hitler, with Poland next on his timetable, also began a cautious rapprochement with the U.S.S.R. On August 23, 1939, the world was stunned by the announcement of a Nazi-Soviet Treaty of friendship. A secret protocol provided that in the event of a "territorial rearrangement" in Eastern Europe the two powers would divide Poland. In addition, Russia would have the Baltic states (Latvia, Lithuania, and Estonia) and Bessarabia (lost to Rumania in 1918) as part of her sphere. Stalin agreed to remain neutral in any German war with Britain or France. World War II began with the German invasion of Poland on September 1, 1939, followed by British and French declarations of war against Germany on September 3.

WORLD WAR II

The German attack (known as the "blitzkrieg" or "lightning war") overwhelmed the poorly equipped Polish army, which could not resist German tanks and airplanes.

On September 17 the Russian armies attacked the Poles from the east. They met the Germans two days later. Stalin's share of Poland extended approximately to the Curzon Line. Later, in June 1940, while Germany was attacking France, Stalin occupied the Baltic states of Latvia, Lithuania, and Estonia.

The only military action of any consequence during the winter of 1939–1940 resulted from Russian demands made on Finland, especially for territory adjacent to Leningrad (then only 20 miles from the border). Finnish refusal led to a Russian attack in November 1939. The Finns resisted with considerable vigor, receiving some supplies from Sweden, Britain, and France, but eventually by March they had to give in to the superior Russian forces.

Finland was forced to cede the Karelian Isthmus, Viipuri, and a naval base at Hangoe.

On May 10, the main German offensive was launched against France. Belgium and the Netherlands were simultaneously attacked. According to plan, British and French forces advanced to aid the Belgians. At this point the Germans departed from the World War I strategy by launching a surprise armored attack through Luxembourg and the Ardennes Forest (considered by the British and French to be impassable for tanks). The Dutch could offer no real resistance and collapsed in four days after the May 13 German bombing of Rotterdam.

Paris fell to the Germans in mid-June. The Pétain government quickly made peace with Hitler, who added to French humiliation by dictating the terms of the armistice to the French at Compiégne in the same railroad car used by Marshal Foch when he gave terms to the Germans at the end of the First World War. The complete collapse of France quickly came as a tremendous shock to the British and Americans.

Mussolini declared war on both France and Britain on June 10. Hitler's forces remained in occupation of the northern part of France, including Paris. He allowed the French to keep their fleet and overseas territories probably in the hope of making them reliable allies. Pétain and his chief minister Pierre Laval established their capital at Vichy and followed a policy of collaboration with their former enemies. A few Frenchmen, however, joined the Free French movement started in London by the then relatively unknown General Charles de Gaulle (1890-1970).

FROM THE FRENCH DEFEAT TO THE INVASION OF RUSSIA

By mid-summer 1940, Germany, together with its Italian ally, dominated most of Western and Central Europe. Germany began with no real plans for a long war, but continued resistance by the British made necessary the belated mobilization of German resources. Hitler's policy included exploiting areas Germany conquered. Collaborators were used to establish governments subservient to German policy. Germany began the policy of forcibly transporting large numbers of conquered Europeans to work in German war industries. Jews especially were forced into slave labor for the German war effort, and increasingly large numbers were rounded up and sent to concentration camps, where they were systematically murdered as the Nazis carried out Hitler's "final solution" of genocide against European Jewry. Although much was known about this during the war, the full horror of these atrocities was not revealed until Allied troops entered Germany in 1945.

With the fall of France, Britain remained the only power of consequence at war with the Axis. Hitler began preparations for invading Britain (Operation "Sea Lion"). Air control over the Channel was vital if an invasion force was to be transported safely to the English Coast. The German Air Force (Luftwaffe) under Herman Göring began its air offensive against the British in the summer of 1940. The Germans concentrated first on British air defenses, then on ports and shipping, and finally in early September they began the attack on London. The Battle of Britain was eventually a defeat for the Germans, who were unable to gain decisive superiority over the British, although they inflicted great damage on both British air defenses and major cities such as London. Despite the damage and loss of life, British morale remained high and necessary war production continued. German losses determined that bombing alone could not defeat Britain. "Operation Sea Lion" was postponed October 12 and never seriously taken up again, although the British did not know this and had to continue for some time to give priority to their coastal and air defenses.

During the winter of 1940–1941, having given up "Operation Sea Lion," Hitler began to shift his forces to the east for an invasion of Russia ("Operation Barbarossa"). Russian expansion towards the Balkans dismayed the Germans, who hoped for more influence there themselves.

The German invasion of Russia began June 22, 1941. The invasion force of three million included Finnish, Rumanian, Hungarian, and Italian contingents along with the Germans and advanced on a broad front of about 2,000 miles. They surrounded the city of Leningrad (although they never managed to actually capture it) and came within about 25 miles of Moscow. In November the enemy actually entered the suburbs, but then the long supply lines, early winter, and Russian resistance (strong despite heavy losses) brought the invasion to a halt. During the winter a Russian counterattack pushed the Germans back from Moscow and saved the capital.

With the coming of the Great Depression and severe economic difficulties, Japanese militarists gained more and more influence over the civilian government. On September 18, 1931, the Japanese occupied all of Manchuria. On July 7, 1937, a full-scale Sino-Japanese war began with a clash between Japanese and Chinese at the Marco Polo Bridge in Peking (now Beijing). An indication of ultimate Japanese aims came on November 3, 1938, when Prince Fumimaro Konoye's (1891–1946) government issued a statement on "A New Order in East Asia." This statement envisaged the integration of Japan, Manchuria (now the puppet state of Manchukuo), and China into one "Greater East Asia Co-Prosperity Sphere" under Japanese leadership. In July 1940, the Konoye government was re-formed with General Hideki Tojo (1884–1948) (Japan's principal leader in World War I) as minister of war.

All of these events led to worsening relations between Japan and the two states in a position to oppose her expansion—the Soviet Union and the United States. Despite border clashes with the Russians, Japan avoided any conflict with that state, and Stalin wanted no war with Japan after he became fully occupied with the German invasion. In the few weeks after attacking the U.S. at Pearl Harbor, Japanese forces were able to occupy strategically important islands (including the Philippines and Dutch East Indies) and territory on the Asian mainland (Malaya, with the British naval base at Singapore, and all of Burma to the border of India).

The Japanese attack brought the United States not only into war in the Pacific, but resulted in German and Italian declarations of war which meant the total involvement of the United States in World War II.

American involvement in the war was ultimately decisive, for it meant that the greatest industrial power of that time was now arrayed against the Axis powers. The United States became, as President Roosevelt put it, "the arsenal of democracy." American aid was crucial to the immense effort of the Soviet Union. Lend-Lease aid was extended to Russia. By 1943 supplies and equipment were reaching Russia in considerable quantities.

The German forces launched a second offensive in the summer of 1942. This attack concentrated on the southern part of the front, aiming at the Caucasus and vital oil fields around the Caspian Sea. At Stalingrad on the Volga River the Germans were stopped. With the onset of winter, Hitler refused to allow the strategic retreat urged by his generals. As a result, the Russian forces crossed the river north and south of the city and surrounded 22 German divisions. On January 31, 1943, following the failure of relief efforts, the German commander Friedrich Paulus (1890–1957) surrendered the remnants of his army. From then on the Russians were almost always on the offensive.

After entering the war in 1940, the Italians invaded British-held Egypt. In December 1940, the British General Archibald Wavell (1883–1950) launched a surprise attack. The Italian forces were driven back about 500 miles and 130,000 were captured. Then Hitler intervened, sending General Erwin Rommel with a small German force (the Afrika Korps) to reinforce the

Italians. Rommel took command and launched a counter-offensive which put his forces on the border of Egypt. By mid-1942 Rommel had driven his troops as far as to El Alamein, only 70 miles from Alexandria.

A change in the British high command now placed General Harold Alexander (1891–1969) in charge of Middle Eastern forces, with General Bernard Montgomery (1887–1976) in immediate command of the British Eighth Army. Montgomery attacked at El Alamein, breaking Rommel's lines and starting a British advance which was not stopped until the armies reached the border of Tunisia.

Meanwhile, the British and American leaders decided that they could launch a second offensive in North Africa ("Operation Torch") which would clear the enemy from the entire coast and make the Mediterranean once again safe for Allied shipping.

The landings resulted in little conflict with the French, and the French forces soon joined the war against the Axis. It was only a matter of time before German troops were forced into northern Tunisia and surrendered. American forces, unused to combat, suffered some reverses at the Battle of the Kasserine Pass, but gained valuable experience. The final victory came in May 1943, about the same time as the Russian victory at Stalingrad.

Relatively safe shipping routes across the North Atlantic to Britain were essential to the survival of Britain and absolutely necessary if a force was to be assembled to invade France and strike at Germany proper. New types of aircraft, small aircraft carriers, more numerous and better-equipped escort vessels, new radar and sonar (for underwater detection), extremely efficient radio direction finding, decipherment of German signals plus the building of more ships turned the balance against the Germans despite their development of improved submarines by early 1943, and the Atlantic became increasingly dangerous for German submarines.

Success in these three campaigns—Stalingrad, North Africa, and the Battle of the Atlantic—gave new hope to the Allied cause and made certain that Allied victory was attainable. With the beginning of an offensive in late 1942 in the Solomon Islands against the Japanese, 1943 became the turning point of the war.

At their conference at Casablanca in January 1943, Roosevelt and Churchill developed a detailed strategy for the further conduct of the war. Sicily was to be invaded, then Italy proper. Rome was not captured by the Allied forces until June 4, 1944. With a new Italian government now supporting the Allied cause, Italian resistance movements in northern Italy became a major force in helping to liberate that area from the Germans.

At the Teheran Conference, held in November 1943 and attended by all three major Allied leaders, the final decision reached by Roosevelt and Churchill some six months earlier to invade France in May 1944 was communicated to the Russians. Stalin promised to open a simultaneous Russian offensive.

The Normandy invasion (Operation "Overlord") was the largest amphibious operation in history. The landings actually took place beginning June 6, 1944. The first day, 130,000 men were successfully landed. Strong German resistance hemmed in the Allied forces for about a month. Then the Allies, now numbering about 1,000,000, managed a spectacular breakthrough. By the end of 1944, all of France had been seized. A second invasion force landed on the Mediterranean coast in August, freed southern France, and linked up with Eisenhower's forces. By the end of 1944, the Allied armies stood on the borders of Germany ready to invade from both east and west.

Stalin's armies crossed into Poland July 23, 1944, and three days later the Russian dictator officially recognized a group of Polish Communists (the so-called Lublin Committee) as the government of Poland. As the Russian armies drew near the eastern suburbs of Warsaw, the London Poles, a resistance group, launched an attack. Stalin's forces waited outside the city while the Germans brought in reinforcements and slowly wiped out the Polish underground army in several weeks of heavy street fighting. The offensive then resumed and the city was liberated by the Red Army, but the influence of the London Poles was now virtually nil. Needless to say, this incident aroused considerable suspicion concerning Stalin's motives and led both Churchill and Roosevelt to begin to think through the political implications of their alliance with Stalin.

By late summer of 1944, the German position in the Balkans began to collapse. The Red Army crossed the border into Rumania leading King Michael (1921–) to seize the opportunity to take his country out of its alliance with Germany and to open the way to the advancing Russians. German troops were forced to make a hasty retreat. At this point Bulgaria changed sides. The German forces in Greece withdrew in October.

From October 9–18, Winston Churchill visited Moscow to try to work out a political arrangement regarding the Balkans and Eastern Europe. Dealing from a position of weakness, he simply wrote out some figures on a sheet of paper: Russia to have the preponderance of influence in countries like

Bulgaria and Rumania; Britain to have the major say in Greece, and a fifty-fifty division in Yugoslavia and Hungary. Stalin agreed. The Americans refused to have anything to do with this "spheres of influence" arrangement.

In Greece, Stalin maintained a hands-off policy when the British used military force to suppress the Communist resistance movement and install a regent for the exiled government.

In early spring of 1945 the Allied armies crossed the Rhine. As the Americans and British and other Allied forces advanced into Germany, the Russians attacked from the east. While the Russian armies were fighting their way into Berlin, Hitler committed suicide in the ruins of the bunker where he had spent the last days of the war. Power was handed over to a government headed by Admiral Karl Dönitz (1891–1980). On May 7, General Alfred Jodl (1890–1946), acting for the German government, made the final uncondi-tional surrender at General Eisenhower's headquarters near Reims.

The future treatment of Germany, and Europe in general, was deter-mined by decisions of the "Big Three" (Churchill, Stalin, and Roosevelt).

A plan to divide Germany into zones of occupation, which had been devised in 1943 by a committee under British Deputy Prime Minister Clement Attlee, was formally accepted with the addition of a fourth zone taken from the British and American zones for the French to occupy. Berlin, which lay within the Russian zone, was divided into four zones of occupation also.

The third summit meeting of the Big Three took place at Potsdam outside Berlin after the end of the European war but while the Pacific war was still going on. The conference began July 17, 1945, with Stalin, Churchill, and the new American President Harry Truman attending. A Potsdam Declaration, aimed at Japan, called for immediate Japanese surrender and hinted at the consequences that would ensue if it were not forthcoming. While at the conference, American leaders received the news of the successful testing of the first atomic bomb in the New Mexico desert, but the Japanese were given no clear warning that such a destructive weapon might be used against them.

On August 6, 1945, the bomb was dropped by a single plane on Hiroshima and an entire city disappeared, with the instantaneous loss of 70,000 lives. In time many other persons died from radiation poisoning and other effects. Since no surrender was received, a second bomb was dropped on Nagasaki, obliterating that city. Even the most fanatical of the Japanese leaders saw what was happening and surrender came quickly. The only departure from unconditional surrender was to allow the Japanese to retain their emperor (Hirohito, 1901–1989), but only with the proviso that he would be subject in every respect to the orders of the occupation commander. The formal surrender took place September 2, 1945, in Tokyo Bay on the deck of the battleship *Missouri*, and the occupation of Japan began under the immediate control of the American commander General Douglas MacArthur (1880–1964).

EUROPE AFTER WORLD WAR II: 1945 TO 1953

Anglo-American ideas about what the postwar world should be like were expressed by Roosevelt and Churchill at their meeting off the coast of Newfoundland in August 1941. The Atlantic Charter was a general statement of goals: restoration of the sovereignty and self-government of nations conquered by Hitler, free access to world trade and resources, cooperation to improve living standards and economic security, and a peace that would ensure freedom from fear and want and stop the use of force and aggression as instruments of national policy.

At the Casablanca Conference, the policy of requiring unconditional surrender by the Axis powers was announced. This ensured that at the end of the war, all responsibility for government of the defeated nations would fall on the victors, and they would have a free hand in rebuilding government in those countries. No real planning was done in detail before the time arrived to meet this responsibility. It was done for the most part as the need arose.

At Teheran, the Big Three did discuss in a general way the occupation and demilitarization of Germany. They also laid the foundation for a post-war organization—the United Nations Organization—which like the earlier League of Nations was supposed to help regulate international relations and keep the peace and ensure friendly cooperation between the nations of the world.

At Potsdam, an agreement was reached to sign peace treaties as soon as possible with former German allies. A Council of Foreign Ministers was established to draft the treaties. Several meetings were held in 1946 and 1947 and treaties were signed with Italy, Rumania, Hungary, Bulgaria, and Finland. These states paid reparations and agreed to some territorial readjustments as a price for peace. No agreement could be reached on Japan or Germany. In 1951, the Western powers led by the U.S. concluded a treaty with Japan without Russian participation. The latter made their own treaty in 1956. A final meeting of the Council of Foreign Ministers broke up in 1947 over Germany, and no peace treaty was ever signed with that country. The division of Germany for purposes of occupation and military government became permanent, with the three Western zones joining and eventually becoming the Federal Republic of Germany and the Russian zone becoming the German Democratic Republic.

Arrangements for the United Nations were confirmed at the Yalta Conference: the large powers would predominate in a Security Council, where they would have permanent seats together with several other powers elected from time to time from among the other members of the U.N. Consent of all the permanent members was necessary for any action to be taken by the Security Council (thus giving the large powers a veto). The General Assembly was to include all members.

EASTERN EUROPE: 1945–1953

Much of European Russia had been devastated, and about 25 million people made homeless. In March 1946 a fourth five-year plan was adopted by the Supreme Soviet intended to increase industrial output to a level 50 percent higher than before the war. A bad harvest and food shortage in 1946 had been relieved by a good harvest in 1947, and in December 1947, the government announced the end of food rationing. At the same time a drastic currency devaluation was put through, which brought immediate hardship to many people but strengthened the Soviet economy in the long run. As a result of these and other forceful and energetic measures, the Soviet Union was able within a few years to make good most of the wartime damage and to surpass pre-war levels of production.

The fate of Eastern Europe (including Poland, Hungary, Rumania, Bulgaria, Czechoslovakia, and the Russian zone of Germany) from 1945 on was determined by the presence of Russian armies in that area.

Communization of Eastern Europe and the establishment of regimes in the satellite areas of the Soviet Union occurred in stages over a three-year period following the end of the war. The timetable of events varied in each country.

As relations broke down between the four occupying powers, the Soviet authorities gradually created a Communist state in their zone. On October 7, 1948, a German Democratic Republic was established. In June 1950, an agreement with Poland granted formal recognition of the Oder-Neisse Line as the boundary between the two states. Economic progress was unsatisfactory for most of the population, and on June 16–17, 1953, riots occurred in East Berlin which were suppressed by Soviet forces using tanks. In East Germany, a program of economic reform was announced which eventually brought some improvement.

In Yugoslavia, Marshal Tito (1892–1980) and his Communist partisan movement emerged from the war in a strong position because of their effective campaign against the German occupation. Tito was able to establish a Communist government in 1945 despite considerable pressure from Stalin, and pursue a course independent of the Soviet Union unique among the countries of Eastern Europe.

WESTERN EUROPE: 1945–1953

The monarchy which had governed Italy since the time of unification in the mid-nineteenth century was now discarded in favor of a republic. King Victor Emmanual III (1869–1947), compromised by his association with Mussolini, resigned in favor of his son, but a referendum in June 1946 established a republic. In simultaneous elections for a constituent assembly, three parties predominated: the Social Democrats, the Communists, and the Christian Democrats.

In the last two years of the war, France recovered sufficiently under the leadership of General Charles de Gaulle to begin playing a significant military and political role once again. In July 1944, the United States recognized de Gaulle's Committee of National Liberation as the de facto government of areas liberated from the German occupation.

In foreign affairs, France occupied Germany. In addition, the Fourth Republic was faced with two major problems abroad when it attempted to assert its authority over Indochina and Algeria. The Indochina situation resulted in a long and costly war against nationalists and Communists under Ho Chi Minh (1890–1969). French involvement ended with the Geneva Accords of 1954 and French withdrawal. The Algerian struggle reached a crisis in 1958 resulting in General de Gaulle's return to power and the creation of a new Fifth Republic.

In May 1945, when Germany surrendered unconditionally, the country lay in ruins. About three-quarters of city houses had been gutted by air raids, industry was in a shambles, and the country was divided into zones of occupation ruled by foreign military governors. Economic chaos was the rule, currency was virtually worthless, food was in short supply, and the black market flourished for those who could afford to buy in it. By the Potsdam agreements, Germany lost about one-quarter of its pre-war territory. In addition, some 12 million people of German origin driven from their homes in countries like Poland and Czechoslovakia had to be fed, housed, and clothed along with the indigenous population.

Demilitarization, denazification, and democratization were the initial goals of the occupation forces in Germany. All four wartime allies agreed on the trial of leading Nazis for a variety of war crimes and "crimes against humanity." An International Military Tribunal was established at Nuremburg to try 22 major war criminals, and lesser courts tried many others. Most of the defendants were executed, although a few like Rudolf Hess were given life imprisonment.

As relations between the three Western powers and the Soviets gradually broke down in Germany, East and West became separate states. In the West, the British and American zones were fused into one in 1946, with the French joining in 1948. Political parties were gradually re-established.

In February 1948, a charter granted further powers of government to the Germans in the American and British zones. Later that year, the Russians and East Germans, in an effort to force the Western powers out of their zones in Berlin, began a blockade of the city which was located within the Russian zone. The response was an allied airlift to supply the city, and eventually, after some months, the blockade was called off.

In 1951 a Conservative majority was returned in Great Britain, and Winston Churchill, who had been defeated in 1945, became prime minister again. The new regime immediately reversed the nationalization of iron and steel. Other measures survived, however, especially the universal health care program which proved to be one of the most popular parts of the Labour achievement. In April 1955, Churchill resigned for reasons of age and health and turned over the prime minister's office to Anthony Eden (1897–1977).

THE MARSHALL PLAN

European recovery from the effects of the war was slow for the first two or three years after 1945. The European Recovery Program (Marshall Plan, named after the American secretary of state and World War II army chief of staff) began in 1948 and showed substantial results in all the Western European countries that took part. The most remarkable gains were in West Germany. The Plan aimed to strengthen Western Europe's resistance to communism.

NATO

In 1949 the United States joined 11 other Atlantic regions in a mutual defense pact called the North American Treaty Organization (NATO).

BRITISH OVERSEAS WITHDRAWAL

Following World War II, there was a considerable migration of Jews who had survived the Nazi Holocaust to Palestine to join Jews who had settled there earlier. Conflicts broke out with the Arabs. The British occupying forces tried to suppress the violence and to negotiate a settlement between the factions. In 1948, after negotiations failed, the British, feeling they could no longer support the cost of occupation, announced their withdrawal. Zionist leaders then proclaimed the independent state of Israel and took up arms to fight the armies of Egypt, Syria, and other Arab states which invaded the Jewish-held area. The new Israeli state quickly proved its technological and military superiority by defeating the invaders.

The Jews of Israel created a modern parliamentary state on the European model with an economy and technology superior to their Arab neighbors. The new state was thought by many Arabs to be simply another manifestation of European imperialism made worse by religious antagonisms.

In 1967, Israel defeated Egypt, Syria, and Jordan in a six-day war, and the Israelis occupied additional territory including the Jordanian sector of the city of Jerusalem. An additional million Arabs came under Israeli rule as a result of this campaign.

Although defeated, the Arabs refused to sign any treaty or to come to terms with Israel. Palestinian refugees living in camps in states bordering Israel created grave problems. A Palestine Liberation Organization (PLO) was formed to fight for the establishment of an Arab Palestinian state on territory taken from Israel on the west bank of the Jordan River. The PLO resorted to terrorist tactics both against Israel and other states in support of their cause.

In October 1973, the Egyptians and Syrians launched an attack on Israel known as the Yom Kippur War. With some difficulty the attacks were repulsed. A settlement was mediated by American Secretary of State Henry Kissinger. The situation has remained unstable, however, with both sides resorting to border raids and other forms of violence short of full-scale war.

The British exercised control over Egypt from the end of the nineteenth century and declared it a British protectorate in December 1914. In 1922 Egypt became nominally independent.

The government under King Farouk I (1920–1965) did little to alleviate the overriding problem of poverty after the war. In 1952, a group of army officers, including Gamal Abdel Nasser (1918–1970) and Anwar Sadat

(1918–1981), plotted against the government, and on July 23 the king was overthrown. Colonel Nasser became premier in April 1954. A treaty with Britain later that year resulted in the withdrawal of all British troops from the Canal Zone.

India under Jawaharlal Nehru (1889–1964) and the Congress party became a parliamentary democracy. The country made economic progress, but gains were largely negated by a population increase to 600 million from 350 million.

THE FRENCH IN INDOCHINA AND ALGERIA

Following World War II, the French returned to Indochina and attempted to restore their rule there. The opposition nationalist movement was led by the veteran Communist Ho Chi Minh. War broke out between the nationalists and the French forces. In 1954 their army was surrounded at Dienbienphu and forced to surrender. This military disaster prompted a change of government in France.

This new government under Premier Pierre Mendès-France (1907–1982) negotiated French withdrawal at a conference held at Geneva, Switzerland in 1954. Cambodia and Laos became independent and Vietnam was partitioned at the 17th parallel. The North, with its capital at Hanoi, became a Communist state under Ho Chi Minh. The South remained non-Communist. Under the Geneva Accords, elections were to be held in the South to determine the fate of that area. However, the United States chose to intervene and support the regime of Ngo Dinh Diem (1901–1963), and elections were never held. Eventually a second Vietnamese war resulted, with the United States playing the role earlier played by France.

In a referendum, on January 8, 1961, the French people approved of eventual Algerian self-determination. In July 1962 French rule ended in Algeria. There was a mass exodus of Europeans from Algeria, but most Frenchmen were grateful to de Gaulle for ending the long Algerian conflict.

THE DUTCH AND INDONESIA

During World War II, the Japanese conquered the Dutch East Indies. At the end of the war, they recognized the independence of the area as Indonesia. When the Dutch attempted to return, four years of bloody fighting ensued against the nationalist forces of Achmed Sukarno (1901–1970). In 1949, the Dutch recognized Indonesian independence. In 1954, the Indonesians dissolved all ties with the Netherlands.

THE COLD WAR AFTER THE DEATH OF STALIN

Following Stalin's death in 1953, Russian leaders appeared more willing than Stalin to be conciliatory and to consider peaceful coexistence.

In the U.S. the atmosphere also changed with the election of President Dwight Eisenhower and conciliatory gestures were not always automatically considered appeasement of the Communists. In 1955 a summit conference of Eisenhower, the British and French leaders, and Khrushchev (1894–1971) met at Geneva in an atmosphere more cordial than any since World War II. The "spirit of Geneva" did not last long, however.

After his return to power in France in 1958, General de Gaulle endeavored to make France a leader in European affairs with himself as spokesman for a Europe that he hoped would be a counter to the "dual hegemony" of the U.S. and U.S.S.R. His policies at times were anti-British or anti-American. Despite his prestige as the last great wartime leader, he did not have great success.

A NEW EUROPE

Joseph Stalin died in March 1953. Eventually a little-known party functionary, Nikita Khrushchev, became Communist Party General Secretary in 1954. Khrushchev's policy of relaxing the regime of terror and oppression of the Stalin years became known as "The Thaw," after the title of a novel by Ilya Ehrenburg (1891–1967).

Change occurred in foreign affairs also. Khrushchev visited Belgrade and re-established relations with Tito, admitting that there was more than one road to socialism. He also visited the United States, met with President Eisenhower, and toured the country. Later, relations became more tense after the U-2 spy plane incident.

Following the loss of face sustained by Russia as a result of the Cuban Missile Crisis and the failure of Khrushchev's domestic agricultural policies, he was forced out of the party leadership and lived in retirement in Moscow until his death in 1971.

After Khrushchev's ouster, the leadership in the Central Committee divided power, making Leonid Brezhnev (1906–1982) party secretary and Aleksei Kosygin chairman of the council of ministers, or premier.

Stalin's successors rehabilitated many of Stalin's victims. They also permitted somewhat greater freedom in literary and artistic matters and even allowed some political criticism. Controls were maintained, however, and sometimes were tightened. Anti-semitism was also still present, and Soviet Jews were long denied permission to emigrate to Israel.

Brezhnev occupied the top position of power until his death in 1982. He was briefly succeeded by Yuri Andropov (1914–1984) (a former secret police chief) and then by Mikhail Gorbachev, who carried out a further relaxation of the internal regime. Gorbachev pushed disarmament and detente in foreign relations, and attempted a wide range of internal reforms known as *perestroika* ("restructuring"). Gorbachev resigned in 1991, and Boris Yeltsin assumed control over the collapsing Soviet Union, which would later become known as the Commonwealth of Independent States, with Yeltsin as Russia's President.

CHANGE IN EASTERN EUROPE

In the 1980s, the Polish trade union movement known as Solidarity and its leader, Lech Walesa, emerged as a political force, organizing mass protests in 1980–1981. Despite government efforts to maintain strong central control and suppress the opposition, the ruling Communists were forced to recognize the opposition and make concessions. In 1990, Lech Walesa was elected president of Poland.

CHANGE IN WESTERN EUROPE

In March 1957 two treaties were signed in Rome creating a European Atomic Energy Commission (Euratom) and a European Economic Community (the Common Market)—which eventually absorbed Euratom. The EEC was to be a customs union creating a free market area with a common external tariff for member nations.

Relations with Northern Ireland proved a burden to successive British governments. The 1922 settlement had left Northern Ireland as a self-governing part of the United Kingdom. Of 1.5 million inhabitants, one-third were Roman Catholic and two-thirds were Protestant. Catholics claimed they were discriminated against and pressed for annexation by the Republic of Ireland. Activity by the Irish Republican Army brought retaliation by Protestant extremists. From 1969 on, there was considerable violence, causing the British to bring in troops to maintain order. Over 1,500 were killed in the next several years in sporadic outbreaks of violence.

Under Prime Minister Thatcher in the 1980s, the British economy improved somewhat. London regained some of its former power as a financial center. In recent years, an influx of people from former colonies in Asia, Africa, and the West Indies has caused some racial tensions.

Prime Minister Thatcher was a partisan of free enterprise. She fought inflation with austerity and let economic problems spur British employers and unions to change for greater efficiency. Conservative victory in the 1987 elections made Thatcher the longest-serving prime minister in modern British history.

Under de Gaulle, a new constitution for France was drafted and approved establishing the Fifth Republic with a much strengthened executive in the form of a president with power to dissolve the legislature and call for elections, to submit important questions to popular referendum, and, if necessary, to assume emergency powers.

In domestic politics, de Gaulle strengthened the power of the president by often using the referendum and bypassing the Assembly. In May 1968, student grievances over conditions in the universities caused hundreds of thousands to revolt. They were soon joined by some 10 million workers, who paralyzed the economy. De Gaulle survived by promising educational reform and wage increases. Promised reforms were begun, but in April 1969, de Gaulle resigned and died about a year later. Economic problems continued to plague France in the 1970s and 1980s.

In Germany, problems with the economy and the environment brought an end to the rule of the Socialists in 1982. An organization called the Greens, which was a loosely organized coalition of environmentalists alienated from society, detracted from Socialist power. In 1982, the German voters turned to the more conservative Christian Democrats again, and Helmut Kohl became chancellor.

In Italy, the Christian Democrats, who were closely allied with the Roman Catholic Church, dominated the national scene. Their organization, though plagued by corruption, did provide some unity to Italian politics by supplying the prime ministers for numerous coalitions.

Italy advanced economically. Natural gas and some oil was discovered in the north and the Po valley area especially benefited. Unfortunately, business efficiency found no parallel in the government or civil service. Italy suffered from terrorism, kidnappings, and assassinations by extreme radical groups such as the Red Brigades. These agitators hoped to create conditions favorable to the overthrow of the democratic constitution.

In Portugal, Europe's longest right-wing dictatorship came to an end in September 1968, when a stroke incapacitated Antonio Salazar, who died two years later. A former collaborator, Marcelo Caetano (1906–1980), became prime minister, and an era of change began. Censorship was relaxed and some freedom was given to political parties.

Portugal went through a succession of governments. Its African colonies of Mozambique and Angola were finally granted independence in 1975. Portugal joined the Common Market in 1986.

Franco, who had been ruler of a fascist regime in Spain since the end of the Civil War in 1939, held on until he was close to 70. He then designated the Bourbon prince, Juan Carlos, to be his successor. In 1975, Franco relinquished power and died three weeks later. Juan Carlos proved a popular and able leader and over the next several years took the country from dictatorship to constitutional monarchy. Basque and Catalan separatist movements, which had caused trouble for so long, were appeased by the granting of local autonomy.

DRILL: WORLD WAR II TO THE DEMISE OF COMMUNISM

1. All of the following statements about Europe at the end of World War II are true EXCEPT

    (A) the border between Germany and Poland was moved westward.

    (B) communist governments assumed control of Eastern European nations.

    (C) a treaty was negotiated with Germany.

    (D) Berlin was made a four-power city in the middle of the communist sector of Germany.

    (E) the border between the Soviet Union and Poland was moved westward.

2. The Yalta conference determined

    I.   the Soviet Union's role as the liberator of Berlin.

    II. the postwar political arrangements in Central and Eastern Europe.

    III. the structure of the United Nations.

IV.   American/British control of Western Europe.

V.   the United States as the only nuclear power.

(A) I, II, and IV only.   (D) I and II only.

(B) I, II, IV, and V only.   (E) I, II, III, IV, and V.

(C) I, II, and III only.

3.   Since the end of the Second World War, separatist movements have led to violence in

(A) Northern Ireland, Spain, and Yugoslavia.

(B) Spain, Greece, and Holland.

(C) Northern Ireland, Holland, and Portugal.

(D) Greece, Yugoslavia, and Spain.

(E) Portugal, Greece, and Northern Ireland.

4.   Which of the following led President Truman to remove MacArthur from command in Korea?

(A) Heavy U.S. casualties

(B) The threat of Japanese involvement

(C) MacArthur's desire to use the atomic bomb on North Korea

(D) Truman's belief that MacArthur's war strategy was too conservative

(E) MacArthur's wish for a naval blockade of China and bombing north of the Yalu River

5.   Which of the following is closely associated with the name of Lech Walesa?

(A) *Glasnost*   (D) Soviet dissidents

(B) The Red Brigade   (E) The Hungarian Uprising of 1956

(C) Solidarity

AMERICAN HISTORY: THE COLONIAL PERIOD (1500–1763)

THE AGE OF EXPLORATION

The Treaty of Tordesillas (1493) drew a line dividing the land in the New World between Spain and Portugal. Lands east of the line were Portuguese. As a result, Brazil eventually became a Portuguese colony, while Spain maintained claims to the rest of the Americas.

To conquer the Americas, the Spanish monarchs used their powerful army, led by independent Spanish adventurers known as conquistadores. The European diseases they unwittingly carried with them devastated the local Native American populations, who had no immunities against such diseases.

Spain administered its new holdings as an autocratic, rigidly controlled empire in which everything was to benefit the parent country. The Spaniards developed a system of large manors or estates (encomiendas), with Indian slaves ruthlessly managed for the benefit of the conquistadores. The encomienda system was later replaced by the similar but somewhat milder hacienda system. As the Indian population died from overwork and European diseases, Spaniards began importing African slaves to supply their labor needs.

ENGLISH AND FRENCH BEGINNINGS

In 1497, the Italian John Cabot (Giovanni Caboto, ca. 1450–1499), sailing under the sponsorship of the king of England in search of a Northwest Passage (a water route to the Orient through or around the North American continent), became the first European since the Vikings more than four centuries earlier to reach the mainland of North America, which he claimed for England. Beginning in 1534, Jacques Cartier (1491–1557), authorized by the king of France, mounted three expeditions to the area of the St. Lawrence River, which he believed might be the hoped for Northwest Passage. He explored up the river as far as the site of Montreal.

When the English finally began colonization, commercial capitalism in England had advanced to the point that the English efforts were supported by private rather than government funds, allowing English colonists to enjoy greater freedom from government interference.

THE BEGINNINGS OF COLONIZATION

Two groups of merchants gained charters from James I, Queen Elizabeth's successor. One group of merchants was based in London and received a charter to North America between what are now the Hudson and the Cape Fear rivers. The other was based in Plymouth and was granted the right to colonize in North America from the Potomac to the northern border of present-day Maine. They were called the Virginia Company of London and the Virginia Company of Plymouth, respectively. They were joint-stock companies that raised their capital by the sale of shares of stock.

The Virginia Company of London settled Jamestown in 1607. It became the first permanent English settlement in North America. During the early years of Jamestown, the majority of the settlers died of starvation, various diseases, or hostile actions by Native Americans. The colony's survival remained in doubt for a number of years.

Impressed by the potential profits from tobacco growing, King James I was determined to have Virginia for himself. In 1624, he revoked the London Company's charter and made Virginia a royal colony. This pattern was followed throughout colonial history; both company colonies and proprietary colonies tended eventually to become royal colonies.

The French opened a lucrative trade in fur with the Native Americans. In 1608, Samuel de Champlain established a trading post in Quebec, from which the rest of what became New France eventually spread.

French exploration and settlement spread through the Great Lakes region and the valleys of the Mississippi and Ohio rivers. French settlements in the Midwest were generally forts and trading posts serving the fur trade.

In 1609, Holland sent an Englishman named Henry Hudson (d. 1611) to search for a Northwest Passage. In this endeavor, Hudson discovered the river that bears his name. Arrangements were made to trade with the Iroquois for furs. In 1624, Dutch trading outposts were established on Manhattan Island (New Amsterdam) and at the site of present-day Albany (Fort Orange).

Many Englishmen came from England for religious reasons. For the most part, these fell into two groups, Puritans and Separatists. Though similar in many respects to the Puritans, the Separatists believed the Church of England was beyond saving and so felt they must separate from it.

Led by William Bradford (1590–1657), a group of Separatists departed in 1620, having obtained from the London Company a charter to settle just south of the Hudson River. Driven by storms, their ship, the *Mayflower*, made landfall at Cape Cod in Massachusetts. This, however, put them outside the jurisdiction of any established government; and so before going ashore they drew up and signed the Mayflower Compact, establishing a foundation for orderly government based on the consent of the governed. After a number of years of hard work, they were able to buy out the investors who had originally financed their voyage, and thus gain greater autonomy.

The Puritans were far more numerous than the Separatists. Charles I determined in 1629 to persecute the Puritans aggressively and to rule without the Puritan-dominated Parliament.

In 1629, they chartered a joint-stock company called the Massachusetts Bay Company. The charter neglected to specify where the company's headquarters should be located. Taking advantage of this unusual omission, the Puritans determined to make their headquarters in the colony itself, 3,000 miles from meddlesome royal officials.

Puritans saw their colony not as a place to do whatever might strike one's fancy, but as a place to serve God and build His kingdom. Dissidents would only be tolerated insofar as they did not interfere with the colony's mission.

One such dissident was Roger Williams (ca. 1603–1683). When his activities became disruptive he was asked to leave the colony. He fled to the wilderness around Narragansett Bay, bought land from the Indians, and founded the settlement of Providence (1636).

Another dissident was Anne Hutchinson (1591–1643), who openly taught things contrary to Puritan doctrine. She was banished from the colony. She also migrated to the area around Narragansett Bay and with her followers founded Portsmouth (1638).

In 1663, Charles II, having recently been restored to the throne moved to reward eight of the noblemen who had helped him regain the crown by granting them a charter for all the lands lying south of Virginia and north of Spanish Florida. The new colony was called Carolina, after the king.

In 1664, Charles gave his brother James, Duke of York, title to all the Dutch lands in America, provided James conquered them first. New Amsterdam fell almost without a shot and became New York.

THE COLONIAL WORLD

New England enjoyed a much more stable and well-ordered society than did the Chesapeake colonies. Puritans placed great importance on the family, which in their society was highly patriarchal. Puritans also placed great importance on the ability to read, since they believed everyone should be able to read the Bible. As a result, New England was ahead of the other colonies educationally and enjoyed extremely widespread literacy. Since New England's climate and soil were unsuited to large-scale farming, the region developed a prosperous economy based on small farming, home industry, fishing, and especially trade and a large shipbuilding industry. Boston became a major international port.

On the bottom rung of Southern society were the black slaves. During the first half of the seventeenth century, blacks in the Chesapeake made up only a small percentage of the population, and were treated more or less as indentured servants. Between 1640 and 1670 this gradually changed, and blacks came to be seen and treated as life-long chattel slaves whose status would be inherited by their children. By 1750, they composed 30 to 40 percent of the Chesapeake population.

While North Carolina tended to follow Virginia in its economic and social development (although with fewer great planters and more small farmers), South Carolina developed a society even more dominated by large plantations and chattel slavery.

Beginning around 1650, British authorities began to take more interest in regulating American trade for the benefit of the mother country. A key idea that underlay this policy was the concept of mercantilism. Each nation's goal was to export more than it imported (i.e., to have a "favorable balance of trade"). To achieve their goals, mercantilists believed economic activity should be regulated by the government. Colonies could fit into England's mercantilist scheme by providing staple crops, such as rice, tobacco, sugar, and indigo, and raw materials, such as timber, that England would otherwise have been forced to import from other countries. Parliament passed a series of Navigation Acts (1651, 1660, 1663, and 1673) to help accomplish these goals.

Pennsylvania was founded as a refuge for Quakers. One of a number of radical religious sects that had sprung up about the time of the English Civil War, the Quakers held many controversial beliefs. They believed all persons had an "inner light" that allowed them to commune directly with God, and, as a result, placed little importance on the church hierarchy. They were also pacifists and declined to show customary deference to those considered to be their social superiors.

Delaware, though at first part of Pennsylvania, was granted a separate legislature by Penn, but until the American Revolution, Pennsylvania's proprietary governors also functioned as governors of Delaware.

THE EIGHTEENTH CENTURY

America's population continued to grow rapidly, both from natural increases due to prosperity and a healthy environment and from large-scale immigration, not only of English but also of other groups such as Scots-Irish and Germans.

It was decided to found a colony as a buffer between South Carolina and Spanish-held Florida. In 1732, a group of British philanthropists, led by General James Oglethorpe (1696–1785), obtained a charter for such a colony which was named Georgia.

England and France continued on a collision course, as France determined to take complete control of the Ohio Valley and western Pennsylvania.

British authorities ordered colonial governors to resist this. George Washington (1732–1799), a young major of the Virginia militia, was sent to western Pennsylvania but was forced by superior numbers to fall back on his hastily built Fort Necessity and then to surrender.

While Washington skirmished with the French, delegates of seven colonies met in Albany, New York, to discuss common plans for defense. Delegate Benjamin Franklin proposed a plan for an intercolonial government. While the other colonies showed no support for the idea, it was an important precedent for the concept of uniting in the face of a common enemy.

Between 1756 and 1763 Britain and France fought the Seven Years War (also known as the French and Indian War). By the Treaty of Paris of 1763, Britain gained all of Canada and all of what is now the United States east of the Mississippi River. France lost all of its North American holdings.

DRILL: AMERICAN HISTORY: THE COLONIAL PERIOD

1. The purpose of the Treaty of Tordesillas was

    (A) to divide the non-European world between Spain and Portugal.

    (B) to specify which parts of North America should be French and which parts should be Spanish.

    (C) to create an alliance of France, Holland, and England against Spanish designs in the New World.

    (D) to divide the New World between France and Spain.

    (E) to exclude any Portuguese colonization from the Western Hemisphere.

2.   The chief significance of French explorer Samuel de Champlain's alienation of the Iroquois Indians was

    (A) to prevent the French from establishing a profitable fur trade in Canada.

    (B) to prevent Champlain from founding any permanent settlement along the St. Lawrence River.

    (C) to prevent Champlain from making it back to France alive.

    (D) to prevent New France from expanding southward into what is now the United States.

    (E) the creation of an alliance of British and French colonists against the Iroquois.

3.   Explorers who established French claims to the eastern United States included

    I.   Giovanni da Verrazano.   IV. John Cabot.

    II.   Martin Frobisher.   V. Henry Hudson.

    III. Jacques Cartier.

    (A) I only.   (D) I, III, IV, and V.

    (B) I and III.   (E) II only.

    (C) I, II, and V.

4.   The primary motive for European exploration in the fifteenth and sixteenth centuries was

    (A) to gain access to the wealth of the Far East.

    (B) to relieve population overcrowding.

(C) to find a place outside of Europe for religious dissidents to be relocated.

(D) to establish bases for defense against other European powers.

(E) scientific curiosity.

5. In the sixteenth and seventeenth centuries, the Europeans' greatest impact on the Americas was the

(A) introduction of Christianity to American Indian tribes.

(B) destruction of the massive American forests to make room for farms.

(C) introduction of modern technology to American Indian tribes, allowing them to compete effectively with Europe.

(D) introduction of European diseases to America, devastating many American Indian tribes.

(E) introduction of slavery to the Americas.

THE AMERICAN REVOLUTION (1763–1787)

THE COMING OF THE AMERICAN REVOLUTION

In 1763, George Grenville (1712–1770) became prime minister of Britain and set out to solve some of the empire's more pressing problems. Chief among these was the large national debt incurred in the recent war.

In 1764, Grenville pushed through Parliament the Sugar Act (also known as the Revenue Act), which aimed at raising revenue by taxing goods imported by the Americans.

The Stamp Act (1765) imposed a direct tax on Americans for the first time. It required Americans to purchase revenue stamps on everything from newspapers to legal documents, and would have created an impossible drain on hard currency in the colonies.

Americans reacted first with restrained and respectful petitions and pamphlets in which they pointed out that "taxation without representation is tyranny." From there, resistance progressed to stronger protests that eventually became violent.

In October 1765, delegates from nine colonies met as the Stamp Act Congress, and passed moderate resolutions against the act, asserting that Americans could not be taxed without the consent of their representatives. The Stamp Act Congress showed that representatives of the colonies could work together, and gave political leaders in the various colonies a chance to become acquainted with each other.

Colonial merchants' boycott of British goods spread throughout the colonies and had a powerful effect on British merchants and manufacturers, who began clamoring for the act's repeal.

Meanwhile, the fickle King George III had dismissed Grenville over an unrelated disagreement and replaced him with a cabinet headed by Charles Lord Rockingham (1730–1782). In March 1766 Parliament repealed the Stamp Act. At the same time, however, it passed the Declaratory Act, which claimed the power to tax or make laws for the Americans "in all cases whatsoever."

The Rockingham ministry was replaced with a cabinet dominated by Chancellor of the Exchequer Charles Townshend (1725–1767). In 1766, Parliament passed his program of taxes on items imported into the colonies. These taxes came to be known as the Townshend duties.

American reaction was at first slow, but the sending of troops, aroused them to resistance. Nonimportation was again instituted, and soon British merchants were calling on Parliament to repeal the acts. In March 1770, Parliament, under the new prime minister, Frederick Lord North (1737–1792), repealed all of the taxes except that on tea, which was retained to prove Parliament had the right to tax the colonies if it so desired.

A relative peace was brought to an end by the Tea Act of 1773. In desperate financial condition—partially because the Americans were buying smuggled Dutch tea rather than the taxed British product—the British East India Company sought and obtained from Parliament concessions that allowed it to ship tea directly to the colonies rather than only by way of Britain. The result would be that East India Company tea, even with the tax, would be cheaper than smuggled Dutch tea. The colonists would thus, it was hoped, buy the tea, tax and all. The East India Company would be saved, and the Americans would be tacitly accepting Parliament's right to tax them.

The Americans, however, proved resistant to this approach; rather than seem to admit Parliament's right to tax, they vigorously resisted the cheaper tea. Various methods, including tar and feathers, were used to prevent the collection of the tax on tea. In most ports, Americans did not allow the tea to be landed.

In Boston, however, pro-British Governor Thomas Hutchinson (1711–1780) forced a confrontation by ordering Royal Navy vessels to prevent the tea ships from leaving the harbor. After 20 days, this would, by law, result in the cargoes being sold at auction and the tax paid. The night before the time was to expire, December 16, 1773, Bostonians thinly disguised as Native Americans boarded the ships and threw the tea into the harbor.

The British responded with four acts collectively titled the Coercive Acts. First, the Boston Port Act closed the port of Boston to all trade until local citizens would agree to pay for the lost tea (they would not). Secondly, the Massachusetts Government Act greatly increased the power of Massachusetts's royal governor at the expense of the legislature. Thirdly, the Administration of Justice Act provided that royal officials accused of crimes in Massachusetts could be tried elsewhere, where chances of acquittal might be greater. Finally, a strengthened Quartering Act allowed the new governor, General Thomas Gage (1721–1787), to quarter his troops anywhere, including unoccupied private homes.

THE WAR FOR INDEPENDENCE

The British government paid little attention to the First Continental Congress, having decided to teach the Americans a military lesson. More troops were sent to Massachusetts, which was officially declared to be in a state of rebellion. Orders were sent to General Gage to arrest the leaders of the resistance, or failing that, to provoke any sort of confrontation that would allow him to turn British military might loose on the Americans.

Gage decided on a reconnaissance-in-force to find and destroy a reported stockpile of colonial arms and ammunition at Concord. Seven hundred British troops set out on this mission on the night of April 18, 1775, which resulted in skirmishes with the colonists at Lexington and Concord.

Open warfare had begun, and the myth of British invincibility was destroyed. Militia came in large numbers from all the New England colonies to join the force besieging Gage and his army in Boston. The following month the Americans tightened the noose around Boston by fortifying Breed's Hill (a spur of Bunker Hill).

The British determined to remove them by a frontal attack. Twice the British were thrown back, but they finally succeeded when the Americans ran out of ammunition. Over a thousand British soldiers were killed or wounded in what turned out to be the bloodiest battle of the war (June 17, 1775). Yet the British had gained very little and remained bottled up in Boston.

Meanwhile in May 1775, American forces under Ethan Allen (1738–1789) and Benedict Arnold (1741–1801) took Fort Ticonderoga on Lake Champlain.

While these events were taking place in New England and Canada, the Second Continental Congress met in Philadelphia in May 1775. Congress was divided into two main factions. One was composed mostly of New Englanders and leaned toward declaring independence from Britain. The other drew its strength primarily from the Middle Colonies and was not yet ready to go that far.

The Declaration of Independence was primarily the work of Thomas Jefferson (1743–1826) of Virginia. It was a restatement of political ideas by then commonplace in America and showed why the former colonists felt justified in separating from Great Britain. It was formally adopted by Congress on July 4, 1776.

The British landed that summer at New York City, where they hoped to find many loyalists. Washington narrowly avoided being trapped there (an escape partially due to British General Howe's slowness). Defeated again at the Battle of Washington Heights (August 29–30, 1776) in Manhattan, Washington was forced to retreat across New Jersey with the aggressive British General Lord Charles Cornwallis (1738–1805) in pursuit.

With his victory almost complete, General Howe decided to wait till spring to finish annihilating Washington's army. Scattering his troops in small detachments so as to hold all of New Jersey, he went into winter quarters.

Washington, with his small army melting away as demoralized soldiers deserted, decided on a bold stroke. On Christmas night 1776, his army crossed the Delaware River and struck the Hessians at Trenton. The Hessians, still groggy from their hard-drinking Christmas party, were easily defeated. A few days later, Washington defeated a British force at Princeton (January 3, 1777). Much of New Jersey was regained, and Washington's army was saved from disintegration.

Hoping to weaken Britain, France began making covert shipments of arms to the Americans early in the war. Shipments from France were vital for the Americans. The American victory at Saratoga convinced the French to join openly in the war against England. Eventually the Spanish (1779) and the Dutch (1780) joined as well.

Howe was replaced by General Henry Clinton (1738–1795), who was ordered to abandon Philadelphia and march to New York. Clinton maintained New York as Britain's main base. In November 1778, the British easily conquered Georgia. Late the following year, Clinton moved on South Carolina and in May 1780 Charleston surrendered. Clinton then returned to New York, leaving Cornwallis to continue the Southern campaign.

In the west, George Rogers Clark (1752–1818) led an expedition down the Ohio River and into the area of present-day Illinois and Indiana, defeating a British force at Vincennes, Indiana, and securing the area north of the Ohio River for the United States.

In the south, Cornwallis began to move northward toward North Carolina, but on October 7, 1780, a detachment of his force was defeated by American frontiersmen at the Battle of Kings Mountain in northern South Carolina. Cornwallis unwisely moved north without bothering to secure South Carolina first. The result was that the British would no sooner leave an area than American militia or guerilla bands, such as that under Francis Marion "the Swamp Fox" (ca. 1732–1795), were once again in control.

American commander Nathaniel Greene's (1742–1786) brilliant southern strategy led to a crushing victory at Cowpens, South Carolina (January 17, 1781), by troops under Greene's subordinate, General Daniel Morgan (1736–1802) of Virginia. It also led to a near victory by Greene's own force at Guilford Court House, North Carolina (March 15, 1781).

The frustrated and impetuous Cornwallis now abandoned the southern strategy and moved north into Virginia, taking a defensive position at Yorktown. With the aid of a French fleet which took control of Chesapeake Bay and a French army which joined him in sealing off the land approaches to Yorktown, Washington succeeded in trapping Cornwallis. After three weeks of siege, Cornwallis surrendered (October 17, 1781).

News of the debacle at Yorktown brought the collapse of Lord North's ministry, and the new cabinet opened peace negotiations.

The final agreement became known as the Treaty of Paris of 1783. Its terms stipulated the following: 1) The United States was recognized as an independent nation by the major European powers, including Britain. 2) Its western boundary was set at the Mississippi River. 3) Its southern boundary was set at 31° north latitude (the northern boundary of Florida). 4) Britain retained Canada, but had to surrender Florida to Spain. 5) Private British creditors would be free to collect any debts owed by United States citizens. 6) Congress was to recommend that the states restore confiscated loyalist property.

THE CREATION OF NEW GOVERNMENTS

After the collapse of British authority in 1775, it became necessary to form new state governments. By the end of 1777, ten new state constitutions had been formed. Most state constitutions included bills of rights—lists of things the government was not supposed to do to the people.

In the summer of 1776, Congress appointed a committee to begin devising a framework for a national government. The end result preserved the sovereignty of the states and created a very weak national government.

The Articles of Confederation provided for a unicameral Congress in which each state would have one vote, as had been the case in the Continental Congress. Executive authority under the articles would be vested in a committee of 13, with one member from each state. In order to amend the articles, the unanimous consent of all the states was required.

The Articles of Confederation government was empowered to make war, make treaties, determine the amount of troops and money each state should contribute to the war effort, settle disputes between states, admit new states to the Union, and borrow money. But it was not empowered to levy taxes, raise troops, or regulate commerce.

Ratification of the Articles of Confederation was delayed by disagreements over the future status of the lands that lay to the west of the original 13 states. Maryland, which had no such claim, withheld ratification until, in 1781, Virginia agreed to surrender its western claims to the new national government.

DRILL: THE AMERICAN REVOLUTION

1. Which of the following was a response to the Stamp Act?

    (A) The Boston Tea Party

    (B) The Battle of Lexington

    (C) The Paxton Boys' march on Philadelphia

(D) Nonimportation of British goods

(E) The Boston Massacre

2. During the 1760s and 1770s the most effective American tactic in gaining the repeal of the Stamp and Townshend Acts was

(A) tarring and feathering British tax agents.

(B) sending petitions to the king and Parliament.

(C) boycotting British goods.

(D) destroying private property, such as tea, on which a tax was to be levied.

(E) using death threats to intimidate British tax agents.

3. George Washington's army faced which of the following problems during the American Revolution?

(A) The British public unanimously supported the policy of its government.

(B) Two-thirds of the colonists opposed the war.

(C) The army was dependent on poorly trained militia.

(D) The army used conventional military tactics.

(E) The British government was able to give its full attention to the war.

4. Which of the following was NOT a provision of the Paris Peace Treaty ending the American Revolution?

(A) Louisiana was returned to French control.

(B) Florida was returned to Spanish control.

(C) The United States was recognized as an independent nation.

(D) The lands between the Mississippi and the Appalachians were given to the U.S. in disregard for the rights of Indian tribes living in those regions.

     (E) The British granted the Americans fishing rights off the coast of Newfoundland.

5.   Which Revolutionary War battle is considered the "turning point" in the war because it led to direct French assistance for the Americans?

     (A) Trenton   (D) Yorktown

     (B) Bunker Hill   (E) Saratoga

     (C) Princeton

THE UNITED STATES CONSTITUTION (1787–1789)

DEVELOPMENT AND RATIFICATION

As time went on, the inadequacy of the Articles of Confederation became increasingly apparent. It was decided in 1787 to call for a convention of all the states to meet in Philadelphia for the purpose of revising the Articles of Confederation.

The men who met in Philadelphia in 1787 were remarkably able, highly educated, and exceptionally accomplished. For the most part they were lawyers, merchants, and planters. Though representing individual states, most thought in national terms.

George Washington was unanimously elected to preside, and the enormous respect that he commanded helped hold the convention together through difficult times.

The delegates shared a basic belief in the innate selfishness of man, which must somehow be kept from abusing the power of government. For this purpose, the document that they finally produced contained many checks and balances, designed to prevent the government, or any one branch of the government, from gaining too much power.

Benjamin Franklin played an important role in reconciling the often heated delegates and in making various suggestions that eventually helped the convention arrive at the "Great Compromise," proposed by Roger Sherman (1721–1793) and Oliver Ellsworth (1745–1807). The Great (or Connecticut) Compromise provided for a presidency, a Senate with all states represented equally (by two senators each), and a House of Representatives with representation according to population.

Another crisis involved North-South disagreement over the issue of slavery. Here also a compromise was reached. Slavery was neither endorsed nor condemned by the Constitution. Each slave was to count as three-fifths of a person for purposes of apportioning representation and direct taxation on the states (the Three-Fifths Compromise). The federal government was prohibited from stopping the importation of slaves prior to 1808.

The third major area of compromise was the nature of the presidency. The result was a strong presidency with control of foreign policy and the power to veto Congress's legislation. Should the president commit an actual crime, Congress would have the power to impeach him. Otherwise, the president would serve for a term of four years and be reelectable without limit. As a check to the possible excesses of democracy, the president was to be elected by an electoral college, in which each state would have the same number of electors as it did senators and representatives combined. The person with the second highest total in the electoral college would be vice president. If no one gained a majority in the electoral college, the president would be chosen by the House of Representatives.

The new Constitution was to take effect when nine states, through special state conventions, had ratified it.

As the struggle over ratification got under way, those favoring the Constitution astutely named themselves Federalists (i.e., advocates of centralized power) and labeled their opponents Antifederalists.

By June 21, 1788, the required nine states had ratified, but the crucial states of New York and Virginia still held out. Ultimately, the promise of the addition of a bill of rights helped win the final states. In March 1789, George Washington was inaugurated as the nation's first president.

DRILL: THE UNITED STATES CONSTITUTION

1. Those who supported ratification of the Constitution were called

    (A) Federalists.   (D) Antifederalists.

    (B) Democrats.   (E) Republicans.

    (C) Whigs.

2. Which of the following groups tended to support the Federalists?

    (A) Small farmers   (D) Baptist and Methodist ministers

    (B) Small businessmen   (E) Skilled craftsmen

    (C) Wealthy merchants

3. Alexander Hamilton believed that the United States should

    (A) repudiate the debts of the Confederation but assume those of the states.

    (B) assume the debts of the Confederation but not those of the states.

    (C) assume the debts of both the Confederation and the states.

    (D) repudiate the debts of both the Confederation and the states.

    (E) assume the debts of the Confederation, the states, and local governments.

4. The Constitutional Convention took place in

    (A) 1776.   (D) 1781.

    (B) 1789.   (E) 1800.

    (C) 1787.

5. When no presidential candidate obtains a majority of the electoral vote, who chooses the president?

    (A) The Senate

    (B) The House of Representatives

    (C) The Supreme Court

    (D) The Senate and the House of Representatives combined

    (E) The electoral college

THE NEW NATION (1789–1824)

THE FEDERALIST ERA

Few Antifederalists were elected to Congress, and many of the new legislators had served as delegates to the Philadelphia Convention two years before.

George Washington received virtually all the votes of the presidential electors, and John Adams received the next highest number, thus becoming the vice president. After a triumphant journey from Mount Vernon, Washington was inaugurated in New York City, the temporary seat of government (April 30, 1789).

Ten amendments were ratified by the states by the end of 1791 and became the Bill of Rights. The first nine spelled out specific guarantees of personal freedoms, and the Tenth Amendment reserved to the states all those powers not specifically withheld or granted to the federal government.

The Judiciary Act of 1789 provided for a Supreme Court with six justices, and invested it with the power to rule on the constitutional validity of state laws. It was to be the interpreter of the "supreme law of the land." A system of district courts was set up to serve as courts of original jurisdiction, and three courts of appeal were established.

Congress established three departments of the executive branch—state, treasury, and war—as well as the offices of attorney general and postmaster general.

WASHINGTON'S ADMINISTRATION (1789–1797)

Treasury Secretary Alexander Hamilton, in his "Report on the Public Credit," proposed the funding of the national debt at face value, federal assumption of state debts, and the establishment of a national bank. In his "Report on Manufactures," Hamilton proposed an extensive program for federal stimulation of industrial development through subsidies and tax incentives. The money needed to fund these programs would come from an excise tax on distillers and from tariffs on imports.

Thomas Jefferson, Secretary of State, and others objected to the funding proposal because they believed it would enrich a small elite group at the expense of the more worthy common citizen.

Hamilton interpreted the Constitution as having vested extensive powers in the federal government. This "implied powers" stance claimed that the government was given all powers that were not expressly denied to it. This is the "broad" interpretation.

Jefferson and Madison held the view that any action not specifically permitted in the Constitution was thereby prohibited. This is the "strict" interpretation, and the Republicans opposed the establishment of Hamilton's national bank based on this view of government. The Jeffersonian supporters, primarily under the guidance of James Madison, began to organize political groups in opposition to the Federalist program. They called themselves Republicans.

The Federalists, as Hamilton's supporters were called, received their strongest support from the business and financial groups in the commercial centers of the Northeast and from the port cities of the South. The strength of the Republicans lay primarily in the rural and frontier areas of the South and West.

FOREIGN AND FRONTIER AFFAIRS

The U.S. proclaimed neutrality when France went to war with Europe in 1792, and American merchants traded with both sides. In retaliation, the British began to seize American merchant ships and force their crews into service with the British navy.

John Jay negotiated a treaty with the British that attempted to settle the conflict at sea, as well as to curtail English agitation of their Native American allies on the western borders in 1794.

In the Pinckney Treaty, ratified by the Senate in 1796, the Spanish opened the Mississippi River to American traffic and recognized the 31st parallel as the northern boundary of Florida.

INTERNAL PROBLEMS

In 1794, western farmers refused to pay the excise tax on whiskey which formed the backbone of Hamilton's revenue program. When a group of Pennsylvania farmers terrorized the tax collectors, President Washington sent out a federalized militia force of some 15,000 men and the rebellion evaporated, thus strengthening the credibility of the young government.

JOHN ADAMS' ADMINISTRATION (1797–1801)

In the Election of 1796 John Adams was the Federalist candidate, and Thomas Jefferson the Republican. Jefferson received the second highest number of electoral votes and became vice president.

REPRESSION AND PROTEST

The elections in 1798 increased the Federalists' majorities in both houses of Congress and they used their "mandate" to enact legislation to stifle foreign influences. The Alien Act raised new hurdles in the path of immigrants trying to obtain citizenship, and the Sedition Act widened the powers of the Adams administration to muzzle its newspaper critics.

Republican leaders were convinced that the Alien and Sedition Acts were unconstitutional, but the process of deciding on the constitutionality of federal laws was as yet undefined. Jefferson and James Madison decided that state legislatures should have that power, and they drew up a series of resolutions which were presented to the Kentucky and Virginia legislatures. They proposed that state bodies could "nullify" federal laws within those states. These resolutions were adopted only in these two states, and so the issue died, but the principle of states' rights would have great force in later years.

THE REVOLUTION OF 1800

Thomas Jefferson and Aaron Burr (1756–1836) ran on the Republican ticket, though not together, against John Adams and Charles Pinckney (1746–1825) for the Federalists. All ran for the presidency; the candidate garnering the second-highest number of electoral votes would become vice president. Both Jefferson and Burr received the same number of electoral votes, so the election went to the House of Representatives. After a lengthy deadlock, Alexander Hamilton threw his support to Jefferson and Burr had to accept the vice presidency, the result obviously intended by the electorate. Jefferson appointed James Madison as secretary of state and Albert Gallatin (1761–1849) secretary of the treasury.

The Federalist Congress passed a new Judiciary Act early in 1801, and President Adams filled the newly created vacancies with party supporters, many of them with last-minute commissions. John Marshall (1755–1835) was then appointed chief justice of the United States Supreme Court, thus guaranteeing continuation of Federalist policies from the bench of the high court.

THE JEFFERSONIAN ERA

Thomas Jefferson and his Republican followers envisioned a nation of independent farmers living under a central government that exercised a minimum of control and served merely to protect the individual liberties guaranteed by the Constitution. This agrarian paradise would be free of the industrial smoke and urban blight of Europe, and would serve as a beacon light of Enlightenment rationalism to a world searching for direction. But Jefferson presided over a nation that was growing more industrialized and urban, and which seemed to need an ever-stronger president.

DOMESTIC AFFAIRS

The Twelfth Amendment was adopted and ratified in 1804, ensuring that a tie vote between candidates of the same party could not again cause the confusion of the Jefferson-Burr affair.

Following the Constitutional mandate, the importation of slaves was stopped by law in 1808.

The Louisiana Purchase: An American delegation purchased the trans-Mississippi territory from Napoleon for $15 million in April 1803, even though they had no authority to buy more than the city of New Orleans.

Exploring the West: Meriwether Lewis (1774–1809) and William Clark's (1770–1838) group left St. Louis in 1804 and returned two years later with a wealth of scientific and anthropological information. At the same time, Zebulon Pike and others had been traversing the middle parts of Louisiana and mapping the land.

MADISON'S ADMINISTRATION (1809–1817)

The Election of 1808: Republican James Madison won the election over Federalist Charles Pinckney, but the Federalists gained seats in both houses of the Congress.

The Native American tribes of the Northwest and the Mississippi Valley were resentful of the government's policy of pressured removal to the West, and the British authorities in Canada exploited their discontent by encouraging border raids against the American settlements.

At the same time, the British interfered with American transatlantic shipping, including impressing sailors and capturing ships.

The Congress in 1811 contained a strong prowar group called the War Hawks led by Henry Clay (1777–1852) and John C. Calhoun (1782–1850). They gained control of both houses and began agitating for war with the British. On June 1, 1812, President Madison asked for a declaration of war and Congress complied.

After three years of inconclusive war, in 1815 the Treaty of Ghent provided for the acceptance of the status quo that had existed at the beginning of hostilities, and both sides restored their wartime conquests to the other.

The Federalists had increasingly become a minority party. They vehemently opposed the war, and Daniel Webster (1782–1852) and other New England congressmen consistently blocked the Administration's efforts to prosecute the war effort. On December 15, 1814, delegates from the New England states met in Hartford, Connecticut, and drafted a set of resolutions suggesting nullification—and even secession—if their interests were not protected against the growing influence of the South and the West.

Soon after the convention adjourned, the news of Andrew Jackson's victory over the British on January 8, 1815 at New Orleans was announced and their actions were discredited. The Federalist party ceased to be a political force from this point on.

POSTWAR DEVELOPMENTS

Protective Tariff (1816): The first protective tariff in the nation's history was passed in 1816 to slow the flood of cheap British manufactures into the country.

Rush-Bagot Treaty (1817): An agreement was reached in 1817 between Britain and the United States to stop maintaining armed fleets on the Great Lakes. This first "disarmament" agreement is still in effect.

The Adams-Onis Treaty (1819): Spain had decided to sell the remainder of the Florida territory to the Americans before they took it anyway. Under this agreement, the Spanish surrendered all their claims to Florida. The United States agreed to assume $5 million in debts owed to American merchants.

THE MONROE DOCTRINE

As Latin American nations began declaring independence, British and American leaders feared that European governments would try to restore the former New World colonies to their erstwhile royal owners.

In December 1823, President James Monroe (1758–1831) included in his annual message to Congress a statement that the peoples of the American hemisphere were "henceforth not to be considered as subjects for future colonization by any European powers."

INTERNAL DEVELOPMENT (1820–1830)

The years following the War of 1812 were years of rapid economic and social development, followed by a severe depression in 1819. But this slump was temporary, and it became obvious that the country was moving rapidly from its agrarian origins toward an industrial, urban future.

The Monroe Presidency (1817–1823): James Monroe, the last of the "Virginia dynasty," had been handpicked by the retiring Madison and he was elected with only one electoral vote opposed—a symbol of national unity.

THE MARSHALL COURT

John Marshall delivered the majority opinions in a number of critical decisions in these formative years, all of which served to strengthen the power of the federal government and restrict the powers of state governments. These are two key examples:

Marbury v. Madison (1803): This case established the Supreme Court's power of judicial review over federal legislation.

Gibbons v. Ogden (1824): In a case involving competing steamboat companies, Marshall ruled that commerce included navigation, and that only Congress has the right to regulate commerce among states. Thus, the state-granted monopoly was voided.

STATEHOOD: A BALANCING ACT

The Missouri Compromise (1820): The Missouri Territory, the first to be organized from the Louisiana Purchase, applied for statehood in 1819. Since the Senate membership was evenly divided between slaveholding and free states at that time, the admission of a new state would give the voting advantage either to the North or to the South.

As the debate dragged on, the northern territory of Massachusetts applied for admission as the state of Maine. The two admission bills were combined, with Maine coming in free and Missouri coming in as a slave state. To make the package palatable for the House, a provision was added that prohibited slavery in the remainder of the Louisiana Territory north of the southern boundary of Missouri (latitude 36°30').

DRILL: THE NEW NATION

1. A revolution in what country made American neutrality an issue in the 1790s?

(A) Great Britain   (D) France

(B) Spain   (E) Germany

(C) Netherlands

2. The Whiskey Rebellion of 1794 protested

   (A) Prohibition.

   (B) a 25% tax on whiskey.

   (C) government regulation of whiskey production.

   (D) the lifting of import duties on whiskey.

   (E) a 30% drop in whiskey prices.

3. Which of the following does NOT describe the Louisiana Purchase of 1803?

   (A) The United States purchased Louisiana from France for $15 million.

   (B) Jefferson expanded the powers of the presidency.

   (C) French power expanded in the Western Hemisphere.

   (D) The United States doubled in size.

   (E) The treaty of cession left some of the boundaries vague.

4. The *Marbury v. Madison* decision of 1803 established the principle that

   (A) the federal government had the power to regulate commerce.

   (B) the Supreme Court had the power to declare acts of Congress unconstitutional.

   (C) the federal government had the power to protect property rights under the contract clause.

   (D) a state lacked the power to block the operation of a federal agency.

   (E) states had the power to determine whether acts of Congress applied within their borders.

5. The Monroe Doctrine stated that the United States

    (A) was not concerned with the type of government other countries might have.

    (B) was concerned only with the type of government that the countries of the Western Hemisphere might have.

    (C) would not tolerate any new European colonization in the New World.

    (D) claimed the Western Hemisphere as its exclusive zone of influence.

    (E) was prepared to drive out by force any European power that did not give up its colonies in the Western Hemisphere.

JACKSONIAN DEMOCRACY AND WESTWARD EXPANSION (1824–1850)

JACKSONIAN DEMOCRACY (1829–1841)

The Election of 1824

Although John Quincy Adams, through the controversial action of the House of Representatives, became president in the 1824 election, Andrew Jackson instigated a campaign for the presidency immediately. He won the election of 1828.

Jackson was popular with the common man. He seemed to be the prototype of the self-made westerner: rough-hewn, violent, vindictive, with few ideas but strong convictions. He ignored his appointed cabinet officers and relied instead on the counsel of his "Kitchen Cabinet," a group of partisan supporters.

Jackson expressed the conviction that government operations could be performed by untrained, common folk, and he threatened to dismiss large numbers of government employees and replace them with his supporters.

He exercised his veto power more than any other president before him.

The War on the Bank

The Bank of the United States had operated under the direction of

Nicholas Biddle (1786–1844) since 1823. He was a cautious man, and his conservative economic policy enforced conservatism among the state and private banks—which many bankers resented. In 1832 Jackson vetoed the Bank's renewal, and it ceased being a federal institution in 1836.

Jackson had handpicked his Democratic successor, Martin Van Buren (1782–1862) of New York. The opposition Whig party had emerged from the ruins of the National Republicans and other groups who opposed Jackson's policies.

Van Buren, inherited all the problems and resentments generated by his mentor. He spent most of his term in office dealing with the financial chaos left by the death of the Second Bank. The best he could do was to eventually persuade Congress to establish an Independent Treasury to handle government funds. It began functioning in 1840.

The Election of 1840

The Whigs nominated William Henry Harrison, "Old Tippecanoe," a western fighter against the Native Americans. Their choice for vice president was John Tyler (1790–1862), a former Democrat from Virginia. The Democrats put up Van Buren again.

Harrison won but died only a month after the inauguration, having served the shortest term in presidential history.

The Meaning of Jacksonian Politics

The Age of Jackson was the beginning of the modern two-party system. Popular politics, based on emotional appeal, became the accepted style. The practice of meeting in mass conventions to nominate national candidates for office was established during these years.

The Democrats opposed big government and the requirements of modernization: urbanization and industrialization. Their support came from the working classes, small merchants, and small farmers.

The Whigs promoted government participation in commercial and industrial development, the encouragement of banking and corporations, and a cautious approach to westward expansion. Their support came largely from northern business and manufacturing interests and large southern planters. Calhoun, Clay, and Webster dominated the Whig party during the early decades of the nineteenth century.

REMAKING SOCIETY: ORGANIZED REFORM

The early antislavery movement advocated only the purchase and colonization of slaves. The American Colonization Society was organized in 1817, and established the colony of Liberia in 1830, but by that time the movement had reached a dead end.

In 1831, William Lloyd Garrison (1805–1879) started his paper, *The Liberator*, and began to advocate total and immediate emancipation. He founded the New England Anti-slavery Society in 1832 and the American Anti-slavery Society in 1833. Theodore Weld (1803–1895) pursued the same goals, but advocated more gradual means.

The movement split into two wings: Garrison's radical followers, and the moderates who favored "moral suasion" and petitions to Congress. In 1840, the Liberty party, the first national antislavery party, fielded a presidential candidate on the platform of "free soil" (nonexpansion of slavery into the new western territories).

DIVERGING SOCIETIES—LIFE IN THE NORTH

As the nineteenth century progressed, the states seemed to polarize more into the two sections we call the North and the South, with the expanding West becoming ever more identified with the North.

THE ROLE OF MINORITIES

The women's rights movement focused on social and legal discrimination, and women like Lucretia Mott (1793–1880) and Sojourner Truth (ca. 1797–1883) became well-known figures on the speakers' circuit.

By 1850, 200,000 free blacks lived in the North and West. Their lives were restricted everywhere by prejudice, and "Jim Crow" laws separated the races. Black citizens organized separate churches and fraternal orders. The economic security of the free blacks was constantly threatened by the newly arrived immigrants, who were willing to work at the least desirable jobs for lower wages. Racial violence was a daily threat.

THE GROWTH OF INDUSTRY

By 1850, the value of industrial output had surpassed that of agricultural production. The Northeast produced more than two-thirds of the manufactured goods. Between 1830 and 1850, the number of patents issued for industrial inventions almost doubled.

DIVERGING SOCIETIES—LIFE IN THE SOUTH

The southern states experienced dramatic growth in the second quarter of the nineteenth century. The economy grew more productive and more prosperous, but still the section called the South was basically agrarian, with few important cities and only scattered industry. The plantation system, with its cash-crop production driven by the use of slave labor, remained the dominant institution.

The most important economic phenomenon of the early decades of the nineteenth century was the shift in population and production from the old "upper South" of Virginia and the Carolinas to the "lower South" of the newly opened Gulf states of Alabama, Mississippi, and Louisiana. In the older Atlantic states, tobacco retained its importance, but shifted westward to the Piedmont. It was replaced in the East by food grains. The southern Atlantic coast continued to produce rice, and southern Louisiana and east Texas retained their emphasis on sugar cane. But the rich black soil of the new Gulf states proved ideal for the production of short-staple cotton, especially after the invention of the "gin." Cotton soon became the center of the southern economy.

CLASSES IN THE SOUTH

The large plantations growing cotton, sugar, or tobacco used the gang system, in which white overseers directed black drivers who supervised large groups of workers in the fields, all performing the same operation. In the culture of rice, and on the smaller farms, slaves were assigned specific tasks, and when those tasks were finished, the worker had the remainder of the day to himself.

House servants usually were considered the most favored since they were spared the hardest physical labor and enjoyed the most intimate relationship with the owner's family.

COMMERCE AND INDUSTRY

The lack of manufacturing and business development has frequently been blamed for the South's losing its bid for independence in 1861–1865. Actually, the South was highly industrialized for its day and compared favorably with most European nations in the development of manufacturing capacity. However, it trailed far behind the North, so much so that when war erupted in 1861, the northern states owned 81 percent of the factory capacity in the United States.

MANIFEST DESTINY AND WESTWARD EXPANSION

Although the term "Manifest Destiny" was not actually coined until 1844, the belief that the American nation was destined to eventually expand all the way to the Pacific Ocean, and to possibly embrace Canada and Mexico, had been voiced for years by many who believed that American liberty and ideals should be shared with everyone possible, by force if necessary. The rising sense of nationalism which followed the War of 1812 was fed by the rapidly expanding population, the reform impulse of the 1830s, and the desire to acquire new markets and resources for the burgeoning economy of "Young America."

The Adams-Onis Treaty of 1819 had set the northern boundary of Spanish possessions near the present northern border of California. The territory north of that line and west of the vague boundaries of the Louisiana Territory had been claimed over the years by Spain, England, Russia, France, and the United States. By the 1820s, all these claims had been yielded to Britain and the United States. The United States claimed all the way north to the 54°40' parallel. Unable to settle the dispute, they had agreed on a joint occupation of the disputed land.

In the 1830s, American missionaries followed the traders and trappers to the Oregon country. They began to publicize the richness and beauty of the land. The result was the "Oregon Fever" of the 1840s, as thousands of settlers trekked across the Great Plains and the Rocky Mountains to settle the new Shangri-la.

Texas had been a state in the Republic of Mexico since 1822, following the Mexican revolution against Spanish control. The new Mexican government invited immigration from the north by offering land grants to Stephen Austin (1793–1836) and other Americans. By 1835, approximately 35,000 "gringos" were homesteading on Texas land.

The Mexican officials saw their power base eroding as the foreigners flooded in, so they moved to tighten control through restrictions on immigration and through tax increases. The Texans responded in 1836 by proclaiming independence and establishing a new republic. The ensuing war was short-lived. The Mexican dictator, Antonia López de Santa Anna (1794–1876), advanced north and annihilated the Texan garrisons at the Alamo and at Goliad. On April 23, 1836, Sam Houston (1793–1863) defeated him at San Jacinto, and the Mexicans were forced to let Texas go its way.

Houston immediately asked the American government for recognition and annexation, but President Andrew Jackson feared the revival of the slavery issue. He also feared war with Mexico and so did nothing. When Van Buren followed suit, the new republic sought foreign recognition and support, which the European nations eagerly provided, hoping thereby to create a counterbalance to rising American power and influence in the Southwest. France and England both quickly concluded trade agreements with the Texans.

The district of New Mexico had, like Texas, encouraged American immigration. Soon that state was more American than Mexican. The Santa Fe Trail, running from Independence, Missouri, to the town of Santa Fe, created a prosperous trade in mules, gold, silver, and furs, which moved north in exchange for manufactured goods. American settlements sprung up all along the route.

TYLER, POLK, AND CONTINUED WESTWARD EXPANSION

A states' rights southerner and a strict constitutionalist who had been placed on the Whig ticket to draw Southern votes, John Tyler, who became president in 1841 upon Harrison's death, rejected the entire Whig program of a national bank, high protective tariffs, and federally funded internal improvements (roads, canals, etc.). In the resulting legislative confrontations, Tyler vetoed a number of Whig-sponsored bills.

The Whigs were furious. In opposition to Tyler over the next few years, the Whigs, under the leadership of Clay, transformed themselves from a loose grouping of diverse factions into a coherent political party with an elaborate organization.

Rejected by the Whigs and without ties to the Democrats, Tyler was a politician without a party. Hoping to gather a political following of his own, he sought an issue with powerful appeal and believed he had found it in the question of Texas annexation. Tyler's new secretary of state, John C. Calhoun, negotiated an annexation treaty with Texas. Calhoun's identification with extreme proslavery forces and his insertion in the treaty of proslavery statements caused the treaty's rejection by the Senate (1844).

THE ELECTION OF 1844

Democratic front-runner Martin Van Buren and Whig front-runner Henry Clay agreed privately that neither would endorse Texas annexation, and that it would not become a campaign issue, but expansionists at the Democratic convention succeeded in dumping Van Buren in favor of James

K. Polk (1795–1849). Polk, called "Young Hickory" by his supporters, was a staunch Jacksonian who opposed protective tariffs and a national bank, but favored territorial expansion, including not only annexation of Texas but also occupation of all the Oregon country (up to latitude 54° 40') hitherto jointly occupied by the United States and Britain.

The Whigs nominated Clay, who continued to oppose Texas annexation. Later, sensing the mood of the country was against him, he began to equivocate.

The antislavery Liberty party nominated James G. Birney. Apparently because of Clay's wavering on the Texas issue, Birney was able to take enough votes away from Clay in New York to give that state, and thus the election, to Polk.

Tyler, as a lame-duck president, made one more attempt to achieve Texas annexation before leaving office. By means of a joint resolution, which unlike a treaty required only a simple majority rather than a two-thirds vote, he was successful in getting the measure through Congress. Texas was finally admitted to the Union in 1845.

As a good Jacksonian, Polk favored a low, revenue-only tariff rather than a high, protective tariff. This he obtained in the Walker Tariff (1846). He also opposed a national debt and a national bank and reestablished Van Buren's Independent Sub-Treasury system, which remained in effect until 1920.

By the terms of the Oregon Treaty (1846), a compromise with Great Britain was reached. The current United States-Canada boundary east of the Rockies (49°) was extended westward to the Pacific. Some northern Democrats were angered and felt betrayed by Polk's failure to insist on all of Oregon, but the Senate readily accepted the treaty.

Though Mexico broke diplomatic relations with the United States immediately upon Texas's admission to the Union, there was still hope of a peaceful settlement. In the fall of 1845, Polk sent John Slidell (1793–1871) to Mexico City with a proposal for a peaceful settlement.

Nothing came of these attempts at negotiation. Racked by coup and counter-coup, the Mexican government refused even to receive Slidell.

Polk thereupon sent United States troops into the disputed territory in southern Texas. A force under General Zachary Taylor (1784–1850) (who was nicknamed "Old Rough and Ready") took up a position just north of the Rio Grande. Eight days later, April 5, 1846, Mexican troops attacked an

American patrol. When news of the clash reached Washington, Polk sought and received from Congress a declaration of war against Mexico on May 13, 1846.

Americans were sharply divided about the war. Some favored it because they felt Mexico had provoked the war, or because they felt it was the destiny of America to spread the blessings of freedom to oppressed peoples. Others, generally northern abolitionists, saw in the war the work of a vast conspiracy of southern slaveholders greedy for more slave territory.

Negotiated peace finally came about when the State Department clerk Nicholas Trist, negotiated and signed the Treaty of Guadalupe-Hidalgo (February 2, 1848), ending the Mexican War. Under the terms of the treaty, Mexico ceded to the United States the southwestern territory from Texas to the California coast.

Although the Mexican War increased the nation's territory by one-third, it also brought to the surface serious political issues that threatened to divide the country, particularly the question of slavery in the new territories.

DRILL: JACKSONIAN DEMOCRACY AND WESTWARD EXPANSION

1. Which of the following opposed rechartering the Second Bank of the United States?

    (A) Nicholas Biddle   (D) Andrew Jackson

    (B) Henry Clay   (E) John Marshall

    (C) Daniel Webster

2. The followers of Andrew Jackson established what political party?

    (A) Whig   (D) Federalist

    (B) Republican   (E) Populist

    (C) Democratic

3.   When President Andrew Jackson's enemies spoke of the "Kitchen Cabinet," they were referring to

(A) a group of old friends and unofficial advisors of the president.

(B) a number of persons of low social standing, including a former cook, who were appointed by Jackson to high cabinet positions.

(C) a suggestion as to where Jackson might keep the federal government's money if he removed it from the Bank of the United States.

(D) a coterie of Jackson supporters in the U.S. Senate.

(E) several state governors who supported Jackson.

4.   Beginning in the 1830s, William Lloyd Garrison called for

(A) colonization of slaves.

(B) immediate emancipation of slaves.

(C) free soil.

(D) step-by-step emancipation of slaves.

(E) popular sovereignty.

5.   What became the South's major cash crop for sale in the international market in the 19th century?

(A) Tobacco   (D) Rice

(B) Cotton   (E) Indigo

(C) Corn

SECTIONAL CONFLICT AND THE CAUSES OF THE CIVIL WAR (1850–1860)

THE CRISIS OF 1850 AND AMERICA AT MIDCENTURY

The Mexican War had no more than started when, on August 8, 1846, freshman Democratic Congressman David Wilmot (1814–1868) of Pennsylvania introduced his Wilmot Proviso as a proposed amendment to a war appropriations bill. It stipulated that "neither slavery nor involuntary servitude shall ever exist" in any territory to be acquired from Mexico. It was passed by the House, and though rejected by the Senate, it was reintroduced again and again amid increasingly acrimonious debate.

The southern position was expressed by John C. Calhoun, now serving as senator from South Carolina. He argued that the territories were the property not of the United States federal government, but of all the states together, and therefore Congress had no right to prohibit in any territory any type of "property" (by which he meant slaves) that was legal in any of the states.

Antislavery northerners, pointing to the Northwest Ordinance of 1787 and the Missouri Compromise of 1820 as precedents, argued that Congress had the right to make what laws it saw fit for the territories, including, if it so chose, laws prohibiting slavery.

A compromise proposal favored by President Polk and many moderate southerners called for the extension of the 36° 30' line of the Missouri Compromise westward through the Mexican Cession to the Pacific, with territory north of the line to be closed to slavery.

Another compromise solution, favored by northern Democrats such as Lewis Cass (1782–1866) of Michigan and Stephen A. Douglas (1813–1861) of Illinois, was known as "squatter sovereignty" and later as "popular sovereignty." It held that the residents of each territory should be permitted to decide for themselves whether to allow slavery.

The Election of 1848: The Democrats nominated Lewis Cass, and their platform endorsed his middle-of-the-road popular sovereignty position with regard to slavery in the territories.

The Whigs dodged the issue even more effectively by nominating General Zachary Taylor, whose fame in the Mexican War made him a strong candidate. Taylor knew nothing of politics, had never voted, and liked to think of himself as above politics. He took no position at all with respect to slavery in the territories.

Some antislavery northern Whigs and Democrats, disgusted with their parties' failure to take a clear stand against the spread of slavery, deserted the party ranks to form an antislavery third party. Their party was called the Free Soil party, since it stood for keeping the soil of new western territories free of slavery. Its candidate was Martin Van Buren.

The election excited relatively little public interest. Taylor won a narrow victory.

The question of slavery's status in the western territories was made more immediate when, on January 24, 1848, gold was discovered not far from Sacramento, California. The next year, gold seekers from the eastern United States and from many foreign countries swelled California's population from 14,000 to 100,000.

In September 1849, having more than the requisite population and being in need of better government, California petitioned for admission to the Union as a free state.

Southerners were furious. Long outnumbered in the House of Representatives, the South would now find itself, should California be admitted as a free state, also outvoted in the Senate.

At this point, the aged Henry Clay proposed an eight-part package. For the North, California would be admitted as a free state; the land in dispute between Texas and New Mexico would go to New Mexico; the New Mexico and Utah territories (all of the Mexican Cession outside of California) would not be specifically reserved for slavery, the status there would be decided by popular sovereignty; and the slave trade would be abolished in the District of Columbia.

For the South, a tougher Fugitive Slave Law would be enacted; the federal government would pay Texas's $10,000,000 preannexation debt; Congress would declare that it did not have jurisdiction over the interstate slave trade and would promise not to abolish slavery itself in the District of Columbia.

President Taylor died (apparently of gastroenteritis) on July 9, 1850, and was succeeded by Vice President Millard Fillmore (1800–1874). In Congress, the fight for the Compromise was taken up by Senator Stephen A. Douglas of Illinois who broke Clay's proposal into its component parts so that he could use varying coalitions to push each part through Congress. The Compromise was adopted.

The 1852 Democratic convention deadlocked between Cass and Douglas and so settled on dark horse Franklin Pierce (1804–1869) of New Hampshire. The Whigs chose General Winfield Scott, a war hero with no political background.

The result was an easy victory for Pierce, largely because the Whig party, badly divided along North-South lines as a result of the battle over the Compromise of 1850, was beginning to come apart.

President Pierce expressed the nation's hope that a new era of sectional peace was beginning. He sought to distract the nation's attention from the slavery issue to an aggressive program of foreign economic and territorial expansion known as "Young America."

In 1853, Commodore Matthew Perry (1794–1858) led a United States naval force into Tokyo Bay on a peaceful mission to open Japan—previously closed to the outside world—to American diplomacy and commerce.

By means of the Reciprocity Treaty (1854), Pierce succeeded in opening Canada to greater United States trade.

From Mexico he acquired in 1853 the Gadsden Purchase, a strip of land in what is now southern New Mexico and Arizona along the Gila River. The purpose of this purchase was to provide a good route for a transcontinental railroad across the southern part of the country.

The chief factor in the economic transformation of America during the 1840s and 1850s was the dynamic rise of the railroads. They helped link the Midwest to the Northeast rather than just the South, as would have been the case had only water transportation been available.

The 1850s was the heyday of the steamboat on inland rivers, and the clipper ship on the high seas. The period also saw rapid and sustained industrial growth, especially in the textile industry.

In the North, the main centers of agricultural production shifted from the Mid-Atlantic states to the more fertile lands of the Midwest. Mechanical reapers and threshers came into wide use.

America's second two-party system, which had developed during the 1830s, was in the process of breaking down. The Whig party was now in the process of complete disintegration. This was partially the result of the slavery issue, which divided the party along North-South lines, and partially the result of the nativist movement.

The collapse of a viable two-party system made it much more difficult for the nation's political process to contain the explosive issue of slavery.

THE RETURN OF SECTIONAL CONFLICT

The strengthened Fugitive Slave Law enraged northerners. So violent was northern feeling against the law that several riots erupted as a result of attempts to enforce it. Some northern states passed personal liberty laws in an attempt to prevent the enforcement of the Fugitive Slave Law.

One northerner who was outraged by the Fugitive Slave Act was Harriet Beecher Stowe. She wrote *Uncle Tom's Cabin*, a fictional book depicting what she perceived as the evils of slavery. Furiously denounced in the South, the book became an overnight bestseller in the North, where it turned many toward active opposition to slavery.

All illusion of sectional peace ended abruptly in 1854 when Senator Stephen A. Douglas of Illinois introduced a bill in Congress to organize the area west of Missouri and Iowa as the territories of Kansas and Nebraska on the basis of popular sovereignty.

The Kansas-Nebraska Act aroused a storm of outrage in the North, where its repeal of the Missouri Compromise was seen as the breaking of a solemn agreement. It hastened the disintegration of the Whig party and divided the Democratic party along North-South lines.

In the North, many Democrats left the party and were joined by former Whigs and Know-Nothings in the newly created Republican party. Springing to life almost overnight as a result of northern fury at the Kansas-Nebraska Act, the Republican party included diverse elements whose sole unifying principle was the firm belief that slavery should be banned from all the nation's territories, confined to the states where it already existed, and allowed to spread no further.

For the next several years Kansas was in chaos, including at various times armed conflict, voter fraud, two governments, and a questionable constitution.

In *Dred Scott v. Sanford*, the Supreme Court attempted to finally settle the slavery question. The case involved a Missouri slave, Dred Scott (ca. 1795–1858), who had been encouraged by abolitionists to sue for his freedom on the basis that his owner had taken him for several years to a free state, Illinois, and then to a free territory, Wisconsin.

Under the domination of aging pro-southern Chief Justice Roger B. Taney of Maryland, the Court attempted to read the extreme southern position on slavery into the Constitution, ruling not only that Scott had no standing to sue in federal court, but also that temporary residence in a free state, even for several years, did not make a slave free, and that the Missouri Compromise (already a dead letter by that time) had been unconstitutional all along because Congress did not have the authority to exclude slavery from a territory. Nor did territorial governments have the right to prohibit slavery.

The 1858 Illinois senatorial campaign produced a series of debates that got to the heart of the issues that were threatening to divide the nation. Incumbent Democratic senator and front-runner for the 1860 presidential nomination Stephen A. Douglas was opposed by a Springfield lawyer, little known outside the state, by the name of Abraham Lincoln.

Lincoln, in a series of seven debates that the candidates agreed to hold during the course of the campaign, stressed that Douglas's doctrine of popular sovereignty failed to recognize slavery for the moral wrong it was.

Douglas, for his part, maintained that his guiding principle was democracy, not any moral standard of right or wrong with respect to slavery.

At the debate held in Freeport, Illinois, Lincoln pressed Douglas to reconcile the principle of popular sovereignty to the Supreme Court's decision in the Dred Scott case. How could the people "vote it up or vote it down," if, as the Supreme Court alleged, no territorial government could prohibit slavery? Douglas, in what came to be called his "Freeport Doctrine," replied that the people of any territory could exclude slavery simply by declining to pass any of the special laws that slave jurisdictions usually passed for their protection.

Douglas's answer was good enough to win him reelection to the Senate, although by the narrowest of margins, but hurt him in the coming presidential campaign.

For Lincoln, despite the failure to win the Senate seat, the debates were a major success, propelling him into the national spotlight, and strengthening the resolve of the Republican party to resist compromise on the free-soil issue.

THE COMING OF THE CIVIL WAR

On the night of October 16, 1859, John Brown, an abolitionist, led 18 followers in seizing the federal arsenal at Harpers Ferry, Virginia, taking hostages, and endeavoring to incite a slave uprising. Quickly cornered by Virginia militia, he was eventually captured by a force under the command of army Colonel Robert E. Lee (1807–1870).

Brown was quickly tried, convicted, sentenced, and on December 2, 1859, hanged. Many northerners looked upon Brown as a martyr.

Though responsible northerners such as Lincoln denounced Brown's raid as a criminal act which deserved to be punished by death, many southerners became convinced that the entire northern public approved of

Brown's action and that the only safety for the South lay in a separate southern confederacy.

As the 1860 presidential election approached, two Democratic conventions failed to reach consensus, and the sundered halves of the party nominated separate candidates. The southern wing of the party nominated Buchanan's vice president, John C. Breckinridge of Kentucky, on a platform calling for a federal slave code in all the territories. What was left of the national Democratic party nominated Douglas on a platform of popular sovereignty.

A third presidential candidate was added by the Constitutional Union party, a collection of aging former Whigs and Know-Nothings from the southern and border states, plus a handful of moderate southern Democrats. It nominated John Bell of Tennessee on a platform that sidestepped the issues and called simply for the Constitution, the Union, and the enforcement of the laws.

The Republicans met in Chicago, confident of victory and determined to do nothing to jeopardize their favorable position. Accordingly, they rejected as too radical front-running New York Senator William H. Seward in favor of Illinois favorite son Abraham Lincoln. The platform called for federal support of a transcontinental railroad and for the containment of slavery.

On election day, the voting went along strictly sectional lines. Breckinridge carried the Deep South; Bell, the border states; and Lincoln, the North. Douglas, although second in popular votes, carried only a single state and part of another. Lincoln led in popular votes, and though he was short of a majority in that category, he did have the needed majority in electoral votes and was elected.

THE SECESSION CRISIS

On December 20, 1860, South Carolina, by vote of a special convention, declared itself out of the Union. By February 1, 1861, six more states (Alabama, Georgia, Florida, Mississippi, Louisiana, and Texas) had followed suit.

Representatives of the seceded states met in Montgomery, Alabama, in February 1861 and declared themselves to be the Confederate States of America. They elected former Secretary of War and United States senator Jefferson Davis of Mississippi as president, and Alexander Stephens (1812–1883) of Georgia as vice president. They also adopted a constitution for the

Confederate states which, while similar to the United States Constitution in many ways, contained several important differences:

1) Slavery was specifically recognized, and the right to move slaves from one state to another was guaranteed.

2) Protective tariffs were prohibited.

3) The president was to serve for a single nonrenewable six-year term.

4) The president was given the right to veto individual items within an appropriations bill.

5) State sovereignty was specifically recognized.

DRILL: SECTIONAL CONFLICT AND THE CAUSES OF THE CIVIL WAR

1. Which of the following was part of the Compromise of 1850?

   (A) Abolition of the slave trade

   (B) A new fugitive slave law

   (C) California's entry into the Union on the basis of popular sovereignty

   (D) Utah and New Mexico territories to be free

   (E) A new eastern border for Texas

2. The main issue of the 1850s Free-Soil party was that

   (A) the federal government should permit no further spread of slavery in the territories.

   (B) a homestead act should be passed, granting 160 acres of government land in the West free to anyone who would settle on it and improve it for five years.

   (C) the federal government should oversee immediate and uncompensated abolition of slavery.

(D) freed slaves should be provided with 40 acres and two mules to provide them the economic means of independent self-support.

(E) the United States should annex Cuba.

3. The Wilmot Proviso was most likely to be supported by

(A) Jacksonian Democrats.

(B) advocates of nullification.

(C) secessionists.

(D) Free-Soilers.

(E) advocates of popular sovereignty.

4. The Wilmot Proviso stipulated that

(A) slavery should be prohibited in the lands acquired as a result of the Mexican War.

(B) no lands should be annexed to the United States as a result of the Mexican War.

(C) California should be a free state while the rest of the Mexican Cession should be reserved for the formation of slave states.

(D) the status of slavery in the Mexican Cession should be decided on the basis of "popular sovereignty."

(E) the Missouri Compromise line should be extended through the Mexican Cession to the Pacific, lands north of it being closed to slavery.

5. The Compromise of 1850 had the effect of

(A) providing a compromise that offered only limited expansion of slavery into territories west of the Mississippi, satisfying both pro-slavery Southerners and abolitionist Northerners, and resolving the issue of slavery west of the Mississippi.

(B) postponing and evading, rather than resolving, the problems related to slavery in American territories west of the Mississippi.

(C) ending Southern demands for the expansion of slavery into American territories west of the Mississippi.

(D) ending Northern demands for the prohibition of slavery in American territories west of the Mississippi.

(E) providing a compromise that allowed all American territories west of the Mississippi to decide the slavery issue for themselves.

THE CIVIL WAR AND RECONSTRUCTION (1860–1877)

HOSTILITIES BEGIN

In his inaugural address, Lincoln urged southerners to reconsider their actions, but warned that the Union was perpetual, that states could not secede, and that he would therefore hold the federal forts and installations in the South.

Only two remained in federal hands: Fort Pickens, off Pensacola, Florida; and Fort Sumter, in the harbor of Charleston, South Carolina. Lincoln soon received word from Major Robert Anderson, commander of the small garrison at Sumter, that supplies were running low. Desiring to send in the needed supplies, Lincoln informed the governor of South Carolina of his intention, but promised that no attempt would be made to send arms, ammunition, or reinforcements unless southerners initiated hostilities.

Confederate General P.G.T. Beauregard (1818–1893), acting on orders from President Davis, demanded Anderson's surrender. Anderson said he would surrender if not resupplied. Knowing supplies were on the way, the Confederates opened fire at 4:30 a.m. on April 12, 1861. The next day, the fort surrendered.

The day following Sumter's surrender, Lincoln declared an insurrection and called for the states to provide 75,000 volunteers to put it down. In response to this, Virginia, Tennessee, North Carolina, and Arkansas declared their secession.

The remaining slave states, Delaware, Kentucky, Maryland, and Missouri, wavered, but stayed with the Union.

The North enjoyed at least five major advantages over the South. It had overwhelming preponderance in wealth and was vastly superior in industry.

The North also had an advantage of almost three to one in manpower; and over one-third of the South's population was composed of slaves, whom Southerners would not use as soldiers. Unlike the South, the North received large numbers of immigrants during the war. The North retained control of the United States Navy, and thus would command the sea and be able to blockade the South. Finally, the North enjoyed a much superior system of railroads.

The South did, however, have several advantages. It was vast in size, making it difficult to conquer. Its troops would be fighting on their own ground, a fact that would give them the advantage of familiarity with the terrain, as well as the added motivation of defending their homes and families. Its armies would often have the opportunity of fighting on the defensive, a major advantage in the warfare of that day.

Though Jefferson Davis had extensive military and political experience, Lincoln was much superior to Davis as a war leader, showing firmness, flexibility, mental toughness, great political skill, and, eventually, an excellent grasp of strategy.

At a creek called Bull Run near the town of Manassas Junction, Virginia, just southwest of Washington, D.C., the Union Army met a Confederate force under generals P.G.T. Beauregard and Joseph E. Johnston, July 21, 1861. In the First Battle of Bull Run (called First Manassas in the South), the Union army was forced to retreat in confusion back to Washington.

EARLY GAINS BY THE SOUTH

To replace the discredited McDowell, Lincoln chose General George B. McClellan (1826–1885). McClellan was a good trainer and organizer and was loved by the troops, but he was unable to effectively use the powerful army (now called the Army of the Potomac) he had built up.

Lee summoned General Thomas J. "Stonewall" Jackson (1824–1863) and his army from the Shenandoah Valley (where Jackson had just finished defeating several superior federal forces), and with the combined forces attacked McClellan.

After two days of bloody but inconclusive fighting, McClellan lost his nerve and began to retreat. In the remainder of what came to be called the Battle of the Seven Days, Lee continued to attack McClellan, forcing him back to his base, though at great cost in lives. McClellan's army was loaded back onto its ships and taken back to Washington.

Before McClellan's army could reach Washington, Lee took the opportunity to thrash Union General John Pope (1822–1892), who was in northern Virginia with another northern army, at the Second Battle of Bull Run.

West of the Appalachian Mountains, matters were proceeding differently. The northern commanders there, Henry W. Halleck (1815–1872) and Don Carlos Buell (1818–1898), were no more enterprising than McClellan, but Halleck's subordinate, Ulysses S. Grant, was.

With permission from Halleck, Grant mounted a combined operation—army troops and navy gunboats—against two vital Confederate strongholds, forts Henry and Donelson, which guarded the Tennessee and Cumberland rivers in northern Tennessee. When Grant captured the forts in February 1862, Johnston was forced to retreat to Corinth in northern Mississippi.

Grant pursued, but ordered by Halleck to wait until all was in readiness before proceeding, halted his troops at Pittsburg Landing on the Tennessee River, 25 miles north of Corinth. On April 6, 1862 General Albert Sidney Johnston, who had received reinforcements and been joined by General P.G.T. Beauregard, surprised Grant there, but in the two-day battle that followed (Shiloh) failed to defeat him. Johnston was among the many killed in what was, up to this point, the bloodiest battle in American history.

Grant was severely criticized in the North for having been taken by surprise. Yet with other Union victories and Farragut's capture of New Orleans, the North had taken all of the Mississippi River except for a 110-mile stretch between the Confederate fortresses of Vicksburg, Mississippi, and Port Hudson, Louisiana.

Many southerners believed Britain and France would rejoice in seeing a divided and weakened America. They also believed the two countries would likewise be driven by the need of their factories for cotton and thus intervene on the Confederacy's behalf.

This view proved mistaken. Britain already had a large supply of cotton, and had other sources besides the U.S. British leaders may also have weighed their country's need to import wheat from the northern United States against its desire for cotton from the southern states. Finally, British public opinion opposed slavery.

Skillful northern diplomacy had a great impact. In this, Lincoln had the extremely able assistance of Secretary of State William Seward, who took a hard line in warning Europeans not to interfere, and of the ambassador to Great Britain Charles Francis Adams (1807–1886). Britain remained neutral, and other European countries, including France, followed its lead.

Congress in 1862 passed two highly important acts dealing with domestic affairs in the North. The Homestead Act granted 160 acres of government land free of charge to any person who would farm it for at least five years. Much of the West was eventually settled under the provisions of this act. The Morrill Land Grant Act offered large amounts of the federal government's land to states that would establish "agricultural and mechanical" colleges. Many of the nation's large state universities were later founded under the provisions of this act.

THE EMANCIPATION PROCLAMATION

By mid-1862, Lincoln, under pressure from radical elements of his own party and hoping to create a favorable impression on foreign public opinion, determined to issue the Emancipation Proclamation, which declared free all slaves in areas still in rebellion as of January 1, 1863. At Seward's recommendation, Lincoln waited to announce the proclamation until the North should win some sort of victory. This was provided by the Battle of Antietam (September 17, 1862).

After his victory at the Second Battle of Bull Run, Lee moved north and crossed into Maryland, where he hoped to win a decisive victory that would force the North to recognize southern independence.

The armies finally met along Antietam Creek, just east of the town of Sharpsburg in western Maryland. In a bloody but inconclusive day-long battle, known as Antietam in the North and Sharpsburg in the South, McClellan's timidity led him to miss another excellent chance to destroy Lee's cornered and badly outnumbered army. After the battle, Lee retreated to Virginia, and Lincoln removed McClellan from command.

To replace him, Lincoln chose General Ambrose E. Burnside (1824–1881), who promptly demonstrated his unfitness by blundering into a lopsided defeat at Fredericksburg, Virginia (December 13, 1862).

Lincoln then replaced Burnside with General Joseph "Fighting Joe" Hooker (1814–1879). He was soundly beaten at the Battle of Chancellorsville (May 5–6, 1863). At this battle, the brilliant Southern general "Stonewall" Jackson was accidentally shot by his own men and died several days later.

Lee received permission from President Davis to invade Pennsylvania. He was pursued by the Army of the Potomac, now under the command of General George G. Meade (1815–1872), who had replaced the discredited Hooker. They met at Gettysburg in a three-day battle (July 1–3, 1863) that was the bloodiest of the war. Lee, who sorely missed the services of Jackson and whose cavalry leader, the normally reliable J.E.B. Stuart (1833–1864), failed to provide him with timely reconnaissance, was defeated. However, he was allowed by the victorious Meade to retreat to Virginia with his army intact if battered, much to Lincoln's disgust.

Meanwhile, Grant moved on Vicksburg, one of the two last Confederate bastions on the Mississippi River. In a brilliant campaign, he bottled up the Confederate forces of General John C. Pemberton (1814–1881) inside the city and placed them under siege. After six weeks, the defenders surrendered on July 4, 1863. Five days later, Port Hudson surrendered, giving the Union complete control of the Mississippi.

After Union forces under General William Rosecrans (1819–1898) suffered an embarrassing defeat at the Battle of Chickamauga in northwestern Georgia (September 19–20, 1863), Lincoln named Grant overall commander of Union forces in the West.

Grant went to Chattanooga, Tennessee, where Confederate forces under General Braxton Bragg (1817–1876) were virtually besieging Rosecrans, and immediately took control of the situation. Gathering Union forces from other portions of the western theater and combining them with reinforcements from the East, Grant won a resounding victory at the Battle of Chattanooga (November 23–25, 1863), in which federal forces stormed seemingly impregnable Confederate positions on Lookout Mountain and Missionary Ridge. This victory put Union forces in position for a drive into Georgia, which began the following spring.

Early in 1864, Lincoln made Grant commander of all Union armies. Grant devised a coordinated plan for constant pressure on the Confederacy. General William T. Sherman would lead a drive toward Atlanta, Georgia, with the goal of destroying the Confederate army under General Joseph E. Johnston (who had replaced Bragg). Grant would accompany Meade and the Army of the Potomac in advancing toward Richmond with the goal of destroying Lee's Confederate army.

In a series of bloody battles (the Wilderness, Spotsylvania, Cold Harbor) in May and June of 1864, Grant drove Lee to the outskirts of Richmond. Still unable to take the city or get Lee at a disadvantage, Grant circled around, attacking Petersburg, Virginia, an important railroad junction just south of Richmond and the key to that city's—and Lee's—supply lines. Once again turned back by entrenched Confederate troops, Grant settled down to besiege Petersburg and Richmond in a stalemate that lasted some nine months.

Sherman had been advancing simultaneously in Georgia. He maneuvered Johnston back to the outskirts of Atlanta with relatively little fighting. At that point, Confederate President Davis lost patience with Johnston and replaced him with the aggressive General John B. Hood (1831–1879). Hood and Sherman fought three fierce but inconclusive battles around Atlanta in late July, and then settled down to a siege of their own during the month of August.

THE ELECTION OF 1864 AND NORTHERN VICTORY

Lincoln ran on the ticket of the National Union party, essentially the Republican party with loyal or "War" Democrats. His vice-presidential candidate was Andrew Johnson (1808–1875), a loyal Democrat from Tennessee.

The Democratic party's presidential candidate was General George B. McClellan, who ran on a platform labeling the war a failure, and calling for a negotiated peace settlement even if that meant southern independence.

In September 1864, word came that Sherman had taken Atlanta. The capture of this vital southern rail and manufacturing center brought an enormous boost to northern morale. Along with other northern victories that summer and fall, it ensured a resounding election victory for Lincoln and the continuation of the war to complete victory for the North.

To speed that victory, Sherman marched through Georgia from Atlanta to the sea, arriving at Savannah in December 1864 and turning north into the Carolinas, leaving behind a 60-mile-wide swath of destruction.

Lee abandoned Richmond (April 3, 1865) and attempted to escape with what was left of his army. Pursued by Grant, he was cornered and forced to surrender at Appomattox, Virginia (April 9, 1865). Other Confederate armies still holding out in various parts of the South surrendered over the next few weeks.

Lincoln did not live to receive news of the final surrenders. On April 14, 1865, he was shot in the back of the head while watching a play in Ford's Theater in Washington.

THE ORDEAL OF RECONSTRUCTION

Reconstruction began well before the fighting of the Civil War came to an end. It brought a time of difficult adjustments in the South.

Among those who faced such adjustments were the recently freed slaves.

To ease the adjustment, Congress in 1865 created the Freedman's Bureau to provide food, clothing, and education, and generally look after the interests of former slaves.

To restore legal governments in the seceded states, Lincoln developed a policy that made it relatively easy for southern states to enter the collateral process.

Tennessee, Arkansas, and Louisiana formed loyal governments under Lincoln's plan, but were refused recognition by a Congress dominated by Radical Republicans.

Radical Republicans such as Thaddeus Stevens (1792–1868) of Pennsylvania believed Lincoln's plan did not adequately punish the South, restructure southern society, or boost the political prospects of the Republican party.

Instead, the radicals in Congress drew up the more stringent Wade-Davis Bill which Lincoln killed with a "pocket veto," and the radicals were furious. When Lincoln was assassinated the radicals rejoiced, believing Vice President Andrew Johnson would be less generous to the South, or at least easier to control.

CONGRESSIONAL RECONSTRUCTION

Determined to reconstruct the South as it saw fit, Congress passed a Civil Rights Act and extended the authority of the Freedman's Bureau, giving it both quasi-judicial and quasi-executive powers.

Johnson vetoed both bills, claiming they were unconstitutional; but Congress overrode the vetoes. Fearing that the Supreme Court would agree with Johnson and overturn the laws, Congress approved and sent on to the states for ratification (June 1866) the Fourteenth Amendment, making constitutional the laws Congress had just passed. The Fourteenth Amendment defined citizenship and forbade states to deny various rights to citizens, reduced the representation in Congress of states that did not allow blacks to vote, forbade the paying of the Confederate debt, and made former Confederates ineligible to hold public office.

To control the president, Congress passed the Army Act, reducing the president's control over the army. Congress also passed the Tenure of Office Act, forbidding Johnson to dismiss cabinet members without the Senate's permission.

Johnson obeyed the letter but not the spirit of the Reconstruction acts, and Congress, angry at his refusal to cooperate, sought in vain for grounds to impeach him, until in August 1867 Johnson violated the Tenure of Office Act in order to test its constitutionality. The matter was not tested in the courts, however, but in Congress, where Johnson was impeached by the House of Representatives and came within one vote of being removed by the Senate.

THE ELECTION OF 1868 AND THE FIFTEENTH AMENDMENT

In 1868, the Republicans nominated Ulysses S. Grant for president, who had no political record and whose views—if any—on national issues were unknown.

The narrow victory of even such a strong candidate as Grant prompted Republican leaders to decide that it would be politically expedient to give the vote to all blacks, Northern as well as Southern. For this purpose, the fifteenth Amendment was drawn up and submitted to the states. Ironically, the idea was so unpopular in the North that it won the necessary three-fourths approval only with its ratification by southern states required to do so by Congress.

Though personally of unquestioned integrity, Grant naively placed his faith in a number of thoroughly dishonest men. His administration was rocked by one scandalous revelation of government corruption after another.

Many of the economic difficulties the country faced during Grant's administration were caused by the necessary readjustments from a wartime economy back to a peacetime economy. The central economic question was deflation versus inflation, or more specifically, whether to retire the unbacked paper money, greenbacks, printed to meet the wartime emergency, or to print more.

Early in Grant's second term, the country was hit by an economic depression known as the Panic of 1873. Brought on by the overexpansive tendencies of railroad builders and businessmen during the immediate post-war boom, the Panic was triggered by economic downturns in Europe, and more immediately, by the failure of Jay Cooke and Company, a major American financial firm.

The Panic led to clamor for the printing of more greenbacks. In 1874, Congress authorized a small new issue of greenbacks, but it was vetoed by Grant. Pro-inflation forces were further enraged when Congress in 1873 demonetized silver, going to a straight gold standard. Silver was becoming more plentiful due to western mining and was seen by some as a potential source of inflation. Pro-inflation forces referred to the demonetization of silver as the "Crime of '73."

In the election of 1876, the Democrats campaigned against corruption and nominated New York Governor Samuel J. Tilden (1814–1886), who had broken the Tweed political machine of New York City.

The Republicans passed over Grant and turned to Governor Rutherford B. Hayes (1822–1893) of Ohio. Like Tilden, Hayes was decent, honest, in favor of hard money and civil service reform, and opposed to government regulation of the economy.

Tilden won the popular vote and led in the electoral vote 184 to 165. However, 185 electoral votes were needed for election, and 20 votes, from the three Southern states still occupied by federal troops and run by Republican governments, were disputed.

A deal was made whereby those 20 votes went to Hayes in return for the removal of federal troops from the South. Reconstruction was over.

DRILL: THE CIVIL WAR AND RECONSTRUCTION

1. By February 1, 1861, what group of states had seceded from the Union?

    (A) Mississippi, Florida, Alabama, Georgia, Louisiana, Texas, and South Carolina

    (B) Mississippi, Arkansas, Missouri, Alabama, Georgia, and Florida

    (C) Arkansas, Tennessee, North Carolina, and Virginia

    (D) Texas, Louisiana, Arkansas, Mississippi, and Alabama

    (E) Kentucky, Mississippi, Arkansas, Missouri, Alabama, and Georgia

2. Which of the following served as president of the Confederate States of America?

    (A) Robert E. Lee   (D) Jefferson Davis

    (B) William T. Sherman   (E) Alexander H. Stephens

    (C) Robert Y. Hayne

3. Which of the following was NOT a Northern advantage in the Civil War?

    (A) It was fighting a defensive war.

    (B) It had greater manufacturing capacity.

    (C) It owned greater railroad trackage.

    (D) It had a larger population.

    (E) The mountain chains ran north and south.

4. Who served as a Union General?

    (A) Joseph Johnston   (D) Robert E. Lee

    (B) Thomas Jackson   (E) J.E.B. Stuart

    (C) William T. Sherman

5. Robert E. Lee surrendered to Ulysses Grant at

    (A) Spotsylvania.   (D) Raleigh.

    (B) Appomattox.   (E) Richmond.

    (C) Cold Harbor.

INDUSTRIALISM, WAR, AND THE PROGRESSIVE ERA (1877–1912)

POLITICS OF THE PERIOD (1877–1882)

The presidencies of Abraham Lincoln and Theodore Roosevelt (1858–1919) mark the boundaries of a half century of relatively weak executive leadership and legislative domination by Congress and the Republican party.

"Stalwarts," led by New York senator Roscoe Conkling (1829–1888), favored the old spoils system of political patronage. "Half-Breeds," headed by Maine senator James G. Blaine (1830–1893), pushed for civil service reform and merit appointments to government posts.

THE ECONOMY (1877–1882)

Between 1860 and 1894, the United States moved from the fourth largest manufacturing nation to the world's leader through capital accumulation, natural resources, especially in iron, oil, and coal, an abundance of labor helped by massive immigration, railway transportation, and communications and major technical innovations such as the development of the modern steel industry and electrical energy.

By 1880, northern capital erected the modern textile industry in the New South by bringing factories to the cotton fields.

SOCIAL AND CULTURAL DEVELOPMENTS (1877–1882)

In time, advocates of the "social gospel" such as Jane Addams (1860–1939) and Washington Gladden (1836–1918) urged the creation of settlement houses and better health and education services to accommodate the new immigrants. In 1881, Booker T. Washington (1856–1915) became president of Tuskegee Institute in Alabama, a school devoted to teaching and vocational education for African-Americans.

THE ECONOMY (1882–1887)

Captains of industry, such as John D. Rockefeller in oil, J. P. Morgan (1837–1919) in banking, Gustavus Swift (1839–1903) in meat processing, Andrew Carnegie in steel, and E. H. Harriman (1848–1909) in railroads, put together major industrial empires.

The concentration of wealth and power in the hands of a relatively small number of giant firms led to a monopoly capitalism that minimized competition. This led to a demand by smaller businessmen, farmers, and laborers for government regulation of the economy in order to promote competition.

The Interstate Commerce Act (1887): Popular resentment of railroad abuses such as price-fixing, kickbacks, and discriminatory freight rates created demands for state regulation of the railway industry. The Interstate Commerce Act was passed providing that a commission be established to oversee fair and just railway rates, prohibit rebates, end discriminatory practices, and require annual reports and financial statements.

American Federation of Labor (1886): Samuel Gompers (1850–1924) and Adolph Strasser put together a combination of national craft unions to represent labor's concerns with wages, hours, and safety conditions. Although militant in its use of the strike and in its demand for collective bargaining in labor contracts with large corporations, it did not promote violence or radicalism.

After graduating from Stevens Institute of Technology in 1883, Frederick W. Taylor (1856–1915), the father of scientific management, introduced modern concepts of industrial engineering, plant management, time and motion studies, efficiency experts, and a separate class of managers in industrial manufacturing.

THE EMERGENCE OF A REGIONAL EMPIRE (1887–1892)

Despite a protective tariff policy, the United States became increasingly international as it sought to export surplus manufactured and agricultural goods. Foreign markets were viewed as a safety valve for labor employment problems and agrarian unrest.

THE ECONOMY (1887–1892)

Corporate monopolies (trusts) which controlled whole industries were subject to federal prosecution if they were found to be combinations or conspiracies in restraint of trade. Although supported by smaller businesses, labor unions, and farm associations, the Sherman Antitrust Act of 1890 was in time interpreted by the Supreme Court to apply to labor unions and farmers' cooperatives as much as to large corporate combinations. Monopoly was still dominant over laissez-faire, free-enterprise economics during the 1890s.

FOREIGN RELATIONS (1887–1892)

As secretary of state, James G. Blaine was concerned with international trade, political stability, and excessive militarism in Latin America. His international Bureau of American Republics was designed to promote a Pan-American customs union and peaceful conflict resolution. To achieve his aims, Blaine opposed U.S. military intervention in the hemisphere.

ECONOMIC DEPRESSION AND SOCIAL CRISIS (1892–1897)

The economic depression that began in 1893 brought about a collective response from organized labor, militant agriculture, and the business community. Each group called for economic safeguards and a more humane free-enterprise system which would expand economic opportunities in an equitable manner.

POLITICS OF THE PERIOD (1892–1897)

The most marked development in American politics was the emergence of a viable third-party movement in the form of the essentially agrarian Populist party.

Democrat Grover Cleveland (New York) regained the White House by defeating Republican president Benjamin Harrison (Indiana). Cleveland's conservative economic stand in favor of the gold standard brought him the support of various business interests. The Democrats won control of both houses of Congress.

The People's party (Populist) nominated James Weaver (Iowa) for president in 1892. The party platform called for the enactment of a program espoused by agrarians, but also for a coalition with urban workers and the middle class. Specific goals were the coinage of silver to gold at a ratio of 16 to 1; federal loans to farmers; a graduated income tax; postal savings banks; public ownership of railroads and telephone and telegraph systems; prohibition of alien land ownership; immigration restriction; a ban on private armies used by corporations to break up strikes; an eight-hour working day; a single six-year term for president and direct election of senators; the right of initiative and referendum; and the use of the secret ballot.

In the election of 1896, the Republicans nominated William McKinley (Ohio) for president on a platform which promised to maintain the gold standard and protective tariffs. The Democratic party repudiated Cleveland's conservative economics and nominated William Jennings Bryan (1860–1925) (Nebraska) for president on a platform similar to the Populists. Bryan delivered one of the most famous speeches in American history when he declared that the people must not be "crucified upon a cross of gold."

The Populist party also nominated Bryan. Having been outmaneuvered by the Silver Democrats, the Populists lost the opportunity to become a permanent political force.

McKinley won a hard-fought election by only about one-half million votes, as Republicans succeeded in creating the fear among business groups and middle-class voters that Bryan represented a revolutionary challenge to the American system. The Republicans retained control over Congress, which they had gained in 1894.

THE ECONOMY (1892–1897)

Homestead Strike (1892): Iron and steel workers went on strike in

Pennsylvania against the Carnegie Steel Company to protest salary reductions.

The primary causes for the depression of 1893 were dramatic growth of the federal deficit, withdrawal of British investments from the American market and the outward transfer of gold, and loss of business confidence. Twenty percent of the work force was eventually unemployed. The depression would last four years.

March of Unemployed (1894): The Populist businessman Jacob Coxey (1854–1951) led a march of hundreds of unemployed workers on Washington asking for a government work-relief program.

Pullman Strike (1894): Eugene Debs's (1855–1926) American Railway Union struck the Pullman Palace Car Co. in Chicago over wage cuts and job losses. The strikes were all ended by force.

Wilson-Gorman Tariff (1894): This protective tariff did little to promote overseas trade as a way to ease the depression.

Dingley Tariff (1897): The Dingley Tariff raised protection to new highs for certain commodities.

SOCIAL AND CULTURAL DEVELOPMENTS (1892–1897)

The Anti-Saloon League was formed in 1893. Women were especially concerned about the increase of drunkenness during the depression.

Immigration declined by almost 400,000 during the depression. Settlement houses helped poor immigrants. Such institutions also lobbied against sweatshop labor conditions and for bans on child labor.

FOREIGN RELATIONS (1892–1897)

The Cuban revolt against Spain in 1895 threatened American business interests in Cuba. Sensational "yellow" journalism, and nationalistic statements from officials such as Assistant Secretary of the Navy Theodore Roosevelt (1858–1919), encouraged popular support for direct American military intervention on behalf of Cuban independence. President McKinley, however, proceeded cautiously through 1897.

THE SINO-JAPANESE WAR (1894–1895)

Japan's easy victory over China signaled to the United States and other nations trading in Asia that China's weakness might result in its colonization by industrial powers, and thus in the closing of the China market. This concern led the United States to announce the Open Door policy with China, designed to protect equal opportunity of trade and China's political independence (1899 and 1900).

FOREIGN POLICY (1897–1902)

On March 27, President McKinley asked Spain to call an armistice, accept American mediation to end the war, and end the use of concentration camps in Cuba. Spain refused to comply. On April 21, Congress declared war on Spain with the objective of establishing Cuban independence (Teller Amendment). The first U.S. forces landed in Cuba on June 22, 1898 and by July 17 had defeated the Spanish forces.

On May 1, 1898, the Spanish fleet in the Philippines was destroyed, and Manila surrendered on August 13. Spain agreed to a peace conference to be held in Paris in October 1898, where it ceded the Philippines, Puerto Rico, and Guam to the United States, in return for a payment of $20 million to Spain for the Philippines. The Treaty of Paris was ratified by the Senate on February 6, 1900.

Filipino nationalists under Emilio Aguinaldo (1869–1964) rebelled against the United States (February 1899) when they learned the Philippines would not be given independence. The United States used 70,000 men to suppress the revolutionaries by June 1902. A special U.S. commission recommended eventual self-government for the Philippines.

During the war with Spain, the United States annexed Hawaii on July 7, 1898. In 1900, the United States claimed Wake Island, 2,000 miles west of Hawaii.

Although Cuba was granted its independence, the Platt Amendment of 1901 guaranteed that it would become a virtual protectorate of the United States. Cuba could not: 1) make a treaty with a foreign state impairing its independence, or 2) contract an excessive public debt. Cuba was required to: 1) allow the United States to preserve order on the island, and 2) lease a naval base for 99 years to the United States at Guantanamo Bay.

POLITICS OF THE PERIOD (1900–1902)

The unexpected death of Vice President Garrett Hobart led the Republican party to choose the war hero and reform governor of New York, Theodore Roosevelt, as President William McKinley's vice-presidential running mate. Riding the crest of victory against Spain, the G.O.P platform called for upholding the gold standard for full economic recovery, promoting economic expansion and power in the Caribbean and the Pacific, and building a canal in Central America. The Democrats once again nominated William Jennings Bryan on a platform condemning imperialism and the gold standard. McKinley easily won reelection and the Republicans retained control of both houses of Congress.

While attending the Pan American Exposition in Buffalo, New York, the president was shot on September 6 by Leon Czolgosz, an anarchist. The president died on September 14. Theodore Roosevelt became the nation's 25th president, and at age 42, its youngest to date.

THEODORE ROOSEVELT AND PROGRESSIVE REFORMS 1902–1907)

President Roosevelt did much to create a bipartisan coalition of liberal reformers whose objective was to restrain corporate monopoly and promote economic competition at home and abroad.

The president pledged strict enforcement of the Sherman Antitrust Act (1890), which was designed to break up illegal monopolies and regulate large corporations for the public good.

Hepburn Act (1906): Membership of the Interstate Commerce Commission was increased from five to seven. The I.C.C. could set its own fair freight rates, had its regulatory power extended over pipelines, bridges, and express companies, and was empowered to require a uniform system of accounting by regulated transportation companies.

Pure Food and Drug Act (1906): This prohibited the manufacture, sale, and transportation of adulterated or fraudulently labeled foods and drugs in accordance with consumer demands.

Meat Inspection Act (1906): This provided for federal and sanitary regulations and inspections in meat-packing facilities. Wartime scandals in 1898 involving spoiled canned meats were a powerful force for reform.

THE ECONOMY (1902–1907)

Antitrust Policy (1902): Attorney General P. C. Knox (1853–1921) first brought suit against the Northern Securities Company, a railroad holding corporation put together by J. P. Morgan (1837–1913), and then moved against Rockefeller's Standard Oil Company. By the time he left office in 1909, Roosevelt had indictments against 25 monopolies.

Department of Commerce and Labor (1903): A new cabinet position was created to address the concerns of business and labor. Within the department, the Bureau of Corporations was empowered to investigate and report on the illegal activities of corporations.

Coal Strike (1902): Roosevelt interceded with government mediation to bring about negotiations between the United Mine Workers union and the anthracite mine owners after a bitter strike over wages, safety conditions, and union recognition. This was the first time that the government intervened in a labor dispute without automatically siding with management.

A brief economic recession and panic occurred in 1907 as a result, in part, of questionable bank speculations, a lack of flexible monetary and credit policies, and a conservative gold standard. This event called attention to the need for banking reform which would lead to the Federal Reserve System in 1913.

SOCIAL AND CULTURAL DEVELOPMENTS (1902–1907)

There was not one unified progressive movement, but a series of reform causes designed to address specific social, economic, and political problems. Progressive reforms might best be described as evolutionary change from above rather than revolutionary upheaval from below.

Muckrakers (a term coined by Roosevelt) were investigative journalists and authors who were often the publicity agents for reforms.

FOREIGN RELATIONS (1902–1907)

Panama Canal: Roosevelt engineered the separation of Panama from Colombia and the recognition of Panama as an independent country. The Hay-Bunau-Varilla Treaty of 1903 granted the United States control of the canal zone in Panama for $10 million and an annual fee of $250,000, beginning nine years after ratification of the treaty by both parties. Construction of the canal began in 1904 and was completed in 1914.

Roosevelt Corollary to the Monroe Doctrine: The United States reserved the right to intervene in the internal affairs of Latin American nations to keep European powers from using military force to collect debts in the Western Hemisphere. The United States by 1905 had intervened in the affairs of Venezuela, Haiti, the Dominican Republic, Nicaragua, and Cuba.

Taft-Katsura Memo (1905): The United States and Japan pledged to maintain the Open Door principles in China. Japan recognized American control over the Philippines, and the United States granted a Japanese protectorate over Korea.

Gentleman's Agreement with Japan (1907): After numerous incidents of racial discrimination against Japanese in California, Japan agreed to restrict the emigration of unskilled Japanese workers to the United States.

THE REGULATORY STATE AND THE ORDERED SOCIETY (1907–1912)

Deciding not to run for reelection, Theodore Roosevelt opened the way for William H. Taft (1857–1930) (Ohio) to run on a Republican platform calling for a continuation of antitrust enforcement, environmental conservation, and a lower tariff policy to promote international trade. The Democrats nominated William Jennings Bryan for a third time on an antimonopoly and low tariff platform. Taft easily won and the Republicans retained control of both houses of Congress. For the first time, the American Federation of Labor entered national politics officially with an endorsement of Bryan. This decision began a long alliance between organized labor and the Democratic party in the twentieth century.

Antitrust Policy: In pursuing anti-monopoly law enforcement, Taft chose as his attorney general George Wickersham (1858–1936), who brought 44 indictments in antitrust suits.

Taft was less successful in healing the Republican split between conservatives and progressives over such issues as tariff reform, conservation, and the almost dictatorial power held by the reactionary Republican Speaker of the House, Joseph Cannon (Illinois).

The 1912 election was one of the most dramatic in American history. President Taft's inability to maintain party harmony led Theodore Roosevelt to return to national politics. When denied the Republican nomination, Roosevelt and his supporters formed the Progressive (Bull Moose) party and nominated Roosevelt for president on a political platform nicknamed "The New Nationalism." It called for stricter regulation on large corporations, creation of a tariff commission, women's suffrage, minimum wages and benefits, direct election of senators, initiative, referendum and recall, presidential primaries, and prohibition of child labor. Roosevelt also called for a Federal Trade Commission to regulate the economy, a stronger executive, and more government planning. Theodore Roosevelt did not see big business as evil, but as a permanent development that was necessary in a modern economy.

The Republicans: President Taft and Vice President Sherman were nominated on a platform of "Quiet Confidence," which called for a continuation of the progressive programs pursued by Taft.

The Democrats: A compromise nominated New Jersey governor Woodrow Wilson for president. Wilson called his campaign the "New Freedom"; it was similar to programs in the Progressive and Republican parties. Wilson called for breaking up large corporations rather than just regulating them. He differed from the other two party candidates by favoring independence for the Philippines, and by advocating the exemption from prosecution of labor unions under the Sherman Antitrust Act. Wilson also supported such measures as lower tariffs, a graduated income tax, banking reform, and direct election of senators.

The Republican split paved the way for Wilson's victory. Although a minority president, Wilson garnered the largest electoral majority in American history up to that time. Democrats won control of both houses of Congress.

THE WILSON PRESIDENCY

Before the outbreak of World War I in 1914, President Wilson, working with cooperative majorities in both houses of Congress, achieved much of the remaining progressive agenda, including lower tariff reform (Underwood-Simmons Act, 1913), the Sixteenth Amendment (graduated income tax, 1913), the Seventeenth Amendment (direct election of senators, 1913), the Federal Reserve banking system (which provided regulation and flexibility to monetary policy, 1913), the Federal Trade Commission (to investigate unfair business practices, 1914), and the Clayton Antitrust Act (improving the old Sherman Act and protecting labor unions and farm cooperatives from prosecution, 1914).

Other goals such as the protection of children in the work force (Keating-Owen Act, 1916), credit reform for agriculture (Federal Farm Loan Act, 1916), and an independent tariff commission (1916) came later. By the end of Wilson's presidency, the New Freedom and the New Nationalism had merged into one government philosophy of regulation, order, and standardization in the interest of an increasingly diverse nation.

SOCIAL AND CULTURAL DEVELOPMENTS (1907–1912)

In 1905, the African-American intellectual militant W. E. B. DuBois (1868–1963) founded the Niagara Movement which called for federal legislation to protect racial equality and for full rights of citizenship. The National Association for the Advancement of Colored People was organized in 1909.

A radical labor organization called the Industrial Workers of the World (I.W.W., or Wobblies, 1905–1924) was active in promoting violence and revolution. The I.W.W. organized effective strikes in the textile industry in 1912, and among a few western miners groups, but had little appeal to the average American worker. After the Red Scare of 1919, the government worked to smash the I.W.W. and deported many of its immigrant leaders and members.

FOREIGN RELATIONS (1907–1915)

President Taft sought to avoid military intervention, especially in Latin America, by replacing "big stick" policies with "dollar diplomacy" in the expectation that American financial investments would encourage economic, social, and political stability. This idea proved an illusion.

Wilson urged Huerta to hold democratic elections and adopt a constitutional government. Huerta refused and Wilson invaded Mexico with troops at Veracruz in 1914. A second U.S. invasion came in northern Mexico in 1916.

The United States kept a military presence in the Dominican Republic and Haiti, and intervened militarily in Nicaragua (1911) to quiet fears of revolution and help manage foreign financial problems.

DRILL: INDUSTRIALISM, WAR, AND THE PROGRESSIVE ERA

1. A member of the Social Gospel movement would probably

    (A) consider such social sins as alcohol abuse and sexual permissiveness as society's most serious problems.

    (B) assert that the poor were themselves at fault for their circumstances.

    (C) maintain that abuses and social degradation resulted solely from a lack of willpower on the part of those who committed them.

    (D) hold that religion is an entirely individualistic matter.

    (E) argue that Christians should work to reorganize the industrial system and bring about international peace.

2. The Sino-Japanese War affected the United States in which of the following ways?

    (A) It led to U.S. aid for Russia.

    (B) It increased the need for rapid naval transportation between the Atlantic and Pacific Oceans.

    (C) It convinced the U.S. that it needed to increase its presence in the Pacific to protect its interests.

    (D) It increased isolationism in the United States.

    (E) It led the U.S. to re-emphasize the Monroe Doctrine.

3. The Roosevelt corollary to the Monroe Doctrine established which of the following?

    (A) The right of European nations to forcefully collect debts in the Western Hemisphere.

    (B) The right of the United States to build and fortify an Atlantic-Pacific canal.

    (C) The independence of Panama from Colombia.

    (D) The right of the U.S. to act as a police power in the Western Hemisphere nations.

    (E) The right of the United States to act as an arbitrator in European conflicts with Western Hemisphere nations.

4. The "Wisconsin Idea" of Robert LaFollette included which of the following?

    (A) Close cooperation with the University of Wisconsin in the writing of legislation

    (B) Strong support of labor unions

    (C) Reduction of business and income taxes

    (D) Subsidies to agriculture

    (E) Establishment of Social Security

5.   Which of the following is true of W.E.B. DuBois?

   (A) He founded the National Association for the Advancement of Colored People.

   (B) He was the chief author of the Atlanta Compromise.

   (C) He was an outspoken critic of the Niagara Movement.

   (D) He believed that blacks should temporarily accommodate themselves to the whites.

   (E) He worked closely with Booker T. Washington.

WILSON AND WORLD WAR I (1912–1920)

IMPLEMENTING THE NEW FREEDOM: THE EARLY YEARS OF THE WILSON ADMINISTRATION

Wilson was only the second Democrat (Cleveland was the first) elected president since the Civil War. Key appointments to the cabinet were William Jennings Bryan as secretary of state and William Gibbs McAdoo (1863–1941) as secretary of the treasury.

The Federal Reserve Act of 1913: The law divided the nation into 12 regions, with a Federal Reserve bank in each region. Federal Reserve banks loaned money to member banks at interest less than the public paid to the member banks, and the notes of indebtedness of businesses and farmers to the member banks were held as collateral. This allowed the Federal Reserve to control interest rates by raising or lowering the discount rate.

The money loaned to the member banks was in the form of a new currency, Federal Reserve notes, which was backed 60 percent by commercial paper and 40 percent by gold. This currency was designed to expand and contract with the volume of business activity and borrowing.

The Federal Reserve system serviced the financial needs of the federal government. The system was supervised and policy was set by a national Federal Reserve Board composed of the secretary of the treasury, the comptroller of the currency, and five other members appointed by the president of the United States.

The Clayton Antitrust Act of 1914: This law supplemented and interpreted the Sherman Antitrust Act of 1890. Under its provisions, stock ownership by a corporation in a competing corporation was prohibited, and the same persons were prohibited from managing competing corporations. Price discrimination (charging less in some regions than in others to undercut the competition) and exclusive contracts which reduced competition were prohibited.

THE ELECTION OF 1916

The minority party nationally in terms of voter registration, the Democrats nominated Wilson and adopted his platform calling for continued progressive reforms and neutrality in the European war.

The Republican convention bypassed Theodore Roosevelt and chose Charles Evans Hughes (1862–1948), an associate justice of the Supreme Court and formerly a progressive Republican governor of New York.

Wilson won the election.

SOCIAL ISSUES IN THE FIRST WILSON ADMINISTRATION

In 1913, Treasury Secretary William G. McAdoo and Postmaster General Albert S. Burleson segregated workers in some parts of their departments with no objection from Wilson. Many northern blacks and whites protested, especially black leader W. E. B. DuBois (1868–1963), who had supported Wilson in 1912.

Wilson opposed immigration restrictions and vetoed a literacy test for immigrants in 1915, but in 1917, Congress overrode a similar veto.

WILSON'S FOREIGN POLICY AND THE ROAD TO WAR

Wilson's Basic Premise: Wilson promised a more moral foreign policy than that of his predecessors, denouncing imperialism and dollar diplomacy, and advocating the advancement of democratic capitalist governments throughout the world.

Wilson signaled his repudiation of Taft's dollar diplomacy by withdrawing American involvement from the six-power loan consortium of China.

In 1912, American marines had landed in Nicaragua to maintain order, and an American financial expert had taken control of the customs station. The Wilson administration kept the marines in Nicaragua and negotiated the Bryan-Chamorro Treaty of 1914, which gave the United States an option to build a canal through the country.

Claiming that political anarchy existed in Haiti, Wilson sent marines in 1915 and imposed a treaty making the country a protectorate, with American control of its finances and constabulary. The marines remained until 1934.

In 1916, Wilson sent marines to the Dominican Republic to stop a civil war and established a military government under an American naval commander.

Wilson feared in 1915 that Germany might annex Denmark and its Caribbean possession, the Danish West Indies or Virgin Islands. After extended negotiations, the United States purchased the islands from Denmark by treaty on August 4, 1916, for $25 million and took possession of them on March 31, 1917.

In 1913, Wilson refused to recognize the government of Mexican military dictator Victoriano Huerta, and offered unsuccessfully to mediate between Huerta and his Constitutionalist opponent, Venustiano Carranza. When the Huerta government arrested several American seamen in Tampico in April 1914, American forces occupied the port of Veracruz, an action condemned by both Mexican political factions. In July 1914, Huerta abdicated his power to Carranza, who was soon opposed by his former general Francisco "Pancho" Villa (1878–1923). Seeking American intervention as a means of undermining Carranza, Villa shot 16 Americans on a train in northern Mexico in January 1916 and burned the border town of Columbus, New Mexico, in March 1916, killing 19 people. Carranza reluctantly consented to Wilson's request that the United States be allowed to pursue and capture Villa in Mexico, but did not expect the force of about 6,000 army troops under the command of General John J. Pershing which crossed the Rio Grande on March 18. The force advanced more than 300 miles into Mexico, failed to capture Villa, and became, in effect, an army of occupation. The Carranza government demanded an American withdrawal, and several clashes with Mexican troops occurred. War threatened, but in January 1917 Wilson removed the American forces.

THE ROAD TO WAR IN EUROPE

When World War I broke out in Europe, Wilson issued a proclamation of American neutrality on August 4, 1914. The value of American trade with the Central Powers fell from $169 million in 1914 to almost nothing in 1916, but trade with the Allies rose from $825 million to $3.2 billion during the same period. In addition, the British and French had borrowed about $3.25 billion from American sources by 1917. The United States had become a major supplier of Allied munitions, food, and raw materials.

The sinking of the British liner *Lusitania* off the coast of Ireland on May 7, 1915, with the loss of 1,198 lives, including 128 Americans, brought strong protests from Wilson. Secretary of State Bryan, who believed Americans should stay off belligerent ships, resigned rather than insist on questionable neutral rights and was replaced by Robert Lansing.

The House-Grey Memorandum: Early in 1915, Wilson sent his friend and adviser Colonel Edward M. House on an unsuccessful visit to Europe to offer American mediation in the war. Late in the year, House returned to London to propose that Wilson call a peace conference; if Germany refused to attend or was uncooperative at the conference, the United States could enter the war on the Allied side. An agreement to that effect, called the House-Grey memorandum, was signed by the British foreign secretary, Sir Edward Grey, on February 22, 1916.

In an address to Congress on January 22, 1917, Wilson made his last offer to serve as a neutral mediator. He proposed a "peace without victory," based not on a "balance of power" but on a "community of power."

Germany announced on January 31, 1917, that it would sink all ships, belligerent or neutral, without warning in a large war zone off the coasts of the Allied nations in the eastern Atlantic and the Mediterranean. Wilson broke diplomatic relations with Germany on February 3. During February and March several American merchant ships were sunk by submarines.

The British intercepted a secret message from the German foreign secretary, Arthur Zimmerman, to the German minister in Mexico, and turned it over to the United States on February 24, 1917. The Germans proposed that, in the event of a war between the United States and Germany, Mexico attack the United States. After the war, the "lost territories" of Texas, New Mexico, and Arizona would be returned to Mexico. When the telegram was released to the press on March 1, many Americans became convinced that war with Germany was necessary.

A declaration of war against Germany was signed by Wilson on April 6.

WORLD WAR I: THE MILITARY CAMPAIGN

The American force of about 14,500, which had arrived in France by September 1917, was assigned a quiet section of the line near Verdun. When the Germans mounted a major drive toward Paris in the spring of 1918, the Americans experienced their first important engagements. In June, they prevented the Germans from crossing the Marne at Chateau-Thierry, and cleared the area of Belleau Woods. In July, eight American divisions aided

French troops in attacking the German line between Reims and Soissons. The American First Army, with over half a million men under Pershing's immediate command, was assembled in August 1918, and began a major offensive at St. Mihiel on the southern part of the front on September 12. Following the successful operation, Pershing began a drive against the German defenses between Verdun and Sedan, an action called the Meuse-Argonne offensive. He reached Sedan on November 7. During the same period the English in the north and the French along the central front also broke through the German lines. The fighting ended with the armistice on November 11, 1918.

MOBILIZING THE HOME FRONT

A number of volunteer organizations sprang up around the country to search for draft dodgers, enforce the sale of bonds, and report any opinion or conversation considered suspicious. Such groups publicly humiliated people accused of not buying war bonds, and persecuted, beat, and sometimes killed people of German descent. The anti-German and antisubversive war hysteria in the United States far exceeded similar public moods in Britain and France during the war.

The Espionage Act of 1917 provided for fines and imprisonment for persons who made false statements which aided the enemy, incited rebellion in the military, or obstructed recruitment or the draft. Printed matter advocating treason or insurrection could be excluded from the mails. The Sedition Act of May 1918 forbade any criticism of the government, flag, or uniform, even if there were not detrimental consequences, and expanded the mail exclusion. The laws were applied in ways that trampled on civil liberties. The Espionage Act was upheld by the Supreme Court in the case of *Shenk v. United States* in 1919. The opinion, written by Justice Oliver Wendell Holmes, Jr. (1841–1935), stated that Congress could limit free speech when the words represented a "clear and present danger," and that a person cannot cry "fire" in a crowded theater. The Sedition Act was similarly upheld in *Abrams v. United States* a few months later. Ultimately 2,168 persons were prosecuted under the laws, and 1,055 were convicted, of whom only 10 were charged with actual sabotage.

WARTIME SOCIAL TRENDS

Large numbers of women, mostly white, were hired by factories and other enterprises in jobs never before open to them. When the war ended, almost all returned to traditional "women's jobs" or to homemaking. Returning veterans replaced them in the labor market.

The labor shortage opened industrial jobs to Mexican-Americans and to African-Americans. W. E. B. DuBois, the most prominent African-American leader of the time, supported the war effort in the hope that the war would make the world safe for democracy and bring a better life for African-Americans in the United States. About half a million rural southern African-Americans migrated to cities, mainly in the North and Midwest, to obtain employment in war and other industries, especially in steel and meatpacking. In 1917, there were race riots in 26 cities in the North and South, with the worst in East St. Louis, Illinois.

In December 1917, a constitutional amendment to prohibit the manufacture and sale of alcoholic beverages in the United States was passed by Congress and submitted to the states for ratification.

PEACEMAKING AND DOMESTIC PROBLEMS (1918–1920)

From the time of the American entry into the war, Wilson had maintained that the war would make the world safe for democracy. He insisted that there should be peace without victory, meaning that the victors would not be vindictive toward the losers, so that a fair and stable international situation in the postwar world would ensure lasting peace. In an address to Congress on January 8, 1918, he presented his specific peace plan in the form of the Fourteen Points. The first five points called for open rather than secret peace treaties, freedom of the seas, free trade, arms reduction, and a fair adjustment of colonial claims. The next eight points were concerned with the national aspirations of various European peoples and the adjustment of boundaries. The fourteenth point, which he considered the most important and had espoused as early as 1916, called for a "general association of nations" to preserve the peace.

Wilson decided that he would lead the American delegation to the peace conference which opened in Paris on January 12, 1919. In doing so he became the first president to leave the country during his term of office. In the negotiations, which continued until May 1919, Wilson found it necessary to make many compromises in forging the text of the treaty.

Following a protest by 39 senators in February 1919, Wilson obtained some changes in the League of Nations structure to exempt the Monroe Doctrine and domestic matters from League jurisdiction. Then, on July 26, 1919, he presented the treaty with the League within it to the Senate for ratification. Almost all of the 47 Democrats supported Wilson and the treaty, but the 49 Republicans were divided. About a dozen were "irreconcilables" who thought that the United States should not be a member of the League under any circumstances. The remainder included 25 "strong" and 12 "mild" reservationists who would accept the treaty with some changes. The main objection centered on Article X of the League Covenant, where the reservationists wanted it understood that the United States would not go to war to defend a League member without the approval of Congress.

On September 3, 1919, Wilson set out on a national speaking tour to appeal to the people to support the treaty and the League and to influence their senators. He collapsed after a speech in Pueblo, Colorado, on September 25, and returned to Washington, where he suffered a severe stroke on October 2 which paralyzed his left side. He was seriously ill for several months, and never fully recovered. The treaty failed to get a two-thirds majority either with or without the reservations.

Many people, including British and French leaders, urged Wilson to compromise on reservations, including the issue of Article X. Many historians think that Wilson's ill health impaired his judgment, and that he would have worked out a compromise had he not had the stroke. The Senate took up the treaty again in February 1920, and on March 19 it was again defeated both with and without the reservations. The United States officially ended the war with Germany by a resolution of Congress signed on July 2, 1921, and a separate peace treaty was ratified on July 25. The United States did not join the League.

DOMESTIC PROBLEMS AND THE END OF THE WILSON ADMINISTRATION

In January 1919, the Eighteenth Amendment to the Constitution prohibiting the manufacture, sale, transportation, or importation of intoxicating liquors was ratified by the states, and it became effective in January 1920. The Nineteenth Amendment providing for women's suffrage, which had been defeated in the Senate in 1918, was approved by Congress in 1919. It was ratified by the states in time for the election of 1920.

Americans feared the spread of the Russian Communist revolution to the United States, and many interpreted the widespread strikes of 1919 spurred by inflation, as Communist-inspired and the beginning of the revolution. Bombs sent through the mail to prominent government and business leaders in April 1919 seemed to confirm their fears, although the origin of the bombs has never been determined. The anti-German hysteria of the war years was transformed into the anti-Communist and antiforeign hysteria of 1919 and 1920, and continued in various forms through the 1920s.

Attorney General A. Mitchell Palmer, who aspired to the 1920 presidential nomination, was one of the targets of the anonymous bombers in the spring of 1919. In August 1919, he named J. Edgar Hoover (1895–1972) to head a new Intelligence Division in the Justice Department to collect information about radicals. After arresting nearly 5,000 people in late 1919 and early 1920, Palmer announced that huge Communist riots were planned for major cities on May Day (May 1, 1920). Police and troops were alerted, but the day passed with no radical activity. Palmer was discredited and the Red Scare subsided.

White hostility based on competition for lower-paid jobs and black encroachment into neighborhoods led to race riots in 26 cities, with hundreds killed or wounded and millions of dollars in property damage. Fear of returning African-American veterans in the South led to an increase of lynchings from 34 in 1917 to 60 in 1918 and 70 in 1919. Some of the victims were veterans still in uniform.

DRILL: WILSON AND WORLD WAR I

1. All of the following contributed to American entrance into World War I EXCEPT

   (A) German submarine warfare.

   (B) cultural and economic ties with Great Britain.

   (C) the Zimmerman telegram.

   (D) the presidential election of 1916.

   (E) the February 1917 revolution in Russia.

2. Which of the following had the greatest effect in moving the United States toward participation in the First World War?

   (A) The German disregard of treaty obligations in violating Belgian neutrality

(B) Germany's declaration of its intent to wage unrestricted submarine warfare

(C) A German offer to reward Mexico with U.S. territory should it join Germany in a war against the United States

(D) The beginning of the Russian Revolution

(E) situation for the Allies

3. In 1913 Woodrow Wilson withheld recognition of the Huerta government of Mexico for which of the following reasons?

(A) Huerta did not really control the country.

(B) Huerta was unwilling to carry out his country's obligations to other countries.

(C) Wilson disapproved of Huerta's actions.

(D) Pancho Villa had raided Columbus, New Mexico.

(E) American sailors had been arrested at Tampico.

4. What was the major factor which brought the United States into WW I?

(A) Unrestricted submarine warfare by the British against shipping in German waters

(B) Terror bombing of British cities by German airplanes and zeppelins

(C) Reports of war atrocities by the German army such as the mass murders of British and French prisoners of war and the executions of millions of German Jews by the Kaiser

(D) The belief that the British and French would eventually lose a war of attrition against Germany and that the U.S. had a moral obligation to prevent that from happening

(E) Unrestricted submarine warfare by the Germans against shipping in British waters

5. The Eighteenth Amendment to the United States Constitution

(A) prohibits the sale of alcoholic beverages.

(B)   recognizes women's right to vote.

(C)   limits the president to two terms.

(D)   establishes the direct election of United States senators.

(E)   establishes the federal income tax.

THE ROARING TWENTIES AND ECONOMIC COLLAPSE (1920–1929)

THE ELECTION OF 1920

The Republican Convention: Senator Warren G. Harding (1865–1923) of Ohio was nominated as a dark-horse candidate, and Governor Calvin Coolidge (1872–1933) of Massachusetts was chosen as the vice presidential nominee. The platform opposed the League and promised low taxes, high tariffs, immigration restriction, and aid to farmers.

The Democratic Convention: Governor James Cox was nominated on the 44th ballot, and Franklin D. Roosevelt (1882–1945), an assistant secretary of the Navy and distant cousin of Theodore, was selected as his running mate. The platform endorsed the League, but left the door open for reservations.

THE TWENTIES: ECONOMIC ADVANCES AND SOCIAL TENSIONS

The principal driving force of the economy of the 1920s was the automobile. Automobile manufacturing stimulated supporting industries such as steel, rubber, and glass, as well as gasoline refining and highway construction. During the 1920s, the United States became a nation of paved roads. The Federal Highway Act of 1916 started the federal highway system and gave matching funds to the states for construction.

Unlike earlier boom periods, which had involved large expenditures for capital investments such as railroads and factories, the prosperity of the 1920s depended heavily on the sale of consumer products. Purchases of "big ticket" items such as automobiles, refrigerators, and furniture were made possible by installment or time payment credit. The idea was not new, but the availability of consumer credit expanded tremendously during the 1920s. Consumer interest and demand was spurred by the great increase in professional advertising, which used newspapers, magazines, radio, billboards, and other media.

There was a trend toward corporate consolidation during the 1920s. In most fields, an oligopoly of two to four firms dominated. This is exemplified by the automobile industry, where Ford, General Motors, and Chrysler produced 83 percent of the vehicles in 1929. Government regulatory agencies such as the Federal Trade Commission and the Interstate Commerce Commission were passive and generally controlled by persons from the business world.

There was also a trend toward bank consolidation. Because corporations were raising much of their money through the sale of stocks and bonds, the demand for business loans declined. Commercial banks then put more of their funds into real estate loans, loans to brokers against stocks and bonds, and the purchase of stocks and bonds themselves.

AMERICAN SOCIETY IN THE 1920s

By 1920, for the first time, a majority of Americans (51 percent) lived in an urban area with a population of 2,500 or more. A new phenomenon of the 1920s was the tremendous growth of suburbs and satellite cities, which grew more rapidly than the central cities. Streetcars, commuter railroads, and automobiles contributed to the process, as well as the easy availability of financing for home construction. The suburbs had once been the domain of the wealthy, but the technology of the 1920s opened them to working-class families.

Traditional American moral standards regarding premarital sex and marital fidelity were widely questioned for the first time during the 1920s. The automobile, by giving people mobility and privacy, was generally considered to have contributed to sexual license. Birth control, though illegal, was promoted by Margaret Sanger (1883–1966) and others and was widely accepted.

When it became apparent that women did not vote as a block, political leaders gave little additional attention to the special concerns of women. Divorce laws were liberalized in many states at the insistence of women. Domestic service was the largest job category. Most other women workers were in traditional female occupations such as secretarial and clerical work, retail sales, teaching, and nursing. Rates of pay were below those for men. Most women still pursued the traditional role of housewife and mother, and society accepted that as the norm.

The migration of southern rural African-Americans to the cities continued, with about 1.5 million moving during the 1920s. By 1930, about 20 percent of American blacks lived in the North, with the largest concentrations in New York, Chicago, and Philadelphia. While they were generally better off economically in the cities than they had been as tenant farmers, they generally held low-paying jobs and were confined to segregated areas of the cities.

A native of Jamaica, Marcus Garvey (1887–1940) founded the Universal Negro Improvement Association, advocating African-American racial pride and separatism rather than integration, and called for a return of African-Americans to Africa. In 1921, he proclaimed himself the provisional president of an African empire, and sold stock in the Black Star Steamship Line which would take migrants to Africa. The line went bankrupt in 1923, and Garvey was convicted and imprisoned for mail fraud in the sale of the line's stock and then deported. His legacy was an emphasis on African-American pride and self-respect.

Many writers of the 1920s were disgusted with the hypocrisy and materialism of contemporary American society. Often called the "Lost Generation," many of them, such as novelists Ernest Hemingway (1899–1961) and F. Scott Fitzgerald (1896–1940) and poets Ezra Pound (1885–1972) and T. S. Eliot (1888–1965), moved to Europe.

SOCIAL CONFLICTS

Many white Protestant families saw their traditional values gravely threatened. The traditionalists were largely residents of rural areas and small towns, and the clash of farm values with the values of an industrial society of urban workers was evident. The traditionalist backlash against modern urban industrial society expressed itself primarily through intolerance.

On Thanksgiving Day in 1915, the Knights of the Ku Klux Klan, modeled on the organization of the same name in the 1860s and 1870s, was founded near Atlanta by William J. Simmons. Its purpose was to intimidate African-Americans, who were experiencing an apparent rise in status during World War I. By 1923, the Klan had about five million members throughout the nation. The largest concentrations of members were in the South, the Southwest, the Midwest, California, and Oregon.

There had been calls for immigration restriction since the late nineteenth century. Labor leaders believed that immigrants depressed wages and impeded unionization. Some progressives believed that they created social problems. In June 1917, Congress, over Wilson's veto, had imposed a literacy test for immigrants and excluded many Asian nationalities. In 1921, Congress passed the Emergency Quota Act. In practice, the law admitted about as many as wanted to come from such nations as Britain, Ireland, and Germany, while severely restricting Italians, Greeks, Poles, and east European Jews. It became effective in 1922 and reduced the number of immigrants annually to about 40 percent of the 1921 total. Congress then passed the National Origins Act of 1924, which further reduced the number of south and east Europeans, and cut the annual immigration to 20 percent of the 1921 figure. In 1927, the annual maximum was reduced to 150,000.

Fundamentalist Protestants, under the leadership of William Jennings Bryan, began a campaign in 1921 to prohibit the teaching of evolution in the schools, and thus protect belief in the literal biblical account of creation. The idea was especially well received in the South.

Sacco and Vanzetti: On April 15, 1920, two unidentified gunmen robbed a shoe factory and killed two men in South Braintree, Massachusetts. Nicola Sacco and Bartolomeo Vanzetti, Italian immigrants and admitted anarchists, were tried for the murders. After they were convicted and sentenced to death in July 1921, there was much protest in the United States and in Europe that they had not received a fair trial. After six years of delays, they were executed on August 23, 1927. The pair were ultimately vindicated by Massachusetts Governor Michael Dukakis in 1977.

GOVERNMENT AND POLITICS IN THE 1920s: THE HARDING ADMINISTRATION

Harding was a handsome and amiable man of limited intellectual and organizational abilities. He had spent much of his life as the publisher of a newspaper in the small city of Marion, Ohio. He recognized his limitations, but hoped to be a much-loved president.

Harding appointed some outstanding persons to his cabinet, including Secretary of State Charles Evans Hughes, a former Supreme Court justice and presidential candidate; Secretary of the Treasury Andrew Mellon (1855–1937), a Pittsburgh aluminum and banking magnate and reportedly the richest man in America; and Secretary of Commerce Herbert Hoover, a dynamic multimillionaire mine owner famous for his wartime relief efforts. Less impressive was his appointment of his cronies Albert B. Fall as secretary of the interior and Harry M. Daugherty as attorney general.

The Teapot Dome Scandal began when Secretary of the Interior Albert B. Fall in 1921 secured the transfer of several naval oil reserves to his jurisdiction. In 1922, he secretly leased reserves at Teapot Dome in Wyoming to Harry F. Sinclair of Monmouth Oil and at Elk Hills in California to Edward Doheny of Pan-American Petroleum. Sinclair and Doheny were acquitted in 1927 of charges of defrauding the government, but in 1929, Fall was convicted, fined, and imprisoned for bribery.

Vice President Calvin Coolidge became president upon Harding's death in 1923.

THE ELECTION OF 1924

The Republicans: Calvin Coolidge was nominated. The platform endorsed business development, low taxes, and rigid economy in government. The party stood on its record of economic growth and prosperity since 1922.

The Progressives: Robert M. LaFollette, after failing in a bid for the Republican nomination, formed a new Progressive party, with support from Midwest farm groups, socialists, and the American Federation of Labor. The platform attacked monopolies, and called for the nationalization of railroads, the direct election of the president, and other reforms.

The Democrats: John W. Davis was nominated and presented little contrast with the Republicans.

THE ELECTION OF 1928

The Republicans: Coolidge did not seek another term, and the convention quickly nominated Herbert Hoover, the secretary of commerce, for president. The platform endorsed the policies of the Harding and Coolidge administrations.

The Democrats: Governor Alfred E. Smith (1873–1944) of New York, a Catholic and an antiprohibitionist, controlled most of the nonsouthern delegations. Southerners supported his nomination with the understanding that the platform would not advocate repeal of prohibition. The platform differed little from the Republican, except in advocating lower tariffs.

THE GREAT DEPRESSION: THE CRASH

Herbert Hoover, an Iowa farm boy and an orphan, graduated from Stanford University with a degree in mining engineering. He became a multimillionaire from mining and other investments around the world. After serving as the director of the Food Administration under Wilson, he became secretary of commerce under Harding and Coolidge. He believed that cooperation between business and government would enable the United States to abolish poverty through continued economic growth.

Stock prices increased throughout the decade. The boom in prices and volume of sales was especially active after 1925, and was intensive during 1928–29.

Careful investors, realizing that stocks were overpriced, began to sell to take their profits. During October 1929, prices declined as more stock was sold. On "Black Thursday," October 24, 1929, almost 13 million shares were traded, a large number for that time, and prices fell precipitously. Investment banks tried to boost the market by buying, but on October 29, "Black Tuesday," the market fell about 40 points, with 16.5 million shares traded.

DRILL: THE ROARING TWENTIES AND ECONOMIC COLLAPSE

1. Which of the following appealed to black pride and urged separation of the races?

   (A) Paul Robeson

   (B) A. Philip Randolph

   (C) Marcus Garvey

   (D) Claude McKay

   (E) Langston Hughes

2. All of the following were characteristic of the 1920s EXCEPT

   (A) voting rights for women.

   (B) prohibition and bootlegging.

   (C) consumerism and easy credit.

   (D) Progressivist reform and union growth.

   (E) Ku Klux Klan power and popularity.

3. At the time of his death, Warren G. Harding was

   (A) at a low point in his popularity.

   (B) in the midst of a well-publicized scandal.

(C) still popular but gradually losing his hold on the people.

(D) one of the most unpopular presidents in U.S. history.

(E) in serious danger of impeachment.

4. As president, Calvin Coolidge generally

(A) favored large government building projects.

(B) urged Congress to raise taxes.

(C) kept government spending low and encouraged private business.

(D) took an active role in pushing legislation through Congress.

(E) argued that the protective tariff should be lowered in order to provide a more healthy economic environment.

5. Which of the following factors led to the crash of the stock market in 1929?

(A) The mass purchase of underpriced stocks

(B) The selling off of overpriced stocks by investors

(C) The election of Herbert Hoover

(D) The passage of the Revenue Act of 1926

(E) The accumulation of debt from World War I loans

THE GREAT DEPRESSION AND THE NEW DEAL (1929–1941)

REASONS FOR THE DEPRESSION

A stock-market crash does not mean that a depression must follow. In 1929, a complex interaction of many factors caused the decline of the economy.

Many people had bought stock on a margin of 10 percent, meaning that they had borrowed 90 percent of the purchase through a broker's loan and put up the stock as collateral. When the price of a stock fell more than 10 percent, the lender sold the stock for whatever it would bring and thus further depressed prices. The forced sales brought great losses to the banks and businesses that had financed the broker's loans, as well as to the investors.

There were already signs of recession before the market crash in 1929. The farm economy, which involved almost 25 percent of the population, had been depressed throughout the decade. Coal, railroads, and New England textiles had not been prosperous. After 1927, new construction declined and auto sales began to sag. Many workers had been laid off before the crash of 1929.

During the early months of the depression, most people thought it was just an adjustment in the business cycle which would soon be over. As time went on, the worst depression in American history set in, reaching its bottom point in early 1932.

HOOVER'S DEPRESSION POLICIES

The Agricultural Marketing Act: Passed in June 1929, before the market crash, this law, proposed by the president, created the Federal Farm Board. It had a revolving fund of $500 million to lend agricultural cooperatives to buy commodities, such as wheat and cotton, and hold them for higher prices.

The Hawley-Smoot Tariff: This law, passed in June 1930, raised duties on both agricultural and manufactured imports.

The Reconstruction Finance Corporation: Chartered by Congress in 1932, the RFC loaned money to railroads, banks, and other financial institutions. It prevented the failure of basic firms, on which many other elements of the economy depended, but was criticized by some as relief for the rich.

The Federal Home Loan Bank Act: This law, passed in July 1932, created home-loan banks, to make loans to building and loan associations, savings banks, and insurance companies to help them avoid foreclosures on homes.

ELECTION OF 1932

The Republicans renominated Hoover while the Democrats nominated Franklin D. Roosevelt, governor of New York. Although calling for a cut in spending, Roosevelt communicated optimism and easily defeated Hoover.

THE FIRST NEW DEAL

In February 1933, before Roosevelt took office, Congress passed the Twenty-first Amendment to repeal prohibition, and sent it to the states. In March, the new Congress legalized light beer. The amendment was ratified by the states and took effect in December 1933.

When Roosevelt was inaugurated on March 4, 1933, the American economic system seemed to be on the verge of collapse. Roosevelt assured the nation that "the only thing we have to fear is fear itself," called for a special session of Congress to convene on March 9, and asked for "broad executive powers to wage war against the emergency." Two days later, he closed all banks and forbade the export of gold or the redemption of currency in gold.

LEGISLATION OF THE FIRST NEW DEAL

The special session of Congress, from March 9 to June 16, 1933, passed a great body of legislation which has left a lasting mark on the nation. The period has been referred to ever since as the "Hundred Days." Historians have divided Roosevelt's legislation into the First New Deal (1933–1935) and a new wave of programs beginning in 1935 called the Second New Deal.

The Emergency Banking Relief Act was passed on March 9, the first day of the special session. The law provided additional funds for banks from the RFC and the Federal Reserve, allowed the Treasury to open sound banks after 10 days and to merge or liquidate unsound ones, and forbade the hoarding or export of gold. Roosevelt, on March 12, assured the public of the soundness of the banks in the first of many "fireside chats," or radio addresses. People believed him, and most banks were soon open with more deposits than withdrawals.

The Banking Act of 1933, or the Glass-Steagall Act, established the Federal Deposit Insurance Corporation (FDIC) to insure individual deposits in commercial banks, and separated commercial banking from the more speculative activity of investment banking.

The Truth-in-Securities Act required that full information about stocks and bonds be provided by brokers and others to potential purchasers.

The Home Owners Loan Corporation (HOLC) had authority to borrow money to refinance home mortgages and thus prevent foreclosures. Eventually it lent more than three billion dollars to more than one million home owners.

Gold was taken out of circulation following the president's order of

March 6, and the nation went off the gold standard. Eventually, on January 31, 1934, the value of the dollar was set at $35 per ounce of gold, 59 percent of its former value. The object of the devaluation was to raise prices and help American exports.

The Securities and Exchange Commission was created in 1934 to supervise stock exchanges and to punish fraud in securities trading.

The Federal Housing Administration (FHA) was created by Congress in 1934 to insure long-term, low-interest mortgages for home construction and repair.

These programs, intended to provide temporary relief for people in need, were to be disbanded when the economy improved.

The Federal Emergency Relief Act appropriated $500 million for aid to the poor to be distributed by state and local governments. It also established the Federal Emergency Relief Administration under Harry Hopkins (1890–1946).

The Civilian Conservation Corps enrolled 250,000 young men aged 18 to 24 from families on relief to go to camps where they worked on flood control, soil conservation, and forest projects under the direction of the War Department.

The Public Works Administration, under Secretary of the Interior Harold Ickes, had $3.3 billion to distribute to state and local governments for building projects such as schools, highways, and hospitals.

In November 1933, Roosevelt established the Civil Works Administration to hire four million unemployed workers. The temporary and makeshift nature of the jobs, such as sweeping streets, brought much criticism, and the experiment was terminated in April 1934.

The Agricultural Adjustment Act of 1933 created the Agricultural Adjustment Administration (AAA). Farmers agreed to reduce production of principal farm commodities and were paid a subsidy in return. The money came from a tax on the processing of the commodities. Farm prices increased, but tenants and sharecroppers were hurt when owners took land out of cultivation. The law was repealed in January 1936 on the grounds that the processing tax was not constitutional.

The Federal Farm Loan Act consolidated all farm credit programs into the Farm Credit Administration to make low-interest loans for farm mortgages and other agricultural purposes.

The Commodity Credit Corporation was established in October 1933 by the AAA to make loans to corn and cotton farmers against their crops so that they could hold them for higher prices.

The Frazier-Lemke Farm Bankruptcy Act of 1934 allowed farmers to defer foreclosure on their land while they obtained new financing, and helped them to recover property already lost through easy financing.

National Industrial Recovery Act: This law was viewed as the corner-stone of the recovery program. It sought to stabilize the economy by preventing extreme competition, labor-management conflicts, and overpro-duction. A board composed of industrial and labor leaders in each industry or business drew up a code for that industry which set minimum prices, minimum wages, maximum work hours, production limits, and quotas. The antitrust laws were temporarily suspended.

The TVA, a public corporation under a three-member board, was proposed by Roosevelt as the first major experiment in regional public planning. Starting from the nucleus of the government's Muscle Shoals property on the Tennessee River, the TVA built 20 dams in an area of 40,000 square miles to stop flooding and soil erosion, improve navigation, and generate hydroelectric power. It also manufactured nitrates for fertilizer, conducted demonstration projects for farmers, engaged in reforestation, and attempted to rehabilitate the whole area.

The economy improved but did not recover. The GNP, money supply, salaries, wages, and farm income rose. Unemployment dropped from about 25 percent of nonfarm workers in 1933 to about 20.1 percent, or 10.6 million, in 1935.

THE SECOND NEW DEAL: OPPOSITION

The Share Our Wealth Society was founded in 1934 by Senator Huey "The Kingfish" Long (1893–1935) of Louisiana. Long was a populist demagogue who was elected governor of Louisiana in 1928, established a practical dictatorship over the state, and moved to the United States Senate in 1930. He supported Roosevelt in 1932, but then broke with him, calling him a tool of Wall Street for not doing more to combat the depression. Long called for the confiscation of all fortunes over five million dollars and a tax of one hundred percent on annual incomes over one million. His society had more than five million members when he was assassinated on the steps of the Louisiana Capitol on September 8, 1935.

THE SECOND NEW DEAL BEGINS

The Works Progress Administration (WPA) was started in May 1935, following the passage of the Emergency Relief Appropriations Act of April 1935. The WPA employed people from the relief rolls for 30 hours of work a week at pay double the relief payment but less than private employment.

The National Youth Administration (NYA) was established as part of the WPA in June 1935 to provide part-time jobs for high school and college students to enable them to stay in school, and to help young adults not in school to find jobs.

The Rural Electrification Administration (REA) was created in May 1935 to provide loans and WPA labor to electric cooperatives so they could build lines into rural areas not served by private companies.

The Social Security Act was passed in August 1935. It established a retirement plan for persons over age 65, which was to be funded by a tax on wages paid equally by employee and employer. The first benefits, ranging from $10 to $85 per month, were paid in 1942. Another provision of the act had the effect of forcing the states to initiate unemployment insurance programs.

The Banking Act of 1935 created a strong central Board of Governors of the Federal Reserve system with broad powers over the operations of the regional banks.

THE ELECTION OF 1936

Roosevelt had put together a coalition of followers who made the Democratic party the majority party in the nation for the first time since the Civil War. While retaining the Democratic base in the South and among white ethnics in the big cities, Roosevelt also received strong support from midwestern farmers. Two groups that made a dramatic shift into the Democratic ranks were union workers and African-Americans.

THE LAST YEARS OF THE NEW DEAL

Frustrated by a conservative Supreme Court which had overturned much of his New Deal legislation, Roosevelt, in February 1937, proposed to Congress the Judicial Reorganization Bill, which would allow the president to name a new federal judge for each judge who did not retire by the age of $70\frac{1}{2}$. The appointments would be limited to a maximum of 50, with no more than six added to the Supreme Court. The president was astonished by the wave of opposition from Democrats and Republicans alike, but he uncharacteristically refused to compromise. In doing so, he not only lost the bill but control of the Democratic Congress, which he had dominated since 1933. Nonetheless, the Court changed its position, as Chief Justice Charles Evans Hughes and Justice Owen Roberts began to vote with the more liberal members.

Most economic indicators rose sharply between 1935 and 1937. Roosevelt decided that the recovery was sufficient to warrant a reduction in relief programs and a move toward a balanced budget. The budget for fiscal year 1938 was reduced from $8.5 billion to $6.8 billion, with the WPA experiencing the largest cut. During the winter of 1937–1938, the economy slipped rapidly and unemployment rose to 12.5 percent. In April 1938, Roosevelt requested and received from Congress an emergency appropriation of about $3 billion for the WPA, as well as increases for public works and other programs. In July 1938, the economy began to recover, and it regained the 1937 levels in 1939.

SOCIAL DIMENSIONS OF THE NEW DEAL ERA

Unemployment for African-Americans was much higher than for the general population, and before 1933 they were often excluded from state and local relief efforts. Roosevelt seems to have given little thought to the special problems of African-Americans, and he was afraid to endorse legislation such as an antilynching bill for fear of alienating the southern wing of the Democratic party. More African-Americans were appointed to government positions by Roosevelt than ever before, but the number was still small. Roosevelt issued an executive order on June 25, 1941, establishing the Fair Employment Practices Committee to ensure consideration for minorities in defense employment.

John Collier, the commissioner of the Bureau of Indian Affairs, persuaded Congress to repeal the Dawes Act of 1887 by passing the Indian Reorganization Act of 1934. The law restored tribal ownership of lands, recognized tribal constitutions and government, and provided loans to tribes for economic development.

LABOR UNIONS

Labor unions lost members and influence during the 1920s and early 1930s. The National Industrial Recovery Act gave them new hope when it guaranteed the right to unionize, and during 1933 about 1.5 million new members joined unions.

The passage of the National Labor Relations or Wagner Act in 1935 resulted in a massive growth of union membership, but at the expense of bitter conflict within the labor movement. The American Federation of Labor was made up primarily of craft unions. Some leaders wanted to unionize the mass-production industries, such as automobiles and rubber, with industrial unions. In November 1935, John L. Lewis and others established the Committee for Industrial Organization to unionize basic industries, presumably within the AFL. President William Green of the AFL ordered the CIO to disband in January 1936. When the rebels refused, they were expelled by the AFL in March 1937. The insurgents then reorganized the CIO as the independent Congress of Industrial Organizations.

During its organizational period, the CIO sought to initiate several industrial unions, particularly in the steel, auto, rubber, and radio industries. In late 1936 and early 1937, it used a tactic called the sit-down strike, with the strikers occupying the workplace to prevent any production. By the end of 1941, the CIO was larger than the AFL. Union members comprised about 11.5 percent of the work force in 1933 and 28.2 percent in 1941.

NEW DEAL DIPLOMACY AND THE ROAD TO WAR

Roosevelt and Secretary of State Cordell Hull continued the policies of their predecessors by endeavoring to improve relations with Latin American nations, and formalized their position by calling it the Good Neighbor Policy.

At the Montevideo Conference of American Nations in December of 1933, the United States renounced the right of intervention in the internal affairs of Latin American countries. In 1936, in the Buenos Aires Convention, the United States agreed to submit all American disputes to arbitration.

UNITED STATES NEUTRALITY LEGISLATION

Belief that the United States should stay out of foreign wars and problems began in the 1920s and grew in the 1930s. Examinations of World War I profiteering and revisionist history that asserted Germany had not been responsible for World War I and that the United States had been misled were also influential during the 1930s. A Gallup poll in April 1937 showed that almost two-thirds of those responding thought that American entry into World War I had been a mistake.

The Johnson Act of 1934: This law prohibited any nation in default on World War I payments from selling securities to any American citizen or corporation.

The Neutrality Acts of 1935: On outbreak of war between foreign nations, all exports of American arms and munitions to them would be embargoed for six months. In addition, American ships were prohibited from carrying arms to any belligerent, and the president was to warn American citizens not to travel on belligerent ships.

The Neutrality Acts of 1936: The laws gave the president authority to determine when a state of war existed, and prohibited any loans or credits to belligerents.

The Neutrality Acts of 1937: The laws gave the president authority to determine if a civil war was a threat to world peace and if it was covered by the Neutrality Acts. It also prohibited all arms sales to belligerents, and allowed the cash-and-carry sale of nonmilitary goods to belligerents.

THE AMERICAN RESPONSE TO THE WAR IN EUROPE

In August 1939, Roosevelt created the War Resources Board to develop a plan for industrial mobilization in the event of war. The next month, he established the Office of Emergency Management in the White House to centralize mobilization activities.

The Neutrality Act of 1939: Roosevelt officially proclaimed the neutrality of the United States on September 5, 1939. The Democratic Congress, in a vote that followed party lines, passed a new Neutrality Act in November. It allowed the cash-and-carry sale of arms and short-term loans to belligerents, but forbade American ships to trade with belligerents or Americans to travel on belligerent ships.

Almost all Americans recognized Germany as a threat. They divided on whether to aid Britain or to concentrate on the defense of America. The Committee to Defend America by Aiding the Allies was formed in May 1940, and the America First Committee, which opposed involvement, was incorporated in September 1940.

In April 1940, Roosevelt declared that Greenland, a possession of conquered Denmark, was covered by the Monroe Doctrine, and he supplied military assistance to set up a coastal patrol there.

In May 1940, Roosevelt appointed a Council of National Defense, chaired by William S. Knudson (1879–1948), the president of General Motors, to direct defense production and to build 50,000 planes. The Office of Production Management was created to allocate scarce materials, and the Office of Price Administration was established to prevent inflation and protect consumers.

Congress approved the nation's first peacetime draft, the Selective Service and Training Act, in September 1940.

Roosevelt determined that to aid Britain in every way possible was the best way to avoid war with Germany. In September 1940, he signed an agreement to give Britain 50 American destroyers in return for a 99-year lease on air and naval bases in British territories in Newfoundland, Bermuda, and the Caribbean.

THE ELECTION OF 1940

The Republicans: The Republicans nominated Wendell L. Willkie (1892–1944) of Indiana, a dark-horse candidate. The platform supported a strong defense program, but severely criticized New Deal domestic policies.

The Democrats: Roosevelt was nominated for a third term, breaking a tradition which had existed since George Washington. The platform endorsed the foreign and domestic policies of the administration.

The Election: Roosevelt won by a much narrower margin than in 1936.

AMERICAN INVOLVEMENT WITH THE EUROPEAN WAR

The Lend-Lease Act: This let the United States provide supplies to Britain in exchange for goods and services after the war. It was signed on March 11, 1941.

In April 1941, Roosevelt started the American Neutrality Patrol. The American navy would search out but not attack German submarines in the western half of the Atlantic and warn British vessels of their location. Also in April, U.S. forces occupied Greenland, and in May, the president declared a state of unlimited national emergency.

American marines occupied Iceland, a Danish possession, in July 1941 to protect it from seizure by Germany. The American navy began to convoy American and Icelandic ships between the United States and Iceland.

On August 9, 1941, Roosevelt and Winston Churchill issued the Atlantic Charter.

Germany invaded Russia in June 1941, and in November the United States extended lend-lease assistance to the Russians.

The American destroyer *Greer* was attacked by a German submarine near Iceland on September 4, 1941. Roosevelt ordered the American military forces to shoot on sight any German or Italian vessel in the patrol zone. An undeclared naval war had begun. The American destroyer *Kearny* was attacked by a submarine on October 16, and the destroyer *Reuben James* was sunk on October 30, with 115 lives lost. In November, Congress authorized the arming of merchant ships.

THE ROAD TO PEARL HARBOR

In late July 1941, the United States placed an embargo on the export of aviation gasoline, lubricants, and scrap iron and steel to Japan, and granted an additional loan to China. In December, the embargo was extended to include iron ore and pig iron, some chemicals, machine tools, and other products.

In October 1941, a new military cabinet headed by General Hideki Tojo took control of Japan. The Japanese secretly decided to make a final effort to negotiate, and to go to war if no solution was found by November 25. A new round of talks followed in Washington, but neither side would make a substantive change in its position, and on November 26, Hull repeated the American demand that the Japanese remove all their forces from China and Indochina immediately. The Japanese gave final approval on December 1 for an attack on the United States.

The Japanese planned a major offensive to take the Dutch East Indies, Malaya, and the Philippines in order to obtain the oil, metals, and other raw materials they needed. At the same time, they would attack Pearl Harbor in Hawaii to destroy the American Pacific fleet to keep it from interfering with their plans.

The United States had broken the Japanese diplomatic codes and knew that trouble was imminent. Between December 1 and December 6, 1941, it became clear to administration leaders that Japanese task forces were being ordered into battle. American commanders in the Pacific were warned of possible aggressive action there, but not forcefully.

At 7:55 a.m. on Sunday, December 7, 1941, the first wave of Japanese carrier-based planes attacked the American fleet in Pearl Harbor. A second wave followed at 8:50 a.m. The United States suffered the loss of two battleships sunk, six damaged and out of action, three cruisers and three destroyers sunk or damaged, and a number of lesser vessels destroyed or damaged. All of the 150 aircraft at Pearl Harbor were destroyed on the ground. Worst of all, 2,323 American servicemen were killed and about 1,100 wounded. The Japanese lost 29 planes, five midget submarines, and one fleet submarine.

DRILL: THE GREAT DEPRESSION AND THE NEW DEAL

1. The United States began mobilizing for war after September 1939 through which of the following?

    (A) The Neutrality Act of 1939

    (B) The Selective Service Acts of 1940 and 1941

    (C) The establishment of Lend-Lease in 1941

    (D) The Declaration of Panama

    (E) The exchange of American destroyers for British naval bases in the Caribbean

2. At the time of the Japanese attack on Pearl Harbor, the United States found itself

    (A) partially prepared by over a year of the nation's first peacetime draft.

    (B) fully prepared through complete mobilization and training beginning at the outbreak of the war in Europe.

    (C) almost completely unprepared, with one of the smallest armies in the world.

    (D) with a large and modern navy but an army of under 100,000 men.

    (E) with a large but untrained army of conscripts called up within the past six weeks.

3. All of the following New Deal agencies were created during the Great Depression to provide jobs for the unemployed EXCEPT

    (A) Farm Security Administration (FSA).

    (B) Civil Works Administration (CWA).

    (C) Civilian Conservation Corps (CCC).

    (D) Works Progress Administration (WPA).

    (E) National Youth Administration (NYA).

4.   All of the following are true of Hoover's response to the Great Depression EXCEPT

   (A) he at first stressed the desirability of localism and private initiative rather than government intervention.

   (B) he saw the depression as akin to an act of nature, about which nothing could be done except to ride it out.

   (C) he urged the nation's business leaders to maintain wages and full employment.

   (D) his strategy for ending the depression was a failure.

   (E) he was not able to avoid increasing unpopularity.

5.   All of the following contributed to the Great Depression EXCEPT

   (A) excessive stocks and securities speculation.

   (B) protectionist trade measures.

   (C) huge farm debts resulting from collapsed crop prices.

   (D) lack of credit to help consumers sustain economic growth.

   (E) an imbalance of distribution of wealth in which the rich controlled far too much of the available income.

WORLD WAR II AND THE POSTWAR ERA (1941–1960)

DECLARED WAR BEGINS

On December 8, 1941, Congress declared war on Japan, with one dissenting vote. On December 11, Germany and Italy declared war on the United States. Great Britain and the United States then established the Combined Chiefs of Staff, headquartered in Washington, to direct Anglo-American military operations.

On January 1, 1942, representatives of 26 nations met in Washington, D.C., and signed the Declaration of the United Nations, pledging themselves to the principles of the Atlantic Charter and promising not to make a separate peace with their common enemies.

THE HOME FRONT

War Production Board: The WPD was established in 1942 by President Franklin D. Roosevelt for the purpose of regulating the use of raw materials.

Wage and Price Controls: In April 1942, the General Maximum Price Regulation Act froze prices and extended rationing. In April 1943, prices, wages, and salaries were frozen.

Revenue Act of 1942: The Revenue Act of 1942 extended the income tax to the majority of the population. Payroll deduction for the income tax began in 1944.

Social Changes: Rural areas lost population, while population in coastal areas increased rapidly. Women entered the work force in increasing numbers. African-Americans moved from the rural South to northern and western cities, with racial tensions often resulting, most notably in the June 1943 racial riot in Detroit.

Smith-Connolly Act: Passed in 1943, the Smith-Connolly Antistrike Act authorized government seizure of a plant or mine idled by a strike if the war effort was impeded. It expired in 1947.

Korematsu v. United States: In 1944, the Supreme Court upheld President Roosevelt's 1942 order that Issei (Japanese-Americans who had emigrated from Japan) and Nisei (native born Japanese-Americans) be relocated to concentration camps. The camps were closed in March 1946.

Presidential Election of 1944: President Franklin D. Roosevelt, together with new vice-presidential candidate Harry S. Truman (1884–1972) of Missouri, defeated his Republican opponent, Governor Thomas E. Dewey of New York.

Roosevelt died on April 12, 1945, at Warm Springs, Georgia. Harry S. Truman became president.

THE NORTH AFRICAN AND EUROPEAN THEATRES

The United States joined in the bombing of the European continent in July 1942. Bombing increased during 1943 and 1944 and lasted to the end of the war.

The Allied army under Dwight D. Eisenhower attacked French North Africa in November 1942. The Vichy French forces surrendered.

In the Battle of Kassarine Pass, North Africa, February 1943, the Allied army met General Erwin Rommel's Africa Korps. Although the battle is variously interpreted as a standoff or a defeat for the United States, Rommel's forces were soon trapped by the British moving in from Egypt. In May 1943, Rommel's Africa Korps surrendered.

Allied armies under George S. Patton (1885–1945) invaded Sicily from Africa in July 1943, and gained control by mid-August. Moving from Sicily, the Allied armies invaded the Italian mainland in September. The Germans, however, put up a stiff resistance, with the result that Rome did not fall until June 1944.

In March 1944, the Soviet Union began pushing into Eastern Europe.

On "D-Day," June 6, 1944, Allied armies under Dwight D. Eisenhower, now commander-in-chief of the Allied Expeditionary Forces, began an invasion of Normandy, France.

Allied armies liberated Paris in August. By mid-September, they had arrived at the Rhine, on the edge of Germany.

Beginning on December 16, 1944, at the Battle of the Bulge, the Germans counterattacked, driving the Allies back about 50 miles into Belgium. By January, the Allies were once more advancing toward Germany. The Allies crossed the Rhine in March 1945. In the last week of April, Eisenhower's forces met the Soviet army at the Elbe. On May 7, 1945, Germany surrendered.

THE PACIFIC THEATRE

By the end of December 1941, Guam, Wake Island, the Gilbert Islands, and Hong Kong had fallen to the Japanese. In January 1942, Raboul, New Britain, fell, followed in February by Singapore and Java, and in March by Rangoon, Burma. U.S. forces surrendered at Corregidor, Philippines, on May 6, 1942.

The Battle of the Coral Sea, May 7–8, 1942, stopped the Japanese advance on Australia.

The Battle of Midway, June 4–7, 1942, proved to be the turning point in the Pacific.

A series of land, sea, and air battles took place around Guadalcanal in the Solomon Islands from August 1942 to February 1943, stopping the Japanese.

The Allied strategy of island hopping, begun in 1943, sought to neutralize Japanese strongholds with air and sea power and then move on.

U.S. forces advanced into the Gilberts (November 1943), the Marshalls (January 1944), and the Marianas (June 1944). After the American capture of the Marianas, General Tojo resigned as premier of Japan.

The Battle of Leyte Gulf, October 25, 1944, resulted in Japan's loss of most of its remaining naval power. Forces under General Douglas MacArthur (1880–1964) liberated Manila in March 1945.

Between April and June 1945, in the battle for Okinawa, nearly 50,000 American casualties resulted from the fierce fighting, but the battle virtually destroyed Japan's remaining defenses.

THE ATOMIC BOMB

The Manhattan Engineering District was established by the army engineers in August 1942 for the purpose of developing an atomic bomb (it eventually became known as the Manhattan Project). J. Robert Oppenheimer directed the design and construction of a transportable atomic bomb at Los Alamos, New Mexico.

On December 2, 1942, Enrico Fermi (1901–1954) and his colleagues at the University of Chicago produced the first atomic chain reaction.

On July 16, 1945, the first atomic bomb was exploded at Alamogordo, New Mexico.

The *Enola Gay* dropped an atomic bomb on Hiroshima, Japan, on August 6, 1945, killing about 78,000 persons and injuring 100,000 more. On August 9, a second bomb was dropped on Nagasaki, Japan.

On August 8, 1945, the Soviet Union entered the war against Japan.

Japan surrendered on August 14, 1945. The formal surrender was signed on September 2.

DIPLOMACY

Casablanca Conference: On January 14–25, 1943, Franklin D. Roosevelt and Winston Churchill, prime minister of Great Britain, declared a policy of unconditional surrender for "all enemies."

Moscow Conference: In October 1943, Secretary of State Cordell Hull obtained Soviet agreement to enter the war against Japan after Germany was defeated, and to participate in a world organization after the war was over.

Declaration of Cairo: Issued on December 1, 1943, after Roosevelt met with General Chiang Kai-shek in Cairo from November 22 to 26, the Declaration of Cairo called for Japan's unconditional surrender and stated that all Chinese territories occupied by Japan would be returned to China and that Korea would be free and independent.

THE EMERGENCE OF THE COLD WAR AND CONTAINMENT

In 1947, career diplomat and Soviet expert George F. Kennan wrote an anonymous article for *Foreign Affairs* in which he called for a counterforce to Soviet pressures, for the purpose of "containing" communism.

Truman Doctrine: In February 1947, Great Britain notified the United States that it could no longer aid the Greek government in its war against Communist insurgents. The next month President Harry S. Truman asked Congress for $400 million in military and economic aid for Greece and Turkey. In what became known as the "Truman Doctrine," he argued that the United States must support free peoples who were resisting Communist domination.

Marshall Plan: Secretary of State George C. Marshall (1880–1959) proposed in June 1947 that the United States provide economic aid to help rebuild Europe. The following March, Congress passed the European Recovery Program, popularly known as the Marshall Plan, which provided more than $12 billion in aid.

After the United States, France, and Great Britain announced plans to create a West German Republic out of their German zones, the Soviet Union in June 1948 blocked surface access to Berlin. The United States then instituted an airlift to transport supplies to the city until the Soviets lifted their blockade in May 1949.

NATO

In April 1949, the North Atlantic Treaty Organization was signed by the United States, Canada, Great Britain, and nine European nations. The signatories pledged that an attack against one would be considered an attack against all. The Soviets formed the Warsaw Treaty Organization in 1955 to counteract NATO.

INTERNATIONAL COOPERATION

Representatives from Europe and the United States, at a conference held July 1–22, 1944, signed agreements for an international bank and a world monetary fund to stabilize international currencies and rebuild the economies of war-torn nations.

From April to June 1945, representatives from 50 countries met in San Francisco to establish the United Nations. The U.N. charter created a General Assembly composed of all member nations which would act as the ultimate policy-making body. A Security Council, made up of 11 members, including the United States, Great Britain, France, the Soviet Union, and China as permanent members and six additional nations elected by the General Assembly for two-year terms, would be responsible for settling disputes among U.N. member nations.

CONTAINMENT IN ASIA

General Douglas MacArthur headed a four-power Allied Control Council which governed Japan, allowing it to develop economically and politically.

Between 1945 and 1948, the United States gave more than $2 billion in aid to the Nationalist Chinese under Chiang Kai-shek, and sent George C. Marshall to settle the conflict between Chiang's Nationalists and Mao Tsetung's Communists. In 1949, however, Mao defeated Chiang and forced the Nationalists to flee to Formosa (Taiwan). Mao established the People's Republic of China on the mainland.

KOREAN WAR

On June 25, 1950, North Korea invaded South Korea. President Truman committed U.S. forces commanded by General MacArthur, but under United Nations auspices. By October, the U.N. forces (mostly American) had driven north of the 38th parallel, which divided North and South Korea. Chinese troops attacked MacArthur's forces on November 26, pushing them south of the 38th parallel, but by spring 1951, the U.N. forces had recovered their offensive.

In June 1953, an armistice was signed, leaving Korea divided along virtually the same boundary that had existed prior to the war.

EISENHOWER-DULLES FOREIGN POLICY

Dwight D. Eisenhower, elected president in 1952, chose John Foster Dulles (1888–1959) as secretary of state. Dulles talked of a more aggressive foreign policy, calling for "massive retaliation" and "liberation" rather than containment. He wished to emphasize nuclear deterrents rather than conventional armed forces.

After several years of nationalist war against French occupation, France, Great Britain, the Soviet Union, and China signed the Geneva Accords in July 1954, dividing Vietnam along the 17th parallel. The North would be under Ho Chi Minh and the South under Emperor Bao Dai. Elections were scheduled for 1956 to unify the country, but Ngo Dinh Diem overthrew Bao Dai and prevented the elections from taking place. The United States supplied economic aid to South Vietnam.

Dulles attempted to establish a Southeast Asia Treaty Organization parallel to NATO, but was able to obtain only the Philippine Republic, Thailand, and Pakistan as signatories in September 1954.

President Eisenhower announced in January 1957 that the United States was prepared to use armed force in the Middle East against Communist aggression. Under this doctrine, U.S. marines entered Beirut, Lebanon, in July 1958 to promote political stability during a change of governments. The marines left in October.

The United States supported the overthrow of President Jacobo Arbenz Guzman of Guatemala in 1954 because he began accepting arms from the Soviet Union.

In January 1959, Fidel Castro overthrew Fulgencio Batista, dictator of Cuba. Castro soon began criticizing the United States and moved closer to the Soviet Union, signing a trade agreement with the Soviets in February 1960. The United States prohibited the importation of Cuban sugar in October 1960, and broke off diplomatic relations in January 1961.

THE POLITICS OF AFFLUENCE: DEMOBILIZATION AND DOMESTIC POLICY

Harry S. Truman, formerly a senator from Missouri and vice president of the United States, became president on April 12, 1945.

Congress created the Atomic Energy Commission in 1946, establishing civilian control over nuclear development and giving the president sole authority over the use of atomic weapons in warfare.

Taft-Hartley Act (1947): The Republicans, who had gained control of Congress in 1946, sought to control the power of the unions through the Taft-Hartley Act. This act made the "closed-shop" illegal; labor unions could no longer force employers to hire only union members. The act slowed down efforts to unionize the South, and by 1954, 15 states had passed "right to work" laws, forbidding the "union-shop."

In 1948, the president banned racial discrimination in federal government hiring practices and ordered desegregation of the armed forces.

The Presidential Succession Act of 1947 placed the Speaker of the House and the president pro tempore of the Senate ahead of the secretary of state and after the vice president in the line of succession. The Twenty-second Amendment to the Constitution, ratified in 1951, limited the president to two terms.

ELECTION OF 1948

Truman was the Democratic nominee, but the Democrats were split by the States' Rights Democratic party (Dixiecrats) which nominated Governor Strom Thurmond of South Carolina, and the Progressive party, which nominated former Vice President Henry Wallace. The Republicans nominated Governor Thomas E. Dewey of New York. After traveling widely, and attacking the "do-nothing Congress," Truman won a surprise victory.

ANTICOMMUNISM

In 1950, Julius and Ethel Rosenberg and Harry Gold were charged with giving atomic secrets to the Soviet Union. The Rosenbergs were convicted and executed in 1953.

On February 9, 1950, Senator Joseph R. McCarthy (1908–1957) of Wisconsin stated that he had a list of known Communists who were working in the State Department. He later expanded his attacks. After making charges against the army, he was censured and discredited by the Senate in 1954.

EISENHOWER'S DYNAMIC CONSERVATISM

The Republicans nominated Dwight D. Eisenhower, most recently NATO commander, for the presidency. The Democrats nominated Governor Adlai E. Stevenson (1900–1965) of Illinois for president. Eisenhower won by a landslide; for the first time since Reconstruction, the Republicans won some southern states.

Eisenhower sought to balance the budget and lower taxes but did not attempt to roll back existing social and economic legislation. Eisenhower first described his policy as "dynamic conservatism," and then as "progressive moderation." The administration abolished the Reconstruction Finance Corporation, ended wage and price controls, and reduced farm price supports. It cut the budget and in 1954 lowered tax rates for corporations and individuals with high incomes; an economic slump, however, made balancing the budget difficult.

Social Security was extended in 1954 and 1956 to an additional 10 million people, including professionals, domestic and clerical workers, farm workers, and members of the armed services.

The Rural Electrification Administration announced in 1960 that 97 percent of American farms had electricity.

In 1954, Eisenhower obtained congressional approval for joint Canadian-U.S. construction of the St. Lawrence Seaway, which was to give oceangoing vessels access to the Great Lakes. In 1956, Congress authorized construction of the Interstate Highway System, with the federal government supplying 90 percent of the cost and the states 10 percent.

The launching of the Soviet space satellite *Sputnik* on October 4, 1957, created fear that America was falling behind technologically. Although the United States launched *Explorer I* on January 31, 1958, the concern continued. In 1958, Congress established the National Aeronautics and Space Administration (NASA) to coordinate research and development, and passed the National Defense Education Act to provide grants and loans for education.

On January 3, 1959, Alaska became the 49th state, and on August 21, 1959, Hawaii became the 50th.

CIVIL RIGHTS

Eisenhower completed the formal integration of the armed forces, desegregated public services in Washington, D.C., naval yards, and veterans' hospitals, and appointed a Civil Rights Commission.

Brown v. Board of Education of Topeka: In this 1954 case, NAACP lawyer Thurgood Marshall challenged the doctrine of "separate but equal" (*Plessy v. Ferguson*, 1896). The Court declared that separate educational facilities were inherently unequal. In 1955, the Court ordered states to integrate "with all deliberate speed."

Although he did not personally support the Supreme Court decision, Eisenhower sent 10,000 National Guardsmen and 1,000 paratroopers to Little Rock, Arkansas, to control mobs and enable African-Americans to enroll at Central High in September 1957.

On December 11, 1955, in Montgomery, Alabama, Rosa Parks, a black woman, refused to give up her seat on a city bus to a white and was arrested. Under the leadership of Martin Luther King (1929–1968), an African-American pastor, African-Americans of Montgomery organized a bus boycott that lasted for a year, until, in December 1956, the Supreme Court refused to review a lower court ruling that stated that separate but equal was no longer legal.

In 1959, state and federal courts nullified Virginia laws that prevented state funds from going to integrated schools. This proved to be the beginning of the end for "massive resistance."

In February 1960, four African-American students who had been denied service staged a sit-in at a segregated Woolworth lunch counter in Greensboro, North Carolina. This inspired sit-ins elsewhere in the South and led to the formation of the Student Nonviolent Coordinating Committee (SNCC), one of whose chief aims would be to end segregation in public accommodations.

THE ELECTION OF 1960

Vice President Richard M. Nixon won the Republican presidential nomination, and the Democrats nominated Senator John F. Kennedy (1917–1963) for the presidency, with Lyndon B. Johnson (1908–1973), majority leader of the Senate, as his running mate.

Kennedy won the election by slightly more than 100,000 popular votes and 94 electoral votes, based on majorities in New England, the Middle Atlantic, and the South.

DRILL: WORLD WAR II AND THE POSTWAR ERA

1. Which of the following is NOT associated with the atomic bomb?

    (A) The Manhattan Project   (D) Nagasaki and Hiroshima

    (B) J. Robert Oppenheimer   (E) Los Alamos, New Mexico

    (C) General Billy Mitchell

2. At the Casablanca Conference in January 1943, President Franklin Roosevelt and British Prime Minister Winston Churchill agreed

    (A) to concentrate on beating the Germans first before dealing with the Japanese.

(B) to shift Allied efforts from the European to the Pacific Theater of the war.

(C) to demand unconditional surrender of the Axis powers.

(D) to grant a general amnesty to Axis leaders who would surrender.

(E) to land troops in France in the summer of 1943.

3. The battle that marked the shift of power in the naval struggle between the United States and Japan in World War II was

(A) Leyte Gulf.   (D) Coral Sea.

(B) Guadalcanal.   (E) Midway.

(C) Pearl Harbor.

4. The Korean War was fought to

(A) stop an invasion of North Korea by the Communist-led South.

(B) end U.S. imperialism in Southeast Asia.

(C) stop an invasion of South Korea by Japan.

(D) eliminate taxation without representation in South Korea.

(E) stop an invasion of South Korea by the Communist-led North.

5. Which of the following statements is correct about the case of Julius and Ethel Rosenberg?

(A) They were accused of giving atomic secrets to Germany during World War II.

(B) They were exposed as spies by former Communist agent Whitaker Chambers.

(C) They were convicted of espionage, condemned, and electrocuted.

(D) They were convicted but were later pardoned by President Eisenhower because public opinion did not favor harsh treatment of accused Communist spies.

(E) They confessed to having carried out espionage on behalf of the Soviet Union.

THE NEW FRONTIER, VIETNAM, AND SOCIAL UPHEAVAL (1960–1972)

KENNEDY'S "NEW FRONTIER" AND THE LIBERAL REVIVAL

Kennedy was unable to get much of his program through Congress because of an alliance of Republicans and southern Democrats.

Kennedy did gain congressional approval for raising the minimum wage from $1.00 to $1.25 an hour and extending it to 3 million more workers.

The 1961 Housing Act provided nearly $5 billion over four years for the preservation of open urban spaces, development of mass transit, and the construction of middle-class housing.

In May 1961, blacks and whites boarded buses in Washington, D.C., and traveled across the South to New Orleans to test federal enforcement of regulations prohibiting discrimination. They met violence in Alabama but continued to New Orleans.

The Justice Department, under Attorney General Robert F. Kennedy (1925–1968), began to push for civil rights, including desegregation of interstate transportation in the South, integration of schools, and supervision of elections.

In the fall of 1962, President Kennedy called the Mississippi National Guard to federal duty to enable an African-American, James Meredith, to enroll at the University of Mississippi.

Kennedy presented a comprehensive civil rights bill to Congress in 1963. With the bill held up in Congress, 200,000 people marched, demonstrating on its behalf on August 28, 1963, in Washington, D.C. Martin Luther King gave his "I Have a Dream" speech.

THE COLD WAR CONTINUES

Under Eisenhower, the Central Intelligence Agency had begun training some 2,000 men for an invasion of Cuba to overthrow Fidel Castro, the left-leaning revolutionary who had taken power in 1959. On April 19, 1961, this force invaded at the Bay of Pigs, but was pinned down and forced to surrender. Some 1,200 men were captured.

In August 1961, Khrushchev closed the border between East and West Berlin and ordered the erection of the Berlin Wall.

The Soviet Union began the testing of nuclear weapons in September 1961. Kennedy then authorized resumption of underground testing by the United States.

On October 14, 1962, a U-2 reconnaissance plane brought photographic evidence that missile sites were being built in Cuba. Kennedy, on October 22, announced a blockade of Cuba and called on Khrushchev to dismantle the missile bases and remove all weapons capable of attacking the United States from Cuba. Six days later, Khrushchev backed down, withdrew the missiles, and Kennedy lifted the blockade.

In July 1963, a treaty banning the atmospheric testing of nuclear weapons was signed by all the major powers except France and China.

The early sixties weren't only about saber rattling and nuclear one-upmanship, however. In 1961, Kennedy announced the Alliance for Progress, which would provide $20 million in aid to Latin America.

JOHNSON AND THE GREAT SOCIETY

On November 22, 1963, Kennedy was assassinated by Lee Harvey Oswald in Dallas, Texas. Jack Ruby, a nightclub owner, killed Oswald two days later.

Succeeding Kennedy, Lyndon B. Johnson had extensive experience in both the House and Senate, and as a Texan, was the first southerner to serve as president since Woodrow Wilson.

A tax cut of more than $10 billion passed Congress in 1964, and an economic boom resulted.

The 1964 Civil Rights Act outlawed racial discrimination by employers and unions, created the Equal Employment Opportunity Commission to enforce the law, and eliminated the remaining restrictions on black voting.

Michael Harrington's *The Other America* (1962) showed that 20 to 25 percent of American families were living below the governmentally defined poverty line. The Economic Opportunity Act of 1964 sought to address the problem by establishing a Job Corps, community action programs, educational programs, work-study programs, job training, loans for small businesses and farmers, and Volunteers in Service to America (VISTA), a "domestic peace corps." The Office of Economic Opportunity administered many of these programs.

ELECTION OF 1964

Lyndon Johnson was nominated for president by the Democrats. The Republicans nominated Senator Barry Goldwater, a conservative from Arizona. Johnson won more than 61 percent of the popular vote and could now launch his own "Great Society" program.

The Medicare Act of 1965 combined hospital insurance for retired people with a voluntary plan to cover physicians' bills. Medicaid provided grants to states to help the poor below retirement age.

EMERGENCE OF BLACK POWER

In 1965, Martin Luther King announced a voter registration drive. With help from the federal courts, he dramatized his effort by leading a march from Selma to Montgomery, Alabama, between March 21 and 25. The Voting Rights Act of 1965 authorized the attorney general to appoint officials to register voters.

Seventy percent of African-Americans lived in city ghettos. In 1966, New York and Chicago experienced riots, and the following year there were riots in Newark and Detroit. The Kerner Commission, appointed to investigate the riots, concluded that they were directed at a social system that prevented African-Americans from getting good jobs and crowded them into ghettos.

Stokely Carmichael, in 1966, called for the civil rights movements to be "black-staffed, black-controlled, and black-financed." Later, he moved on to the Black Panthers, self-styled urban revolutionaries based in Oakland, California. Other leaders such as H. Rap Brown also called for Black Power.

On April 4, 1968, Martin Luther King was assassinated in Memphis by James Earl Ray (Ray, an escaped convict, pled guilty to the murder and was sentenced to 99 years). Riots in more than 100 cities followed.

THE NEW LEFT

In 1964 students at the University of California at Berkeley staged sit-ins to protest the prohibition of political canvassing on campus. In December, police broke up a sit-in; protests spread to other campuses around the nation.

Student protests began focusing on the Vietnam War. In the spring of 1967, 500,000 gathered in Central Park in New York City to protest the war, many burning their draft cards. SDS (Students for a Democratic Society) became more militant and willing to use violence.

More than 200 large campus demonstrations took place in the spring, culminating in the occupation of buildings at Columbia University to protest the university's involvement in military research and what they deemed as its poor relations with minority groups. Police wielding clubs eventually broke up the demonstration. In August, thousands gathered in Chicago to protest the war during the Democratic convention.

Beginning in 1968, SDS began breaking up into rival factions. By the early 1970s, the New Left had lost political influence, having abandoned its original commitment to democracy and nonviolence.

WOMEN'S LIBERATION

In *The Feminine Mystique* (1963), Betty Friedan argued that middle-class society stifled women and did not allow them to use their individual talents. She attacked the cult of domesticity.

In 1966, Friedan and other feminists founded the National Organization for Women (NOW), which called for equal employment opportunities and equal pay.

VIETNAM

After the French defeat in 1954, the United States sent military advisors to South Vietnam to aid the government of Ngo Dinh Diem. The pro-Communist Vietcong forces gradually grew in strength, partly because Diem failed to follow through on promised reforms. They received support from North Vietnam, the Soviet Union, and China.

In August 1964—after claiming that North Vietnamese gunboats had fired on American destroyers in the Gulf of Tonkin—Lyndon Johnson pushed the Gulf of Tonkin resolution through Congress, authorizing him to use military force in Vietnam. After a February 1965 attack by the Vietcong on Pleiku, Johnson ordered operation "Rolling Thunder," the first sustained bombing of North Vietnam. Johnson then sent combat troops to South Vietnam; under the leadership of General William C. Westmoreland, they conducted search and destroy operations. The number of troops increased to 184,000 in 1965, 385,000 in 1966, 485,000 in 1967, and 538,000 in 1968.

"Hawks" defended the president's policy and, drawing on containment theory, said that the nation had the responsibility to resist aggression. If

Vietnam should fall, it was said, all Southeast Asia would eventually go. The administration stressed its willingness to negotiate the withdrawal of all "foreign" forces from the war.

Opposition began quickly, with "teach-ins" at the University of Michigan in 1965 and a 1966 congressional investigation led by Senator J. William Fulbright. Antiwar demonstrations were attracting large crowds by 1967. "Doves" argued that the war was a civil war in which the United States should not meddle.

On January 31, 1968, the first day of the Vietnamese new year (Tet), the Vietcong attacked numerous cities and towns, American bases, and even Saigon. Although they suffered large losses, the Vietcong won a psychological victory, as American opinion began turning against the war.

THE ELECTION OF 1968

In November 1967, Senator Eugene McCarthy of Minnesota announced his candidacy for the 1968 Democratic presidential nomination, running on the issue of opposition to the war.

In February, McCarthy won 42 percent of the Democratic vote in the New Hampshire primary, compared with Johnson's 48 percent. Robert F. Kennedy then announced his candidacy for the Democratic presidential nomination.

Lyndon Johnson withdrew his candidacy on March 31, 1968, and Vice President Hubert H. Humphrey took his place as a candidate for the Democratic nomination.

After winning the California primary over McCarthy, Robert Kennedy was assassinated by Sirhan Sirhan, a young Palestinian. This event assured Humphrey's nomination.

The Republicans nominated Richard M. Nixon. Governor George C. Wallace of Alabama ran for the presidency under the banner of the American Independent party, appealing to fears generated by protestors and the idea that government has grown too large.

Johnson suspended air attacks on North Vietnam shortly before the election. Nonetheless, Nixon, who emphasized stability and order, defeated Humphrey by a margin of one percentage point. Wallace's 13.5 percent was the best showing by a third-party candidate since 1924.

THE NIXON CONSERVATIVE REACTION

The Nixon administration sought to block renewal of the Voting Rights Act and delay implementation of court-ordered school desegregation in Mississippi.

In 1969, Nixon appointed Warren E. Burger, a conservative, as chief justice. Although more conservative than the Warren court, the Burger court did declare the death penalty, as used at the time, unconstitutional in 1972, and struck down state antiabortion legislation in 1973.

VIETNAMIZATION

The president turned to "Vietnamization," the effort to build up South Vietnamese forces while withdrawing American troops. In 1969, Nixon reduced American troop strength by 60,000, but at the same time ordered the bombing of Cambodia, a neutral country.

In April 1970, Nixon announced that Vietnamization was succeeding but a few days later, he sent troops into Cambodia to clear out Vietcong sanctuaries and resumed bombing of North Vietnam.

Protests against escalation of the war were especially strong on college campuses. After several students were killed during protests, several hundred colleges were closed down by student strikes, as moderates joined the radicals. Congress repealed the Gulf of Tonkin Resolution.

The publication in 1971 of classified Defense Department documents, called "The Pentagon Papers," revealed that the government had misled the Congress and the American people regarding its intentions in Vietnam during the mid-1960s.

Nixon drew American forces back from Cambodia but increased bombing. In March 1972, after stepped-up aggression from the North, Nixon ordered the mining of Haiphong and other northern ports.

In the summer of 1972, negotiations between the United States and North Vietnam began in Paris. A few days before the 1972 presidential election, Henry Kissinger, the president's national security advisor, announced that "peace was at hand."

Nixon resumed bombing of North Vietnam in December 1972, claiming that the North Vietnamese were not bargaining in good faith. In January 1973, the opponents reached a settlement in which the North Vietnamese retained control over large areas of the South and agreed to release American prisoners of war within 60 days. Nearly 60,000 Americans had been killed and 300,000 more wounded and the war had cost Americans $109 billion. On March 29, 1973, the last American combat troops left South Vietnam.

FOREIGN POLICY

With his national security advisor, Henry Kissinger, Nixon took some bold diplomatic initiatives. In February 1972, Nixon and Kissinger went to China to meet with Mao Tse-tung and his associates. The United States agreed to support China's admission to the United Nations and to pursue economic and cultural exchanges.

Nixon and Kissinger called their policy *détente*, a French term meaning a relaxation in the tensions between two governments.

THE ELECTION OF 1972

Richard M. Nixon, who had been renominated by the Republicans, won a landslide victory over the Democratic nominee, Senator George McGovern.

DRILL: THE NEW FRONTIER, VIETNAM, AND SOCIAL UPHEAVAL

1. The Bay of Pigs incident involved

    (A) the presence of Soviet nuclear missiles in Cuba.

    (B) a CIA plot to overthrow Chilean leader Salvador Allende.

    (C) a confrontation between U.S. and Soviet troops in Europe.

    (D) a clash between a U.S. Navy destroyer and North Vietnamese patrol boats.

    (E) a U.S.-sponsored attempt by free Cubans to overthrow Communist dictator Fidel Castro.

2. All of the following events took place during the Kennedy administration EXCEPT

    (A) the Bay of Pigs invasion.

    (B) the building of the Berlin Wall.

(C) a limited test ban treaty signed by the United States, the Soviet Union, and Great Britain.

(D) the Cuban missile crisis.

(E) the U-2 incident.

3. In 1968 who challenged President Lyndon Johnson in the New Hampshire primary, ultimately forcing him to withdraw from the presidential race?

(A) Hubert H. Humphrey   (D) Eugene McCarthy

(B) Robert Kennedy   (E) George C. Wallace

(C) Edmund Muskie

4. All of the following were legislative failures of the Kennedy Administration EXCEPT

(A) urban renewal.   (D) medical care for the aged

(B) raising of the minimum wage. (E) tax reductions.

(C) federal aid to education.

5. Johnson's "Great Society" program was aimed primarily at

(A) spurring advances in American science and technical education and increasing funding to high-tech research facilities.

(B) sending American volunteers to impoverished foreign nations to help educate their people and build their economic base.

(C) securing civil rights for all Americans and eliminating poverty.

(D) providing minimum wage jobs for all unemployed Americans and shifting tax dollars from the military to the civilian sector of the economy.

(E) retraining adults who had dropped out of school and increasing the number of Americans who attended college.

WATERGATE, CARTER, AND THE NEW CONSERVATISM (1972–1991)

WATERGATE

What became known as the Watergate crisis began during the 1972 presidential campaign. Early on the morning of June 17, James McCord, a security officer for the Committee to Reelect the President (sometimes known as CREEP), and four other men broke into Democratic headquarters at the Watergate apartment complex in Washington, D.C., and were caught while going through files and installing electronic eavesdropping devices.

In March 1974, a grand jury indicted Haldeman, Ehrlichman, former Attorney General John Mitchell, and four other White House aides and named Nixon an unindicted co-conspirator.

Meanwhile, the House Judiciary Committee televised its debate over impeachment, adopting three articles of impeachment. It charged the president with obstructing justice, misusing presidential power, and failing to obey the committee's subpoenas.

Before the House began to debate impeachment, Nixon announced his resignation on August 8, 1974, to take effect at noon the following day. Gerald Ford then became president.

THE FORD PRESIDENCY

Gerald Ford was in many respects the opposite of Nixon. Although a partisan Republican, he was well liked and free of any hint of scandal. Ford almost immediately encountered controversy when in September 1974 he offered to pardon Nixon. Nixon accepted the offer, although he admitted no wrongdoing and had not yet been charged with a crime.

VIETNAM

As North Vietnamese forces pushed back the South Vietnamese, Ford asked Congress to provide more arms for the South. Congress rejected the request, and in April 1975 Saigon fell to the North Vietnamese.

CARTER'S MODERATE LIBERALISM

Ronald Reagan, a former movie actor and governor of California, opposed Ford for the Republican presidential nomination in 1976, but Ford won by a slim margin. The Democrats nominated James Earl Carter, formerly governor of Georgia, who ran on the basis of his integrity and lack of Washington connections. Carter narrowly defeated Ford in the election.

Carter offered amnesty to Americans who had fled the draft and gone to other countries during the Vietnam War. He established the Departments of Energy and Education and placed the civil service on a merit basis. He created a "superfund" for cleanup of chemical waste dumps, established controls over strip mining, and protected 100 million acres of Alaskan wilderness from development.

CARTER'S FOREIGN POLICY

Carter negotiated a controversial treaty with Panama, affirmed by the Senate in 1978, that provided for the transfer of ownership of the canal to Panama in 1999 and guaranteed its neutrality.

Carter ended official recognition of Taiwan and in 1979 recognized the People's Republic of China. Conservatives called the decision a "sell-out."

In 1978, Carter negotiated the Camp David Accords between Israel and Egypt. Israel promised to return occupied land in the Sinai to Egypt in exchange for Egyptian recognition, a process completed in 1982. An agreement to negotiate the Palestinian refugee problem proved ineffective.

THE IRANIAN CRISIS

In 1978, a revolution forced the shah of Iran to flee the country, replacing him with a religious leader, Ayatollah Ruhollah Khomeini. Because the United States had supported the shah with arms and money, the revolutionaries were strongly anti-American, calling the United States the "Great Satan."

After Carter allowed the exiled shah to come to the United States for medical treatment in October 1979, some 400 Iranians broke into the American embassy in Teheran on November 4, taking the occupants captive. They demanded that the shah be returned to Iran for trial and that his wealth be confiscated and given to Iran. Carter rejected these demands; instead, he froze Iranian assets in the United States and established a trade embargo against Iran.

THE ELECTION OF 1980

Republican Ronald Reagan defeated Carter by a large electoral majority, and the Republicans gained control of the Senate and increased their representation in the House.

After extensive negotiations with Iran, in which Algeria acted as an intermediary, the American hostages were freed on January 20, 1981. It was the day of Reagan's inaugural.

THE REAGAN PRESIDENCY: ATTACKING BIG GOVERNMENT

An ideological though pragmatic conservative, Ronald Reagan acted quickly and forcefully to change the direction of government policy. He placed priority on cutting taxes. His approach was based on "supply-side" economics, the idea that if government left more money in the hands of the people, they would invest rather then spend the excess on consumer goods. The results would be greater production, more jobs, and greater prosperity, and thus more income for the government despite lower tax rates.

Reagan asked for a 30 percent tax cut, and despite fears of inflation on the part of Congress, in August 1983 obtained a 25 percent cut, spread over three years.

Congress passed the Budget Reconciliation Act in 1981, cutting $39 billion from domestic programs, including education, food stamps, public housing, and the National Endowments for the Arts and Humanities. While cutting domestic programs, Reagan increased the defense budget by $12 billion.

From a deficit of $59 billion in 1980, the federal budget was running $195 billion in the red by 1983.

Because of rising deficits, Reagan and Congress increased taxes in various ways. The 1982 Tax Equity and Fiscal Responsibility Act reversed some concessions made to business in 1981. Social Security benefits became taxable income in 1983. In 1984, the Deficit Reduction Act increased taxes by another $50 billion. But the deficit continued to increase.

Reagan ended ongoing antitrust suits against IBM and AT&T, thereby fulfilling his promise to reduce government interference with business.

ASSERTING AMERICAN POWER

Reagan took a hard line against the Soviet Union, calling it an "evil empire." He placed new cruise missiles in Europe, despite considerable opposition from Europeans.

Reagan concentrated on obtaining funding for the development of a computer-controlled Strategic Defense Initiative (SDI) system, popularly called "Star Wars" after the movie of that name. The concept behind SDI was that it would destroy enemy missiles from outer space.

In Nicaragua, Reagan encouraged the opposition (*contras*) to the leftist Sandinista government with arms, tactical support, and intelligence, and supplied aid to the government of El Salvador in its struggles against left-wing rebels. In October 1983, the president also sent American troops into the Caribbean island nation of Grenada to overthrow a newly established Cuban-backed regime.

THE ELECTION OF 1984

Walter Mondale, a former senator from Minnesota and vice president under Carter, won the Democratic nomination. Mondale criticized Reagan for his budget deficits, high unemployment and interest rates, and reduction of spending on social services. However, Reagan was elected to a second term in a landslide. Mondale's selection of Geraldine Ferraro as his running mate marked the first time a woman ran for the office of vice president.

SECOND-TERM FOREIGN CONCERNS

After Mikhail S. Gorbachev became the premier of the Soviet Union in March 1985 and took a more flexible approach toward both domestic and foreign affairs, Reagan softened his anti-Soviet stance.

Reagan and Gorbachev had difficulty reaching an agreement on arms limitations at summit talks in 1985 and 1986. Finally, in December 1987, they signed an agreement eliminating medium-range missiles from Europe.

IRAN-CONTRA

In 1985 and 1986, several Reagan officials sold arms to the Iranians in hopes of encouraging them to use their influence in getting American hostages in Lebanon released. Profits from these sales were then diverted to the Nicaraguan *contras* in an attempt to get around congressional restrictions on funding the *contras*. The attorney general was forced to appoint a special prosecutor, and Congress held hearings on the affair in May 1987.

SECOND-TERM DOMESTIC AFFAIRS: THE ECONOMY

The Tax Reform Act of 1986 lowered tax rates. At the same time, it removed many tax shelters and tax credits. The law did away with the concept of progressive taxation, the requirement that the percentage of income taxed increased as income increased.

The federal deficit reached $179 billion in 1985. At about the same time, the United States experienced trade deficits of more than $100 billion annually.

Black Monday: On October 19, 1987, the Dow Jones Industrial Average dropped more than 500 points, or over 20 percent. Between August 25 and October 20, the market lost over a trillion dollars in paper value.

NASA: The explosion of the space shuttle *Challenger* soon after take-off on January 28, 1986, damaged NASA's credibility and reinforced doubts about the complex technology required for the SDI program. All aboard the ill-fated shuttle perished, including a New Hampshire teacher.

Supreme Court: Reagan reshaped the Court in 1986, replacing Chief Justice Warren C. Burger with Associate Justice William H. Rehnquist, probably the most conservative member of the Court. Although failing in his nomination of Robert Bork for associate justice, Reagan did appoint other conservatives to the Court: Sandra Day O'Connor, Antonin Scalia, and Anthony Kennedy.

THE ELECTION OF 1988

Vice President George Bush won the Republican nomination. Bush easily defeated Michael Dukakis, the Democratic nominee, but the Republicans were unable to make any inroads in Congress.

THE BUSH ADMINISTRATION

Soon after George Bush took office, the budget deficit for 1990 was estimated at $143 billion. In September, the administration and Congress agreed to increase taxes on gasoline, tobacco, and alcohol, establish an excise tax on luxury items, and raise medicare taxes. Cuts were also to be made in medicare and other domestic programs. In a straight party vote, Republicans voting against and Democrats voting in favor, Congress in December transferred the power to decide whether new tax and spending proposals violated the deficit cutting agreement from the White House Office of Management and Budget to the Congressional Budget Office.

The Commission on Base Realignment and Closure proposed in December 1989 that 54 military bases be closed. In June 1990, Secretary of Defense Richard Cheney sent to Congress a plan to cut military spending by 10 percent and the armed forces by 25 percent over the next five years. The following April, Cheney recommended the closing of 43 domestic military bases, plus many more abroad.

With the savings and loan industry in financial trouble in 1989, largely because of bad real-estate loans, Bush signed a bill which created the Resolution Trust Corporation to oversee the closure and merging of S&Ls, and which provided $166 billion over 10 years to cover the bad debts. Estimates of the total costs of the debacle ran to more than $300 billion.

BUSH'S ACTIVIST FOREIGN POLICY

Since coming to office, the Bush administration had been concerned that Panamanian dictator Manuel Noriega was providing an important link in the drug traffic between South America and the United States. After economic sanctions, diplomatic efforts, and an October 1989 coup failed to oust Noriega, Bush ordered 12,000 troops into Panama on December 20. On January 3, 1990, Noriega surrendered to the Americans and was taken to the United States to stand trial on drug-trafficking charges. Found guilty in 1992, he was sentenced to 40 years. Twenty-three United States soldiers and three American civilians were killed in the Panamanian operation. Panama lost nearly 300 soldiers and more than 500 civilians.

After years of civil war, Nicaragua held a presidential election in February 1990. Violetta Barrios de Chamorro of the National Opposition Union defeated Daniel Ortega of the Sandinistas (who had come to power in 1979), thereby fulfilling a longstanding American objective. The United States lifted its economic sanctions in March and put together an economic aid package for Nicaragua. In September 1991, the Bush administration forgave Nicaragua most of its debt to the United States.

In 1989 the Chinese government violently suppressed a pro-democracy movement centered in Beijing. Although establishing sanctions on China in 1991 on high-technology satellite-part exports, Bush continued to support renewal of China's Most Favored Nation trading status.

END OF THE COLD WAR

Amid the collapse of communism in Eastern Europe, Bush met with Mikhail Gorbachev in Malta from where the two leaders appeared to agree that the Cold War was over. On July 30 and 31, Bush met Gorbachev in Moscow where they signed the START treaty, which cut United States and Soviet nuclear arsenals by 30 percent, and pushed for Middle Eastern talks.

PERSIAN GULF CRISIS

On August 2, 1990, Iraq invaded Kuwait, an act that Bush denounced as "naked aggression." The United States quickly banned most trade with Iraq, froze Iraq's and Kuwait's assets in the United States, and sent aircraft carriers to the Persian Gulf. After the U.N. Security Council condemned the invasion, on August 6, Bush ordered the deployment of air, sea, and land forces to Saudi Arabia, dubbing the operation "Desert Shield."

On February 23, the allied air assault began. Four days later, Bush announced that Kuwait had been liberated and he ordered offensive operations to cease. The United Nations established the terms for the cease-fire: Iraqi annexation of Kuwait to be rescinded, Iraq to accept liability for damages and return Kuwaiti property, Iraq to end all military actions and identify mines and booby traps, and Iraq to release captives. Iraq accepted U.N. terms on April 6.

COLLAPSE OF SOVIET COMMUNISM

In the aftermath of the Soviet coup attempt on August 19, 1991, much of the Communist structure came crashing down; the Communist party itself was prohibited in Russia. The remaining Baltic republics of Latvia and Estonia declared their independence, which was recognized by the United States several days after other nations had done so. Most of the other Soviet republics then followed suit in declaring their independence.

In September 1991, Bush announced unilateral removal and destruction of ground-based tactical nuclear weapons in Europe and Asia, removal of nuclear-armed Tomahawk cruise missiles from surface ships and submarines, immediate destruction of intercontinental ballistic missiles covered by START, and an end to the 24-hour alert for strategic bombers that the United States had maintained for decades. Gorbachev responded the next month by announcing the immediate deactivation of intercontinental ballistic missiles covered by START, removal of all short-range missiles from Soviet ships, submarines, and aircraft, and destruction of all ground-based tactical nuclear weapons. He also said that the Soviet Union would reduce its forces by 700,000 troops, and he placed all long-range nuclear missiles under a single command.

LOS ANGELES RIOTS

The 1991 videotaped beating of African-American motorist Rodney King by Los Angeles police officers resulted in a trial which acquitted the police in April 1992. Violence erupted in South-Central Los Angeles, lasting from April 29 to May 1 and resulting in 52 deaths, the destruction of 600 buildings, and over $1 billion in damages. Army, Marine, and National Guard units were called in to quell the riot. In 1993 two of the police officers were convicted in federal court of violating King's civil rights.

TAILHOOK SCANDAL

A 1991 convention of the Tailhook Association of Navy and Marine fliers produced complaints of sexual harassment. An investigation revealed that 26 women had been abused. In 1994 the chief of naval operations, Admiral Frank B. Kelso II, retired early after being accused of manipulating the investigation.

CRISIS IN EDUCATION

The National Commission on Excellence in Education, appointed in 1981, argued in "A Nation at Risk" that a "rising tide of mediocrity" characterized the nation's schools. In the wake of the report many states instituted reforms, including higher teacher salaries, competency tests for teachers, and an increase in required subjects for high school graduation. In September 1989, Bush met with the nation's governors in Charlottesville, Va., to work on a plan to improve the schools. The meeting called for the establishment of national performance goals to be measured by achievement tests. In February 1990, the National Governors Association then adopted specific performance goals, stating that achievement tests should be administered in grades four, eight, and twelve.

DRILL: WATERGATE, CARTER, AND THE NEW CONSERVATISM

1. All of the following correctly describe Gerald Ford as president EX-CEPT

    (A) he pardoned Richard Nixon.

    (B) he was the first president not elected to a national executive office.

    (C) he gave federal help when New York City faced bankruptcy.

    (D) he aided South Vietnam militarily when it was about to collapse.

    (E) he cut inflation from 12 percent to 6 percent.

2. The American hostage crisis in Iran was precipitated by

    (A) the American government allowing the deposed Shah of Iran to come to the United States for cancer treatment.

(B) Jimmy Carter's involvement in arranging the Camp David accords between the Egyptians and the Israelis.

(C) American air strikes against Iran's ally, Libya.

(D) American support for Israel's 1980 invasion of southern Lebanon.

(E) American attempts to overthrow the newly emplaced government of Ayatollah Khomeini.

3. The savings and loan crisis resulted in

(A) higher real estate prices in the Southwest.

(B) the creation of a corporation to manage the crisis.

(C) the end of federal insurance for bank deposits.

(D) wider use of "junk bonds" in financial markets.

(E) depositors losing all or most of their savings in these institutions.

4. Which of the following was a controversial Bush appointee to the Supreme Court?

(A) Sandra Day O'Connor   (D) Howard Metzenbaum

(B) Anita Hill   (E) Clarence Thomas

(C) James Baker

5. Which of the following was NOT an ally of the United States during the Gulf Crisis?

(A) France   (D) Israel

(B) Saudi Arabia   (E) Iran

(C) Japan

THE COLLAPSE OF COMMUNISM TO THE CLINTON PRESIDENCY

THE ELECTION OF 1992

The Democrats

William (Bill) Clinton, governor of Arkansas, overcame several rivals in the primaries to win the Democratic nomination. He chose Senator Albert Gore of Tennessee as his vice presidential running mate.

The Republicans

President George Bush and Vice President J. Danforth (Dan) Quayle easily won the Republican nomination, despite a challenge from conservative columnist Patrick Buchanan.

Ross Perot

Entrepreneur Ross Perot entered the campaign as an independent, making effective use of television and pledging to reduce the deficit and make government work.

The Campaign

Clinton and Perot emphasized the economy, particularly the deficit and the need to create more jobs. Bush called for a return to "traditional values" and publicized his foreign policy achievements.

The Election

Clinton won 43 percent (44,909,889) of the popular vote and 370 electoral votes while Bush gained 37 percent (39,104,545) of the popular vote and 168 electoral votes. Although he won no electoral votes, Perot achieved 19 percent (19, 742,267) of the popular vote.

THE CLINTON PRESIDENCY (1993 –)

Homosexuality in the Military

Clinton created a storm of controversy when he proposed in January 1993 lifting the ban on gays and lesbians in the military. In July 1993, a compromise "don't ask, don't tell" policy was adopted, requiring gays and lesbians to be discreet about their sexual orientation and not to engage in homosexual acts.

Abortion

In January 1993 Clinton lifted restrictions on abortion established by the Bush administration, including the "gag rule" forbidding discussion of abortion with patients at federally funded family planning clinics and the ban on use of fetal tissue for research. In 1993 and 1994 abortion rights opponents killed two abortion doctors in Pensacola, Florida.

Family Leave Bill

Vetoed earlier by Bush, the Family Leave Bill, which Clinton signed in February 1993, required large companies to provide up to 12 weeks' unpaid leave for family and medical emergencies.

World Trade Center Bombing

In one of the most devastating acts of terrorism ever perpetrated on U.S. soil, a bomb blast at New York's World Trade Center in February 1993 killed six people, injured more than 1,000, and caused extensive damage. Four Islamic militants were convicted in 1994 in connection with the incident on conspiracy, explosives, and assault charges. In a second trial in the fall of 1997, a federal jury convicted two others, one of whom masterminded the bombing.

"Motor-Voter" Bill

Passed in 1993, the "Motor-Voter" bill required states to allow citizens to register to vote while applying for driver's licenses and to adopt standardized procedures for voter registration by mail.

Branch Davidians

In February 1993 the U.S. Bureau of Alcohol, Tobacco, and Firearms raided the headquarters of the Branch Davidian religious cult near Waco, Texas, resulting in the deaths of four federal agents. After a 51-day standoff, from February 28 to April 26, the F.B.I. attacked the compound with tear gas and began destroying walls of the compound. Cult members apparently started a fire; at least 72 Branch Davidians, including their leader, David Koresh, died.

Budget Deficit

The Omnibus Budget Reconciliation Act of 1993 sought to reduce the federal deficit by $496 billion by 1998. It combined $225 billion in spending cuts with $241 billion in new taxes over five years. The tax increases affected incomes over $115,000.

NAFTA

The North American Free Trade Agreement (NAFTA), negotiated by the Bush administration, eliminated most tariffs and other trade barriers between the United States, Canada, and Mexico. Passed by Congress and signed by Clinton—for whom it had been a major campaign issue—in 1993, NAFTA became law in January 1994. Standing in opposition were organized labor and the Reform Party's Ross Perot, while Republicans stood shoulder-to-shoulder with the Democratic president.

Gun Control

The Brady Handgun Violence Prevention Act, adopted in 1993, established a five-day waiting period for the purchase of handguns while local law-enforcement officials checked the background of prospective buyers.

Economy

By the end of 1993 unemployment had dropped to 6.4 percent, the lowest since January 1991, and inflation stood at 2.7 percent. The GNP grew at an annual rate of 5.9 percent in the fourth quarter of 1993. In 1994, the Federal Reserve, fearing an increase in inflation, began a series of interest rate increases. But inflation retreated and stayed quiescent for the rest of the decade, unemployment by February 1999 had fallen to 4.4 percent, and the U.S. economy continued its robust expansion—despite layoffs at several major U.S. companies and faltering economies in Asia and Latin America.

Crime Bill

Adopted in 1994 the crime bill authorized spending $13.45 billion for state, local, and federal police, with an emphasis on community policing, $9.85 billion for prisons, and $6.9 billion for crime prevention programs. It also banned 19 types of assault weapons, imposed life sentences for third-time violent felons and drug offenders convicted in federal courts, and created over 50 new federal death penalty crimes.

Supreme Court Appointments

Clinton named moderates Ruth Bader Ginsburg (1993) and Stephen Breyer (1994) to the Supreme Court.

Health Care Reform

In October 1993, the Clinton administration proposed legislation to reform the health care system which included universal coverage with a guaranteed benefits package, managed competition through health care alliances which would bargain with insurance companies, and employer mandates to provide health insurance for employees. Opposed by most Republicans, small business, and insurance and medical-business interests, Senate Majority Leader George Mitchell of Maine dropped his attempt at compromise legislation in September 1994.

Whitewater Probe, a Sex Scandal, Impeachment, and Acquittal

Clinton was criticized for alleged wrongdoing in connection with the Whitewater real estate development, in which he had been an investor with James B. and Susan McDougal, owners of a failed savings and loan institution, while governor of Arkansas. The Justice Department appointed Robert B. Fiske in January 1994 as a "special counsel" to probe the allegations. After Congress renewed the independent counsel law, a three-judge panel appointed Kenneth W. Starr to replace Fiske in the new role of "independent prosecutor." The Starr investigation yielded massive findings in late 1998, roughly midway into Clinton's second term, but they were far afield of Whitewater or of any of the several matters of alleged misconduct that Starr had said he'd been looking into. Instead, the Starr Report focused on an adulterous affair that Clinton had had with Monica Lewinsky, a White House intern. It was on charges stemming from this report that Clinton was impeached by the House of Representatives in December 1998. The Senate acquitted him in February 1999, with most Senators voting along party lines.

1994 Elections

Voters in the 1994 off-year election gave Republicans, most of whom were conservative, control of both houses of Congress. It was the first time since 1952 that the GOP had won a majority in the House of Representatives. The South, once a Democratic stronghold, was now clearly moving into the Republican camp. On the state level, Republicans dominated the races for governorships.

Oklahoma City Bombing

On April 19, 1995, a rental truck loaded with explosives was detonated at the Alfred P. Murrah federal building in Oklahoma City, Okla. The blast—the deadliest act of terrorism ever committed in the U.S.—killed 168 people, including 19 children in the building's day care center, and injured more than 500 others. Two members of a right-wing, paramilitary militia were arrested as suspects in the bombing. Timothy James McVeigh was convicted and sentenced to death in June 1997. A second defendant, Terry Nichols, was convicted on conspiracy charges.

FOREIGN POLICY

Somalia

In May 1993 the United Nations took control of relief efforts in Somalia from United States troops. The last U.S. soldiers left in 1994.

Middle East

Yitzhak Rabin, Prime Minister of Israel, and Yasir Arafat, Chairman of the Palestine Liberation Organization, signed an accord in 1994 establishing Palestinian self-rule in the Gaza Strip and Jericho. The PLO began establishing control over its territory in the summer of 1994. In October 1994 Israel and Jordan signed a treaty to begin the process of establishing full diplomatic relations.

Haiti

In an attempt to force the ouster of the military government that had overthrown the democratically elected Jean-Bertrand Aristide in 1991, the Clinton administration succeeded in pushing the United Nations to establish an oil and arms embargo against Haiti in 1993. The embargo was extended the following year to include virtually everything except food and medicine. The United States banned all commercial flights to Haiti in 1994. Refugees from Haiti into the United States continued to be a major problem for the administration, which refused to let most of them enter the country. In September, after threats that an invasion was imminent, Lt. General Raoul Cedras and the remainder of the military junta agreed to relinquish power. The U.S. then led a multinational force that occupied the island to ensure social stability during the period of transition and Aristide resumed the presidency in October.

North Korea

North Korea threatened in 1993 to withdraw from the Nuclear Nonproliferation Treaty which led to several months of tensions over international inspection of its nuclear sites. Diplomatic discussions between North Korea and the United States, although delayed by the death of North Korean leader Kim Il Sung in July 1994, led to an agreement which included American financial and technological assistance for North Korean nuclear energy. In return, North Korea accepted the Nuclear Nonproliferation Treaty.

NATO

In 1994 the North Atlantic Treaty Organization—at the urging of the United States—offered former members of the Warsaw Pact limited association to enhance European security. Then, on March 16, 1999, in what NATO Secretary-General Javier Solana described as "the triumph of justice over history," Poland, the Czech Republic, and Hungary were admitted into the alliance at a ceremony hosted in Independence, Mo., by U.S. Secretary of State Madeleine Albright.

Vietnam

The Clinton administration in 1994 lifted the trade embargo against Vietnam because of its cooperation with efforts to find the remains of U.S. military personnel.

China

In 1994, China's "Most Favored Nation" status was continued, despite Clinton's oft-made election campaign statements regarding a lack of improvement in political freedom in that country.

Iraq

On October 7, 1994, in response to an Iraqi military buildup on its border with Kuwait, Clinton ordered American troops, ships, and aircraft to the region and demanded that Saddam Hussein pull his forces back from the border. Four days later, the Iraqi troops began withdrawing. Hussein apparently had been hoping to force the United Nations to lift its sanctions against his country. In the ensuing years, Hussein continued to skirmish diplomatically with an international team of inspectors charged with checking that Iraq was meeting its obligation to the U.N. not to produce weapons of mass destruction. After warning Hussein of the price he would pay for not allowing the inspectors to do their job, Clinton ordered a brief, sustained air attack on suspected weapons-related sites in late 1998. Periodic bombing raids continued into 1999, as Hussein refused to let the inspectors do their U.N.-mandated job.

DRILL: THE COLLAPSE OF COMMUNISM TO THE CLINTON PRESIDENCY

1. All of the following contributed to the collapse of Communism EXCEPT

    (A) Soviet economic problems

    (B) Anti-Communist demonstrations in Eastern Europe

    (C) Internal liberalization of Soviet society

    (D) American violations of trade agreements

    (E) Free elections in Poland

2.   Nicolae Ceaucescu was the dictator of which nation?

    (A) Poland   (D) Romania

    (B) Czechoslovakia   (E) Yugoslavia

    (C) Hungary

3.   The Crime Bill of 1994 included all of the following provisions EXCEPT

    (A) increased spending for federal, state, and local police forces

    (B) a ban on 19 types of assault weapons

    (C) the death penalty for third-time violent offenders

    (D) life imprisonment for drug offenders convicted in federal courts

    (E) creation of 50 new federal death penalty crimes

4.   In 1994, China's "Most Favored Nation" trade status was renewed, despite the Clinton administration's dissatisfaction with

    (A) China's continuing human rights violations.

    (B) the multi-million dollar trade deficit between China and the U.S.

    (C) China's refusal to allow inspection of nuclear sites.

    (D) China's continuing trade with American adversaries, such as Iraq.

    (E) threats to the safety of Americans traveling in China.

5.   American reaction to the overthrow of Haiti's democratically elected president, Jean-Bertrande Aristide, included all of the following EXCEPT

    (A) an oil and arms embargo.

    (B) a food and medicine embargo.

    (C) a ban on commercial flights to Haiti.

    (D) refusal to admit refugees.

    (E) leadership of a multi-national force created to ensure stability.

HISTORICAL AND SOCIAL SCIENTIFIC AWARENESS REVIEW

ANSWER KEY TO DRILL QUESTIONS

THE ANCIENT AND MEDIEVAL WORLDS

1.	**(A)**	3.	**(B)**	5.	**(A)**
2.	**(C)**	4.	**(D)**		

THE LATE MIDDLE AGES AND THE RENAISSANCE

1.	**(A)**	3.	**(D)**	5.	**(C)**
2.	**(E)**	4.	**(D)**		

BOURBON, BAROQUE AND THE ENLIGHTENMENT

1.	**(D)**	3.	**(A)**	5.	**(A)**
2.	**(B)**	4.	**(B)**		

REVOLUTION AND THE NEW WORLD ORDER

1.	**(D)**	3.	**(E)**	5.	**(B)**
2.	**(C)**	4.	**(A)**		

REALISM AND MATERIALISM

1.	**(C)**	3.	**(D)**	5.	**(B)**
2.	**(D)**	4.	**(E)**		

WORLD WAR I AND EUROPE IN CRISIS

1.	**(A)**	3.	**(E)**	5.	**(E)**
2.	**(E)**	4.	**(C)**		

WORLD WAR II TO THE DEMISE OF COMMUNISM

1.	**(C)**	3.	**(A)**	5.	**(C)**
2.	**(C)**	4.	**(C)**		

THE COLONIAL PERIOD

1.	**(A)**	3.	**(A)**	5.	**(D)**
2.	**(D)**	4.	**(A)**		

THE AMERICAN REVOLUTION

1.	**(D)**	3.	**(C)**	5.	**(E)**
2.	**(C)**	4.	**(A)**		

THE UNITED STATES CONSTITUTION

1.	**(A)**	3.	**(C)**	5.	**(B)**
2.	**(C)**	4.	**(C)**		

THE NEW NATION

1.	**(D)**	3.	**(C)**	5.	**(C)**
2.	**(B)**	4.	**(B)**		

JACKSONIAN DEMOCRACY AND WESTWARD EXPANSION

1.	**(D)**	3.	**(A)**	5.	**(B)**
2.	**(C)**	4.	**(B)**		

SECTIONAL CONFLICT AND THE CAUSES OF THE CIVIL WAR

1.	**(B)**	3.	**(D)**	5.	**(B)**
2.	**(A)**	4.	**(A)**		

THE CIVIL WAR AND RECONSTRUCTION

1.	**(A)**	3.	**(A)**	5.	**(B)**
2.	**(D)**	4.	**(C)**		

INDUSTRIALISM, WAR, AND THE PROGRESSIVE ERA

1. **(E)**   3. **(D)**   5. **(A)**
2. **(C)**   4. **(A)**

WILSON AND WORLD WAR I

1. **(D)**   3. **(C)**   5. **(A)**
2. **(B)**   4. **(E)**

THE ROARING TWENTIES AND ECONOMIC COLLAPSE

1. **(C)**   3. **(B)**   5. **(B)**
2. **(D)**   4. **(C)**

THE GREAT DEPRESSION AND THE NEW DEAL

1. **(B)**   3. **(A)**   5. **(D)**
2. **(A)**   4. **(B)**

WORLD WAR II AND THE POSTWAR ERA

1. **(C)**   3. **(E)**   5. **(C)**
2. **(C)**   4. **(E)**

THE NEW FRONTIER, VIETNAM, AND SOCIAL UPHEAVAL

1. **(E)**   3. **(D)**   5. **(C)**
2. **(E)**   4. **(B)**

WATERGATE, CARTER, AND THE NEW CONSERVATISM

1. **(D)**   3. **(E)**   5. **(E)**
2. **(A)**   4. **(E)**

THE COLLAPSE OF COMMUNISM TO THE CLINTON PRESIDENCY

1. **(D)**   3. **(C)**   5. **(B)**
2. **(D)**   4. **(A)**

Chapter 4

Artistic Expression and the Humanities Review

The Artistic Expression and the Humanities section of the LAST is designed to assess your ability to comprehend, interpret, and contextualize works of art. You will be expected to understand basic elements of form and content in the visual and performing arts from various time periods and cultures. You should be able to respond to themes and motifs in literature and the arts, as well as analyze religious and philosophical ideas and their significance in shaping various cultures. This review will give you the background you need to do well on this section of the exam.

AESTHETIC PERCEPTION AND CREATIVE EXPRESSION

The visual and performing arts have served to express humanity's basic spiritual beliefs and the need to organize its environment from prehistoric times to the present. Seventeen thousand years ago, before cities and settled villages, Paleolithic people at Lascaux (modern France)—and at Altimira (modern Spain) about 2,000 years later—produced realistic animal paintings on cave walls in an attempt to capture the essences of the creatures they hunted and encountered. The urge to create art existed even earlier in the Paleolithic period, and numerous small female figures (now called Venuses) and carved weapons dating from perhaps as early as 30,000 B.C. have been discovered in Europe. Megalithic structures, such as Stonehenge in England, and monuments of ancient civilizations, such as the Egyptian pyramids, were precisely calculated architectural forms that answered sophisticated needs of astronomical calculation, paid homage to the mysteries and power of the sun and stars, and attempted to master the passage to the afterlife. Tribal people throughout history have used dance and music to control their environment,

Venus of Willendorf
c. 25,000–20,000 BC Stone Museum of Natural History, Vienna

communicate with animals, and comprehend the unseen world, as well as to merely celebrate, and have produced masks, weavings, textiles, pottery, and jewelry of harmonious form and color and complex abstract patterns.

Beginning with the first great civilized society, the Sumerians in Mesopotamia more than 5,000 years ago, the peoples of the world have continued on a consistent path in the area of fine, applied, and performing arts. Visual fine art has come to mean a self-conscious creation of aesthetically sophisticated works, usually by one individual, in an attempt to further knowledge, expand style and technology, and create beauty. Applied art is practical and often evolves directly from the needs, culture, and tastes of a community; crafts and decorative art, utilitarian or commercial objects in which quality of technique is primary, are examples. Increasingly, the lines between fine art and craft have become blurred, so that it is no longer necessary to arbitrarily enthrone a work of art merely because it is, for example, a painting rather than a piece of pottery or jewelry. In the performing arts, folk dance and music are a natural outgrowth of a community's recreational, entertainment, celebratory, and ritualistic needs. The great masterpieces of ballet, opera, and classical music each represent the conscious manipulation of form and idea in a new way to create an individualistic work, usually for the purposes of an audience's edification and amusement.

All of the arts on all levels may be judged as either successful or not, as good or mediocre, and have a beauty and legitimacy that operates on an aesthetic level and arises from its culture.

The visual and performing arts basically encompass the categories of sculpture, architecture, painting and graphics, music, dance, and theater. Each of these has its own rules and requirements and aesthetic appeal, its own distinct way of satisfying a basic human means of expression.

Sculpture is concerned with molding shapes in three-dimensional forms. Sculptures may be cast—molten metals poured into molds to create cast-bronze figures—and such works would include ancient Greek statues of warriors, equestrian monuments of the Italian Renaissance, Auguste Rodin's *Thinker*, and Frederic Bartholdi's enormous Statue of Liberty. They may also be carved—from wood, stone, or marble—shaped from clay, or in the twentieth century, welded together from metal pieces.

Painting is a two-dimensional means of re-creating reality or arranging abstract forms in color on a flat surface. Surfaces have traditionally been walls, wooden panels, canvas, paper and parchment, even decorative objects such as vases. The color is usually applied with a brush, using pigments mixed with media such as linseed oil or water. Types of painting include watercolor, oil, tempera, and acrylic; for frescoes, pigments are applied directly over wet plaster to seal in the art on a wall or ceiling. Other two-dimensional art, in color or black and white, includes *drawing*—with graphite (pencil), ink applied by pen or brush, and chalk or crayons—and *printmaking*. In etching, woodcuts, lithographs, and the many variations on these methods, multiple copies of a drawing are made by creating either a raised or recessed surface (metal, wood, or stone) that takes ink and pressing paper against the surface.

Architecture is the conscious organization of space and form to provide a structure for living, working, worshipping, or for other residential or civic needs. Great architecture has always been intimately connected with new technologies and building materials, as well as with the immediate cultural needs of a community, city, or nation. Gothic cathedrals, for example, soar to the heavens with massive vertical elements to reflect the religious devotion of medieval Europe. The simple shapes and unadorned facades of many twentieth-century buildings reveal a fascination with the era's ease of using such materials as glass, steel, and concrete and a rejection of what was considered the overly decorated architecture of the previous century.

Dance is an art form based on physical movement and expression—by humans singly, or in couples or groups. Folk and tribal dancing are often related to communal celebration or religious ritual. Dance created to entertain an audience by one person may be choreographed and worked out in strict steps and gestures, such as in ballet or musical theater.

Music is the arrangement of sounds for voice and musical instruments, and, like dance, requires training and repetitive practice. For most of history, music has been an outgrowth of a community's or an ethnic group's need to celebrate, and has often been linked to story-telling or poetry. Traditional instruments have been indigenous variations on drums, horns, pipes (such as flutes), and hollow boxes fitted with vibrating strings (such as lyres or lutes). In Europe, a system of musical notation developed during the Middle Ages, and the use of notation (written symbolic indications of pitch and duration of tones) is a convenient way to distinguish "art" (or classical, or complexly composed) music from folk music. Since the seventeenth century, orchestral instruments of the West have multiplied to include pianos, saxophones, clarinets, cellos, and in our own era, electronic synthesizers.

Theater is the performance, for the sake of an audience's education or entertainment, of a story, usually of drama, comedy, or some combination thereof. The West's tradition of theater originated chiefly with the ancient Greeks—the tragedies of Aeschylus and Sophocles, the comedies of Aristophanes—and many feel reached its high point in the late sixteenth and early seventeenth centuries in England with the plays of William Shakespeare, who is revered throughout the world for his mastery of the form. Theater requires vocal declamation, acting, costumes, sometimes masks, usually a scenic backdrop or constructed set, and poetic expression. Music is often an integral part of the performance as well. Theater may be said to encompass all the art forms, since a theatrical production of ballet, opera, or musical drama/comedy can include all the disciplines, employing set decoration, costuming, dance, song, and instrumental music.

CULTURAL HERITAGE

Artistic expression in dance, theater, music, and the visual arts has undergone many stylistic changes in the passing centuries of the world's civilizations. It can be affected by the era's spirit, by evolving economic and social changes, and by religion. The form the art takes, and the way it fits into the lives of a people, depends on its geographical source and the ethnic group from which it originates. For example, one form of dance in Europe by the seventeenth century evolved into the sophisticated high-art form of ballet, which is both entertaining and cerebral. In India, four types of dance are considered classical, but these have very different forms and purposes than European ballet. Even within a society, the representations and needs of an art form change with the cultural forces of an age. While the religious-symbolic paintings, sculptures, and manuscript illuminations of the Middle Ages saw no need to relate human beings realistically to each other in size, or place them in a natural-looking environment or realistic space, the Renaissance artists, seeing humans as the center of the universe and seeking rational knowledge, depicted a world of visual beauty, of perfectly observed persons in perfectly proportioned environments.

In theater, twentieth-century drama may emphasize psychological portraits of individuals and realistic dialogue. But the ancient Greeks sought to portray—using masks and chorus (a group of dancer-singers) commentary on the main action—great themes of fate, honor, and pride. In the tradition of Japanese Noh plays, which originated in the fifteenth century and derive from Zen Buddhism, five plays separated by three comic interludes are marked by stylized acting, masks, mime, and folk dance.

In music, the system of tonal scales and preferences are often unique to a culture: for example, the Chinese prefer the pentatonic scale of five notes, while the West has primarily used a scale of seven notes (eight with the repeated first note for an octave). Indian musical pieces are often built upon *ragas* (meaning "mood" or "color"), which are melodic patterns of five to seven tones. Indian compositions feature repetitive patterns and use scales whose octaves have 22 intervals, or steps.

Architecture is related to the most basic needs of a society and the technology and materials available to a culture or in a geographic location. Because the ancient Egyptians needed grandeur in their funerary monuments and they were able to master the complicated calculations to perfectly cut and arrange huge stones, the magnificent pyramids were created. Architecture is the measure of the prevailing philosophy of an age. The Renaissance architects, for example, sought to express their rediscovery of ancient humanism and search for knowledge, as well as their new-found joy in earthly life and beauty, through the application of perfect proportions, the use of classical engineering techniques, and by perfecting of the art of constructing domes.

HISTORICAL SURVEY

VISUAL ARTS

Paleolithic people in Europe painted animal pictures on the cave walls at Lascaux and Altimira about 15,000-13,000 B.C. Some examples of even older art, dating from 30,000 to 20,000 B.C., are the various "Venuses"—small stylized stone carvings of women as symbols of fertility, found in modern France, Italy, and Austria. The artists of the ancient civilizations of Sumer, Babylon, and Assyria were skilled in carving even the hardest rocks, such as granite and basalt, into narratives of battles and historical records. Egyptian statues, like their architectural monuments the pyramids, were often of colossal size, to further exalt the power of the society's leaders and gods. The art of ancient Greece has its roots in the Minoan civilization on the island of Crete, which flourished about 2500-1400 B.C.: the palace at Knossos is known for characteristic wall paintings revealing a people enamored of games, leisure, and the beauty of the sea. The mainland Greeks of the classical period, about a thousand years later, were fascinated by physical beauty. Their Olympian gods were fashioned in the human image, and a universe of perfection, guided by a master plan, was re-created in their idealized and gracefully proportioned sculptures, architecture, and paintings. In the Hellenistic period, these various objects came to be appreciated as art, for their beauty alone.

The culture of Rome excelled in engineering and building, whose purpose it was to efficiently organize a vast empire and provide an aesthetic environment for private and public use. The Romans built temples, roads, bath complexes, civic buildings, palaces, and aqueducts. One of the greatest of their artistic and engineering accomplishments was the massive-domed temple of all the gods, the Pantheon, which is today one of the most perfectly preserved of all classical-period buildings.

The early Christian period era borrowed the basilica form of Roman architecture for its churches, particularly evident in churches in the town of Ravenna in northeast Italy. The seventh-century church of San Vitale echoes the mosaic mastery of the eastern Roman, or Byzantine, empire in Constantinople (which flourished as a center of civilization for a thousand years after the decline of Rome). Its grandiose apse mosaic depicts Emperor Justinian and Empress Theodora.

The Romanesque style of art and architecture was preeminent from about 800 to 1200. By then many local styles, including the decorative arts of

View from the Apse of Sanvitale, Ravenna, Italy 526–547 A.D.

the Byzantines, the Near East, and the German and Celtic tribes, were contributing to European culture. Common features of Romanesque churches are round arches, vaulted ceilings, and heavy walls that are profusely decorated—primarily with symbolic figures of Christianity, the realism of which for its creators had became less and less important and was, instead, subordinate to the message.

Gothic art flourished in Europe for the next 300 years. The cathedrals in this style are some of the purest expressions of an age. They combine a continued search for engineering and structural improvement with stylistic features that convey a relentless verticality, a reach toward heaven, and the unbridled adoration of God. Soaring and airy, these cathedrals were constructed using such elements as flying buttresses and pointed arches and vaults, and were decorated by a profusion of sculptures and stained-glass windows that were, for the worshippers, visual encyclopedias of Christian teachings and stories.

The Italian Renaissance's roots are found as early as the 1300s, when the painter Giotto began to compose his figures into groups and depict expressive human gestures. During the fifteenth century, art, architecture, literature, and music were invigorated. Renaissance artists developed new forms and revived classical styles and values, with the belief in the importance of human experience on Earth. Great sculptors approached true human characterization and realism. Lorenzo Ghiberti created the bronze doors of the Florence Baptistry (early fifteenth century) and Donatello produced *Gattamelata*, the first equestrian statue since the Roman era.

Architecture, in the hands of Filippo Brunelleschi and Leon Battista Alberti, revived the Greek elements and took a scientific, ordered approach, one similarly expressed in painting, with the emphasis on the calculated composition of figures in space known as perspective. The Renaissance artists sought to produce works of perfect beauty and engaged in a constant search for knowledge, most often portraying religious subjects and wealthy patrons. The stylistic innovations of such fifteenth-century painters as Masaccio, Paolo Uccello, Fra Angelico, Piero della Francesca, Andrea Mantegna, and Sandro Botticelli were built upon in the High Renaissance of the next century.

Art became more emotional and dramatic, color and movement were heightened, compositions were more vigorous, and there were increased references to classical iconography and the pleasures of an idyllic golden age. These aspects can be seen in Michelangelo's magnificent Sistine Chapel frescoes and his powerful sculptures of *David* and *Moses,* Leonardo's *Mona Lisa,* Raphael's *School of Athens* fresco, and the increasingly dramatic and colorful works of the Venetian and northern Italian masters Titian, Correggio, Giorgione, and Bellini. The northern European Renaissance also emphasized a renewed interest in the visible world, and works by Albrecht Durer, Lucas Cranach, Matthias Grunewald, and Albrecht Altdorfer reveal an emphasis on the symbolism of minutely observed details and accurate realism based on observation of reality rather than prescribed rules.

Presaged by the works of the Venetian artist Tintoretto (the radiating *Last Supper*) and El Greco in Spain (*View of Toledo; The Immaculate Conception*), the baroque period of the seventeenth century produced artists who added heightened drama to the forms of Renaissance art. Caravaggio (*The Calling of Saint Matthew; The Conversion of Saint Paul*) and the

The Death of Marat
Jacques Louis David, 1793. Royal Museums of Fine Arts, Brussels.

sculptor Gianlorenzo Bernini (*Saint Teresa in Ecstasy*) in Italy; the Flemish masters Peter Paul Rubens (*Marie de Medici Lands at Marseilles)* and Jacob Jordaens portrayed figures in constant motion, draperies of agitated angles, and effects of lighting and shadow that amplified emotional impact and mystery.

In this spirit followed such painters of court life and middle-class portraiture as Velazquez, Rembrandt, Anthony Van Dyck, and Frans Hals. Rembrandt used expressive brushwork and mysterious light contrasts to enliven genre painting and portraiture, particularly of groups. Rembrandt's influence has remained potent, since his art appears to impart universal truths, and sections of his compositions glow with a mysterious inner light often unrelated to realistic effects (*The Night Watch*, many self-portraits).

The art of the early eighteenth century is often called rococo. Painters like Jean-Antoine Watteau (*Embarkation for Cythera*), Giambattista Tiepolo (frescoes of the Wurzberg Residenz), Francois Boucher, and Jean-Honore Fragonard, often for decorative wall and ceiling schemes, turned the agitated drama of the baroque into light, pastel-toned, swirling compositions that seem placed in an idyllic land of a golden age. In the seventeenth and eighteenth centuries, European artists also responded to middle-class life and everyday objects and created genre paintings (Jan Vermeer, Adriaen van Ostade, Jean-Baptiste Chardin). Jean-Baptiste Greuze in France and William Hogarth in England endowed their everyday subjects with a wealth of narrative detail that aimed to impart a specific moral message.

Such narrative art combined in the nineteenth century with romantic literature—Goethe, Byron, Shelley, Scott, Wordsworth, and others—and political events to produce works with a political point of view or a story to tell, in a variety of styles. Jacques-Louis David used a severe classical sculptural style (neoclassical) in his paintings to revive classical art and ennoble images of the French Revolution and Napoleon's empire (*The Death of Marat; The Oath of the Horatii; Napoleon in His Study*). Neoclassical sculpture revived the aloof severity and perfection of form of ancient art (Jean-Antoine Houdon, Antonio Canova, Bertel Thorvaldsen, Horatio Greenough)—a style also reflected in Thomas Jefferson's architectural designs for his Monticello home and the University of Virginia.

The Spanish painter Francisco de Goya commented powerfully on political events in his painting *May 3, 1808*. In France, Eugene Delacroix (*The Death of Sardanapalus; Liberty Leading the People*) and Theodore Gericault (*The Raft of the Medusa*) imbued subjects from literature, the Bible, exotic lands, and current events with dramatic and heroic intensity. The grandeur and transcendence of nature, the emotional reaction to inner dreams and metaphysical truths of romanticism are seen in the work of such mystical artists as England's William Blake, Henry Fuselli, and John Martin, and America's Thomas Cole. Caspar David Friedrich in Germany and the English Pre-Raphaelites (William Holman Hunt, John Everett Millais, Dante Gabriel Rossetti, Ford Madox Brown, Arthur Hughes, and others) endowed their keenly observed, minutely detailed works with a romantic spirit of poetic yearning and literary references, and accurately re-created the natural world in brilliantly colored landscapes.

In the first half of the nineteenth century, landscape painting in England reached a zenith with the works with Constable and Turner. Turner's awe-inspiring landscapes form a bridge between the spirit of romanticism and the expressionistic brushwork and realism of the Barbizon School in France, whose chief painters were Charles Daubigny and Jean-Baptiste-Camille Corot. Beginning with Barbizon, the French painters of the nineteenth century concentrated more and more on the reporterlike depiction of every-day life and the natural environment in a free, painterly (gesture and brushwork) style.

The realist pioneers were Gustave Courbet (*The Stone Breakers; A Burial at Ormans*), Jean-Francois Millet (*The Sower; The Angelus*), and Honore Daumier (*The Third-Class Carriage*). Renowned as a political caricaturist, Daumier's chief medium was the lithograph and paved the way for the stylistic and subject innovations of the Impressionists. Traditional means of composing a picture, academic methods of figure modeling, of color relations, and accurate and exact rendering of people and objects, were rejected in favor of an art that emphasized quickly observed and sketched moments from life, the relation of shapes and forms and colors, the effects of light, and the act of painting itself.

Beginning with Edouard Manet (*Le Dejeuner sur l'Herbe; Olympia*) in the 1860s, French artists continually blurred the boundaries of realism and abstraction, and the landscapes and everyday-life paintings of such Impressionist artists as Claude Monet, Camille Pissarro, Auguste Renoir, Alfred Sisley, and Edgar Degas gave way to the more experimental arrangements of form and color of the great Postimpressionists—Paul Gauguin, Vincent Van Gogh, Georges Seurat, and Toulouse-Lautrec. Auguste Rodin produced powerful sculptures with the freedom of Impressionist style.

Greatly influenced by Japanese art and particularly the flattened space, distinctive shapes, and strong colors of Japanese woodblock prints, artists from Manet and Degas to the American Impressionist Mary Cassatt, from Toulouse-Lautrec to the Nabis (Edouard Vuillard, Pierre Bonnard, and Maurice Denis) used paintings, pastels, and lithography to further break down the boundaries between representational art and abstraction. The new freer form of art, centered around the personality of the artist and celebrating personal style and the manipulation of form and color, in the late nineteenth and early twentieth century evolved in a number of directions.

Some artists turned inward to explore mystical, symbolic, and psychological truths: Symbolists, Expressionists, and exponents of art nouveau, such as Odilon Redon, Jan Toorop, Edvard Munch (*The Scream*), James Ensor (*The Entry of Christ into Brussels*), Gustav Klimt (*The Kiss*), Ernst Kirchner, Max Pechstein. Others pursued formal innovations, among them Paul Cezanne, Henri Matisse, Pablo Picasso, Georges Braque, and Juan Gris. Picasso's Cubism (*Les Demoiselles d'Avignon*) seemed the most direct call for the total

Shop Block, The Bauhaus.
Walter Gropius. 1925–26, Dessau Germany

destruction of realistic depiction; his use of African and Oceanic tribal art, and his emphasis on taking objects apart and reassembling them—thus showing a subject's multiplicity of aspects and dissolving time and space—led to similar experiments by Fernand Leger, Marcel Duchamp, the sculptors Alexander Archipenko and Jacques Lipchitz, and the Italian Futurist Umberto Boccioni (*Unique Forms of Continuity in Space*).

Pure abstraction, with little or no relation to the outside world, was approached in the more emotional, expressionistic, and color-oriented paintings of Wassily Kandinsky, Roger Delauney, and Paul Klee. More cerebral arrangements of abstract geometrical shapes and colors were the mark of Kasimir Malevich, Piet Mondrian, and the Bauhaus School of Design in Germany, whose stripped-down, simplified, and usually geometrically-oriented aesthetic influenced architecture, industrial and commercial design, sculpture, and the graphic arts for half a century.

In architecture can be seen the most obvious results of this new tradition, from the simplified, sleek structures of Le Corbusier and Walter Gropius to the boxlike glass skyscrapers of Philip Johnson. The pioneering giant of twentieth-century architecture was Frank Lloyd Wright, whose rejection of eclectic decorative styles of the previous century's architecture and use of new engineering techniques paralleled the Bauhaus aesthetic. From the early

Three Flags
Jasper Johns, 1958. Collection of Mr. and Mrs. Burton Tremaine, Meriden, CT.

1900s, Wright's buildings (the Robie House, Fallingwater, and Tokyo's Imperial Hotel) exhibited a personal and bold originality, based on a philosophy of "organic architecture," a belief that the form of a structure should be dictated by its natural surroundings, purpose, and building materials.

Inspired by the psychoanalytic writings of Sigmund Freud and Carl Jung, the subconscious and the metaphysical became another important element in art, especially in the work of the Surrealist artists Salvador Dali (*The Persistence of Memory*), Giorgio de Chirico, Max Ernst, Rene Magritte, Juan Miro, and Yves Tanguy. Important sculptors who manipulated abstract shapes and were influenced by tribal arts in the twentieth century include Constantin Brancusi, Henry Moore, Hans Arp, and Alberto Giacometti; Alexander Calder created floating assemblies called mobiles, and Louise Nevelson made constructions and wall sculptures from scraps of everyday objects.

Obsession with self and with abstraction also led to the major American art movement after World War II, know as Abstract Expressionism. The chief proponents of this style were Clifford Still, Jackson Pollock, Willem de Kooning, and Robert Motherwell. Other Americans took this movement into the area of color-field painting, a cooler, more reserved formalism of simple shapes and experimental color relationships. Artists in this movement include Mark Rothko, Barnett Newman, Joseph Albers, and Ad Reinhardt.

Other important trends in American art in the twentieth century were reflective of a democratic and consumer society. The muralists and social realists between the wars created art that was physically interesting, and whose subjects were accessible to the average person. John Sloan, George Bellows, Edward Hopper, Thomas Hart Benton, Grant Wood, and John Stuart Curry were among those who celebrated the American scene in paintings, and frequently in murals for public buildings and through widely available fine prints. The great Mexican muralists, who usually concentrated on political themes—Diego Rivera, Jose Clemente Orozco, and David Siqueiros— brought their work to the public both in Mexico and in the United States. The icons of American popular culture found their way, in the movement known as Pop Art, into canvases by Andy Warhol, Robert Indiana, Larry Rivers, Jasper Johns, Roy Lichtenstein, and Robert Rauschenberg.

MUSIC

In the ancient world, Egyptian, Sumerian, and Hebrew cultures used song and such instruments as lyres, harps, drums, flutes, cymbals, and trumpets. The ancient Greeks accompanied the recitation of poetry with the stringed lyre, and Athenian drama was accompanied by the *aulos* or double-piped oboe (an instrument used in the worship of Dionysus), and choral songs were heard between recited passages.

In the early Christian era, plainsong, or unaccompanied religious chant, was codified and arranged, with early forms of music notation, by Pope Gregory the Great (late sixth century). This is the origin of Gregorian chant. By the twelfth and thirteenth centuries, the important form of polyphony, upon which the distinctive art music of the West is based, enabled supportive melodies to be added to the main chant. The basic form of music notation, representing pitch through the use of a staff, was invented by the Italian Benedictine monk Guido d'Arezzo. Throughout the later Middle Ages both religious and secular polyphonic music was composed, and melodies and rhythms became more diversified: new musical forms included the ballade, the rondeau, and the virelai of the troubadours. The first polyphonic setting of the Catholic mass was composed by Guillaume de Machaut in the fourteenth century.

During the Renaissance, the spirit of humanism and rationalism per-vaded polyphonic music, technical problems of composition were eagerly resolved, and music began to be seen as a mark of culture. More and more emphasis was placed upon secular music and dance and instrumental music ensembles, as well as on increasingly complex combinations of voices and instruments. Major composers were Giovanni da Palestrina, Josquin des Pres, Orlando di Lasso, William Byrd, and Giovanni Gabrieli.

Baroque music of the seventeenth and early eighteenth centuries employed a greater complexity of contrapuntal, or multimelodic, form, and the beginnings of harmony, the use of colorful instrumental ensembles, and great drama and emotion. The new dramatic forms became popular entertainment, particularly the operas of Claudio Monteverdi (*The Coronation of Poppea*). Other innovative forms included the oratorio, the cantata, the sonata, the suite, the concerto, and the fugue. The great works of baroque music were composed by Dietrich Buxtehude, Johann Pachelbel, Alessandro Scarlatti, Antonio Vivaldi (*The Four Seasons*), Henry Purcell, Jean Phillipe Rameau, George Frideric Handel (*The Messiah; Israel in Egypt*) and Johann Sebastian Bach (Brandenberg concertos*).

The greatest composers of the classical period of the latter half of the eighteenth century, marked by clarity of form, logical thematic development, and strict adherence to sonata form, were Franz Joseph Haydn and Wolfgang Amadeus Mozart. Mozart's structurally exquisite works approach perfection of form while adding to music inventive melodic diversity. Mozart wrote 41 symphonies, as well as such innovative operas as *The Marriage of Figaro* and *The Magic Flute*. The German composer Ludwig van Beethoven (Fifth and Ninth symphonies, *Moonlight* and *Pathetique* sonatas) ushered in the romantic school of symphonic music. His symphonies and piano sonatas, concertos, and string quartets explode with dramatic passion, expressive melodies and harmonies, and complex thematic development.

Much of the romantic music that followed was less formal and more expressive, often associated with grandiose concepts and literary themes, and increasingly more colorful instrumentally. Art songs, piano concertos and sonatas, and symphonic poems (which seek to paint a musical picture or tell a story) became important forms for romantic composers. These included Frédéric Chopin (mainly piano music, some of which he called nocturnes), Hector Berlioz (*Symphonie Fantastique; Les Troyans*), Franz Liszt (*Mephisto Waltz,* piano concertos), Richard Strauss (*Also Sprach Zarathustra, Don Juan*, the operas *Salome* and *Elektra)*, and Felix Mendelssohn (four symphonies, incidental music to *A Midsummer Night's Dream)*. Other important symphonic composers of the nineteenth century were Robert Schumann, Johannes Brahms, Peter Ilich Tchaikovsky, and Gustav Mahler.

Throughout the century, musical development continued in the direction of a greater richness of harmony, a more varied use of musical instruments and orchestral color, and a greater use of chromaticism (the freedom to use tones not related to the key of the composition).

Other important influences in nineteenth-century music include the use of ethnic influences or folk melodies and music of a nationalistic vein, as well as of popular song—often linked to composers who were outstanding melodists and harmonic innovators—pieces such as this were written by Giacomo Rossini (*The Barber of Seville; William Tell*), Georges Bizet (*Carmen),* Giuseppe Verdi (*Aida; La Traviata*), Giacomo Puccini (*La Boheme; Tosca*), and the American Louis Moreau Gottschalk (*A Night in the Tropics; The Banjo*), and the Russians—Mikhail Glinka (*A Life for the Tsar*), Alexander Borodin (*Prince Igor, In the Steppes of Central Asia*), Modest Mussorgsky (*Boris Gudonov, A Night on Bald Mountain*), and Nicholas Rimsky-Korsakov (*Russian Easter Overture, Sherherazade*).

One of the great innovators in opera, Richard Wagner, sought to create a new form of music drama, using continuous music and relentless, swirling harmonies to underlie massive spectacle and recitative, or sung dialogue. Mussorgky and Wagner's idiomatic and chromatic harmonies greatly influenced the French "impressionist" composers, Claude Debussy (*La Mer; Prelude to the Afternoon of a Faun; Children's Corner Suite*) and Maurice Ravel (*Rhapsodie Espagnole; Mother Goose Suite; Tombeau de Couperin*), who for the most part eschewed the traditional larger forms and wrote emotional, dramatic, and colorful tone pictures and sonatas, using oriental tonalities and free rhapsodic forms.

The concert music of the twentieth century increasingly endeavored to enlarge the boundaries of rhythm, form, and harmony, seemingly parallel to the direction in the visual arts away from traditional structure and melodic-harmonic connections with listeners and toward more personal or intellectual experiments in abstraction. Thus, Igor Stravinsky may be seen as the musical equivalent of Picasso; the composer who, during the years before World War I, broke apart rhythms and introduced radical harmonies in works like *The Rite of Spring* and *Petrushka,* which set the stage for further trends away from traditional ideas of tonality and harmony. Francis Poulenc (*Les Biches*) and Stravinsky himself sought to use the new rhythms and harmonies in more structurally clear, and less orchestrally dense, neoclassical pieces. The Austrian composers Arnold Schoenberg, Anton von Webern, and Alban Berg employed a new, 12-tone system, which was a highly intellectualized method of composing music without a fixed key and by establishing an arbitrary "tone row."

Ethnic and popular influences continued to exert an important pull in the creation of twentieth-century music. Folk music was a major element in the works of the English composers Ralph Vaughan Williams and Gustav Holst, of the Hungarian composers Bela Bartok and Zoltan Kodaly, and often in the music of Stravinsky and the Soviet Union's Sergei Prokofiev and Aram Khachaturian. Ragtime, blues, jazz, and other popular folk, dance, and commercial music provided material for some of the most innovative and exciting work in twentieth-century music: Stravinsky's *Ragtime for Eleven Instruments* and *A Soldier's Tale;* Ravel's *Les Enfants et Les Sortileges* and Piano Concerto in G; Darius Milhaud's *La Creation du Monde* and *Le Boeuf sur le Toit*; Kurt Weill's *Threepenny Opera;* Erik Satie's *Parade;* George Gershwin's *Rhapsody in Blue* and *Porgy and Bess;* and many pieces by Poulenc, Paul Hindemith, Leonard Bernstein, and Bohuslav Martinu. Composers after World War II continued to employ the intellectual methods of Schoenberg and to experiment with tape-recorded sound (Edgard Varese) and conceptual music based on indeterminacy or chance (John Cage). Since the 1970s, American music has seen a return to romanticism, reflected in the renewed interest in the music of Samuel Barber and David Diamond and in the lush scores of David Del Tredici *(Final Alice)*. The minimalists, whose work is built upon gradual shifts of consistently repeated melodies and harmonies, include Philip Glass *(Einstein on the Beach)* and John Adams *(Nixon in China)*.

DANCE, THEATER, OPERA, POPULAR MUSICAL THEATER, AND ETHNIC/FOLK TRADITIONS

Many tribal peoples believe that through imitative dance they can gain knowledge of the mysterious powers of nature and influence the unseen world. Most dancing of this kind is communal. Dances of the ancient civilizations were often reserved for priests and religious rituals. But even the pharoahs of ancient Egypt enjoyed dancing as spectacle, and the ancient Greeks held dancing in high esteem, establishing many different styles for different purposes: the *gymnopedia,* for example, was a vigorous dance for athletic young men, and the *dithyramb* was a processional dance employing poetry and narrative, from which Greek drama arose. Romans enjoyed dancing as entertainment and pioneered the use of pantomime.

During the Middle Ages, the common folk enjoyed dancing, much of it related to fertility or seasonal rituals such as Maypole and wedding dances. The frenzied dance of death was the popular response to the spread of the plague in Europe, and dances in parades and pageants were also popular.

Secular dance with more formalized steps and forms became important among the upper classes after the Renaissance period. Stylized and formalized dances included the pavanne, the galliard, the sarabande, the gigue, the minuet, the gavotte, and the chaconne.

Eastern Music and Dance

Among Western and non-Western cultures alike the folk traditions of the performing arts often link the disciplines of dance, theater, and music. Ethnic dance with the longest and most sophisticated tradition is the classical dance of India, of which there are four main schools. Kathakali is the most theatrical of the Indian dances: actor-dancers perform stories based on mythological tales, and extensive use is made of costumes, masks, drums, makeup, and shouts.

Bharata Natyam, of southern India, is the oldest form, whose principles were described in Hindu scriptures 2,000 years ago. It requires extensive body movements, complex rhythms for the feet, and complex facial movements and hand gestures. Kathek is the Moslem-influenced dance of northern India, which values virtuosity and emotional expression. Manipuri dancing is strictly religious, and one of the annual village dance festivals is a ballet of the creation of the world. Indian dance has exerted great influence over the court and temple dances of Indonesia, Thailand, Japan, and other Asian countries.

Dance is primarily linked with theatrical entertainments in China (the opera) and Japan. Japanese Kabuki theater employs masks, singing, and dancing in a highly stylized manner, and the Noh plays of Japan are dance-dramas with stylized scenery and acting. In Indonesia, the Javanese *gamalen,* an orchestra of tuned percussion instruments consisting of up to 80 pieces, is played softly to accompany song and gentle dancing, and powerfully for heroic dances. Native American tribal dances are essentially ritualistic (such as the ghost dance of the Paiutes), but the hoop and eagle dances of the western Indian peoples are theatrical and intricate.

Folk dancing for pure recreation is also an important tradition, and in the West among the most significant dances are the Scottish Highland fling, the Italian tarantella, the American Virginia reel and square dances, and the Argentine tango. Popular American social dancing, usually requiring two persons, in the twentieth century has adopted many Latin American dances, including the rhumba, mambo, and tango, and is related to both popular songs and jazz-band arrangements—first spread through sales of sheet music, then records, and often derived from musical theater and films.

The importance of social dancing and the continual interest in new popular dance steps was essentially begun by the American dance team of Irene and Vernon Castle in the period during and after World War I. Popular dances have included the Charleston, the jitterbug, the fox trot, the twist and, increasingly after the 1950s, other youth-oriented dances related to rock music.

Self-consciously created dance, expressive and entertaining, as a form of theater and as ballet has often been used alone or as part of a wider production. Ballet has origins in both the ancient Roman pantomime and the Italian *commedia dell'arte*. France led the way in establishing the essentials of the classical ballet, beginning with the founding of the Royal Academy of Dancing in Paris in 1661. France created a theatrical tradition of opera ballets, and dance rules and steps were strictly formalized.

Into the nineteenth century it was nearly impossible for an acceptable opera not to include a ballet section. In Italy the ballet was affiliated with the opera company at La Scala in Milan, and in Russia academies of ballet in Moscow and St. Petersburg won worldwide fame. By the end of the nineteenth century significant ballets were being composed by Tchaikovsky (*Swan Lake; The Nutcracker*). It was another Russian, Sergei Diaghilev, who made ballet one of the most important independent art forms of the twentieth century. Diaghilev, who was essentially a producer, brought together such great choreographers and dancers as Michael Fokine, Leonide Massine, and Vasilav Nijinsky with composers such as Stravinsky, Prokofiev, Debussy, Poulenc, and Satie.

One of Diaghilev's greatest Ballet Russe choreographers, George Balanchine, became the most important American choreographer, director of the New York City Ballet, after World War II. The traditional elements of ballet were enlarged by the use of more abstract patterns, nontraditional steps and forms, greater individual expression, less virtuosic display, greater athleticism, and more incorporation of folk/popular-dance elements. Pioneering choreographers in the first half of the twentieth century include Isadora Duncan, Ruth St. Denis, Ted Shawn, Martha Graham, Agnes De Mille, and Jerome Robbins.

Agnes De Mille and Jerome Robbins were the leading figures of ballet-dance as used in American musical theater. Their folk- and jazz-inflected dances added significantly to the ballet idiom and revolutionized the American musical—De Mille with Rodgers and Hammerstein's *Oklahoma* and Robbins with Leonard Bernstein's *West Side Story*.

Music and theater have always been linked, and the traditions of opera, operetta, and musical comedy/drama in Europe and America have produced enduring theatrical masterpieces: the operas of Rossini, Verdi, Puccini, Bizet, Wagner, Weill, and Gershwin; the operettas of Gilbert and Sullivan (*The Pirates of Penzance; The Mikado; Patience*), Johann Strauss, Jr. (*Die Fledermaus*), Jacques Offenbach (*Tales of Hoffmann*), and Franz Lehar (*The Merry Widow)*; the musical comedies (a term loosely applied; musical theater is more accurate) of Jerome Kern (*Show Boat*), Richard Rodgers (*Carousel; Oklahoma; The King and I*), George Gershwin (*Strike Up the Band; Of Thee I Sing*), Leonard Bernstein (*On the Town; West Side Story*), and Stephen Sondheim (*Follies; Sweeney Todd*).

Drama and comedy have sought without music to portray humanity's deepest passions and most universal concerns, and simply to amuse or entertain. Medieval drama was primarily religious, the stylized mystery and miracle plays; where often presented in cathedrals and monasteries. Most theatrical performances in Europe until the sixteenth century took place in booths or courtyards or an outside open area. The great plays of Shakespeare and his contemporaries were presented in theaters, but these were merely stages set against the side of a building with spectators gathered around the stage on three sides in the yard or in galleries, with no provisions for scenery. Over the next hundred years, theaters were gradually enclosed and a separated stage, demarcated by a proscenium opening, hosted theatricals with elaborate scenery and even indoor lighting. Moliere in the seventeenth century and Beaumarchais in the eighteenth wrote comedies of manners and farces; the latter's *Barber of Seville* and *Marriage of Figaro* were adapted for operas by Rossini and Mozart, respectively.

Similar plays, with somewhat more realism and characters reflecting the interests and values of the middle class, were written in the nineteenth century by Oscar Wilde (*The Importance of Being Earnest; Lady Windemere's Fan*), George Bernard Shaw (*Pygmalion*), and Anton Chekov (*The Cherry Orchard*). Drama became more psychological and sought to reveal truths about real people and their inner and interpersonal conflicts with the dramas of August Strindberg (*Miss Julie*) and Henrik Ibsen (*A Doll's House*). Great American twentieth-century playwrights include Eugene O'Neill (*Long Day's Journey into Night; The Iceman Cometh*), Tennessee Williams (*The Glass Menagerie; A Streetcar Named Desire)*, and Arthur Miller (*Death of a Salesman; The Crucible*).

AESTHETIC VALUING

In addition to understanding the history of the visual and performing arts, it is important to be able to confront a work and judge its aesthetic merits—regardless of whether we specifically recognize it from memory. Questions one may ask are: A) What is the purpose of the work? Religious? Entertainment? Philosophical? Emotional? Didactic? Pure form? Social or political commentary? B) To what culture does it belong, and to what geographical region and time period—and how does it reflect these? C) Is its origin and/or function popular or commercial? Does it derive organically from the needs or celebratory functions of a community, or is it a self-conscious artistic creation of one individual? D) What style is it in? For example: Is this music baroque, classical, or romantic? Is it influenced by ethnic or popular music? Often after answering such questions, one may even be able to determine the specific artist—by putting all the clues together as in a detective story.

In looking at a work of visual art, in order to judge its quality—whether it is or isn't good art—we need to assess: A) whether it succeeds in its purpose; B) if the artist has spoken with a unique voice—regardless of style—or could this artwork just as easily be the work of someone else? C) if the style is appropriate to the expressed purpose of the work; D) if the work is memorable and distinctive; E) if the artist has used the technical elements available to the particular discipline with accomplished skill.

Although such basic questions as these can be applied in evaluating all good art, it is important to remember that beyond these kinds of questions there are other criteria that apply only to certain art forms, for certain purposes, in certain cultures. For example, it is inappropriate to look for the use of perspective of the Western-realist tradition in Japanese or Chinese art. In music, the improvisitory style and variation forms of American jazz, and other musical vocabulary unique to the jazz (as played by such musician/composers as Duke Ellington and King Oliver) allows its quality to be judged on equal but different terms than a symphony by Beethoven. In Islamic art, the beauties of manuscripts and textiles and architectural decoration are normally limited to exquisite patterns, beautiful script for texts, and stylized naturalistic forms for ornamentation; in the religious tradition, the realistic representation of human figures is purposely avoided.

The intensity of the Hindu religious feeling in India, the workings of the universe, the endless cycles of rebirth, the goal of the ultimate blissful union with the divine, especially the intense experience of erotic love—all are embodied in Kandarya Mahaveda and other temples at Khajuraho. The profusion of sculptures rising up the temple walls at Khajuraho occupy the senses and mind in ways similar to the religious instruction afforded by the vast number of sculptural and stained-glass stories and images of the European Gothic cathedrals, such as Rheims, Chartres, and Naumberg.

In opera, the masterful works by Puccini and Weill succeed on very different levels, and were created using different styles and for different purposes. While Puccini's *La Boheme, Tosca, Madama Butterfly,* and *La Fanciulla del West* are affecting melodramas of the highest order, with ravishing music serving drama and emotion in a perfect union, Kurt Weill's and Bertolt Brecht's *Threepenny Opera* and *The Rise and Fall of the City of Mahagonny* excoriate the excesses of modern societies built on greed and bloated bourgeois values—by using oblique satire and austerely constructed music that incorporates jazz rhythms and harmonies and popular-music-type melodies. Similarly, style and purpose are served brilliantly by the naturalism and accurate depiction of observed nature in the works of such masters as Rembrandt, Gainsborough, van Dyck, Courbet, and Renoir.

Just as successful and affecting is the personal, mystical vision of William Blake appropriately expressed in his watercolors and hand-colored prints of symbolic, contorted figures. And just as aesthetically brilliant are the agitated woodcuts and paintings depicting the psychological introspection and emotional turmoil of expressionist artists such as Edvard Munch, Oskar Kokoschka, Egon Schiele, and Max Beckman.

PROSE

GENERAL RULES AND IDEAS

Why do people write prose? Certainly such a question has a built-in counter: As opposed to writing what, poetry? One possible answer is that the person is a poor poet. The requirements and restrictions of the various genres make different demands upon a writer; most writers find their niche and stay there, secure in their private "comfort zone." Shakespeare stuck with poetry; Hemingway made his name writing novels. If either did venture outside of his literary domain, the world took little note.

Students are sometimes confused as to what exactly prose is. Basically, prose is **not** poetry. Prose is what we write and speak most of the time in our everyday intercourse: unmetered, unrhymed language. Which is not to say that prose does not have its own rhythms—language, whether written or spoken, has cadence and balance. And certainly prose can have instances of rhyme or assonance, alliteration or onomatopoeia. Language is, after all, phonic.

Furthermore, prose may be either *fiction* or *non-fiction*. A novel (like a short story) is fiction; an autobiography is non-fiction. While a novel (or short story) may have autobiographical elements, an autobiography is presumed to be entirely factual. Essays are usually described in other terms: expository, argumentative, persuasive, critical, narrative. Essays may have elements of either fiction or non-fiction, but are generally classed as a separate subgenre.

Satire, properly speaking, is not a genre at all, but rather a *mode*, elements of which can be found in any category of literature—from poetry and drama to novels and essays. Satire is a manifestation of authorial attitude (tone) and purpose. Our discussion of satire will be limited to its use in prose.

But we have not addressed the initial question: "Why do people write prose?" The answer depends, in part, on the writer's intent. If he or she wishes to tell a rather long story, filled with many characters and subplots, interlaced with motifs, symbols, and themes, with time and space to develop interrelationships and to present descriptive passages, the writer generally chooses the novel as his or her medium. If he or she believes the story can be presented more compactly and less complexly, he or she may choose the novella or the short story.

These subgenres require from the reader a different kind of involvement than does the essay. The essay, rather than presenting a story from which the reader may discern meaning through the skillful analysis of character, plot, symbol, and language, presents a relatively straightforward account of the writer's opinion(s) on an endless array of topics. Depending upon the type of essay, the reader may become informed (expository), provoked (argumentative), persuaded, enlightened (critical), or, in the case of the narrative essay, better acquainted with the writer who wishes to illustrate a point with his or her story, whether it is autobiographical or fictitious.

Encountering satire in prose selections demands that the reader be sensitive to the nuances of language and form, that he or she detect the double-edged sword of irony, and that they correctly assess both the writer's tone and his purpose.

Readers of prose, like readers of poetry, seek aesthetic pleasure, entertainment, and knowledge, not necessarily in that order. Fiction offers worlds—real and imagined—in which characters and ideas, events and language, interact in ways familiar and unfamiliar. As readers, we take delight in the wisdom we fancy we have acquired from a novel or short story. Non-fiction offers viewpoints which we may find comforting or horrifying, amusing or sobering, presented by the author rather than by a once-removed persona. Thus, we are tempted to believe that somehow the truths presented in non-fiction are more "real" than the truths revealed by fiction. But we must resist! Truth is not "genre-specific."

READING NOVELS

Most literary handbooks will define a novel as an extended fictional prose narrative, derived from the Italian *novella*, meaning "tale" or "piece of news." The term "novelle," meaning short tales, was applied to works such as Boccaccio's *The Decameron*, a collection of stories which had an impact on later works such as Chaucer's *Canterbury Tales*. In most European countries, the word for novel is *roman*, short for *romance*, which was applied to longer verse narratives (Malory's *Morte d'Arthur*), which were later written in prose. Early romances were associated with "legendary, imaginative, and poetic material"—tales "of the long ago or the far away or the imaginatively improbable"; novels, on the other hand, were felt to be "bound by the facts of the actual world and the laws of probability" (*A Handbook to Literature*, C. Hugh Holman, p. 354).

The novel has, over some 600 years, developed into many special forms which are classified by subject matter: detective novel, psychological novel, historical novel, regional novel, picaresque novel, Gothic novel, stream-of-consciousness novel, epistolary novel, and so on. These terms, of course, are not exhaustive nor mutually exclusive. Furthermore, depending on the conventions of the author's time period, his style, and his outlook on life, his *mode* may be termed *realism, romanticism, impressionism, expressionism, naturalism,* or *neo-classicism* (Holman, p. 359).

Our earlier description of a novel ("...a rather long story, filled with many characters and subplots, interlaced with motifs, symbols, and themes, with time and space to develop interrelationships and to present descriptive passages") is satisfactory for our purposes here. The works generally included on the LAST are those which have stood the test of time in significance, literary merit, and reader popularity. New works are incorporated into the canon which is a reflection of what works are being taught in literature classes. Teachers begin to teach those works which are included frequently among the questions. So the process is circular, but the standards remain high for inclusion.

Analyzing novels is a bit like asking the journalist's five questions: what? who? why? where? and how? The what? is the story, the narrative, the plot and subplots. Most students are familiar with Freytag's Pyramid, originally designed to describe the structure of a five-act drama but now widely used to analyze fiction as well. The stages generally specified are *introduction* or *exposition*, *complication*, *rising action*, *climax*, *falling action*, and *denouement* or *conclusion*. As the novel's events are charted, the "change which structures the story" should emerge. There are many events in a long narrative; but generally only one set of events comprises the "real" or "significant" story.

Subplots often parallel or serve as counterpoints to the main plot line, serving to enhance the central story. Minor characters sometimes have essentially the same conflicts and goals as the major characters, but the consequences of the outcome seem less important. Sometimes the parallels involve reversals of characters and situations, creating similar yet distinct differences in the outcomes. Nevertheless, seeing the parallels makes understanding the major plot line less difficult.

Sometimes an author divides the novel into chapters—named or unnamed, perhaps just numbered. Or he or she might divide the novel into "books" or "parts," with chapters as subsections. Readers should take their cue from these divisions; the author must have had some reason for them. Take note of what happens in each larger section, as well as within the smaller chapters. Whose progress is being followed? What event or occurrence is being foreshadowed or prepared for? What causal or other relationships are there between sections and events? Some writers, such as Steinbeck in *The Grapes of Wrath*, use intercalary chapters, alternating between the "real" story (the Joads) and peripheral or parallel stories (the Okies and migrants in general). Look for the pattern of such organization; try to see the interrelationships of these alternating chapters.

Of course, plots cannot happen in isolation from characters, the *who?* element of a story. Not only are there major and minor characters to consider; we need to note whether the various characters are *static* or *dynamic*. Static characters do not change in significant ways—that is, in ways which relate to the story which is structuring the novel. A character may die, i.e., change from alive to dead, and still be static, unless his death is central to the narrative. For instance, in Golding's *Lord of the Flies*, the boy with the mulberry birthmark apparently dies in a fire early in the novel. Momentous as any person's death is, this boy's death is not what the novel is about. However, when Simon is killed, and later Piggy, the narrative is directly impacted because the reason

NYSTCE – New York State Teacher Certification Exam

for their deaths is central to the novel's theme regarding man's innate evil. A dynamic character may change only slightly in his attitudes, but those changes may be the very ones upon which the narrative rests. For instance, Siddhartha begins as a very pure and devout Hindu but is unfulfilled spiritually. He eventually does achieve spiritual contentment, but his change is more a matter of degree than of substance. He is not an evil man who attains salvation, nor a pious man who becomes corrupt. It is the process of his search, the stages in his pilgrimage, which structure the novel *Siddhartha*.

We describe major characters or "actors" in novels as *protagonists* or *antagonists*. Built into those two terms is the Greek word *agon,* meaning "struggle." The *pro*tagonist struggles toward or for someone or something; the *ant(i)*agonist struggles against someone or something. The possible conflicts are usually cited as man against himself, man against man, man against society, man against nature. Sometimes more than one of these conflicts appears in a story, but usually one is dominant and is the structuring device.

A character can be referred to as *stock*, meaning that he exists because the plot demands it. For instance, a Western with a gunman who robs the bank will require a number of stock characters: the banker's lovely daughter, the tough but kindhearted barmaid, the cowardly white-shirted citizen who sells out the hero to save his own skin, and the young freckle-faced lad who shoots the bad guy from a second-story hotel window.

Or a character can be a *stereotype*, without individuating characteristics. For instance, a sheriff in a small Southern town; a football player who is all brawn; a librarian clucking over her prized books; the cruel commandant of a POW camp.

Characters often serve as *foils* for other characters, enabling us to see one or more of them better. A classic example is Tom Sawyer, the Romantic foil for Huck Finn's Realism. Or, in Lee's *To Kill a Mockingbird*, Scout as the naive observer of events which her brother Jem, four years older, comes to understand from the perspective of the adult world.

Sometimes characters are *allegorical*, standing for qualities or concepts rather than for actual personages. For instance, Jim Casey (initials "J. C.") in *The Grapes of Wrath* is often regarded as a Christ figure, pure and self-sacrificing in his aims for the migrant workers. Or Kamala, Siddhartha's teacher in the art of love, whose name comes from the tree whose bark is used as a purgative; purges him of his ascetic ways on his road to self-hood and spiritual fulfillment.

Other characters are fully three-dimensional, "rounded," "mimetic" of humans in all their virtue, vice, hope, despair, strength and weakness. This verisimilitude aids the author in creating characters who are credible and plausible, without being dully predictable and mundane.

The interplay of plot and characters determines in large part the *theme* of a work, the why? of the story. First of all, we must distinguish between a mere topic and a genuine theme or thesis; and then between a theme and contributing *motifs*. A *topic* is a phrase, such as "man's inhumanity to man"; or "the fickle nature of fate." A *theme*, however, turns a phrase into a statement: "Man's inhumanity to man is barely concealed by 'civilization.'" Or "Man is a helpless pawn, at the mercy of fickle fate." Many writers may deal with the same topic, such as the complex nature of true love; but their themes may vary widely, from "True love will always win out in the end," to "Not even true love can survive the cruel ironies of fate."

To illustrate the relationship between plot, character, and theme, let's examine two familiar fairy tales. In "The Ugly Duckling," the structuring story line is "Once upon a time there was an ugly duckling, who in turn became a beautiful swan." In this case, the duckling did nothing to merit either his ugliness nor his eventual transformation; but he did not curse fate. He only wept and waited, lonely and outcast. And when he became beautiful, he did not gloat; he eagerly joined the other members of his flock, who greatly admired him. The theme here essentially is: "Good things come to him who waits," or "Life is unfair—you don't get what you deserve, nor deserve what you get"? What happens to the theme if the ugly duckling remains an ugly duckling: "Some guys just never get a break"?

Especially rewarding to examine for the interdependence of plot and theme is "Cinderella": "Once upon a time, a lovely, sweet-natured young girl was forced to labor for and serve her ugly and ungrateful stepmother and two stepsisters. But thanks to her fairy godmother, Cinderella and the Prince marry, and live happily ever after."

We could change events (plot elements) at any point, but let's take the penultimate scene where the Prince's men come to the door with the single glass slipper. Cinderella has been shut away so that she is not present when the other women in the house try on the slipper. Suppose that the stepmother or either of the two stepsisters tries on the slipper—and it fits! Cinderella is in the back room doing the laundry, and her family waltzes out the door to the palace and she doesn't even get an invitation to the wedding. And imagine the Prince's dismay when the ugly, one-slippered lady lifts her wedding veil for the consummating kiss! Theme: "There is no justice in the world, for those of low or high station"; or "Virtue is not its own reward"?

Or let's say that during the slipper-test scene, the stepsisters, stepmother, and finally Cinderella all try on the shoe, but to no avail. And then in sashays the Fairy Godmother, who gives them all a knowing smirk, puts out her slipper-sized foot and cackles hysterically, like the mechanical witch in the penny arcade. Theme: "You can't trust anybody these days"; or, a favorite statement of theme, "Appearances can be deceiving." The link between plot and theme is very strong, indeed.

Skilled writers often employ *motifs* to help unify their works. A motif is a detail or element of the story which is repeated throughout, and which may even become symbolic. Television shows are ready examples of the use of motifs. A medical show, with many scenes alternately set in the hospital waiting room and operating room, uses elements such as the pacing, anxious parent or loved one, the gradually filling ashtray, the large wall clock whose hands melt from one hour to another. And in the operating room, the half-masked surgeon whose brow is frequently mopped by the nurse; the gloved hand open-palmed to receive scalpel, sponge, and so on; the various oscilloscopes giving read-outs of the patient's very fragile condition; the expanding and collapsing bladder manifesting that the patient is indeed breathing; and, again, the wall clock, assuring us that this procedure is taking forever. These are all motifs, details which in concert help convince the reader that this story occurs in a hospital, and that the mood is pretty tense, that the medical team is doing all it can, and that Mom and Dad will be there when Junior or Sissy wakes up.

But motifs can become symbolic. The oscilloscope line quits blipping, levels out, and gives off the ominous hum. And the doctor's gloved hand sets down the scalpel and shuts off the oscilloscope. In the waiting room, Dad crushes the empty cigarette pack; Mom quits pacing and sinks into the sofa. The door to the waiting room swings shut silently behind the retreating doctor. All these elements signal "It's over, finished."

This example is very crude and mechanical, but motifs in the hands of a skillful writer are valuable devices. And in isolation, and often magnified, a single motif can become a controlling image with great significance. For instance, Emma Bovary's shoes signify her obsession with material things; and when her delicate slippers become soiled as she crosses the dewy grass to meet her lover, we sense the impurity of her act as well as its futility. Or when wise Piggy, in *Lord of the Flies,* is reduced to one lens in his specs, and finally to no specs at all, we see the loss of insight and wisdom on the island, and chaos follows.

Setting is the where? element of the story. But setting is also the *when* element: time of day, time of year, time period or year; it is the dramatic moment, the precise intersection of time and space when this story is being told. Setting is also the atmosphere: positive or negative ambiance, calm, chaotic, Gothic, Romantic. The question for the reader to answer is whether the setting is ultimately essential to the plot/theme, or whether it is incidental; i.e., could this story/theme have been told successfully in another time and/or place? For instance, could the theme in *Lord of the Flies* be made manifest if the boys were not on an island? Could they have been isolated in some other place? Does it matter whether the "war" which they are fleeing is WWII or WWIII or some other conflict, in terms of the theme?

Hopefully, the student will see that the four elements of plot, character, theme, and setting are intertwined and largely interdependent. A work must really be read as a whole, rather than dissected and analyzed in discrete segments.

The final question, how?, relates to an author's style. Style involves language (word choice), syntax (word order, sentence type and length), the balance between narration and dialogue, the choice of narrative voice (first person participant, third person with limited omniscience), use of descriptive passages, and other aspects of the actual words on the page which are basically irrelevant to the first four elements (plot, character, theme, and setting). Stylistic differences are fairly easy to spot among such diverse writers as Jane Austen, whose style is—to today's reader—very formal and mannered; Mark Twain, whose style is very casual and colloquial; William Faulkner, whose prose often spins on without punctuation or paragraphs far longer than the reader can hold either the thought or his breath; and Hemingway, whose dense but spare, pared-down style has earned the epithet, "Less is more."

READING SHORT STORIES

The modern short story differs from earlier short fiction such as the parable, fable, and tale, in its emphasis on character development through scenes rather than summary: through *showing* rather than *telling*. Gaining popularity in the 19th century, the short story generally was realistic, presenting detailed accounts of the lives of middle-class personages. This tendency toward realism dictates that the plot be grounded in *probability*, with causality fully in operation. Furthermore, the characters are human with recognizable human motivations, both social and psychological. Setting—time and place—is realistic rather than fantastic. And, as Poe stipulated, the elements of plot, character, setting, style, point of view, and theme all work toward a single *unified* effect.

However, some modern writers have stretched these boundaries and have mixed in elements of nonrealism—such as the supernatural and the fantastic—sometimes switching back and forth between realism and nonrealism, confusing the reader who is expecting conventional fiction. Barth's "Lost in the Funhouse" and Allen's "The Kugelmass Episode" are two stories which are not, strictly speaking, *realistic*. However, if the reader will approach and accept this type of story on its own terms, he or she will be better able to understand and appreciate them fully.

Unlike the novel, which has time and space to develop characters and interrelationships, the short story must rely on flashes of insight and revelation to develop plot and characters. The "slice of life" in a short story is of necessity much narrower than that in a novel; the time span is much shorter, the focus much tighter. To attempt anything like the panoramic canvas available to the novelist would be to view fireworks through a soda straw: occasionally pretty, but ultimately not very satisfying or enlightening.

The elements of the short story are those of the novel, discussed earlier. However, because of the compression of time and concentration of effect, probably the short story writer's most important decision is *point of view*. A narrator may be *objective*, presenting information without bias or comment. Hemingway frequently uses the objective *third-person* narrator, presenting scenes almost dramatically, i.e., with a great deal of dialogue and very little narrative, none of which directly reveals the thoughts or feelings of the characters. The third-person narrator may, however, be less objective in presentation, directly revealing the thoughts and feelings, of one or more of the characters, as Chopin does in "The Story of an Hour." We say that such a narrator is fully or partially *omniscient*, depending on how complete its knowledge is of the characters' psychological and emotional makeup. The least objective narrator is the *first-person* narrator, who presents information from the perspective of a single character who is a participant in the action. Such a narrative choice allows the author to present the discrepancies between the writer's/reader's perceptions and those of the narrator.

One reason the choice of narrator, the point of view from which to tell the story, is immensely important in a short story is that the narrator reveals character and event in ways which affect our understanding of theme. For instance, in Faulkner's "A Rose for Emily," the unnamed narrator who seems to be a townsperson recounts the story out of chronological order, juxtaposing events whose causality and significance are uncertain. The narrator withholds information which would explain events being presented, letting the reader puzzle over Emily Grierson's motivations, a device common in detective fiction. In fact, the narrator presents contradictory information, making the reader alternately pity and resent the spinster. When we examine the imagery and conclude that Miss Emily and her house represent the decay and decadence of the Old South which resisted the invasion of "progress" from the North, we see the importance of setting and symbol in relation to theme.

Similarly, in Mansfield's "Bliss," the abundant description of setting creates the controlling image of the lovely pear tree. But this symbol of fecundity becomes ironic when Bertha Young belatedly feels sincere and overwhelming desire for her husband. The third-person narrator's omniscience is limited to Bertha's thoughts and feelings; otherwise we would have seen her husband's infidelity with Miss Fulton.

In O'Connor's "Good Country People," the narrator is broadly omniscient, but the reader is still taken by surprise at the cruelty of the Bible salesman who seduces Joy-Hulga. That he steals her artificial leg is perhaps poetic justice, since she (with her numerous degrees) had fully intended to seduce him ("just good country people"). The story's title, the characters' names—Hopewell, Freeman, Joy; the salesman's professed Christianity, the Bibles hollowed out to hold whiskey and condoms, add to the irony of Mrs. Freeman's final comment on the young man: "Some can't be that simple… I know I never could."

The *initiation story* frequently employs the first-person narrator. To demonstrate the subtle differences which can occur in stories which ostensibly have the same point of view and general theme, let's look at three: "A Christmas Memory" (Capote), "Araby" (Joyce), and "A & P" (Updike).

Early in "A Christmas Memory," Capote's narrator identifies himself:

> The person to whom she is speaking is myself. I am seven; she is sixty-something. We are cousins, very distant ones, and we have lived together—well, as long as I can remember. Other people inhabit the house, relatives; and though they have power over us, and frequently make us cry, we are not, on the whole, too much aware of them. We are each other's best friend. She calls me Buddy, in memory of a boy who was formerly her best friend. The other Buddy died in the 1880's, when she was still a child. She is still a child.

Buddy and his cousin, who is called only "my friend," save their meager earnings throughout the year in order to make fruitcakes at Christmas to give mainly to "persons we've met maybe once, perhaps not at all… Like President Roosevelt…. Or Abner Packer, the driver of the six o'clock bus from Mobile, who exchanges waves with us everyday…." Their gifts to one another each year are always handmade, often duplicates of the year before, like the kites they present on what was to be their last Christmas together.

Away at boarding school, when Buddy receives word of his friend's death, it "merely confirms a piece of news some secret vein had already received, severing from me an irreplaceable part of myself, letting it loose like a kite on a broken string. That is why, walking across a school campus on this particular December morning, I keep searching the sky. As if I expected to see, rather like hearts, a lost pair of kites hurrying toward heaven."

Buddy's characterizations of his friend are also self-revelatory. He and she are peers, equals, despite their vast age difference. They are both totally unselfish, joying in the simple activities mandated by their economic circumstances. They are both "children."

The story is told in present tense, making the memories from the first paragraphs seem as "real" and immediate as those from many years later. And Buddy's responses from the early years ("Well, I'm disappointed. Who wouldn't be? With socks, a Sunday school shirt, some handkerchiefs, a hand-me-down sweater and a year's subscription to a religious magazine for children. *The Little Shepherd*. It makes me boil. It really does.") are as true to his seven-year-old's perspective, as are those when he, much older, has left home ("I have a new home too. But it doesn't count. Home is where my friend is, and there I never go.").

The youthful narrator in "A & P" also uses present tense, but not consistently, which gives his narrative a very colloquial, even unschooled flavor. Like Buddy, Sammy identifies himself in the opening paragraph: "In walks these three girls in nothing but bathing suits. I'm in the third checkout slot, with my back to the door, so I don't see them until they're over by the bread." And later, "Stokesie's married, with two babies chalked up on his fuselage already, but as far as I can tell that's the only difference. He's twenty-two, and I was nineteen this April." The girls incur the wrath of the store manager, who scolds them for their inappropriate dress. And Sammy, in his adolescent idealism, quits on the spot; although he realizes that he does not want to "do this" to his parents, he tells us "… it seems to me that once you begin a gesture it's fatal not to go through with it." But his *beau geste* is ill-spent: "I look around for my girls, but they're gone, of course.... I could see Lengel in my place in the slot, checking the sheep through. His face was dark gray and his back stiff, as if he'd just had an injection of iron, and my stomach kind of fell as I felt how hard the world was going to be to me hereafter."

Like Buddy, Sammy tells his story from a perch not too distant from the events he recounts. Both narrators still feel the immediacy of their rites of passage very strongly. Buddy, however, reveals himself to be a more admirable character, perhaps because his story occurs mainly when he is seven—children tend not to be reckless in the way that Sammy is. Sammy was performing for an audience, doing things he knew would cause pain to himself and his family, for the sake of those three girls who never gave him the slightest encouragement and whom he would probably never even see again.

In "Araby," the unnamed narrator tells of a boyhood crush he had on the older sister of one of his chums: "I thought little of the future. I did not know whether I would ever speak to her or not or, if I spoke to her, how I could tell her of my confused adoration. But my body was like a harp and her words and gestures were like fingers running upon the wires." She asks the boy if he is going to Araby, a "splendid bazaar," and reveals that she cannot. He promises to go himself and bring her something. But his uncle's late homecoming delays the boy's excursion until the bazaar is nearly closed for the night, and he is unable to find an appropriate gift. Forlornly, "I turned away slowly and walked down the middle of the bazaar.... Gazing up into the darkness I saw myself as a creature driven and derided by vanity; and my eyes burned with anguish and anger." This narrator is recounting his story from much further away than either Buddy or Sammy tells his own. The narrator of "Araby" has the perspective of an adult, looking back at a very important event in his boyhood. His "voice" reflects wisdom born of experience. The incident was very painful then; but its memory, while poignant, is no longer devastating. Like Sammy, this narrator sees the dichotomy between his adolescent idealism and the mundane reality of "romance." However, the difference is in the narrator's ability to turn the light on himself; Sammy is still so close to the incident that he very likely would whip off his checker's apron again if the girls returned to the A & P. The "Araby" narrator has "mellowed," and can see the futility—and the necessity—of adolescent love.

READING ESSAYS

Essays fall into four rough categories: *speculative*, *argumentative*, *narrative*, and *expository*. Depending on the writer's purpose, his essay will fit more or less into one or these groupings.

The speculative essay is so named because, as its Latin root suggests, it *looks* at ideas; explores them rather than explains them. While the speculative essay may be said to be *meditative*, it often makes one or more points. But the thesis may not be as obvious or clear-cut as that in an expository or argumentative essay. The writer deals with ideas in an associative manner, playing with ideas in a looser structure than he would in an expository or argumentative essay. This "flow" may even produce *intercalary* paragraphs, which present alternately a narrative of sorts and thoughtful responses to the events being recounted, as in White's "The Ring of Time."

The purposes of the argumentative essay, on the other hand, are always clear: to present a point and provide evidence, which may be factual or anecdotal, and to support it. The structure is usually very formal, as in a debate, with counterpositions and counterarguments. Whatever the organizational pattern, the writer's intent in an argumentative essay is to persuade his reader of the validity of some claim, as Bacon does in "Of Love."

Narrative and expository essays have elements of both the speculative and argumentative modes. The narrative essay may recount an incident or a series of incidents and is almost always autobiographical, in order to make a point, as in Orwell's "Shooting an Elephant." The informality of the storytelling makes the narrative essay less insistent than the argumentative essay, but more directed than the speculative essay.

Students are probably most familiar with the expository essay, the primary purpose of which is to explain and clarify ideas. While the expository essay may have narrative elements, that aspect is minor and subservient to that of explanation. Furthermore, while nearly all essays have some element of persuasion, argumentation is incidental in the expository essay. In any event, the four categories—speculative, argumentative, narrative, and expository— are neither exhaustive nor mutually exclusive.

As non-fiction, essays have a different set of elements from novels and short stories: *voice, style, structure*, and *thought*.

Voice in non-fiction is similar to the narrator's tone in fiction; but the major difference is in who is "speaking." In fiction, the author is not the speaker—the narrator is the speaker. Students sometimes have difficulty with this distinction, but it is necessary if we are to preserve the integrity of the fictive "story." In an essay, however, the author speaks directly to the reader, even if he is presenting ideas which he may not actually espouse personally— as in a satire. This directness creates the writer's tone, his or her attitude toward his subject.

Style in non-fiction derives from the same elements as style in fiction: word choice, syntax, balance between dialogue and narration, voice, use of description—those things specifically related to words on the page. Generally speaking, an argumentative essay will be written in a more formal style than will a narrative essay, and a meditative essay will be less formal than an expository essay. But such generalizations are only descriptive, not prescriptive.

Structure and thought, the final elements of essays, are so intertwined as to be inextricable. We must be aware that to change the structure of an essay will alter its meaning. For instance, in White's "The Ring of Time," to abandon the *intercalary* paragraph organization, separating the paragraphs which narrate the scenes with the young circus rider from those which reflect on the circularity and linearity of time, would alter our understanding of the essay's thesis. Writers signal structural shifts with alterations in focus, as well as with visual clues (spacing), verbal clues—(*but, therefore, however*), or shifts in the kind of information being presented (personal, scientific, etc).

Thought is perhaps the single element which most distinguishes non-fiction from fiction. The essayist chooses this form not to tell a story but to present an idea. Whether he or she chooses the speculative, narrative, argumentative, or expository format, the essayist has something on his or her mind that he or she wants to convey to the reader. It is this idea which we are after when we analyze an essay.

Often anthologized is Orwell's "Shooting an Elephant," a narrative essay (presumably) recounting the writer's experience in Burma as an officer of the British law that ruled the poverty-ridden people of a small town. Orwell begins with two paragraphs which explain that, as a white, European authority figure, he was subjected to taunts and abuse by the natives. Ironically, he sympathized with the Burmese and harbored fairly strong anti-British feelings, regarding the imperialists as the oppressors rather than the saviors. He tells us that he felt caught, trapped between his position of authority which he himself resented, and the hatred of those he was required to oversee.

The body of the essay—some eleven paragraphs—relates the incident with an otherwise tame elephant gone "must" which had brought chaos and destruction to the village. Only occasionally does Orwell interrupt the narrative to reveal his reactions directly, but his descriptions of the Burmese are sympathetically drawn. The language is heavily connotative, revealing the helplessness of the villagers against both the elephant and the miserable circumstances of their lives.

Orwell recounts how, having sent for an elephant gun, he found that he was compelled to shoot the animal, even though its destruction was by now unwarranted and even ill-advised, given the value of the elephant to the village. But the people expected it, demanded it; the white man realized that he did not have dominion over these people of color after all. They were in charge, not he.

To make matters worse, Orwell bungles the "murder" of the beast, which takes half an hour to die in great agony. And in the aftermath of discussions of the rightness or wrongness of his action, Orwell wonders if anyone realizes he killed the elephant only to save face. It is the final sentence of the final paragraph which directly reveals the author's feelings, although he has made numerous indirect references to them throughout the essay. Coupled with the opening paragraphs, this conclusion presents British imperialism of the period in a very negative light: "the unable doing the unnecessary to the ungrateful."

Having discovered Orwell's main idea, we must look at the other elements (voice, style, structure) to see *how* he communicates it to the reader. The voice of the first-person narrative is fairly formal, yet remarkably candid, using connotation to color our perception of the events. Orwell's narrative has many complex sentences, with vivid descriptive phrases in series, drawing our eye along the landscape and through the crowds as he ponders his next move. Structurally, the essay first presents a premise about British imperialism, then moves to a gripping account of the officer's reluctant shooting of the elephant; and ends with an admission of his own culpability as an agent of the institution he detests. Orwell frequently signals shifts between his role as officer and his responses as a humane personage with *but*, or with dashes to set off his responses to the events he is recounting.

READING SATIRE

Satire, is a *mode* which may be employed by writers of various genres: poetry, drama, fiction, non-fiction. It is more a perspective than a product.

Satire mainly exposes and ridicules, derides and denounces vice, folly, evil, stupidity, as these qualities manifest themselves in persons, groups of persons, ideas, institutions, customs, or beliefs. While the satirist has many techniques at his disposal, there are basically only two types of satire: gentle or harsh, depending on the author's intent, his audience, and his methods.

The terms *romanticism, realism,* and *naturalism* can help us understand the role of *satire*. Romanticism sees the world idealistically, as perfectible if not perfect. Realism sees the world as it is, with healthy doses of both good and bad. Naturalism sees the world as imperfect, with evil often triumphing over good. The satirist is closer to the naturalist than he is to the romantic or realist, for both the satirist and the naturalist focus on what is wrong with the world, intending to expose the foibles of man and his society. The difference between them lies in their techniques. The naturalist is very direct and does not necessarily employ humor; the satirist is more subtle, and does.

For instance, people plagued with overpopulation and starvation is not, on first glance, material for humor. Many works have treated such conditions with sensitivity, bringing attention to the plight of the world's unfortunate. Steinbeck's *Grapes of Wrath* is such a work. However, Swift's "A Modest Proposal" takes essentially the same circumstances and holds them up for our amused examination. How does the satirist make an un-funny topic humorous? And why would he do so?

The satirist's techniques— weapons—include *irony, parody, reversal* or *inversion, hyperbole, understatement, sarcasm, wit, invective.* By exaggerating characteristics, by saying the opposite of what he or she means, by using cleverness to make cutting or even cruel remarks at the expense of the subject, the writer of satire can call the reader's attention to those things he or she believes are repulsive, despicable, or destructive.

Whether he or she uses more harsh (Juvenalian) or more gentle (Horatian) satire depends upon the writer's attitude and intent. Is he or she merely flaunting clever intellect, playing with words for our amusement or to inflate his or her own sense of superiority? Is he or she probing the psychological motivations for the foolish or destructive actions of some person(s)? Is he or she determined to waken an unenlightened or apathetic audience, moving its members to thought or action? Are the flaws which the satirist is pointing out truly destructive or evil, or are they the faults we would all recognize in ourselves if we glanced in the mirror, not admirable but not really harmful to ourselves or society? Is the author amused, sympathetic, objective, irritated, scornful, bitter, pessimistic, mocking? The reader needs to identify the satirist's purpose and tone. Its subtlety sometimes makes satire a difficult mode to detect and to understand.

Irony is perhaps the satirist's most powerful weapon. The basis of irony is inversion or reversal, doing or saying the opposite or the unexpected. Shakespeare's famous sonnet beginning "My mistress' eyes are nothing like the sun…" is an ironic tribute to the speaker's beloved, who, he finally declares is "as rare/As any she belied with false compare." At the same time,

Shakespeare is poking fun at the sonnet form as it was used by his contemporaries—himself included—-to extol the virtues of their ladies. By selecting a
woman who, by his own description, is physically unattractive in every way
imaginable, and using the conventions of the love sonnet to present her many
flaws, he has inverted the sonnet tradition. And then by asserting that she
compares favorably with any of the other ladies whose poet-lovers have lied
about their virtues, he presents us with the unexpected twist. Thus, he satirizes
both the love sonnet form and its subject by using irony.

Other notable poetic satires include Koch's "Variations on a Theme by
William Carlos Williams," in which he parodies Williams "This is Just to
Say." Koch focuses on the simplicity and directness of Williams' imagery and
makes the form and ideas seem foolish and trivial. In "Boom!," Nemerov
takes issue with a pastor's assertion that modern technology has resulted in
a concomitant rise in religious activities and spiritual values. Nemerov
catalogues the instant, disposable, and extravagant aspects of Americans'
lifestyles, which result in "pray as you go... pilgrims" for whom religion is
another convenience, commercial rather than spiritual.

Satire in drama is also common; Wilde's "The Importance of Being
Earnest" is wonderfully funny in its constant word play (notably on the name
Earnest) and its relentless ridiculing of the superficiality which Wilde saw as
characteristic of British gentry. Barrie's "The Admirable Chrichton" has a
similar theme, with the added assertion that it is the "lower" or servant class
which is truly superior—again, the ironic reversal so common in satire. Both
of these plays are mild in their ridicule; the authors do not expect or desire any
change in society or in the viewer. The satire is gentle; the satirists are amused,
or perhaps bemused at the society whose foibles they expose.

Classic novels that employ satire include Swift's *Gulliver's Travels* and
Voltaire's *Candide*, both of which fairly vigorously attack aspects of the
religions, governments, and prevailing intellectual beliefs of their respective
societies. A modern novel which uses satire is Heller's *Catch-22*, which is
basically an attack on war and the government's bureaucratic bungling of men
and material, specifically in WWII. But by extension, Heller is also viewing
with contempt the unmotivated, illogical, capricious behavior of all institutions which operate by that basic law, "catch-22." Like Swift and Voltaire,
Heller is angry. And although his work, like the other two, has humor and wit,
exaggeration and irony, his purpose is more than intellectual entertainment
for his readers. Heller hopes for reform.

Heller's attack is frontal, his assault direct. Swift chose to couch his tale in a fantastic setting with imaginary creatures in order to present his views with impunity. The audience, as well as the times, also affect the satirist's work. If the audience is hostile, the writer must veil his theme; if the audience is indifferent, he must jolt them with bitter and reviling language if he desires change. If he does not fear reprisals, the satirist may take any tone he pleases.

We can see satire in operation in two adaptations of the biblical story of King Solomon, who settled the dispute between two mothers regarding an infant: Cut the baby in two and divide it between you, he told them. The rightful mother protested, and was promptly awarded the child. The story is meant to attest to the King's wisdom and understanding of parental love, in this case.

However, Twain's Huck Finn has some difficulty persuading runaway slave Jim that Solomon was wise. Jim insists that Solomon, having fathered "'bout five million chillen," was "waseful…. *He* as soon chop a chile in two as a cat. Dey's plenty mo'. A chile er two, mo' er less, warn't no consekens to Solermun, dad fetch him!" Twain is ridiculing not only Jim's ingenuousness, as he does throughout the novel; he is also deflating time-honored beliefs about the Bible and its traditional heroes, as he earlier does with the account of Moses and the "bulrushers." While Twain's tone is fairly mild, his intent shows through as serious; Twain was disgusted with traditional Christianity and its hypocritical followers, as we see later in *Huck Finn* when young Buck Grangerford is murdered in the feud with the Shepherdsons: "I wished I hadn't ever come ashore that night to see such things."

A second satiric variation on the Solomon theme appears in Asprin's *Myth Adventures*, in the volume *Hit or Myth*. Skeebe, the narrator, realizes that he, as King pro-tem, must render a decision regarding the ownership of a cat. Hoping to inspire them to compromise, he decrees that they divide the cat between them: "Instead they thanked me for my wisdom, shook hands, and left smiling, presumably to carve up their cat." He concludes that many of the citizens of this realm "don't have both oars in the water," a conclusion very like Huck's: "I never see such a nigger. If he got a notion in his head once, there warn't no getting it out again." The citizens' unthinking acceptance of the infallibility of authority is as laughable as Jim's out-of-hand rejection of Solomon's wisdom because no wise man would "want to live in the mids' er sich a blim-blammin' all de time" as would prevail in the harem with the King's "million wives."

POETRY

Opening a book to study for an examination is perhaps the worst occasion on which to read poetry, or about poetry, because above all, poetry should be enjoyed; it is definitely "reading for pleasure." This last phrase seems to have developed recently to describe the reading we do other than for information or for study. Perhaps you personally would not choose poetry as pleasure reading because of the bad name poetry has received over the years. Some students regard the "old" poetry such as Donne's or Shelley's as effete (for "wimps" and "nerds" only, in current language), or modern poetry as too difficult or weird. It is hard to imagine that poetry was the "current language" for students growing up in the Elizabethan or Romantic eras. Whereas in our world information can be retrieved in a nanosecond, in those worlds time was plentiful to sit down, clear the mind and let poetry take over. Very often the meaning of a poem does not come across in a nanosecond and for the modern student this proves very frustrating. Sometimes it takes years for a poem to take on meaning—the reader simply knows that the poem sounds good and it provokes an emotional response that cannot be explained. With time, more emotional experience, more reading of similar experiences, more life, the reader comes to a meaning of that poem that satisfies for the time being. In a few more years that poem may take on a whole new meaning.

This is all very well for reading for pleasure but you are now called upon, in your present experience, to learn poetry for an important examination. Perhaps the first step in the learning process is to answer the question, "Why do people write poetry?" An easy answer is that they wish to convey an experience, an emotion, an insight, or an observation in a startling or satisfying way, one that remains in the memory for years. But why not use a straightforward sentence or paragraph? Why wrap up that valuable insight in fancy words, rhyme, paradox, meter, allusion, symbolism and all the other seeming mumbo-jumbo that explicators of poetry use? Why not just come right out and say it like "normal people" do? An easy answer to these questions is that poetry is not a vehicle for conveying meaning alone. Gerard Manley Hopkins, one of the great innovators of rhythm in poetry, claimed that poetry should be "heard for its own sake and interest even over and above its interest or meaning." Poetry provides intellectual stimulus of course, one of the best ways of studying a poem is to consider it a jigsaw puzzle presented to you whole, an integral work of art, which can be taken apart piece by piece (word by word), analyzed scientifically, labelled, and put back together again into a whole, and then the meaning is complete. But people write poetry to convey more than meaning.

T.S. Eliot maintained that the meaning of the poem existed purely to distract us "while the poem did its work." One interpretation of a poem's "work" is that it changes us in some way. We see the world in a new way because of the way the poet has seen it and told us about it. Maybe one of the reasons people write poetry is to encourage us to *see* things in the first place. Simple things like daffodils take on a whole new aspect when we read the way Wordsworth saw them. Why did Wordsworth write that poem? His sister had written an excellent account of the scene in her journal. Wordsworth not only evokes nature as we have never seen it before, alive, joyous, exuberant, he shows nature's healing powers, its restorative quality as the scene flashes "upon that inward eye/Which is the bliss of solitude." Bent over your books studying, how many times has a similar quality of nature's power in the memory come to you? Maybe for you a summer beach scene rather than daffodils by the lake is more meaningful, but the poet captures a moment that we have all experienced. The poet's magic is to make that moment new again.

If poets enhance our power of sight they also awaken the other senses as powerfully. We can hear Emily Dickinson's snake in the repeated "s" sound of the lines:

His notice sudden is—
The Grass divides as with a Comb—
A spotted shaft is seen—

and because of the very present sense of sound, we experience the indrawn gasp of breath of fear when the snake appears. We can touch the little chimneysweep's hair "that curled like a lamb's back" in William Blake's poetry and because of that tactile sense we are even more shocked to read that the child's hair is all shaved off so that the soot will not spoil its whiteness. We can smell the poison gas as Wilfred Owen's soldiers fumble with their gas masks; we can taste the blood gurgling in the poisoned lungs.

Poets write, then, to awaken the senses. They have crucial ideas but the words they use are often more important than the meaning. More important still than ideas and sense awakening is the poet's appeal to the emotions. And it is precisely this area that disturbs a number of students. Our modern society tends to block out emotions—we need reviews to tell us if we enjoyed a film, a critic's praise to see if a play or novel is worth our time. Poets write to overcome that blocking (very often it is their own blocking of emotion they seek to alleviate), but that is not to say that poetry immediately sets us laughing, crying, loving, hating. The important fact about the emotional release in poetry is that poets help us explore our own emotions, sometimes by shocking us, sometimes by drawing attention to balance and pattern, sometimes by cautioning us to move carefully in this inner world.

Poets tell us nothing really new. They tell us old truths about human emotions that we begin to restructure anew, to reread our experiences in light of theirs, to reevaluate our world view. Whereas a car manual helps us understand the workings of a particular vehicle, a poem helps us understand the inner workings of human beings. Poets frequently write to help their emotional life—the writing then becomes cathartic, purging or cleansing the inner life, feeding that part of us that separates us from the animal. Many poets might paraphrase Byron, who claimed that he had to write or go mad. Writer and reader of poetry enter into a collusion, each helping the other to find significance in the human world, to find safety in a seemingly alien world.

This last point brings any reader of poetry to ask the next question: Why read poetry? One might contend that a good drama, novel or short story might provide the same emotional experience. But a poem is much more accessible. Apart from the fact that poems are shorter than other genres, there is a unique directness to them which hinges purely on language. Poets can say in one or two lines what may take novelists and playwrights entire works to express. For example, Keats' lines—

Beauty is truth, truth beauty,—that is all
Ye know on earth, and all ye need to know—

Poetry can be studied, pondered, open to each reader's interpretations, linger in the memory with more emphasis than George Eliot's *Middlemarch*, or Ibsen's *The Wild Duck*, which endeavor to make the same point.

In your reading of poems remember that poetry is perhaps the oldest art and yet surrounds us without our even realizing it. Listeners thrilled to Homer's poetry; tribes chanted invocations to their gods; today we listen to pop-song lyrics and find ourselves, sometimes despite ourselves, repeating certain rhythmic lines. Advertisements we chuckle over or say we hate have a way of repeating themselves as we use the catchy phrase or snappy repetition. Both lyricists and advertisers cleverly use language, playing on the reader's/listener's/watcher's ability to pick up on a repeated sound or engaging rhythm or inner rhyme. Think of a time as a child when you thoroughly enjoyed poetry: nursery rhymes, ball-game rhythms, jump-rope patterns. Probably you had no idea of the meaning of the words ("Little Miss Muffet sat on a tuffet..." a tuffet?!) but you responded to the sound, the pattern. As adults we read poetry for that sense of sound and pattern. With more experience at reading poetry there is an added sense of pleasure as techniques are recognized: alliteration, onomatopoeia; forms of poetry become obvious—the sonnet, the rondelle. Even greater enjoyment comes from watching a poet's development, tracing themes and ideas, analyzing maturity in growth of imagery, use of rhythm.

To the novice reader of poetry, a poem can speak to the reader at a particular time and become an experience in itself. A freshman's experience after her mother's death exemplifies this. Shortly after the death, the student found Elizabeth Jenning's poem "Happy Families." Using the familiar names of the cards, Mrs. Beef and Master Bun, the poet describes how strangers try to help the family carry on their lives normally although one of the "happy family" is "missing." The card game continues although no one wants it to. At the end the players go back to their individual rooms and give way to their individual grief. The student described the relief at knowing that someone else had obviously experienced her situation where everyone in the family was putting up a front, strangers were being very kind, and a general emptiness prevailed because of that one missing family member. The poem satisfied. The student saw death through another's eyes; the experience was almost the same, yet helped the reader to reevaluate, to view a universal human response to grief as well as encourage her to deal with her own.

On reading a poem the brain works on several different levels: it responds to the sounds; it responds to the words themselves and their connotations; it responds to the emotions; it responds to the insights or learning of the world being revealed. For such a process poetry is a very good training ground—a boot camp—for learning how to read literature in general. All the other genres have elements of poetry within them. Learn to read poetry well and you will be a more accomplished reader, even of car manuals! Perhaps the best response to reading poetry comes from a poet herself, Emily Dickinson, who claimed that reading a book of poetry made her feel "as if the top of [her] head were taken off!"

Before such a process happens to you, here are some tips for reading poetry before and during the examination.

BEFORE THE EXAM

1. Make a list of poets and poems you remember; analyze poems you liked, disliked, loved, hated, and were indifferent to. Find the poems. Reread them and for each one analyze your *feelings*, first of all, about the poetry itself. Have your feelings changed? Now what do you like or hate? Then paraphrase the *meaning* of each poem.

Notice how the "magic" goes from the poem, i.e., "To Daffodils:" the poet sees many daffodils by the side of a lake and then thinks how the sight of them later comforts him.

2. Choose a poem at random from an anthology or one mentioned in this introduction. Read it a couple of times, preferably aloud, because the speaking voice will automatically grasp the rhythm and that will help the meaning. Do not become bogged-down in individual word connotation or the meaning of the poem—let the poetry do its "work" on you; absorb the poem as a whole jigsaw puzzle.

3. Now take the puzzle apart. Look carefully at the title. Sometimes a straightforward title helps you focus. Sometimes a playful title helps you get an angle on the meaning. "Happy Families," of course, is an ironic title because the family playing the card game of that name is not happy.

4. Look carefully at the punctuation. Does the sense of a line carry from one to another? Does a particular mark of punctuation strike you as odd? Ask why that mark was used.

5. Look carefully at the words. Try to find the meaning of words with which you are not familiar within the context. Familiar words may be used differently: ask why that particular use. Having tapped into your memory bank of vocabulary and you are still at a loss, go to a dictionary. Once you have the *denotation* of the word, start wondering about the *connotation*. Put yourself in the poet's position and think why that word was used.

6. Look carefully at all the techniques being used. You will gain these as you progress through this section and through the test preparation. As soon as you come across a new idea—"caesura" perhaps— learn the word, see how it applies to poetry, where it is used. Be on the lookout for it in other poetry. Ask yourself questions such as why the poet used alliteration here; why the rhythm changes there; why the poet uses a sonnet form and which sonnet form is in use. Forcing yourself to ask the WHY questions, and answering them, will train the brain to read more perceptively. Poetry is not accidental; poets are deliberate people; they do things for specific reasons. Your task under a learning situation is to discover WHY.

7.   Look carefully at the speaker. Is the poet using another persona? Who is that persona? What is revealed about the speaker? Why use that particular voice?

8.   Start putting all the pieces of the puzzle together. The rhythm helps the meaning. The word choice helps the imagery. The imagery adds to the meaning. Paraphrase the meaning. Ask yourself simple questions: What is the poet saying? How can I relate to what is being said? What does this poet mean to me? What does this poem contribute to human experience?

9.   Find time to read about the great names in poetry. Locate people within time areas and analyze what those times entailed. For example, the Elizabethans saw a contest between secular love and love of God. The Romantics (Wordsworth, Coleridge, Keats, Shelley, Byron) loved nature and saw God within nature. The Victorians (Tennyson, Blake) saw nature as a threat to mankind and God, being replaced by the profit cash-nexus of the Industrial Age. The moderns (T.S. Eliot, Pound, Yeats) see God as dead and man as hollow, unwanted and unsafe in an alien world. The Post-Moderns see life as "an accident," a comic/cosmic joke, fragmented, purposeless—often their topics will be political: apartheid, abortion, unjust imprisonment.

10.   Write a poem of your own. Choose a particular style; use the sonnet form; parody a famous poem; express yourself in free verse on a crucial, personal aspect of your life. Then analyze your own poetry with the above ideas.

DURING THE EXAM

You will have established a routine for reading poetry, but now you are under pressure, must work quickly, and will have no access to a dictionary. You cannot read aloud but you can:

1.   Internalize the reading—hear the reading in your head. Read through the poem two or three times following the absorbing procedure.

2.   If the title and poet are supplied, analyze the title as before and determine the era of the poetry. Often this pushes you toward the meaning.

3. Look carefully at the questions which should enable you to "tap into" your learning process. Answer the ones that are immediately clear to you: form, technique, language perhaps.

4. Go back for another reading for those questions that challenge you—theme or meaning perhaps—analyze the speaker or the voice at work—paraphrase the meaning—ask the simple question "What is the poet saying?"

5. If a question asks you about a specific line, metaphor, opening or closing lines, highlight or underline them to force your awareness of each crucial word. Internalize another reading emphasizing the highlighted area—analyze again the options you have for your answers.

6. Do not waste time on an answer that eludes you. Move onto another section and let the poetry do its "work." Very often the brain will continue working on the problem on another level of consciousness. When you go back to the difficult question, it may well become clear.

7. If you still are not sure of the answer, choose the option that you *feel* is the closest to correct.

Go home, relax, forget about the examination—read your favorite poem!

VERSE AND METER

As children reading or learning poetry in school, we referred to each section of a poem as a verse. We complained we had ten verses to learn for homework. In fact the word *verse* strictly refers to a line of poetry, perhaps from the original Latin word "versus": a row or a line, and the notion of turning, "vertere," to turn or move to a new idea. In modern use we refer to poetry often as "verse" with the connotation of rhyme, rhythm and meter but we still recognize verse because of the positioning of lines on the page, the breaking of lines that distinguish verse from prose.

The verses we learned for homework are in fact known as *stanzas:* a grouping of lines with a metrical order and often a repeated rhyme which we know as the *rhyme scheme.* Such a scheme is shown by letters to show the repeating sounds. Byron's "Stanzas" will help you recall the word, see the use of a definite rhyme and how to mark it:

"Stanzas"

(When a man hath no freedom to fight for at home)	
When a man hath no freedom to fight for at home,	*a*
Let him combat for that of his neighbors;	*b*
Let him think of the glories of Greece and of Rome,	*a*
And get knocked on the head for his labors.	*b*
To do good to mankind is the chivalrous plan,	*c*
And is always as nobly requited;	*d*
Then battle for freedom wherever you can,	*c*
And, if not shot or hanged, you'll get knighted.	*d*

The rhyme scheme is simple: *abab* and your first question should be "Why such a simple, almost sing-song rhyme?" The simplicity reinforces the tone of the poem: sarcastic, cryptic, cynical. There is almost a sneer behind the words "And get knocked on his head for his labors." It is as if the poet sets out to give a lecture or at least a homily along the lines of: "Neither a lender nor a borrower be," but then undercuts the seriousness. The irony of the poem rests in the fact that Byron joined a freedom fighting group in Greece and died, not gloriously, but of a fever. We shall return to this poem for further discussion.

Certain types of rhyme are worth learning. The most common is the *end rhyme*, which has the rhyming word at the end of the line, bringing the line to a definite stop but setting up for a rhyming word in another line later on, as in "Stanzas": home… Rome, a perfect rhyme. *Internal rhyme* includes at least one rhyming word within the line, often for the purpose of speeding the rhythm or making it linger. Look at the effect of Byron's internal rhymes mixed with half-rhymes: "combat… for that"; "Can/And… hanged" slowing the rhythm, making the reader dwell on the harsh long "a" sound, prolonging the sneer which almost becomes a snarl of anger. *Slant rhyme*, sometimes referred to as half, off, near or approximate rhyme, often jolts a reader who expects a perfect rhyme; poets thus use such a rhyme to express disappointment or a deliberate let-down. *Masculine rhyme* uses one-syllable words or stresses the final syllable of polysyllabic words, giving the feeling of strength and impact. *Feminine rhyme* uses a rhyme of two or more syllables, the stress not falling upon the last syllable, giving a feeling of softness and lightness; one can see that these terms for rhyme were written in a less enlightened age! The terms themselves for the rhymes are less important than realizing or at least appreciating the effects of the rhymes.

If the lines from "Stanzas" had been unrhymed and varying in metrical pattern, the verse would have been termed *free*, or to use the French term,

"Vers libre," not to be confused with *blank verse*, which is also unrhymed but has a strict rhythm. The Elizabethan poets Wyatt and Surrey introduced blank verse, which Shakespeare uses to such good effect in his plays, and later, Milton in the great English epic, *Paradise Lost*. Free verse has become associated with "modern" poetry, often adding to its so-called obscurity because without rhyme and rhythm, poets often resort to complicated syntactical patterns, repeated phrases, awkward cadences and parallelism. Robert Frost preferred not to use it because, as he put it, "Writing free verse is like playing tennis with the net down," suggesting that free verse is easier than rhymed and metrical. However, if you have ever tried writing such verse, you will know the problems. (Perhaps a good exercise after your learning about meter is to write some "free" verse.) T.S. Eliot, who uses the form most effectively in "The Journey of the Magi," claimed that no *"vers"* is *"libre"* for the poet who wanted to do a good job.

Such a claim for the artistry and hard work behind a poem introduces perhaps the most difficult of the skills for a poet to practice and a reader to learn: meter. This time the Greeks provide the meaning of the word from *"metron,"* meaning measure. *Meter* simply means the pattern or measure of stressed or accented words within a line of verse. When studying meter a student should note where stresses fall on syllables—that is why reading aloud is so important, because it catches the natural rhythm of the speaking voice—and if an absence of stressed syllables occurs there is always an explanation why. We "expect" stressed and unstressed syllables because that is what we use in everyday speech. We may stress one syllable over another for a certain effect, often using the definite article "THE well known author..." or the preposition "Get OUT of here!" Usually, however, we use a rising and falling rhythm, known as *iambic rhythm*. A line of poetry that alternates stressed and unstressed syllables is said to have *iambic meter*. A line of poetry with ten syllables of rising and falling stresses is known as *iambic pentameter*, best used by Shakespeare and Milton in their blank verse. The basic measuring unit in a line of poetry is called a *foot*. An iambic foot has one unstressed syllable followed by a stressed marked by ∪ /. Pentameter means "five-measure." Therefore iambic pentameter has five groups of two syllables, or ten beats, to the line. Read aloud the second and fourth, sixth and eighth lines of "Stanzas," tapping the beat on your desk or your palm, and the ten beat becomes obvious. Read again with the stresses unstressed and stressed (or soft and loud, short or long, depending on what terminology works for you) and the iambic foot becomes clear.

Tapping out the other alternate lines in this poem you will not find ten beats but twelve. The term for this line is **hexameter,** or six feet, rather than five. Other line-length names worth learning are:

monometer	one foot	**dimeter**	two feet
trimeter	three feet	**tetrameter**	four feet
heptameter	seven feet	**octameter**	eight feet

Other foot names worth learning are:

the **anapest** marked ∪ ∪ / the most famous anapestic line being:

"Twas the night before Christmas, when all through the house..."

the **trochee,** marked / ∪, the most memorable trochaic line being:

"Double double toil and trouble..."

the **dactyl** marked / ∪ ∪ / ∪ ∪, the most often quoted dactylic line being:

"Take her up tenderly..."

Old English poetry employs a meter known as accentual meter, with four stresses to the line without attention to the unstressed syllables. Contemporary poets tend not to use it, but one of the greatest innovators in rhythm and meter, Gerard Manley Hopkins, used it as the "base line" for his counterpointed "Sprung Rhythm." Living in the 19th century, Hopkins produced poetry that even today strikes the reader as "modern," in that the rhymes and rhythms often jar the ear, providing stressed syllables where we expect unstressed and vice versa. The rhythm was measured by feet of from one to four syllables, and any number of unstressed syllables. Underneath the rhythm we hear the "regular" rhythm we are used to in speech, and an intriguing counterpoint develops. One stanza from "The Caged Skylark" will show the method at work:

> As a dare-gale skylark scanted in a dull cage
> Man's mounting spirit in his bone-house, mean house, dwells—
> That bird beyond the remembering his free fells;
> This in drudgery, day-labouring-out life's age.

The stress on "That" and "This" works particularly well to draw attention to the two captives: the skylark and Man. The accentual meter in the second line reinforces the wretchedness of the human condition. No reader could possibly read that line quickly, nor fail to put the full length of the syllable on "dwells." The dash further stresses the length and the low pitch of the last word.

If at first the terms for meter are new and strange, remember that what is most important is not that you mindlessly memorize the terminology but are able to recognize the meter and analyze why the poet has used it in the particular context of the poem. For example, Shakespeare did not want the lyrical fall and rise of the iamb for his witches around the cauldron, so he employs the much more unusual trochee to suggest the gloom and mystery of the heath in "Macbeth." Many poets will "mix and match" their meter and your task as a student of poetry is to analyze why. Perhaps the poet sets up the regular greeting card meter, rising and falling rhythm, regular end-stopped rhyme. If the poet abruptly changes that pattern, there is a reason. If the poet subtly moves from a disruptive meter into a smooth one, then analyze what is going on in the meaning. If the poet is doing "a good job" as T.S. Eliot suggested, then the rhyme, rhythm and meter should all work together in harmony to make the poem an integral whole.

FIGURATIVE LANGUAGE AND POETIC DEVICES

It will be becoming ever more obvious that a poem is not created from mere inspiration. No doubt the initial movement for a poem has something of divine intervention: the ancients talked of being visited by the Muse of Poetry; James Joyce coined the word "epiphany" for the clear moment of power of conception in literature, but then the poet sets to working at the expression to make it the best it can be.

Perhaps what most distinguishes poetry from any other genre is the use of figurative language—figures of speech—used through the ages to convey the poet's own particular world-view in a unique way. Words have *connotation* and *denotation*, *figurative* and *literal* meanings. We can look in the dictionary for denotation and literal meaning, but figurative language works its own peculiar magic, tapping into shared experiences within the psyche. A simple example involves the word "home." If we free-associated for awhile among a group of twenty students we would find a number of connotations for the word, depending on the way home was for us in our experiences: comforting, scary, lonely, dark, creepy, safety, haven, hell…. However, the denotation is quite straightforward: a house or apartment or dwelling that provides shelter for an individual or family. Poets include in their skill various figures of speech to "plug into" the reader's experiences, to prompt the reader to say "I would have never thought of it in those terms but now I see!"

The most important of these skills is perhaps the *metaphor*, which compares two unlike things, feelings, objects, and the *simile*. Metaphors are more difficult to find than similes, which also compare two dissimilar things but always use the words "as if" (for a clause) or "like" (for a word or phrase). Metaphors suggest the comparison, the meaning is implicit. An easy way to distinguish between the two is the simple example of the camel. **Metaphor**: the camel is the ship of the desert. **Simile**: a camel is like a ship in the desert. Both conjure up the camel's almost sliding across the desert, storing up its water as a ship must do for survival for its passengers, and the notion of the vastness of the desert parallels the sea. The metaphor somehow crystallizes the image. Metaphors can be *extended* so that an entire poem consists of a metaphor or unfortunately they can be *mixed*. The latter rarely happens in poetry unless the poet is deliberately playing with his readers and provoking humor.

Start thinking of how many times you use similes in your own writing or speech. The secret is, as Isaac Babel once said, that similes must be "as precise as a slide rule and as natural as the smell of dill." The precision and naturalness coming together perfectly often set up an equation of comparison. A student once wrote "I felt torn apart by my loyalty to my mother and grandmother, like the turkey wishbone at Thanksgiving." We have all experienced divided loyalties. Using the graphic wishbone-tearing idea, something we have all done at Thanksgiving or have seen done lets us more easily relate to the student's experience. Another student wrote of his friends waiting for the gym class to begin "like so many captive gazelles." Again the visual point of comparison is important but also the sense of freedom in the idea of gazelle, the speed, the grace; juxtaposing that freedom with the word "captive" is a master stroke that makes a simile striking.

The same student went on to an *extended simile* to state precisely and naturally his feelings upon going into a fistfight: "I was like the kid whose parents were killed by the crooked sheriff, waiting for high noon and the showdown that would pit a scared kid with his father's rusty old pistol against the gleaming steel of a matched pair, nestled in the black folds of the sheriff's holsters. I knew there was no way out. Surrounded by friends, I marched out into the brilliant sun, heading for the back fields of the playground, desperately trying to polish the rusty old gun." Although this student was writing in prose, his use of figurative language is poetic. He plugs into readers' movie experience with the central idea of the showdown at high noon, an *allusion* that involves the reader on the same plane as the writer. The notion of the black holster extends the allusion of the old cowboy films where the "baddies" wore black hats and rode black horses. The use of the word "nestled" provokes some interesting connotations of something soft and sweet like a kitten nestling into something. But then the gun is an implement of destruction and death; maybe "nestles" takes on the connotation of how a snake might curl in the sun at the base of a tree. The metaphor then ends with the child going out into the sun. The "rusty gun" in context of the essay was in fact the outmoded ideas and morals his father and old books had inculcated in him. All in all a very clever use of figurative language in prose. If the same concept had been pursued in poetry, the metaphor would have moved more speedily, more subtly—a poet cannot waste words—and of course would have employed line breaks, rhythm and meter.

Personification is a much easier area than metaphor to detect in poetry. Usually the object that is being personified—referred to as a human with the personal pronoun sometimes, or possessing human attributes—is capitalized, as in this stanza from Thomas Gray's "Ode on a Distant Prospect of Eton College":

> Ambition this shall tempt to rise,
> Then whirl the wretch from high,
> To bitter Scorn a sacrifice,
> And grinning Infamy.
> The stings of Falsehood those shall try,
> And hard Unkindness' altered eye,
> That mocks the tear it forced to flow;
> And keen Remorse with blood defiled,
> And moody Madness laughing wild
> Amid severest woe.

As the poet watches the young Eton boys, he envisions what the years have to offer them, and the qualities he sees he gives human status. Thus Ambition is not only capable of tempting, an amoral act, but also of "whirling," a physical act. Scorn is bitter, Infamy grinning, and so on. Coleridge employs a more visual personification in "The Ancient Mariner," for the sun whom he describes as:

> ...the Sun (was) flecked with bars
> (Heaven's Mother send us grace!)
> As if through a dungeon-grate he peered
> With broad and burning face.

More so than with Gray's more formal personification, Coleridge's supplies an image that is precise—we can see the prisoner behind the bars, and what's more this particular prisoner has a broad and burning face... of course because he is the sun! The personification brings us that flash of recognition when we can say "Yes, I see that!"

The word *image* brings us to another important aspect of figurative language. Not a figure of speech in itself, the image plays a large role in poetry because the reader is expected to imagine what the poet is evoking, through the senses. The image can be literal, wherein the reader has little adjustment to make to see or touch or taste the image; a figurative image demands more from readers, almost as if they have to be inside the poet's imagination to understand the image. Very often this is where students of poetry, modern poetry particularly, find the greatest problems because the poetry of *imagism*, a term coined by Ezra Pound, is often intensely personal, delving into the mind of the poet for the comparison and connection with past memories that many readers cannot possibly share. Such an image is referred to as *free*, open to many interpretations. This concept suits the post-modern poet who feels that life is fragmented, open to multi-interpretations—there is no fixed order. Poets of the Elizabethan and Romantic eras saw the world as whole, steady, *fixed*, exactly the word used for their type of images. Readers of this poetry usually share the same response to the imagery. For example, the second stanza of Keats' "Ode to a Nightingale" sets up the taste imagery of a

> draught of vintage that hath been
> Cooled a long age in the deep-delvéd earth,
> Tasting of Flora and the country green,
> Dance, and Provençal song, and sunburnt mirth!
> O for a beaker of the warm South,
> Full of the true, the blushful Hippocrene,
> With beaded bubbles winking at the brim,
> And purple-stainéd mouth;

Even though Flora and Hippocrene are not names we are readily familiar with, the image of the cool wine, the taste, the look, the feeling evoked of the South and warmth, all come rushing into our minds as we enter the poet's imagination and find images in common.

Blake's imagery in "London" works in a similar way but as readers we have to probe a little harder, especially for the last line of the last stanza:

> But, most thro' midnight streets I hear
> How the youthful Harlot's curse
> Blasts the new-born Infant's tear,
> And blights with plagues the Marriage hearse.

Notice how the "Marriage hearse" immediately sets up a double image. Marriage we associate with happiness and joy; hearse we associate with death and sorrow. The image is troubling. We go back to the previous lines. The harlot curses her (?) new-born—the curse of venereal disease—that child marries and carries the disease to marriage? Or the young man consorting with the harlot passes on the disease to his marriage partner? Marriage then becomes death? The image is intriguing and open to interpretation.

Image in figurative language inevitably leads to symbol. When an object, an image, a feeling, takes on larger meaning outside of itself, then a poet is employing a symbol, something which stands for something greater. Because mankind has used symbols for so long many have become stock or conventional: the rose standing for love; the flag standing for patriotism, love of one's country (thus the controversy over flag-burning today); the color yellow standing for corruption (hence Gatsby's Daisy Buchanan—the white-dressed virginal lady with the center core of carelessness); the bird for freedom; the sea for eternity; the cross for suffering and sacrifice. If you are not versed in the Christian tradition it might be useful to read its symbols because the older poetry dwells on the church and the trials of loving God and loving Woman—the latter also has become a symbol deteriorating over the ages from Eve to the Madonna to Whore.

If the symbol is not conventional then it may carry with it many interpretations, depending on the reader's insight. Some students "get carried away" with symbolism, seeing more in the words than the poets do! If the poet is "doing a good job" the poetry will steer you in the "right" direction of symbolism. Sometimes we are unable to say what "stands for" what, but simply that the symbol evokes a mood; it suggests an idea to you that is difficult to explain.

The best way to approach symbolism is to understand a literal meaning first and then shift the focus, as with a different camera lens, and see if the poet is saying something even more meaningful. Blake again supplies an interesting example. In his poem "The Chimney Sweeper" he describes the young child's dream of being locked up in "coffins of black." Literally of course coffins are brown wood, the color of mourning is black. Shift the focus then to the young child chimney sweeper, so young he can barely lisp the street cry "Sweep" so it comes out "'weep! 'weep! 'weep! 'weep!" (a symbolic line in itself). Your reading of the Industrial Age's cruelty to children who were exploited as cheap, plentiful, and an expendable labor force will perhaps have taught you that children were used as chimney brushes—literally thrust up the thin black chimneys of Victorian houses and factories, where very often they became trapped, suffocated, sometimes burned to death if fires were set by unknowing owners. Now the black coffins stand for the black-with-soot chimneys the little children had to sweep, chimneys which sometimes became their coffins.

The realization of the symbol brings a certain horror to the poem. In the dream an Angel releases the children who then run down "a green plain leaping, laughing…/And wash in a river, and shine in the sun." The action is of course symbolic in that in real life the children's movements were restricted, living in monstrous cities where green plains would be enjoyed only by the rich, and totally limited by the size of the chimneys. They were always black with soot. They rarely saw the sun, never mind shone in it! Again the symbolism adds something to the poem. In many students there have been reactions of tears and anger when they *see* the symbolism behind such simple lines.

The idea of reading about the Industrial Age brings us to an important part of figurative language, briefly mentioned before: *allusion*. Poets tap into previous areas of experience to relate their insights, to draw their readers into shared experiences. Remember how the student writer alluded to old cowboy movies, the classic "High Noon." Poets will refer to history, myth, other older poems, plays, music, heroes, famous people. Allusion is becoming more and more difficult for the modern student because reading is becoming more and more a lost art. Core courses in schools have become hotbeds of controversy about what students should know. Fortunately modern poets are shifting their allusions so that contemporary readers can appreciate and join in with their background of knowledge.

If we now return to more specific figures of speech and other poetic devices, you may feel you can immediately get to grips with these rather than read for background. Alphabetical order may help in your studying:

Alliteration: the repetition of consonants at the beginning of words that are next door to each other or close by. The Hopkins' stanza quoted earlier provides some fine examples: "skylark scanted"; "Man's mounting… mean house"; "free fells"; "drudgery, day-labouring-out life's age." Always try to understand the reason for the alliteration. Does it speed or slow the rhythm? Is it there for emphasis? What does the poet want you to focus on?

Apostrophe: the direct address of someone or something that is not present. Many odes begin this way. Keats' "Ode to a Grecian Urn" for example: "Thou still unravished bride of quietness," and "Ode to Psyche": "O Goddess! hear these tuneless numbers."

Assonance: the repetition of vowel sounds usually internally rather than initially. "Her goodly eyes like sapphires shining bright." Here the poet, Spenser, wants the entire focus on the blue eyes, the crispness, and the light.

Bathos: deliberate anticlimax to make a definite point or draw attention to a falseness. The most famous example is from Pope's "Rape of the Lock": "Here thou, great Anna! whom three realms obey, /Dost sometimes counsel take—and sometimes tea."

The humor in the bathos is the fact that Anna is the Queen of England—she holds meetings in the room Pope describes but also indulges in the venerable English custom of afternoon tea. The fact that tea should rhyme with obey doubles the humor as the elongated vowel of the upper-class laconic English social group is also mocked.

Caesura: the pause, marked by punctuation (/) or not within the line. Sometimes the caesura (sometimes spelled cesura) comes at an unexpected point in the rhythm and gives the reader pause for thought.

Conceits: very elaborate comparisons between unlikely objects. The metaphysical poets such as John Donne were criticized for "yoking" together outrageous terms, describing lovers in terms of instruments, or death in terms of battle.

Consonance: similar to slant rhyme—the repetition of consonant sounds without the vowel sound repeated. Hopkins again frequently uses this as in "Pied Beauty": "All things counter, original, spare, strange;… adazzle, dim."

Diction: the word for word choice. Is the poet using formal or informal language? Does the poetry hinge on slang or a dialect? If so what is the purpose? Are the words "highfalutin" or low-brow?

Enjambment: the running-on of one line of poetry into another. Usually the end of lines are rhymed so there is an end-stop. In more modern poetry, without rhyme, often run-on lines occur to give a speedier flow, the sound of the speaking voice or a conversational tone.

Hyperbole: refers to large overstatement often used to draw attention to a mark of beauty or a virtue or an action that the poet disagrees with. Donne's instruction to the woman he is trying to seduce not to kill the flea, by contrasting her reluctance with "a marriage" of blood within a flea, reinforces the hyperbole used throughout the poem:

Oh stay, three lives in one flea spare,
Where we almost, yea, more than married are.

The example is also good for an unexpected caesura for emphasis at the second pause.

Irony: plays an important role in voice or tone, inferring a discrepancy between what is said and what is meant. A famous example is Shelley's "Ozymandias," which tells of the great ruler who thought that he and his name would last forever, but the traveller describes the huge statue in ruins with the inscription speaking truer than the ruler intended: "My name is Ozymandias, king of kings: /Look on my works, ye Mighty, and despair!"

Metonymy: the name for something closely related to it which then takes on a larger meaning. "You can't fight City Hall" has taken on the meaning of fighting against an entire bureaucracy. "You can't go home again" suggests that you can never emotionally return to your roots.

Onomatopoeia: a device in which the word captures the sound. In many poems the words are those in general use: the whiz of fireworks; the crashing of waves on the shore; the booming of water in a underground sea-cave. However, poets like Keats use the device to superb effect in, for example, " To Autumn,'' when he describes the gleaner sitting by the cider press watching the last "oozings hours by hours"… one can hear the last minute drops squeezed from the apples.

Oxymoron: a form of paradox in which contradictory words are used next to each other: "painful pleasure," "sweet sorrow."

Paradox: a situation or action or feeling that appears to be contradictory but on inspection turns out to be true or at least make sense. "The pen is mightier than the sword" at first glance is a contradiction of reality. One can hardly die by being stabbed by a pen… but in the larger world view the words of men, the signing of death warrants, the written issuing of commands to the gas chambers have killed. Or reason has prevailed by men writing out their grievances and as a result lives have been saved. Paradox always opens up the doors of thinking.

Pun: a play on words often for humorous or sarcastic effect. The Elizabethans were very fond of them; many of Shakespeare's comedies come from punning. Much of Donne's sexual taunting involves the use of the pun.

Sarcasm: when verbal irony is too harsh it moves into the sarcastic realm. It has been termed the "lowest form of wit" but can be used to good effect in the tone of a poem. Browning's dramatic monologues make excellent use of the device.

Synecdoche: when a part of an object is used to represent the entire thing or vice versa. When we ask someone to give us a hand we would be horrified if they cut off the hand, what we want is the person's help, from all of the body!

Syntax: the ordering of words into a particular pattern. If a poet shifts words from the usual word order you know you are dealing with an older style of poetry (Shakespeare, Milton) or a poet who wants to shift emphasis onto a particular word.

Tone: the voice or attitude of the speaker. Remember that the voice need not be that of the poet's. He or she may be adopting a particular tone for a purpose. Your task is to analyze if the tone is angry, sad, conversational, abrupt, wheedling, cynical, affected, satiric, etc. Is the poet including you in a cozy way by using "you," or is he accusing "you" of what he is criticizing? Is the poet keeping you at a distance with coldness and third person pronouns. If so, why? The most intriguing of voices is Browning's in his *dramatic monologues*: poems that address another person who remains silent. Browning brought this type of poetry to an art.

TYPES OF POETRY

Having begun to grasp that poetry contains a great deal more than initially meets the eye, you should now start thinking about the various types of poetry. Certainly in discussing a poem it is also useful to know what "breed" you are dealing with because the form may dictate certain areas of rhyme or meter and may enhance the meaning.

The pattern or design of a poem is known as *form*, and even the strangest, most experimental poetry will have some type of form to it. Allen Ginsberg's "A Supermarket in California" caused a stir because it didn't read like poetry, but on the page there is a certain form to it. Some poets even try to match the shape of the poem to the subject. Find in anthologies John Hollander's "Swan and Shadow," and Dorthi Charles' "Concrete Cat." Such visual poems are not just fun to look at and read but the form adds to the subject and helps the reader appreciate the poet's world view. *Closed form* will be immediately recognizable because lines can be counted, shape determined. The poet must keep to the recognized form, in number of lines, rhyme scheme, and/or meter. *Open form* developed from "vers libre," which name some poets objected to as it suggested that there was little skill or craft behind the poem, simply creativity, as the name suggests, gives a freedom of pattern to the poet.

The most easily recognized closed form of poetry is the *sonnet*, sometimes referred to as a *fixed form*. The sonnet always has fourteen lines but there are two types of sonnets, the Petrarchan or Italian, and the Shakespearean or English. The word sonnet in fact comes from the Italian word "sonnetto" meaning a "little song," and Petrarch, the 14th century Italian poet, took the form to its peak with his sonnets to his loved one Laura. This woman died before he could even declare his love, and such poignant, unrequited love became the theme for many Elizabethan sonnets. As a young man might telephone a young woman for a date in today's society, the Elizabethan would send a sonnet. The Petrarchan sonnet is organized into two groups: eight lines and six: the *octave* and the *sestet*. Usually the rhyme scheme is abbaabba-cdecde, but the sestet can vary in its pattern. The octave may set up a problem or a proposition, and then the answer or resolution follows in the sestet after a turn or a shift. The Shakespearean sonnet organizes the lines into three groups of four lines: *quatrains* and a *couplet*: two rhyming lines. The rhyming scheme is always abab cdcd efef gg, and the turn or shift can happen at one of three places or leave the resolution or a "twist in the tail" at the end.

Couplet, mentioned earlier, leads us to a closed form of poetry that is very useful for the poet. It is a two-line stanza that usually rhymes with an end rhyme. If the couplet is firmly end-stopped and written in iambic pentameter it is known as an *heroic couplet*, after the use was made of it in the English translations of the great classical or heroic epics such as *The Iliad* and *The Odyssey*. Alexander Pope became a master of the heroic couplet, sometimes varying to the twelve- syllable line from the old French poetry on Alexander the Great. The line became known as the *Alexandrine*. Pope gained fame first as a translator of the epics and then went on to write mock-heroic poems like "The Rape of the Lock," written totally in heroic couplets which never become monotonous, as a succession of regularly stepped-out couplets can, because he varied the place of the caesura and masterfully employed enjambment.

Rarely in an exam will you be presented with an epic because part of the definition of the word is vastness of size and range. However, you may be confronted with an excerpt and will need to recognize the structure. The translation will usually be in couplets, the meter regular with equal line lengths, because originally these poems were sung aloud or chanted to the beat of drums. Because of their oral quality, repetition plays an important part, so that if the bard, or singer, forgot the line, the audience, who had heard the stories many times before, could help him out. The subject deals with great deeds of heroes: Odysseus (Ulysses), Hector, and Aeneus, their adventures and their trials; the theme will be of human grief or pride, divided loyalties— but all "writ large." The one great English epic, *Paradise Lost* is written by

Milton and deals with the story of Adam and Eve and the Fall. Adam thus becomes the great hero. The huge battle scenes of *The Iliad* are emulated in the War of the Heavens when Satan and his crew were expelled into Hell; the divided loyalties occur when Adam must choose between obedience to God and love for his wife.

On much simpler lines are the *ballads*, sometimes the earliest poems we learn as children. Folk or popular ballads were first sung as early as the 15th century and then handed down through generations until finally written down. Usually the ballads are anonymous and simple in theme, having been composed by working folk who originally could not read or write. The stories—a ballad is a story in a song—revolve around love and hate and lust and murder, often rejected lovers, knights, and the supernatural. As with the epic, and for the same reason, repetition plays a strong part in the ballad and often a repeated refrain holds the entire poem together. The form gave rise to the *ballad stanza*, four lines rhyming abcb with lines 1 and 3 having 8 syllables and lines 2 and 4 having 6. Poets who later wrote what are known as *literary ballads* kept the same pattern. Read Coleridge's "Ancient Mariner" and all the elements of the ballad come together as he reconstructs the old folk story but writes it in a very closed form.

The earlier poetry dealt with narrative. The "father of English poetry," Geoffrey Chaucer, told stories within a story for the great *Canterbury Tales*. The Elizabethans turned to love and the humanistic battle between love of the world and love of God. Wordsworth and Coleridge marked a turning point by not only using "the language of men" in poetry but also by moving away from the narrative poem to the *lyric*. The word comes again from the Greek, meaning a story told with the poet playing upon a lyre. Wordsworth moves from story to emotion, often "emotion recollected in tranquillity" as we saw in "Daffodils." Although sometimes a listener is inferred, very often the poet seems to be musing aloud.

Part of the lyric "family" is the *elegy,* a lament for someone's death or the passing of a love or concept. One of the most famous is Thomas Gray's "Elegy Written in a Country Churchyard," which mourns not only the passing of individuals but of a past age and the wasted potential within every human being, no matter how humble. Often *ode* and elegy become synonymous, but an ode, also part of the lyric family, is usually longer, dealing with more profound areas of human life than simply death. Keats' odes are perhaps the most famous and most beloved in English poetry.

More specialized types of poetry need mentioning so that you may recognize and be able to explicate how the structure of the poem enhances the meaning or theme. For example the *villanelle*: a courtly love poem structure from medieval times, built on five three-line stanzas known as *tercets*, with the rhyme scheme aba, followed by a four-line stanza, a *quatrain* which ends the poem abaa. As if this were not pattern and order enough, the poem's first line appears again as the last line of the 2nd and 4th tercets; *and* the third line appears again in the last line of the 3rd and 5th tercets; *and* these two lines appear again as rhyming lines at the end of the poem! The most famous and arguably the best villanelle, as some of the older ones can be so stiff in their pattern that the meaning is inconsequential, is Dylan Thomas' "Do not go gentle into that good night." The poem stands on its own with a magisterial meaning of mankind raging against death, but when one appreciates the structure also, the rage is even more emphatic because it is so controlled. A poem well worth finding for "reading for pleasure." In James Joyce's *A Portrait of the Artist as a Young Man*, writing a villanelle on an empty cigarette packet turns the young boy, Stephen Daedalus, dreaming of being an artist, into a poet, a "real" artist.

Said to be the most difficult of all closed forms is the *sestina*, also French, sung by medieval troubadours, a "song of sixes." The poet presents six six-line stanzas, with six end-words in a certain order, then repeats those six repeated words in any order in a closing tercet. Find Elizabeth Bishop's "Sestina" or W.H. Auden's "Hearing of Harvests Rotting in the Valleys" and the idea of six images running through the poet's head and being skillfully repeated comes across very clearly. You might even try working out a sestina for yourself.

Perhaps at this stage an *epigram* might be more to your liking and time scale because it is short, even abrupt, a little cynical and always to the point. The cynical Alexander Pope mastered the epigram, as did Oscar Wilde centuries later. Perhaps at some stage we have all written *doggerel*, rhyming poetry that becomes horribly distorted to fit the rhymes, not through skill but the opposite. In contrast *limericks* are very skilled: five lines using the anapest meter with the rhyme scheme: aabba. Unfortunately they can deteriorate into types such as "There was a young lady from....," but in artful hands such as Shakespeare's (see Ophelia's mad song in *Hamlet*: "And will he not come again?"), and Edward Lear's, limericks display fine poetry. Finally, if you are trying to learn all the different types of closed-form poetry, you might try an *aubade*—originally a song or piece of music sung or played at dawn—a poem written to the dawn or about lovers at dawn—the very time when poetic creation is extremely high!

Although the name might suggest open-form, *blank verse* is in fact closed-form poetry. As we saw earlier, lines written in blank verse are unrhymed and in iambic pentameter. Open-form poets can arrange words on the page in any order, not confined by any rhyme pattern or meter. Often it seems as if words have spilled onto the page at random with a direct address to the readers, as if the poets are cornering them in their room, or simply chatting over the kitchen table. The lines break at any point—the dash darts in and out—the poets are talking to the audience with all the "natural" breaks that the speaking voice will demonstrate. Open-form poets can employ rhyme, but sometimes it seems as if the rhyme has slipped into the poem quite easily—there is no wrenching of the word "to make it rhyme." Very often there is more internal rhyme as poets play with words, often giving the sensation they are thinking aloud. Open-form poetry is usually thought of as "modern," at least post-World War I, but the use of space on the page, the direct address of the voice and the use of the dash clearly marks Emily Dickinson as an open-form poet, but she lived from 1830-1886.

LEARNING ABOUT THE "OTHER" LITERATURE

In his recent book, *The Rhetoric of the "Other" Literature*, noted scholar W. Ross Winterowd argues that literature has been much too narrowly defined. Traditional genres (fiction, poetry, and drama) do not accommodate the huge volume of nonfictional texts that have been written over the past several centuries. According to Winterowd, any text of enduring value, regardless of its genre, is worthy of the name "literature."

Indeed, students may be exposed to a variety of these "other" literatures. Students may read the works of autobiographers, diarists, biographers, historians, critics, essayists, journalists, political commentators, scientific writers, and nature writers, among others. Whatever the discipline, excellent prose pieces share certain characteristics of style and arrangement. Similarly, there are strategies for critical reading that are useful for any prose passage.

A BRIEF LOOK AT THE SIGNIFICANCE OF THE ESSAY

The "other" literature most often takes the form of an essay. Students will study essays written by writers from a variety of disciplines and periods. Over the last 400 years, many compelling essays have captured the audiences of their day with their powerful ideas and styles. The development of the essay as an art form is particularly interesting precisely because great essay writers have sprung from fields as diverse as politics and biology, education and art history. This fact speaks to the importance of conveying ideas in writing. The literary tradition of the essay has been shaped by thinkers who, regardless of their training, felt strongly about issues and ideas, and who had an impact on their audiences.

Despite its power to change people's thinking, the essay has not enjoyed the prestige of fiction, poetry, and drama. Montaigne, a sixteenth-century lawyer and writer, generally agreed upon by scholars as the father of the essay, helps us understand why. Montaigne articulated the problematic nature of the form when he defined the essay very loosely, saying anything could be included in it and that it could start and stop wherever it pleased. An essay could consequently include history and personal experience, fact and fiction, scientific discovery and philosophical musing. The "proper" length of an essay is nowhere specified, though it is generally read in one sitting. Essays are often written in the first person, and thus are easily seen as an expression of the author's persona or voice as well as the author's thoughts. An essay's style, therefore, is as significant as the information and opinion it contains. Essays are often superb examples of the marriage of form and content, the hallmark of great literature. It is indeed appropriate to consider essays the "other" literature.

STRATEGIES FOR CRITICAL READING OF PROSE PASSAGES

Critical reading is a demanding process. Linguists and language philosophers speak passionately of the importance of true literacy in human affairs. It is not enough to merely comprehend: true literacy lies in the ability to make critical judgments, to analyze, and to evaluate. It is with this end in mind—true literacy—that any reader should approach a text.

WHAT CRITICAL READERS DO

If you can summarize the main points of an essay, that's a start. If you can recall the plot twists in a short story, or articulate the line of reasoning in an argument, that's a start. But if you are able to offer an informed opinion about the purpose and merits of a text, then you are on the road to true literacy.

The LAST seeks to identify critical readers, readers who not only can describe *what* happened in a text they've read, but *why* it happened and *how* it happened.

More specifically, as a critical reader, you will:

- summarize and outline complex material,

- critically examine a text's reasoning,

- analyze the way a text achieves its effects, especially through stylistic choice,

- evaluate a text, deciding whether it is accurate, authoritative, and convincing,

- determine a text's significance,

- compare and contrast different texts,

- synthesize information from one or more related texts, and

- apply concepts in one text to other texts.

As a critical reader, you'll be an active participant, not a passive recipient. It may help to envision yourself in a dialogue with the author and other critical readers. As rhetorician and critic Mikhail Bahktin argues, language operates in a dialogic mode, where receivers are just as essential to effective transmission of messages as senders.

There are six strategies a critical reader can employ to participate fully in the "re-creative act" that is reading.

1. Get the facts straight.

2. Analyze the argument.

3. Identify basic features of style.

4. Explore your personal response.

5. Evaluate the text overall and determine its significance.

6. Compare and contrast related texts.

1. *Get the Facts Straight*

Listen and read actively, pencil in hand, underlining important phrases or noting key points in the margin. Briefly record your reactions, questions, and conclusions. Though you may not have time to thoroughly annotate a prose passage during a test, if you rigorously practice annotating beforehand, you'll begin to do it less laboriously and with less written back-up.

Your first task as a critical reader is to learn everything you can about the text. You can begin by scrutinizing the implications of the title, trying to identify the author and general time period in which the text was written, and identifying the thesis. In short, a good reader looks for the main ideas, but also looks for other information (author, era, form) that may help him or her determine the slant of those ideas.

Once you've identified the essence of a passage, try to jot it down in your own words in a single sentence. This will help you focus on a text's meaning and purpose, a skill extremely useful when the detailed multiple-choice questions present you with "blind alleys" or slightly off-base interpretations of a text.

There are really four activities you perform in order to "get the facts straight:"

a. **Previewing** – looking over a text to learn all you can *before* you start reading (This is, of course, much more difficult with excerpts.)

b. **Annotating** – marking up the text to record reactions, questions, and conclusions (Hint: It's especially useful to underline what you think the thesis is.)

c. **Outlining** – identifying the sequence of main ideas, often by *numbering* key phrases

d. **Summarizing** – stating the purpose and main idea, the "essence" of a text

Once you've got the facts straight, you're ready to tackle the analytic and evaluative aspects of critical reading. Before addressing those, let's test your ability to get the facts.

Here's an essay titled "Education of Women" by William Hazlitt, an essayist and scholar who wrote during the early nineteenth century. Try your hand at previewing, annotating, outlining, and summarizing it. Then look at the following pages, where a proficient critical reader has done those operations for you. Compare your responses and see where you can improve. Remember, you don't have to take copious notes to get to the essence of a text.

"Education of Women"

We do not think a classical education proper for women. It may pervert their minds, but it cannot elevate them. It has been asked, Why a woman should not learn the dead languages as well as the modern ones? For this plain reason, that the one are still spoken, and may have immediate associations connected with them, and the other not. A woman may have a lover who is a Frenchman, or an Italian, or a Spaniard; and it is well to be provided against every contingency in that way. But what possible interest can she feel in those old-fashioned persons, the Greeks and Romans, or in what was done two thousand years ago? A modern widow would doubtless prefer Signor Tramezzani to Aeneas, and Mr. Conway would be a formidable rival to Paris.[1] No young lady in our days, in conceiving an idea of Apollo, can go a step beyond the image of her favorite poet: nor do we wonder that our old friend, the Prince Regent,[2] passes for a perfect Adonis in the circles of beauty and fashion. Women in general have no ideas, except personal ones. They are mere egoists. They have no passion for truth, nor any love of what is purely ideal. They hate to think, and they hate every one who seems to think of anything but themselves. Everything is to them a perfect nonentity which does not touch their senses, their vanity, or their interest. Their poetry, their criticism, their politics, their morality, and their divinity, are downright affectation. That line in Milton is very striking—

'He for God only, she for God in him.'

Such is the order of nature and providence; and we should be sorry to see any fantastic improvements on it. Women are what they were meant to be; and we wish for no alteration in their bodies or their minds. They are the creatures of the circumstances in which they are placed, of sense, of sympathy and habit. They are exquisitely susceptible of the passive impressions of things: but to form an idea of pure understanding or imagination, to feel an interest in the true and the good beyond themselves, requires an effort of which they are incapable. They want principle, except that which consists in an adherence to established custom; and this is the reason of the severe laws which have been set up as a barrier against every infringement of decorum and propriety in women. It has been observed by an ingenious writer of the present day, that women want imagination. This requires explanation. They have less of that imagination which depends on intensity of passion, on the accumulation of ideas and feelings round one object, on bringing all nature and all art to bear on a particular purpose, on continuity and comprehension of mind; but for the same reason, they have more fancy, that is greater flexibility of mind, and can more readily vary and separate their ideas at pleasure. The reason of the greater presence of mind which has been remarked in women is, that they are less in the habit of speculating on what is best to be done, and the first suggestion is decisive. The writer of this article confesses that he never met with any woman who could reason, and with but one reasonable woman. There is no instance of a woman having been a great mathematician or metaphysician or poet or painter: but they can dance and sing and act and write novels and fall in love, which last quality alone makes more than angels of them. Women are no judges of the characters of men, except as men. They have no real respect for men, or they never respect them for those qualities, for which they are respected by men. They in fact regard all such qualities as interfering with their own pretensions, and creating a jurisdiction different from their own. Women naturally wish to have their favourites all to themselves, and flatter their weaknesses to make them more dependent on their own good opinion, which, they think, is all they want. We have, indeed, seen instances of men, equally respectable and amiable, equally admired by the women and esteemed by the men, but who have been ruined by an excess of virtues and accomplishments.

—William Hazlitt (1815)

[1] Hazlitt was a theatre critic and had accused a popular Italian tenor, Tramezzani, of overacting in his love scenes. He also criticized actor William Conway in the role of Romeo.

[2] The Prince Regent was George, Prince of Wales, recently declared insane.

A. Previewing "Education of Women"

A quick look over the text of "Education of Women" reveals a few items worth mentioning. This short essay is probably most closely related to an Op-Ed (Opinion-Editorial) piece written in a newspaper. Published in the *Examiner* in 1815, the essay begins with a proclamation, "We do not think a classical education proper for women." The term "we" suggests the assurance of numbers and power. It's safe to assume Hazlitt believes he speaks for a significant group (perhaps educated men?). And lastly, the year 1815 is relevant to our reading because it suggests a time when women did not enjoy the rights and privileges that are commonplace in the late twentieth century, at least in most of the major industrialized cultures. If the year were not stated, you could infer from the debate over educating women that the piece was written before the late twentieth century.

B. Annotating "Education of Women"

An annotation records reactions, questions, and conclusions. Underlining key phrases may help you find the theme. Here are excerpts from Hazlitt's essay with underlining and annotations alongside to facilitate easy reference.

"Education of Women"

We do not think a classical education proper for women. It may pervert their minds, but it cannot elevate them. It has been asked, Why a woman should not learn the dead languages as well as the modern ones? For this plain reason, that the one are still spoken, and may have immediate associations connected with them, and the other not. A woman may have a lover who is a Frenchman, or an Italian, or a Spaniard; and it is well to be provided against every contingency in that way. But what possible interest can she feel in those old-fashioned persons, the Greeks and Romans, or in what was done two thousand years ago? A modern widow would doubtless prefer Signor Tramezzani to Aeneas, and Mr. Conway would be a formidable rival to Paris.[1] No young lady in our days, in conceiving an idea of Apollo, can go a step beyond the image of her favorite poet: nor do we wonder that our old friend, the Prince Regent[2], passes for a perfect Adonis in the circles of beauty and fashion. Women in general have no ideas, except personal ones. They are mere egoists. They have no passion for

1. The Thesis! But, what was a "classical" education in 1815? Probably Latin and Greek, philosophy and the "classics" of literature.

2. Perversion, not elevation, is the result of education of women—learning "taints" women.

3. Women learn modern languages only to be able to speak to their lovers—women have a shallow purpose for education.

4. Allusion to "poor" actors of the day (see footnote) who are preferable to historical figures (Aeneas, Paris)—women have little interest in history or politics, only romantic self-gratification.

truth, nor any love of what is purely ideal. They hate to think, and they hate every one who seems to think of anything but themselves. Everything is to them a perfect nonentity which does not touch their senses, their vanity, or their interest. Their poetry, their criticism, their politics, their morality, and their divinity, are downright affectation. That line in Milton is very striking—

'He for God only, she for God in him.'

Such is the order of nature and providence; and we should be sorry to see any fantastic improvements on it. Women are what they were meant to be; and we wish for no alteration in their bodies or their minds. They are the creatures of the circumstances in which they are placed, of sense, of sympathy and habit. They are exquisitely susceptible of the passive impressions of things: but to form an idea of pure understanding or imagination, to feel an interest in the true and the good beyond themselves, requires an effort of which they are incapable. They want principle, except that which consists in an adherence to established custom; and this is the reason of the severe laws which have been set up as a barrier against every infringement of decorum and propriety in women. It has been observed by an ingenious writer of the present day, that women want imagination. This requires explanation. They have less of that imagination which depends on intensity of passion, on the accumulation of ideas and feelings round one object, on bringing all nature and all art to bear on a particular purpose, on continuity and comprehension of mind; but for the same reason, they have more fancy, that is greater flexibility of mind, and can more readily vary and separate

5. Women don't think, are selfish, frivolous.

6. Women's destiny—creatures of circumstance, habit. Women can't change.

7. They have impressions, not ideas. So women only feel, can't think? They aren't interested in any truths beyond what is true for them.

8. They "want principle...They "want" imagination...Want means lack, not desire.

their ideas at pleasure. The reason of that greater presence of mind which has been remarked in women is, that they are <u>less in the habit of speculating on what is best to be done, and the first suggestion is decisive. The writer of this article confesses that he never met with any woman who could reason, and with but one reasonable woman. There is no instance of a woman having been a great mathematician or metaphysician or poet or painter: but they can dance and sing and act and write novels and fall in love,</u> which last quality alone makes more than angels of them. <u>Women are no judges of the characters of men, except as men. They have no real respect for men, or they never respect them for those qualities, for which they are respected by men.</u> They in fact regard all such qualities as interfering with their <u>own pretensions,</u> and creating a jurisdiction different from their own. Women naturally wish to have their favourites all to themselves, and flatter their weaknesses to make them more dependent on their own good opinion, which, they think, is all they want. We have, indeed, seen instances of <u>men,</u> equally respectable and amiable, equally admired by the women and esteemed by the men, but <u>who have been ruined by an excess of virtues and accomplishments.</u>

As these annotations illustrate, a reader approaching Hazlitt's text would have several questions and perhaps express surprise at Hazlitt's opinionated judgments. Your notes should, as the sample annotations do, reflect your reactions as the text progresses. Make sure you include any conclusions you have drawn as well as the questions that occur to you. The lines you underline or highlight, places where the text makes statement of "fact," will help you identify the main ideas later.

9. They don't synthesize ideas but rather "separate" them. Does this mean they can't compare issues, seeing things only in isolation?

10. Women go with the first idea, don't reason through alternatives. Where is his evidence?

11. Oh, here's the proof…he's met only one reasonable women.

12. Women have accomplished little. Falling in love is their greatest skill. The double-standard in action; women are restricted to "non-cognitive" activity. The most they can aspire to: performing arts, romance.

13. Women ruin men.

C. *Outlining "Education of Women"*

Go back to the statements you have underlined. Paraphrase and list them in numerical order, with supporting statements subsumed under key statements. Hazlitt's essay could be said to have the following key points, extrapolated from the underlining and written in outline form.

1. Classical education not proper for women
    a. modern language study better suits their romances
    b. no interest in history

2. Education is wasted on them because
    a. women have no ideas
    b. women have no passion for truth
    c. women hate to think

3. Women are what they are meant to be: frivolous, superficial
    a. creatures of circumstance, sympathy, and habit
    b. can't form ideas of understanding or imagination
    c. they lack principle
    d. they have fancy, flexibility of mind
    e. they can't synthesize ideas, but see ideas separately
    f. they take the first suggestion rather than speculate on what's best
    g. women can't reason

4. There are no examples of great women thinkers

5. Women are frivolous creatures
    a. women are only able to dance, sing, act, write novels, fall in love
    b. women cannot judge character
    c. women don't respect men for qualities considered good in women themselves (they're hypocrites)

D. *Summarizing "Education of Women"*

Read in this outline form, Hazlitt's essay is clearly an opinionated discussion of why women are not suited to education. Women are "born to" certain frivolous qualities of mind and behavior, and lack the mental capacity to reason, particularly in any principled fashion. The outline of key points and supporting statements lead the reader rather pointedly to this conclusion.

Though at first Hazlitt's essay seems a disjointed litany of complaints, a sequence of reasons becomes more apparent after annotating and outlining the essay. It also becomes clearer how much Hazlitt relies on "accepted" opinion and his own experience rather than demonstrable proof.

We have just undertaken previewing, annotating, outlining, and summarizing the elements of "Get the Facts Straight." Very often at the conclusion of this stage of critical reading, the reader begins to get a handle on the text. The remaining five strategies after "Get the Facts Straight" seem to flow readily and speedily. Let's apply these remaining five strategies to Hazlitt's "Education of Women."

2. Analyze the Argument

An analysis examines a whole as the sum of its parts. Another brief look at the outline of "Education of Women" reveals the parts of Hazlitt's argument. In short, women should not be educated because they lack the qualities education enhances. They lack the capacity to entertain ideas because they have no passion for truth and hate to think. Women are naturally predisposed to acting precipitously rather than thoughtfully, with the use of reasoning. Evidence for these statements may be found in the lack of female contributions to human knowledge. Women can "perform" (and write novels, a less-than-respectable literary endeavor in 1815), and fall in love, but do little else. In short, things that require judgment are not suitable activities for women.

Hazlitt's essay has a rather simple argumentative structure. He asserts women are not educable and then provides "reasons" why. Hazlitt's "reasons" are primarily opinions, offered without any backing except the assertion that women have achieved little. The essay concludes with a final comment on the ability of women to ruin men, chiefly through flattery.

Analysis reveals that Hazlitt's essay has little to offer in support of the opinion it presents. Further, its statements seem more an emotional outpouring than a reasonable explanation. (The careful reader will also make note of how difficult it is to view Hazlitt's remarks in an unprejudiced fashion—the twentieth-century reader will, in all probability, find his assertions a bit ridiculous.)

3. Identify Basic Features of Style

Stylistically, Hazlitt's essay may be described as a series of blunt statements followed by reflection on how the statement is manifested in his culture. Hazlitt draws on anecdotal support—his observations of the women of his day, a line from Milton, and his own knowledge of the absence of women's accomplishments. Hazlitt's essay seems a collection of accepted or common knowledge: he writes as though his "reasons" are generally agreed upon, undisputed statements of fact. This structure suggests that because something is widely believed, readers should accept it. In all probability readers in 1815 did. Thus, the tone is both authoritative and perhaps a bit annoyed—annoyed with the problems women present.

Hazlitt's diction is largely straightforward, more plain than flowery. A few of the words and phrases he chooses have powerful or dramatic connotations, such as "pervert," "mere egoists," "perfect nonentity," "downright affectation," "hate to think," and "no passion for truth." But he relies largely on ordinary language and sentence structure. Only occasionally does he indulge in a syntactic permutation. For example, in the sentence "The writer of this article confesses that he never met with any woman who could reason, and with but one reasonable woman," Hazlitt shifts the modal verb "could reason" to the adjective "reasonable" with memorable effect. By and large, however, his sentences are simple declaratives, not difficult to read or interpret and not especially memorable stylistically.

4. *Explore Your Personal Response*

While nineteenth-century readers would probably have nodded in agreement as Hazlitt offered reasons why women shouldn't be educated, contemporary readers are probably surprised, dismayed, perhaps even angry. Review your responses in the annotations to the text. They will help recreate your personal reactions and the causes for those reactions. Do not always expect to agree with, or even appreciate a writer's point of view. You will find yourself disagreeing with texts rather regularly. The important thing is to be certain you can account for the sources and causes of your disagreement. Much of reader disagreement with Hazlitt's essay rests in what we would consider a more enlightened perspective on the abilities of women. An awareness of historical context does help explain "Education of Women," but probably doesn't increase twentieth-century sympathy for Hazlitt's position.

5. *Evaluate the Text Overall and Determine its Significance*

Hazlitt's essay "Education of Women" was a product of early nineteenth-century sensibilities. Its chief significance today is as a representative of its time, an indicator of a social and intellectual climate much different than our own. As a citizen of the Romantic period preceding the Victorian age,

Hazlitt expresses an understanding of women that today we would deem, at the very least, incomplete.

6. *Compare and Contrast Related Texts*

A complete analysis of Hazlitt's essay would include a comparison of other essays of his, if available, on the subject of women and education. It would also be useful to examine other early nineteenth-century essays on this subject, and lastly, to contrast Hazlitt's essay with contemporary (i.e., late twentieth-century) essays that argue for and against the education of women. Through such comparison, a more complete understanding of Hazlitt's essay is possible. Occasionally you might be asked on the exam to contrast opposing (or similar) views on a single subject, but only within very narrow parameters. For instance, you might be questioned about two distinct styles used to approach the same subject and the resulting effects.

Although you may experience certain points of departure from the above discussion, most skilled readers will agree, in general, with its broad conclusions. This is because the text has been kept in mind and referred to throughout the discussion. If you read attentively, that is, if you attend to the text carefully, you are much more likely to reflect judiciously upon it. Thus, the components of our good reading definition—to read attentively, reflectively, and judiciously—are all present in the six broad strategies described and employed above.

The very *active* reading strategies employed on Hazlitt's essay "Education of Women" can be used with any text to help you "re-create" it with optimal effectiveness. That is to say, you as a reader should be able to very closely approximate the original authorial intentions, as well as understand the general audience response and your more particular individual response. Remember to work with the six strategies in sequence. They are:

1.   Get the facts straight.
     a.   Preview
     b.   Annotate
     c.   Outline
     d.   Summarize

2.   Analyze the argument.

3.   Identify basic features of style.

4. Explore your personal response.

5. Evaluate the text overall and determine its significance.

6. Compare and contrast related texts.

DRILL: ARTISTIC EXPRESSION AND THE HUMANITIES

1. The graphic art of the early nineteenth century poet-artist William Blake is a product of

   (A) neoclassical style

   (B) Pre-Raphaelitism.

   (C) political events following the French Revolution.

   (D) a mystical, personal, metaphysical vision.

2. The plays of Shakespeare were performed

   (A) on a stage in an open area.

   (B) in fields.

   (C) in a large amphitheater.

   (D) in the courts of English nobility.

3. The operas of Puccini were written in a style called verismo, or realist. *La boheme,* for example, takes place

   (A) in China.

   (B) in Bohemia.

   (C) among the starving artists in Paris.

   (D) among cowboys in the American West.

4. Intaglio, relief, and planographic all describe what kind of art technique?

    (A) Printmaking

    (B) Sculpture

    (C) Carved monument inscriptions

    (D) Frescoes

5. Albrecht Durer's Renaissance paintings in Germany differed from those of the Italian Renaissance in that they

    (A) depicted only common people.

    (B) observed nature more closely.

    (C) were not religious.

    (D) never depicted animals.

Questions 6–11 are based on the following passage. Read the passage carefully before choosing your answers.

1   We laymen have always been intensely curious to know—like the cardinal who put a similar question to Ariosto—from what sources that strange being, the creative writer, draws his material, and how he manages to make such an impression on us with it and to arouse in us
5   emotions of which, perhaps, we had not even thought ourselves capable. Our interest is only heightened the more by the fact that, if we ask him, the writer himself gives us no explanation, or none that is satisfactory, and it is not at all weakened by our knowledge that not even the clearest insight into the determinants of his choice of material and into the nature
10   of the art of creating imaginative form will ever help to make creative writers of us.

    If we could at least discover in ourselves or in people like ourselves an activity which was in some way akin to creative writing! An examination of it would then give us a hope of obtaining the beginnings
15   of an explanation of the creative work of writers. And, indeed, there is some prospect of this being possible. After all, creative writers themselves like to lessen the distance between their kind and the common run of humanity; they so often assure us that every man is a poet at heart and that the last poet will not perish till the last man does.

20   Should we not look for the first traces of imaginative activity as
early as in childhood? The child's best-loved and most intense occupation is with his play or games. Might we not say that every child at play
behaves like a creative writer, in that he creates a world of his own, or,
rather, rearranges the things of his world in a new way which pleases
25   him? It would be wrong to think he does not take that world seriously;
on the contrary, he takes play very seriously and he expends large
amounts of emotion on it. The opposite of play is not what is serious but
what is real. In spite of all the emotion with which he cathects his world
of play, the child distinguishes it quite well from reality; and he likes to
30   link his imagined objects and situations to the tangible and visible things
of the real world. This linking is all that differentiates the child's "play"
from "fantasying."

6.   What is the effect of the speaker's use of "we"?

(A) It separates the speaker and his/her colleagues from the reader.

(B) It involves the reader in the search for, yet distinguishes him/her
     from, the creative writer.

(C) It creates a royal and authoritative persona for the speaker.

(D) It makes the speaker the stand-in for all men.

7.   What is the antecedent of "it" (line 8)?

(A) "explanation"   (C) "interest"

(B) "fact"   (D) "impression"

8.   Which of the following statements would the speaker be most likely to
     DISAGREE with?

(A) A lay person cannot become a creative writer by studying the
     writer's methods.

(B) All men are writers at heart.

(C) Creative writers are fundamentally different from nonwriters.

(D) Children understand the distinction between imagination and real-
     ity.

9. "Cathects" (line 28) can best be defined as

    (A) constructs.   (C) fantasizes.

    (B) distances.   (D) discourages.

10. The structure of the passage can best be described as

    (A) an initial paragraph that introduces an idea and two paragraphs that digress from that idea.

    (B) a series of paragraphs that answer the questions with which they begin.

    (C) a series of questions ascending in their inability to be answered.

    (D) paragraphs whose length or brevity parallel their depth or narrowness of inquiry.

11. It can be inferred that the speaker believes that creative writing is

    (A) an opposite of childhood play.

    (B) unrelated to childhood play.

    (C) a continuation of childhood play.

    (D) similar to the fantasizing of childhood play.

Questions 12–15 are based on the following passage.

1   Under the strange nebulous envelopment, wherein our Professor has now shrouded himself, no doubt but his spiritual nature is nevertheless progressive, and growing: for how can the "Son of Time," in any case, stand still? We behold him, through those dim years, in a state of
5   crisis, of transition: his mad Pilgrimings, and general solution into aimless Discontinuity, what is all this but a mad Fermentation; wherefrom, the fiercer it is, the clearer product will one day evolve itself.

    Such transitions are ever full of pain: thus the Eagle when he moults is sickly; and, to attain his new beak, must harshly dash-off the old one
10 upon rocks. What Stoicism soever our Wanderer, in his individual acts

and motions, may affect, it is dear that there is a hot fever of anarchy and misery raging within; coruscations of which flash out: as, indeed, how could there be other? Have we not seen him disappointed, bemocked of Destiny, through long years? All that the young heart might desire and
15 pray for has been denied; nay, as in the last worst instance, offered and then snatched away. Ever an "excellent Passivity"; but of useful, reasonable Activity, essential to the former as Food to Hunger, nothing granted: till at length, in this wild Pilgrimage, he must forcibly seize for himself an Activity, though useless, unreasonable. Alas, his cup of
20 bitterness, which had been filling drop by drop, ever since that first "ruddy morning" in the Hinterschlag Gymnasium, was at the very lip; and then with that poison drop, of the Towngood-andBlumine business, it runs over, and even hisses over in a deluge of foam.

He himself says once, with more justice than originality: "Man is,
25 properly speaking, based upon Hope, he has no other possession but Hope; this world of his is emphatically the Place of Hope." What, then, was our Professor's possession? We see him, for the present, quite shutout from Hope; looking not into the golden orient, but vaguely all round into a dim copper firmament, pregnant with earthquake and
30 tornado.

12. All of the following name the main character of the passage EXCEPT

   (A) our Wanderer.   (C) he/him.

   (B) the Eagle.   (D) our Professor.

13. Which phrase best summarizes the speaker's intent in examining this stage of the main character's life?

   (A) "Such transitions are ever full of pain" (line 8)

   (B) "Have we not seen him disappointed, bemocked of Destiny, through long years" (lines 12–13)

   (C) "there is a hot fever of anarchy and misery raging within" (line 11)

   (D) "what is all this but a mad Fermentation; wherefrom, the fiercer it is, the clearer product will one day evolve itself" (lines 6–7)

14. The accumulative painfulness of this time for the main character is illustrated primarily by the use of

(A) metaphors.

(C) hyperbole.

(B) digressions.

(D) oxymoron.

15. What is the function of the clause introduced by "nay" in line 14?

(A) It negates the clause that precedes it.

(B) It contradicts the clause that precedes it.

(C) It intensifies the clause that precedes it.

(D) It restates the clause that precedes it.

ANSWER KEY TO DRILL QUESTIONS

1.	(D)	6.	(B)	11.	(D)
2.	(A)	7.	(C)	12.	(B)
3.	(C)	8.	(C)	13.	(D)
4.	(A)	9.	(A)	14.	(D)
5.	(B)	10.	(B)	15.	(C)

Chapter 5

Communications Skills Review

This review was developed to prepare you for the Communications Skills Section of the LAST. You will be guided through a step-by-step approach to attacking reading passages and questions. Also included are tips to help you quickly and accurately answer the questions which will appear in this section. By studying our review, you will greatly increase your chances of achieving a passing score on the Communications Skills Section of the LAST.

Remember, the more you know about the skills tested, the better you will perform on the test. In this section, the skills you will be tested on are

- determining what a word or phrase means;

- determining main ideas;

- recognizing supporting details;

- determining purpose;

- determining point of view;

- organizing ideas in the passage; and

- evaluating the validity of the author's argument.

To help you master these skills, we present examples of the types of questions you will encounter and explanations of how to answer them. A drill section is also provided for further practice. Even if you are sure you will perform well on this section, make sure to complete the drills, as they will help sharpen your skills.

A FOUR-STEP APPROACH

When you take the Communication Skills section of the LAST, you will have two tasks:

1. to read the passage, and

2. to answer the questions.

Of the two, carefully reading the passage is the most important; answering the questions is based on an understanding of the passage. Here is a four-step approach to reading:

Step 1: preview,

Step 2: read actively,

Step 3: review the passage, and

Step 4: answer the questions.

You should study the following exercises and use these four steps when you complete the Communications Skills section of the LAST.

STEP 1: PREVIEW

A preview of the reading passage will give you a purpose and a reason for reading; previewing is a good strategy to use in test-taking. Before beginning to read the passage (usually a four-minute activity if you preview and review), you should take about 30 seconds to look over the passage and questions. An effective way to preview the passage is to read quickly the first sentence of each paragraph, the concluding sentence of the passage, and the questions — not all the answers — following the passage. A passage is given below. Practice previewing the passage by reading the first sentence of each paragraph and the last line of the passage.

PASSAGE

That the area of obscenity and pornography is a difficult one for the Supreme Court is well documented. The Court's numerous attempts to define obscenity have proven unworkable and left the decision to the subjective preferences of the justices. Perhaps Justice Stewart put it best when, after refusing to define obscenity, he declared, "But I know it when I see it." Does the Court literally have to see it to know it? Specifically, what role does the fact-pattern, including the materials' medium, play in the Court's decision?

Several recent studies employ fact-pattern analysis in modeling the Court's decision making. These studies examine the fact-pattern or case characteristics, often with ideological and attitudinal factors, as a determinant of the decision reached by the Court. In broad terms, these studies owe their theoretical underpinnings to attitude theory. As the name suggests, attitude theory views the Court's attitudes as an explanation of its decisions.

These attitudes, however, do not operate in a vacuum. As Spaeth explains, "the activation of an attitude involves both an object and the situation in which that object is encountered." The objects to which the court directs its attitudes are litigants. The situation — the subject matter of the case — can be defined in broad or narrow terms. One may define the situation as an entire area of the law (e.g., civil liberties issues). On an even broader scale the situation may be defined as the decision to grant certiorari or whether to defect from a minimum-winning coalition.

Defining the situation with such broad strokes, however, does not allow one to control for case content. In many specific issue areas, the cases present strikingly similar patterns. In examining the Court's search and seizure decisions, Segal found a relatively small number of situational and case characteristic variables explain a high proportion of the Court's decisions.

Despite Segal's success, efforts to verify the applicability of fact-pattern analysis in other issue areas and using broad-based factors have been slow in forthcoming. Renewed interest in obscenity and pornography by federal and state governments, the academic community, and numerous antipornography interest groups indicates the Court's decisions in this area deserve closer examination.

The Court's obscenity and pornography decisions also present an opportunity to study the Court's behavior in an area where the Court has granted significant decision-making authority to the states. In *Miller vs. California* (1973) the Court announced the importance of local community standards in obscenity determinations. The Court's subsequent behavior may suggest how the Court will react in other areas where it has chosen to defer to the states (e.g., abortion).

QUESTIONS

1. The main idea of the passage is best stated in which of the following?

   (A) The Supreme Court has difficulty convicting those who violate obscenity laws.

(B) The current definitions for obscenity and pornography provided by the Supreme Court are unworkable.

(C) Fact-pattern analysis is insufficient for determining the attitude of the Court toward the issues of obscenity and pornography.

(D) Despite the difficulties presented by fact-pattern analysis, Justice Segal found the solution in the patterns of search and seizure decisions.

2. The main purpose of the writer in this passage is to

(A) convince the reader that the Supreme Court is making decisions about obscenity based on their subjective views only.

(B) explain to the reader how fact-pattern analysis works with respect to cases of obscenity and pornography.

(C) define obscenity and pornography for the layperson.

(D) demonstrate the role fact-pattern analysis plays in determining the Supreme Court's attitude about cases in obscenity and pornography.

3. Of the following, which fact best supports the writer's contention that the Court's decisions in the areas of obscenity and pornography deserve closer scrutiny?

(A) The fact that a Supreme Court Justice said, "I know it when I see it."

(B) Recent studies that employ fact-pattern analysis in modeling the Court's decision-making process.

(C) The fact that attitudes do not operate in a vacuum.

(D) The fact that federal and state governments, interest groups, and the academic community show renewed interest in the obscenity and pornography decisions by the Supreme Court.

4. Among the following statements, which states an opinion expressed by the writer rather than a fact?

(A) That the area of obscenity and pornography is a difficult one for the Supreme Court is well documented.

(B) The objects to which a court directs its attitudes are the litigants.

(C) In many specific issue areas, the cases present strikingly similar patterns.

(D) The Court's subsequent behavior may suggest how the Court will react in other legal areas.

5. The list of topics below that best reflects the organization of the topics of the passage is

(A) I.   The difficulties of the Supreme Court

    II.   Several recent studies

    III. Spaeth's definition of "attitude"

    IV. The similar patterns of cases

    V.   Other issue areas

    VI. The case of *Miller vs. California*

(B) I   The Supreme Court, obscenity, and fact-pattern analysis

    II.   Fact-pattern analyses and attitude theory

    III. The definition of "attitude" for the Court

    IV. The definition of "situation"

    V.   The breakdown in fact-pattern analysis

    VI. Studying Court behavior

(C) I.   Justice Stewart's view of pornography

    II.   Theoretical underpinnings

    III. A minimum-winning coalition

    IV. Search and seizure decisions

    V.   Renewed interest in obscenity and pornography

    VI. The importance of local community standards

(D) I.   The Court's numerous attempts to define obscenity

    II.   Case characteristics

    III. The subject matter of cases

    IV. The Court's proportion of decisions

    V.   Broad-based factors

    VI. Obscenity determination

6. Which paragraph below is the best summary of the passage?

    (A) The Supreme Court's decision-making process with respect to obscenity and pornography has become too subjective. Fact-pattern analyses, used to determine the overall attitude of the Court, reveal only broad-based attitudes on the part of the Court toward the situations of obscenity cases. But these patterns cannot fully account for the Court's attitudes toward case content. Research is not conclusive that fact-pattern analyses work when applied to legal areas. Renewed public and local interest suggests continued study and close examination of how the Court makes decisions. Delegating authority to the states may reflect patterns for Court decisions in other socially sensitive areas.

    (B) Though subjective, the Supreme Court decisions are well documented. Fact-pattern analyses reveal the attitude of the Supreme Court toward its decisions in cases. Spaeth explains that an attitude involves both an object and a situation. For the Court, the situation may be defined as the decision to grant certiorari. Cases present strikingly similar patterns, and a small number of variables explain a high proportion of the Court's decisions. Segal has made an effort to verify the applicability of fact-pattern analysis with some success. The Court's decisions on obscenity and pornography suggest weak Court behavior, such as in *Miller vs. California*.

    (C) To determine what obscenity and pornography mean to the Supreme Court, we must use fact-pattern analysis. Fact-pattern analysis reveals the ideas that the Court uses to operate in a vacuum. The litigants and the subject matter of cases is defined in broad terms (such as an entire area of law) to reveal the Court's decision-making process. Search and seizure cases reveal strikingly similar patterns, leaving the Court open to grant certiorari effectively. Renewed public interest in the Court's decisions proves how the Court will react in the future.

    (D) Supreme Court decisions about pornography and obscenity are under examination and are out of control. The Court has to see the case to know it. Fact-pattern analyses reveal that the Court can only define cases in narrow terms, thus revealing individual egotism on the part of the Justices. As a result of strikingly similar patterns in search and seizure cases, the Court should be studied further for its weakness in delegating authority to state courts, as in the case of *Miller vs. California*.

7. Based on the passage, the rationale for fact-pattern analyses arises out of what theoretical groundwork?

    (A) Subjectivity theory

    (B) The study of cultural norms

    (C) Attitude theory

    (D) Cybernetics

8. Based on data in the passage, what would most likely be the major cause for the difficulty in pinning down the Supreme Court's attitude toward cases of obscenity and pornography?

    (A) The personal opinions of the Court Justices

    (B) The broad nature of the situations of the cases

    (C) The ineffective logistics of certiorari

    (D) The inability of the Court to resolve the variables presented by individual case content

9. In the context of the passage, *subjective* might be most nearly defined as

    (A) personal.

    (B) wrong.

    (C) focussed.

    (D) objective.

    By previewing the passage, you should have read the following:

    • That the area of obscenity and pornography is a difficult one for the Supreme Court is well documented.

    • Several recent studies employ fact-pattern analysis in modeling the Court's decision making.

    • These attitudes, however, do not operate in a vacuum.

    • Defining the situation with such broad strokes, however, does not allow one to control for case content.

    • Despite Segal's success, efforts to verify the applicability of fact-pattern analysis in other issue areas and using broad-based factors have been slow in forthcoming.

- The Court's obscenity and pornography decisions also present an opportunity to study the Court's behavior in an area where the Court has granted significant decision-making authority to the states.

- The Court's subsequent behavior may suggest how the Court will react in other areas where it has chosen to defer to the states (e.g., abortion).

These few sentences tell you much about the entire passage.

As you begin to examine the passage, you should first determine the main idea of the passage and underline it, so that you can easily refer back to it if a question requires you to do so (see question 1). The main idea should be found in the first paragraph of the passage, and may even be the first sentence. From what you have read thus far, you now know that the main idea of this passage is that: the Supreme Court has difficulty in making obscenity and pornography decisions.

In addition, you also know that recent studies have used fact-pattern analysis in modeling the Court's decision. You have learned also that attitudes do not operate independently and that case content is important. The feasibility of using fact-pattern analysis in other areas and broad-based factors have not been quickly verified. To study the behavior of the Court in an area in which they have granted significant decision-making authority to the states, one has only to consider the obscenity and pornography decisions. In summary, the author suggests that the Court's subsequent behavior may suggest how the Court will react in those other areas in which decision-making authority has previously been granted to the states. As you can see, having this information will make the reading of the passage much easier.

You should have also looked at the stem of the question in your preview. You do not necessarily need to spend time reading the answers to each question in your preview. The stem alone can help to guide you as you read.

The stems in this case are:

1.   The main idea of the passage is best stated in which of the following?

2.   The main purpose of the writer in this passage is to

3.   Of the following, which fact best supports the writer's contention that the Court's decisions in the areas of obscenity and pornography deserve closer scrutiny?

4. Among the following statements, which states an opinion expressed by the writer rather than a fact?

5. The list of topics below that best reflects the organization of the topics of the passage is

6. Which paragraph below is the best summary of the passage?

7. Based on the passage, the rationale for fact-pattern analyses arises out of what theoretical groundwork?

8. Based on data in the passage, what would most likely be the major cause for the difficulty in pinning down the Supreme Court's attitude toward cases of obscenity and pornography?

9. In the context of the passage, *subjective* might be most nearly defined as

STEP 2: READ ACTIVELY

After your preview, you are now ready to read actively. This means that as you read, you will be engaged in such things as underlining important words, topic sentences, main ideas, and words denoting tone of the passage. If you think underlining can help you save time and help you remember the main ideas, feel free to use your pencil.

Read carefully the first sentence of each paragraph since this often contains the topic of the paragraph. You may wish to underline each topic sentence.

During this stage, you should also determine the writer's purpose in writing the passage (see question 2), as this will help you focus on the main points and the writer's key points in the organization of a passage. You can determine the author's purpose by asking yourself, "Does *the relationship* between the writer's main idea plus evidence the writer uses answer one of four questions":

* What is the writer's overall primary goal or objective?

* Is the writer trying primarily to persuade you by proving or using facts to make a case for an idea? (P)

* Is the writer trying only primarily to inform and enlighten you about an idea, object, or event? (I)

* Is the writer attempting primarily to amuse you? Keep you fascinated? Laughing? (A)

Read these examples and see if you can decide what the primary purpose of the following statements might be.

(A) Jogging too late in life can cause more health problems than it solves. I will allow that the benefits of jogging are many: lowered blood pressure, increased vitality, better cardiovascular health, and better muscle tone. However, an older person may have a history of injury or chronic ailments that makes jogging counterproductive. For example, the elderly jogger may have hardening of the arteries, emphysema, or undiscovered aneurysms just waiting to burst and cause stroke or death. Chronic arthritis in the joints will only be aggravated by persistent irritation and use. Moreover, for those of us with injuries sustained in our youth — such as torn Achilles' tendons or torn knee cartilage — jogging might just make a painful life more painful, cancelling out the benefits the exercise is intended to produce.

(B) Jogging is a sporting activity that exercises all the main muscle groups of the body. That the arms, legs, buttock, and torso voluntary muscles are engaged goes without question. Running down a path makes you move your upper body as well as your lower body muscles. People do not often take into account, however, how the involuntary muscle system is also put through its paces. The heart, diaphragm, even the eye and face muscles, take part as we hurl our bodies through space at speeds up to five miles per hour over distances as long as 26 miles.

(C) It seems to me that jogging styles are as identifying as fingerprints! People seem to be as individual in the way they run as they are in personality. Here comes the Duck, waddling down the track, little wings going twice as fast as the feet in an effort to stay upright. At about the quarter mile mark, I see the Penguin, quite natty in the latest jogging suit, body stiff as a board from neck to ankles and the ankles flexing a mile a minute to cover the yards. And down there at the half-mile post — there comes the Giraffe — a tall fellow in a spotted electric yellow outfit, whose long strides cover about a dozen yards each, and whose neck waves around under some old army camouflage hat that probably served its time in a surplus store in the Bronx rather than in Desert Storm. Once you see the animals in the jogger woods once, you can identify them from miles away just by seeing their gait. And by the way, be careful whose hoof you're stepping on, it may be mine!

In (A) the writer makes a statement that a number of people would debate and which isn't clearly demonstrated in science or common knowledge. In fact, common wisdom usually maintains the opposite thesis. Many would say that jogging improves the health of the aging — even slows down the aging process. As soon as you see a writer point to or identify *an issue open to debate* and standing in need of proof, s/he is setting out to persuade you of one side or the other. You'll notice, too, that the writer in this case takes a stand, here. It's almost as if s/he is saying, "I have concluded that . . . ." But a thesis or arguable idea is only a *hypothesis* until evidence is summoned by the writer to prove it. Effective arguments are based on serious, factual, or demonstrable evidence, not opinion.

In (B) the writer is just stating a fact. This is not a matter for debate. From here, the writer's evidence is to *explain* and *describe* what is meant by the fact. S/he proceeds to *analyze* (break down into its elements) the way the different muscle groups come into play or do work when jogging, thus explaining the fact stated as a main point in the opening sentence. That jogging exercises all the muscle groups is not in question or a matter of debate. Besides taking the form of explaining how something works, what parts it is made of (for example, the basic parts of a bicycle are...), writers may show how the idea, object, or event functions. A writer may use this information to prove something. But if s/he doesn't argue to prove a debatable point, then the purpose must be either to inform (as here) or to entertain.

In (C) the writer is taking a stand, but s/he is not attempting to prove anything, merely pointing to a lighthearted observation. Moreover, all of the examples s/he uses to support the statement are either fanciful, funny, odd, or peculiar to the writer's particular vision. Joggers aren't really animals, after all.

Make sure to examine all of the facts that the author uses to support his/her main idea. This will allow you to decide whether or not the writer has made a case, and what sort of purpose s/he supports. Look for supporting details — facts, examples, illustrations, the testimony or research of experts, that are about the topic in question and *show* what the writer *says* is so. In fact, paragraphs and theses consist of *show* and *tell*. The writer *tells* you something is so or not so and then *shows* you facts, illustrations, expert testimony, or experience to back up what s/he says is or is not so. As you determine where the author's supporting details are, you may want to label them with an "S" so that you can refer back to them easily when answering questions (see question 3).

It is also important for you to be able to recognize the difference between the statements of fact presented and statements of the author's opinion. You will be tested on this skill in this section of the test (see question 4). Let's look at the following examples. In each case ask yourself if you are reading a fact or an opinion.

1.   Some roses are red.

2.   Roses are the most beautiful flower on earth.

3.   After humans smell roses, they fall in love.

4.   Roses are the worst plants to grow in your backyard.

Number 1 is a fact. All you have to do is go look at the evidence. Go to a florist. You will see that number 1 is true. A fact is anything which can be demonstrated to be true in reality or which has been demonstrated to be true in reality and is documented by others. For example, the moon is in orbit about 250,000 miles from the earth.

Number 2 is an opinion. The writer claims this as truth, but since it is an abstract quality (beauty), it remains to be seen. Others will hold different opinions. This is a matter of taste, not fact.

Number 3 is an opinion. There is probably some time-related coincidence between these two, but there is no verifiable or repeatable and observable evidence that this is always true — at least not the way it is true that if you throw a ball into the air, it will always come back down to earth if left on its own without interference. Opinions have a way of sounding absolute, are held by the writer with confidence, but are not backed up by factual evidence.

Number 4, though perhaps sometimes true, is a matter of opinion. Many variables contribute to the health of a plant in a garden: soil, temperature range, amount of moisture, number, and kinds of bugs. This is a debatable point that the writer would have to prove.

As you read, you should note the structure of the passage. There are several common structures for the passages. Some of these structures are described below.

Main Types of Paragraph Structures

1.   The structure is a main idea plus supporting arguments.

2.   The structure is a main idea plus examples.

3.   The structure includes comparisons or contrasts.

4. There is a pro and a con structure.

5. The structure is chronological.

6. The structure has several different aspects of one idea.

For example, a passage on education in the United States in the 1600s and 1700s might first define education, then describe colonial education, then give information about separation of church and state, and then outline the tax opposition and support arguments. Being able to recognize these structures will help you recognize how the author has organized the passage.

Examining the structure of the passage will help you answer questions that ask you to organize (see question 5) the information in the passage, or to summarize (see question 6) the information presented in that passage.

For example, if you see a writer using a transitional pattern that reflects a sequence moving forward in time, such as "In 1982 . . . Then, in the next five years . . . A decade later, in 1997, the xxxx will . . ." chances are the writer is telling a story, history, or the like. Writers often use transitions of classification to analyze an idea, object, or event. They may say something like, "The first part . . . Secondly . . . Thirdly . . . Finally." You may then ask yourself what is this analysis for? To explain or to persuade me of something? These transitional patterns may also help reveal the relationship of one part of a passage to another. For example, a writer may be writing "on the one hand, . . . on the other hand . . ." This should alert you to the fact that the writer is comparing two things or contrasting them. What for? Is one better than the other? Worse?

By understanding the *relationship* among the main point, transitions, and supporting information, you may more readily determine the pattern of organization as well as the writer's purpose in a given piece of writing.

As with the paragraph examples above showing the difference among possible purposes, you must look at the relationship between the facts or information presented (that's the show part) and what the writer is trying to point out to you (that's the tell part) with that data. For example, in the data given in number 6 above, the discussion presented about education in the 1600s might be used

- to prove that it was a failure (a form of argument),

- to show that it consisted of these elements (an analysis of the status of education during that time), or

- to show that education during that time was silly.

To understand the author's purpose, the main point and the evidence that supports it must be considered together to be understood. In number 6, no statement appears which controls these disparate areas of information. To be meaningful, a controlling main point is needed. You need to know that that main point is missing. You need to be able to distinguish between the writer showing data and the writer telling or making a point.

In the two paragraphs below, consider the different relationship between the same data above and the controlling statement, and how that controlling statement changes the discussion from explanation to argument:

(A) Colonial education was different than today's and consisted of several elements. Education in those days meant primarily studying the three "r's" (reading, 'riting, and 'rithmetic) and the Bible. The church and state were more closely aligned with one another — education was, after all, for the purpose of serving God better, not to make more money.

(B) Colonial "education" was really just a way to create a captive audience for the Church. Education in those days meant studying the three "r's" in order to learn God's word — the Bible — not commerce. The Church and state were closely aligned with one another, and what was good for the Church was good for the state — or else you were excommunicated, which kept you out of Heaven for sure.

The same information areas are brought up in both cases, but in (A) the writer treats it analytically (. . ."consisted of several elements" . . .), not taking any real debatable stand on the issue. What is, is. However, the controlling statement in (B) puts forth a volatile hypothesis, and then uses the same information to support that hypothesis.

STEP 3: REVIEW THE PASSAGE

After you finish reading actively, take 10 or 20 seconds to look over the main idea and the topic sentences that you have underlined, and the key words and phrases you have marked. Now you are ready to enter Step 4 and answer the questions.

STEP 4: ANSWER THE QUESTIONS

In Step 2, Read Actively, you gathered enough information from the passage to answer questions dealing with main idea, purpose, support, fact vs. opinion, organization, and summarization. Let's look again at these questions.

Main Idea Questions

Looking back at the questions which follow the passage, you see that question 1 is a "main idea" question:

1.   The main idea of the passage is best stated in which of the following?

(A) The Supreme Court has difficulty convicting those who violate obscenity laws.

(B) The current definitions for obscenity and pornography provided by the Supreme Court are unworkable.

(C) Fact-pattern analysis is insufficient for determining the attitude of the Court toward the issues of obscenity and pornography.

(D) Despite the difficulties presented by fact-pattern analysis, Justice Segal found the solution in the patterns of search and seizure decisions.

In answering the question, you see that answer choice (C) is correct. The writer uses the second, third, fourth, and fifth paragraphs to show how fact-pattern analysis is an ineffective determinant of Court attitude toward obscenity and pornography.

Answer (A) is incorrect. Nothing is ever said directly about "convicting" persons accused of obscenity, only that the Court has difficulty defining it.

Choice (B) is also incorrect. Though it is stated as a fact by the writer, it is only used as an effect that leads the writer to examine how fact-pattern analysis does or does not work to reveal the "cause" or attitude of the Court toward obscenity and pornography.

Finally, answer choice (D) is incorrect. The statement is contrary to what Segal found when he examined search and seizure cases.

Purpose Questions

In examining question 2, you see that you must determine the author's purpose in writing the passage:

2.   The main purpose of the writer in this passage is to

(A) convince the reader that the Supreme Court is making decisions about obscenity based on their subjective views only.

(B) explain to the reader how fact-pattern analysis works with respect to cases of obscenity and pornography.

(C) define obscenity and pornography for the layperson.

(D) demonstrate the role fact-pattern analysis plays in determining the Supreme Court's attitude about cases in obscenity and pornography.

Looking at the answer choices, you see that choice (D) is correct. Though the writer never states it directly, s/he summons data consistently to show that fact-pattern analysis only gives us part of the picture, or "broad strokes" about the Court's attitude, but cannot account for the attitude toward individual cases.

Choice (A) is incorrect. The writer doesn't try to convince us of this fact, but merely states it as an opinion resulting from the evidence derived from the "well-documented" background to the problem.

(B) is also incorrect. The writer does more than just explain the role of fact-pattern analysis, but rather shows how it cannot fully apply.

The passage is about the Court's difficulty in defining these terms, not the man or woman in the street. Nowhere do definitions for these terms appear. Therefore, choice (C) is incorrect.

Support Questions

Question 3 requires you to analyze the author's supporting details:

3. Of the following, which fact best supports the writer's contention that the Court's decisions in the areas of obscenity and pornography deserve closer scrutiny?

(A) The fact that a Supreme Court Justice said, "I know it when I see it."

(B) Recent studies that employ fact-pattern analysis in modeling the Court's decision-making process.

(C) The fact that attitudes do not operate in a vacuum.

(D) The fact that federal and state governments, interest groups, and the academic community show renewed interest in the obscenity and pornography decisions by the Supreme Court.

To answer this question, let's look at the answer choices. Choice (D) must be correct. In the fifth paragraph, the writer states that the "renewed interest" — a real and observable fact — from these groups "indicates the Court's decisions . . . deserve closer examination," another way of saying scrutiny.

Answer (A) is incorrect. The writer uses this remark to show how the Court cannot effectively define obscenity and pornography, relying on "subjective preferences" to resolve issues.

In addition, choice (B) is incorrect because the writer points to the data in (D), not fact-pattern analyses, to prove this.

(C), too, is incorrect. Although it is true, the writer makes this point to show how fact-pattern analysis doesn't help clear up the real-world "situation" in which the Court must make its decisions.

Fact vs. Opinion Questions

By examining question 4, you can see that you are required to know the difference between fact and opinion:

4. Among the following statements, which states an opinion expressed by the writer rather than a fact?

    (A) That the area of obscenity and pornography is a difficult one for the Supreme Court is well documented.

    (B) The objects to which a court directs its attitudes are the litigants.

    (C) In many specific issue areas, the cases present strikingly similar patterns.

    (D) The Court's subsequent behavior may suggest how the Court will react in other legal areas.

Keeping in mind that an opinion is something that cannot be proven to hold true in all circumstances, you can determine that choice (D) is correct. It is the only statement among the four for which the evidence is yet to be gathered. It is the writer's opinion that this may be a way to predict the Court's attitudes.

(A), (B), and (C) are all taken from data or documentation in existence already in the world, and are, therefore, incorrect.

Organization Questions

Question 5 asks you to organize given topics to reflect the organization of the passage:

5. The list of topics below that best reflects the organization of the topics of the passage is

    (A) I.   The difficulties of the Supreme Court

         II. Several recent studies

         III. Spaeth's definition of "attitude"

         IV. The similar patterns of cases

         V.   Other issue areas

         VI. The case of *Miller vs. California*

    (B) I.   The Supreme Court, obscenity, and fact-pattern analysis

         II. Fact-pattern analyses and attitude theory

         III. The definition of "attitude" for the Court

         IV. The definition of "situation"

         V.   The breakdown in fact-pattern analysis

         VI. Studying Court behavior

    (C) I.   Justice Stewart's view of pornography

         II. Theoretical underpinnings

         III. A minimum-winning coalition

         IV. Search and seizure decisions

         V.   Renewed interest in obscenity and pornography

         VI. The importance of local community standards

    (D) I.   The Court's numerous attempts to define obscenity

         II. Case characteristics

         III. The subject matter of cases

         IV. The Court's proportion of decisions

         V.   Broad-based factors

         VI. Obscenity determination

    After examining all of the choices, you will determine that choice (B) is the correct response. These topical areas lead directly to the implied thesis that the "role" of fact-pattern analysis is insufficient for determining the attitude of the Supreme Court in the areas of obscenity and pornography. (See question 1.)

Answer (A) is incorrect because the first topic stated in the list is not the topic of the first paragraph. It is too global. The first paragraph is about the difficulties the Court has with defining obscenity and how fact-pattern analysis might be used to determine the Court's attitude and clear up the problem.

(C) is incorrect because each of the items listed in this topic list are supporting evidence or data for the real topic of each paragraph. (See the list in (B) for correct topics.) For example, Justice Stewart's statement about pornography is only cited to indicate the nature of the problem with obscenity for the Court. It is not the focus of the paragraph itself.

Finally, (D) is incorrect. As with choice (C) these are all incidental pieces of information or data used to make broader points.

Summarization Questions

To answer question 6, you must be able to summarize the passage:

6.   Which paragraph below is the best summary of the passage?

(A) The Supreme Court's decision-making process with respect to obscenity and pornography has become too subjective. Fact-pattern analyses, used to determine the overall attitude of the Court, reveal only broad-based attitudes on the part of the Court toward the situations of obscenity cases. But these patterns cannot fully account for the Court's attitudes toward case content. Research is not conclusive that fact-pattern analyses work when applied to legal areas. Renewed public and local interest suggests continued study and close examination of how the Court makes decisions. Delegating authority to the states may reflect patterns for Court decisions in other socially sensitive areas.

(B) Though subjective, the Supreme Court decisions are well documented. Fact-pattern analyses reveal the attitude of the Supreme Court toward its decisions in cases. Spaeth explains that an attitude involves both an object and a situation. For the Court, the situation may be defined as the decision to grant certiorari. Cases present strikingly similar patterns, and a small number of variables explain a high proportion of the Court's decisions. Segal has made an effort to verify the applicability of fact-pattern analysis with some success. The Court's decisions on obscenity and pornography suggest weak Court behavior, such as in *Miller vs. California.*

(C) To determine what obscenity and pornography mean to the Supreme Court, we must use fact-pattern analysis. Fact-pattern analysis reveals the ideas that the Court uses to operate in a vacuum. The litigants and the subject matter of cases is defined in broad terms (such as an entire area of law) to reveal the Court's decision-making process. Search and seizure cases reveal strikingly similar patterns, leaving the Court open to grant certiorari effectively. Renewed public interest in the Court's decisions proves how the Court will react in the future.

(D) Supreme Court decisions about pornography and obscenity are under examination and are out of control. The Court has to see the case to know it. Fact-pattern analyses reveal that the Court can only define cases in narrow terms, thus revealing individual egotism on the part of the Justices. As a result of strikingly similar patterns in search and seizure cases, the Court should be studied further for its weakness in delegating authority to state courts, as in the case of *Miller vs. California*.

The paragraph that best and most accurately reports what the writer demonstrated based on the implied thesis (see question 1) is answer choice (C) which is correct.

Choice (A) is incorrect. While it reflects some of the evidence presented in the passage, the passage does not imply that all Court decisions are subjective, just the ones about pornography and obscenity. Similarly, the writer does not suggest that delegating authority to the states as in *Miller vs. California* is a sign of some weakness, but merely that it is worthy of study as a tool for predicting or identifying the Court attitude.

Response (B) is also incorrect. The writer summons information over and over to show how fact-pattern analysis cannot pin down the Court's attitude toward case content.

(D) is incorrect. Nowhere does the writer say or suggest that the justice system is "out of control" or that the justices are "egotists," only that they are liable to be reduced to being "subjective" rather than based on an identifiable shared standard.

At this point, the four remaining question types must be discussed: recall questions (see question 7), cause/effect questions (see question 8), and definition questions (question 9). They are as follows:

Recall Questions

To answer question 7, you must be able to recall information from the passage:

7. Based on the passage, the rationale for fact-pattern analyses arises out of what theoretical groundwork?

(A) Subjectivity theory

(B) The study of cultural norms

(C) Attitude theory

(D) Cybernetics

The easiest way to answer this question is to refer back to the passage. In the second paragraph, the writer states that recent studies using fact-pattern analyses, "owe their theoretical underpinnings to attitude theory." Therefore, we can conclude that response (C) is correct.

Answer choices (A), (B), and (D) are incorrect, as they are never discussed or mentioned by the writer.

Cause/Effect Questions

Question 8 requires you to analyze a cause-and-effect relationship:

8. Based on data in the passage, what would most likely be the major cause for the difficulty in pinning down the Supreme Court's attitude toward cases of obscenity and pornography?

(A) The personal opinions of the Court Justices

(B) The broad nature of the situations of the cases

(C) The ineffective logistics of certiorari

(D) The inability of the Court to resolve the variables presented by individual case content

Choice (D) is correct, as it is precisely what fact-pattern analyses cannot resolve.

Response (A) is incorrect because no evidence is presented for this, only that they do make personal decisions.

Answer choice (B) is incorrect because this is one way in which fact-pattern analysis can be helpful.

Finally, (C) is only a statement about certiorari being difficult to administer, and this was never claimed about them by the writer in the first place.

Definition Questions

9. In the context of the passage, *subjective* might be most nearly defined as

    (A) personal.

    (B) wrong.

    (C) focussed.

    (D) objective.

Choice (A) is best. By taking in and noting the example of Justice Stewart provided by the writer, we can see that Justice Stewart's comment is an example not of right or wrong. (He doesn't talk about right or wrong. He uses the verb "know" — whose root points to *know*ledge, understanding, insight, primarily, not ethical considerations.) He probably doesn't mean focussed by this since the focus is provided by the appearance or instance of the case itself. By noting the same word ending and the appearance of the root "object" — meaning an observable thing exiting outside of ourselves in time and space, and comparing it with the root of subjective, "subject" — often pointing to something personally studied, we can begin to rule out "objective" as perhaps the opposite of "subjective." Most of the time if we are talking about people's "preferences," they are usually about taste or quality, and they are usually not a result of scientific study or clear reasoning, but arise out of a combination of personal taste and idiosyncratic intuitions. Thus, (A) becomes the most likely choice.

(C) is incorrect because the Court's focus is already in place: on obscenity and pornography.

Answer (B) is incorrect. Nothing is implied or stated about the rightness or wrongness of the decisions themselves. Rather it is the definition of obscenity that seems "unworkable."

(D) is also incorrect. Objective is the direct opposite of subjective. To reason based on the object of study is the opposite of reasoning based upon the beliefs, opinions, or ideas of the one viewing the object, rather than the evidence presented by the object itself independent of the observer.

You may not have been familiar with the word subjective, but from your understanding of the writer's intent, you should have been able to figure out what s/he was after. Surrounding words and phrases almost always offer you some clues in determining the meaning of a word. In addition, any examples that appear in the text may also provide some hints.

VOCABULARY ENHANCER

It is important to understand the meanings of all words — not just the ones you are asked to define. A good vocabulary is a strength that can help you perform well on all sections of this test. The following information will build your skills in determining the meanings of words.

SIMILAR FORMS AND SOUNDS

The complex nature of language sometimes makes reading difficult. Words often become confusing when they have similar forms and sounds. Indeed the author may have a correct meaning in mind, but an incorrect word choice can alter the meaning of the sentence or even make it totally illogical.

NO: Martha was always part of that *cliché*.

YES: Martha was always part of that *clique*.

(A *cliché* is a trite or hackneyed expression; a *clique* is an exclusive group of people.)

NO: The minister spoke of the soul's *immorality*.

YES: The minister spoke of the soul's *immortality*.

(*Immorality* means wickedness; *immortality* means imperishable or unending life.)

NO: Where is the nearest *stationary* store?

YES: Where is the nearest *stationery* store?

(*Stationary* means immovable; *stationery* is paper used for writing.)

Below are groups of words that are often confused because of their similar forms and sounds.

1.   accent – *v.* – to stress or emphasize (You must *accent* the last syllable.)

ascent – *n.* – a climb or rise (John's *ascent* of the mountain was dangerous.)

assent – *n.* – consent; compliance (We need your *assent* before we can go ahead with the plans.)

2. accept – *v.* – to take something offered (She *accepted* the gift.)

   except – *prep.* – other than; but (Everyone was included in the plans *except* him.)

3. advice – *n.* – opinion given as to what to do or how to handle a situation (Her sister gave her *advice* on what to say at the interview.)

   advise – *v.* – to counsel (John's guidance counselor *advised* him on which colleges to apply to.)

4. affect – *v.* – to influence (Mary's suggestion did not *affect* me.)

   effect – 1. *v.*– to cause to happen (The plan was *effected* with great success.); 2. *n.* – result (The *effect* of the medicine is excellent.)

5. allusion – *n.* – indirect reference (In the poem, there are many biblical *allusions*.)

   illusion – *n.* – false idea or conception; belief or opinion not in accord with the facts (Greg was under the *illusion* that he could win the race after missing three weeks of practice.)

6. already – *adv.* – previously (I had *already* read that novel.)

   all ready – *adv.* + *adj.* – prepared (The family was *all ready* to leave on vacation.)

7. altar – *n.* – table or stand used in religious rites (The priest stood at the *altar*.)

   alter – *v.* – to change (Their plans were *altered* during the strike.)

8. capital – 1. *n.* – a city where the government meets (The senators had a meeting in Albany, the *capital* of New York.); 2. money used in business (They had enough *capital* to develop the industry.)

   capitol – *n.* – building in which the legislature meets (Senator Brown gave a speech at the *capitol* in Washington.)

9. choose – *v.* – to select (Which camera did you *choose*?)

   chose – (past tense, *choose*) (Susan *chose* to stay home.)

10. cite – *v.* – to quote (The student *cited* evidence from the text.)

    site – *n.* – location (They chose the *site* where the house would be built.)

11. clothes – *n.* – garments (Because she got caught in the rain, her *clothes* were wet.)

    cloths – *n.* – pieces of material (The *cloths* were used to wash the windows.)

12. coarse – *adj.* – rough; unrefined (Sandpaper is *coarse.*)

    course – 1. *n.* – path of action (She did not know what *course* would solve the problem.); 2. passage (We took the long *course* to the lake.); 3. series of studies (We both enrolled in the physics *course.*); 4. part of a meal (She served a five *course* meal.)

13. consul – *n.* – a person appointed by the government to live in a foreign city and represent the citizenry and business interests of his native country there (The *consul* was appointed to Naples, Italy.)

    council – *n.* – a group used for discussion, advisement (The *council* decided to accept his letter of resignation.)

    counsel – *v.* – to advise (Tom *counsels* Jerry on tax matters.)

14. decent – *adj.* – proper; respectable (He was very *decent* about the entire matter.)

    descent – 1. *n.* – moving down (In Dante's *Inferno*, the *descent* into Hell was depicted graphically.); 2. ancestry (He is of Irish *descent.*)

15. device – 1. *n.* – plan; scheme (The *device* helped her win the race.); 2. invention (We bought a *device* that opens the garage door automatically.)

    devise – *v.* – to contrive (He *devised* a plan so John could not win.)

16. emigrate – *v.* – to go away from a country (Many Japanese *emigrated* from Japan in the late 1800s.)

    immigrate – *v.* – to come into a country (Her relatives *immigrated* to the United States after World War I.)

17. eminent – *n.* – prominent (He is an *eminent* member of the community.)

    imminent – *adj.* – impending (The decision is *imminent.*)

    immanent – *adj.* – existing within (Maggie believed that religious spirit is *immanent* in human beings.)

18. fair – 1. *adj.* – beautiful (She was a *fair* maiden.); 2. just (She tried to be *fair.*); 3. *n* – festival (There were many games at the *fair.*)

    fare – *n.* – amount of money paid for transportation (The city proposed that the subway *fare* be raised.)

19. forth – *adv.* – onward (The soldiers moved *forth* in the blinding snow.)

fourth – *n., adj.* – 4th (She was the *fourth* runner-up in the beauty contest.)

20. its – possessive form of *it* (Our town must improve *its* roads.)

it's – contraction of it is (*It's* time to leave the party.)

21. later – *adj., adv.* – at a subsequent date (We will take a vacation *later* this year.)

latter – *n.* – second of the two (Susan can visit Monday or Tuesday. The *latter,* however, is preferable.)

22. lead – 1. *n.* – (led) a metal (The handgun was made of *lead.*); 2. *v.t.* – (leed) to show the way (The camp counselor *leads* the way to the picnic grounds.)

led – past tense of *lead* (#2 above) (The dog *led* the way.)

23. loose – *adj.* – free; unrestricted (The dog was let *loose* by accident.)

lose – *v.* – to suffer the loss of (He was afraid he would *lose* the race.)

24. moral – 1. *adj.* – virtuous (She is a *moral* woman with high ethical standards.); 2. *n.* – lesson taught by a story, incident, etc. (Most fables end with a *moral.*)

morale – *n.* – mental condition (After the team lost the game, their *morale* was low.)

25. of – *prep.* – from (She is *of* French descent.)

off – *adj.* – away; at a distance (The television fell *off* the table.)

26. passed – *v.* – having satisfied some requirement (He *passed* the test.)

past – 1. *adj.* – gone by or elapsed in time (His *past* deeds got him in trouble.); 2. *n.* – a period of time gone by (His *past* was shady.); 3. *prep.* – beyond (She ran *past* the house.)

27. personal – *adj.* – private (Jack was unwilling to discuss his childhood; it was too *personal.*)

personnel – *n.* – staff (The *personnel* at the department store was made up of young adults.)

28. principal – *n.* – head of a school (The *principal* addressed the graduating class.)

principle – *n.* – the ultimate source, origin, or cause of something; a law, truth (The *principles* of physics were reviewed in class today.)

29. prophecy – *n.* – prediction of the future (His *prophecy* that he would become a doctor came true.)

    prophesy – *v.* – to declare or predict (He *prophesied* that we would win the lottery.)

30. quiet – *adj.* – still; calm (At night all is *quiet.*)

    quite – *adv.* – really; truly (She is *quite* a good singer.)

    quit – *v.* – to free oneself (Peter had little time to spare so he *quit* the chorus.)

31. respectfully – *adv.* – with respect, honor, esteem (He declined the offer *respectfully.*)

    respectively – *adv.* – in the order mentioned (Jack, Susan and Jim, who are members of the club, were elected president, vice-president, and secretary *respectively.*)

32. stationary – *adj.* – immovable (The park bench is *stationary.*)

    stationery – *n.* – paper used for writing (The invitations were printed on yellow *stationery.*)

33. straight – *adj.* – not curved (The road was *straight.*)

    strait – 1. *adj.* – restricted; narrow; confined (The patient was put in a *strait* jacket.); 2. *n.* – narrow waterway (He sailed through the *Straits* of Magellan.)

34. than – *conj.* – used most commonly in comparisons (Maggie is older *than* I.)

    then – *adv.* – soon afterward (We lived in Boston, *then* we moved to New York.)

35. their – possessive form of *they* (That is *their* house on Tenafly Drive.)

    they're – contraction of they are (*They're* leaving for California next week.)

    there – *adv.* – at that place (Who is standing *there* under the tree?)

36. to – *prep.* – in the direction of; toward; as (She made a turn *to* the right on Norman Street.)

    too – 1. *adv.* – more than enough (She served *too* much for dinner.); 2. also (He is going to Maine *too.*)

    two – *n.* – 2; one and one (We have *two* pet rabbits.)

37. weather – *n.* – the general condition of the atmosphere (The *weather* is expected to be clear on Sunday.)

   whether – *conj.* – if it be a case or fact (We don't know *whether* the trains are late.)

38. who's – contraction of who is or who has (*Who's* willing to volunteer for the night shift?)

   whose – possessive form of *who* (*Whose* book is this?)

39. your – possessive form of *you* (Is this *your* seat?)

   you're – contraction of you and are (I know *you're* going to do well on the test.)

MULTIPLE MEANINGS

In addition to words that sound alike, you must be careful when dealing with words that have multiple meanings. For example:

> The boy was thrilled that his mother gave him a piece of chewing *gum*.

> Dentists advise people to floss their teeth to help prevent *gum* disease.

As you can see, one word can have different meanings depending on the context in which it is used.

CONNOTATION AND DENOTATION

Language can become even more complicated. Not only can a single word have numerous definitions and subtle meanings, it may also take on added meanings through implication. The **connotation** is the idea suggested by its place near or association with other words or phrases. The **denotation** of a word is the direct explicit meaning.

CONNOTATION

Sometimes, you will be asked to tell the meaning of a word in the context of the paragraph. You may not have seen the word before, but from your understanding of the writer's intent, you should be able to figure out what it is s/he's after. For example, read the following paragraph:

Paris is a beautiful city, perhaps the most beautiful on earth. Long, broad avenues are lined with seventeenth and eighteenth century apartments, office buildings, and cafes. Flowers give the city a rich and varied look. The bridges and the river lend an air of lightness and grace to the whole urban landscape.

1. In this paragraph, "rich" most nearly means

    (A) wealthy.

    (B) polluted.

    (C) colorful.

    (D) dull.

If you chose "colorful" you would be right. Although "rich" literally means "wealthy" (that is its *denotation*, its literal meaning), here the writer means more than the word's literal meaning, and seems to be highlighting the variety and color that the flowers add to the avenues, that is, richness in a figurative sense.

The writer is using a non-literal meaning, or *connotation* that we associate with the word "rich" to show what s/he means. When we think of something "rich," we usually also think of abundance, variety, color, and not merely numbers.

DENOTATION

Determining the denotation of a word is different from determining a word's connotation. Read this paragraph:

Many soporifics are on the market to help people sleep. Take a glass of water and two *Sleepeze* and you get the "zzzzz" you need. *Sominall* supposedly helps you get the sleep you need so you can go on working. With *Morpho*, your head hits the pillow and you're asleep before the light goes out.

1. From this paragraph, a "soporific" is probably

    (A) a drug that stimulates you to stay awake.

    (B) a kind of sleeping bag.

    (C) a kind of bed.

    (D) a drug that helps you sleep.

What is a soporific? You can figure out what it means by looking at what is said around it. People take these "soporifics" to go to sleep, not to wake up. So it can't be (A). You can't take two beds and a glass of water to go to sleep, either. So, it can't be (C). Anyway, you might be able to identify what a soporific is because you recognize the brand names used as examples. So, it must be some sort of pill that you take to sleep. Well, pills are usually drugs of some kind. Therefore, the answer is (D).

VOCABULARY BUILDER

Although the context in which a word appears can help you determine the meaning of the word, one sure-fire way to know a definition is to learn it. By studying the following lists of words and memorizing their definition(s), you will be better equipped to answer Communication Skills questions that deal with word meanings.

To benefit most from this vocabulary list, study the words and their definitions, then answer all of the drill questions making sure to check your answers with the answer key that appears at the end of the review.

GROUP 1

abstract – *adj.* – not easy to understand; theoretical

acclaim – *n.* – loud approval; applause

acquiesce – *v.* – agree or consent to an opinion

adamant – *adj.* – not yielding; firm

adversary – *n.* – an enemy; foe

advocate – 1. *v.* – to plead in favor of; 2. *n.* – supporter; defender

aesthetic – *adj.* – showing good taste; artistic

alleviate – *v.* – to lessen or make easier

aloof – *adj.* – distant in interest; reserved; cool

altercation – *n.* – controversy; dispute

altruistic – *adj.* – unselfish

amass – *v.* – to collect together; accumulate

ambiguous – *adj.* – not clear; uncertain; vague

ambivalent – *adj.* – undecided

ameliorate – *v.* – to make better; to improve

amiable – *adj.* – friendly

amorphous – *adj.* – having no determinate form

anarchist – *n.* – one who believes that a formal government is unnecessary

antagonism – *n.* – hostility; opposition

apathy – *n.* – lack of emotion or interest

appease – *v.* – to make quiet; to calm

apprehensive – *adj.* – fearful; aware; conscious

arbitrary – *adj.* – based on one's preference or whim

arrogant – *adj.* – acting superior to others; conceited

articulate – 1. *v.* – to speak distinctly; 2. *adj.* – eloquent; fluent; 3. *adj.* – capable of speech; 4. *v* – to hinge; to connect; 5. *v.* – to convey; to express effectively

Drill 1

DIRECTIONS: Match each word in the left column with the word in the right column that is most *opposite* in meaning.

Word		Match	
1. ___ articulate	6. ___ abstract	A. hostile	F. disperse
2. ___ apathy	7. ___ acquiesce	B. concrete	G. enthusiasm
3. ___ amiable	8. ___ arbitrary	C. selfish	H. certain
4. ___ altruistic	9. ___ amass	D. reasoned	I. resist
5. ___ ambivalent	10. ___ adversary	E. ally	J. incoherent

DIRECTIONS: Match each word in the left column with the word in the right column that is most *similar* in meaning.

Word		Match	
11. ___ adamant	14. ___ antagonism	A. afraid	D. insistent
12. ___ aesthetic	15. ___ altercation	B. disagreement	E. hostility
13. ___ apprehensive		C. tasteful	

GROUP 2

assess – *v.* – to estimate the value of

astute – *adj.* – cunning; sly; crafty

atrophy – *v.* – to waste away through lack of nutrition

audacious – *adj.* – fearless; bold

augment – *v.* – to increase or add to; to make larger

austere – *adj.* – harsh; severe; strict

authentic – *adj.* – real; genuine; trustworthy

authoritarian – *adj.* – acting as a dictator; demanding obedience

banal – *adj.* – common; petty; ordinary

belittle – *v.* – to make small; to think lightly of

benefactor – *n.* – one who helps others; a donor

benevolent – *adj.* – kind; generous

benign – *adj.* – mild; harmless

biased – *adj.* – prejudiced; influenced; not neutral

blasphemous – *adj.* – irreligious; away from acceptable standards

blithe – *adj.* – happy; cheery; merry

brevity – *n.* – briefness; shortness

candid – *adj.* – honest; truthful; sincere

capricious – *adj.* – changeable; fickle

caustic – *adj.* – burning; sarcastic; harsh

censor – *v.* – to examine and delete objectionable material

censure – *v.* – to criticize or disapprove of

charlatan – *n.* – an imposter; fake

coalesce – *v.* – to combine; come together

collaborate – *v.* – to work together; cooperate

Drill 2

DIRECTIONS: Match each word in the left column with the word in the right column that is most *opposite* in meaning.

Word		Match	
1. ___ augment	6. ___ authentic	A. permit	F. malicious
2. ___ biased	7. ___ candid	B. heroine	G. neutral
3. ___ banal	8. ___ belittle	C. praise	H. mournful
4. ___ benevolent	9. ___ charlatan	D. diminish	I. unusual
5. ___ censor	10. ___ blithe	E. dishonest	J. genuine

DIRECTIONS: Match each word in the left column with the word in the right column that is most *similar* in meaning.

Word		Match	
11. ___ collaborate	14. ___ censure	A. harmless	D. cooperate
12. ___ benign	15. ___ capricious	B. cunning	E. criticize
13. ___ astute		C. changeable	

GROUP 3

compatible – *adj.* – in agreement; harmonious

complacent – *adj.* – content; self-satisfied; smug

compliant – *adj.* – yielding; obedient

comprehensive – *adj.* – all-inclusive; complete; thorough

compromise – *v.* – to settle by mutual adjustment

concede – 1. *v.* – to acknowledge; admit; 2. to surrender; to abandon one's position

concise – *adj.* – in few words; brief; condensed

condescend – *v.* – to come down from one's position or dignity

condone – *v.* – to overlook; to forgive

conspicuous – *adj.* – easy to see; noticeable

consternation – *n.* – amazement or terror that causes confusion

consummation – *n.* – the completion; finish

contemporary – *adj.* – living or happening at the same time; modern

contempt – *n.* – scorn; disrespect

contrite – *adj.* – regretful; sorrowful

conventional – *adj.* – traditional; common; routine

cower – *v.* – crouch down in fear or shame

defamation – *n.* – any harm to a name or reputation; slander

deference – *n.* – a yielding to the opinion of another

deliberate – 1. *v.* – to consider carefully; weigh in the mind; 2. *adj.* – intentional

denounce – *v.* – to speak out against; condemn

depict – *v.* – to portray in words; present a visual image

deplete – *v.* – to reduce; to empty

depravity – *n.* – moral corruption; badness

deride – *v.* – to ridicule; laugh at with scorn

Drill 3

<u>**DIRECTIONS:**</u> Match each word in the left column with the word in the right column that is most *opposite* in meaning.

Word		**Match**	
1. ____ deplete	6. ____ condone	A. unintentional	F. support
2. ____ contemporary	7. ____ conspicuous	B. disapprove	G. beginning
3. ____ concise	8. ____ consummation	C. invisible	H. ancient
4. ____ deliberate	9. ____ denounce	D. respect	I. virtue
5. ____ depravity	10. ____ contempt	E. fill	J. verbose

> **DIRECTIONS:** Match each word in the left column with the word in the right column that is most *similar* in meaning.

	Word			Match		
11. ___ compatible		14. ___ comprehensive	A. portray		D. thorough	
12. ___ depict		15. ___ complacent	B. content		E. common	
13. ___ conventional			C. harmonious			

GROUP 4

desecrate – *v.* – to violate a holy place or sanctuary

detached – *adj.* – separated; not interested; standing alone

deter – *v.* – to prevent; to discourage; hinder

didactic – 1. *adj.* – instructive; 2. dogmatic; preachy

digress – *v.* – stray from the subject; wander from topic

diligence – *n.* – hard work

discerning – *adj.* – distinguishing one thing from another

discord – *n.* – disagreement; lack of harmony

discriminating – 1. *v.* – distinguishing one thing from another; 2. *v.* – demonstrating bias; 3. *adj.* – able to distinguish

disdain – 1. *n.* – intense dislike; 2. *v.* – look down upon; scorn

disparage – *v.* – to belittle; undervalue

disparity – *n.* – difference in form, character, or degree

dispassionate – *adj.* – lack of feeling; impartial

disperse – *v.* – to scatter; separate

disseminate – *v.* – to circulate; scatter

dissent – *v.* – to disagree; differ in opinion

dissonance – *n.* – harsh contradiction

diverse – *adj.* – different; dissimilar

document – 1. *n.* – official paper containing information; 2. *v.* – to support; substantiate; verify dogmatic – *adj.* – stubborn; biased; opinionated

dubious – *adj.* – doubtful; uncertain; skeptical; suspicious

eccentric – *adj.* – odd; peculiar; strange

efface – *v.* – wipe out; erase

effervescence – 1. *n.* – liveliness; spirit; enthusiasm; 2. bubbliness

egocentric – *adj.* – self-centered

Drill 4

DIRECTIONS: Match each word in the left column with the word in the right column that is most *opposite* in meaning.

Word				Match			
1. ___ detached	6. ___ dubious	A. agree	F. respect
2. ___ deter	7. ___ diligence	B. certain	G. compliment
3. ___ dissent	8. ___ disdain	C. lethargy	H. sanctify
4. ___ discord	9. ___ desecrate	D. connected	I. harmony
5. ___ efface	10. ___ disparage	E. assist	J. restore

DIRECTIONS: Match each word in the left column with the word in the right column that is most *similar* in meaning.

Word				Match		
11. ___ effervescence	14. ___ document	A. violate	D. liveliness
12. ___ efface	15. ___ eccentric	B. distribute	E. odd
13. ___ disseminate		C. substantiate	

GROUP 5

elaboration – *n.* – act of clarifying; adding details

eloquence – *n.* – the ability to speak well

elusive – *adj.* – hard to catch; difficult to understand

emulate – *v.* – to imitate; copy; mimic

endorse – *v.* – support; to approve of; recommend

engender – *v.* – to create; bring about

enhance – *v.* – to improve; compliment; make more attractive

enigma – *n.* – mystery; secret; perplexity

ephemeral – *adj.* – temporary; brief; short-lived

equivocal – *adj.* – doubtful; uncertain

erratic – *adj.* – unpredictable; strange

erroneous – *adj.* – untrue; inaccurate; not correct

esoteric – *adj.* – incomprehensible; obscure

euphony – *n.* – pleasant sound

execute – 1. *v.* – put to death; kill; 2. to carry out; fulfill

exemplary – *adj.* – serving as an example; outstanding

exhaustive – *adj.* – thorough; complete

expedient – *adj.* – advisable; convenient; makeshift

expedite – *v.* – speed up

explicit – *adj.* – specific; definite

extol – *v.* – praise; commend

extraneous – *adj.* – irrelevant; not related; not essential

facilitate – *v.* – make easier; simplify

fallacious – *adj.* – misleading

fanatic – *n.* – enthusiast; extremist

Drill 5

DIRECTIONS: Match each word in the left column with the word in the right column that is most *opposite* in meaning.

Word		Match	
1. ___ extraneous	6. ___ erratic	A. incomplete	F. eternal

2. ___ ephemeral	7. ___ explicit	B. delay	G. abridge
3. ___ exhaustive	8. ___ euphony	C. dependable	H. relevant
4. ___ expedite	9. ___ elusive	D. comprehensible	I. indefinite
5. ___ erroneous	10. ___ elaborate	E. dissonance	J. accurate

DIRECTIONS: Match each word in the left column with the word in the right column that is most *similar* in meaning.

Word		Match	
11. ___ endorse	14. ___ fallacious	A. enable	D. convenient
12. ___ expedient	15. ___ engender	B. recommend	E. deceptive
13. ___ facilitate		C. create	

GROUP 6

fastidious – *adj.* – fussy; hard to please

fervor – *n.* – passion; intensity

fickle – *adj.* – changeable; unpredictable

fortuitous – *adj.* – accidental; happening by chance; lucky

frivolity – *n.* – giddiness; lack of seriousness

fundamental – *adj.* – basic; necessary

furtive – *adj.* – secretive; sly

futile – *adj.* – worthless; unprofitable

glutton – *n.* – overeater

grandiose – *adj.* – extravagant; flamboyant

gravity – *n.* – seriousness

guile – *n.* – slyness; deceit

gullible – *adj.* – easily fooled

hackneyed – *adj.* – commonplace; trite

hamper – *v.* – interfere with; hinder

haphazard – *adj.* – disorganized; random

hedonistic – *adj.* – pleasure seeking

heed – *v.* – obey; yield to

heresy – *n.* – opinion contrary to popular belief

hindrance – *n.* – blockage; obstacle

humility – *n.* – lack of pride; modesty

hypocritical – *adj.* – two-faced; deceptive

hypothetical – *adj.* – assumed; uncertain

illuminate – *v.* – make understandable

illusory – *adj.* – unreal; false; deceptive

Drill 6

DIRECTIONS: Match each word in the left column with the word in the right column that is most *opposite* in meaning.

	Word				Match		
1.	___ heresy	6.	___ fervent	A.	predictable	F.	beneficial
2.	___ fickle	7.	___ fundamental	B.	dispassionate	G.	orthodoxy
3.	___ illusory	8.	___ furtive	C.	simple	H.	organized
4.	___ frivolity	9.	___ futile	D.	extraneous	I.	candid
5.	___ grandiose	10.	___ haphazard	E.	real	J.	seriousness

> **DIRECTIONS:** Match each word in the left column with the word in the right column that is most *similar* in meaning.

Word		**Match**	
11. ____ glutton	14. ____ hackneyed	A. hinder	D. overeater
12. ____ heed	15. ____ hindrance	B. obstacle	E. obey
13. ____ hamper		C. trite	

GROUP 7

immune – *adj.* – protected; unthreatened by

immutable – *adj.* – unchangeable; permanent

impartial – *adj.* – unbiased; fair

impetuous – 1. *adj.* – rash; impulsive; 2. forcible; violent

implication – *n.* – suggestion; inference

inadvertent – *adj.* – not on purpose; unintentional

incessant – *adj.* – constant; continual

incidental – *adj.* – extraneous; unexpected

inclined – 1. *adj.* – apt to; likely to; 2. angled

incoherent – *adj.* – illogical; rambling

incompatible – *adj.* – disagreeing; disharmonious

incredulous – *adj.* – unwilling to believe; skeptical

indifferent – *adj.* – unconcerned

indolent – *adj.* – lazy; inactive

indulgent – *adj.* – lenient; patient

inevitable – *adj.* – sure to happen; unavoidable

infamous – *adj.* – having a bad reputation; notorious

infer – *v.* – form an opinion; conclude

initiate – 1. *v.* – begin; admit into a group; 2. *n.* – a person who is in the process of being admitted into a group

innate – *adj.* – natural; inborn

innocuous – *adj.* – harmless; innocent

innovate – *v.* – introduce a change; depart from the old

insipid – *adj.* – uninteresting; bland

instigate – *v.* – start; provoke

intangible – *adj.* – incapable of being touched; immaterial

Drill 7

DIRECTIONS: Match each word in the left column with the word in the right column that is most *opposite* in meaning.

	Word				Match		
1. ___	immutable	6. ___	innate	A.	intentional	F.	changeable
2. ___	impartial	7. ___	incredulous	B.	articulate	G.	avoidable
3. ___	inadvertent	8. ___	inevitable	C.	gullible	H.	harmonious
4. ___	incoherent	9. ___	intangible	D.	material	I.	learned
5. ___	incompatible	10. ___	indolent	E.	biased	J.	energetic

DIRECTIONS: Match each word in the left column with the word in the right column that is most *similar* in meaning.

	Word				Match		
11. ___	impetuous	14. ___	instigate	A.	lenient	D.	conclude
12. ___	incidental	15. ___	indulgent	B.	impulsive	E.	extraneous
13. ___	infer			C.	provoke		

GROUP 8

ironic – *adj.* – contradictory; inconsistent; sarcastic

irrational – *adj.* – not logical

jeopardy – *n.* – danger

kindle – *v.* – ignite; arouse

languid – *adj.* – weak; fatigued

laud – *v.* – to praise

lax – *adj.* – careless; irresponsible

lethargic – *adj.* – lazy; passive

levity – *n.* – silliness; lack of seriousness

lucid – 1. *adj.* – shining; 2. easily understood

magnanimous – *adj.* – forgiving; unselfish

malicious – *adj.* – spiteful; vindictive

marred – *adj.* – damaged

meander – *v.* – wind on a course; go aimlessly

melancholy – *n.* – depression; gloom

meticulous – *adj.* – exacting; precise

minute – *adj.* – extremely small; tiny

miser – *n.* – penny pincher; stingy person

mitigate – *v.* – alleviate; lessen; soothe

morose – *adj.* – moody; despondent

negligence – *n.* – carelessness

nostalgic – *adj.* – longing for the past; filled with bittersweet memories

novel – *adj.* – new

Drill 8

DIRECTIONS: Match each word in the left column with the word in the right column that is most *opposite* in meaning.

Word				**Match**	
1. ___ irrational	6. ___ magnanimous		A. extinguish		F. ridicule
2. ___ kindle	7. ___ levity		B. jovial		G. kindly
3. ___ meticulous	8. ___ minute		C. selfish		H. sloppy
4. ___ malicious	9. ___ laud		D. logical		I. huge
5. ___ morose	10. ___ novel		E. seriousness		J. stale

DIRECTIONS: Match each word in the left column with the word in the right column that is most *similar* in meaning.

Word		Match	
11. ____ ironic	14. ____ jeopardy	A. lessen	D. carelessness
12. ____ marred	15. ____ negligence	B. damaged	E. danger
13. ____ mitigate		C. sarcastic	

GROUP 9

nullify – *v.* – cancel; invalidate

objective – 1. *adj.* – open-minded; impartial; 2. *n.* – goal

obscure – *adj.* – not easily understood; dark

obsolete – *adj.* – out of date; passe

ominous – *adj.* – threatening

optimist – *n.* – person who hopes for the best; sees the good side

orthodox – *adj.* – traditional; accepted

pagan – 1. *n.* – polytheist; 2. *adj.* – polytheistic

partisan – 1. *n.* – supporter; follower; 2. *adj.* – biased; one sided

perceptive – *adj.* – full of insight; aware

peripheral – *adj.* – marginal; outer

pernicious – *adj.* – dangerous; harmful

pessimism – *n.* – seeing only the gloomy side; hopelessness

phenomenon – 1. *n.* – miracle; 2. occurrence

philanthropy – *n.* – charity; unselfishness

pious – *adj.* – religious; devout; dedicated

placate – *v.* – pacify

plausible – *adj.* – probable; feasible

pragmatic – *adj.* – matter-of-fact; practical

preclude – *v.* – inhibit; make impossible

predecessor – *n.* – one who has occupied an office before another

prodigal – *adj.* – wasteful; lavish

prodigious – *adj.* – exceptional; tremendous

profound – *adj.* – deep; knowledgeable; thorough

profusion – *n.* – great amount; abundance

Drill 9

DIRECTIONS: Match each word in the left column with the word in the right column that is most *opposite* in meaning.

Word			Match		
1. ___ objective	6. ___ plausible		A. scanty	F. minute
2. ___ obsolete	7. ___ preclude		B. assist	G. anger
3. ___ placate	8. ___ prodigious		C. superficial	H. pessimism
4. ___ profusion	9. ___ profound		D. biased	I. modern
5. ___ peripheral	10. ___ optimism		E. improbable	J. central

DIRECTIONS: Match each word in the left column with the word in the right column that is most *similar* in meaning.

Word			Match	
11. ___ nullify	14. ___ pernicious		A. invalidate	D. threatening
12. ___ ominous	15. ___ prodigal		B. follower	E. harmful
13. ___ partisan			C. lavish	

GROUP 10

prosaic – *adj.* – tiresome; ordinary

provincial – *adj.* – regional; unsophisticated

provocative – 1. *adj.* – tempting; 2. irritating

prudent – *adj.* – wise; careful; prepared

qualified – *adj.* – experienced; indefinite

rectify – *v.* – correct

redundant – *adj.* – repetitious; unnecessary

refute – *v.* – challenge; disprove

relegate – *v.* – banish; put to a lower position

relevant – *adj.* – of concern; significant

remorse – *n.* – guilt; sorrow

reprehensible – *adj.* – wicked; disgraceful

repudiate – *v.* – reject; cancel

rescind – *v.* – retract; discard

resignation – 1. *n.* – quitting; 2. submission

resolution – *n.* – proposal; promise; determination

respite – *n.* – recess; rest period

reticent – *adj.* – silent; reserved; shy

reverent – *adj.* – respectful

rhetorical – *adj.* – having to do with verbal communication

rigor – *n.* – severity

sagacious – *adj.* – wise; cunning

sanguine – 1. *adj.* – optimistic; cheerful; 2. red

saturate – *v.* – soak thoroughly; drench

scanty – *adj.* – inadequate; sparse

Drill 10

DIRECTIONS: Match each word in the left column with the word in the right column that is most *opposite* in meaning.

	Word			Match	
1. ___ provincial		6. ___ remorse	A. inexperienced	F. affirm
2. ___ reticent		7. ___ repudiate	B. joy	G. extraordinary
3. ___ prudent		8. ___ sanguine	C. pessimistic	H. sophisticated

4. ____ qualified   9. ____ relevant   D. unrelated   I. forward

5. ____ relegate   10. ____ prosaic   E. careless   J. promote

---

DIRECTIONS: Match each word in the left column with the word in the right column that is most *similar* in meaning.

	Word			**Match**	
11. ____ provocative	14. ____ rescind		A. drench	D. severity
12. ____ rigor	15. ____ reprehensible		B. tempting	E. blameworthy
13. ____ saturate			C. retract	

GROUP 11

scrupulous – *adj.* – honorable; exact

scrutinize – *v.* – examine closely; study

servile – *adj.* – slavish; groveling

skeptic – *n.* – doubter

slander – *v.* – defame; maliciously misrepresent

solemnity – *n.* – seriousness

solicit – *v.* – ask; seek

stagnant – *adj.* – motionless; uncirculating

stanza – *n.* – group of lines in a poem having a definite pattern

static – *adj.* – inactive; changeless

stoic – *adj.* – detached; unruffled; calm

subtlety – 1. *n.* – understatement; 2. propensity for understatement; 3. sophistication; 4. cunning

superficial – *adj.* – on the surface; narrow-minded; lacking depth

superfluous – *adj.* – unnecessary; extra

surpass – *v.* – go beyond; outdo

sycophant – *n.* – flatterer

symmetry – *n.* – correspondence of parts; harmony

taciturn – *adj.* – reserved; quiet; secretive

tedious – *adj.* – time-consuming; burdensome; uninteresting

temper – *v.* – soften; pacify; compose

tentative – *adj.* – not confirmed; indefinite

thrifty – *adj.* – economical; pennywise

tranquility – *n.* – peace; stillness; harmony

trepidation – *n.* – apprehension; uneasiness

trivial – *adj.* – unimportant; small; worthless

Drill 11

DIRECTIONS: Match each word in the left column with the word in the right column that is most *opposite* in meaning.

Word   **Match**

1. ___ scrutinize   6. ___ tentative   A. frivolity   F. skim

2. ___ skeptic   7. ___ thrifty   B. enjoyable   G. turbulent

3. ___ solemnity   8. ___ tranquility C. prodigal   H. active

4. ___ static   9. ___ solicit   D. chaos   I. believer

5. ___ tedious   10. ___ stagnant   E. give   J. confirmed

DIRECTIONS: Match each word in the left column with the word in the right column that is most *similar* in meaning.

Word   **Match**

11. ___ symmetry   14. ___ subtle   A. understated   D. fear

12. ___ superfluous 15. ___ trepidation B. unnecessary   E. flatterer

13. ___ sycophant   C. balance

GROUP 12

tumid – *adj.* – swollen; inflated

undermine – *v.* – weaken; ruin

uniform – *adj.* – consistent; unvaried; unchanging

universal – *adj.* – concerning everyone; existing everywhere

unobtrusive – *adj.* – inconspicuous; reserved

unprecedented – *adj.* – unheard of; exceptional

unpretentious – *adj.* – simple; plain; modest

vacillation – *n.* – fluctuation

valid – *adj.* – acceptable; legal

vehement – *adj.* – intense; excited; enthusiastic

venerate – *v.* – revere

verbose – *adj.* – wordy; talkative

viable – 1. *adj.* – capable of maintaining life; 2. possible; attainable

vigor – *n.* – energy; forcefulness

vilify – *v.* – slander

virtuoso – *n.* – highly skilled artist

virulent – *adj.* – deadly; harmful; malicious

vital – *adj.* – important; spirited

volatile – *adj.* – changeable; undependable

vulnerable – *adj.* – open to attack; unprotected

wane – *v.* – grow gradually smaller

whimsical – *adj.* – fanciful; amusing

wither – *v.* – wilt; shrivel; humiliate; cut down

zealot – *n.* – believer; enthusiast; fan

zenith – *n.* – point directly overhead in the sky

Drill 12

DIRECTIONS: Match each word in the left column with the word in the right column that is most *opposite* in meaning.

	Word			Match		
1. ____ uniform		6. ____ vigorous	A. amateur		F. support	
2. ____ virtuoso		7. ____ volatile	B. trivial		G. constancy	
3. ____ vital		8. ____ vacillation	C. visible		H. lethargic	
4. ____ wane		9. ____ undermine	D. placid		I. wax	
5. ____ unobtrusive		10. ____ valid	E. unacceptable		J. varied	

DIRECTIONS: Match each word in the left column with the word in the right column that is most *similar* in meaning.

	Word		Match	
11. ____ wither		14. ____ vehement	A. intense	D. possible
12. ____ whimsical		15. ____ virulent	B. deadly	E. shrivel
13. ____ viable			C. amusing	

KNOWING YOUR WORD PARTS

Memorization and practice are not the only ways to learn the meanings of new words. While taking this test, you will have nothing but your own knowledge and context clues to refer to when you come into contact with unfamiliar words. Even though we have provided you with a comprehensive list of words, there is a very good chance that you will come across words that you still do not know. Therefore, you will need to study our list of prefixes, roots, and suffixes in order to be prepared.

PREFIXES

Prefix	Meaning	Example
ab-, a-, abs-	away, from	absent – away, not present abstain – keep from doing, refrain
ad-	to, toward	adjacent – next to address – to direct towards
ante-	before	antecedent – going before in time anterior – occurring before
anti-	against	antidote – remedy to act against an evil antibiotic – substance that fights against bacteria
be-	over, thoroughly	bemoan – to mourn over belabor – to exert much labor upon
bi-	two	bisect – to divide biennial – happening every two years
cata-, cat-, cath-	down	catacombs – underground passage ways
circum-	around	circumscribe – to draw a circle around circumspect – watchful on all sides
com-	with	combine – join together communication – to have dealing with
contra-	against	contrary – opposed contrast – to stand in opposition

de-	down, from	decline – to bend downward
		decontrol – to release from government control
di-	two	dichotomy – cutting in two
		diarchy – system of government with two authorities
dis-, di-	apart, away	discern – to distinguish as separate
		digress – to turn away from the subject of attention
epi-, ep-, eph-	upon, among	epidemic – happening among many people
		episode – one in a series of events
ex-, e-	from, out	exceed – go beyond the limit
		emit – to send forth
extra-	outside, beyond	extraordinary – beyond or out of the common method
		extrasensory – beyond the senses
hyper-	beyond, over	hyperactive – over the normal activity level
		hypercritic – one who is critical beyond measure
hypo-	beneath, lower	hypodermic – parts beneath the skin
		hypocrisy – to be under a pretense of goodness
in-, il-, im-, ir-	not	inactive – not active
		irreversible – not reversible
in-, il-, im-, ir-	in, on, into	instill – to put in slowly
		impose – to lay on
inter-	among, between	intercom – to exchange conversations between people
		interlude – performance given between parts in a play
intra-	within	intravenous – within a vein
		intramural – within a single college or its students

meta-	beyond, over, along with	metamorphosis – change over in form or nature
		metatarsus – part of foot beyond the flat of the foot
mis-	badly, wrongly	misconstrue – to interpret wrongly
		misappropriate – to use wrongly
mono-	one	monogamy – to be married to one person at a time
		monotone – a single, unvaried tone
multi-	many	multiple – of many parts
		multitude – a great number
non-	no, not	nonsense – lack of sense
		nonentity – not existing
ob-	against	obscene – offensive to modesty
		obstruct – to hinder the passage of
para-, par-	beside	parallel – continuously at equal distance apart
		parenthesis – sentence inserted within a passage
per-	through	persevere – to maintain an effort
		permeate – to pass through
poly-	many	polygon – a plane figure with many sides or angles
		polytheism – belief in existence of many gods
post-	after	posterior – coming after
		postpone – to put off till a future time
pre-	before	premature –occuring before the proper time
		premonition – a previous warning
pro-	in favor of, forward	prolific – bringing forth offspring
		project – throw or cast forward

re-	back, again	reimburse – pay back
		retract – to draw back
semi-	half	semicircle – half a circle
		semiannual – half-yearly
sub-	under	subdue – to bring under one's power
		submarine – travel under the surface of the sea
super-	above	supersonic – above the speed of sound
		superior – higher in place or position
tele-, tel-	across	telecast – transmit across a distance
		telepathy – communication between minds
trans-	across	transpose – to change the position of two things
		transmit – to send from one person to another
ultra-	beyond	ultraviolet – light beyond the limit of visibility
		ultramarine – beyond the sea
un-	not	undeclared – not declared
		unbelievable – not believable
uni-	one	unity – state of oneness
		unison – sounding together
with-	away, against	withhold – to hold back
		withdraw – to take away

ROOTS

Root	Meaning	Example
act, ag	do, act, drive	activate – to make active
		agile – having quick motion
alt	high	altitude – height
		alto – highest singing voice
alter, altr	other, change	alternative – choice between two things
		altruism – living for the good of others
am, ami	love, friend	amiable – worthy of affection
		amity – friendship
anim	mind, spirit	animated – spirited
		animosity – violent hatred
annu, enni	year	annual – every year
		centennial – every hundred years
aqua	water	aquarium – tank for water animals and plants
		aquamarine – semiprecious stone of sea-green color
arch	first, ruler	archenemy – chief enemy
		archetype – original pattern from which things are copied
aud	hear	audible – capable of being heard
		audience – assembly of hearers
auto	self	automatic – self-acting
		autobiography –story one writes about oneself
bell	war	belligerent – a party taking part in a war
		bellicose – war-like

ben, bene	good	benign – kindly disposition
		beneficial – advantageous
bio	life	biotic – relating to life
		biology – the study of life
brev	short	abbreviate – make shorter
		brevity – shortness
cad, cas	fall	cadence – fall in voice
		casualty – loss caused by death
capit, cap	head	captain – the head or chief
		decapitate – to cut off the head
cede, ceed, cess	to go, to yield	recede – to move or fall back
		proceed – to move onward
cent	hundred	century – hundred years
		centipede – insect with a hundred legs
chron	time	chronology – science dealing with historical dates
		chronicle – register of events in order of time
cide, cis	to kill, to cut	homicide – murder
		incision – a cut
clam, claim	to shout	acclaim – receive with applause
		proclamation – announce publicly
cogn	to know	recognize – to know again
		cognition – awareness
corp	body	incorporate – combine into one body
		corpse – dead body
cred	to trust, to believe	incredible – unbelievable
		credulous – too prone to believe
cur, curr, curs	to run	current – flowing body of air or water
		excursion – short trip
dem	people	democracy – government formed for the people

dic, dict	to say	dictate – to read aloud for another to transcribe
		verdict – decision of a jury
doc, doct	to teach	docile – easily instructed
		indoctrinate – to instruct
domin	to rule	dominate – to rule
		dominion – territory of rule
duc, duct	to lead	conduct – act of guiding
		induce – to overcome by persuasion
eu	well, good	eulogy – speech or writing in praise
		euphony – pleasantness or smoothness of sound
fac, fact, fect, fic	to do, to make	factory – location of production
		fiction – something invented or imagined
fer	to bear, to carry	transfer – to move from one place to another
		refer – to direct to
fin	end, limit	infinity – unlimited
		finite – limited in quantity
flect, flex	to bend	flexible – easily bent
		reflect – to throw back
fort	luck	fortunate – lucky
		fortuitous – happening by chance
fort	strong	fortify – strengthen
		fortress – stronghold
frag, fract	break	fragile – easily broken
		fracture – break
fug	flee	fugitive – fleeing
		refugee – one who flees to a place of safety

gen	class, race	engender – to breed
		generic – of a general nature in regard to all members
grad, gress	to go, to step	regress – to go back
		graduate – to divide into regular steps
gram, graph	writing	telegram – message sent by telegraph
		autograph – person's handwriting or signature
ject	to throw	projectile – capable of being thrown
		reject – to throw away
leg	law	legitimate – lawful
		legal – defined by law
leg, lig, lect	to choose, gather, read	illegible – incapable of being read
		election – the act of choosing
liber	free	liberal – favoring freedom of ideas
		liberty – freedom from restraint
log, logy	study, speech	archaeology – study of human antiquities
		prologue – address spoken before a performance
luc, lum	light	translucent – slightly transparent
		illuminate – to light up
magn	large, great	magnify – to make larger
		magnificent – great
mal, male	bad, wrong	malfunction – to operate incorrectly
		malevolent – evil
mar	sea	marine – pertaining to the sea
		submarine – below the surface of the sea
mater, matr	mother	maternal – motherly
		matriarchy – government exercised by a mother

mit, miss	to send	transmit – to send from one person or place to another
		mission – the act of sending
morph	shape	metamorphosis – a changing in shape
		anthropomorphic – assuming a human shape
mut	change	mutable – subject to change
		mutate – to change
nat	born	innate – inborn
		native – a person born in a given place
neg	deny	negative – expressing denial
		renege – to deny
nom	name	nominate – to put forward a name
		anonymous – no name given
nov	new	novel – new
		renovate – to make as good as new
omni	all	omnipotent – all powerful
		omnipresent – all present
oper	to work	operate – to work on something
		cooperate – to work with others
pass, path	to feel	pathetic – affecting the tender emotions
		passionate – moved by strong emotion
pater, patr	father	paternal – fatherly
		patriarchy – government exercised by a father
ped, pod	foot	pedestrian – one who travels on foot
		podiatrist – foot doctor
pel, puls	to drive, to push	impel – to drive forward
		compulsion – irresistible force
phil	love	philharmonic – loving harmony or music

		philanthropist – one who loves and seeks to do good for others
port	carry	export – to carry out of the country
		portable – able to be carried
psych	mind	psychology – study of the mind
		psychiatrist – specialist in mental disorders
quer, ques, quir, quis	to ask	inquiry – to ask about
		question – that which is asked
rid, ris	to laugh	ridiculous – laughable
		derision – to mock
rupt	to break	interrupt – to break in upon
		erupt – to break through
sci	to know	science – systematic knowledge of physical or natural phenomena
		conscious – having inward knowledge
scrib, script	to write	transcribe – to write over again
		script – text of words
sent, sens	to feel, to think	sentimental – feel great emotion
		sensitive – easily affected by changes
sequ, secut	to follow	sequence – connected series
		consecutive – following one another in unbroken order
solv, solu, solut	to loosen	dissolve – to break up
		absolute – without restraint
spect	to look at	spectator – one who watches
		inspect – to look at closely
spir	to breathe	inspire – to breathe in
		respiration – process of breathing

string, strict	to bind	stringent – binding strongly
		restrict – to restrain within bounds
stru, struct	to build	misconstrue – to interpret wrongly
		construct – to build
tang, ting,		
tact, tig	to touch	tangent – touching, but not intersecting
		contact – touching
ten, tent, tain	to hold	tenure – holding of office
		contain – to hold
term	to end	terminate – to end
		terminal – having an end
terr	earth	terrain – tract of land
		terrestrial – existing on earth
therm	heat	thermal – pertaining to heat
		thermometer – instrument for measuring temperature
tort, tors	to twist	contortionist – one who twists violently
		torsion – act of turning or twisting
tract	to pull, to draw	attract – draw toward
		distract – to draw away
vac	empty	vacant – empty
		evacuate – to empty out
ven, vent	to come	prevent – to stop from coming
		intervene – to come between
ver	true	verify – to prove to be true
		veracious – truthful
verb	word	verbose – use of excess words
		verbatim – word for word
vid, vis	to see	video – picture phase of television
		vision – act of seeing external objects

vinc, vict,		
vang	to conquer	invincible – unconquerable
		victory – defeat of enemy
viv, vit	life	vital – necessary to life
		vivacious – lively
voc	to call	provocative – serving to excite or stimulate to action
		vocal – uttered by voice
vol	to wish, to will	involuntary – outside the control of will
		volition – the act of willing or choosing

SUFFIXES

Suffix	Meaning	Example
-able, -ble	capable of	believable – capable of believing
		legible – capable of being read
-acious, -icious, -ous	full of	vivacious – full of life
		wondrous – full of wonder
-ant, -ent	full of	eloquent – full of eloquence
		expectant – full of expectation
-ary	connected with	honorary – for the sake of honor
		disciplinary – enforcing instruction
-ate	to make	ventilate – to make public
		consecrate – to dedicate
-fy	to make	magnify – to make larger
		testify – to make witness
-ile	pertaining to, capable of	docile – capable of being managed easily
		civil – pertaining to a city or state

-ism	belief, ideal	conservationism – ideal of keeping safe
		sensationalism – matter, language designed to excite
-ist	doer	artist – one who creates art
		pianist – one who plays the piano
-ose	full of	verbose – full of words
		grandiose – striking, imposing
-osis	condition	neurosis – nervous condition
		psychosis – psychological condition
-tude	state	magnitude – state of greatness
		multitude – state of quantity

Drill 13: Reading Comprehension

DIRECTIONS: Read the passage and answer the questions that follow.

Water

The most important source of sediment is earth and rock material carried to the sea by rivers and streams; the same materials may also have been transported by glaciers and winds. Other sources are volcanic ash and lava, shells and skeletons of organisms, chemical precipitates formed in seawater, and particles from outer space.

Water is a most unusual substance because it exists on the surface of the earth in its three physical states: ice, water, and water vapor. There are other substances that might exist in a solid and liquid or gaseous state at temperatures normally found at the earth's surface, but there are no other substances which occur in all three states.

Water is odorless, tasteless, and colorless. It is the only substance known to exist in a natural state as a solid, liquid, or gas on the surface of the earth. It is a universal solvent. Water does not corrode, rust, burn, or separate into its components easily. It is chemically indestructible. It can corrode almost any metal and erode the most solid rock. A unique property of water is that it expands and floats on water when frozen or in the solid state. Water has a freezing point of 0°C and a boiling point of 100°C. Water has the capacity for absorbing great quantities of heat with relatively little increase in temperature. When *distilled*, water is a poor conductor of electricity but when salt is added, it is a good conductor of electricity.

Sunlight is the source of energy for temperature change, evaporation, and currents for water movement through the atmosphere. Sunlight controls the rate of photosynthesis for all marine plants, which are directly or indirectly the source of food for all marine animals. Migration, breeding, and other behaviors of marine animals are affected by light.

Water, as the ocean or sea, is blue because of the molecular scattering of the sunlight. Blue light, being of short wavelength, is scattered more effectively than light of longer wavelengths. Variations in color may be caused by particles suspended in the water, water depth, cloud cover, temperature, and other variable factors. Heavy concentrations of dissolved materials cause a yellowish hue, while algae will cause the water to look green. Heavy populations of plant and animal materials will cause the water to look brown.

1. Which of the following lists of topics best organizes the information in the selection?

    (A) I. Water as vapor

         II. Water as ice

         III. Water as solid

    (B) I. Properties of seawater

         II. Freezing and boiling points of water

         III. Photosynthesis

         IV. Oceans and seas

    (C) I. Water as substance

         II. Water's corrosion

         III. Water and plants

         IV. Water and algae coloration

    (D) I. Water's physical states

         II. Properties of water

         III. Effects of the sun on water

         IV. Reasons for color variation in water

2. According to the passage, what is the most unique property of water?

    (A) Water is odorless, tasteless, and colorless.

    (B) Water exists on the surface of the earth in three physical states.

    (C) Water is chemically indestructible.

    (D) Water is a poor conductor of electricity.

3. Which of the following best defines the word *distilled* as it is used in the last sentence of the third paragraph?

    (A) Free of salt content

    (B) Free of electrical energy

    (C) Dehydrated

    (D) Containing wine

4. The writer's main purpose in this selection is to

   (A) explain the colors of water.

   (B) examine the effects of the sun on water.

   (C) define the properties of water.

   (D) describe the three physical states of all liquids.

5. The writer of this selection would most likely agree with which of the following statements?

   (A) The properties of water are found in most other liquids on this planet.

   (B) Water should not be consumed in its most natural state.

   (C) Water might be used to serve many different functions.

   (D) Water is too unpredictable for most scientists.

DIRECTIONS: Read the passage and answer the questions that follow.

The Beginnings of the Submarine

A submarine was first used as an offensive weapon during the American Revolutionary War. The Turtle, a one-man submersible designed by an American inventor named David Bushnell and hand-operated by a screw propeller, attempted to sink a British man-of-war in New York Harbor. The plan was to attach a charge of gunpowder to the ship's bottom with screws and explode it with a time fuse. After repeated failures to force the screws through the copper sheathing of the hull of H.M.S. *Eagle*, the submarine gave up and withdrew, exploding its powder a short distance from the *Eagle*. Although the attack was unsuccessful, it caused the British to move their blockading ships from the harbor to the outer bay.

On 17 February 1864, a Confederate craft, a hand-propelled submersible, carrying a crew of eight men, sank a Federal corvette that was blockading Charleston Harbor. The hit was accomplished by a torpedo suspended ahead of the Confederate *Hunley* as she rammed the Union frigate *Housatonic*, and is the first recorded instance of a submarine sinking a warship.

The submarine first became a major component in naval warfare during World War I, when Germany demonstrated its full potential. Wholesale sinking of Allied shipping by the German U-boats almost swung the war in favor of the Central Powers. Then, as now, the submarine's greatest advantage was that it could operate beneath the ocean surface where detection was difficult. Sinking a submarine was comparatively easy, once it was found — but finding it before it could attack was another matter.

During the closing months of World War I, the Allied Submarine Devices Investigation Committee was formed to obtain from science and technology more effective underwater detection equipment. The committee developed a reasonably accurate device for locating a submerged submarine. This device was a trainable hydrophone, which was attached to the bottom of the ASW ship, and used to detect screw noises and other sounds that came from a submarine. Although the committee disbanded after World War I, the British made improvements on the locating device during the interval between then and World War II, and named it ASDIC after the committee.

American scientists further improved on the device, calling it SONAR, a name derived from the underlined initials of the words sound navigation and ranging.

At the end of World War II, the United States improved the snorkel (a device for bringing air to the crew and engines when operating submerged on diesels) and developed the Guppy (short for greater underwater propulsion power), a conversion of the fleet-type submarine of World War II fame. The superstructure was changed by reducing the surface area, streamlining every protruding object, and enclosing the periscope shears in a streamlined metal faring. Performance increased greatly with improved electronic equipment, additional battery capacity, and the addition of the snorkel.

6. The passage implies that one of the most pressing modifications needed for the submarine was to

(A) streamline its shape.

(B) enlarge the submarine for accommodating more torpedoes and men.

(C) reduce the noise caused by the submarine.

(D) add a snorkel.

7. It is inferred that

(A) ASDIC was formed to obtain technology for underwater detection.

(B) ASDIC developed an accurate device for locating submarines.

(C) the hydrophone was attached to the bottom of the ship.

(D) ASDIC was formed to develop technology to defend U.S. shipping.

8. SONAR not only picked up the sound of submarines moving through the water but also

(A) indicated the speed at which the sub was moving.

(B) gave the location of the submarine.

(C) indicated the speed of the torpedo.

(D) placed the submarine within a specified range.

9. According to the passage, the submarine's success was due in part to its ability to

(A) strike and escape undetected.

(B) move swifter than other vessels.

(C) submerge to great depths while being hunted.

(D) run silently.

10. From the passage, one can infer

(A) David Bushnell was indirectly responsible for the sinking of the Federal corvette in Charlestown Harbor.

(B) David Bushnell invented the Turtle.

(C) the Turtle was a one-man submarine.

(D) the Turtle sank the *Eagle* on February 17, 1864.

ANSWER KEY TO DRILL QUESTIONS

Drill 1
1.	(J)	9.	(F)
2.	(G)	10.	(E)
3.	(A)	11.	(D)
4.	(C)	12.	(C)
5.	(H)	13.	(A)
6.	(B)	14.	(E)
7.	(I)	15.	(B)
8.	(D)		

Drill 2
1.	(D)	9.	(B)
2.	(G)	10.	(H)
3.	(I)	11.	(D)
4.	(F)	12.	(A)
5.	(A)	13.	(B)
6.	(J)	14.	(E)
7.	(E)	15.	(C)
8.	(C)		

Drill 3
1.	(E)	9.	(F)
2.	(H)	10.	(D)
3.	(J)	11.	(C)
4.	(A)	12.	(A)
5.	(I)	13.	(E)
6.	(B)	14.	(D)
7.	(C)	15.	(B)
8.	(G)		

Drill 4
1.	(D)	9.	(H)
2.	(E)	10.	(G)
3.	(A)	11.	(D)
4.	(I)	12.	(A)
5.	(J)	13.	(B)
6.	(B)	14.	(C)
7.	(C)	15.	(E)
8.	(F)		

Drill 5
1.	(H)	9.	(D)
2.	(F)	10.	(G)
3.	(A)	11.	(B)
4.	(B)	12.	(D)
5.	(J)	13.	(A)
6.	(C)	14.	(E)
7.	(I)	15.	(C)
8.	(E)		

Drill 6
1.	(G)	9.	(F)
2.	(A)	10.	(H)
3.	(E)	11.	(D)
4.	(J)	12.	(E)
5.	(C)	13.	(A)
6.	(B)	14.	(C)
7.	(D)	15.	(B)
8.	(I)		

Drill 7
1.	(F)	9.	(D)
2.	(E)	10.	(J)
3.	(A)	11.	(B)
4.	(B)	12.	(E)
5.	(H)	13.	(D)
6.	(I)	14.	(C)
7.	(C)	15.	(A)
8.	(G)		

Drill 8
1.	(D)	9.	(F)
2.	(A)	10.	(J)
3.	(H)	11.	(C)
4.	(G)	12.	(B)
5.	(B)	13.	(A)
6.	(C)	14.	(E)
7.	(E)	15.	(D)
8.	(I)		

Drill 9

1.	(D)	9.	(C)
2.	(I)	10.	(H)
3.	(G)	11.	(A)
4.	(A)	12.	(D)
5.	(J)	13.	(B)
6.	(E)	14.	(E)
7.	(B)	15.	(C)
8.	(F)		

Drill 10

1.	(H)	9.	(D)
2.	(I)	10.	(G)
3.	(E)	11.	(B)
4.	(A)	12.	(D)
5.	(J)	13.	(A)
6.	(B)	14.	(C)
7.	(F)	15.	(E)
8.	(C)		

Drill 11

1.	(F)	9.	(E)
2.	(I)	10.	(G)
3.	(A)	11.	(C)
4.	(H)	12.	(B)
5.	(B)	13.	(E)
6.	(J)	14.	(A)
7.	(C)	15.	(D)
8.	(D)		

Drill 12

1.	(J)	6.	(H)
2.	(A)	7.	(D)
3.	(B)	8.	(G)
4.	(I)	9.	(F)
5.	(C)	10.	(E)

READING COMPREHENSION—DETAILED EXPLANATIONS OF ANSWERS

1. **(D)** The correct response is (D) because its precepts are summations of each of the composition's main paragraphs. (A) only mentions points made in the second paragraph. (B) and (C) only mention scattered points made throughout the passage, each of which does not represent a larger body of information within the passage.

2. **(B)** The second paragraph states that this is the reason that water is a most unusual substance. (A) and (C) list unusual properties of water, but are not developed in the same manner as the property stated in (B). (D) is not even correct under all circumstances.

3. **(A)** The sentence contrasts distilled water to that which contains salt, so (A) is correct. (B), (C), and (D) are not implied by the passage.

4. **(C)** The writer's didactic summary of water's properties is the only perspective found in the passage. (A) and (B) are the subjects of individual paragraphs within the passage, but hardly represent the entire passage itself. An in-depth discussion of the physical states of liquids (D) is not offered within the passage.

5. **(C)** The correct choice is (C) because of the many properties of water ascribed to it in the passage, each of which might serve one practical purpose or another. (A) and (D) are contradicted within the passage, while (B) is not implied at all by the passage.

6. **(A)** Answer (A) is correct because of the importance of streamlining mentioned in the final paragraph. (B) and (C) are not suggested in the paragraph, and (D) is secondary in importance to (A).

7. **(D)** Since it may be inferred from the general purpose of underwater detection equipment, (D) is correct. While (A) and (B) are true statements, they are not inferences. (C) is not implied in the passage.

8. **(D)** Answer (D) is correct because the "R" in SONAR stands for "Ranging." (A), (B), and (C) are neither mentioned nor implied by the passage.

9. **(A)** As was mentioned in the third sentence of the third paragraph, (A) is correct. (B), (C), and (D) are not mentioned in the passage.

10. **(A)** It may be inferred that Bushnell's invention led to the success of the later version of the submarine. (B) and (C) are true, but are not inferences because they are directly stated in the first paragraph. (D) is not a true statement; the Turtle had no direct link to the 1864 incident.

Chapter 6

Writing Skills Review

The requirements for informal spoken English are much more relaxed than the rigid rules for "standard written English." While slang, colloquialisms, and other informal expressions are acceptable and sometimes very appropriate in casual speech, they are inappropriate in academic and business writing. More often than not, writers, especially student writers, do not make a distinction between the two: they use the same words, grammar, and sentence structure from their everyday speech in their college papers, albeit unsuccessfully.

The NYSTCE does not require you to know grammatical terms such as *gerund*, *subject complement*, or *dependent clause*, although general familiarity with such terms may be helpful to you in determining whether a sentence or part of a sentence is correct or incorrect. You should watch for errors in grammar, spelling, punctuation, capitalization, sentence structure, and word choice. Remember: this is a test of written language skills; therefore, your responses should be based on what you know to be correct for written work, not what you know to be appropriate for a casual conversation. For instance, in informal speech, you might say "Who are you going to choose?" But in formal academic writing, you would write "Whom are you going to choose?" Your choices, then, should be dictated by requirements for *written*, not *conversational* English.

WORD CHOICE SKILLS

CONNOTATIVE AND DENOTATIVE MEANINGS

The denotative meaning of a word is its *literal*, dictionary definition: what the word denotes or "means." The connotative meaning of a word is what the word connotes or "suggests"; it is a meaning apart from what the word literally means. A writer should choose a word based on the tone and context of the sentence; this ensures that a word bears the appropriate connotation while still conveying some exactness in denotation. For example, a gift might be described as "cheap," but the directness of this word has a negative connotation—something cheap is something of little or no value. The word "inexpensive" has a more positive connotation, though "cheap" is a synonym for "inexpensive." Decisions of this type require you to determine the appropriateness of words and phrases for the context of a sentence.

WORDINESS AND CONCISENESS

Effective writing is concise. Wordiness, on the other hand, decreases the clarity of expression by cluttering sentences with unnecessary words.

Effective writing demands that you avoid redundancies (unnecessary repetitions), circumlocution (failure to get to the point), and padding with loose synonyms.

Notice the difference in impact between the first and second sentences in the following pairs:

INCORRECT: The medical exam that he gave me was entirely complete.

CORRECT: The medical exam he gave me was complete.

INCORRECT: Larry asked his friend John, who was a good, old friend, if he would join him and go along with him to see the foreign film made in Japan.

CORRECT: Larry asked his good, old friend John if he would join him in seeing the Japanese film.

INCORRECT: I was absolutely, totally happy with the present that my parents gave to me at 7 a.m. on the morning of my birthday.

CORRECT: I was happy with the present my parents gave me on the morning of my birthday.

Drill: Word Choice Skills

<u>DIRECTIONS</u>: Choose the correct option.

1. His <u>principal</u> reasons for resigning were his <u>principles</u> of right and wrong.

    (A) principal ... principals   (C) principle ... principles

    (B) principle ... principals   (D) No change is necessary.

2. The book tells about Alzheimer's disease—how it <u>affects</u> the patient and what <u>effect</u> it has on the patient's family.

    (A) effects ... affect   (C) effects ... effects

    (B) affects ... affect   (D) No change is necessary.

3. The <u>amount</u> of homeless children we can help depends on the <u>number</u> of available shelters.

    (A) number ... number   (C) number ... amount

    (B) amount ... amount   (D) No change is necessary.

4. All students are <u>suppose to</u> pass the test before <u>achieving</u> upper-division status.

    (A) suppose to ... acheiving

    (B) suppose to ... being achieved

    (C) supposed to ... achieving

    (D) No change is necessary.

5. The reason he <u>succeeded</u> is <u>because</u> he worked hard.

    (A) succeeded ... that   (C) succede ... because of

    (B) seceded ... that   (D) No change is necessary.

> **DIRECTIONS:** Select the sentence that clearly and effectively states the idea and has no structural errors.

6. (A) South of Richmond, the two roads converge together to form a single highway.

   (B) South of Richmond, the two roads converge together to form an interstate highway.

   (C) South of Richmond, the two roads converge to form an interstate highway.

   (D) South of Richmond, the two roads converge to form a single interstate highway.

7. (A) The student depended on his parents for financial support.

   (B) The student lacked the ways and means to pay for his room and board, so he depended on his parents for this kind of money and support.

   (C) The student lacked the ways and means or the wherewithal to support himself, so his parents provided him with the financial support he needed.

   (D) The student lacked the means to pay for his room and board, so he depended on his parents for financial support.

8. (A) Vincent van Gogh and Paul Gauguin were close personal friends and companions who enjoyed each other's company and frequently worked together on their artwork.

   (B) Vincent van Gogh and Paul Gauguin were friends who frequently painted together.

   (C) Vincent van Gogh was a close personal friend of Paul Gauguin's, and the two of them often worked together on their artwork because they enjoyed each other's company.

   (D) Vincent van Gogh, a close personal friend of Paul Gauguin's, often worked with him on their artwork.

9. (A) A college education often involves putting away childish thoughts, which are characteristic of youngsters, and concentrating on the future, which lies ahead.

(B) A college education involves putting away childish thoughts, which are characteristic of youngsters, and concentrating on the future.

(C) A college education involves putting away childish thoughts and concentrating on the future.

(D) A college education involves putting away childish thoughts and concentrating on the future which lies ahead.

10. (A) I had the occasion to visit an Oriental pagoda while I was a tourist on vacation and visiting in Kyoto, Japan.

(B) I visited a Japanese pagoda in Kyoto.

(C) I had occasion to visit a pagoda when I was vacationing in Kyoto, Japan.

(D) On my vacation, I visited a Japanese pagoda in Kyoto.

SENTENCE STRUCTURE SKILLS

PARALLELISM

Parallel structure is used to express matching ideas. It refers to the grammatical balance of a series of any of the following:

Phrases:

The squirrel ran *along the fence, up the tree,* and *into his burrow* with a mouthful of acorns.

Adjectives:

The job market is flooded with *very talented, highly motivated,* and *well-educated* young people.

Nouns:

You will need a *notebook, pencil,* and *dictionary* for the test.

Clauses:

The children were told to decide *which toy they would keep* and *which toy they would give away.*

Verbs:

The farmer *plowed*, *planted*, and *harvested* his corn in record time.

Verbals:

Reading, *writing*, and *calculating* are fundamental skills that all of us should possess.

Correlative conjunctions:

Either you will do your homework *or* you will fail.

Repetition of structural signals:

(such as articles, auxiliaries, prepositions, and conjunctions)

INCORRECT: I have quit my job, enrolled in school, and am looking for a reliable babysitter.

CORRECT: I *have quit* my job, *have enrolled* in school, and *am looking* for a reliable babysitter.

Note: Repetition of prepositions is considered formal and is not necessary.

You can travel *by car, by plane, or by train*; it's all up to you.

OR

You can travel *by car, plane, or train*; it's all up to you.

When a sentence contains items in a series, check for both punctuation and sentence balance. When you check for punctuation, make sure the commas are used correctly. When you check for parallelism, make sure that the conjunctions connect similar grammatical constructions, such as all adjectives or all clauses.

MISPLACED AND DANGLING MODIFIERS

A misplaced modifier is one that is in the wrong place in the sentence. Misplaced modifiers come in all forms—words, phrases, and clauses. Sentences containing misplaced modifiers are often very comical: *Mom made me eat the spinach instead of my brother*. Misplaced modifiers, like the one in this sentence, are usually too far away from the word or words they modify. This sentence should read: *Mom made me, instead of my brother, eat the spinach.*

Modifiers like *only*, *nearly*, and *almost* should be placed next to the word they modify and not in front of some other word, especially a verb, that they are not intended to modify.

A modifier is misplaced if it appears to modify the wrong part of the sentence or if we cannot be certain what part of the sentence the writer intended it to modify. To correct a misplaced modifier, move the modifier next to the word it describes.

> INCORRECT: She served hamburgers to the men on paper plates.

> CORRECT: She served hamburgers on paper plates to the men.

Split infinitives also result in misplaced modifiers. Infinitives consist of the marker *to* plus the plain form of the verb. The two parts of the infinitive make up a grammatical unit that should not be split. Splitting an infinitive is placing an adverb between the *to* and the verb.

> INCORRECT: The weather service expects temperatures to not rise.

> CORRECT: The weather service expects temperatures not to rise.

Sometimes a split infinitive may be natural and preferable, and though it may still bother some readers, it has become acceptable in formal writing.

> EX: Several U.S. industries expect *to* more than *triple* their use of robots within the next decade.

A squinting modifier is one that may refer to either a preceding or a following word, leaving the reader uncertain about what it is intended to modify. Correct a squinting modifier by moving it next to the word it is intended to modify.

> INCORRECT: Snipers who fired on the soldiers often escaped capture.

> CORRECT: Snipers who often fired on the soldiers escaped capture.

> OR   Snipers who fired on the soldiers escaped capture often.

A dangling modifier is a modifier or verb in search of a subject: the modifying phrase (usually an *-ing* word group, an *-ed* or *-en* word group, or a *to + a verb* word group—participle phrase or infinitive phrase respectively) either appears to modify the wrong word or has nothing to modify. It is literally dangling at the beginning or the end of a sentence. The sentences often look and sound correct: *To be a student government officer, your grades must be above average.* (However, the verbal modifier has nothing to describe. Who is *to be a student government officer*? Your grades?) Questions of this type require you to determine whether a modifier has a headword or whether it is dangling at the beginning or the end of the sentence.

To correct a dangling modifier, reword the sentence by either: 1) changing the modifying phrase to a clause with a subject, or 2) changing the subject of the sentence to the word that should be modified. The following are examples of a dangling gerund, a dangling infinitive, and a dangling participle:

INCORRECT: Shortly after leaving home, the accident occurred.

                Who is <u>leaving home</u>, the accident?

CORRECT: Shortly after we left home, the accident occurred.

INCORRECT: To get up on time, a great effort was needed.

                <u>To get up</u> needs a subject.

CORRECT: To get up on time, I made a great effort.

FRAGMENTS

A fragment is an incomplete construction which may or may not have a subject and a verb. Specifically, a fragment is a group of words pretending to be a sentence. Not all fragments appear as separate sentences, however. Often, fragments are separated by semicolons.

INCORRECT: Traffic was stalled for ten miles on the freeway. Because repairs were being made on potholes.

CORRECT: Traffic was stalled for ten miles on the freeway because repairs were being made on potholes.

INCORRECT: It was a funny story; one that I had never heard before.

CORRECT: It was a funny story, one that I had never heard before.

RUN-ON/FUSED SENTENCES

A run-on/fused sentence is not necessarily a long sentence or a sentence that the reader considers too long; in fact, a run-on may be two short sentences: *Dry ice does not melt it evaporates.* A run-on results when the writer fuses or runs together two separate sentences without any correct mark of punctuation separating them.

INCORRECT: Knowing how to use a dictionary is no problem each dictionary has a section in the front of the book telling how to use it.

CORRECT: Knowing how to use a dictionary is no problem. Each dictionary has a section in the front of the book telling how to use it.

Even if one or both of the fused sentences contains internal punctuation, the sentence is still a run-on.

INCORRECT: Bob bought dress shoes, a suit, and a nice shirt he needed them for his sister's wedding.

CORRECT: Bob bought dress shoes, a suit, and a nice shirt. He needed them for his sister's wedding.

COMMA SPLICES

A comma splice is the unjustifiable use of only a comma to combine what really is two separate sentences.

INCORRECT: One common error in writing is incorrect spelling, the other is the occasional use of faulty diction.

CORRECT: One common error in writing is incorrect spelling; the other is the occasional use of faulty diction.

Both run-on sentences and comma splices may be corrected in one of the following ways:

RUN-ON: Neal won the award he had the highest score.

COMMA SPLICE: Neal won the award, he had the highest score.

Separate the sentences with a period:

Neal won the award. He had the highest score.

Separate the sentences with a comma and a coordinating conjunction (*and, but, or, nor, for, yet, so*):

Neal won the award for he had the highest score.

Separate the sentences with a semicolon:

Neal won the award; he had the highest score.

Separate the sentences with a subordinating conjunction such as *although, because, since, if*:

Neal won the award because he had the highest score.

SUBORDINATION, COORDINATION, AND PREDICATION

Suppose, for the sake of clarity, you wanted to combine the information in these two sentences to create one statement:

I studied a foreign language. I found English quite easy.

How you decide to combine this information should be determined by the relationship you'd like to show between the two facts. *I studied a foreign language, and I found English quite easy* seems rather illogical. The **coordination** of the two ideas (connecting them with the coordinating conjunction *and* is ineffective. Using **subordination** instead (connecting the sentences with a subordinating conjunction) clearly shows the degree of relative importance between the expressed ideas:

After I studied a foreign language, I found English quite easy.

When using a conjunction, be sure that the sentence parts you are joining are in agreement.

INCORRECT: She loved him dearly but not his dog.

CORRECT: She loved him dearly but she did not love his dog.

A common mistake that is made is to forget that each member of the pair must be followed by the same kind of construction.

INCORRECT: They complimented them both for their bravery and they thanked them for their kindness.

CORRECT: They both complimented them for their bravery and thanked them for their kindness.

While refers to time and should not be used as a substitute for *although*, *and*, or *but*.

INCORRECT: While I'm usually interested in Fellini movies, I'd rather not go tonight.

CORRECT: Although I'm usually interested in Fellini movies, I'd rather not go tonight.

Where refers to time and should not be used as a substitute for *that*.

INCORRECT: We read in the paper where they are making great strides in DNA research.

CORRECT: We read in the paper that they are making great strides in DNA research.

After words like reason and explanation, use *that*, not *because*.

> INCORRECT: His explanation for his tardiness was because his alarm did not go off.

> CORRECT: His explanation for his tardiness was that his alarm did not go off.

Drill: Sentence Structure Skills

> **DIRECTIONS:** Choose the sentence that expresses the thought most clearly and that has no error in structure.

1. (A) Many gases are invisible, odorless, and they have no taste.

   (B) Many gases are invisible, odorless, and have no taste.

   (C) Many gases are invisible, odorless, and tasteless.

2. (A) Everyone agreed that she had neither the voice or the skill to be a speaker.

   (B) Everyone agreed that she had neither the voice nor the skill to be a speaker.

   (C) Everyone agreed that she had either the voice nor the skill to be a speaker.

3. (A) The mayor will be remembered because he kept his campaign promises and because of his refusal to accept political favors.

   (B) The mayor will be remembered because he kept his campaign promises and because he refused to accept political favors.

   (C) The mayor will be remembered because of his refusal to accept political favors and he kept his campaign promises.

4. (A) While taking a shower, the doorbell rang.

   (B) While I was taking a shower, the doorbell rang.

   (C) While taking a shower, someone rang the doorbell.

5. (A) He swung the bat, while the runner stole second base.

   (B) The runner stole second base while he swung the bat.

   (C) While he was swinging the bat, the runner stole second base.

DIRECTIONS: **Choose the correct option.**

---

6. Nothing grows as well in Mississippi as <u>cotton. Cotton</u> being the state's principal crop.

    (A) cotton, cotton   (C) cotton cotton

    (B) cotton; cotton   (D) No change is necessary.

7. It was a heartwrenching <u>movie; one</u> that I had never seen before.

    (A) movie and   (C) movie. One

    (B) movie, one   (D) No change is necessary.

8. Traffic was stalled for three miles on the <u>bridge. Because</u> repairs were being made.

    (A) bridge because   (C) bridge, because

    (B) bridge; because   (D) No change is necessary.

9. The ability to write complete sentences comes with <u>practice writing</u> run-on sentences seems to occur naturally.

    (A) practice, writing   (C) practice and

    (B) practice. Writing   (D) No change is necessary.

10. Even though she had taken French classes, she could not understand native French <u>speakers they</u> all spoke too fast.

    (A) speakers, they   (C) speaking

    (B) speakers. They   (D) No change is necessary.

VERBS

VERB FORMS

This section covers the principal parts of some irregular verbs including troublesome verbs like *lie* and *lay*. The use of regular verbs like *look* and *receive* poses no real problem to most writers since the past and past participle forms end in *-ed*; it is the irregular forms which pose the most serious problems—for example, *seen, written*, and *begun*.

VERB TENSES

Tense sequence indicates a logical time sequence.

Use Present Tense

in statements of universal truth:

> I learned that the sun *is* 90 million miles from the earth.

in statements about the contents of literature and other published works:

> In this book, Sandy *becomes* a nun and *writes* a book on psychology.

Use Past Tense

in statements concerning writing or publication of a book:

> He *wrote* his first book in 1949, and it *was published* in 1952.

Use Present Perfect Tense

for an action that began in the past but continues into the future:

> I *have lived* here all my life.

Use Past Perfect Tense

for an earlier action that is mentioned in a later action:

> Cindy ate the apple that she *had picked*.

(First she picked it, then she ate it.)

Use Future Perfect Tense

for an action that will have been completed at a specific future time:

> By May, I *shall have graduated*.

Use a Present Participle

for action that occurs at the same time as the verb:

> *Speeding* down the interstate, I saw a cop's flashing lights.

Use a Perfect Participle

for action that occurred before the main verb:

> *Having read* the directions, I started the test.

Use the Subjunctive Mood

to express a wish or state a condition contrary to fact:

> *If it were not raining,* we could have a picnic.

in *that* clauses after verbs like *request, recommend, suggest, ask, require,* and *insist*; and after such expressions as *it is important* and *it is necessary*:

> It is necessary that all papers *be* submitted on time.

SUBJECT-VERB AGREEMENT

Agreement is the grammatical correspondence between the subject and the verb of a sentence: *I do; we do; they do; he, she, it does.*

Every English verb has five forms, two of which are the bare form (plural) and the *-s* form (singular). Simply put, singular verb forms end in *-s;* plural forms do not.

Rules Governing Subject-Verb Agreement:

A verb must agree with its subject, not with any additive phrase in the sentence such as a prepositional or verbal phrase. Ignore such phrases.

> Your *copy* of the rules *is* on the desk.

> Ms. Craig's *record* of community service and outstanding teaching *qualifies* her for a promotion.

In an inverted sentence beginning with a prepositional phrase, the verb still agrees with its subject.

> At the end of the summer *come* the best *sales.*

> Under the house *are* some old Mason *jars.*

Prepositional phrases beginning with compound prepositions such as *along with, together with, in addition to,* and *as well as* should be ignored, for they do not affect subject-verb agreement.

> *Gladys Knight,* as well as the Pips, *is* riding the midnight train to Georgia.

A verb must agree with its subject, not its subject complement.

> *Taxes are* a problem.

> A *problem is* taxes.

When a sentence begins with an expletive such as *there, here,* or *it,* the verb agrees with the subject, not the expletive.

> Surely, there *are* several *alumni* who would be interested in forming a group.

> There *are* 50 *students* in my English class.

> There *is* a horrifying *study* on child abuse in *Psychology Today.*

Indefinite pronouns such as *each, either, one, everyone, everybody,* and *everything* are singular.

> *Somebody* in Detroit *loves* me.

> *Does either* [one] of you have a pencil?

> *Neither* of my brothers *has* a car.

Indefinite pronouns such as *several, few, both,* and *many* are plural.

> *Both* of my sorority sisters *have* decided to live off campus.

> *Few seek* the enlightenment of transcendental meditation.

Indefinite pronouns such as *all, some, most,* and *none* may be singular or plural depending on their referents.

> *Some* of the food *is* cold.

> *Some* of the vegetables *are* cold.

> I can think of some retorts, but *none seem* appropriate.

> *None* of the children *is* as sweet as Sally.

Fractions such as *one-half* and *one-third* may be singular or plural depending on the referent.

> *Half* of the mail *has* been delivered.

> *Half* of the letters *have* been read.

Subjects joined by *and* take a plural verb unless the subjects are thought to be one item or unit.

> *Jim* and *Tammy were* televangelists.

> *Operation Ivy is* my favorite group.

In cases when the subjects are joined by *or, nor, either . . . or,* or *neither . . . nor,* the verb must agree with the subject closer to it.

> Either the teacher or the *students are* responsible.

> Neither the students nor the *teacher is* responsible.

Relative pronouns, such as *who, which,* or *that,* which refer to plural antecedents require plural verbs. However, when the relative pronoun refers to a singular subject, the pronoun takes a singular verb.

> She is one of the girls *who cheer* on Friday nights.

> She is the only cheerleader *who has* a broken leg.

Subjects preceded by *every, each,* and *many a* are singular.

> *Every* man, woman, and child *was* given a life preserver.

> *Each* undergraduate *is* required to pass a proficiency exam.

> *Many a* tear *has* to fall before one matures.

A collective noun, such as *audience, faculty, jury,* etc., requires a singular verb when the group is regarded as a whole, and a plural verb when the members of the group are regarded as individuals.

> The *jury has* made its decision.

> The *faculty are* preparing their grade rosters.

Subjects preceded by *the number of* or *the percentage of* are singular, while subjects preceded by *a number of* or *a percentage of* are plural.

> The *number of* vacationers in Florida *increases* every year.

> *A number of* vacationers *are* young couples.

Titles of books, companies, name brands, and groups are singular or plural depending on their meaning.

> *Great Expectations is* my favorite novel.

> The *Rolling Stones are* performing in the Super Dome.

Certain nouns of Latin and Greek origin have unusual singular and plural forms.

Singular	Plural
criterion	criteria
alumnus	alumni
datum	data
medium	media

> The *data are* available for inspection.

> The only *criterion* for membership *is* a high GPA.

Some nouns such as *deer*, *shrimp*, and *sheep* have the same spellings for both their singular and plural forms. In these cases, the meaning of the sentence will determine whether they are singular or plural.

> *Deer are* beautiful animals.

> The spotted *deer is* licking the sugar cube.

Some nouns like *scissors*, *jeans*, and *wages* have plural forms but no singular counterparts. These nouns almost always take plural verbs.

> The *scissors are* on the table.

> My new *jeans fit* me like a glove.

Words used as examples, not as grammatical parts of the sentence, require singular verbs.

> *Can't is* the contraction for "cannot."

> *Cats is* the plural form of "cat."

Mathematical expressions of subtraction and division require singular verbs, while expressions of addition and multiplication take either singular or plural verbs.

> Ten *divided* by two *equals* five.

> Five *times* two *equals* ten.

> OR   Five *times* two *equal* ten.

Nouns expressing time, distance, weight, and measurement are singular when they refer to a unit and plural when they refer to separate items.

> *Fifty yards is* a short distance.

> *Ten years have* passed since I finished college.

Expressions of quantity are usually plural.

> *Nine out of ten* dentists *recommend* that their patients floss.

Some nouns ending in *-ics,* such as *economics* and *ethics*, take singular verbs when they refer to principles or a field of study; however, when they refer to individual practices, they usually take plural verbs.

> *Ethics is* being taught in the spring.

> His unusual business *ethics are* what got him into trouble.

Some nouns like *measles*, *news*, and *calculus* appear to be plural but are actually singular in number. These nouns require singular verbs.

> *Measles is* a very contagious disease.

> *Calculus requires* great skill in algebra.

A verbal noun (infinitive or gerund) serving as a subject is treated as singular, even if the object of the verbal phrase is plural.

> *Hiding* your mistakes *does* not make them go away.

> *To run* five miles *is* my goal.

A noun phrase or clause acting as the subject of a sentence requires a singular verb.

> What I need is to be loved.

> Whether there is any connection between them is unknown.

Clauses beginning with *what* may be singular or plural depending on the meaning, that is, whether *what* means "the thing" or "the things."

> What I want for Christmas is a new motorcycle.

> What matters are Clinton's ideas.

A plural subject followed by a singular appositive requires a plural verb; similarly, a singular subject followed by a plural appositive requires a singular verb.

> When the girls throw a party, *they* each bring a *gift.*

> The *board*, all ten members, *is* meeting today.

Drill: Verbs

DIRECTIONS: Choose the correct option.

1. If you <u>had been concerned</u> about Marilyn, you <u>would have went</u> to greater lengths to ensure her safety.

    (A) had been concern . . . would have gone

    (B) was concerned . . . would have gone

    (C) had been concerned . . . would have gone

    (D) No change is necessary.

2. Susan <u>laid</u> in bed too long and missed her class.

    (A) lays (C) lied

    (B) lay (D) No change is necessary.

3. The Great Wall of China <u>is</u> fifteen hundred miles long; it <u>was built</u> in the third century B.C.

   (A) was . . . was built
   (B) is . . . is built
   (C) has been . . . was built
   (D) No change is necessary.

4. Joe stated that the class <u>began</u> at 10:30 a.m.

   (A) begins
   (B) had begun
   (C) was beginning
   (D) No change is necessary.

5. The ceiling of the Sistine Chapel <u>was</u> painted by Michelangelo; it <u>depicted</u> scenes from the Creation in the Old Testament.

   (A) was . . . depicts
   (B) is . . . depicts
   (C) has been . . . depicting
   (D) No change is necessary.

6. After Christmas <u>comes</u> the best sales.

   (A) has come
   (B) come
   (C) is coming
   (D) No change is necessary.

7. The bakery's specialty <u>are</u> wedding cakes.

   (A) is
   (B) were
   (C) be
   (D) No change is necessary.

8. Every man, woman, and child <u>were given</u> a life preserver.

   (A) have been given
   (B) had gave
   (C) was given
   (D) No change is necessary.

9. Hiding your mistakes <u>don't</u> make them go away.

   (A) doesn't
   (B) do not
   (C) have not
   (D) No change is necessary.

10. The Board of Regents <u>has recommended</u> a tuition increase.

   (A) have recommended
   (B) has recommend
   (C) had recommended
   (D) No change is necessary.

PRONOUNS

PRONOUN CASE

Appropriate pronoun case is essential to effective, understandable essay writing. Pronoun case can either be nominative or objective.

Nominative Case	Objective Case
I	me
he	him
she	her
we	us
they	them
who	whom

This review section answers the most frequently asked grammar questions: when to use *I* and when to use *me*; when to use *who* and when to use *whom*. Some writers avoid *whom* altogether, and instead of distinguishing between *I* and *me*, many writers incorrectly use *myself*.

Use the nominative case (subject pronouns)

for the subject of a sentence:

> *We* students studied until early morning for the final.

> Alan and *I* "burned the midnight oil," too.

for pronouns in apposition to the subject:

> Only two students, Alex and *I*, were asked to report on the meeting.

for the predicate nominative/subject complement:

> The actors nominated for the award were *she* and *I*.

for the subject of an elliptical clause:

> Molly is more experienced than *he*.

for the subject of a subordinate clause:

> Robert is the driver *who* reported the accident.

for the complement of an infinitive with no expressed subject:

> I would not want to be *he*.

Use the objective case (object pronouns)

for the direct object of a sentence:

> Mary invited *us* to her party.

for the object of a preposition:

> The books that were torn belonged to *her*.

> Just between you and *me*, I'm bored.

for the indirect object of a sentence:

> Walter gave a dozen red roses to *her*.

for the appositive of a direct object:

> The committee elected two delegates, Barbara and *me*.

for the object of an infinitive:

> The young boy wanted to help *us* paint the fence.

for the object of a gerund:

> Enlisting *him* was surprisingly easy.

for the object of a past participle:

> Having called the other students and *us*, the secretary went home for the day.

for a pronoun that precedes an infinitive (the subject of an infinitive):

> The supervisor told *him* to work late.

for the complement of an infinitive with an expressed subject:

> The fans thought the best player to be *him*.

for the object of an elliptical clause:

> Bill tackled Joe harder than *me*.

for the object of a verb in apposition:

> Charles invited two extra people, Carmen and *me*, to the party.

When a conjunction connects two pronouns or a pronoun and a noun, remove the "and" and the other pronoun or noun to determine what the correct pronoun form should be:

> Mom gave ~~Tom and~~ myself a piece of cake.

> Mom gave ~~Tom and~~ I a piece of cake

> Mom gave ~~Tom and~~ me a piece of cake.

NYSTCE – New York State Teacher Certification Exam

Removal of these words reveals what the correct pronoun should be:

Mom gave *me* a piece of cake.

The only pronouns that are acceptable after *between* and other prepositions are: *me, her, him, them,* and *whom.* When deciding between *who* and *whom,* try substituting *he* for *who* and *him* for *whom;* then follow these easy transformation steps:

1. Isolate the *who* clause or the *whom* clause:

   whom we can trust

2. Invert the word order, if necessary. Place the words in the clause in the natural order of an English sentence, subject followed by the verb:

   we can trust whom

3. Read the final form with the *he* or *him* inserted:

   We can trust ~~whom~~ him.

When a pronoun follows a comparative conjunction like *than* or *as,* complete the elliptical construction to help you determine which pronoun is correct.

EX: She has more credit hours than me [do].

She has more credit hours than I [do].

PRONOUN-ANTECEDENT AGREEMENT

Appropriate pronoun antecedent is very important to the effective essay. Pronouns must agree with their antecedent in number, gender and person. An antecedent is a noun or pronoun to which another noun or pronoun refers.

Here are the two basic rules for pronoun reference-antecedent agreement:

1. Every pronoun must have a conspicuous antecedent.

2. Every pronoun must agree with its antecedent in number, gender, and person.

When an antecedent is one of dual gender like *student, singer, artist, person, citizen,* etc., use *his* or *her.* Some careful writers change the antecedent to a plural noun to avoid using the sexist, singular masculine pronoun *his:*

INCORRECT: Everyone hopes that he will win the lottery.

CORRECT: Most people hope that they will win the lottery.

Ordinarily, the relative pronoun *who* is used to refer to people, *which* to refer to things and places, *where* to refer to places, and *that* to refer to places or things. The distinction between *that* and *which* is a grammatical distinction (see the section on Word Choice Skills).

Many writers prefer to use *that* to refer to collective nouns.

EX: A family *that* traces its lineage is usually proud of its roots.

Many writers, especially students, are not sure when to use the reflexive case pronoun and when to use the possessive case pronoun. The rules governing the usage of the reflexive case and the possessive case are quite simple.

Use the possessive case

before a noun in a sentence:

Our friend moved during the semester break.

My dog has fleas, but *her* dog doesn't.

before a gerund in a sentence:

Her running helps to relieve stress.

His driving terrified her.

as a noun in a sentence:

Mine was the last test graded that day.

to indicate possession:

Karen never allows anyone else to drive *her* car.

Brad thought the book was *his,* but it was someone else's.

Use the reflexive case

as a direct object to rename the subject:

I kicked *myself.*

as an indirect object to rename the subject:

Henry bought *himself* a tie.

as an object of a prepositional phrase:

Tom and Lillie baked the pie for *themselves.*

as a predicate pronoun:

She hasn't been *herself* lately.

Do not use the reflexive in place of the nominative pronoun:

INCORRECT: Both Randy and *myself* plan to go.

CORRECT: Both Randy and *I* plan to go.

INCORRECT: *Yourself* will take on the challenges of college.

CORRECT: *You* will take on the challenges of college.

INCORRECT: Either James or *yourself* will paint the mural.

CORRECT: Either James or *you* will paint the mural.

Watch out for careless use of the pronoun form:

INCORRECT: George *hisself* told me it was true.

CORRECT: George *himself* told me it was true.

INCORRECT: They washed the car *theirselves.*

CORRECT: They washed the car *themselves.*

Notice that reflexive pronouns are not set off by commas:

INCORRECT: Mary, *herself*, gave him the diploma.

CORRECT: Mary *herself* gave him the diploma.

INCORRECT: I will do it, *myself.*

CORRECT: I will do it *myself.*

PRONOUN REFERENCE

Pronoun reference requires you to determine whether the antecedent is conspicuously written in the sentence or whether it is remote, implied, ambiguous, or vague, none of which results in clear writing. Make sure that every italicized pronoun has a conspicuous antecedent and that one pronoun substitutes only for another noun or pronoun, not for an idea or a sentence.

Pronoun reference problems occur

when a pronoun refers to either of two antecedents:

> INCORRECT: Joanna told Tim that *she* was getting fat.

> CORRECT: Joanna told Tim, "I'm getting fat."

when a pronoun refers to a remote antecedent:

> INCORRECT: A strange car followed us closely, and *he* kept blinking his lights at us.

> CORRECT: A strange car followed us closely, and its driver kept blinking his lights at us.

when *this*, *that*, and *which* refer to the general idea of the preceding clause or sentence rather than the preceding word:

> INCORRECT: The students could not understand the pronoun reference handout, which annoyed them very much.

> CORRECT: The students could not understand the pronoun reference handout, a fact which annoyed them very much.

> OR   The students were annoyed because they could not understand the pronoun reference handout.

when a pronoun refers to an unexpressed but implied noun:

> INCORRECT: My husband wants me to knit a blanket, but I'm not interested in it.

> CORRECT: My husband wants me to knit a blanket, but I'm not interested in knitting.

when *it* is used as something other than an expletive to postpone a subject:

> INCORRECT: It says in today's paper that the newest shipment of cars from Detroit, Michigan, seems to include outright imitations of European models.

> CORRECT: Today's paper says that the newest shipment of cars from Detroit, Michigan, seems to include outright imitations of European models.

> INCORRECT: The football game was canceled because it was bad weather.

> CORRECT: The football game was canceled because the weather was bad.

when *they* or *it* is used to refer to something or someone indefinitely, and there is no definite antecedent:

INCORRECT: At the job placement office, they told me to stop wearing ripped jeans to my interviews.

CORRECT: At the job placement office, I was told to stop wearing ripped jeans to my interviews.

when the pronoun does not agree with its antecedent in number, gender, or person:

INCORRECT: Any graduate student, if they are interested, may attend the lecture.

CORRECT: Any graduate student, if he or she is interested, may attend the lecture.

OR   All graduate students, if they are interested, may attend the lecture.

INCORRECT: Many Americans are concerned that the overuse of slang and colloquialisms is corrupting the language.

CORRECT: Many Americans are concerned that the overuse of slang and colloquialisms is corrupting their language.

INCORRECT: The Board of Regents will not make a decision about tuition increase until their March meeting.

CORRECT: The Board of Regents will not make a decision about tuition increase until its March meeting.

when a noun or pronoun has no expressed antecedent:

INCORRECT: In the President's address to the union, he promised no more taxes.

CORRECT: In his address to the union, the President promised no more taxes.

Drill: Pronouns

DIRECTIONS: Choose the correct option.

1. My friend and <u>myself</u> bought tickets for *Cats*.

   (A) I

   (B) me

   (C) us

   (D) No change is necessary.

2. Alcohol and tobacco are harmful to <u>whomever</u> consumes them.

   (A) whom

   (B) who

   (C) whoever

   (D) No change is necessary.

3. Everyone is wondering <u>whom</u> her successor will be.

   (A) who

   (B) whose

   (C) who'll

   (D) No change is necessary.

4. Rosa Lee's parents discovered that it was <u>her who</u> wrecked the family car.

   (A) she who

   (B) she whom

   (C) her whom

   (D) No change is necessary.

5. A student <u>who</u> wishes to protest <u>his or her</u> grades must file a formal grievance in the Dean's office.

   (A) that . . . their

   (B) which . . . his

   (C) whom . . . their

   (D) No change is necessary.

6. One of the best things about working for this company is that <u>they pay</u> big bonuses.

   (A) it pays

   (B) they always pay

   (C) they paid

   (D) No change is necessary.

7. Every car owner should be sure that <u>their</u> automobile insurance is adequate.

   (A) your

   (B) his or her

   (C) its

   (D) No change is necessary.

8. My mother wants me to become a teacher, but I'm not interested in <u>it</u>.

   (A) this   (C) that

   (B) teaching   (D) No change is necessary.

9. Since I had not paid my electric bill, <u>they</u> sent me a delinquent notice.

   (A) the power company   (C) it

   (B) he   (D) No change is necessary.

10. Margaret seldom wrote to her sister when <u>she</u> was away at college.

   (A) who   (C) her sister

   (B) her   (D) No change is necessary.

ADJECTIVES AND ADVERBS

CORRECT USAGE

Adjectives are words that modify nouns or pronouns by defining, describing, limiting, or qualifying those nouns or pronouns.

Adverbs are words that modify verbs, adjectives, or other adverbs and that express such ideas as time, place, manner, cause, and degree. Use adjectives as subject complements with linking verbs; use adverbs with action verbs.

EX: The old man's speech was *eloquent*.   ADJECTIVE

     Mr. Brown speaks *eloquently*.   ADVERB

     Please be *careful*.   ADJECTIVE

     Please drive *carefully*.   ADVERB

Good or well

Good is an adjective; its use as an adverb is colloquial and nonstandard.

   INCORRECT: He plays *good*.

   CORRECT: He looks *good* to be an octogenarian.

           The quiche tastes very *good*.

Well may be either an adverb or an adjective. As an adjective, *well* means "in good health."

| CORRECT: | He plays *well*. | ADVERB |
| | My mother is not *well*. | ADJECTIVE |

Bad or badly

Bad is an adjective used after sense verbs such as *look, smell, taste, feel*, or *sound*, or after linking verbs (*is, am, are, was, were*).

INCORRECT: I feel *badly* about the delay.

CORRECT: I feel *bad* about the delay.

Badly is an adverb used after all other verbs.

INCORRECT: It doesn't hurt very *bad*

CORRECT: It doesn't hurt very *badly*.

Real or really

Real is an adjective; its use as an adverb is colloquial and nonstandard. It means "genuine."

INCORRECT: He writes *real* well.

CORRECT: This is *real* leather.

Really is an adverb meaning "very."

INCORRECT: This is *really* diamond.

CORRECT: Have a *really* nice day.

EX:	This is *real* amethyst.	ADJECTIVE
	This is *really* difficult.	ADVERB
	This is a *real* crisis	ADJECTIVE
	This is *really* important.	ADVERB

Sort of and kind of

Sort of and *kind of* are often misused in written English by writers who actually mean *rather* or *somewhat*.

INCORRECT: Jan was *kind of* saddened by the results of the test.

CORRECT: Jan was *somewhat* saddened by the results of the test.

FAULTY COMPARISONS

Sentences containing a faulty comparison often sound correct because their problem is not one of grammar but of logic. Read these sentences closely to make sure that like things are being compared, that the comparisons are complete, and that the comparisons are logical.

When comparing two persons or things, use the comparative, not the superlative form, of an adjective or an adverb. Use the superlative form for comparison of more than two persons or things. Use *any*, *other*, or *else* when comparing one thing or person with a group of which it/he or she is a part.

Most one- and two-syllable words form their comparative and superlative degrees with *-er* and *-est* suffixes. Adjectives and adverbs of more than two syllables form their comparative and superlative degrees with the addition of *more* and *most*.

Positive	Comparative	Superlative
good	better	best
old	older	oldest
friendly	friendlier	friendliest
lonely	lonelier	loneliest
talented	more talented	most talented
beautiful	more beautiful	most beautiful

A double comparison occurs when the degree of the modifier is changed incorrectly by adding both *-er* and *more* or *-est* and *most* to the adjective or adverb.

INCORRECT: He is the *most nicest* brother.

CORRECT: He is the *nicest* brother.

INCORRECT: She is the *more meaner* of the sisters.

CORRECT: She is the *meaner* sister.

Illogical comparisons occur when there is an implied comparison between two things that are not actually being compared or that cannot be logically compared.

INCORRECT: The interest at a loan company is higher *than* a bank.

CORRECT: The interest at a loan company is higher *than* that *at* a bank.

OR The interest at a loan company is higher *than at* a bank.

Ambiguous comparisons occur when elliptical words (those omitted) create for the reader more than one interpretation of the sentence.

INCORRECT: I like Mary better than you. (than you *what*?)

CORRECT: I like Mary better than I like you.

OR   I like Mary better than you do.

Incomplete comparisons occur when the basis of the comparison (the two categories being compared) is not explicitly stated.

INCORRECT: Skywriting is *more* spectacular.

CORRECT: Skywriting is *more* spectacular *than* billboard advertising.

Do not omit the words *other, any,* or *else* when comparing one thing or person with a group of which it/he or she is a part.

INCORRECT: Joan writes better *than any* student in her class.

CORRECT: Joan writes better *than any other* student in her class.

Do not omit the second *as* of *as . . . as* when making a point of equal or superior comparison.

INCORRECT: The University of West Florida is *as large* or larger than the University of North Florida.

CORRECT: The University of West Florida is *as large as* or larger than the University of Northern Florida.

Do not omit the first category of the comparison, even if the two categories are the same.

INCORRECT: This is one of the best, if not the best, college in the country.

CORRECT: This is one of the best colleges in the country, if not the best.

The problem with the incorrect sentence is that *one of the best* requires the plural word *colleges*, not *college*.

Drill: Adjectives and Adverbs

> **DIRECTIONS:** Choose the correct option.

1.   Although the band performed <u>badly</u>, I feel <u>real bad</u> about missing the concert.

(A) badly . . . real badly   (C) badly . . . very bad

(B) bad . . . badly   (D) No change is necessary.

2. These reports are <u>relative simple</u> to prepare.

    (A) relatively simple   (C) relatively simply

    (B) relative simply   (D) No change is necessary.

3. He did <u>very well</u> on the test although his writing skills are not <u>good</u>.

    (A) real well . . . good   (C) good . . . great

    (B) very good . . . good   (D) No change is necessary.

4. Shake the medicine bottle <u>good</u> before you open it.

    (A) very good   (C) well

    (B) real good   (D) No change is necessary.

5. Though she speaks <u>fluently</u>, she writes <u>poorly</u> because she doesn't observe <u>closely</u> or think <u>clear</u>.

    (A) fluently . . . poorly . . . closely . . . clearly

    (B) fluent . . . poor . . . close . . . clear

    (C) fluently . . . poor . . . closely . . . clear

    (D) No change is necessary.

DIRECTIONS: Select the sentence that clearly and effectively states the idea and has no structural errors.

---

6. (A) Los Angeles is larger than any city in California.

    (B) Los Angeles is larger than all the cities in California.

    (C) Los Angeles is larger than any other city in California.

7. (A) Art history is as interesting as, if not more interesting than, music appreciation.

    (B) Art history is as interesting, if not more interesting than, music appreciation.

    (C) Art history is as interesting as, if not more interesting, music appreciation.

8. (A) The baseball team here is as good as any other university.

    (B) The baseball team here is as good as all the other universities.

    (C) The baseball team here is as good as any other university's.

9. (A) I like him better than you.

    (B) I like him better than I like you.

    (C) I like him better.

10. (A) You are the most stingiest person I know.

    (B) You are the most stingier person I know.

    (C) You are the stingiest person I know.

PUNCTUATION

COMMAS

Commas should be placed according to standard rules of punctuation for purpose, clarity, and effect. The proper use of commas is explained in the following rules and examples:

In a series:

When more than one adjective describes a noun, use a comma to separate and emphasize each adjective. The comma takes the place of the word *and* in the series.

the long, dark passageway

another confusing, sleepless night

an elaborate, complex, brilliant plan

the old, grey, crumpled hat

Some adjective-noun combinations are thought of as one word. In these cases, the adjective in front of the adjective-noun combination needs no comma. If you inserted *and* between the adjective-noun combination, it would not make sense.

a stately oak tree

an exceptional wine glass

my worst report card

a china dinner plate

The comma is also used to separate words, phrases, and whole ideas (clauses); it still takes the place of *and* when used this way.

an apple, a pear, a fig, and a banana

a lovely lady, an elegant dress, and many admirers

She lowered the shade, closed the curtain, turned off the light, and went to bed.

The only question that exists about the use of commas in a series is whether or not one should be used before the final item. It is standard usage to do so, although many newspapers and magazines have stopped using the final comma. Occasionally, the omission of the comma can be confusing.

INCORRECT: He got on his horse, tracked a rabbit and a deer and rode on to Canton.

We planned the trip with Mary and Harold, Susan, Dick and Joan, Gregory and Jean and Charles.

With a long introductory phrase:

Usually if a phrase of more than five or six words or a dependent clause precedes the subject at the beginning of a sentence, a comma is used to set it off.

After last night's fiasco at the disco, she couldn't bear the thought of looking at him again.

Whenever I try to talk about politics, my wife leaves the room.

Provided you have said nothing, they will never guess who you are.

It is not necessary to use a comma with a short sentence.

In January she will go to Switzerland.

After I rest I'll feel better.

During the day no one is home.

If an introductory phrase includes a verb form that is being used as another part of speech (a *verbal*), it must be followed by a comma.

INCORRECT: When eating Mary never looked up from her plate.

CORRECT: When eating, Mary never looked up from her plate.

INCORRECT: Because of her desire to follow her faith in James wavered.

CORRECT: Because of her desire to follow, her faith in James wavered.

INCORRECT: Having decided to leave Mary James wrote her a letter.

CORRECT: Having decided to leave Mary, James wrote her a letter.

To separate sentences with two main ideas:

To understand this use of the comma, you need to be able to recognize compound sentences. When a sentence contains more than two subjects and verbs (clauses), and the two clauses are joined by a conjunction (*and, but, or, nor, for, yet*), use a comma before the conjunction to show that another clause is coming.

> I thought I knew the poem by heart, but he showed me three lines I had forgotten.

> Are we really interested in helping the children, or are we more concerned with protecting our good names?

> He is supposed to leave tomorrow, but he is not ready to go.

> Jim knows you are disappointed, and he has known it for a long time.

If the two parts of the sentence are short and closely related, it is not necessary to use a comma.

> He threw the ball and the dog ran after it.

> Jane played the piano and Michael danced.

Be careful not to confuse a sentence that has a compound verb and a single subject with a compound sentence. If the subject is the same for both verbs, there is no need for a comma.

INCORRECT: Charles sent some flowers, and wrote a long letter explaining why he had not been able to attend.

CORRECT: Charles sent some flowers and wrote a long letter explaining why he had not been able to attend.

INCORRECT: Last Thursday we went to the concert with Julia, and afterwards dined at an old Italian restaurant.

CORRECT: Last Thursday we went to the concert with Julia and afterwards dined at an old Italian restaurant.

INCORRECT: For the third time, the teacher explained that the literacy level for high school students was much lower than it had been in previous years, and, this time, wrote the statistics on the board for everyone to see.

CORRECT: For the third time, the teacher explained that the literacy level for high school students was much lower than it had been in previous years and this time wrote the statistics on the board for everyone to see.

In general, words and phrases that stop the flow of the sentence or are unnecessary for the main idea are set off by commas.

Abbreviations after names:

Did you invite John Paul, Jr., and his sister?

Martha Harris, Ph.D., will be the speaker tonight.

Interjections (an exclamation without added grammatical connection):

Oh, I'm so glad to see you.

I tried so hard, alas, to do it.

Hey, let me out of here.

Direct address:

Roy, won't you open the door for the dog?

I can't understand, Mother, what you are trying to say.

May I ask, Mr. President, why you called us together?

Hey, lady, watch out for that car!

Tag questions:

I'm really hungry, aren't you?

Jerry looks like his father, doesn't he?

Geographical names and addresses:

The concert will be held in Chicago, Illinois, on August 12.

The letter was addressed to Mrs. Marion Heartwell, 1881 Pine Lane, Palo Alto, California 95824.

(Note: No comma is needed before the zip code, because it is already clearly set off from the state name.)

Transitional words and phrases:

On the other hand, I hope he gets better.

In addition, the phone rang constantly this afternoon.

I'm, nevertheless, going to the beach on Sunday.

You'll find, therefore, that no one is more loyal than I am.

Parenthetical words and phrases:

You will become, I believe, a great statesman.

We know, of course, that this is the only thing to do.

In fact, I planted corn last summer.

The Mannes affair was, to put it mildly, a surprise.

Unusual word order:

The dress, new and crisp, hung in the closet.

Intently, she stared out the window.

With nonrestrictive elements:

Parts of a sentence that modify other parts are sometimes essential to the meaning of the sentence and sometimes not. When a modifying word or group of words is not vital to the meaning of the sentence, it is set off by commas. Since it does not restrict the meaning of the words it modifies, it is called "nonrestrictive." Modifiers that are essential to the meaning of the sentence are called "restrictive" and are not set off by commas.

ESSENTIAL: The girl *who wrote the story* is my sister.

NONESSENTIAL: My sister, *the girl who wrote the story*, has always loved to write.

ESSENTIAL: John Milton's famous poem *Paradise Lost* tells a remarkable story.

NONESSENTIAL: Dante's greatest work, *The Divine Comedy,* marked the beginning of the Renaissance.

ESSENTIAL: The cup *that is on the piano* is the one I want.

NONESSENTIAL: The cup, *which my brother gave me last year*, is on the piano.

ESSENTIAL: The people *who arrived late* were not seated.

NONESSENTIAL: George, *who arrived late*, was not seated.

To set off direct quotations:

Most direct quotes or quoted materials are set off from the rest of the sentence by commas.

> "Please read your part more loudly," the director insisted.

> "I won't know what to do," said Michael, "if you leave me."

> The teacher said sternly, "I will not dismiss this class until I have silence."

> Who was it who said "Do not ask for whom the bell tolls; it tolls for thee"?

Note: Commas always go inside the closing quotation mark, even if the comma is not part of the material being quoted.

Be careful not to set off indirect quotes or quotes that are used as subjects or complements.

> "To be or not to be" is the famous beginning of a soliloquy in Shakespeare's *Hamlet*. (subject)

> She said she would never come back. (indirect quote)

> Back then my favorite poem was "Evangeline." (complement)

To set off contrasting elements:

> Her intelligence, not her beauty, got her the job.

> Your plan will take you a little further from, rather than closer to, your destination.

> It was a reasonable, though not appealing, idea.

> He wanted glory, but found happiness instead.

In dates:

Both forms of the date are acceptable.

> She will arrive on April 6, 1998.

> He left on 5 December 1980.

> In January 1967, he handed in his resignation.

> On October 22, 1992, Frank and Julie were married.

Usually, when a subordinate clause is at the end of a sentence, no comma is necessary preceding the clause. However, when a subordinate clause introduces a sentence, a comma should be used after the clause.

Some common subordinating conjunctions are:

after	so that
although	though
as	till
as if	unless
because	until
before	when
even though	whenever
if	while
inasmuch as	since

SEMICOLONS

Correct semicolon usage requires you to be able to distinguish between the semicolon and the comma, and the semicolon and the colon. This review section covers the basic uses of the semicolon: to separate independent clauses not joined by a coordinating conjunction, to separate independent clauses separated by a conjunctive adverb, and to separate items in a series with internal commas. It is important to be consistent; if you use a semicolon between *any* of the items in the series, you must use semicolons to separate *all* of the items in the series.

Usually, a comma follows the conjunctive adverb. Note also that a period can be used to separate two sentences joined by a conjunctive adverb. Some common conjunctive adverbs are:

accordingly	nevertheless
besides	next
consequently	nonetheless
finally	now
furthermore	on the other hand
however	otherwise
indeed	perhaps
in fact	still
moreover	therefore

Then is also used as a conjunctive adverb, but it is not usually followed by a comma.

Use the semicolon

to separate independent clauses which are not joined by a coordinating conjunction:

> I understand how to use commas; the semicolon I have not yet mastered.

to separate two independent clauses connected by a conjunctive adverb:

> He took great care with his work; *therefore*, he was very successful.

to combine two independent clauses connected by a coordinating conjunction if either or both of the clauses contain other internal punctuation:

> Success in college, some maintain, requires intelligence, industry, and perseverance; *but* others, fewer in number, assert that only personality is important.

to separate items in a series when each item has internal punctuation:

> I bought an old, dilapidated chair; an antique table which was in beautiful condition; and a new, ugly, blue and white rug.

> Call our customer service line for assistance: Arizona, 1-800-555-6020; New Mexico, 1-800-555-5050; California, 1-800-555-3140; or Nevada, 1-800-555-3214.

Do not use the semicolon

to separate a dependent and an independent clause:

> INCORRECT: You should not make such statements; even though they are correct.

> CORRECT: You should not make such statements even though they are correct.

to separate an appositive phrase or clause from a sentence:

> INCORRECT: His immediate aim in life is centered around two things; becoming an engineer and learning to fly an airplane.

> CORRECT: His immediate aim in life is centered around two things: becoming an engineer and learning to fly an airplane.

to precede an explanation or summary of the first clause:

Note: Although the sentence below is punctuated correctly, the use of the semicolon provides a miscue, suggesting that the second clause is merely an extension, not an explanation, of the first clause. The colon provides a better clue.

>WEAK: The first week of camping was wonderful; we lived in cabins instead of tents.

>BETTER: The first week of camping was wonderful: we lived in cabins instead of tents.

to substitute for a comma:

>INCORRECT: My roommate also likes sports; particularly football, basketball, and baseball.

>CORRECT: My roommate also likes sports, particularly football, basketball, and baseball.

to set off other types of phrases or clauses from a sentence:

>INCORRECT: Being of a cynical mind; I should ask for a recount of the ballots.

>CORRECT: Being of a cynical mind, I should ask for a recount of the ballots.

>INCORRECT: The next meeting of the club has been postponed two weeks; inasmuch as both the president and vice-president are out of town.

>CORRECT: The next meeting of the club has been postponed two weeks, inasmuch as both the president and vice-president are out of town.

Note: The semicolon is not a terminal mark of punctuation; therefore, it should not be followed by a capital letter unless the first word in the second clause ordinarily requires capitalization.

COLONS

While it is true that a colon is used to precede a list, one must also make sure that a complete sentence precedes the colon. The colon signals the reader that a list, explanation, or restatement of the preceding will follow. It is like an arrow, indicating that something is to follow. The difference between the colon and the semicolon and between the colon and the period is that the colon is an introductory mark, not a terminal mark. Look at the following examples:

>The Constitution provides for a separation of powers among the three branches of government.

government. The period signals a new sentence.

government; The semicolon signals an interrelated sentence.

government, The comma signals a coordinating conjunction followed by another independent clause.

government: The colon signals a list.

The Constitution provides for a separation of powers among the three branches of *government*: executive, legislative, and judicial.

Ensuring that a complete sentence precedes a colon means following these rules:

Use the colon to introduce a list (one item may constitute a list):

I hate this one course: English.

Three plays by William Shakespeare will be presented in repertory this summer at the University of Michigan: *Hamlet, Macbeth,* and *Othello.*

To introduce a list preceded by *as follows* or *the following*:

The reasons he cited for his success are as follows: integrity, honesty, industry, and a pleasant disposition.

To separate two independent clauses, when the second clause is a restatement or explanation of the first:

All of my high school teachers said one thing in particular: college is going to be difficult.

To introduce a word or word group which is a restatement, explanation, or summary of the first sentence:

These two things he loved: an honest man and a beautiful woman.

To introduce a formal appositive:

I am positive there is one appeal which you can't overlook: money.

To separate the introductory words from a quotation which follows, if the quotation is formal, long, or paragraphed separately:

The actor then stated: "I would rather be able to adequately play the part of Hamlet than to perform a miraculous operation, deliver a great lecture, or build a magnificent skyscraper."

The colon should only be used after statements that are grammatically complete.

Do *not* use a colon after a verb:

> INCORRECT: My favorite holidays are: Christmas, New Year's Eve, and Halloween.

> CORRECT: My favorite holidays are Christmas, New Year's Eve, and Halloween.

Do *not* use a colon after a preposition:

> INCORRECT: I enjoy different ethnic foods such as: Greek, Chinese, and Italian.

> CORRECT: I enjoy different ethnic foods such as Greek, Chinese, and Italian.

Do *not* use a colon interchangeably with the dash:

> INCORRECT: Mathematics, German, English: These gave me the greatest difficulty of all my studies.

> CORRECT: Mathematics, German, English—these gave me the greatest difficulty of all my studies.

Information preceding the colon should be a complete sentence regardless of the explanatory information following the clause.

Do *not* use the colon before the words *for example, namely, that is,* or *for instance* even though these words may be introducing a list.

> INCORRECT: We agreed to it: namely, to give him a surprise party.

> CORRECT: There are a number of well-known American women writers: for example, Nikki Giovanni, Phillis Wheatley, Emily Dickinson, and Maya Angelou.

Colon usage questions test your knowledge of the colon preceding a list, restatement, or explanation. These questions also require you to be able to distinguish between the colon and the period, the colon and the comma, and the colon and the semicolon.

APOSTROPHES

Apostrophes require you to know when an apostrophe has been used appropriately to make a noun possessive, not plural. Remember the following rules when considering how to show possession.

Add *'s* to singular nouns and indefinite pronouns:

> Tiffany's flowers
>
> a dog's bark
>
> everybody's computer
>
> at the owner's expense
>
> today's paper

Add *'s* to singular nouns ending in *s*, unless this distorts the pronunciation:

> Delores's paper
>
> the boss's pen
>
> Dr. Yots' class
>
> for righteousness' sake
>
> Dr. Evans's office OR Dr. Evans' office

Add *an apostrophe* to plural nouns ending in *s* or *es*:

> two cents' worth
>
> ladies' night
>
> thirteen years' experience
>
> two weeks' pay

Add *'s* to plural nouns not ending in *s:*

> men's room
>
> children's toys

Add *'s* to the last word in compound words or groups:

> brother-in-law's car
>
> someone else's paper

Add *'s* to the last name when indicating joint ownership:

> Joe and Edna's home
>
> Julie and Kathy's party
>
> women and children's clinic

Add *'s* to both names if you intend to show ownership by each person:

> Joe's and Edna's trucks
>
> Julie's and Kathy's pies

Ted's and Jane's marriage vows

Possessive pronouns change their forms *without* the addition of an apostrophe:

her, his, hers

your, yours

their, theirs

it, its

Use the possessive form of a noun preceding a gerund:

His driving annoys me.

My bowling a strike irritated him.

Do you mind our stopping by?

We appreciate your coming.

Add *'s* to words and initials to show that they are plural:

no if's, and's, or but's

the do's and don't's of dating

three A's

IRA's are available at the bank.

Add *s* to numbers, symbols, and letters to show that they are plural:

TVs

VCRs

the 1800s

the returning POWs

QUOTATION MARKS

These kinds of decisions test your knowledge of the proper use of quotation marks with other marks of punctuation, with titles, and with dialogue.

The most common use of double quotation marks (") is to set off quoted words, phrases, and sentences.

"If everybody minded their own business," said the Duchess in a hoarse growl, "the world would go round a great deal faster than it does."

"Then you would say what you mean," the March Hare went on.

"I do," Alice hastily replied: "at least—at least I mean what I say—that's the same thing, you know."

—from Lewis Carroll's *Alice in Wonderland*

Single quotation marks are used to set off quoted material within a quote.

"Shall I bring 'Rhyme of the Ancient Mariner' along with us?" she asked her brother.

Mrs. Green said, "The doctor told me, 'Go immediately to bed when you get home!'"

"If she said that to me," Katherine insisted, "I would tell her, 'I never intend to speak to you again! Goodbye, Susan!'"

When writing dialogue, begin a new paragraph each time the speaker changes.

"Do you know what time it is?" asked Jane.

"Can't you see I'm busy?" snapped Mary.

"It's easy to see that you're in a bad mood today!" replied Jane.

Use quotation marks to enclose words used as words (sometimes italics are used for this purpose).

"Judgment" has always been a difficult word for me to spell.

Do you know what "abstruse" means?

"Horse and buggy" and "bread and butter" can be used either as adjectives or as nouns.

If slang is used within more formal writing, the slang words or phrases should be set off with quotation marks.

Harrison's decision to leave the conference and to "stick his neck out" by flying to Jamaica was applauded by the rest of the conference attendees.

When words are meant to have an unusual or specific significance to the reader, for instance irony or humor, they are sometimes placed in quotation marks.

For years, women were not allowed to buy real estate in order to "protect" them from unscrupulous dealers.

The "conversation" resulted in one black eye and a broken nose.

To set off titles of TV shows, poems, stories, and book chapters, use quotation marks. (Book, motion picture, newspaper, and magazine titles are underlined when handwritten.)

> The article "Moving South in the Southern Rain," by Jergen Smith in the *Southern News*, attracted the attention of our editor.

> The assignment is "Childhood Development," Chapter 18 of *Human Behavior*.

> My favorite essay by Montaigne is "On Silence."

> "Happy Days" led the TV ratings for years, didn't it?

> You will find Keats' "Ode to a Grecian Urn" in Chapter 3, "The Romantic Era," in Lastly's *Selections from Great English Poets*.

Errors to avoid:

Be sure to remember that quotation marks always come in pairs. Do not make the mistake of using only one set.

> INCORRECT: "You'll never convince me to move to the city, said Thurman. I consider it an insane asylum."

> CORRECT: "You'll never convince me to move to the city," said Thurman. "I consider it an insane asylum."

> INCORRECT: "Idleness and pride tax with a heavier hand than kings and parliaments," Benjamin Franklin is supposed to have said. If we can get rid of the former, we may easily bear the latter."

> CORRECT: "Idleness and pride tax with a heavier hand than kings and parliaments," Benjamin Franklin is supposed to have said. "If we can get rid of the former, we may easily bear the latter."

When a quote consists of several sentences, do not put the quotation marks at the beginning and end of each sentence; put them at the beginning and end of the entire quotation.

> INCORRECT: "It was during his student days in Bonn that Beethoven fastened upon Schiller's poem." "The heady sense of liberation in the verses must have appealed to him." "They appealed to every German." —John Burke

> CORRECT: "It was during his student days in Bonn that Beethoven fastened upon Schiller's poem. The heady sense of liberation in the verses must have appealed to him. They appealed to every German." —John Burke

Instead of setting off a long quote with quotation marks, if it is longer than five or six lines you may want to indent and single space it. If you do indent, do not use quotation marks.

> In his *First Inaugural Address,* Abraham Lincoln appeals to the war-torn American people:
>
> > We are not enemies, but friends. We must not be enemies. Though passion may have strained, it must not break, our bonds of affection. The mystic chords of memory, stretching from every battlefield and patriot grave to every living heart and hearthstone all over this broad land, will yet swell the chorus of the Union when again touched, as surely they will be, by the better angels of our nature.

Be careful not to use quotation marks with indirect quotations.

INCORRECT: Mary wondered "if she would get over it."

CORRECT: Mary wondered if she would get over it.

———————————

INCORRECT: The nurse asked "how long it had been since we had visited the doctor's office."

CORRECT: The nurse asked how long it had been since we had visited the doctor's office.

When you quote several paragraphs, it is not sufficient to place quotation marks at the beginning and end of the entire quote. Place quotation marks at the *beginning of each paragraph,* but only at the *end of the last paragraph.* Here is an abbreviated quotation for an example:

> "Here begins an odyssey through the world of classical mythology, starting with the creation of the world . . .
>
> "It is true that themes similar to the classical may be found in any corpus of mythology . . . Even technology is not immune to the influence of Greece and Rome . . .
>
> "We need hardly mention the extent to which painters and sculptors . . . have used and adapted classical mythology to illustrate the past, to reveal the human body, to express romantic or antiromantic ideals, or to symbolize any particular point of view."

Remember that commas and periods are *always* placed inside the quotation marks even if they are not actually part of the quote.

INCORRECT: "Life always gets colder near the summit", Nietzsche is purported to have said, "—the cold increases, responsibility grows".

CORRECT: "Life always gets colder near the summit," Nietzsche is purported to have said, "—the cold increases, responsibility grows."

INCORRECT: "Get down here right away", John cried. "You'll miss the sunset if you don't."

CORRECT: "Get down here right away," John cried. "You'll miss the sunset if you don't."

INCORRECT: "If my dog could talk", Mary mused, "I'll bet he would say, 'Take me for a walk right this minute'".

CORRECT: "If my dog could talk," Mary mused, "I'll bet he would say, 'Take me for a walk right this minute'."

Other marks of punctuation, such as question marks, exclamation points, colons, and semicolons, go inside the quotation marks if they are part of the quoted material. If they are not part of the quotation, however, they go outside the quotation marks. Be careful to distinguish between the guidelines for the comma and period, which always go inside the quotation marks, and those for other marks of punctuation.

INCORRECT: "I'll always love you"! he exclaimed happily.

CORRECT: "I'll always love you!" he exclaimed happily.

INCORRECT: Did you hear her say, "He'll be there early?"

CORRECT: Did you hear her say, "He'll be there early"?

INCORRECT: She called down the stairs, "When are you going"?

CORRECT: She called down the stairs, "When are you going?"

INCORRECT: "Let me out"! he cried. "Don't you have any pity"?

CORRECT: "Let me out!" he cried. "Don't you have any pity?"

Remember to use only one mark of punctuation at the end of a sentence ending with a quotation mark.

INCORRECT: She thought out loud, "Will I ever finish this paper in time for that class?".

CORRECT: She thought out loud, "Will I ever finish this paper in time for that class?"

INCORRECT: "Not the same thing a bit!", said the Hatter. "Why, you might just as well say that 'I see what I eat' is the same thing as 'I eat what I see'!".

CORRECT: "Not the same thing a bit!" said the Hatter. "Why, you might just as well say that 'I see what I eat' is the same thing as 'I eat what I see'!"

Drill: Punctuation

DIRECTIONS: Choose the correct option.

1. Indianola, <u>Mississippi, where B.B. King and my father grew up,</u> has a population of less than 50,000 people.

   (A) Mississippi where, B.B. King and my father grew up,

   (B) Mississippi where B.B. King and my father grew up,

   (C) Mississippi; where B.B. King and my father grew up,

   (D) No change is necessary.

2. John Steinbeck's best known novel *The Grapes of Wrath* is the story of the <u>Joads an Oklahoma family</u> who were driven from their dustbowl farm and forced to become migrant workers in California.

   (A) Joads, an Oklahoma family

   (B) Joads, an Oklahoma family,

   (C) Joads; an Oklahoma family

   (D) No change is necessary.

3. All students who are interested in student teaching next <u>semester, must submit an application to the Teacher Education Office.</u>

   (A) semester must submit an application to the Teacher Education Office.

   (B) semester, must submit an application, to the Teacher Education Office.

    (C)   semester: must submit an application to the Teacher Education Office.

    (D)   No change is necessary.

4.   Whenever you travel by <u>car, or plane, you</u> must wear a seatbelt.

    (A)   car or plane you   (C)   car or plane, you

    (B)   car, or plane you   (D)   No change is necessary.

5.   Wearing a seatbelt is not just a good <u>idea, it's</u> the law.

    (A)   idea; it's   (C)   idea. It's

    (B)   idea it's   (D)   No change is necessary.

6.   Senators and representatives can be reelected <u>indefinitely; a</u> president can only serve two terms.

    (A)   indefinitely but a   (C)   indefinitely a

    (B)   indefinitely, a   (D)   No change is necessary.

7.   Students must pay a penalty for overdue library <u>books, however, there</u> is a grace period.

    (A)   books; however, there   (C)   books: however, there

    (B)   books however, there   (D)   No change is necessary.

8.   Among the states that seceded from the Union to join the Confederacy in 1860-1861 <u>were:</u> Mississippi, Florida, and Alabama.

    (A)   were   (C)   were.

    (B)   were;   (D)   No change is necessary.

9.   The art exhibit displayed works by many famous <u>artists such as:</u> Dali, Picasso, and Michelangelo.

    (A)   artists such as;   (C)   artists. Such as

    (B)   artists such as   (D)   No change is necessary.

10. The National Shakespeare Company will perform <u>the following plays:</u> *Othello, Macbeth, Hamlet,* and *As You Like It.*

    (A)   the following plays,   (C)   the following plays

    (B)   the following plays;   (D)   No change is necessary.

CAPITALIZATION

When a word is capitalized, it calls attention to itself. This attention should be for a good reason. There are standard uses for capital letters. In general, capitalize (1) all proper nouns, (2) the first word of a sentence, and (3) the first word of a direct quotation.

You should also capitalize

Names of ships, aircraft, spacecraft, and trains:

Apollo 13	*Mariner IV*
DC-10	S.S. *United States*
Sputnik II	Boeing 707

Names of deities:

God	Jupiter
Allah	Holy Ghost
Buddha	Venus
Jehovah	Shiva

Geological periods:

Neolithic age	Cenozoic era
late Pleistocene times	Ice Age

Names of astronomical bodies:

Mercury	Big Dipper
the Milky Way	Halley's comet
Ursa Major	North Star

Personifications:

Reliable Nature brought her promised Spring.

Bring on Melancholy in his sad might.

She believed that Love was the answer to all her problems.

Historical periods:

the Middle Ages	World War I
Reign of Terror	Great Depression
Christian Era	Roaring Twenties
Age of Louis XIV	Renaissance

Organizations, associations, and institutions:

Girl Scouts	North Atlantic Treaty Organization
Kiwanis Club	League of Women Voters
New York Yankees	Unitarian Church
Smithsonian Institution	Common Market
Library of Congress	Franklin Glen High School
New York Philharmonic	Harvard University

Government and judicial groups:

United States Court of Appeals	Senate
Committee on Foreign Affairs	Parliament
New Jersey City Council	Peace Corps
Arkansas Supreme Court	Census Bureau
House of Representatives	Department of State

A general term that accompanies a specific name is capitalized only if it follows the specific name. If it stands alone or comes before the specific name, it is put in lowercase:

Washington State	the state of Washington
Senator Dixon	the senator from Illinois
Central Park	the park
Golden Gate Bridge	the bridge
President Clinton	the president of the United States
Pope John XXIII	the pope
Queen Elizabeth I	the queen of England
Tropic of Capricorn	the tropics
Monroe Doctrine	the doctrine of expansion
the Mississippi River	the river
Easter Day	the day
Treaty of Versailles	the treaty
Webster's Dictionary	the dictionary
Equatorial Current	the equator

Use a capital to start a sentence:

>Our car would not start.
>
>When will you leave? I need to know right away.
>
>Never!
>
>Let me in! Please!

When a sentence appears within a sentence, start it with a capital letter:

>We had only one concern: When would we eat?
>
>My sister said, "I'll find the Monopoly game."
>
>He answered, "We can only stay a few minutes."

The most important words of titles are capitalized. Those words not capitalized are conjunctions (*and*, *or*, *but*) and short prepositions (*of*, *on*, *by*, *for*). The first and last word of a title must always be capitalized:

A Man for All Seasons	*Crime and Punishment*
Of Mice and Men	*Rise of the West*
Strange Life of Ivan Osokin	"Sonata in G Minor"
"Let Me In"	"Ode to Billy Joe"
"Rubaiyat of Omar Khayyam"	"All in the Family"

Capitalize newspaper and magazine titles:

>*U.S. News & World Report*
>
>*National Geographic*
>
>the *New York Times*
>
>the *Washington Post*

Capitalize radio and TV station call letters:

ABC	NBC
WNEW	WBOP
CNN	HBO

Do not capitalize compass directions or seasons:

west	north
east	south
spring	winter
autumn	summer

Capitalize regions:

the South	the Northeast
the West	Eastern Europe

> BUT: the south of France
>
> the east part of town

Capitalize specific military units:

the U.S. Army

the 7th Fleet

the German Navy

the 1st Infantry Division

Capitalize political groups and philosophies:

Democrat	Communist
Marxist	Nazism
Whig	Federalist
Existentialism	Transcendentalism

BUT do not capitalize systems of government or individual adherents to a philosophy:

democracy	communism
fascist	agnostic

Drill: Capitalization

> **DIRECTIONS:** Choose the correct option.

1. Mexico is the southernmost country in <u>North America</u>. It borders the United States on the north; it is bordered on the <u>south</u> by Belize and Guatemala.

    (A) north America . . . South

    (B) North America . . . South

    (C) North america . . . south

    (D) No change is necessary.

2.   (A)   Until 1989, Tom Landry was the only Coach the Dallas cow-
           boys ever had.

     (B)   Until 1989, Tom Landry was the only coach the Dallas Cow-
           boys ever had.

     (C)   Until 1989, Tom Landry was the only Coach the Dallas Cow-
           boys ever had.

3.   The <u>Northern Hemisphere</u> is the half of the <u>earth</u> that lies north of the
     <u>Equator.</u>

     (A)   Northern hemisphere . . . earth . . . equator

     (B)   Northern hemisphere . . . Earth . . . Equator

     (C)   Northern Hemisphere . . . earth . . . equator

     (D)   No change is necessary.

4.   (A)   My favorite works by Ernest Hemingway are "The Snows of
           Kilamanjaro," *The Sun Also Rises,* and *For Whom the Bell
           Tolls.*

     (B)   My favorite works by Ernest Hemingway are "The Snows Of
           Kilamanjaro," *The Sun Also Rises,* and *For Whom The Bell
           Tolls.*

     (C)   My favorite works by Ernest Hemingway are "The Snows of
           Kilamanjaro," *The Sun also Rises,* and *For whom the Bell
           Tolls.*

5.   Aphrodite (<u>Venus in Roman Mythology</u>) was the <u>Greek</u> goddess of
     love.

     (A)   Venus in Roman mythology . . . greek

     (B)   venus in roman mythology . . . Greek

     (C)   Venus in Roman mythology . . . Greek

     (D)   No change is necessary.

6.   The <u>Koran</u> is considered by <u>Muslims</u> to be the holy word.

     (A)   koran . . . muslims   (C)   Koran . . . muslims

     (B)   koran . . . Muslims   (D)   No change is necessary.

7. (A) The freshman curriculum at the community college includes english, a foreign language, Algebra I, and history.

    (B) The freshman curriculum at the community college includes English, a foreign language, Algebra I, and history.

    (C) The Freshman curriculum at the Community College includes English, a foreign language, Algebra I, and History.

8. At the <u>spring</u> graduation ceremonies, the university awarded over 2,000 <u>bachelor's</u> degrees.

    (A) Spring . . . Bachelor's   (C) Spring . . . bachelor's

    (B) spring . . . Bachelor's   (D) No change is necessary.

9. The fall of the <u>Berlin wall</u> was an important symbol of the collapse of <u>Communism</u>.

    (A) berlin Wall . . . communism

    (B) Berlin Wall . . . communism

    (C) berlin wall . . . Communism

    (D) No change is necessary.

10. A photograph of <u>mars</u> was printed in <u>the *New York Times*</u>.

    (A) Mars . . . *The New York Times*

    (B) mars . . . *The New York times*

    (C) mars . . . *The New York Times*

    (D) No change is necessary.

SPELLING

Spelling questions test your ability to recognize misspelled words. This section reviews spelling tips and rules to help you spot incorrect spellings. Problems such as the distinction between *to* and *too* and *lead* and *led* are covered under the Word Choice Skills section of this review.

- Remember, *i* before *e* except after *c*, or when sounded as "a" as in *neighbor* and *weigh*.

- There are only three words in the English language that end in *-ceed*:

proceed, succeed, exceed

- There are several words that end in *-cede*:

    secede, recede, concede, precede

- There is only one word in the English language that ends in *-sede*:

    supersede

Many people learn to read English phonetically; that is, by sounding out the letters of the words. However, many English words are not pronounced the way they are spelled, and those who try to spell English words phonetically often make spelling *errors*. It is better to memorize the correct spelling of English words rather than relying on phonetics to spell correctly.

FREQUENTLY MISSPELLED WORDS

The following list of words are frequently misspelled words. Study the spelling of each word by having a friend or teacher drill you on the words. Then mark down the words that you misspelled and study those select ones again. (The words appear in their most popular spellings.)

a lot	across	all right
ability	address	almost
absence	addressed	already
absent	adequate	although
abundance	advantage	altogether
accept	advantageous	always
acceptable	advertise	amateur
accident	advertisement	American
accommodate	advice	among
accompanied	advisable	amount
accomplish	advise	analysis
accumulation	advisor	analyze
accuse	aerial	angel
accustomed	affect	angle
ache	affectionate	annual
achieve	again	another
achievement	against	answer
acknowledge	aggravate	antiseptic
acquaintance	aggressive	anxious
acquainted	agree	apologize
acquire	aisle	apparatus

apparent

appear

appearance

appetite

application

apply

appreciate

appreciation

approach

appropriate

approval

approve

approximate

argue

arguing

argument

arouse

arrange

arrangement

article

artificial

ascend

assistance

assistant

associate

association

attempt

attendance

attention

audience

August

author

automobile

autumn

auxiliary

available

avenue

awful

awkward

bachelor

balance

balloon

bargain

basic

beautiful

because

become

before

beginning

being

believe

benefit

benefited

between

bicycle

board

bored

borrow

bottle

bottom

boundary

brake

breadth

breath

breathe

brilliant

building

bulletin

bureau

burial

buried

bury

bushes

business

cafeteria

calculator

calendar

campaign

capital

capitol

captain

career

careful

careless

carriage

carrying

category

ceiling

cemetery

cereal

certain

changeable

characteristic

charity

chief

choose

chose

cigarette

circumstance

citizen

clothes

clothing

coarse

coffee

collect

college

column

comedy

comfortable

commitment

committed

committee

communicate

company

comparative

compel

competent

competition

compliment

conceal

conceit

conceivable

conceive

concentration

conception

condition

conference
confident
congratulate
conquer
conscience
conscientious
conscious
consequence
consequently
considerable
consistency
consistent
continual
continuous
controlled
controversy
convenience
convenient
conversation
corporal
corroborate
council
counsel
counselor
courage
courageous
course
courteous
courtesy
criticism
criticize
crystal
curiosity
cylinder
daily
daughter
daybreak
death
deceive
December
deception
decide

decision
decisive
deed
definite
delicious
dependent
deposit
derelict
descend
descent
describe
description
desert
desirable
despair
desperate
dessert
destruction
determine
develop
development
device
dictator
died
difference
different
dilemma
dinner
direction
disappear
disappoint
disappointment
disapproval
disapprove
disastrous
discipline
discover
discriminate
disease
dissatisfied
dissection
dissipate

distance
distinction
division
doctor
dollar
doubt
dozen
earnest
easy
ecstasy
ecstatic
education
effect
efficiency
efficient
eight
either
eligibility
eligible
eliminate
embarrass
embarrassment
emergency
emphasis
emphasize
enclosure
encouraging
endeavor
engineer
English
enormous
enough
entrance
envelope
environment
equipment
equipped
especially
essential
evening
evident
exaggerate

exaggeration
examine
exceed
excellent
except
exceptional
exercise
exhausted
exhaustion
exhilaration
existence
exorbitant
expense
experience
experiment
explanation
extreme
facility
factory
familiar
fascinate
fascinating
fatigue
February
financial
financier
flourish
forcibly
forehead
foreign
formal
former
fortunate
fourteen
fourth
frequent
friend
frightening
fundamental
further
gallon
garden

gardener
general
genius
government
governor
grammar
grateful
great
grievance
grievous
grocery
guarantee
guess
guidance
half
hammer
handkerchief
happiness
healthy
heard
heavy
height
heroes
heroine
hideous
himself
hoarse
holiday
hopeless
hospital
humorous
hurried
hurrying
ignorance
imaginary
imbecile
imitation
immediately
immigrant
incidental
increase
independence

independent
indispensable
inevitable
influence
influential
initiate
innocence
inoculate
inquiry
insistent
instead
instinct
integrity
intellectual
intelligence
intercede
interest
interfere
interference
interpreted
interrupt
invitation
irrelevant
irresistible
irritable
island
its
it's
itself
January
jealous
journal
judgment
kindergarten
kitchen
knew
knock
know
knowledge
labor
laboratory
laid

language	mistake	optimistic
later	momentous	origin
latter	monkey	original
laugh	monotonous	oscillate
leisure	moral	ought
length	morale	ounce
lesson	mortgage	overcoat
library	mountain	paid
license	mournful	pamphlet
light	muscle	panicky
lightning	mysterious	parallel
likelihood	mystery	parallelism
likely	narrative	particular
literal	natural	partner
literature	necessary	pastime
livelihood	needle	patience
loaf	negligence	peace
loneliness	neighbor	peaceable
loose	neither	pear
lose	newspaper	peculiar
losing	newsstand	pencil
loyal	niece	people
loyalty	noticeable	perceive
magazine	o'clock	perception
maintenance	obedient	perfect
maneuver	obstacle	perform
marriage	occasion	performance
married	occasional	perhaps
marry	occur	period
match	occurred	permanence
material	occurrence	permanent
mathematics	ocean	perpendicular
measure	offer	perseverance
medicine	often	persevere
million	omission	persistent
miniature	omit	personal
minimum	once	personality
miracle	operate	personnel
miscellaneous	opinion	persuade
mischief	opportune	persuasion
mischievous	opportunity	pertain
misspelled	optimist	picture

piece	proceed	repetition
plain	produce	representative
playwright	professional	requirements
pleasant	professor	resemblance
please	profitable	resistance
pleasure	prominent	resource
pocket	promise	respectability
poison	pronounce	responsibility
policeman	pronunciation	restaurant
political	propeller	rhythm
population	prophet	rhythmical
portrayal	prospect	ridiculous
positive	psychology	right
possess	pursue	role
possession	pursuit	roll
possessive	quality	roommate
possible	quantity	sandwich
post office	quarreling	Saturday
potatoes	quart	scarcely
practical	quarter	scene
prairie	quiet	schedule
precede	quite	science
preceding	raise	scientific
precise	realistic	scissors
predictable	realize	season
prefer	reason	secretary
preference	rebellion	seize
preferential	recede	seminar
preferred	receipt	sense
prejudice	receive	separate
preparation	recipe	service
prepare	recognize	several
prescription	recommend	severely
presence	recuperate	shepherd
president	referred	sheriff
prevalent	rehearsal	shining
primitive	reign	shoulder
principal	relevant	shriek
principle	relieve	siege
privilege	remedy	sight
probably	renovate	signal
procedure	repeat	significance

significant	sweat	unusual
similar	sweet	useful
similarity	syllable	usual
sincerely	symmetrical	vacuum
site	sympathy	valley
soldier	synonym	valuable
solemn	technical	variety
sophomore	telegram	vegetable
soul	telephone	vein
source	temperament	vengeance
souvenir	temperature	versatile
special	tenant	vicinity
specified	tendency	vicious
specimen	tenement	view
speech	therefore	village
stationary	thorough	villain
stationery	through	visitor
statue	title	voice
stockings	together	volume
stomach	tomorrow	waist
straight	tongue	weak
strength	toward	wear
strenuous	tragedy	weather
stretch	transferred	Wednesday
striking	treasury	week
studying	tremendous	weigh
substantial	tries	weird
succeed	truly	whether
successful	twelfth	which
sudden	twelve	while
superintendent	tyranny	whole
suppress	undoubtedly	wholly
surely	United States	whose
surprise	university	wretched
suspense	unnecessary	

Drill: Spelling

DIRECTIONS: Identify the misspelled word in each set.

1. (A) probly
   (B) accommodate
   (C) acquaintance

2. (A) auxiliary
   (B) atheletic
   (C) beginning

3. (A) environment
   (B) existence
   (C) Febuary

4. (A) ocassion
   (B) occurrence
   (C) omitted

5. (A) perspiration
   (B) referring
   (C) priviledge

DIRECTIONS: Choose the correct option.

6. <u>Preceding</u> the <u>business</u> session, lunch will be served in a <u>separate</u> room.

   (A) preceeding . . . business . . . seperate
   (B) proceeding . . . bussiness . . . seperate
   (C) proceeding . . . business . . . seperite
   (D) No change is necessary.

7. Monte <u>inadvertently</u> left <u>several</u> of his <u>libary</u> books in the cafeteria.

   (A) inadverdently . . . serveral . . . libery

   (B) inadvertently . . . several . . . library

   (C) inadvertentely . . . several . . . librery

   (D) No change is necessary.

8. Sam wished he had more <u>liesure</u> time so he could <u>persue</u> his favorite hobbies.

   (A) leisure . . . pursue   (B) Liesure . . . pursue

   (C) leisure . . . persue   (D) No change is necessary.

9. One of my <u>favrite charecters</u> in <u>litrature</u> is Bilbo from *The Hobbit*.

   (A) favrite . . . characters . . . literature

   (B) favorite . . . characters . . . literature

   (C) favourite . . . characters . . . literature

   (D) No change is necessary.

10. Even <u>tho</u> Joe was badly hurt in the <u>accidant</u>, the company said they were not <u>lible</u> for damages.

   (A) though . . . accidant . . . libel

   (B) though . . . accident . . . liable

   (C) though . . . acident . . . liable

   (D) No change is necessary.

ESSAY WRITING REVIEW

The NYSTCE contains two writing exercises: one in the LAST, and one in the ATS-W. You must pace yourself on the multiple choice sections, so that you will have enough time to produce an adequate essay.

Writing under pressure can be frustrating, but if you study this review, practice and polish your essay skills, and have a realistic sense of what to expect, you can turn problems into possibilities. The following review will show you how to plan and write a logical, coherent, and interesting essay.

PRE-WRITING/PLANNING

Before you begin to actually write, there are certain preliminary steps you need to take. A few minutes spent planning pays off—your final essay will be more focused, well-developed, and clearer. For a 20-minute essay, you should spend about five minutes on the pre-writing process.

Understand the Question

Read the essay question very carefully and ask yourself the following questions:

- What is the meaning of the topic statement?

- Is the question asking me to persuade the reader of the validity of a certain opinion?

- Do I agree or disagree with the statement? What will be my thesis (main idea)?

- What kinds of examples can I use to support my thesis? Explore personal experiences, historical evidence, current events, and literary subjects.

Consider Your Audience

Essays would be pointless without an audience. Why write an essay if no one wants or needs to read it? Why add evidence, organize your ideas, or correct bad grammar? The reason to do any of these things is because someone out there needs to understand what you mean or say.

What does the audience need to know to believe you or to come over to your position? Imagine someone you know listening to you declare your position or opinion and then saying, "Oh, yeah? Prove it!" This is your audience—write to them. Ask yourself the following questions so that you will not be confronted with a person who says, "Prove it!"

- What evidence do I need to prove my idea to this skeptic?

- What would s/he disagree with me about?

- What does he or she share with me as common knowledge? What do I need to tell the reader?

WRITING YOUR ESSAY

Once you have considered your position on the topic and thought of several examples to support it, you are ready to begin writing.

Organizing Your Essay

Decide how many paragraphs you will write. In a 30-minute exercise, you will probably have time for no more than four or five paragraphs. In such a format, the first paragraph will be the introduction, the next two or three will develop your thesis with specific examples, and the final paragraph should be a strong conclusion.

The Introduction

The focus of your introduction should be the thesis statement. This statement allows your reader to understand the point and direction of your essay. The statement identifies the central idea of your essay and should clearly state your attitude about the subject. It will also dictate the basic content and organization of your essay. If you do not state your thesis clearly, your essay will suffer.

The thesis is the heart of the essay. Without it, readers won't know what your major message or central idea is in the essay.

The thesis must be something that can be argued or needs to be proven, not just an accepted fact. For example, "Animals are used every day in cosmetic and medical testing," is a fact—it needs no proof. But if the writer says, "Using animals for cosmetic and medical testing is cruel and should be stopped," we have a point that must be supported and defended by the writer.

The thesis can be placed in any paragraph of the essay, but in a short essay, especially one written for evaluative exam purposes, the thesis is most effective when placed in the last sentence of the opening paragraph.

Consider the following sample question:

ESSAY TOPIC:

"That government is best which governs least."

ASSIGNMENT: Do you agree or disagree with this statement? Choose a specific example from current events, personal experience, or your reading to support your position.

After reading the topic statement, decide if you agree or disagree. If you agree with this statement, your thesis statement could be the following:

> "Government has the right to protect individuals from interference but no right to extend its powers and activities beyond this function."

This statement clearly states the writer's opinion in a direct manner. It also serves as a blueprint for the essay. The remainder of the introduction should give two or three brief examples that support your thesis.

Supporting Paragraphs

The next two or three paragraphs of your essay will elaborate on the supporting examples you gave in your introduction. Each paragraph should discuss only one idea. Like the introduction, each paragraph should be coherently organized, with a topic sentence and supporting details.

The topic sentence is to each paragraph what the thesis statement is to the essay as a whole. It tells the reader what you plan to discuss in that paragraph. It has a specific subject and is neither too broad nor too narrow. It also establishes the author's attitude and gives the reader a sense of the direction in which the writer is going. An effective topic sentence also arouses the reader's interest.

Although it may occur in the middle or at the end of the paragraph, the topic sentence usually appears at the beginning of the paragraph. Placing it at the beginning is advantageous because it helps you stay focused on the main idea.

The remainder of each paragraph should support the topic sentence with examples and illustrations. Each sentence should progress logically from the previous one and be centrally connected to your topic sentence. Do not include any extraneous material that does not serve to develop your thesis.

Conclusion

Your conclusion should briefly restate your thesis and explain how you have shown it to be true. Since you want to end your essay on a strong note, your conclusion should be concise and effective.

Do not introduce any new topics that you cannot support. If you were watching a movie that suddenly shifted plot and characters at the end, you would be disappointed or even angry. Similarly, conclusions must not drift away from the major focus and message of the essay. Make sure your conclusion is clearly on the topic and represents your perspective without any confusion about what you really mean and believe. The reader will respect you for staying true to your intentions.

The conclusion is your last chance to grab and impress the reader. You can even use humor, if appropriate, but a dramatic close will remind the reader you are serious, even passionate, about what you believe.

EFFECTIVE USE OF LANGUAGE

Clear organization, while vitally important, is not the only factor the graders of your essay consider. You must also demonstrate that you can express your ideas clearly, using correct grammar, diction, usage, spelling, and punctuation. For rules on grammar, usage, and mechanics, consult the Communications Skills Review in this book.

Point-of-View

Depending on the audience, essays may be written from one of three points of view:

1. *Subjective/Personal* Point of View:

    "I think . . ."

    "I believe cars are more trouble than they are worth."

    "I feel . . ."

2. *Second Person* Point of View (We . . . You; I . . . You):

    "If *you* own a car, *you* will soon find out that it is more trouble than it is worth."

3. *Third Person* Point of View (focuses on the idea, not what "I" think of it):

    "*Cars* are more trouble than *they* are worth."

It is very important to maintain a consistent point of view throughout your essay. If you begin writing in the first-person ("I"), do not shift to the second- or third-person in the middle of the essay. Such inconsistency is confusing to your reader and will be penalized by the graders of your essay.

Tone

A writer's tone results from his or her attitude towards the subject and the reader. If the essay question requires you to take a strong stand, the tone of your essay should reflect this.

Your tone should also be appropriate for the subject matter. A serious topic demands a serious tone. For a more light-hearted topic, you may wish to inject some humor into your essay.

Whatever tone you choose, be consistent. Do not make any abrupt shifts in tone in the middle of your essay.

Verb Tense

Make sure to remain in the same verb tense in which you began your essay. If you start in the past, make sure all verbs are past tense. Staying in the same verb tense improves the continuity and flow of ideas. Avoid phrases such as "now was," a confusing blend of present and past. Consistency of time is essential to the reader's understanding.

Transitions

Transitions are like the links of a bracelet, holding the beads or major points of your essay together. They help the reader follow the smooth flow of your ideas and show a connection between major and minor ideas. Transitions are used either at the beginning of a paragraph, or to show the connections among ideas within a single paragraph. Without transitions, you will jar the reader and distract him from your true ideas.

Here are some typical transitional words and phrases:

Linking similar ideas

again	for example	likewise
also	for instance	moreover
and	further	nor
another	furthermore	of course
besides	in addition	similarly
equally important	in like manner	too

Linking dissimilar/contradictory ideas

although	however	on the other hand
and yet	in spite of	otherwise
as if	instead	provided that
but	nevertheless	still
conversely	on the contrary	yet

Indicating cause, purpose, or result

as	for	so
as a result	for this reason	then
because	hence	therefore
consequently	since	thus

Indicating time or position

above	before	meanwhile
across	beyond	next
afterwards	eventually	presently
around	finally	second
at once	first	thereafter
at the present time	here	thereupon

Indicating an example or summary

as a result	in any event	in other words
as I have said	in brief	in short
for example	in conclusion	on the whole
for instance	in fact	to sum up

COMMON WRITING ERRORS

The four writing errors most often made by beginning writers are run-ons (also known as fused sentences), fragments, lack of subject-verb agreement, and incorrect use of the object:

1. **Run-ons**: "She swept the floor it was dirty" is a run-on, because the pronoun "it" stands as a noun subject and starts a new sentence. A period or semicolon is needed after "floor."

2. **Fragments**: "Before Jimmy learned how to play baseball" is a fragment, even though it has a subject and verb (Jimmy learned). The word "before" fragmentizes the clause, and the reader needs to know what happened before Jimmy learned how to play baseball.

3. **Problems with subject-verb agreement**: "Either Maria or Robert are going to the game" is incorrect because either Maria is going or Robert is going, but not both. The sentence should say, "Either Maria or Robert is going to the game."

4. **Incorrect object**: Probably the most common offender in this area is saying "between you and I," which sounds correct, but isn't. "Between" is a preposition that takes the objective case "me." The correct usage is "between you and me."

The NYSTCE test graders also cite lack of thought and development, misspellings, incorrect pronouns or antecedents, and lack of development as frequently occurring problems. Finally, keep in mind that clear, coherent handwriting always works to your advantage. Readers will appreciate an essay they can read with ease.

FIVE WORDS WEAK WRITERS OVERUSE

Weak and beginning writers overuse the vague pronouns "you, we, they, this," and "it" often without telling exactly who or what is represented by the pronoun.

1. Beginning writers often shift to second person **"you,"** when the writer means "a person." This shift confuses readers and weakens the flow of the essay. Although "you" is commonly accepted in creative writing, journalism, and other arenas, in a short, formal essay, it is best to avoid "you" altogether.

2. **"We"** is another pronoun that should be avoided. If by "we" the writer means "Americans," "society," or some other group, then he or she should say so.

3. **"They"** is often misused in essay writing, because it is overused in conversation: "I went to the doctor, and they told me to take some medicine." Tell the reader who "they" are.

4. **"This"** is usually used incorrectly without a referent: "She told me she received a present. This sounded good to me." This what? This idea? This news? This present? Be clear—don't make your readers guess what you mean. The word "this" should be followed by a noun or referent.

5. **"It"** is a common problem among weak writers. To what does "it" refer? Your readers don't appreciate vagueness, so take the time to be clear and complete in your expression of ideas.

USE YOUR OWN VOCABULARY

Is it a good idea to use big words that sound good in the dictionary or thesaurus, but that you don't really use or understand? No. So whose vocabulary should you use? Your own. You will be most comfortable with your own level of vocabulary.

This "comfort zone" doesn't give you license to be informal in a formal setting or to violate the rules of standard written English, but if you try to write in a style that is not yours, your writing will be awkward and lack a true voice.

You should certainly improve and build your vocabulary at every opportunity, but remember: you should not attempt to change your vocabulary level at this point.

AVOID THE PASSIVE VOICE

In writing, the active voice is preferable because it is emphatic and direct. A weak passive verb leaves the doer unknown or seemingly unimportant. However, the passive voice is essential when the action of the verb is more important than the doer, when the doer is unknown, or when the writer wishes to place the emphasis on the receiver of the action rather than on the doer.

PROOFREADING

Make sure to leave yourself enough time at the end to read over your essay for errors such as misspellings, omitted words, or incorrect punctuation. You will not have enough time to make large-scale revisions, but take this chance to make any small changes that will make your essay stronger. Consider the following when proofreading your work:

- Are all your sentences really sentences? Have you written any fragments or run-on sentences?

- Are you using vocabulary correctly?

- Did you leave out any punctuation? Did you capitalize correctly?

- Are there any misspellings, especially of difficult words?

If you have time, read your essay backwards from end to beginning. By doing so, you may catch errors that you missed reading forward only.

Drill: Essay Writing

DIRECTIONS: You have 30 minutes to plan and write an essay on the topic below. You may write only on the assigned topic.

Make sure to give specific examples to support your thesis. Proofread your essay carefully and take care to express your ideas clearly and effectively.

ESSAY TOPIC:

In the last 20 years, the deterioration of the environment has become a growing concern among both scientists and ordinary citizens.

ASSIGNMENT: Choose one pressing environmental problem, explain its negative impact, and discuss possible solutions.

ANSWERS TO DRILL QUESTIONS

Drill: Word Choice Skills

1.	(D)	4.	(C)	7.	(A)	10.	(B)
2.	(D)	5.	(A)	8.	(B)		
3.	(A)	6.	(C)	9.	(C)		

Drill: Sentence Structure Skills

1.	(C)	4.	(B)	7.	(B)	10.	(B)
2.	(B)	5.	(A)	8.	(A)		
3.	(B)	6.	(A)	9.	(B)		

Drill: Verbs

1.	(C)	4.	(A)	7.	(A)	10.	(D)
2.	(D)	5.	(A)	8.	(C)		
3.	(D)	6.	(B)	9.	(A)		

Drill: Pronouns

1.	(A)	4.	(A)	7.	(B)	10.	(C)
2.	(C)	5.	(D)	8.	(B)		
3.	(A)	6.	(A)	9.	(A)		

Drill: Adjectives and Adverbs

1.	(C)	4.	(C)	7.	(A)	10.	(C)
2.	(A)	5.	(A)	8.	(C)		
3.	(D)	6.	(C)	9.	(B)		

Drill: Punctuation

1.	(D)	4.	(C)	7.	(A)	10.	(D)
2.	(A)	5.	(A)	8.	(A)		
3.	(A)	6.	(D)	9.	(B)		

Drill: Capitalization

1.	(D)	4.	(A)	7.	(B)	10.	(A)
2.	(B)	5.	(C)	8.	(D)		
3.	(C)	6.	(D)	9.	(B)		

Drill: Spelling

1.	(A)	4.	(A)	7.	(B)	10.	(B)
2.	(B)	5.	(C)	8.	(A)		
3.	(C)	6.	(D)	9.	(B)		

Drill: Essay Writing

This Answer Key provides three sample essays which represent possible responses to the essay topic. Compare your own response to those given on the next few pages. Allow the strengths and weaknesses of the sample essays help you to critique your own essay and improve your writing skills.

ESSAY I (SCORE: 5–6)

There are many pressing environmental problems facing both this country and the world today. Pollution, the misuse and squandering of resources, and the cavalier attitude many people express all contribute to the problem. But one of the most pressing problems this country faces is the apathetic attitude many Americans have towards recycling.

Why is recycling so imperative? There are two major reasons. First, recycling previously used materials conserves precious national resources. Many people never stop to think that reserves of metal ores are not unlimited. There is only so much gold, silver, tin, and other metals in the ground. Once it has all been mined, there will never be any more unless we recycle what has already been used.

Second, the United States daily generates more solid waste than any other country on earth. Our disposable consumer culture consumes fast food meals in paper or styrofoam containers, uses disposable diapers with plastic liners that do not biodegrade, receives pounds, if not tons, of unsolicited junk mail every year, and relies more and more on prepackaged rather than fresh food.

No matter how it is accomplished, increased recycling is essential. We have to stop covering our land with garbage, and the best ways to do this are to reduce our dependence on prepackaged goods and to minimize the amount of solid waste disposed of in landfills. The best way to reduce solid waste is to recycle it. Americans need to band together to recycle, to preserve our irreplaceable natural resources, reduce pollution, and preserve our precious environment.

ANALYSIS

This essay presents a clearly defined thesis, and the writer elaborates on this thesis in a thoughtful and sophisticated manner. Various aspects of the problem under consideration are presented and explored, along with possible solutions. The support provided for the writer's argument is convincing and logical. There are few usage or mechanical errors to interfere with the writer's ability to communicate effectively. This writer demonstrates a comprehensive understanding of the rules of written English.

ESSAY II (SCORE: 3–4)

A pressing environmental problem today is the way we are cutting down too many trees and not planting any replacements for them. Trees are beneficial in many ways, and without them, many environmental problems would be much worse.

One of the ways trees are beneficial is that, like all plants, they take in carbon dioxide and produce oxygen. They can actually help clean the air this way. When too many trees are cut down in a small area, the air in that area is not as good and can be unhealthy to breath.

Another way trees are beneficial is that they provide homes for many types of birds, insects, and animals. When all the trees in an area are cut down, these animals lose their homes and sometimes they can die out and become extinct that way. Like the spotted owls in Oregon, that the loggers wanted to cut down the trees they lived in. If the loggers did cut down all the old timber stands that the spotted owls lived in, the owls would have become extinct.

But the loggers say that if they can't cut the trees down then they will be out of work, and that peoples' jobs are more important than birds. The loggers can do two things—they can either get training so they can do other jobs, or they can do what they should have done all along, and start replanting trees. For every mature tree they cut down, they should have to plant at least one tree seedling.

Cutting down the trees that we need for life, and that lots of other species depend on, is a big environmental problem that has a lot of long term consaquences. Trees are too important for all of us to cut them down without thinking about the future.

ANALYSIS

This essay has a clear thesis, which the author does support with good examples. But the writer shifts between the chosen topic, which is that indiscriminate tree-cutting is a pressing environmental problem, and a list of the ways in which trees are beneficial and a discussion about the logging profession. Also, while there are few mistakes in usage and mechanics, the writer does have some problems with sentence structure. The writing is pedestrian and the writer does not elaborate on the topic as much as he or she could have. The writer failed to provide the kind of critical analysis that the topic required.

ESSAY III (SCORE: 1–2)

The most pressing environmental problem today is that lots of people and companies don't care about the environment, and they do lots of things that hurt the environment.

People throw litter out car windows and don't use trash cans, even if their all over a park, soda cans and fast food wrappers are all over the place. Cigarette butts are the worst cause the filters never rot. Newspapers and junk mail get left to blow all over the neighborhood, and beer bottles too.

Companies pollute the air and the water. Sometimes the ground around a company has lots of toxins in it. Now companies can buy credits from other companies that let them pollute the air even more. They dump all kinds of chemicals into lakes and rivers that kill off the fish and causes acid rain and kills off more fish and some trees and small animals and insects and then noone can go swimming or fishing in the lake.

People need to respect the environment because we only have one planet, and if we keep polluting it pretty soon nothing will grow and then even the people will die.

ANALYSIS

The writer of this essay does not define his or her thesis for this essay. Because of this lack of a clear thesis, the reader is left to infer the topic from the body of the essay. It is possible to perceive the writer's intended thesis; however, the support for this thesis is very superficial. The writer presents a list of common complaints about polluters, without any critical discussion of the problems and possible solutions. Many sentences are run-ons and the writer has made several spelling errors. While the author manages to communicate his or her position on the issue, he or she does so on such a superficial level and with so many errors in usage and mechanics that the writer fails to demonstrate an ability to effectively communicate.

Chapter 7 → STARTS "ATS" Review

Knowledge of the Learner

In order for teachers to successfully teach students of all ages and in all disciplines, it is necessary that teachers understand learners. Benjamin Bloom (1976) has suggested that students' cognitive entry skills and intelligence (or IQ) account for about 50 percent of what students achieve academically; 25 percent can be attributed to the quality of instruction students receive; 25 percent can be attributed to affective characteristics of the students. Those affective characteristics include such things as the learner's personality, self-concept, locus of control, attitudes, level of anxiety, and study habits. Therefore, although it is important that teachers acquire and utilize effective teaching techniques and provide quality instruction to students, it can be argued that it is even more important in terms of educational outcomes that teachers understand cognitive and affective factors which influence student performance.

The traditional view of education saw the learner as a *tabula rasa*, a blank slate, upon which the teacher wrote knowledge. In this model, the student was assumed to be an empty vessel; he or she came into the classroom knowing nothing. It was the teacher's responsibility, as the expert, to impart knowledge or to fill the empty vessel.

Today, cognitive psychologists have corrected this faulty notion. Educators now recognize that students bring to the classroom an array of personal characteristics and experiences upon which they base their present knowledge. Those characteristics and experiences may or may not be congruent to the teacher's background; nonetheless, they constitute a knowledge base for the learner. Therefore, the teacher's role is to activate the learner's prior knowledge and help the student connect new information with what is known already. Thus, in today's educational model, the student is seen as an active learner who brings much to the classroom.

The effective teacher, then, must go beyond assuming the role of a "sage on the stage." The effective teacher must be more than just an expert who has mastered a discipline or body of knowledge. The effective teacher must be a facilitator of learning; an effective teacher empowers students to learn for and by themselves. The effective teacher, in other words, is a "guide by the side" of students, assisting them in the process of learning and enhancing that process for students.

It is also important that teachers appreciate a dynamic and interactive view of human development. This approach to understanding human development is one which recognizes that human beings do not develop in a vacuum. People exist in an environment which, friendly or unfriendly, supportive or nonsupportive, evokes and provokes reactions from individuals; moreover, it is not a one-way street with the environment doing all the driving. People also act in certain ways to shape and form their environment. There is a constant interaction or interplay between people and their environments. Thus, effective teachers must be sensitive to and knowledgeable of both personal characteristics of students and characteristics of their environment.

STUDENT DEVELOPMENT AND MATURATION

A teacher does not have to be an expert in anatomy and physiology to see the physical changes that accompany students' growth and maturity. The preschool child has trouble grasping pencils or crayons in a manner to facilitate handwriting; however, even most two-year olds can grasp crayons sufficiently to make marks on papers and, thus, enjoy the creative excitement of art.

Physiological changes play a significant role in the development of children as they increase their control of bodily movements and functions and refine their motor skills. Their ability to engage in simple to complex classroom and playground activities increases as they develop. Classroom and playground activities must be adjusted and adapted in order to be developmentally appropriate for the skill levels of the children.

As students enter junior high or begin their secondary education, they again experience important physiological changes with the onset of puberty. With puberty comes changes in primary sexual characteristics and the emergence of secondary sexual characteristics. In addition to bodily characteristics, there is a change in bodily feelings, and there is an increase in sex drive.

Girls, on average, reach maturational milestones before boys. Physical changes may cause embarrassment to both females and males when they draw unwelcome attention; moreover, these changes almost always create some discomfort as adolescents find the body they were familiar and comfortable with to be quite different, sometimes seemingly overnight.

David Elkind has noted two developmental characteristics of adolescence which share a relationship to the physiological changes accompanying maturation. These two characteristics are the *imaginary audience* and the *personal fable*. First, adolescents, preoccupied with their own physiological changes, often assume that others are equally intrigued by these changes in appearance and behavior; they may feel that others are staring at them, watching their every move, scrutinizing their behavior for one misstep or their appearance for any flaws. If everyone is watching, then it's imperative to be, to act, and to look just right. In today's culture, that means wearing the right clothes and having all the right brand names and status symbols. Because of adolescents' sensitivity to attention (especially the wrong kind of attention, that is, not fitting in, not being "right"), it is especially important that teachers of this age group be aware of the *imaginary audience* phenomenon and be sensitive to social interactions in the classroom. It, indeed, is important that teachers not contribute to creating unwanted attention or to stigmatizing or stereotyping students.

Personal fable refers to the belief that "My life is different from everyone else's; therefore, no one can understand how I feel or what I think. No one has ever felt or thought what I feel and think." This out-of-focus view tends to support both a feeling of isolation (which may be precipitated by the changing sensations from a body that is undergoing biological changes) and a willingness to engage in risky behaviors (thinking that only others have car accidents when they drive dangerously—"It won't happen to me"—or, only other girls get pregnant when they have unprotected sexual relations—"It won't happen to me.").

In sum, these two characteristics of adolescence are examples of how physical changes accompany and, perhaps even evoke, emotional and cognitive changes as individuals grow and mature. Both phenomena of *imaginary audience* and *personal fable* have emotional features (fear of rejection, fear of isolation, fear of difference, shame, guilt from increased sexual feelings, frustration, and so forth) and both describe a feature of adolescent cognitive ability: the ability to think about one's self as an object of one's own and of other's thought. The developmental epistemologist Jean Piaget explained that this way of thinking represents the cognitive stage of formal operations.

Cognition is a term commonly used to refer to all the processes whereby knowledge is acquired; the term can be used to cover very basic perceptual processes, such as smell, touch, sound, and so forth, to very advanced operations, such as analysis, synthesis, and critical thinking.

THEORIES OF COGNITIVE DEVELOPMENT

Until his death in 1980, Jean Piaget was a predominant figure in the field of cognitive psychology. It is safe to postulate that perhaps no other single individual has had greater influence on educational practices than Piaget. Basically, his theory of cognitive development is based on the notion that cognitive abilities (or one's ability to think) are developed as individuals mature physiologically, and they have opportunities to interact with their environment. Piaget described these interactions as the *equilibration* of *accommodation* and *assimilation* cycles or processes. In other words, when individuals (who, according to Piaget, are innately endowed with certain cognitive predispositions and capabilities) encounter a new or novel stimulus, they are brought into a state of *disequilibrium*.

That is a way of saying that they are thrown off balance; they do not know or understand that which is new or unfamiliar. However, through the complementary processes of *accommodation* (or adjusting prior knowledge gained through former experiences and interactions) and *assimilation* (fitting together the new information with what has been previously known or understood), individuals come to know or understand that which is new. Once again, individuals are returned to a state of *equilibrium* where they remain until the next encounter with an unfamiliar something. For Piaget, this is how learners learn.

Piaget also predicted that certain behaviors and ways of thinking characterize individuals at different ages. For this reason, his theory is considered a *stage* theory. *Stage* theories share the common tenet that certain characteristics will occur in predictable sequences and at certain times in the life of the individual.

According to Piaget, there are four stages of cognitive development, beginning with the *sensorimotor* stage describing individuals from birth to around the age of two. The second stage, *preoperational* (describing cognitive behavior between the ages of two and seven), is characterized by egocentrism, rigidity of thought, semilogical reasoning, and limited social cognition; some cognitive psychologists have observed that this stage seems to describe how individuals think more in terms of what they can't do than what they can do. This stage describes the way that children in preschool and kindergarten go about problem-solving; also, many children in the primary grades may be at this stage in their cognitive development.

The next two stages, however, may be most important for elementary and secondary school teachers since they describe cognitive development during the times that most students are in school. The third stage, *concrete operations,* is the beginning of operational thinking and describes the thinking of children between the ages of 7 and 11. Learners at this age begin to decenter. They are able to take into consideration viewpoints other than their own. They can perform transformations, meaning that they can understand reversibility, inversion, reciprocity, and conservation. They can group items into categories. They can make inferences about reality and engage in inductive reasoning; they increase their quantitative skills, and they can manipulate symbols if they are given concrete examples with which to work. This stage of cognitive development is the threshold to higher-level learning for students.

Finally, *formal operations* is the last stage of cognitive development and opens wide the door for higher-ordered, critical thinking. This stage describes the way of thinking for learners between the ages of 11 and 15, and for Piaget, constitutes the ultimate stage of cognitive development (thus also describing adult thinking). Learners at this stage of cognitive development can engage in logical, abstract, and hypothetical thought; they can use the scientific method, meaning they can formulate hypotheses, isolate influences, and identify cause-and effect-relationships. They can plan and anticipate verbal cues. They can engage in both deductive and inductive reasoning, and they can operate on verbal statements exclusive of concrete experiences or examples. These cognitive abilities characterize the highest levels of thought.

Another theoretical approach to understanding human development is offered by Erik Erikson, another important stage theorist, who described psychosocial development. For each of eight stages, he identified a developmental task explained in terms of two polarities. For the purposes of this discussion, only those stages describing school-age individuals will be included.

According to Erikson, preschoolers and primary-school aged children must be able to function in the outside world independently of parents; when children are able to do this, they achieve a sense of *initiative*; when children are not able to move away from total parental attachment and control, they experience a sense of *guilt*. Thus, this stage of psychosocial development is the stage of initiative versus guilt. The child's first venture away from home and into the world of school has considerable significance when viewed in light of this theory; it is imperative that teachers assist students in their first experiences on their own, away from parental control.

Erikson's next stage of development is one involving a tension between *industry* and *inferiority*. For example, if the child who enters school (thus achieving initiative) acquires the skills (including academic skills such as reading, writing, and computation, as well as social skills in playing with others, communicating with others, forming friendships, and so forth) which enable her or him to be successful in school, then the child achieves a sense of *industry;* failure to achieve these skills leads to a sense of *inferiority*.

IDENTITY ACHIEVEMENT AND DIFFUSION

Around the time students enter junior high, they begin the developmental task of achieving *identity*. According to Erikson, the struggle to achieve identity is one of the most important developmental tasks and one which creates serious psychosocial problems for adolescents. For example, even the individual who has successfully achieved all the important developmental milestones (such as initiative and industry) now finds him- or herself in a state of flux: Everything (body, feelings, thoughts) is changing. The adolescent starts to question, "Who am I?" Erikson believed that if adolescents find out what they believe in, what their goals, ideas, and values are, then they attain identity achievement; failure to discover these things leads to identity diffusion.

By the time many students reach high school, they are entering a stage of young adulthood, for Erikson, a psychosocial stage characterized by the polarities of *intimacy* and *isolation*. Individuals at this stage of development begin to think about forming lasting friendships, even marital unions. Erikson would argue that many psychosocial problems experienced by young adults have their origin in the individual's failure to achieve identity during the preceding stage; the young man or woman who does not know who he or she really is cannot achieve true intimacy.

For the classroom teacher, knowledge of psychosocial stages of human development can result in greater effectiveness. For example, the effective teacher realizes the importance of helping students to achieve skills necessary to accomplish crucial developmental tasks. According to Erikson's theory, teachers of elementary school-aged learners would do well to focus on teaching academic and social skills, helping students to gain proficiency in skills that will enable learners to be productive members of society. On the other hand, secondary school teachers would do well to keep in mind, as they engage students in higher-ordered thinking activities appropriate to their stage of cognitive development, that students have pressing psychological and social needs in their struggle to achieve identity and to attain intimacy.

By understanding key principles of human development in its multiple dimensions, effective teachers provide students with both age-appropriate and developmentally-appropriate instruction. This, in sum, is the best instruction. It is instruction that addresses all the needs of students, their physical, emotional, and social needs, as well as their cognitive (or intellectual) needs.

MASLOW'S HIERARCHY OF NEEDS

Abraham Maslow's hierarchy of human needs is a model applicable to many diverse fields, including education, business and industry, health and medical professions, and more. Maslow identified different levels of individuals' needs in a hierarchical sequence, meaning that lower level needs must be satisfied before individuals could ascend to higher levels of achievement. He identified the fulfillment of basic physiological needs as fundamental to individuals' sense of well-being and their ability to engage in any meaningful activity. Simply stated, students' physiological needs (to have hunger and thirst satisfied, to have sleep needs met, to be adequately warm, and so forth) must be met before students can perform school tasks. Today's schools provide students with breakfast and lunch when needed, and great effort and expense is often directed towards heating and cooling school buildings.

Maslow's second level of need concerned safety. Again, students must feel safe from harm and danger before they are ready to learn. Today, schools often are equipped with metal detectors to increase students' sense of safety. In some schools, guards and security officers patrol the halls.

The third level of need, according to Maslow's theory, is the need for affiliation or the need to belong and to be accepted by others. Although this need may, at first glance, seem less related to the student's environment, it does, indeed, refer to the student's social environment. Students need the opportunity to develop social relationships and to establish friendships among their peers. In essence, Maslow, through his theory, determined that environmental factors are important in education.

Another significant principle of human development arises from a long debate between those experts who believed that innate characteristics (those the individual is born with) play the most important role in determining who the individual will become and what he or she will do versus those who believed that environmental characteristics are most important. This argument is referred to in the literature as the *nature* versus *nurture* debate.

NATURE AND NURTURE

After experts on both sides of the argument stated their positions, the conclusion seemed to be that both *nature* (the internal variables) and *nurture* (the environment) play equally important roles in determining the outcome of individuals' growth and maturation. Again, it is important to remember the interaction of the individual with her or his environment, recalling that this view is the *dynamic* view of human development.

Before proceeding, teachers would do well to understand that perception plays an important role for learners to the extent that perception creates our individual reality. The world as we know it is a result of our selective perception. We cannot attend to all events and variables in our environment. We select certain events and variables to notice, to attend to, and these phenomena which we observe form our perceptions; thus, we create our own reality. External and internal phenomena grab our attention and shape reality for each of us.

Thus, it is one thing for teachers to be aware of and sensitive to the students' environment; it is, however, impossible for teachers to see, feel, and understand the individual's environment in exactly the same way that it is seen, felt, and understood by the student.

Carol Tavris, a social psychologist and author of the book, *Anger the Misunderstood Emotion*, notes that emotion plays a significant role in students' perceptions. For example, guilt is an emotion aroused by thoughts such as, "I should study or my parents will kill (be disappointed in) me." This is easily contrasted with the emotion of fear generated by the thought, "I should study or I will be a failure in life." Furthermore, guilt and fear can be compared to the emotion of anger which is prompted by thoughts such as, "Why should I study when my teacher is out to get me?" Today's student often sees the teacher as an enemy, not as an authority figure or a friend. Tavris has identified anger as a primary emotion experienced by many students today and one which plays a significant role in shaping their academic perceptions which, in turn, forms their reality of classroom experiences.

Explaining further, Tavris observes that unfulfilled expectations lead to anger. For example, if a student is led to believe (by teachers, school administrators, their peers, or by parents and siblings) that attending class is somehow irrelevant to academic achievement, then the student who is frequently absent still has the expectation of being successful. The student's perception is that absenteeism is compatible with academic achievement. If, because of absenteeism, the student fails to master essential elements of the curriculum and does not succeed, then the student will feel anger, the appropriate and anticipated emotion.

Anger, however, can be diffused by addressing perceptions, correcting false impressions, and establishing appropriate and realistic expectations. To illustrate, if all those significant individuals to the student emphasize the importance of class attendance, then students acquire the correct perception (in this case) that attendance is important for academic achievement and that absenteeism leads to academic failure.

For the sake of illustration only, let's consider what might happen if the teacher stresses attendance and the parents do not. In this case, the best route for the teacher to take is to show empathy for the student's dilemma. The teacher can acknowledge how difficult it is for the student to attend class when the parents are not supporting attendance, but the teacher also must seek to empower the student to make choices and to take responsibility for her or his own behavior.

In the situation described here, the student undergoes stress because of conflicting messages, and stress is faced by students and faculty alike. In fact, in the above example, the teacher is stressed too in that the teacher faces the conflict between supporting the parents of the student and supporting that which is in the best educational interests of the student.

Stress is the product of any change; both negative and positive changes produce stress. Environmental, physiological, and psychological factors cause stress. For example, environmental factors such as noise, air pollution, and crowding (among others) create stress; physiological factors such as sickness and physical injuries create stress; and, finally, psychological factors such as self-deprecating thoughts and negative self-image cause stress. In addition to the normal stressors that everyone experiences, some students are living in dysfunctional families; some students are dealing with substance abuse and addictions; some are experiencing sexual abuse. There are numerous sources of stress in the lives of students.

Since life is a stressful process, it is important that students and faculty learn acceptable ways to cope with stress. The first step in coping with stress is to recognize the role that stress plays in our lives. A teacher might lead a class through a brainstorming activity to help the students become aware of the various sources of stress affecting them. Next, the teacher could identify positive ways of coping with stress such as the importance of positive self-talk, physical exercise, proper nutrition, adequate sleep, balanced activities, time-management techniques, good study habits, and relaxation exercises.

Students who are stressed often become angry rather easily; however, students are not just angry. They experience a wide range of emotions, and may be sad, depressed, frustrated, afraid, and, on the positive side, happy and surprised. Effective teachers realize that students' emotions, as explained in this section and the preceeding section on human development, play a significant role in students' classroom performance and achievement. Thus, effective teachers seek to create a classroom environment supportive of students' emotional needs. They have appropriate empathy and compassion for the emotional conflicts facing students, yet their concern is tempered by a realistic awareness of the importance of students attaining crucial academic and social skills that will grant them some control over their environment as they become increasingly independent and, eventually, must be prepared to be productive citizens.

Effective teachers recognize the effects of students' perceptions on the learning process and the effects of many environmental factors; as a result, they plan instruction to enhance students' self-esteem and to promote realistic expectations. It is important that teachers be able to differentiate positive and negative environmental factors, maximizing the positive variables and minimizing the negative ones. The teacher has the primary responsibility of creating a classroom environment that recognizes the different environmental factors affecting each student and that encourages each learner to excel, to achieve her or his personal best. Effective teachers work hard at creating learning environments in which all students are ready to learn—where students feel safe, accepted, competent, and productive.

DIVERSITY IN THE CLASSROOM

Effective teachers realize that students bring to the classroom a variety of characteristics, both personal and social, that create within the classroom a microcosm reflective of American society at large. Indeed, America has long held to the notion of being a "melting pot" whereby members of various racial, ethnic, religious, and national origin groups have contributed to the wealth of our culture.

Ethnocentrism is a sociological term used to describe the natural tendency of viewing one's own cultural or familial way of doing things as the right, correct, or best way. Because ethnocentrism is a natural tendency, all people are likely to engage in ethnocentric thinking and behaviors at times.

Some social critics have pointed out that ethnocentrism has played a notable role in American education. They assert that educational institutions often have been guilty of assuming a Eurocentric viewpoint, that is, solely recognizing the contributions of European writers, artists, scientists, philosophers, and so forth, at the expense of those from other cultures. These critics have also noted that the contributions of men often are disproportionately recognized over like achievements of women (Sadker & Sadker, 1994).

In fact, David and Myra Sadker (1994) have found that teachers, both male and female, at all grade levels, are more likely to call on male than female students, are more likely to give positive reinforcement to males' correct responses than to those of females, and to provide coaching or instructional help to males when their responses are incorrect than to females. Their research has led them to conclude that teachers are usually unaware of gender bias in their teaching, but that such bias is pervasive in American schools. Their research also has persuaded them that bias can be eliminated once teachers become sensitive to its debilitating effects on students.

The point made here is that ethnocentrism, in any form, can be damaging because it is exclusive rather than inclusive. Eurocentric, Afrocentric, and other ethnocentric perspectives are equally limited in that they narrowly focus attention on one set of ideas at the neglect of others. Therefore, effective teachers will wisely expend a degree of effort in avoiding ethnocentric thinking and behaviors. Effective teachers will attempt to include all students in all classroom activities. The race, ethnicity, religion, national origin, and gender of learners will be viewed as strengths which enable students to learn with and from each other.

Historically speaking, educational experiments have demonstrated the importance of teachers' avoiding bias and ethnocentric thinking. The *Hawthorne effect,* or the phenomenon whereby what teachers expected became reality, was demonstrated when teachers were told that some students in their classes were extremely intelligent whereas others were extremely slow or mentally retarded. In fact, all students had normal range intelligence. Nonetheless, at the end of the experiment, students who had been identified to the teachers as being extremely intelligent all had made significant academic progress and were not only at the top of their class, but also performing at the top on national achievement tests. Those students who had been identified as retarded had made no progress at all; in fact, they had lost previously-made gains. Thus, it was demonstrated that teachers' expectations for students often become self-fulfilling prophecies.

In today's society, there is considerable reference to multiculturalism. Multiculturalism, if it serves merely to separate and distinguish the accomplishments of select cultural and ethnic groups, has the potential of separating and alienating Americans. To view multiculturalism in a positive light is to acknowledge a kind of multiculturalism which embraces the accomplishments of all cultural and ethnic groups, thereby strengthening our country and society, and promoting a sense of unity in the classroom.

Because multiculturalism and/or cultural diversity can be a controversial issue with many sides to consider, another approach to diversity for the classroom teacher is to acknowledge both cultural diversity and learning diversity and to focus on diversity in learning. This approach transcends cultural boundaries and recognizes that all people have distinct learning preferences and tendencies. Furthermore, this approach acknowledges that all preferences and tendencies are equally valid and that each style of learning has strengths. The teacher who understands learning styles can validate all students in the class.

ENVIRONMENTAL FACTORS

Many factors play a role in determining a student's learning style. Among those most often cited in the research literature on learning style are environmental, emotional, sociological, physiological, and psychological factors (Dunn & Dunn, 1993). Although there are several different models for understanding learning differences and many good instruments for assessing learning styles, the Dunn and Dunn (1993) model is one widely used in public schools with versions suitable for students in elementary and secondary classrooms. It will serve as the basis for the following discussion.

Environmental factors include students' reactions to such stimuli as sound, light, temperature, and room design. Do students prefer to study and learn with or without sound, with bright or soft lights, in warm or cool rooms, with standard classroom furniture or alternative seating? Classroom teachers observe that some students are easily distracted by any noise and require absolute quiet when studying or working on assignments. On the other hand, some students seem to learn best when they can listen to music. Some researchers have found evidence that students who prefer sound learn best when classical or instrumental music is played in the background.

Light is another environmental factor with students' preferences for light appearing to be basically inherited, with family members often exhibiting the same preference. Some students prefer bright, direct illumination while others prefer dim, indirect lighting.

Temperature and design are two other environmental factors affecting learning style. Some students will prefer warmer temperatures whereas others will prefer cooler temperatures. Finally, some students will prefer to sit in straight-backed chairs at desks while others may prefer to sit on soft, comfy chairs or to sit or recline on the floor.

Although traditional classrooms are structured to provide quiet, brightly illuminated study and work areas with straight-backed chairs and desks, classroom teachers will observe that this environment meets the needs of only some of the learners in the class. An effective teacher will take into consideration the learning styles of all students and experiment with different room designs, study centers, and creating different environments in the classroom. Although classroom temperature may seem to be beyond the control of the teacher, students can be advised to dress in layers so that they can remove outer garments when they are too warm and put on more layers when they are too cool.

EMOTIONAL FACTORS

According to Rita and Kenneth Dunn, emotional factors include motivation, persistence, responsibility, and structure. To explain, some students are motivated intrinsically: they undertake and complete tasks because they see the value in doing so. Other students are motivated extrinsically: They undertake and complete tasks because they desire to please others or to earn good marks. In regard to persistence, some students, when they undertake assignments, become totally and completely engaged in their work; they seem to lose track of time and can work for long periods without interruption or without feeling fatigued. Other students seem to work in short spurts of energy, needing to take frequent breaks.

When it comes to responsibility, some students are nonconforming, always doing the unexpected (and sometimes unwanted), whereas other students are conforming, always following the rules. Structure refers to whether or not students need detailed and precise instructions. Some students have lots of questions about how assignments should be done, and they desire detailed, step-by-step instructions on each phase of the assignment. Other students, however, seem to work from general concepts and are usually eager to begin assignments, often beginning their work before the directions have been given.

Sociological factors include whether or not students are social learners—preferring to work in pairs or in groups—or whether they are independent learners—preferring to work alone. Another sociological factor is whether or not students work best under the close guidance and supervision of an authority figure, be it teacher or parent, or whether they work best with a minimum of adult guidance and are best left primarily on their own to do their work.

Physiological factors include students' preferences for food or drink while they study, what time of day they learn best, their mobility needs, and their perceptual strengths. Briefly, some students may need to eat or drink in order to effectively and efficiently learn. Rita Dunn says that to make sure that students do not abuse this privilege, she allows them to eat only carrot or celery sticks (cooked so that the snacks will not crunch when eaten by students) and to drink water. This way, she is certain that only students who really need intake when they are learning will take advantage of this concession.

Some students may learn best early in the morning, some later in the morning, some in early afternoon, and some later in the afternoon. Researchers have found that merely manipulating the time of day that certain students take tests can significantly affect their test performance.

Mobility needs refer to the fact that some students need to move around when they study, whereas other students can sit still for longer periods of time. Although all of these factors are important, and a growing body of literature tends to support the idea that these factors play a significant role in increasing students' performance and in increasing teachers' effectiveness with students, perhaps one of the most important elements in understanding learning style is to identify students' perceptual strengths. Perceptual strengths refer to students' learning modalities, such as whether they are visual, auditory, tactile, or kinesthetic learners. Basically, these perceptual modalities refer to whether students learn best by seeing, hearing, or doing.

Some students can be given a book or handout to read and then perform a task well based on what they have read. These students tend to have visual (iconic or semantic) perceptual strength. Other students are visual learners, too, but they tend to learn best from images. These are the students who seem to recall every event, even minor details, from films, videos, or classroom demonstrations.

Although evidence indicates that less than 15 percent of the school-age population is auditory (Dunn, 1993), much of the classroom instruction takes the form of teachers telling students information. Most students do not learn auditorially. Therefore, these students must be taught how to listen and learn from oral instructions and lecture.

Teachers who rely on telling students the information that is important would do well to remember that females are more likely to learn auditorially than males. Teachers should also keep in mind that whether or not students benefit from lectures is likely to depend on several other elements as well as whether or not the students are auditory learners, such as whether or not the students like the teacher, whether or not they think the information being presented is important, or whether or not they think that listening to the teacher will help them to achieve their goals (Baxter-Magolda, 1992).

On the other hand, there are students who do not seem to benefit much from lectures, textbook assignments, or visual aids. These students' perceptual strengths are tactile and kinesthetic. They learn from movement and motion, from being able to touch, handle, and manipulate objects. Often these students may have been identified as having learning disabilities. Sometimes they have been relegated to shop or cooking classes or have found their success in athletics, music, or art. Interestingly, many of the "hands on" skills that often identify a student for a career as an auto mechanic are also important skills for mechanical engineers and surgeons.

LEARNING STYLES

The obvious benefit of knowing whether or not students are auditory, visual, tactile, or kinesthetic learners is not simply to cater to the learners' preferences or strengths. The significance is that once strengths are identified, then teachers can teach students to use those strengths in situations which are not easy or natural. For example, students who are not auditory learners (but tactile and kinesthetic) must learn responsibility for their own learning; they must learn to become involved in lecture classes. Becoming involved means that they learn to take copious notes, participate in class discussions, ask questions, and answer questions posed by the teacher.

Visual learners must sit where they can see what's going on in class, where they can see the teacher and the board. They need opportunities to draw pictures, to diagram, to take good notes, to create mind maps, and to use flashcards. They must be taught how to visualize the abstract concepts they are being taught, and they need opportunities to practice all these techniques.

For visual learners who learn best by reading, teachers can provide adequate opportunities to read in class. Students need to learn specific note-taking methods, and reading and comprehension strategies. They also can be taught to use supplemental readings, to use the library effectively, and to use workbooks.

Auditory learners need to learn attention-directing activities. They can learn to use audio cassettes as learning aids. They can learn to ask questions in class and to participate in class discussions. They must be taught how to summarize and paraphrase—especially how to state in their own words the concepts they are trying to master. They may need the teacher to repeat or to restate ideas. Students must learn to pay close attention to verbal cues such as voice tone and inflection. Reciting what they have heard (or read) is an important strategy for auditory learners as is finding someone to whom they can explain ideas they have acquired. It may be helpful for auditory learners to work on some assignments with students who are visual learners (Nolting, 1993).

Tactile, kinesthetic learners may benefit from study groups, discussion groups, role-playing situations, lab settings, computer activities, learning games, and using flashcards and other manipulatives. They must get involved in class by asking questions and participating in discussions. They learn best when they can convert what they are learning into real-life, concrete experiences; for example, they may learn fractions by cutting a pizza into slices. Often, they need to work math problems immediately after being shown examples to check their understanding. They often need to move around while they are studying, reviewing ideas while exercising, or doing chores. Many times, they do their best work when they are using tools such as computers, calculators, or even their fingers.

When classroom teachers assess students' learning styles and then begin to teach to empower students to learn more effectively and perform tasks with greater proficiency, the result is that students also learn a tremendous lesson about diversity. They learn that not everyone learns in the same way, but that everyone can achieve. The products of learning can meet the same high standards although the processes for learning may be different for different students.

This is a rich lesson for students and faculty alike. It tells students that it is okay to be different; in fact, everyone is different. It tells students that it is okay to be the way they are. Apart from their race, ethnicity, religious beliefs, national origin, or gender, they are special, and they are good. They can learn. This may be one of the most important lessons that students ever learn and one that all teachers can be proud and eager to teach.

UNDERSTANDING LEARNERS

It is one thing for teachers to have command of their subject matter. It is a given that English teachers will be able to write well, that math teachers will be able to compute and calculate, that science teachers will know and understand science, and so forth. However, it is something else—and something at least as important—that teachers know how to teach.

When teachers understand learners, that is, when teachers understand developmental processes common to all learners, and how environmental features and learning styles, varied and diverse, affect learning, then teachers are better able to design and deliver effective instruction. Although there may be some intuitive aspects to teaching (and it seems that some people were born to teach), teaching skills can be acquired through processes of introspection, observation, direct instruction, self-evaluation, and experimentation.

How teachers teach should be directly related to how learners learn. Theories of cognitive development describe how learners learn new information and acquire new skills. There are many theories of cognitive development, two of which will be included in this review; they are (a) the Piagetian (or Neo-Piagetian) theory, and (b) information processing theory.

Piagetian theory (including Neo-Piagetian theory) describes learning in discrete and predictable stages. Therefore, teachers who understand this theory can provide students with developmentally-appropriate instruction. This theory also describes learners moving from simpler ways of thinking to more complex ways of problem-solving and thinking. For teachers, there are many important implications of this theoretical perspective. For example, teachers must create enriched environments that present learners with multiple opportunities to encounter new and unfamiliar stimuli—be they objects or ideas. Teachers must also provide learners with opportunities to engage in extended dialogue with adults; according to Piaget's theory, conversational interactions with adults are a key component in cognitive development, especially the acquisition of formal operations (or higher-ordered thinking skills). Moreover, it is important that adults (and teachers in particular) model desired behaviors; teachers must reveal their own complex ways of thinking and solving problems to students.

On the other hand, information processing theories of human development take a different approach to describing and understanding how learners learn. Based on a computer metaphor and borrowing computer imagery to describe how people learn, information processing theories begin by determining the processing demands of a particular cognitive challenge (or problem to solve) necessitating a detailed task-analysis of how the human mind changes external objects or events into a useful form according to certain, precisely-specified rules or strategies, similar to the way a computer programmer programs a computer to perform a function. Thus, information processing theories focus on the process, how the learner arrives at a response or answer.

A brief analysis of one information processing theory will serve to illustrate this point. Sternberg's (1985) triarchic theory of intelligence is a theory taking into account three features of learning. Those three features are (a) the mechanics or components of intelligence (including both higher-ordered thinking processes, such as planning, decision making and problem solving, and lower-ordered processes, such as making inferences, mapping, selectively encoding information, retaining information in memory, transferring new information in memory, and so forth); (b) the learner's experiences; and (c) the learner's context (including the adaptation to and the shaping and selecting of environments).

According to Sternberg, learners' use of the mechanics of intelligence is influenced by learners' experiences. To illustrate, some cognitive processes (such as those required in reading) become automatized as a result of continued exposure to and practice of those skills. Learners who come from homes where parents read and where there are lots of different reading materials tend to be more proficient readers; certainly, learners who read a lot become more proficient readers. Those learners who are exposed to reading activities and who have ample opportunities to practice reading have greater skill and expertise in reading; and in a cyclical manner, students who have skills in reading like to read. Conversely, those who lack reading skills don't like to read. Students who don't like to read, don't read; thus, their reading skills, lacking practice, fail to improve.

An information processing approach acknowledges that not only are individuals influenced by their environments and adapt to those environments, individuals also are active in shaping their own environments. In other words, a child who wants to read but who has no books at home may ask parents to buy books, or may go to the library to read, or check out books to read at home.

Information processing theory is of interest to educators because of its insistence on the idea that intelligent performance can be facilitated through instruction and direct training. In sum, intelligent thinking can be taught. Sternberg has urged teachers to identify the mental processes that academic tasks require and to teach learners those processes; he challenges teachers to teach learners what processes to use, when and how to use them, and how to combine them into strategies for solving problems and accomplishing assignments.

Teachers who wish to follow Sternberg's advice might choose to begin teaching by identifying *instructional objectives*, that is, what should students be able to do as a result of instruction. Second, teachers would analyze the objectives in terms of identifying the *instructional outcomes,* those being the tasks or assignments that students can perform as a result of achieving the instructional objectives. Third, teachers would analyze instructional outcomes in terms of the *cognitive skills* or mental processes required to perform those tasks or assignments. After following these three steps and identifying instructional objectives, instructional outcomes, and cognitive skills involved, the teacher is ready to conduct a *preassessment* (or pretest) to determine what students already know.

Instruction is then based on the results of the preassessment with teachers focusing on teaching directly the cognitive skills needed in order for students to perform the task(s). Following instruction, teachers would conduct a *post-assessment* (or post-test) to evaluate the results of instruction. Further instruction would be based on the results of the post-assessment, that is, whether or not students had achieved expected outcomes and whether or not teachers had achieved instructional objectives.

Regardless of which theoretical perspective is adopted by teachers, and, at times, teachers may find themselves taking a rather eclectic approach and borrowing elements from several theoretical bases, it is helpful for teachers to consider if they are structuring their classrooms to satisfy learners' needs or merely their own needs as teachers. Furthermore, if the teachers' goal is to increase teaching effectiveness by facilitating learners' knowledge and skill acquisition, then teachers will engage continuously in a process of self-examination and self-evaluation.

METACOGNITION

Self-examination and self-evaluation are both types of *metacognitive* thinking. *Metacognition* is a term used to describe what, how, and why people know what they know when they know it. In short, it is thinking about thinking and knowing about knowing. Cognitive psychologists describe metacognition as a characteristic of higher-ordered, mature, and sophisticated thinking. Generally speaking, as learners achieve higher levels of cognitive skills, they also increase their metacognitive skills. Therefore, not only should teachers engage in metacognitive thinking, they should model that thinking for their students, and encourage their students to develop metacognitive skills.

Metacognition can be understood in terms of (a) metacognitive knowledge and (b) metacognitive control (Flavell, 1987). Basically, metacognitive knowledge is what learners need to know and metacognitive control is what learners need to do. Metacognitive control, therefore, is in the hands of the learner. Teachers cannot control learners' behavior although they can encourage and admonish. The best that teachers can do is help learners expand their metacognitive awareness and knowledge.

Awareness can be increased by talking about metacognition. Flavell has explained that there are three kinds of metacognitive knowledge, those three kinds being (a) person knowledge, (b) task knowledge, and (c) strategy knowledge.

Person knowledge falls into one of three categories: (a) intraindividual knowledge, (b) interindividual knowledge, and (c) universal knowledge. First, intraindividual knowledge is what the learner knows or understands about him- or herself. Therefore, it is important that learners have opportunities to learn about themselves, about their interests, abilities, propensities, and so forth. For this reason (among others), it is important that learners have opportunities to learn about their own learning style and their perceptual strengths. It is also helpful for them to have opportunities to examine their personalities, values, and goals.

Furthermore, in a model that recognizes the dynamic nature of instruction, that is, one which recognizes that the learner also knows certain things and can contribute to the classroom, the teacher realizes that she or he is a learner, too. Teachers, then, can benefit from examining their own learning style, perceptual strengths, personalities, values, and goals. Moreover, it can be extremely beneficial for teachers to consider their own instructional style.

INSTRUCTIONAL STYLE ASSESSMENT

One instrument that assesses instructional style, the Instructional Style Inventory (Canfield & Canfield, 1988), identifies instructional styles in four general categories (although there also can be combinations of different styles). The four categories are *social*, *independent*, *applied*, and *conceptual*. Briefly stated, the social style is one which describes the teacher who values classroom interactions, who stresses teamwork and group work; the independent style describes the teacher who emphasizes working alone and is likely to rely on self-paced, individualized, and programmed instruction; the applied style is one which stresses real-world experiences and avoids lecture and preparatory reading, but focuses on practicums and site visits, and so forth; finally, the conceptual style is one describing the teacher who is language-oriented and likes highly organized materials and tends to depend on lectures and readings.

Returning to the discussion on metacognitive knowledge, the second kind of person knowledge is interindividual knowledge, how learners are alike and how they are different. Again, this is another reason why the recognition of diversity brought about by studying learning styles can inform learners and improve their cognitive performance. As they learn about their own learning style, learners also observe that their classmates have some similarities and some differences when it comes to the various elements or factors in determining learning style. Interindividual knowledge is increased as students realize that there are many different ways to learn.

Finally, the third kind of personal knowledge is universal knowledge, the knowledge that there are degrees of understanding. Examples are the realization that short-term memory is fallible and has limited capacity, that people can make mistakes, that it is easier to remember things if they are written down, that memory work requires repetition, and so forth. To examine students' understanding of universal knowledge, teachers might ask students to identify what they know about learning. They might, for example, ask students to write down on notecards what they know about how people learn things or by brainstorming the question in class.

The second broad category of metacognitive knowledge, according to Flavell, is task knowledge. Task knowledge includes several different variables, such as whether information is interesting or boring, or if it is new or familiar, or if it is easy or difficult. Task knowledge enables learners to plan appropriately for undertaking tasks (for example, if something is hard to learn, then it may take more time, more concentration, and more effort) and tells them how to go about accomplishing the task (for example, if the task requires memory, then a memory strategy is needed).

Specific tasks relevant to academic disciplines can be identified by classroom teachers; however, there are academic tasks that are generally applicable to all content areas. These academic tasks include what are broadly referred to as study skills, which are foundational skills for all learning. They include such tasks as time management, directing attention, processing information, finding main ideas, studying, and taking tests, among others (Weinstein, Schulte, & Palmer, 1988).

Flavell's final category of metacognitive knowledge is strategy knowledge, which takes into account how learners can best accomplish particular tasks and how they can be reasonably certain that they have reached their cognitive goals. Strategy knowledge also equips learners to monitor their cognitive activities and to gain confidence in their abilities. To illustrate, if the task is to find main ideas, then learners need strategies for finding main ideas. Strategies for this task include learning (a) to preview or survey reading assignments (reading headings, words in bold print; looking at illustrations and graphic aids); (b) to ask questions (What is this about? Who is this about? When did it happen? Where did it happen? How did it happen? Why did it happen?); and (c) to read the first and last sentences in each paragraph (knowing that the first and last sentences in paragraphs are most likely to be topic sentences).

STUDY STRATEGIES

If the task is to study, then learners need specific strategies for studying. These strategies can include, among others, (a) outlining, mapping, or summarizing text (from books or notes); (b) marking text (using margins for notetaking and summarizing); (c) participating in group review sessions; (d) comparing notes with a friend, tutor, or teacher; (e) getting extra help (from a tutor, teacher, or parent); and, (f) going to the library (to get additional information from alternative sources). Of course, strategies such as outlining can be further delineated into specific steps for various kinds of outlines.

Obviously, there is an interaction between person, task, and strategy knowledge. For example, if the task is studying, then a visual learner who learns well by reading (individual characteristic) might choose to go to the library to find an alternative source of information (strategy characteristic); in this example, there is a three-way interaction involving task, individual, and strategy.

Although teachers willingly expend considerable energy teaching students about tasks, they often erroneously assume that students will automatically or tacitly acquire learning strategies. However, the fact is that many students do not acquire these strategies and that even those who may learn some strategies would benefit from direct instruction in the use of specific learning strategies. The research literature indicates that the use of think-aloud protocols, spontaneous private speech, skimming, rereading, context clues, error-detection, grouping skills, examination/evaluation skills (distinguishing between conceptual versus superficial features, or between major themes and minor details and between decoding and comprehension, between verbatim recall and recall for gist) can significantly enhance learners' performance.

Teachers who incorporate an understanding of the role played by metacognition (especially in teaching middle-school and older students) into their instruction will find that they are preparing their students well for a lifetime of learning. Flavell (1979) explained that metacognition is necessary for the oral communication of information, oral persuasion, oral comprehension, reading comprehension, writing, language acquisition, attention, memory, problem-solving, social cognition, self-control, and self-instruction. It is hard to imagine a task that one might do that wouldn't require metacognition.

A recent critique of education in America includes the observation that the movement to teach basic academic skills in America's schools may have resulted in more students performing well on tests of basic skills; however, thinking skills, not just basic skills, are needed in the real world of jobs, families, and citizenship. To better prepare students for the real world, teachers need to focus on the *process* of learning, teaching students *how to think and learn*. Teaching metacognitive awareness and fostering the development of metacognitive knowledge are steps in the right direction.

MOTIVATING STUDENTS

Students often say that they like teachers who can motivate students when, in fact, teachers are not responsible for students' motivation. Motivation is a student's responsibility; motivation comes from within the student. However, effective teachers will help students develop self-discipline, self-control, and self-motivation. These skills of self-management can be taught, yet they require a great deal of effort and practice in order for students to gain true proficiency.

When students say that they like or want teachers who motivate them, they are probably referring to some characteristics that teachers possess which are attractive and interesting to learners. So, while it is true that teachers are not responsible for students' motivation, it is also true that teachers can influence motivation, that teachers can promote and/or inhibit motivation in the classroom by their attitudes and their actions.

One researcher has offered three principles to guide teachers that will lead to greater effectiveness in the classroom (Baxter-Magolda, 1992). Interestingly, each of these principles leads to empowering students and, thus, are motivational in nature.

The first principle is to *validate students as knowers*. This principle is based on the idea of the active learner who brings much to the classroom (the dynamic view of human development). How can teachers validate students? Baxter-Magolda suggests that teachers display a caring attitude towards students. This means that it's appropriate for teachers to take an interest in students, to learn about their likes and dislikes, their interests and hobbies, both in school and outside school. This also means that it's okay for teachers to show enthusiasm and excitement for their classes, not only the subject-matter they teach, but the students they teach as well. It also means, as Carol Tavris (1994) noted, that it's good for teachers to show empathy for students' emotional needs.

Baxter-Magolda also recommends that teachers question authority by example and let students know that they, as teachers, can also be questioned. This means that teachers model critical thinking skills in the classroom. Teachers can question authority when they examine and evaluate readings— whether from textbooks or other sources. Teachers can question authorities when they teach propaganda techniques, exposing advertising claims and gimmicks. Teachers can question authority when they discuss the media and how so-called news sources shape and form public opinion. There are numerous opportunities for teachers in dealing with current affairs and public opinion to question authority and inculcate in their students, critical thinking and higher-ordered reasoning skills.

Also, when teachers allow students to question them, teachers are acknowledging that everyone is a learner. Everyone should participate in a lifelong process of continuous learning. It is no shame or disgrace for the teacher to admit that sometimes he or she doesn't know the answer to every question. This gives the teacher the opportunity to show students how adults think, how they have a level of awareness (metacognition) when they don't know something, and about how they go about finding answers to their questions. Teachers who admit that they don't have all the answers thus have the opportunity to show students how answers can be found and/or to reveal to students that there are no easy answers to some of life's most difficult questions.

Third, to validate students as knowers, teachers can value students' opinions, ideas, and comments. Teachers' affirmations include smiles and nods of approval, positive comments (such as, "That's a good answer."), and encouraging cues (such as, "That may seem like a reasonable answer, but can you think of a better answer?" or "Can you explain what you mean by that answer?"). Validating students as knowers also means supporting students' voices, that is, giving them ample opportunities to express their own ideas, to share their opinions, to make their own contributions to the classroom. These opportunities can include times of oral discussion as well as written assignments.

JOINTLY CONSTRUCTED MEANING

Another principle in Baxter-Magolda's guidelines for teaching effectiveness is for teachers and students to recognize that learning is *a process of jointly-constructing meaning*. To explain, Baxter-Magolda says that it is important for teachers to dialogue with students (also an important concept in Piagetian theory) and that teachers emphasize mutual learning. Also in agreement with Piagetian principles, Baxter-Magolda recommends that teachers reveal their own thinking processes as they approach subjects and as they analyze and understand new subjects and as they solve problems and reach decisions. She further advises that teachers share leadership and promote collegial learning (group work), acknowledging that individual achievement is not the sole purpose or focus for learning. By allowing students to collaborate, they also will learn significant lessons directly applicable to work situations where most accomplishments are the result of team efforts, not the sole efforts of individuals.

Baxter-Magolda's final principle for teachers is to *situate learning in the students' own experiences.* She suggests that this be done by letting students know that they are wanted in class, by using inclusive language (avoiding ethnic and cultural bias and stereotyping, instead using gender-neutral and inclusive language), and focusing on activities. Activities are important for motivation because they give learners things to do, to become actively involved in, arousing their attention and interest, and giving them an outlet for their physical and mental energy. Activities can have an additional positive benefit in that they can serve to connect students to each other, especially when students are given opportunities to participate in collaborative learning (the way things happen in the "real world") and to work in groups. Finally, in situating learning in students' own experiences, it is important to consider the use of personal stories in class, as appropriate (that is, without violating anyone's right to privacy and confidentiality). Moreover, teachers can share personal stories which allow them to connect with students in a deeper and more personal way.

The child psychologist, Harvard professor, and author of numerous scholarly and popular books, Robert Coles, recently wrote of his experiences teaching in a Boston inner-city high school. He told of his disillusionment and his struggle to claim students' respect and attention so that he could teach them. Finally, there was a classroom confrontation, followed by a self-revelation (that being to show his students what he was like as a person). He shared some of his thoughts and feelings about loneliness. He told about his own boyhood experiences of visiting museums with his mother and what she taught him about art. In the end, he, too, had a revelation; he concluded that when teachers share what we have learned about ourselves with our students, we often can transcend the barriers of class and race. A teacher can change a "me" and a "them" (the students) into an "us." Building camaraderie this way then becomes an optimal starting point for teaching and learning (Coles, 1993). Dr. Coles' experience was that telling his story to the class was a step towards helping his students claim some motivation of their own.

When students assume responsibility for their own motivation, they are learning a lesson of personal empowerment. Unfortunately, although personal empowerment is probably one of the most important lessons anyone ever learns, it is a lesson infrequently taught in classrooms across the country.

Empowerment has at least four components, one of which is self-esteem. A good definition of self-esteem is that it is my opinion of me, your opinion of you. It is what we think and believe to be true about ourselves, not what we think about others and not what they think about us. Self-esteem appears to be a combination of self-efficacy and self-respect as seen against a background of self-knowledge.

Self-efficacy, simply stated, is one's confidence in one's own ability to cope with life's challenges. Self-efficacy refers to having a sense of control over life or, better, over one's responses to life. Experts say that ideas about self-efficacy get established by the time children reach the age of four. Because of this early establishment of either a feeling of control or no control, classroom teachers may find that even primary grade students believe that they have no control over their life, that it makes no difference what they do or how they act. Therefore, it is all the more important that teachers attempt to help all students achieve coping skills and a sense of self-efficacy.

Control, in this definition of self-efficacy, can be examined in regard to external or internal motivators. For example, external motivators include such things as luck and the roles played by others in influencing outcomes. Internal motivators are variables within the individual. To explain, if a student does well on a test and is asked, "How did you do so well on that test?," a student who relies on external motivators might reply, "Well, I just got lucky," or "The teacher likes me." If the student failed the test and is asked why, the student dependent on external motivators might answer, "Well, it wasn't my lucky day," or "The teacher doesn't like me," or "My friends caused me to goof off and not pay attention so I didn't know the answers on the test." A student who relies on internal motivators and who does well on a test may explain, "I am smart and always do well on tests," or "I studied hard and that's why I did well." On the other hand, even the student who relies on internal motivators can do poorly on tests and then may explain, "I'm dumb and that's why I don't do well," or "I didn't think the test was important and I didn't try very hard." Even though students have similar experiences, in regard to issues of control, what is important is how students explain their experiences. If students have external motivators, they are likely to either dismiss their performance (success or failure) as matters of luck or to credit or blame the influence of others. If students have internal motivators, then they are likely to attribute their performance to either their intelligence and skills (ability) or their effort.

Students who have external motivators need help understanding how their behavior contributes to and influences outcomes in school. Students need clarification as to how grades are determined and precise information about how their work is evaluated. Students who have internal motivators but low self-esteem (such as thinking, "I'm dumb") need help identifying their strengths and assets (something that can be accomplished when students are given information about learning styles). Self-efficacy can be enhanced.

Another factor in empowerment is self-respect. Self-respect is believing that one deserves happiness, achievement, and love. Self-respect is treating one's self at least as nicely as one treats other people. Many students are not aware of their internal voices (which are established at an early age). Internal voices are constantly sending messages, either positive or negative. Psychologists say that most of us have either a generally positive outlook on life, and our inner voice sends generally positive messages ("You're okay," "People like you," "Things will be all right," and so forth) or a generally negative outlook on life, and an inner voice sending negative messages ("You're not okay," "You're too fat, skinny, ugly, stupid," and so forth).

Many students need to become aware of their inner voice and how it can be setting them up for failure. They need to learn that they can tell their inner voice to stop sending negative messages, and that they can reprogram their inner voice to be kinder, gentler, and to send positive messages. However, it does require effort, practice, and time to reprogram the inner voice.

Two tools which can help students in the reprogramming process are affirmations and visualizations (Ellis, 1991). Affirmations are statements describing what students want. Affirmations must be personal, positive, and written in the present tense. What makes affirmations effective are details. For example, instead of saying, "I am stupid," students can be encouraged to say, "I am capable. I do well in school because I am organized, I study daily, I get all my work completed on time, and I take my school work seriously." Affirmations must be repeated until they can be said with total conviction.

Visualizations are images students can create whereby they see themselves the way they want to be. For example, if a student wants to improve his or her typing skills, then the student evaluates what it would look like, sound like, and feel like to be a better typist. Once the student identifies the image, then the student has to rehearse that image in her or his mind, including as many details and sensations as possible. Both visualization and affirmation can restructure attitudes and behaviors. They can be tools for students to use to increase their motivation.

Finally, the fourth component of empowerment is self-knowledge. Self-knowledge refers to an individual's strengths and weaknesses, assets and liabilities; self-knowledge comes about as a result of a realistic self-appraisal (and can be achieved by an examination of learning styles). Achieving self-knowledge also requires that students have opportunities to explore their goals and values.

Students who know what their goals and values are can more easily see how education will enable them to achieve those goals and values. Conversely, students cannot be motivated when they do not have goals and values, or when they do not know what their goals and values are. In other words, without self-knowledge, motivation is impossible. Therefore, teachers who follow Baxter-Magolda's guidelines for effective instruction and who teach their students about personal empowerment are teachers who realize the importance of motivation and who set the stage for students to claim responsibility for their own successes and failures. Such teachers help students to become motivated to make changes and to accomplish more.

DRILL: KNOWLEDGE OF THE LEARNER

1. Rueben Stein is a middle-school teacher who wants to teach his class about the classification system in the animal kingdom. He decides to introduce this unit to his class by having the students engage in general classification activities. He brings to class a paper bag filled with 30 household items. He dumps the contents of the bag onto a table and then asks the students, in groups of three or four, to put like items into piles and then to justify or explain why they placed certain items into a particular pile.

   By assigning this task to his students, Mr. Stein is providing his students with a developmentally-appropriate task because

   (A) middle-school students like to work in groups.

   (B) the items in the bag are household items with which most students will be familiar.

   (C) the assignment gives students the opportunity to practice their skills at categorizing.

   (D) the assignment will give students a task to perform while the teacher finishes grading papers.

   The correct response is (C); According to Piaget's theory of cognitive development, students in middle school would be at the stage of *concrete operational* thought. Students at this stage of cognitive development would be able to categorize items. Choices (A), (B), and (D) are inappropriate for the following reasons. Choice (A) is a false statement. Although some students will like to work in groups, some students will prefer to work alone — at this and at any age group or cognitive stage. Preferring to learn in groups (or socially) or to learn alone (or independently) is a characteristic of learning style or preference, not a characteristic of cognitive or affective development. Choice (B) is irrelevant to the teacher's intent in assigning the task. Students could just as easily work with unfamiliar items, grouping them by observable features independent of their use or function. Choice (D) is not a good choice under any circumstances. Teachers should assiduously avoid giving students assignments merely to keep them busy while the teacher does something else. All assignments should have an instructional purpose.

2. Maria Smith is a high school English teacher who is concerned about a student who is failing her junior English class. The student has not turned in any outside assignments, and Ms. Smith has noticed a definite decline in the quality of work the student completes in class. Ms. Smith also has observed that the student has great difficulty staying awake in class and that she seems irritable and distracted most of the time.

    In her efforts to help the student, Ms. Smith decides to ask the student

    (A) if she has been having family problems.

    (B) if she realizes that the quality of her classwork is suffering and if she knows of any reasons for the decline.

    (C) to work on better time-management skills.

    (D) to start coming in early or to stay after class to receive extra help with her work.

    The correct response is **(B)**. This question opens the door for dialogue with the student about a range of possible problems. This response shows that the teacher is concerned about the student and her welfare without making assumptions, jumping to conclusions, and/or intruding into the private affairs of the student. Choice (A) presumes that the source of all problems lies with the family. Although the student may be having family-related difficulties, there are other possibilities to consider as well. The student may have taken a job that is taking too much of her time away from her studies or the student may be having health problems. It is unwise for the teacher to conclude that the student is having family problems. Choice (C) is inappropriate because it too narrowly identifies one possible coping mechanism as the solution to the student's problem. Although the student may benefit from acquiring better time-management skills, it also is possible that the student's present problems have little or nothing to do with time-management. Choice (D) is equally inappropriate in that it demands that the student devote even more time to school although she currently is having trouble with present demands. If the student is unwell, then certainly spending more time at school is not the solution to her problem. Clearly, choice (B) is the best alternative to helping the student identify her problem(s) and find a solution.

3.   Elva Rodriguez teaches fourth grade. She has structured her class so that students can spend thirty minutes daily, after lunch, in sustained, silent reading activities with books and reading materials of their own choosing.

In order to maximize this reading opportunity and to recognize differences among learners, Ms. Rodriguez

(A) allows some students to sit quietly at their desks while others are allowed to move to a reading area where they sit on floor cushions or recline on floor mats.

(B) makes sure that all students have selected appropriate reading materials.

(C) plays classical music on a tape player to enhance student learning.

(D) dims the lights in the classroom in order to increase students' reading comprehension.

The correct response is (A). Only choice (A) takes into account differences among learners by giving them options as to how and where they will read. Choice (B) violates the students' freedom to select reading materials which they find interesting and wish to read. When students are allowed to choose their own reading materials, it may seem that some students select materials beyond their present reading comprehension. However, reading research indicates that students can comprehend more difficult material when their interest level is high.

Therefore, any efforts by the teacher to interfere with students' selection of their own reading material would be ill-advised. Choices (C) and (D) are equally poor in that they both describe a concession to only one group of learners. For example, with choice (C), while some students may prefer to read with music playing in the background, other students will find music distracting. The best action for the teacher to take would be for her to allow some students to listen to music on earphones while others read in quiet. In regard to choice (D), some students will prefer bright illumination just as some students will read better with the lights dimmed. Ms. Rodriguez would do well to attempt to accommodate various learner needs by having one area of the room more brightly illuminated when lights are dimmed in another area.

4. Karla Dixon is a second-grade teacher who has selected a book to read to her class after lunch. She shows the students the picture on the cover of the book and reads the title of the book to them. She then asks, "What do you think this book is about?"

    By asking this question, Ms. Dixon is

    (A) learning which students are interested in reading strategies.

    (B) trying to keep the students awake since she knows they usually get sleepy after lunch.

    (C) encouraging students to make a prediction, a precursor of hypothetical thinking.

    (D) finding out which students are good readers.

    The correct response is **(C)**. The teacher is encouraging students to become actively engaged in the learning process by making a prediction based on limited information given in the book title and cover illustration. When students can generate their own predictions or formulate hypotheses about possible outcomes on the basis of available (although limited) data, they are gaining preparatory skills for formal operations (or abstract thinking). Although second-grade students would not be expected to be at the level of cognitive development characterized by formal operations, Piagetian theory would indicate that teachers who model appropriate behaviors and who give students opportunities to reach or stretch for new cognitive skills are fostering students' cognitive growth. Choice (A) is a poor choice because students' responses to this one question posed by the teacher cannot be used to assess adequately their interest in reading activities. Choice (B), likewise, is a poor choice in that it implies no instructional intent for asking the question. Choice (D) is incorrect because students' responses to a single question cannot allow the instructor to determine which students are good readers and which ones are not.

5. Ben Douglas is a high school history teacher. His class is studying the Korean Conflict when a student brings up a question about the morality of the war in Vietnam. This is not a subject that Mr. Douglas is prepared to teach at the time.

    In response to the student's question, Mr. Douglas

    (A) tells the student that the day's topic is the Korean Conflict and suggests that the student bring up the question later on in the term.

    (B) invites the class to respond to the student's question.

    (C) gives the student a cursory response, eliminating the need for any further discussion.

    (D) disciplines the student for not paying attention to the topic under discussion.

The correct response is (**B**). This is the best answer because it acknowledges the student's curiosity and legitimizes the student's right to pursue information by asking questions. It gives approval and recognition to the student's voice of inquiry, *and* it allows other students to voice their opinions and/or to make relevant comments. The teacher does not have to have a ready answer to every question, and this answer choice recognizes that also. The other three choices (A), (C), and (D) all have the opposite effect of ignoring students' voices and missing an opportunity for students to become active learners, learning something about which they may be genuinely interested. All three of the incorrect choices reflect an autocratic attitude towards teaching which is the opposite of what Baxter-Magolda recommends for teaching effectiveness.

References

Baxter-Magolda, M. B. (1992). *Knowing and reasoning in college: Gender-related patterns in students' intellectual development.* San Francisco: Jossey Bass.

Bloom, B. (1976). *Human characteristics and school learning.* New York: McGraw-Hill.

Canfield, A. A. & Canfield, J. S. (1988). Instructional styles inventory. Los Angeles: Western Psychological Services.

Coles, R. (1993). Point of view: When earnest volunteers are solely tested. *Chronicle of Higher Education*, May 5, A52.

Dunn, R. (1993). Presentation on the Productivity Environmental Preferences Scale (PEPS) at Learning Styles Institute, Lubbock, Texas, June 5-9. (Sponsored by Education Service Center, Region XVII.)

Dunn, R., & Dunn, K. (1993). Presentation on Using Learning Styles Information to Enhance Teaching Effectiveness at Learning Styles Institute, Lubbock, Texas, June 5-9. (Sponsored by Education Service Center, Region XVII.)

Elkind, D. (1967). Egocentrism in adolescence. *Child Development*, 38, 1025-34.

Ellis, D. (1991). *Becoming a master student.* Rapid City, SD: College Survival.

Erikson, E. (1963). *Childhood and society.* New York: Horton.

Flavell, J. H. (1979). Metacognition and cognitive monitoring: A new area of cognitive-developmental inquiry. *American Psychologist*, 34, 906-911.

Flavell, J. H. (1987). Speculations about the nature and development of metacognition. In R. H. Kluwe & F. E. Weinert (Eds.), *Metacognition, motivation, and learning* (pp. 21-30). Hillsdale, NJ: Erlbaum.

Maslow, A. (1968). *Toward a psychology of being.* New York: Van Nostrand Reinhold.

Nolting, P. (1993). Presentation on Meeting Learners' Special Needs at West Texas Regional TASP Workshop, Lubbock, Texas, August 7. (Sponsored by Texas Tech University.)

Piaget, J. (1950). *The psychology of intelligence*. London: Routledge and Kegan Paul.

Sadker, M., & Sadker, D. (1994). *Failing at fairness: How America's schools cheat girls*. New York: Charles Scribner's Sons.

Sternberg, R. J. (1985). *Beyond IQ: A triarchic theory of human intelligence*. Cambridge: Cambridge University Press.

Tavris, C. (1994). Presentation on Coping with Student Conflict Inside and Outside the Classroom at Texas Junior College Teachers Conference, San Antonio, February 25.

Weinstein, C. E., Schulte, A.C., & Palmer, D. R. (1988). The learning and study strategies inventory. Clearwater, FL: H & H Publishing.

Chapter 8

Instructional Planning, Delivery, and Assessment

Teachers are responsible for creating a classroom environment that is conducive to learning. Although students must make their own commitment to learning, the professional educator must make the commitment to do everything in his or her power to ensure that all students learn what they need to learn. He or she is responsible for making classes interesting instead of dull, appropriate instead of irrelevant, and challenging instead of boring. Students will learn more if the class is interesting, appropriate, and challenging. If students aren't learning, then no teaching has occurred, no matter how many lectures and activities are provided.

The professional educator is responsible for careful planning, alone or with others, so the class has purpose and direction. He or she also teaches students how to make their own goals and objectives so they may become self-directed learners. Although students may provide suggestions and make plans for classroom activities, the teacher is ultimately responsible for what goes on in the classroom. The teacher must be an effective communicator, using both spoken and written language to convey ideas and serve as a model for student communication. Knowing how to ask questions and what questions to ask is essential. The word educate comes from root words that mean to draw out. Skillful questioning can draw out from students more ideas and work than they ever thought possible.

The professional educator must use a variety of teaching methods, choosing different methods for different goals. He must expand his repertoire from lecture (with which the new teacher is most familiar) to a wide variety of methods, including cooperative learning, inquiry or discovery, discussion, synectics, and other deductive and inductive methods. Today's educator must use all available resources in order to meet a variety of learning styles. He or she must be able to use computers to enhance instruction in a variety of ways.

Assessment must be authentic, that is appropriate to the learning task and reflective of what the student has actually learned or accomplished. Essay questions, portfolios, projects, and peer and self-assessment are usually more authentic measures than true/false or multiple-choice tests.

The professional educator must also master the art of organizing a classroom so that maximum use is made of available time and resources. He or she must use classroom rules, consequences, and procedures which enforce consistency. Although he may allow students suggestions about rules, the educator is responsible for seeing that no one interferes with another's learning.

In short, in order to enhance each student's achievement to their full potential, the professional educator must be a master planner, communicator, teacher, facilitator, organizer, guide, and role model.

OUTCOME-ORIENTED LEARNING

In outcome-oriented learning, teachers define outcomes, or what they want students to know, do, and be when they complete a required course of study. The teachers set high but realistic goals and objectives for their students, then plan instructional activities which will assist students in achieving these goals.

The key to effective outcome-oriented planning is to consider what outcomes must be achieved, then determine which teacher behaviors and which student behaviors will improve the probability that students will achieve the outcomes.

Outcome-based planning starts with the end product—what must be learned or accomplished in a particular course or grade level. For example, an algebra teacher may decide that the final outcome of his or her algebra course would be that students use quadratic equations to solve problems. He or she then works "backward" to determine prerequisite knowledge and skills students need to have in order to accomplish this outcome. By continuing to ask these questions about each set of prerequisites, the teacher finds a starting point for the subject or course, then develops goals and objectives. The outcomes should be important enough to be required of all students.

An outcome-oriented system means that students are given sufficient time and practice to acquire the knowledge and skills. It also means that teachers take into account students' various learning styles and time required for learning and make adaptations by providing a variety of educational opportunities.

SOURCES OF DATA

Information about what outcomes are important for students comes from several sources. Ralph Tyler has defined three basic sources of needs: students, society, and content area. Consideration of these sources leads to a draft of outcomes, which are further refined by screening them through our philosophy and through what we know about educational psychology. Society makes ever-changing demands upon the educational system. Businesses are focusing more on workers who can solve problems. Other national issues—health problems, environmental concerns, etc.—can provide data for educators.

A look at student needs determines the current level of achievement through a study of evaluation results, whether teacher-made, district-developed, or standardized. Comparing where students are, with where they need to be, will show teachers where to start. A consideration of student needs also involves understanding their diverse learning styles, developmental levels, achievement levels, and special adaptations for learning-disabled students. This understanding assists the effective teacher in planning a variety of activities to meet these diverse needs.

Considering content area needs involves reading current research to determine trends in the subject areas. For example, science teachers are heavily involved in providing hands-on experiences in labs. English teachers have moved in the direction of whole-language activities at all levels and an integrated approach to composition and grammar. National and state curriculum committees in mathematics have endorsed a problem-solving approach for all math classes.

PLANNING PROCESSES

Madeline Hunter describes a planning model which requires teacher decisions about content, teacher behavior, and student behavior. The three parts of this model overlap and are related to each other; a decision in one category influences a decision in another. Decisions about content are often made at the state or district level. Teachers use frameworks from the state, curriculum documents developed by the district, and materials from district-chosen textbooks as bases for planning lessons.

A teacher using this model would make decisions about content, including goals and objectives for a lesson or unit, length of lesson/unit, emphasis of lesson, textbooks, and additional resource materials.

Decisions about his or her own behavior include teaching strategies, accommodations for various learning styles, types of activities, sizes of groups, uses of technology and other resources, and room arrangements.

Decisions about their students' behavior include individual or group responses, format of responses, ways students will demonstrate learning, and products of activities.

Robert Gagné delineates nine external events which are important in planning an appropriate sequence of instruction. They are: gaining attention, informing students of the lesson objectives, stimulating recall of previous learning, presenting stimuli with distinctive features, guiding learning, eliciting student performance, providing informative feedback, assessing student performance, and enhancing the retention and transfer of learning.

The term lesson cycle has been applied to processes of lesson planning developed by a variety of people. Planning is cyclical because the process repeats itself continually. These planning processes usually include the development of objectives and a focus for attention, a design for instructional input, constant monitoring of student understanding, provision for rehearsal and practice of knowledge, and opportunities for enrichment or follow-up.

Teachers choose objectives for a lesson from a curriculum guide or develop their own from their knowledge of their subject area and the needs of students. These objectives are clearly communicated to the students in terms of what they will learn (not activities they will do) during the lesson. In a deductive lesson, these objectives are explained to students at the beginning; in an inductive lesson, objectives are clarified at the end of the lesson. Teachers develop a focus or introduction to the lesson (called anticipatory set by Hunter) which should hook the students' interest and focus attention toward the upcoming activities. Instruction may take a variety of forms. The teacher provides instructional activities which will produce the desired outcomes in the students. A wide variety of instructional methods may be used for input, from mastery lectures or labs to cooperative learning or several different types of inductive strategies. The teacher is constantly monitoring student behavior, checking for understanding, and modifying the instruction as necessary.

After or during instructional input, the students rehearse or apply what they've learned. In guided practice, the teacher watches carefully to make sure students have grasped the material correctly. Because the teacher is on hand to assess student responses, she is able to provide correction or additional input if necessary. During independent practice, students work independently. At the end of each lesson (or at the end of the class), the teacher or students summarize or review what has been learned. An additional feature is enrichment, which should be for all students, not only the faster ones. Enrichment means that students either delve deeper into a subject they've been studying or broaden their understanding of the general topic. For example, students who have been studying the stock market could research the history of its development, or they could study the market in other countries.

Lesson cycles are repeated for additional blocks of content. A "lesson" may last anywhere from a few minutes to several days; it isn't limited by the period or the bell.

SELF-DIRECTED LEARNING

Effective teachers not only set goals for their students, but also teach students to set and accomplish their own goals, both individually and in groups. Students need to learn how to plan for their individual learning as well as for learning of a group of students. If students are unaccustomed to setting goals, the effective teacher begins by modeling the process. The teacher explains how he or she develops goals and objectives for the class. One way of encouraging students to set goals is to ask students to set a performance standard for themselves in regard to time needed to complete a project. For example, students might determine they will need 15 minutes to answer five questions, writing one paragraph of at least five sentences for each question. In order to accomplish this goal, the students must focus their attention very carefully and limit themselves to about three minutes per question. The teacher should then ask questions to help students determine whether their goal was realistic, and if not, what adjustments they need to make.

Other steps could be to ask students to develop their own questions about material to be learned or to plan activities to accomplish the goals of the lesson. The highest level is to have students determine the goals for their own learning. For example, a science teacher might introduce the topic of earthquakes, then help students determine what they need to know about earthquakes and the activities and resources which will help them learn. Students also need to develop plans for products which will show that they have met their goals.

Another way to encourage self-directed thinking and learning is to use higher-level questioning strategies and to teach students to use them as well.

COLLABORATIVE LEARNING

Collaborative or cooperative learning strategies provide important ways students learn to work and plan together. David and Roger Johnson and Robert Slavin are three of several educators who have researched cooperative learning and have developed strategies, materials, and resources to assist teachers and students in learning how to work together.

Cooperative groups are formed heterogeneously, so that students of various achievement levels can learn from each other. Lower-achieving students are challenged to keep up with and contribute to their groups; advanced students gain a deeper understanding when they discuss concepts with others. The groups vary in size from three to five members, who usually work with each other for several months in order to develop profitable relationships.

There are five basic elements associated with collaborative learning. The first is *face-to-face interaction*. Group members should be sitting very close to each other so they can look each other in the eye while they discuss. It is important that students begin to form working relationships with their peers. This closeness also helps reduce the noise level of talking.

Another element is *positive interdependence*, which means that students must learn to depend on each other to complete a project or achieve a goal. This is often achieved by providing only one set of resources or one answer sheet. Students must work together in order to perform the task. Another is to provide incentives, such as five extra points on individual tests if everyone in the group makes at least 80 percent. This encourages students to help each other learn so that all will do well on the assessment.

The third element is *individual accountability*. This means that each student in the group is held accountable for everything that is to be learned. One way of encouraging this is to give individual tests. Although students work and study together, each must pass a test for himself. Another method is to give the same grade to each person in the group. This encourages interdependence because students hold each other accountable for learning and performing the assigned part. It encourages individual accountability because the group is successful only if all members perform well. A common error teachers make with this element is neglecting to make sure that all students do their part. Success of the group should not depend on one diligent student or be undermined because of one lazy student.

The next element is *social skills*. The effective teacher has two types of objectives for collaborative learning: cognitive and affective. The cognitive objectives relate to the content which students must understand and master;

the affective objectives relate to social skills which are necessary for students to be able to function in their groups. Examples of social skills include listening actively to others, listening without interrupting, encouraging each other, and using polite language and manners. In addition, teachers assign roles to each member of the group. For example, one student may have the role of group recorder, responsible for writing and turning in any papers or products. Another may have the role of resource clerk, responsible for obtaining and returning materials. Each group member should have a different role; the effective teacher rotates role assignments so that each member has an opportunity to become proficient in each role.

The final element is very important, but it is often omitted. During *group processing*, students reflect on how well their group worked together. They also determine what they can do to function more effectively during the next group assignment. Students learn to set goals for their collaborative groups, in terms of achievement and products. They learn to evaluate their own performance so they can improve it during future projects. The effective teacher helps students set their goals, then monitors to make sure they are making progress. If they are, she will positively reinforce their goal-oriented behavior; if they are not, she will steer them back on course, usually by asking questions which lead students to decide what they need to do next.

THEMATIC CURRICULUM

The effective teacher knows how to collaborate with peers to plan instruction. Collaboration may be as simple as planning and sharing ideas, or as complex as developing a multidisciplinary thematic unit in which teachers of several subject areas will teach around a common theme.

Planning thematic curriculum often involves teachers from several areas—such as math, English, history, science, and health—although an individual teacher could plan thematic units for her own class. Based on a system developed by Sandra Kaplan, the team of teachers develops a one-word universal theme which is applied in all areas, e.g., survival, conflict, traditions, frontiers, or changes. The team lists a series of key words associated with universal themes, e.g., significance, relationships, types, functions, origins, value, or causes. They develop a generalization for the unit, then each teacher plans outcomes for his/her subject area and class. For example, for the theme "Conflict," the team may choose as the generalization, "Conflict is an inherent part of life." The English teacher then develops a literature and composition unit which encourages students to describe conflicts and how they are solved in literature.

The history teacher might focus on conditions which tend to lead to conflict or the effects of conflict. A science unit could explore conflicts between people and the environment. The math teacher might focus on research methods which attempt to resolve conflicts. The health teacher could address constructive ways of solving conflict between good health practices and unhealthy life-styles.

All teachers would plan learning experiences to lead students to understand the generalization as it applies to their particular subject and to the students' personal lives. These experiences may be carried out using a wide variety of instructional strategies and resources.

Effective communication is an obvious mark of an effective teacher. Communication occurs only when someone sends a message and another person receives it. Teachers may "teach" and think they're sending a message, but if students aren't listening, there has been no communication because the receivers are not tuned in.

PRINCIPLES OF VERBAL COMMUNICATION

There are several principles which apply to written and oral messages in the classroom.

The message must be accurate. As Mark Twain said, "The difference between the right word and the almost right word is the difference between lightning and the lightning bug." Teachers in particular must be careful to use very specific words that carry the appropriate denotation (literal meaning) as well as connotation (feelings, associations, and emotions associated with the word). Content teachers must carefully teach vocabulary related to the subject area.

It is possible to be completely accurate, however, without being clear. At times a teacher may use an excessive amount of jargon from his or her subject area. While students must learn vocabulary related to the subject area, the teacher must ensure that she teaches the words and then reviews them so the students have practice using them. At other times a teacher may assume that students understand difficult words. Many students are hesitant to ask what a word means; teachers must be alert to nonverbal signs that students don't understand a word (confused looks, pauses in writing a word down, failure to answer a question containing the word, etc.). Taking a couple of seconds to ask students to define a word will help them understand the larger content area concepts.

Words should also be specific or concrete. The more abstract a word, the more ambiguous it will be. For example, "physical activity" is very general;

"Little League baseball" is much more specific. Although students need to learn abstract words, explaining them in a concrete manner will increase their understanding. Saying that a war causes economic difficulties is general; being more specific would be to say that it reduces the amount of tax money available to cities because of money spent on munitions.

A teacher's communications must also be organized. Students will not be able to follow directions which are given in jumbled order, interrupted with, "Oh, I forgot to tell you." Effective teachers plan their directions carefully, writing them down for the students or making notes for themselves so they will give directions or explain concepts in appropriate order.

Other communication strategies include monitoring the effects of a message, or making sure that the audience actually received and understood the message. A teacher may encourage students to be active and reflective listeners by having each student summarize what another has said before making his or her own contribution.

NONVERBAL COMMUNICATION

Even when the verbal or written message is accurate, clear, specific, and organized, nonverbal communication can confuse the message. Sometimes the nonverbal aspect of communication can carry more weight than the verbal. Nonverbal messages can be sent by the way teachers dress, the way they use their facial expressions, and the way they use their voice. Experienced educators realize that students respond better when teachers dress professionally. Most people find it easier to take seriously someone dressed in neat, clean clothes than someone in wrinkled, ill-fitting clothing. Also, students behave better when they themselves are dressed better.

EYE CONTACT

Facial expressions communicate a world of emotions and ideas. Teachers use many voluntary facial expressions. All students have seen "the look" from a teacher, usually when a student does something out of order. A frown or raised eyebrows can also be very effective. Although positive involuntary expressions such as smiles and laughter are appropriate, teachers should guard against involuntary negative facial expressions that convey contempt, anger, or dislike to a student.

Eye contact can be used to control interactions. Teachers often look directly at students when to encourage them to speak or look away to discourage them from speaking. "The stare" can be part of "the look" which teachers use for discipline reasons. Making eye contact with students is important when the teacher is giving instructions, sharing information, or answering questions. Many people make a habit of scanning the room with their eyes, pausing briefly to meet the gaze of many members of an audience. However, eye contact should last about four seconds to assure the person in the audience (or classroom) that the speaker has actually made contact.

Students also use their eyes, making contact with the teacher when they want to answer a question, but often looking at the floor or ceiling when they want to avoid being called on. However, teachers must be careful in making assumptions about eye contact. Research has revealed that students who are visually oriented tend to look upward while they are thinking about a response; kinesthetic learners tend to look down while they are thinking; auditory learners may look to the side. The teacher who says to a student, "The answer's not written on the floor!" may not understand the student's mode of thinking. Effective teachers who are encouraging higher-level thinking may find a classroom filled with eyes that look in various directions.

Cultural factors may also contribute to confusion about eye contact. Many cultures teach children that it is very disrespectful to look an adult in the eye; therefore, these students may stand or sit with downcast eyes as a gesture of respect. Forcing the issue only makes the students and teacher uncomfortable and actually hinders communication.

Body language can also convey feelings and emotions to students. A teacher can emphasize points and generalizations by gesturing or tapping something on the chalkboard. If a teacher gestures too often or too wildly, students find it difficult to determine what the teacher is trying to emphasize. Too many gestures can also cause the students to watch the gestures instead of attending to the information.

Beginning teachers especially need to convey a relaxed but formal body posture, which denotes strength, openness, and friendliness. Hiding behind the desk or crossing the arms indicate timidity or even fear. A teacher who meets students at the door with a smile and even a handshake shows students he or she is confident and in control.

The way a teacher uses the voice conveys prejudices, feelings, and emotions. When a teacher's words convey one meaning and her tone of voice conveys another, the students will believe the tone rather than the meaning. Students immediately know the difference between "That's a great idea" said in a low voice with a shrug, and "That's a great idea!" said with energy and a smile. A teacher's tone of voice can tell a student, "I'm asking you, but I don't think you can answer this." Messages can be modified by varying the loudness or softness, by varying the tone, by using high or low pitch, and by changing the quality of speech.

A teacher's expectations for student behavior can be revealed through a combination of verbal and nonverbal communication. Jere Brophy and others have researched the relationship between teacher expectations and student behavior. This research shows that teachers often communicate differently when dealing with high-achievers and low-achievers. This behavior is not always deliberate or conscious on the part of the teacher, but it can communicate negative expectations. When dealing with high-achievers as opposed to low-achievers, teachers tend to listen more carefully, give them more time to answer, prompt or assist them more, call on them more often, give more feedback, and look more interested. The effective communicator will be careful not to differentiate communication based on a student's achievement level.

Media communication has become a vital part of the classroom process. Effective teachers use a variety of audio-visuals in every class, including posters, graphs, overhead transparencies, films, videos, CD-ROMs, and laser disks.

QUESTIONING

There are many ways that teachers can ask questions that elicit different levels of thinking, although studies of teachers' skills in questioning often reveal frequent use of lower-level questions and infrequent use of higher-level ones.

A simple method is to divide questions into two types: closed and open. An example of a closed question is, "What was the main character's name?" There is usually only one right answer to a closed question. Often students can point to a phrase or sentence in a book to answer a closed question.

An open-ended question requires students to think carefully about the answer. There may be more than one appropriate answer to an open-ended question. An example is, "What do you think was the most important contribution of Pascal to the field of mathematics?" Teachers who ask open-ended questions are not looking for one specific answer, rather they are looking for well-supported responses. Asking an open-ended question but requiring one specific answer will discourage rather than encourage thinking.

An example of a closed question is, "What is five times five?" An example of an open-ended math question is, "What is the best way to solve this problem?" The open-ended question assumes that the teacher will accept all reasonable methods of solving the problem, provided the students can explain why their method is best.

There are other ways to categorize questions. Benjamin Bloom, et al., developed a taxonomy of educational objectives for the cognitive domain. Teachers have used this taxonomy for a variety of purposes in addition to writing objectives, including categorizing questions and activities.

THE SIX LEVELS OF TAXONOMY

There are six levels in the taxonomy, each one building on the previous level. The first level is knowledge. This is similar to the closed question, with one right answer which should be obvious to students who have read or studied. Words which often elicit recall or memory answers include who, what, when, and where. Examples of knowledge-level questions include: Who developed the first microscope? What were the names of Columbus' ships? In what year was South Carolina first settled? Where is Tokyo?

The next level is comprehension, which also elicits lower-level thinking and answers. The primary difference from the first level is that students must show that they understand a concept, perhaps by explaining in their own words. The question "What does obfuscate mean?" would be answered on a knowledge level if students repeat a memorized definition from the dictionary and on a comprehension level if students explain the term in their own words.

The first higher-level category is application. Students take what they've learned and use this knowledge in a different way or in a different situation. A simple example of this level is using mathematics operations—add, subtract, multiply, and divide—to solve problems. Another example is translating an English sentence into Spanish, or applying what the students have learned about Spanish vocabulary and grammar to develop an appropriate and correct response. Another form of application is changing the format of information, e.g., create a graph from a narrative description of a survey. The key to this level is the use or application of knowledge and skills in a similar but new situation.

The next level is analysis, which involves taking something apart, looking at all the pieces, and then making a response. An example of an analytical question is, "How are these two characters alike and how are they different?" This question requires students to examine facts and characteristics of each individual, then put the information together in an understandable comparison. Another example is, "What are the advantages and disadvantages of each of these two proposals?" Another example might be, "Compare the wolves in *The Three Little Pigs* and *Little Red Riding Hood*."

The next level is synthesis, which involves putting information together in a new, creative way. Developing a new way of solving problems, writing a short story, designing an experiment—these are all creative ways of synthesizing knowledge. For example, fourth-grade science students may develop and conduct research on food waste in the cafeteria and make recommendations for changes. An example of a synthesis question is, "What do you predict will happen if we combine these two chemicals?" This question assumes students will have factual knowledge. Their predictions must be reasonable and based on prior reading and/or discussion.

The highest level is evaluation. This level involves making value judgments and very often involves the question "Why?" or a request to "Justify your answer." For example, students may be asked to use their analysis of two possible solutions to a problem to determine which is the better solution. Their response must be reasonable and well-supported.

Evaluation-level activities must build on previous levels. Skipping from knowledge-level to evaluation-level questions will result in ill-conceived and poorly-supported responses. Although teachers might use an evaluation question to provoke interest in a topic, they should make sure that students have opportunities to work at other levels as they develop their responses.

This type of questioning promotes risk-taking and problem-solving, if the teacher has established a safe environment where students are encouraged and not ridiculed for creative or unusual responses. The teacher does not expect only one specific answer, but allows students to ponder several reasonable possibilities.

Effective teachers also appreciate cultural dimensions of communication and are aware that some cultures teach their children not to question adults. These teachers explain to students that they expect questions, encourage students to ask them, but do not force the issue if students are very uncomfortable. Sometimes students may be willing to write down and turn in questions for the teacher. Teacher attitude can promote or deter questions, even by so simple a tactic as changing, "Does anybody have any questions?" to "What questions do you have?" The first question implies that no one should have questions; the second assumes that there will be questions.

CLASSROOM CLIMATE

All of the elements of effective communication can be used to promote an atmosphere of active inquiry in the classroom. Teachers can present an idea to students, ask a real question that they are interested in, then guide exploration, using effective communication skills to encourage and lead the students.

Effective teachers also teach students to use the elements of communication so they can work together to explore concepts and then make effective presentations to the rest of the class (or other classrooms). Structured cooperative learning activities can promote collaborative learning and effective communication. The elements of communication are social skills which can be addressed during cooperative activities.

METHODS OF ENHANCEMENT

Effective teachers use not one but many methods and strategies to enhance student learning. Teachers choose different strategies to meet different purposes and the needs of the content and the students. If the purpose is to provide a foundation for future investigations, the teacher might choose to use a short mastery lecture with questions. If the purpose is to encourage creative thinking, the teacher might choose a synectic strategy. If the purpose is to encourage expression of a variety of viewpoints about a topic, the teacher might choose structured discussion. If the purpose is to investigate current problems without specific answers, the teacher might choose an inquiry lesson.

DEDUCTIVE STRATEGIES

Methods can be divided into two categories: deductive and inductive. Deductive methods are those in which teachers present material through mastery lecture, or students teach each other through presentations. In deductive lessons, the generalizations or rules are taught from the beginning, then examples and elaboration are developed which support the generalizations or rules. Deductive thinking often requires students to make assessments based on specific criteria which they or others develop. Inductive methods are those in which teachers encourage students to study, research, and analyze data they collect, then develop generalizations and rules based on their findings.

During inductive lessons, a hypothesis or concept is introduced at the beginning, but generalizations are developed later in the lesson and are based on inferences from data.

The lecture is a deductive method, whereby information is presented to students by the teacher. New teachers are especially attuned to lecture because that is the usual mode of instruction in college classes. An advantage of lecture is that large amounts of information can be presented in an efficient manner; however, effective teachers avoid dumping loads of information through lectures. Mastery lectures should be short, usually no more than 10 or 15 minutes at a time, and constantly interrupted with questions to and from students. Questions during a lecture tend to be lower-level ones, when the teacher is building a foundation of knowledge for students to use in later activities. The effective teacher, however, uses higher-level questions even during lectures.

Information sessions must also be supplemented with an array of visual materials that will appeal to visual learners as well as auditory ones. Putting words or outlines on the board or a transparency is very helpful; however, this is still basically a verbal strategy. Drawings, diagrams, cartoons, pictures, caricatures, and graphs are visual aids for lectures. Teacher drawings need not be highly artistic, merely memorable. Often a rough or humorous sketch will be more firmly etched in students' minds than elaborate drawings. Using a very simple sketch provides a better means of teaching the critical attributes than a complicated one. The major points stand out in a simple sketch; details can be added once students understand the basic concepts. For example, a very simple sketch of the shapes of the snouts of alligators and crocodiles can fix the difference in students' memory; identification from pictures then becomes easier.

Teachers should also be careful to include instruction on how to take notes while listening to a speaker, a skill that will be useful during every student's career, whether listening to instructions from a supervisor or a speaker at meetings and conferences. One way a teacher can do this is to show students notes or an outline from the mini-lecture he or she is about to present or to write notes or an outline on the board or overhead while she is presenting the information. This activity requires careful planning by the teacher and will result in a more organized lecture. This type of structure is especially helpful for sequential learners, who like organization. It will also help random learners develop organizational skills. A web or map or cluster is a more right-brained method of connecting important points in a lecture or a chapter. The effective teacher will use both systems and teach both to students, so they have a choice of strategies.

INDUCTIVE STRATEGIES

Inquiry or discovery lessons are inductive in nature. Inquiry lessons start with a thought-provoking question for which students are interested in finding an explanation. The question can be followed by brainstorming a list of what the students already know about the topic, then categorizing the information. The categories can then be used as topics for group or individual research. Deductive presentations by students of their research can follow.

Some advantages of inductive lessons are that they generally require higher-level thinking by both teacher and students, and they usually result in higher student motivation, interest, and retention. They are also more interesting to the teacher, who deals with the same concepts year after year. Disadvantages include the need for additional preparation by the teacher, the need for access to a large number of resources, and additional time for students to research the concepts. The teacher spends a great amount of time in planning the lessons, then acts as facilitator during classes.

Generally, the greater the amount of planning and prediction by the teacher, the greater the success of the students. This does not mean that the activity must be tightly structured or set in concrete, but the effective teacher tries to predict student responses and his or her reactions to them. The need for purchasing additional resources has been moderated by computerized bibliographic services, interlibrary loan, and CD-ROMs with all types of information. Because inductive, research-oriented units require more class time, subject-area teachers must work together to determine what concepts are essential for students to understand; other nonessential concepts are omitted.

An English teacher wishing to introduce an inductive study of *Julius Caesar* might ask students what would happen if a group of United States senators and representatives banded together to kill the current president and take control of the government. After brainstorming ideas about causes and effects of the assassination, students could categorize the ideas (political, irrational, economic, etc.), then work in cooperative groups to develop their predictions about each area. Groups could also research the assassinations of Lincoln, McKinley, and Kennedy, then study *Julius Caesar* for comparison of motives and effects. A culminating activity could be to write a scenario of what might happen in an assassination of the current president. English and history teachers who want to team teach could develop this project together.

A computer science teacher could ask students if they think there will ever be a computer that's smarter than a human being. This would lead to a definition of terms, then investigation into human intelligence, artificial intelligence, computer languages, films such as *2001: A Space Odyssey*, along with demonstrations of computer programs related to artificial intelligence.

Books such as *The Timetables of History* or *The People's Chronology* can be used as a reference for history, English, science, business, and the arts. Students can analyze ten-year periods to discover what was happening in several of the seven topics, then look for connections. Is literature connected to political events? Do art and music reflect current events? What effects do scientific discoveries have on economics? Does the U.S. "Black Friday" of October 28, 1929, have any relationship to the "Black Friday" in Germany in 1927? What predictions does William Beveridge make in his 1942 "Report on Social Security"? A major class project could be to extend a section of the timetables to include African and Asian events through research into each of the seven topics. Over a period of several years, this could become a valuable resource for the school.

A science teacher has numerous opportunities for inductive approaches; in fact, he or she could develop his or her complete curriculum around problems to solve. He or she could ask students to brainstorm a list of everything they can think of that runs by electrical power, then to predict what the world might be like today if electricity had not yet been discovered, or if it hadn't been discovered until 1950. Would there have been any world wars? atomic weapons? movies? pollution? Their study could include effects of this discovery on the people in the time it was discovered (including violent reactions), resulting devices which use electricity, ecological issues, possible future uses of electrical power, etc.

Science teachers could also lead discussion of ethical issues in science during a study of cell biology. What would happen if biochemists discover how to clone people, and a dangerous criminal steals the formula and clones himself or warlike leaders of nations? What effects might this have on law and order, peace and war? Should there be laws to stop scientific experiments of certain types?

Teachers of mathematics could introduce a lesson on place value or number systems by asking students how mathematics might be different if people had eight or twelve fingers instead of ten. Students could then investigate number systems and even invent one of their own.

Art or music teachers could show a selection of paintings or play several recordings and ask students in what decade they were painted or written. Students must explain their reasons for giving a particular date. Research could lead to discussion on what paintings or music of a particular decade had in common, their countries of origin, the influence of religion on art or music, and whether political events influence art and music. They could also be asked to predict what art will look like or how music will sound in the year 2050. Students could do projects based on how someone in the year 2050 might write about current art or music. Content area teachers can team with an art teacher to discuss mathematics in art and music, the influence of historical events on the arts, poems or plays related to the art or music world, or the science of sound. Art or music students could develop original projects as part of subject area class assignments.

Business teachers might ask students what kind of business they would like to own, if money were no object. Students would need to explain their reasons, then research the business they chose. The class could brainstorm questions for study, then categorize them to determine general areas of research. Students who choose the same business could work together; resource people from the business community could visit the class to explain business concepts, answer questions, and predict what business will be like in 10 or 20 or 50 years.

COOPERATIVE STRATEGIES

Cooperative learning lessons may be developed as deductive or inductive. Deductive activities include practice and review of information through games or tournaments and presentations made by the teacher or by students. Inductive activities include research, analysis, and synthesis of information.

DISCUSSION STRATEGIES

Discussions are often thought of as unstructured talk by students sitting around in a circle, answering the basic question, "What do you think about _____?" However, profitable discussions are carefully planned, with specific objectives leading to understanding of specific concepts.

Discussion lessons may be deductive or inductive, depending on the emphasis. Deductive lessons will be more structured, often with clear answers which the teacher expects and leads the students to provide. Inductive lessons will be less structured, but very well planned. Teachers ask open-ended questions and accept a variety of answers which are well supported by information or inferences from the text. The effective teacher plans a variety of questions, with learner outcomes in mind, and leads the discussion without dominating it. She also will make certain that all students participate and have an opportunity to contribute. Students may also plan and lead discussions, with careful assistance from the teacher.

An English teacher may plan a discussion of *Our Town*. All students write a variety of questions, e.g., based on levels of Bloom's taxonomy. Half the class discusses among themselves the questions presented by the other half of the class; roles change for the last half of the period or the next class period. The teacher's main role is to facilitate and make sure students follow the guidelines.

An important advantage, which is also a disadvantage, is the amount of time required by genuine discussion. The advantage is that all students have opportunities to contribute to learning and therefore feel a greater sense of ownership; the disadvantage is that productive discussion takes a great deal of time.

COMPARISON/CONTRAST

An important higher-order thinking skill is the ability to compare and contrast two things or concepts which are dissimilar on the surface. Thomas Gordon has described a process of synectics, whereby students are forced to make an analogy between something that is familiar and something that is new; the concepts seem to be completely different, but through a series of steps, students discover underlying similarities. For example, a biology teacher might plan an analogy between a cell (new concept) and a city government (familiar concept). Although they seem impossibly different, they both have systems for transportation, disposal of unwanted materials, and parts that govern these systems. By comparing something new with something familiar, students have a "hook" for the new information which will help them remember it as well as better understand it. For example, students trying to remember functions of a cell would be assisted by remembering parts of the city government.

TEACHER AND STUDENT ROLES

An effective teacher plays many roles in the classroom in addition to the traditional instructor role. In one lesson, a teacher may play several roles as she uses several different strategies. Teachers who use lecture are in the role of an instructor who provides information. Students who listen to lectures are usually in a passive, often inattentive, role of listener. Teachers who use cooperative strategies take on the roles of a coach, who encourages his students to work together, and a facilitator, who helps activities proceed smoothly and provides resources. Students in a collaborative role must learn social and group roles as well as content in order to accomplish learning tasks. Teachers who use inquiry strategies take the role of a facilitator who plans outcomes and provides resources for students as they work. Students in an inquirer role must take more responsibility for their own learning by planning, carrying out, and presenting research and projects. Teachers who listen to student discussions and presentations and evaluate student papers and projects take on the role of an audience who provides constructive feedback. Students in a discussion role must prepare carefully and think seriously about the topic under discussion.

The most natural role for teachers is that of instructor, since that is the role which they have seen modeled most often. The usual role for students is that of passive listener, since that is the role they have practiced most often.

Taking on other roles requires commitment to learning new methods and procedures, as well as practice for perfecting them. Both teachers and students may feel uncomfortable in new roles until they are practiced enough to become familiar.

CURRICULUM PLANNING

The effective teacher includes resources of all types in the curriculum planning process. He or she should be very familiar with the school library, city/county library, education service center resources, and the library of any college or university in the area. She should have a list of all audiovisual aids which may be borrowed, e.g., kits, films, filmstrips, videos, laser disks, and computer software. All audiovisual aids should be related to curricular objectives. Many librarians have keyed their resources to objectives in related subject areas, so the teacher can incorporate them with ease into the lessons. However, resources should never be used with a class unless they have been previewed and approved by the teacher. The list of resources to be used in a lesson or unit should be included in the curriculum guide or the lesson plan for ease of use.

PLANNING FOR RESOURCES

The effective teacher determines the appropriate place in the lesson for audiovisual aids. If the material is especially interesting and thought-provoking, he or she may use it to introduce a unit. For example, a travel video on coral reefs or snorkeling might be an excellent introduction to the study of tropical fish and plants. The same video could be used at the end of the study to see how many fish and plants the students can recognize and name. Computer software that "dissects" frogs or worms may be used after a discussion of what students already know about the animals and how their internal organs compare with those of humans. A video of a Shakespearean play could be intermixed with discussion and class reading of scenes from the play.

Videos, films, and filmstrips may be stopped for discussion. Research reveals that students comprehend better and remember longer if the teacher introduces a video or film appropriately, then stops it frequently to discuss what the students have just seen and heard. This method also helps keep students' attention focused and assists them in learning note-taking skills.

PRINT RESOURCES

The most common print material is the textbook, which has been selected by teachers on the campus from a list of books approved by the state. Textbooks are readily available, economical, and written to match state curriculum requirements. However, the adoption process is a long one, and textbooks (particularly science and history) can become out-of-date quickly; therefore, the teacher must use additional resources with recent dates.

Local, state, and national newspapers and magazines should not be overlooked. Some newspapers and magazines have special programs to help teachers use their products in the classroom for reading and writing opportunities as well as for sources of information. Local newspapers may be willing to send specialists to work with students or act as special resource persons.

A limitation of textbooks is their tendency to provide sketchy or minimal treatment of topics, partly because publishers are required to include such a broad range of topics. An ineffective teacher may use the "chapter a week" theory of "covering" a textbook. This method pays no consideration to the importance of information in each chapter or its relevance to the overall district curriculum. Neither does it promote critical thinking on the part of the teacher or the student. Students tend to believe the textbook is something to be endured and not employed as a tool for learning. The effective teacher chooses sections from the textbook that are relevant to his or her learning goals and omits the rest. He or she also supplements the sketchy treatments by using an abundance of other resources.

VISUAL MATERIALS

The most available tools in classrooms are the chalkboard and the overhead projector. There are several principles which apply to both. The teacher must write clearly and in large letters. Overhead transparencies should never be typed on a regular typewriter, because the print is too small. Computers allow type sizes of at least 18 points, which is the minimum readable size. Also, both boards and transparencies should be free of clutter. Old information should be removed before new information is added. These tools work more effectively if the teacher plans ahead of time what she will write or draw on them. Using different colors will emphasize relationships or differences.

Posters and charts can complement lessons, but the walls should not be so cluttered that students are unable to focus on what's important for the current lesson. Posters and charts can be displayed on a rotating basis. Filmstrips, films, and videos are appealing to students because they are surrounded by visual images on television, computers, and video games.

Films and filmstrips have the advantage of being projected on a large screen, so all students can see clearly. Videos and computers can be connected to large displays or projected on large screens, but these projection devices are rather expensive. If the available screen is too small for large-group viewing, then the teacher might break the class into groups and have several different projects for them to do on a rotating basis.

Some of the best graphic aids will be those developed by individual students or by groups of students. Along with learning about subject area concepts, students will be learning about design and presentation of information. Students can take pictures of their products to put in a portfolio or scrapbook.

VIDEODISK AND INTERACTIVE VIDEO

Videodisks provide a sturdy, compact system of storage for pictures and sound. They can store more than 50,000 separate frames of still images, up to 50 hours of digitized stereo music, or about 325 minutes of motion pictures with sound. An advantage of videodisk over videotape is that each frame can be accessed separately and quickly. The simplest level of use involves commands to play, pause, forward, or reverse. Individual frames can be accessed by inputting their number.

These programs can become interactive by linking them to a computer. The teacher can then individually access, sequence, and pace the information from the interactive system. An art teacher with a collection of pictures of the world's art treasures can choose which pictures to use and the order in which to show them, then design custom-made lessons which can be used repeatedly or easily revised. He or she might decide to develop a program on landscapes as portrayed in art during a certain period of time. By using the videodisk's reference guide, the teacher determines which pictures to use and the length of time he wants each displayed. He or she can develop numerous lessons from one videodisk.

More comprehensive interactive programs can use the computer to present information, access a videodisk to illustrate main points, then ask for responses from the student. A multimedia production run by the computer can include images, text, and sound from a videodisk, CD-ROM, graphics software, word processing software, and a sound effects program. Teachers can develop classroom presentations, but students can also develop learning units as part of a research or inquiry project.

The cost of a multimedia system remains relatively high, but students can use it to develop high-level thought processes, collaborative work, and research skills, as well as content knowledge and understanding.

COMPUTER SOFTWARE TOOLS

There are several software tools which are extremely useful for teachers and students. Word processing allows teachers and students to write, edit, and polish assignments and reports. Most programs have a spelling-checker or even a grammar-checker to enhance written products. Students in all subjects can use word processors to write term papers or reports of their research. Many word processors allow writers to put the text into columns, so that students can produce newsletters with headlines of varying sizes. For example, an English class could write a series of reviews of Shakespeare's plays or sonnets, add information about Shakespeare and his times, then collect everything into a newsletter as a class project. There are also desktop publishing programs which allow text and graphics to be integrated to produce publications, such as a class newsletter and school newspapers and yearbooks.

Databases are like electronic file cards; they allow students to input data, then retrieve it in various ways and arrangements. History students can input data about various countries, e.g., population, population growth rate, infant mortality rate, average income, and average education levels. They then manipulate the database to call out information in a variety of ways. The more important step in learning about databases is dealing with huge quantities of information. Students need to learn how to analyze and interpret the data that they see to discover connections between isolated facts and figures and how to eliminate inappropriate information.

On-line databases are essential tools for research. Students can access databases related to English, history, science—any number of subject areas. Most programs allow electronic mail, so that students can communicate over the computer with people from around the world. There are also massive bibliographic databases which help students and teachers to find the resources they need. Many of the print materials can then be borrowed through interlibrary loan. The use of electronic systems can geometrically increase the materials available to students.

Spreadsheets are similar to teacher gradebooks. Rows and columns of numbers can be linked to produce totals and averages. Formulas can connect information in one cell (the intersection of a row and column) to another cell. Teachers often keep gradebooks on a spreadsheet, because of the ease in updating information. Once formulas are in place, teachers can enter grades and have completely up-to-date averages for all students. Students can use spreadsheets to collect and analyze numerical data which can be sorted in various orders. Some spreadsheet programs also include a chart function, so that teachers could display class averages on a bar chart to provide a visual comparison of the classes' performance. Students can enter population figures from various countries, then draw various types of graphs—bars, columns, scatters, histograms, pies—to convey information. This type of graphic information can also be used in multimedia presentations. There are also various stand-alone graph and chart software packages.

Graphics or paint programs allow users to draw freehand to produce any type of picture or use tools to produce boxes, circles, or other shapes. These programs can illustrate classroom presentations or individual research projects. Many word processing programs have some graphic elements.

COMPUTER-ASSISTED INSTRUCTION

Many early uses of computers tended to be drill-and-practice, where students practiced simple skills such as mathematics operations. Many elaborate systems of practice and testing were developed, with management systems so that teachers could keep track of how well the students were achieving. This type of software is useful for skills which students need to practice. An advantage is immediate feedback so students know if they chose the correct answer. Many of these programs have a game format to make the practice more interesting. A disadvantage is their generally low-level nature.

Tutorials are a step above drill-and-practice programs, because they also include explanations and information. Students are asked to make a response, then the program branches to the most appropriate section, based on the students' answer. Tutorials are often used for remedial work, but are also useful for instruction in English as a second language. Improved graphics and sound allow nonspeakers of English to listen to correct pronunciation while viewing pictures of words. Tutorials are used to supplement, not supplant, teacher instruction.

Simulations or problem-solving programs provide opportunities for students to have experiences which would take too long to experience in real-time, would be too costly or difficult to experience, or would be impossible to experience. For example, one of the most popular early simulations allowed students to see if they could survive the Oregon Trail. Users made several choices about food, ammunition, supplies, etc., then the computer moved them along the trail until they reached their goal or died along the way.

There are several simulations which allow students to "dissect" animals. This saves time and materials, is less messy, and allows students who might be reluctant to dissect real animals to learn about them. Other software might explore the effects of weightlessness on plant growth, a situation which would be impossible to set up in the classroom lab. There are several social studies simulations which allow students to do things like invent a country, then see the effects of their political and economic decisions on the country.

MANIPULATIVES AND LABS

Other types of materials which can be used effectively are manipulatives. Manipulatives are touchable, movable materials which enhance students' understanding of a concept. They are used particularly in mathematics and science to give students a concrete way of dealing with concepts, but tangible materials are appropriate and helpful in all subject areas. Math teachers use plastic shapes in studying geometry. Number lines, place value cubes, and tessellation blocks are used to help students understand math, not only in elementary classes but also in algebra, trigonometry, and calculus. Elementary language arts teachers use wooden letters or cut-outs to help students learn the alphabet; secondary English teachers can make part-of-speech cards for sentence structure, frames for structured poetry, and blocks for essay structure. Science teachers are required to use many manipulatives during hands-on lab activities. Social studies and history teachers can use a wealth of cultural artifacts from countries they are studying.

HUMAN RESOURCES

Parents and other members of the community can be excellent local experts from which students can learn about any subject—mathematics from bankers, art and music from artists, English from public relations persons, history from club or church historians or librarians, business from owners of companies. The list can be endless. Effective teachers make sure that any guest who is invited to speak or perform understands the purpose of the visit and the goals or objectives the teacher is trying to accomplish. Preparation can make the class period more focused and meaningful.

Field trips are excellent sources of information, especially about careers and current issues such as pollution control. One field trip can yield assignments in mathematics, history, science, and English, and often art, architecture, music, or health. Teachers can collaborate with each other to produce thematic assignments for the field trip or simply to coordinate the students' assignments. Often a history report can serve as an English paper as well. Data can be analyzed in math classes and presented with the aid of computers.

SELECTION AND EVALUATION CRITERIA

The effective teacher uses criteria to evaluate audiovisual, multimedia, and computer resources. The first thing to look for is congruence with lesson goals. If the software doesn't reinforce student outcomes, then it shouldn't be used, no matter how flashy or well-done. A checklist for instructional computer software could include appropriate sequence of instruction, meaningful student interaction with the software, learner control of screens and pacing, and motivation. Other factors should be considered, such as ability to control sound and save progress, effective use of color, clarity of text and graphics on the screen, and potential as individual or group assignment.

In addition to congruence with curriculum goals, the teacher considers her students' strengths and needs, their learning styles or preferred modalities, and their interests. Students' needs can be determined through formal or informal assessment. Most standardized tests include an indication of which objectives the student did not master. Mastering these objectives can be assisted with computer or multimedia aids.

Learning styles may be assessed with a variety of instruments and models, including those developed by Rita Dunn and Anthony Gregorc. Students with highly visual learning modes will benefit from audiovisuals. Student interests may be revealed by a questionnaire, either purchased or developed by the district or teacher. A knowledge of student interests will help the teacher provide resources to suit individual needs. The effective teacher can design activity choices which relate to class goals but also to student interests.

Evaluation of resources should be accomplished in advance by the teacher, before purchase whenever possible. Evaluation is also conducted during student use of materials. Assessment after student use may be by considering achievement level of the students and/or by surveys which ask for students' responses.

PURPOSES OF ASSESSMENT

The effective teacher understands the importance of ongoing assessment as an instructional tool for the classroom and uses both informal and formal assessment measures. Informal measures may include observation, journals, written drafts, and conversations. More formal measures may include teacher-made tests, district exams, and standardized tests. Effective teachers use both formative and summative evaluation. Formative evaluation occurs during the process of learning, when the teacher or the students monitor progress in obtaining outcomes, while it is still possible to modify instruction. Summative evaluation occurs at the end of a specific time period or course, usually by a single grade used to represent a student's performance.

TEACHER-MADE TESTS

The effective teacher uses a variety of assessment techniques. Teacher-made instruments are ideally developed at the same time as the goals and outcomes are planned, rather than at the last minute after all the lessons have been taught. Carefully planned objectives and assessment instruments serve as lesson development guides for the teacher.

Paper and pencil tests are the most common method for evaluation of student progress. There are a number of different types of questions: multiple-choice, true/false, matching, fill-in-the-blank, short answer, and longer essay. The first five tend to test the knowledge or comprehension levels. Essays often test at the lower levels, but are suitable for assessing learning at higher levels. Projects, papers, and portfolios can provide assessment of higher-level thinking skills.

If the purpose is to test student recall of factual information, a short objective test (multiple-choice, true/false, matching, fill-in-the blank) would be most effective and efficient. The first three types of questions can be answered on machine-scorable scan sheets to provide quick and accurate scoring. Disadvantages are that they generally test lower levels of knowledge and don't provide an opportunity for an explanation of answers.

If the purpose is to test student ability to analyze an event, compare and contrast two concepts, make predictions about an experiment, or evaluate a character's actions, then an essay question would provide the best paper/pencil opportunity for the student to show what he can do. Teachers should make the question explicit enough so that students will know exactly what she expects. For example, "Explain the results of World War II" is too broad; students won't really understand what the teacher expects. It would be more explicit to say, "Explain three results of World War II that you feel had the most impact on participating nations. Explain the criteria you used in selecting these results."

Advantages of an essay include the possibility for students to be creative in their answers, the opportunity for students to explain their responses, and the potential to test for higher-level thinking skills. Disadvantages of essay questions include the time needed for students to formulate meaningful responses, language difficulties of some students, and the time needed to evaluate the essays. Consistency in evaluation is also a problem for the teacher, but this can be alleviated by using an outline of the acceptable answers. Teachers who write specific questions and who know what they are looking for will be more consistent in grading. Also, if there are several essay questions, the effective teacher grades all student responses to the first question, then moves on to all responses to the second, and so on.

AUTHENTIC ASSESSMENTS

Paper and pencil tests or essays are only one method of assessment. Others include projects, observation, checklists, anecdotal records, portfolios, self-assessment, and peer assessment. Although these types of assessment often take more time and effort to plan and administer, they can often provide a more authentic assessment of student progress.

Projects are common in almost all subject areas. They promote student control of learning experiences and provide opportunities for research into a variety of topics, as well as the chance to use visuals, graphics, videos, or multimedia presentations in place of, or in addition to, written reports. Projects also promote student self-assessment because students must evaluate their progress along each step of the project. Many schools have science or history fairs for which students plan, develop, and display their projects. Projects can also be part of business, English, music, art, mathematics, social sciences, health, or physical education courses.

The teacher must make clear the requirements and the criteria for evaluation of the projects before students begin them. He or she must also assist students in selecting projects which are feasible, for which the school has learning resources, and which can be completed in a reasonable amount of time with little or no expense to students.

Advantages of projects are that students can use visual, graphic, art, or music abilities; students can be creative in their topic or research; and the projects can appeal to various learning styles. Disadvantages include difficulty with grading, although this can be overcome by devising a checklist for required elements and a rating scale for quality.

Observations may be made for individual or group work. This method is very suitable for skills or for affective learning. Teachers usually make a list of competencies, skills, or requirements, then check off the ones that are observed in the student or group. An office skills teacher wishing to emphasize interviewing skills may devise a checklist that includes personal appearance, mannerisms, confidence, and addressing the questions that are asked. A teacher who wants to emphasize careful listening may observe a discussion with a checklist which includes paying attention, not interrupting, summarizing another person's ideas, and asking questions of other students.

Anecdotal records may be helpful in some instances, such as capturing the process a group of students uses to solve a problem. This formative data can be useful during feedback to the group. Students can also be taught to write an explanation of the procedures they use for a project or a science experiment. An advantage of an anecdotal record is that it can include all relevant information. Disadvantages include the amount of time necessary to complete the record and difficulty in assigning a grade. If used for feedback, then no grade is necessary.

Advantages of checklists include the potential for capturing behavior that can't be accurately measured with a paper and pencil test, i.e., shooting free throws on the basketball court, following the correct sequence of steps in a science experiment, or including all important elements in a speech in class. One characteristic of a checklist that is both an advantage and a disadvantage is its structure, which provides consistency but inflexibility. An open-ended comment section at the end of a checklist can overcome this disadvantage.

Portfolios are collections of students' best work. They can be used in any subject area where the teacher wants students to take more responsibility for planning, carrying out, and organizing their own learning. They may be used in the same way that artists, models, or performers use them to provide a succinct picture of their best work. Portfolios may be essays or articles written on paper, video tapes, multimedia presentations on computer disks, or a combination. English teachers often use portfolios as a means of collecting the best samples of student writing over the whole year. Sometimes they pass on the work to the next year's teacher to help her assess the needs of her new students. Any subject area can use portfolios, since they contain documentation that reflects growth and learning over a period of time.

Teachers should provide or assist students in developing guidelines for what materials should be placed in portfolios, since it would be unrealistic to include every piece of work in one portfolio. The use of portfolios requires the students to devise a means of evaluating their own work. A portfolio should be a collection of the student's own best work, not a scrapbook for collecting handouts or work done by other individuals, although it can certainly include work by a group in which the student was a participant.

Some advantages of portfolios over testing are that they provide a clearer picture of a student's progress, they are not affected by one inferior test grade, and they help develop self-assessment skills in students. One disadvantage is the amount of time required to teach students how to develop meaningful portfolios. However, this time can be well spent if students learn valuable skills. Another concern is the amount of time teachers must spend to assess portfolios. However, as students become more proficient at self-assessment, the teacher can spend more time in coaching and advising students throughout the development of their portfolios. Another concern is that parents may not understand how portfolios will be graded. The effective teacher devises a system which the students and parents understand before work on the portfolio begins.

SELF AND PEER ASSESSMENT

One goal of an assessment system is to promote student self-assessment. Since most careers require employees or managers to evaluate their own productivity as well as that of others, self-assessment and peer assessment are important lifelong skills.

Effective teachers use a structured approach to teach self-assessment, helping students set standards at first by making recommendations about standards, then gradually moving toward student development of their own criteria and application of the criteria to their work.

One method of developing self-assessment is to ask students to apply the teacher's own standards to a product. For example, an English teacher who uses a rating scale for essays might have students use that scale on their own papers, then compare their evaluations with those of the teacher. A science teacher who uses a checklist while observing an experiment might ask students to use the checklist, then compare theirs with the teacher's.

The class can set standards for evaluating group work as well as individual work. Collaborative groups are effective vehicles for practicing the skills involved in assessment.

STANDARDIZED TESTING

In *criterion-referenced* tests, each student is measured against uniform objectives or criteria. CRTs allow the possibility that all students can score 100 percent because they understand the concepts being tested. Teacher-made tests should be criterion-referenced, because the teacher should develop them to measure the achievement of predetermined outcomes for the course. If teachers have properly prepared lessons based on the outcomes, and if students have mastered the outcomes, then scores should be high. This type of test may be called noncompetitive, because students are not in competition with each other for a high score, and there is no limit to the number of students who can score well. Some commercially developed tests are criterion-referenced; however, the majority are norm-referenced.

The purpose of a *norm-referenced* test is to provide a way to compare the performance of groups of students. This type of test may be called competitive, because a limited number of students can score well. A plot of large numbers of NRT scores will resemble a bell-shaped curve, with most scores clustering around the center and a few scores at each end. The midpoint is an average of data; therefore, by definition, half of the population will score above average and half below average.

The bell-shaped curve was developed as a mathematical description of the results of tossing coins. As such, it represents the chance or normal distribution of skills, knowledge, or events across the general population. A survey of the height of sixth-grade boys will result in an average height, with half the boys above average and half below. There will be a very small number with heights way above average and a very small number with heights way below average, with most heights clustering around the average.

NRT scores are usually reported in percentile scores (not to be confused with percentages), which indicate the percent of the population whose scores fall at or below the score. For example, a group score at the 80th percentile means that the group scored as well as or better than 80 percent of the students who took the test. A student with a score at the 50th percentile has an average score.

Percentile scores rank students from highest to lowest. By themselves the percentile scores do not indicate how well the student has mastered the content objectives. Raw scores indicate how many questions the student answered correctly and are therefore useful in computing the percentage of questions a student answered correctly.

A national test for biology is designed to include objectives for the widest possible biology curriculum, for the broadest use of the test. Normed scores are reported so that schools can compare the performance of their students with the performance of students which the test developers used as its norm group. The test will likely include more objectives than are included in a particular school's curriculum; therefore, that school's students may score low in comparison to the norm group. Teachers must be very careful in selecting a norm-referenced test, and should look for a test which includes objectives which are the most congruent with the school's curriculum.

Schools must also consider the reliability of a test, or whether the instrument will give consistent results when the measurement is repeated. A reliable bathroom scale, for example, will give identical weights for the same person measured three times in a morning. An unreliable scale, however, may give weights that differ by six pounds. Teachers evaluate test reliability over time when they give the same, or almost the same, test to different groups of students. Because there are many factors which affect reliability, teachers must be careful in evaluating this factor.

Schools must also be careful to assess the validity of a test, or whether the test actually measures what it is supposed to measure. If students score low on a test because they couldn't understand the questions, then the test is not valid because it measures reading ability instead of content knowledge. If students score low because the test covered material which was not studied, the test is not valid for that situation. A teacher assesses the validity of her own tests by examining the questions to see if they measure what was planned and taught in her classroom.

A test must be reliable before it can be valid. However, measurements can be consistent without being valid. A scale can indicate identical weights for three weigh-ins of the same person during one morning, but actually be 15 pounds in error. A history test may produce similar results each time it is given, but not be a valid measure of what was taught and learned. Tests should be both reliable and valid. If the test doesn't measure consistently, then it can't be accurate. If it doesn't measure what it's supposed to measure, then its reliability doesn't matter.

Commercial test producers perform various statistical measures of the reliability and validity of their tests and provide the results in the test administrator's booklet.

PERFORMANCE-BASED ASSESSMENT

Some states and districts are moving toward performance-based testing, which means that students are assessed on how well they perform certain tasks. This allows students to use higher-level thinking skills to apply, analyze, synthesize, and evaluate ideas and data. For example, a biology performance-based assessment may require students to read a problem, design and carry out a laboratory experiment, then write a summary of his or her findings. He or she would be evaluated both on the process she used and the output she produced. A history performance-based assessment may require students to research a specific topic over a period of several days, make presentations of his or her findings to the rest of the class, then write a response which uses what he or she has learned from his own research and that of his classmates. He or she is then evaluated on the process and the product of his or her research. An English performance-based test may require students to read a selection of literature, then write a critical analysis. A mathematics test may state a general problem to be solved, then require the student to invent one or more methods of solving the problem, use one of the methods to arrive at a solution, then write the solution and an explanation of the processes he or she used.

Performance-based assessment allows students to be creative in solutions to problems or questions, and it requires them to use higher-level skills. This type of assessment can be time-consuming; however, students are working on content-related problems, using skills that are useful in a variety of contexts. This type of assessment also requires multiple resources, which can be expensive. It also requires teachers to be trained in how to use this type of assessment. However, many schools consider performance-based testing to be a more authentic measure of student achievement than traditional tests.

PHYSICAL ENVIRONMENT

While there are certain physical aspects of the classroom that cannot be changed (size, shape, number of windows, type of lighting, etc.), there are others that can be. Windows can have shades or blinds which distribute light correctly and which allow for the room to be darkened for video or computer viewing. If the light switches do not allow part of the lights to remain on, sometimes schools will change the wiring system. If not, teachers can use a lamp to provide minimum lighting for monitoring students during videos or films.

Schools often schedule maintenance such as painting and floor cleaning during the summer. Often school administrators will accede to requests for a specific color of paint, given sufficient time for planning.

All secondary school classrooms should have a bulletin board used by the teacher and by the students. The effective teacher has plans for changing the board according to units of study. Space should be reserved for display of student work and projects, either on the bulletin board, the wall, or in the hallway. (Secondary teachers who need creative ideas can visit elementary classrooms.)

Bare walls can be depressing; however, covering the wall with too many posters can be visually distracting. Posters with sayings which promote cooperation, study skills, and content ideas should be displayed, but the same ones should not stay up all year, because they become invisible when too familiar.

Most classrooms have movable desks, which allows for varied seating arrangements. If students are accustomed to sitting in rows, this is sometimes a good way to start the year. Harry K. Wong has described his method of assigning seats on the first day of school, which is to assign each desk a column and row number, then give students assignment cards as they come into the room. Another method is to put seating assignments on an overhead, visible when students enter the room. Once students are comfortable with classroom rules and procedures, the teacher can explain to students how to quickly move their desks into different formations for special activities, then return them to their original positions in the last 60 seconds of class.

The best place for the teacher's desk is often at the back of a room, so there are few barriers between the teacher and the students and between the students and the chalkboards. This encourages the teacher to walk around the classroom for better monitoring of students.

SOCIAL AND EMOTIONAL CLIMATE

The effective teacher maintains a climate which promotes the lifelong pursuit of learning. One way to do this is to practice research skills which will be helpful throughout life. All subject areas can promote the skills of searching for information to answer a question, filtering it to determine what is appropriate, and using what is helpful to solve a problem.

Most English teachers require some type of research project, from middle school through the senior year. Ken Macrorie's books on meaningful research can guide English teachers as they develop a project which can answer a real-life issue for students. For example, a student who is trying to decide which school to attend could engage in database and print research on schools which have the major characteristics he's interested in, telephone or written interviews with school officials and current students, review of school catalogs and other documents, and magazine or journal articles which deal with the school. At the end of the process, students will have engaged in primary as well as secondary research, plus they will have an answer to a personal question.

The English teacher and any other subject area teacher can team up to collaborate on a joint research project. The resulting product satisfies both the need of the English teacher to teach research skills and the need of the subject area teacher to teach content knowledge as well as research skills. Primary research can be done through local or regional resources such as business owners, lawyers, physicians, and the general public. Research questions could include: What effects do artificial sweeteners have on the human body's functioning (biology)? What process is used to develop the platform of a political party (history)? What happens when a business is accused of Title IX violations (business)? What effects have higher medical costs had on family budgets (economics)? How has the popularity of music CDs affected the music industry and businesses which sell records and tapes (music and business)?

The effective teacher also facilitates positive social and emotional atmosphere and promotes a risk-taking environment for students. He or she sets up classroom rules and guidelines for how he or she will treat students, how students will treat him or her, and how students will treat each other. In part this means that he or she doesn't allow ridicule or put-downs, either from the teacher or among the students. It also means that the teacher has an accepting attitude toward student ideas, especially when the idea is not what he or she was expecting to hear. Sometimes students can invent excellent ideas which are not always clear until they are asked to explain how they arrived at them.

Students should feel free to answer and ask any questions that are relevant to the class, without fear of sarcasm or ridicule. Teachers should always avoid sarcasm. Sometimes teachers consider sarcasm to be mere teasing, but because some students often interpret it negatively, effective teachers avoid all types and levels of sarcasm.

ROUTINES AND TRANSITIONS

The effective teacher manages routines and transitions with a minimum of disturbance to students and to learning. Procedures are planned before students come to the first class. A routine is a procedure that has been practiced so that it works automatically. A transition is moving from one activity to another or from one desk arrangement to another.

The teacher needs to consider how he or she wants students to behave in the classroom: how they will ask questions, how they will sharpen pencils, how they will pass in papers, how they will put headings on papers, how they will move to get into groups. She also needs to determine her own behaviors: how he or she will start class, how he or she will take roll, how he or she will call students to attention, how he or she will handle tardiness, how he or she will distribute materials, how he or she will handle materials that can be checked out, and how he or she will deal with late papers or projects.

Some procedures should be taught the first day, such as fire and/or emergency drills. The teacher might also teach students how he or she will call them to attention, how they will start class, and how they will ask questions. It's better not to teach all procedures at once; they can be taught as needed. For example, the best time to teach students how to pass in papers is the first time they need to do so. If students are sitting in groups of four, the teacher may teach the students that the group leader should collect papers from each group member, then bring them to the teacher. This means that only one-fourth of the class is moving around. If students are sitting in rows, the teacher may decide to have students pass papers across instead of up the rows. This allows the teacher to monitor students while he or she walks down one aisle to collect the papers. This method also prevents some forms of student misbehavior.

Effective teachers have the students start class immediately, often by putting instructions for a short activity on the board or the overhead as the class enters the room. He or she teaches the students that they should start work on the activity immediately. Math teachers often put up two or three problems for students to work. English teachers often use several sentences which students must write correctly. Any content area teacher can list several content words which students must define, a few questions to review previous work, a brain-teaser, or a puzzle. While students are completing this activity, the teacher can quickly check roll with a seating chart. The activity can be checked before moving into new activities for the day.

The teacher may decide that all students must raise their hands to be recognized before speaking in the large group. He or she should teach this procedure the first day, then make sure he or she enforces it constantly and consistently, reminding students of the procedure and verbally reinforcing the class for following it. ("I appreciate your remembering to raise your hands to ask a question or make a contribution. That makes the class run more smoothly.")

The teacher who wants students to work collaboratively will also teach procedures for group work. He or she may decide that before a student in a group can ask the teacher a question, he or she must ask everyone else in the group. If no one has an answer, then the group leader for the day can raise his or her hand for teacher assistance. This way, only one-fourth of the class is asking for attention. One member of the group can be assigned the role of materials clerk; only one-fourth of the class is moving around the room.

One method of calling a group back to attention, especially during group work, is for the teacher to raise his or her hand, indicating that all students should raise their own hands, stop talking, and focus attention on the teacher. The reason students raise their hands is that some will have their backs to the teacher, but they will be able to see other students raise hands. This procedure can be taught and practiced in three or four minutes and is effective in a classroom or in a large auditorium. Students should have several opportunities for practice, then the teacher should periodically reinforce the group for following the procedure quickly.

The effective teacher plans all transitions ahead of time, then gives clear instructions and a time limit for students to make the move. A teacher who wants students to move themselves or their desks should give all instructions before allowing students to move. It's easier to maintain students' attention while they are still in the large group, plus they can start work as soon as they are in the new arrangement. Instructions for what students will do in the group should come before making membership assignments, so that student attention will be focused on the task. The best way to make group assignments is by giving students a list of group members or by putting the list on the overhead or wall. After checking for questions, the teacher should give the students a reasonable time limit for moving into groups—five to eight seconds—then count off the seconds for the first transition and praise students for making the quick transition. ("Thank you for moving so quickly. This gives you more time to accomplish your task.")

ACADEMIC LEARNING TIME

The effective teacher maximizes the amount of time spent for instruction. A teacher who loses five minutes at the beginning of class and five minutes at the end of class wastes ten minutes a day that could have been spent in educational activities. This is equivalent to a whole period a week, four classes a month, and 25 periods a year.

Academic learning time is the amount of allocated time that students spend in an activity at the appropriate level of difficulty with the appropriate level of success. The appropriate level of difficulty is one which challenges students without frustrating them. Students who have typically been low achievers need a higher rate of success than those who have typically been higher achievers.

One way to increase academic learning time is to teach students procedures so they will make transitions quickly. Another is to have materials and resources ready for quick distribution and use. Another is to give students a time limit for a transition or an activity. In general, time limits for group work should be slightly shorter than students need, in order to encourage time on task and to prevent off-task behavior and discipline problems. It is essential for the teacher to have additional activities planned should the class finish activities sooner than anticipated. As students complete group work, they should have other group or individual activities so they can work up until the last minute before the end of class.

CLASSROOM DISCIPLINE

The effective teacher realizes that having an interesting, carefully planned curriculum is one of the best ways to prevent most discipline problems. Another way is to have a discipline system of classroom rules, consequences, and rewards, which are applied consistently to every student. All classroom rules, consequences, and rewards must be in compliance with campus requirements. The goals of a classroom system of discipline are that students become self-disciplined and that all but the most serious misbehavior is handled in the classroom by the teacher.

The effective teacher limits rules to four or five essential behaviors by determining the conditions that she must have in order for learning to take place. One might be that students must respect each other by not engaging in sarcasm or cutting remarks. Another might be that students must come to class on time with textbooks, paper, and pencil. Another teacher might insist that students raise their hands to be recognized before speaking. A teacher might have as a general principle that students will not hinder her teaching, their own learning, or the learning of other students. (Class rules should not be confused with classroom procedures, such as how to pass in papers.)

The effective teacher knows what the rules will be before students come to the first class, or develops them with the students during the first couple of days. Many teachers choose to have two or three rules, then ask students for input on two more rules for classroom behavior. Others ask for student input for all four or five rules. Most classes will come up with rules that are acceptable to the teacher and to the class. Often teachers will ask students to come up with one or two rules for the teacher (returning tests within two days, making at least one helpful comment on each paper, etc.).

Once the rules have been determined, the teacher makes sure that each student understands each rule, the consequences for breaking a rule, and the rewards for keeping the rules. Consequences should be spelled out in advance, before rules are broken. Some teachers prefer a system of increasingly serious consequences, such as: (1) name on the board, (2) detention after school, (3) call home to parents, (4) visit to the principal. If being sent to the office is a consequence for repeated misbehavior, then the principal must be aware of and approve the consequence. Most principals also have a system of consequences, once students are sent to their office. In general, additional homework should not be assigned as a consequence, because negative feelings transfer to the idea of learning.

Rewards also help maintain discipline. The goal of a discipline system is that students become self-disciplined; however, external rewards can help the classroom run more smoothly. The reward should not be perceived as a bribe, but as a reward for appropriate behavior. Teachers often ask students for a list of possible rewards. They can include verbal praise, stickers, and positive notes home. They can also include class rewards such as ten minutes of free time on Friday or listening to a radio while doing class work, if no more than five misbehaviors have occurred during the week. Classes can accumulate points to "win" a class reward at the end of the six weeks.

After the system of rules, consequences, and rewards has been determined, the teacher should then put them on a poster in the room and give students copies for their notebooks. Often teachers ask students and a parent or guardian to sign a copy and return it for his or her files, to ensure that both the student and parents understand what type of behavior is expected.

One key to effective discipline is consistency. A teacher who has a rule that students must raise their hands to be called on, but who lets students call out questions or answers, will soon find that no one raises his hand. The rule must also be applied to every student. This is one reason that rules must be carefully chosen. A teacher with a rule that states, "Any student who does not turn in homework at the beginning of the period will get a zero," has no room to make allowances for reasonable excuses for not having homework. The rule might be better stated, "Students should turn in homework at the beginning of each class," with a range of consequences that can be chosen by the teacher, based on whether it is a first or repeated infraction.

CORRECTING STUDENTS

The best way to correct students is usually privately. A teacher who reprimands or criticizes a student in front of the rest of the class will often provoke negative or hostile responses from the student. Harry K. Wong and others have described various methods of confronting students privately. The teacher moves close to the student, calls him or her by name, looks the student in the eye, makes a statement of what behavior needs to stop and what behavior needs to begin, thanks him or her, then moves away. If students are accustomed to having the teacher move around the room to monitor achievement, they often will not even know that a student has been corrected.

The effective teacher also perfects "the look," which can be an unobtrusive way to let a student know he or she needs to change their behavior. Effective teachers also avoid falling into the trap of arguing with students. A student who wants to argue with a teacher can be defused if the teacher doesn't respond to the challenge, but restates the change she expects, then continues what she's doing. No one wins in a struggle to defend his or her own position or authority.

STUDENT OWNERSHIP

One way of promoting student ownership in the classroom is to provide multiple opportunities for their input. Many teachers do this through allowing students to determine two or three rules for the classroom. Sometimes they also have class meetings where students discuss issues or problems which have arisen in an attempt to solve or alleviate them.

Effective teachers also give students choices in what they will study or research, within the parameters of the outcomes for the course. Often this can be accomplished by giving a list of options for assignments, or asking students to brainstorm questions about a topic, then letting them choose from among the ones that are feasible, based on the curriculum and on the available resources. Teachers first determine the overall outcome for the unit, then brainstorm possibilities which would be acceptable.

A history teacher may determine that outcomes of a study of a South American country would be that students could explain how climate affects the development of agriculture and industry, how the form of government affects economic development, how sanitary conditions affect health and population growth, and how religion affects customs and traditions. The teacher could allow students to choose which country, either one country for the entire class or different countries for groups of students. Students can brainstorm questions about the country, then determine which questions they will answer in their research. The teacher, as facilitator, can guide the questions or add some of his own to ensure that the research will address the general areas of business and industry, economic development, health conditions, and religion.

COLLABORATION

The effective teacher promotes student ownership of and membership in a smoothly functioning learning community first by modeling positive, cooperative behavior, then by requiring students to exhibit positive behavior to each other. Cooperative learning strategies also promote an environment in which members are responsible, cooperative, purposeful, and mutually supportive. Collaborative activities provide practice in working together and developing social skills necessary to be successful in future classes, vocational or technical school or college, and careers. They allow students to develop leadership ability through the group roles they are assigned.

DRILL: INSTRUCTIONAL PLANNING, DELIVERY, AND ASSESSMENT

1. Mrs. Rodriguez, a tenth-grade English teacher, has five classes of 25 to 28 students who will begin studying *Julius Caesar* in two weeks. She realizes that today's students may find it difficult to relate to events which took place a long time ago. In previous years, she has asked students to read the play in class, with each student taking different roles. This year she wants to encourage greater student excitement in this unit. Which of the following instructional approaches would be most appropriate for Mrs. Rodriguez to use to encourage students to be self-directed learners?

   (A) Writing a study guide with questions about each act for students to answer in a booklet

   (B) Showing a video of the play and then asking students to role play several scenes

   (C) Developing a list of activities related to the play and having the class vote on which ones they want to do

   (D) Providing a list of objectives and having students develop and carry out two activities to help them meet the objectives

The correct response is (D). The question asks how Mrs. Rodriguez can encourage her students to take control of their own learning. Choice (D) is the best answer because the students are being asked to develop their own learning strategies which match goals of the class. This process requires higher-level thinking by the students. The teacher is determining the basic outcomes, but the students will help determine the methods of achieving these outcomes. Choice (A) is a very structured plan which students may complete at their own pace, but it does not allow for choices or innovations by the students. Viewing a video (choice (B)) would be an excellent visual activity to help students understand the play, but the students aren't asked to plan or make decisions. Their role-playing may not be creative because they may tend to imitate the actions from the video. Choice (C) allows students to choose among several activities, which is a good strategy, but all the planning and goal-setting have been done by the teacher.

2. Miss Bailey teaches fifth-grade social studies in a self-contained class-room with 25 students of various achievement levels. She is starting a unit on history of their local community and wants to stimulate the students' thinking. She also wants to encourage students to develop a project as a result of their study. Which type of project would encourage the most higher-level thinking by the students?

    (A) Giving students a list of questions about people, dates, and events, then having them put the answers on a poster, with appropriate pictures, to display in the class.

    (B) Giving students questions to use to interview older members of the community, then write articles based on the interviews and publish them in a booklet.

    (C) Discussing the influence of the past on the present community, then asking students to project what the community might be like in 100 years.

    (D) Using archived newspapers to collect data, then draw a timeline which includes the major events of the community from its beginning to the current date.

The correct response is (**C**). The question asks for work on the analysis, synthesis, or evaluation level. Choice (C) is the best choice because it asks the students to analyze how past causes have produced current effects, then to predict what future effects might be, based on what they have learned about cause-effect relationships. It requires students to put information together in a new way. Choice (A) may involve some creativity in putting the information on a poster, but in general, answering factual questions calls for lower-level (knowledge or comprehension) thinking. Choice (B) may involve some degree of creativity, but giving students prepared questions requires thinking at a lower level than having students develop their own questions, then determine which answers to write about. Choice (D) is a lower-level activity, although there may be a great deal of research for factual information. All options may be good learning activities, but (A), (B), and (D) do not require as much deep thinking as choice (C). Depending on the depth of the study, a teacher may want to include several of these activities.

3. Mr. Swenson teaches mathematics in high school. He is planning a unit on fractal geometry, using the computer lab for demonstrations and for exploration for his advanced math students. The students have used various computer programs to solve algebra and calculus problems. As Mr. Swenson plans a unit of study, he determines that a cognitive outcome will be that students will design and produce fractals, using a computer program. An affective outcome is that students will become excited about investigating a new field of mathematics and will show this interest by choosing to develop a math project relating to fractals. The most appropriate strategy to use <u>first</u> would be

   (A) lecturing to explain the exciting development of fractal geometry over the past 10 to 15 years.

   (B) demonstrating on the computer the way to input values into formulas to produce fractal designs.

   (C) giving students a few simple fractal designs and asking them to figure out the formulas for producing them.

   (D) showing students color pictures of complex fractals and asking them for ideas about how they could be drawn mathematically.

The correct response is **(D)**. The question relates to appropriate sequencing of activities. Choice (D) is the best introductory activity in order to generate student interest in this new field of mathematics and to get students thinking about how to produce fractals. It would stimulate students to use higher-level thinking skills to make predictions by drawing on their knowledge of how to solve problems mathematically. Choice (A) would be the least appropriate to begin the study. Students who want to learn more could research this topic after they have developed an interest in fractals. Choice (B) would be appropriate as a later step, after students are interested in the process and are ready to learn how to produce fractals. Choice (C) would be appropriate as a subsequent step in the process of learning how to produce fractals. Option B requires students to use preplanned formulas; Choice (C) allows them to develop their own formulas, a very high-level activity.

4. Mr. Roberts' sixth-grade social studies class has developed a research project to survey student use of various types of video games. They designed a questionnaire then administered it to all fourth-, fifth-, and sixth-grade students on their campus. The students plan to analyze their data, then develop a presentation to show at the next parent-teacher meeting. Which types of computer software would be helpful during this class project?

I.   Word processing   III.   Simulation

II. Database   IV.   Graph/chart

(A) I, II, III, and IV   (C)   I and III only

(B) I, II, and IV   (D)   III and IV only

The correct response is (B). This question asks for an evaluation of which software programs will help the students achieve their goals of analyzing data and presenting the results. Item I, word processing, would be used in developing and printing the questionnaire, as well as writing a report on the results. Item II, a database, would be used to sort and print out information in various categories so students could organize and analyze their data. Item III, a simulation, would not be appropriate here because the students' basic purpose is to collect data and analyze it. The project does not call for a program to simulate a situation or event. Item IV, graph or chart, would be very useful in analyzing information and in presenting it to others.

5. Mrs. Johnson teaches middle school reading. She teaches reading skills and comprehension through workbooks and through reading and class discussion of specific plays, short stories, and novels. She also allows students to make some selections according to their own interests. Because she believes there is a strong connection between reading and writing, her students are required to write their responses to literature in a variety of ways. Some of her students have heard their high school brothers and sisters discuss portfolios, and they have asked Mrs. Johnson

if they can use them, also. Which of the following statements are appropriate for Mrs. Johnson to consider in deciding whether to agree to the students' request?

I.   Portfolios will develope skills her student can use in high school.

II.   Portfolios will make Mrs. Johnson's students feel more mature because they would be making the same product as their older brothers and sisters.

III. Portfolios will assist her students in meeting course outcomes relating to reading and writing.

IV.   Portfolios will make grading easier because there will be fewer papers and projects to evaluate.

(A) I, II, and IV

(B) I and III only

(C) II and III only

(D) II and IV only

The correct response is **(B)**. The question asks for appropriate questions for Mrs. Johnson to consider in making an instructional decision. Option I is a valid reason for teaching students how to develop portfolios. Teachers constantly teach students the skills which will be useful in school and in their careers. Although option II may produce positive affective results, feeling mature because students are imitating older siblings is not a sufficient reason to choose portfolios. Option III is the most appropriate reason to decide whether to use portfolios. Most activities and projects that promote achievement of course outcomes would be considered appropriate strategies. Option IV is not necessarily true; portfolio assessment can result in more written work, which can be more time consuming. Even if it were true, emphasizing student achievement is more important than easing the workload of teachers. Options I and III are appropriate; therefore, the correct answer is choice (B).

6.   Mr. Deavers, a high school physical education teacher, usually has from 50 to 60 students in each class. He often has difficulty in checking roll and sometimes doesn't know who is present and who is absent from class. He realizes that he needs to institute a new plan. What would be the best procedure for him to institute?

(A) Have students gather on the bleachers, call each student's name and have each student respond, then put a check on the roll sheet.

(B) Divide students into ten groups of five or six, appoint a leader, and have the leaders report absences.

(C) Design a chart with ten rows, assign each student a specific place to stand or sit at the beginning of class, then check roll visually using the chart.

(D) Have students start an activity, then visually identify each student and put checks on the roll sheet.

The correct response is (C). The question asks for an effective method of taking roll that doesn't detract from class. Choice (C) is the best option. By assigning each student a specific place to stand, Mr. Deavers can quickly check attendance, in a method similar to the one he would use in assigning seats in a classroom. If teachers use seating charts in the classroom, this method would be familiar to the students. By requiring students to take this position immediately, he can also assign students to lead warmup exercises while he checks roll, thus making good use of the time. Choice (A) is a poor choice. Although it might increase his awareness of who is absent and who is present, this method wastes instructional time. Also, without organization, one student may answer for another. Choice (B) may be effective, but it assumes that all student leaders will be present each day and that they will all be responsible. A teacher who wants to teach responsibility may use a similar system, but would need to teach responsibility to the student leaders and to have assistant leaders as a backup. Choice (D) is almost impossible if the students are engaged in an activity that requires movement. It would be very time-consuming as well, distracting the teacher's attention from the activity itself.

Chapter 9

The Professional Environment

The preparation of the teacher—in his or her content field as well as in the understanding of youth, the personal experiences that the teacher brings to the classroom, and the attitude toward the teaching assignment all affect the quality of instruction a teacher is able to deliver. Equally critical to the success of the teacher, however, is his or her ability to fit into the school environment, to be able to relate to the parents and community, and to interpret and support the regulations governing New York teachers as well as the ethical concerns associated with the procedures involved in educating youth. The teacher's growth, as a professional, is nurtured by all of these contacts and experiences.

Often individuals are reminded that "no man is an island." Teachers are especially vulnerable to the vital role of interacting positively and successfully with others. The students in the classroom, the teacher across the hall, the principal of the building, the fellow teachers on special assignment committees and teams, the campus technology expert—these are just a few of the immediate continuing contacts the teacher must deal with on a regular basis. Equally important are the interactions with parents and community members. In addition to the teacher's awareness of his or her personal strengths and needs, the varied professional contacts, as well as communications with people in the community, can assist the teacher in selecting the best professional growth opportunities and experiences to reinforce, enrich, and expand the teacher's skills and knowledge.

Even in the days of the one-room school, teachers had to be sensitive to the expectations of parents and community members. Often these expectations focused upon the social behavior of the teacher as much as the effectiveness of the teacher in the classroom. Since teachers often roomed with a family in the community, close observation of personal behavior was a simple matter. Community members generally agreed upon the rather rigid code of behavior deemed suitable for someone to whom the community entrusted its children each day.

Today, such agreement is not as clearly defined. The teacher's role is still one often considered a model of what should be, no matter how unrealistic the role model may be. For this reason, the teacher's skill in communicating with the parents and leaders of the community is vitally important. The success of conducting conferences with parents, of sending response-seeking notes or telephone messages to parents, and of assisting parents in working out positive study support techniques, for students are all based upon the parents' trust in the teacher and, therefore, in the teacher's recommendations and referrals.

In addition to this concept of the teacher's personal responsibility and effectiveness in working with parents, the teacher needs to understand the environment students experience when they are not at school. In the home, with friends at neighborhood parks or recreation centers, or "hanging out" at the mall—wherever the student is outside of school hours will affect the student when he or she returns to school. Perhaps no other factor can affect the role of the students more than what goes on in their lives during the hours spent with peers, especially when the students are congregating without parent or other adult supervision.

Other members of the community can become strong allies of the effective teacher. The school today, as a center of activity in the community and increasingly as an unpopular factor since it determines the increased tax base on homes within the community, is a focal point of interest to all members of the community—not just those with children or grandchildren attending the school. Patrons of the school district want their "money's worth," be it a school with competitive test scores (equating to a good "product" in the business world), a seat on the school board or at least a voice at the next school board meeting, or a positive contact with a member of the teaching staff—you. This more visible interaction today is two-fold, however, and can bring many benefits to the teacher. The education specialist at the computer store can assist the teacher in understanding the working of established programs and in locating and using software for the classroom. The librarian, always an active friend of the classroom teacher, can share which authors are the popular ones for the summer readers of any age group. Likewise, the video rental clerks will know the hot movies for the various ages. Community workers in specialized fields, such as involvement with drugs or gangs, provide much information for the teacher who has just moved into the community as a workplace.

The teacher, united with the various members of the community, becomes a stronger figure, one who is not only providing classroom instruction but also providing assistance to the students in other ways to be better equipped to meet the demands of life.

Finally, in order to fulfill the role delegated to today's educator, the teacher needs to be aware of the many roles to be enacted while under contract to teach. The local campus and district will have specific expectations for each employee. These expectations will involve matters of legal responsibility as well as ethical considerations. Often the expectations are clearly delineated in a teacher's handbook at the beginning of the school year; however, some expectations are more traditional and can only be learned by observing experienced teachers' behavior. Finding a person who is open and well-informed about the practices and attitudes expected of the professional staff members on the campus is a wise step for a beginner. Such a person may be the teacher across the hall, a counselor, or a secretary.

State rules and regulations associated with education often relate to information that a teacher becomes aware of—matters concerning the privacy of student records, the responsibility to report signs of child abuse, student depression and self-destructive attitudes, special needs of some student populations, equal rights of all children regardless of race, religion, or sexual orientation. The teacher needs to know how to help and how to get help; also, the teacher must be aware of occasions when he or she cannot help but must make referrals for specialized assistance for the student.

Within the work environment, the teacher will constantly be facing decision-making situations that extend well beyond the lesson plans for the day or week. Knowing potential roles, utilizing the various sources of available support services, and exercising communication skills effectively to bring the greatest benefits to the students, the teacher clearly demonstrates an in-depth understanding of the teaching environment.

THE TEACHER'S PERSONAL TRAITS

Knowing one's self is an essential characteristic of a successful person in any area of life. The qualities enabling the teacher to work well in a work situation that is often described by others as stressful or boring are the same qualities that make a businessperson or salesperson successful. The teacher, like the banker or clerk, will never be isolated from others and must use a variety of personal interactive skills on a daily basis. Working with students in the classroom, sharing curriculum ideas in a grade-level meeting, projecting a positive image as a well-trained professional who is planning successfully for his or her assignment, or responding maturely to constructive evaluative comments from a supervisor—in every scenario, the excelling teacher demonstrates certain personal traits that project a strong self image: confidence, competence, dedication, enthusiasm, and a sense of humor. These are all traits that cannot be taught through a teacher education program. They are the result of the experiences of the individual during the developmental stages of his or her life and prepare the individual for a successful career in the area chosen.

Teachers are aware of their personal traits. They feel confident of the skills and content acquired during the years of training to become a teacher. Knowing various ways to modify classwork for a student with special needs or how to bring a highly excited class back to a calmer mode of operation instills a feeling of security in the teacher, a sense of being in control that communicates itself to the students without repetitious reprimand or threat.

The teacher's competence in handling the unexpected as well as the routine is clearly observable, as a professional efficiency of being in control of the situation is demonstrated. Enjoying work with both students and fellow professionals, the self-confident teacher is positive about what is going on in the classroom and meeting with staff members. Enthusiasm is often contagious. When the teacher is excited about the students' work, both younger and older students will respond similarly. Finally, finding laughter a healthy outlet, the teacher shares a sense of humor with the students. Even though students may groan at a teacher's puns, their acceptance of the educator's enjoyment of language will be a further linkage in building a positive working environment in the classroom.

In addition to the personal traits that denote a strong self-image, other traits of the individual identify the person who will have the greatest chance for success in a teaching career. A high energy level is most valuable. The apparently tireless teacher can match, perhaps even surpass, the energy level of the students. A well-organized teacher can achieve equally as much, however, since a plan of accomplishing the endless amount of work also brings about successful outcomes. Teachers described as successful are also understanding. Instead of always doing the talking, they find time to listen to students. In the fine art of communicating, too frequently the vital role of being a good listener is sometimes overlooked. When students have problems, an open attitude and a warmth of response can help the student to work out the solution needed.

Of course, sometimes students misbehave and do not respond to the initial efforts of the teacher to bring the student back into acceptable behavioral patterns. Consistency in disciplining students assists the teacher in promoting students' positive behavior. When students who have dropped out of the class focus know a teacher's warning will be followed by action, the students are much more likely to join the classwork as requested.

One trait that serves as a valuable adjunct to all other traits listed may elude many teachers. This is the trait of creativity. Although some teacher preparation programs promote training in innovative methodology, many teachers either lack time or the type of thinking skill that brings about fresh ideas for the classroom. Good interpersonal skills can come to the rescue as the less original teacher can observe and in various ways emulate ideas from other teachers who tend to be more innovative.

The preceding discussion has mentioned traits and skills to develop if they are not apparent in a teacher's personality. One other group of traits remains—behaviors to avoid. The negative traits of griping, carelessness, belittling others, or giving up on a student or the job assignment are the special afflictions released from Pandora's box just to plague teachers. These energy-draining traits can also be contagious; therefore, stay away from anyone who exhibits signs of infection. Examine your behaviors and attitudes occasionally, working toward ever greater success in your teaching assignment.

TEAM RESPONSIBILITIES IN TEACHING

A second aspect of this competency concerns the teacher's role in serving as a member of a team. Increasingly, teachers find their work affected by the need to coordinate with other teachers—in planning, in delivering the lessons, and in evaluating students and curriculum. Many of the personal traits that make a successful classroom teacher will also enable a teacher to work well with other professionals on various assignments and in self-developed team projects.

Perhaps the strongest team of teachers is one made up of two or more teachers or support staff members, all of whom possess the five basic traits of successful individuals discussed: confidence, competence, dedication, enthusiasm, and a sense of humor. The team members complement one another, sharing the responsibility and fully enjoying their work. Humor responds to humor; therefore, each team member especially appreciates his or her teammates' lack of griping and working toward the final goal—the improved learning of the students.

A successful team often allows the teachers to be more innovative. The immediate feedback of positive, respected peers ensures a teacher of his or her decision-making wisdom. Bringing about change—perhaps the primary charge of a team—can be constantly monitored through more than one perspective.

Even if the team members are not equally strong in the personal traits that create a masterful educator, the teachers can learn to share their strengths for the benefit of the students. When a new teacher is assigned to work with a clearly outstanding professional, the opportunity for the less experienced teacher to move along more rapidly in developing successful strategies and polishing skills of instructing occurs.

TEAMING ASSIGNMENTS

Teaming assignments may be for a variety of purposes. Among the more frequently occurring patterns are the following:

1. Classroom instruction—Teachers may be teaching together for the entire day or for specified periods of time. Usually the class section is larger than the class of a single teacher. The teachers may have the same certification or compatible areas of specialization such as social studies, reading, and language arts.

2. Special needs adaptation for the classroom—Since the students who once were placed in special education classes are now integrated into regular classes of study, the classroom teacher becomes a working partner with the specialist. Ways to modify instruction for specific students are discussed and assistance provided by the expert.

3. Curriculum related committees—Teachers and curriculum specialists work together to evaluate the existing curriculum and plan the changes needed. Often, the teacher tries new materials in the classroom and reports to the team about the effectiveness of the new ideas or resources. One annual committee of this nature is the textbook selection committee. Different teachers review and recommend for adoption a specific textbook each year. Teachers may work on a committee for the new textbook in their own subject area or on the district committee, making the final recommendations for all textbook areas to be selected during a single year.

4. Site-based management planning—One of the newer strategies used in schools, committees to assist in making decisions about the management of the school are made up of a variety of staff members. Curriculum, discipline, school regulations, and other concerns affecting the total campus environment become the focus of each meeting, and the teacher's role is often representative of many other teachers on the staff. Meeting time each month may easily total several hours.

5. Special committees—From the calendar committee for the next school year to the cheer committee concerned with providing appropriate contact with ill or bereaved peers, various concerns necessitate that groups of staff members work together. Most of these assignments require only several hours of meeting time, but a demanding issue can extend that time estimate.

In each of the assignments for working together, teachers have the opportunity to demonstrate their positive skills in communicating with others. Often, as in teaching, listening becomes a vital key to the successful outcome of a team meeting.

PROFESSIONAL GROWTH

As a skilled educator, leader, mediator, and listener, the self-aware teacher can identify shaky or worn traits in order to bring about more effective results in work assignments. Some teachers need to develop new traits to provide greater potential for success in certain work-related encounters. Educational practice allows for this improvement in skills through the staff development programs required for all teachers throughout the year. More and more teachers are able to help design these in-service training sessions so that their specific needs are more adequately met. One major committee assignment of teachers is the planning of staff development within a district on specified days. Sessions that enhance the individual's knowledge in a content field are balanced with other opportunities, such as those that work to improve individuals' interpersonal skills, better understanding of technology, or wider knowledge of the available resources within the community.

In addition to required in-service meetings, many teachers continue advanced study at nearby universities. Many of these courses specialize in the needs expressed by the teachers on a campus. For instance, if several teachers are pursuing gifted and talented certification, a university may bring the required courses to a district campus for the teachers' convenience. Individual teachers often belong to the national organizations of their certified area. The reading of the professional magazines of such organizations and the attendance at state and/or national conferences also provide a chance for gaining new content knowledge and strategies of instruction.

The teacher's growth as a professional is never ending. New ideas, new technology, changing roles—all demand continual renewal. The resulting educator, the fully actualized teacher, leads the way.

DEVELOPING A POSITIVE RELATIONSHIP WITH PARENTS EARLY

The teacher will often have a more difficult time getting to know parents today than one or two generations ago. Often parents' attitudes toward becoming involved with the school have changed. This change is not necessarily due to disinterest but to different conditions in life-style. Many parents work outside the community and have less time and energy to develop an interest in the school than formerly. Also, often, a single parent is the sole responsibility for the child's immediate welfare. The single parent, working to provide the necessities for the family, has little free time. Gone also are the days when many parents, themselves, attended their child's school and even studied under some of the same teachers. Greater mobility in the population and the resulting community instability in both population and shared values have taken their toll as well as have the other factors mentioned. What can the teacher do to establish not only a friendly relationship with the parents but a relationship that has developed a degree of mutual trust and respect?

At the beginning of the school year, before an educational or behavioral problem arises with a student, the teacher can make positive contact with all parents. This contact may be by a written note, telephone call, or even a home visit in the late afternoon if the building administrator is not opposed to such visits. During the visit, the teacher can mention several of the immediate content and skill areas that will be studied during the next five or six weeks. He can ask the parent to describe the student's general attitude toward school, the successes of previous years of study, and special interests of the student, and the child's comments about the beginning of the new year. Finally, the teacher can ask the parents about their goals for their children during the coming year.

PARENT/TEACHER COMMUNICATION

One of the most helpful resources for the teacher to establish continuing dialogue with the parents is to maintain an informal journal for all parental communications. Recording what the teacher brings to the meeting as well as ideas and attitudes the teacher leaves with can assist the teacher in making each contact non-repetitive and highly personalized.

If the teaching load of the teacher is too great for the one-on-one approach described, the teacher can try to set up meetings of small groups of parents immediately after school or at another convenient time. Working parents sometimes like to come in early before school in the morning; others can come during a lunch break where teacher and parents "brownbag" in the teacher's room at noon if no other place to meet is available. The group of four or five parents, although not as individualized in focus, is still small enough for the teacher to begin building a sense of cooperation and respect with each, essential in problem intervention or solution which may be required later in the school year. The initial attitude of the parents' role is one of a partnership, focused upon the child's well-being and awareness of the classroom objectives and strategies. Any step that avoids future adversarial parental response, almost always a negative base of communication, can only serve as a benefit for the teacher.

One concern of most parents is the quality of instruction occurring in the classroom. When the teacher can share his or her goals and indicate a continuity of study from day to day and week to week, parents respond positively. After the initial parental contact, teachers can begin a pattern of sending home papers for parents to see. A variety of papers—those showing strengths as well as weaknesses of students—should be selected for this step. If a student begins to show repeated weaknesses in work or attitude toward work, calling the parent for a conference is indicated.

Before the conference, the teacher needs to gather all of the materials needed—examples of the student's work to indicate the problem(s) under focus, the record of the student's daily effort if failure to accomplish assignments is the problem or part of it, anecdotes of misbehavior if the problem is one related to discipline, attempts made to change the negative performance of a student, and certainly suggestions for solving the problem. The teacher should always allow time for the parent to present his or her perspective of the situation as well as the child's attitude about the problem. Sometimes, having the student present becomes a useful strategy, especially if the student has been omitting part of the story when talking about it at home.

The end of any conference should include writing down the actions each participant—teacher, parent, and student—will take to help improve the situation. A tentative date for meeting again, or at least communicating between teacher and parent, should also be set before the participants leave. Within a few days, the teacher should try to find opportunity to provide feedback to both the parent and the student about the matter discussed, especially if improvement of a negative situation can be noted.

As students progress through school, their parents generally tend to have less interest in pursuing conferences with teachers. The parent of an elementary child is much more responsive to the teacher's initial overture to meet than the parent of a secondary student. Sometimes the parent has been to countless meetings with educators over the years, and the student is still exhibiting the same undesirable traits. The parent in this case tends to give up on helping the child. The secondary teachers, too, are often not as enthusiastic about contacting and arranging meetings with all students' parents. The secondary teacher, with well over 100 students, has a real scheduling dilemma compared to the elementary teacher. Often limiting meetings to parents of students with difficulty becomes the major effort of the secondary teacher. Whatever effort the teacher makes, however, is to his or her credit.

RESPONDING TO NONRESPONSIVE PARENTS

Parents of some students, invited repeatedly to meet with a teacher, never seem to be able to arrange a time when they can come. The scheduling problem may be a genuine one, since many parents work long hours some distance from the home or hold more than one job. Sometimes when parents do attend a meeting, they are tired or distracted by even more stressful personal problems than the school situation.

When the teacher receives no response to an invitation for parent conferencing, a notation of the effort to make contact on a specific date should be made in the teacher's journal. Another attempt can be made six or eight weeks later. If a parent in this group does come to a school visitation program or is met informally in the community, the teacher should make every effort to show his or her pleasure at meeting the student's parent. Ideally, the teacher will have a recent anecdote about the child or some specific positive learning comment to make to the parent.

Certainly, these parents should also be included in any note sent to parents about projects or other classroom activities. Since these notes will usually be Xeroxed, a handwritten line or two is easily added to the nonresponding parents' notes. As always, the assurance to the parent that the child's educational welfare and personal well-being are continuing major concerns of the teacher will reinforce the goal of this competency.

LEARNING ABOUT THE COMMUNITY

The first staff development for new teachers in a school district is often based upon providing insight into the make-up of the community. Many larger districts have developed videotapes about their communities. Information to help the teacher adjust to both a new employment situation as well as possibly a new personal residential and shopping area is most vital. Sometimes, the district school busses load up the teachers, and a tour of the immediate neighborhood of the school itself is viewed firsthand, often with helpful commentary by an experienced professional. If such orientation is not provided, the teacher should solicit an informal tour of the community, preferably by someone who has lived there several years. If other new teachers have joined the staff, together they may solicit a guide from the established staff members—a teacher, a secretary, a para-professional. Sometimes a volunteer from the organized parents' group of a campus may have the orientation of new staff members as one of their goals.

Chamber of Commerce information can always provide data about the community. This public relations material is important since it projects the image of the community that the community values. Directly or indirectly reflected therein will be the expectation for the school. Real estate brochures are equally informative. Are the schools used as an attracting agent for people considering moving into the general area? What positive factors in the community are used to lure prospective home buyers or apartment leasers? If the new teacher is planning to buy or lease living accommodations within the community, calling upon a real estate agent to learn more about the area as well as to assist in locating potential residential areas will be useful.

Once the students have started school, the teacher may ask the students to talk about their community. Their perceptions, although certainly reflecting their age biases, still provide insights not otherwise available to a new teacher. Perhaps the teacher will find several students who will spend an hour or two one afternoon or Saturday morning touring the community and pointing out special places—the neighborhood library, nearby public parks, shopping areas, any favorite hang-outs of the teenagers. If the teacher is an elementary school teacher, a parent, with one or two of the students, may provide the tour.

Finally, becoming a patron of a few businesses within the community can serve as a source of information about the community as well as its expectations of and attitudes toward the school. The teacher can take cleaning to a local cleaning establishment or shop at a grocery store or drugstore, exchanging a few words about the school with the persons who provide service at such establishments. Visiting the local library and talking with the librarian always will provide help as well. If the teacher attends a local church, certainly talking to church workers can be very informative.

Learning as much as possible about the community that a school serves will assist the teacher in numerous ways throughout the teaching assignment in that community. The teacher, at the same time, may be building allies upon whom to call if a need occurs.

UTILIZING STRENGTHS OF THE COMMUNITY

Every community will have established sources of support for the school. Parents' groups such as the Parents and Teachers Association, the Dads Club, the Band Boosters, the Sports Club, and dozens of other groups have been formed to provide both financial and philosophical support. These groups are often searching for projects to undertake as part of their yearly program of goals.

Retired teachers in the community may provide information that can be invaluable to the new teacher. Finding out the names of respected former teachers can be accomplished by asking other teachers or by seeking names from parents and students. In some cases, the retired teachers have not only advice but also substantial teaching suggestions and even materials for an earnest new teacher in search of assistance.

Using the community as subject matter for writing experiences can provide additional information for the teacher's use while teaching the students to do a variety of activities to gather primary and secondary information about their home area. Students can research the history of the area in several ways. A very young student can interview and tape older members of the community as they talk about the past. Often the elders welcome an invitation to visit a class and talk about their earliest days in the area and retell the stories that their parents may have told them. Gathering letters, photographs, magazines, maps, toys, and other artifacts of days gone by can provide primary documentation that is often quite interesting to students and also to parents when displayed at open house.

Sometimes special interest groups within the community welcome the opportunity to share aspects of their interest with a class. A local story-telling group may visit a class and demonstrate techniques to make a story's retelling truly exciting for the listeners; a writing group may judge creative writing of the students and offer tips for expressive writing. Parents will often attend elementary classes and share work experiences to begin the students' awareness of the world of work. More formal Career Days, frequently planned on secondary campuses, utilize a variety of local people to talk about their vocational choices and respond to students' questions.

All subject areas can find useful activities centered in the community to teach the content more effectively and realistically. Teaching early stages of reading, the teacher may request students to bring in slogans and advertisements associated with popular breakfast cereals. Often students who do not formally read have become acquainted with such sayings. Sharing them with the class becomes a stimulating activity for everyone. Older language learners can use the community for a variety of language study assignments. Finding errors in spelling or mechanics in the newspaper or on commercial signs, defining the methods used for naming streets in various residential areas of town, collecting the phrases on signs posted about the town—all make reading a real-life activity, not one merely restricted to a textbook in a classroom.

In social studies and literary study especially, as heroes and heroic values are discussed, the teacher can use the community patterns as well to identify the contemporary local heroes and heroic values. Open discussion of differences in opinion and styles of dress and haircut, conducted in a nonjudgmental environment, allows for the variety of values often found in any community today. Living safely and sanely together is surely an accepted value promoted by most school curricula and cannot be postponed until problems do arise.

COPING WITH PROBLEMS IN THE COMMUNITY

Each community, along with the strengths that can be identified, will have deterrents to the educational process. Some of these negative aspects are not merely local problems but symptomatic of many communities today—drug and alcohol abuse, unemployment, heavy mobility within the community, and crime and violence, especially as reflected in gang conflicts. Accompanied by the apparent apathy of adults in regards to the educational process, the toll of these problems upon the effectiveness of the schools can be heavy, for students of any age may be affected adversely by one or more of these conditions of contemporary society.

Often when a school exists in an environment affected by one or more of the societal ills of today, the in-service programs for teachers will focus on the relevant problems obviously affecting the student population. The teacher will learn ways to help students in the classroom and sources of even greater assistance for students through these staff training sessions. The teacher's good judgment will always be required, however, to know to what extent he or she can help with a pervasive problem area. Working at intervention, before a problem area becomes a critical factor affecting the educational process in the classroom, is always a wise course of action.

Young people's familiarity with drugs and alcohol begins very early in some communities. Often the students have had more actual contact knowledge of substance abuse than a teacher has had, whether the contact is with the child or through a family member of a child. Children as young as nine or ten have become addicted to illegal drugs or alcohol. Certainly by middle school age, most students have had some personal involvement with the pain that these twin false panaceas bring.

Another major factor creating an unstable family structure is the unemployment situation. More and more adults are finding changes in their work necessary. Finding new employment opportunities is seldom easy, and the time during which a parent is searching for work can be most stressful upon all family members. The greater mobility of families throughout the United States is often related to employment changes. Certainly as children move to new schools in new communities, adjustment to a different school can create a problem. Teachers need to find out what a new student has been studying in each content area and try to build upon that familiar base. Records from the former campus often take months to be transferred and may be of little help if the student has moved frequently.

Any community is now vulnerable to greater crime and violence within its boundaries. Such an atmosphere will affect the youth and, therefore, the school environment. Not uncommon today is the requirement for students to enter a school building by passing through a metal detector, one attempt to keep weapons out of the school building. If the community is unfortunate enough to have gangs attracting the teenagers, the rival attitudes and behaviors cannot be blocked out of the building as easily as knives or guns. Staff training in multicultural understanding will assist the new teachers in understanding the characteristics of different ethnic groups. In the classroom, intervention may be successful by studying literary works based upon prejudice. Class discussion may defuse potentially volatile situations in real life as students read about conflicts between rival groups, as in *Light in the Forest*, *When the Legends Die*, *The Chosen*, *Flowers for Algernon*, or other novels based upon religious or ethnic prejudices. The classics can also offer groups in conflict, such as in *Romeo and Juliet*, *A Tale of Two Cities*, or *Animal Farm*. Actual historical incidents, as well as contemporary news stories, provide other examples to discuss in class. The teacher, making good judgment calls, can successfully intervene before a problem occurs in class.

The effective teacher can make a difference, even when the problems in the community seem insurmountable. Using the time and talent available, the teacher can address the problems that seem to affect his or her students in an appropriate way in the classroom and be familiar with sources of more extensive help available on campus and in the community.

THE TEACHER AS A CURRICULUM WORKER

One job that seems never to be completed is the preparation of curriculum guides for grade level and/or content areas of instruction. Evaluation of the existing curriculum is an on-going process by teachers, and the major revision of curriculum is usually a major focus every four or five years, especially as new textbooks are adopted and other resources purchased or made available. Special concepts often become fashionable trends in education. During the last 20 years, all grade levels and content areas have had major revision in curricula to include such matters as writing across the content area, reading in the content area, career education, holistic scoring of writing, inquiry study, multicultural concerns, strands of instruction for gifted and talented students, portfolio assessment, and the ever-popular basic skills instruction. One buzz phrase in the late 1990s, for instance, is values training, not to be confused with the values clarification emphasis of the 1970s. Since the home and community may have lost effectiveness as a strong values support system, the school has been automatically selected as the agent to maintain the values for the society. Whatever the reason for curriculum revision, the individual teacher will be affected.

Of course, since the teachers are the ones who use the curriculum, developing it should be a welcomed assignment. Sometimes districts do allocate in-service time for this purpose; other districts pay teachers for working on curriculum during the summer. With the recent financial crunch, however, some teachers are having to work on the curriculum development assignment whenever they can on their own time. (In reality, no amount of time provided, or budget allocated, has ever been sufficient to provide adequate compensation for the time and effort dedicated teachers will spend in rewriting curriculum.)

Associated with the curriculum work will be the teacher's public presenting of the newly revised curriculum to groups of interested adults. Often an overview of the work is expected by the school board of the district. An active curriculum committee of the local Parent-Teacher Association, a group that may have been involved in earlier stages of revision work, will want to hear about the end product. When a school district has developed innovative, exciting ideas, professional groups will often request a presentation at area or state conferences. The dedicated teacher, again, is the one most familiar with the development and specific working ideas of the new curriculum.

THE TEACHER AS A SPECIALIST

Each teacher has specific certification that defines the areas of assignment he or she expects to receive. This area of specialization will not be addressed at this time. The concern of the teacher as a specialist relates to the teacher's assignment to areas for which he or she is not trained and has little or no interest or skill.

Two generations ago, teachers were often assigned out of their field and frequently stayed in such a teaching assignment for extended periods of time. The current trend is to make teachers' assignments within their certification specialties but to require of every teacher the ability to handle instructional focus for special areas that cross all disciplines. Over the last several years, instructional concepts that overlap subject areas have included drug education, career awareness, reading and writing in the content areas, and values reinforcement. Staff development sessions will focus upon these special expectations of every teacher.

Another specialist area affecting the regular teacher in the late 1990s concerns students formerly designated as special education students. Currently, many such previously segregated students are being re-entered into mainstream classes. The regular classroom teacher has students, therefore, who have previously been taught primarily by special education teachers. The regular teacher must learn to offer modifications of instruction for these students and maintain a record of the various techniques used to meet the students' special needs. Modification may be as simple as allowing more time on a timed activity or accepting oral testing in place of written assessment. However, the teacher must have several strategies for teaching each unit of work and make available to students the method by which the student best learns.

Other areas of specialization expected of the teacher may concern special responsibilities to accompany the regular teaching assignment. Being offered a job may be contingent on the teacher's acceptance of a coaching assignment, although the teacher had not been seeking a coaching position. Serving as a sponsor of a school organization or activity group may also be expected of many teachers. As sponsor of the cheerleaders, the teacher will have hours outside of the regular school day to direct and supervise the practice of the cheerleaders and to attend school functions requiring the cheerleaders' performance. As sponsor of the National Honor Society, directing the process of selecting new members and planning the induction ceremony may be pleasant experiences. Of course, responding to angry parents whose sons and daughters were not selected for the prestigious group can be less satisfying.

Teacher education programs attempt to keep up with the reality of assignments met by new teachers, trying to prepare the teachers for whatever they meet. The diversity of schools and school districts, however, account for sometimes surprising job descriptions facing the teacher with a contract offer.

THE TEACHER AND VALUES IN THE CLASSROOM

Reference has been made to the emphasis upon values instruction occurring in many schools throughout New York in the late 1990s. Not only must the teacher be prepared to support the philosophy of his or her school district in regard to this matter, but also the teacher must be prepared to interact appropriately with the students and parents when certain topics like censorship or sex education become a concern.

Each campus will have an approved approach to values education. The teacher should always work within these guidelines. New York school boards are showing an increased acceptance of character building strategies and expect the teacher to promote the human qualities deemed as admirable. Generally these qualities, once strongly supported by all facets of communities across the state, especially the home and the church, concern the traits of a good, law-abiding citizen and decent human being. The model of self-discipline and hard work, once traits identified with the head of a family, now may be exhibited as a worthy model for some students only by the teacher.

The teaching of values may be best achieved as students and teacher discuss pertinent events in their everyday lives or in their reading for school. The media's tendency to provide sensational coverage of well-known sports figures, politicians, and business leaders in the news brings the ugliest of human motives and behavior to everyone's attention. Appropriate class discussion, carefully moderated and directed toward a greater depth of understanding human nature, can help students struggle with a public hero's or heroine's fall from grace. The stories read in class, or the events recounted from history, offer equally valid opportunities for discussion.

The whole concept of censorship is another aspect of values interchange that a teacher may meet. Even if a teacher limits reading to the state-adopted textbooks, critics of some materials or ideas within these textbooks may be challenged by some parents. A district committee for dealing with problems of censorship may be in effect, and the teacher's responsibility will end once the problem is submitted to the committee. Complaints from parents are generally sincere, directed by their concerns for their own children. Sometimes, however, organized groups exert pressure to remove certain reading from the classroom. In recent years, censorship hearings in New York have reviewed complaints ranging from Shirley Jackson's short story "The Lottery" to the children's fairy tale "Rumpelstiltzkin," from Bram Stoker's *Dracula* to the study of classical Greek mythology. Whenever a matter of censorship arises, the teacher should inform the school administrator promptly and follow the district guidelines for such matters.

Although the problems that are related to sex education are generally limited to teachers of health education or biology, all teachers need to be informed of the district policies regarding this potentially controversial issue. Even very young students are now exposed to early sexual information and even actual experience. Surveys indicate that many middle school students have had intimate relationships of a sexual nature. Each teacher's situation will be different; therefore, teachers need to determine before a situation arises (1) how to handle essays or poems making direct reference to sexual matters, (2) how to help students who have earnest questions of a sexual nature, and (3) how much discussion to allow in the classroom on the subject when it relates to the current study.

THE TEACHER AS A LEADER

The major New York pattern of decision making on school campuses in the late 1990s is one based upon site-based management. The individual teacher may, therefore, have a leadership role early in his or her career. In site-based management, a team of professionals on the campus discusses the needs of the campus, makes recommendations to accomplish these needs, and evaluates the resulting actions taken. As a member of the team, the teacher may lead an inquiry or information-gathering committee, reporting the findings to the other team members—fellow teachers, a school administrator, support staff members, parents, and students. As with many other responsibilities undertaken by the teacher, this leadership role often requires after-hours attendance at meetings and offers no remuneration. The days of the "moonlighting" teacher seem to belong to the past.

Larger campuses are usually departmentalized. Teachers work together for various purposes, organized under a chairperson. Sometimes the role of chairperson may extend over many years; other patterns limit the role to a two- or three-year term of duty. The major budget responsibility for the department is the chairperson's. Each grade level on larger campuses may also have a grade-level chairperson. A new teacher can surprisingly find himself or herself named as the grade-level chairperson, serving as a spokesperson for this grade level.

A completely different area of leadership expected of the teacher is as a participant in the professional organizations of the teacher's certification and assignment areas. Area, regional, state, and national organizations service their teachers in various ways, offering displays of new books and other resources for the instructional area as well as workshops and conferences for teachers of the same discipline or teaching interest. Many of these meetings are held on weekends so that teaching responsibilities will not be interrupted.

THE TEACHER AND LEGAL ISSUES

A fundamental expectation of the school board hiring a teacher is that this individual will be well-informed on the legal issues affecting teaching and always work in compliance with them. Staff development sessions based upon legal requirements for educators will be offered to teachers, and the teacher's district or campus handbook will itemize these concerns.

One of the major concerns of all teachers should be the safety and welfare of their students. Thus, students are not left without supervision while on the campus during the school day. The daily appearance of a student should be noted. Any indication of child neglect or physical abuse must be reported promptly to the principal. More subtle is the alarm revealed by a child's written or oral language. Such evidence of a disturbed state of mind, especially one that could represent suicidal tendencies, should be reported at once.

In working with students in a class, the teacher must be sure to work with each in a manner that shows respect. Certainly, prejudicial treatment due to a student's religious beliefs, race, or sexual orientation is never acceptable in the classroom. The teacher is responsible as well for the unbiased atmosphere within the classroom during class discussion and study. Sexist language or harassment by the teacher or by students is intolerable.

The confidentiality of a student's records, including his or her current performance in a teacher's classroom, is also a protected right by law. Since teachers have access to the permanent records of each student, they must be careful to whom they talk about these records. Idle chatter in the teachers' lounge or over lunch with fellow professionals is never appropriate or legal. Likewise, a teacher cannot discuss a student's performance record with adults other than the student's own parents or guardians.

The teacher is often referred to as a professional, a person who has completed advanced study and is deemed worthy of the highest standards of performance. Continually displaying the integrity associated with the teaching of young people, the new teacher can and will easily earn the respect of co-workers, parents, and teachers.

DRILL: THE PROFESSIONAL ENVIRONMENT

1. Jana Davis's eleventh-grade English classes will participate for the first time in a team research project with the American History classes in her high school. (Two teachers in social studies will be working on the project with Mrs. Davis, teaching the same students that she has in her

English classes.) The project indicates that the students' pre-writing activities will include reading a novel by an American author, researching the historical accuracy and/or relevance of the setting of the novel (time and place), and planning the paper.

After the paper has been written, each student's social studies teacher will evaluate the content accuracy, focusing upon the historical research. Mrs. Davis will focus her evaluation of the paper upon the analytical aspects of the novel as well as the written expression—style, mechanics, sentence structure, and usage.

During staff development time prior to the implementation of the research project, Mrs. Davis has asked the two American History teachers to meet with her. None of the teachers have ever worked on a team project like this one. Mrs. Davis has prepared a list of questions to initiate the meeting of the teachers on the team.

> I'd like us to plan the calendar for our research project so that we won't run into problems or be rushed in grading the final product. I know the students will need at least two weeks to read their novels. I have some other questions though before the project begins.

> What are some of the main points we should use to check progress during the pre-writing and planning stages? Should we both approve the thesis statement of the paper? How will our joint grading be reflected in the evaluation rubric? I know you must have some questions, too. I look forward to our getting together as soon as possible. Will our joint planning period next Tuesday be a good day for us to meet?

Jane Davis's questions are intended to

(A) show her interest in the team research project.

(B) indicate to the other two teachers her control of the project.

(C) demonstrate her willingness to accomplish the team project successfully.

(D) clarify the problems in the proposed team project.

The correct response is (C). Jana Davis has asked questions about concerns and decisions that will have a direct impact upon the success of the proposed project. By seeking clarification of these aspects of teaming with two of her teaching colleagues and inviting them to express their ideas and concerns, she will avoid problems and reduce stress associated with working across disciplines. Her pleasant, clearly worded note indicates confidence in working on this team project and a respect for the other two teachers. Her concern about the timing of various stages of the project indicates a good organizational sense and an awareness of the involved nature of the team project.

Incorrect answers for this question are (A), (B), and (D). Answer (A) expresses Mrs. Davis's interest in the project. Her note, however, indicates much more professional forethought than merely expressing an interest. She is ready to get to work in organizing the project and establishing vital points of agreement for the teaming teachers before the students become involved in their research. When she refers to an evaluation rubric, she demonstrates her professional knowledge of creative and meaningful ways to evaluate, especially a way that may be used by more than one evaluator working on the same product. Answer (B) expresses an attitude that is missing in the communication sent by Mrs. Davis. Her message to the teaming teachers is warm and open to input in determining the answers to considerations she mentions. Her capacity to lead is evident, but no strong overtone of seeking control has been expressed in her note. She speaks as an enthusiastic team member, one ready to contribute her time and talent to the joint venture. Answer (D) centers on clarifying problems with the proposed project. Mrs. Davis's questions and her positive tone indicate a willingness to solve potential problems before they actually appear, not accentuate them at this early stage of planning.

2. John Kelly, a fifth grade teacher, has been having many behavioral problems with a new student in his class, Bryan Underwood. During the four weeks Bryan has been enrolled, he has been unable to stay in his seat during class activities. He repeatedly speaks out during the middle of class to ask questions unrelated to the work underway. He disturbs other students with his aggressive behavior, often pushing or punching them. Mr. Kelly has called Bryan's mother and talked to her about his behavior. Mrs. Underwood, a single parent, has agreed to come before school to a meeting with Mr. Kelly about her son's behavior.

When Mrs. Underwood arrives for the conference, Mr. Kelly should greet her with which words?

(A) "I just don't know what I'm going to do with your son!"

(B) "Can you tell me why Bryan is so aggressive in my classroom? Has he exhibited these traits before?"

(C) "Mrs. Underwood, I think you have a real problem with your son."

(D) "Mrs. Underwood, let's see what we can come up with to help your son feel happier about his move to a new school."

The correct response is **(D)**. Mr. Kelly's response is an opening that establishes the shared responsibility of the teacher and the parent to help Bryan. Recognition of a possible cause of Bryan's behavior is given—his recent move from another school. The basic cause of his aggressive behavior is indicated as a factor not related to the parent's handling of her son. A positive tone has been used and, even though Mr. Kelly may not feel as optimistic about Bryan's change in behavior as his words sound, he is making no promises but is seeking support from Bryan's mother to help bring about the desired change. Mr. Kelly is inviting Mrs. Underwood to enter into a collaborative working relationship with him, having Bryan's welfare as the focus.

Incorrect answers for this question are (A), (B), and (C). Answer (A) expresses a negative tone about Bryan as well as the chances of changing Bryan's aggressive behavior. Mr. Kelly's words do not show the professional confidence that would be expected of an educator truly "in charge" of the situation. Mrs. Underwood, who may well be in need of help in managing her son, cannot be inspired to turn to Mr. Kelly for assistance. Answer (B) immediately places the responsibility upon Mrs. Underwood to explain her son's behavior. Before hearing from the professional educator about the classroom situation, she is asked to tell what is happening. Also, she is asked, rather bluntly, to tell about previous aggressive traits Bryan has exhibited.

Of course, we do not know the depth of the telephone conversation between Mr. Kelly and Mrs. Underwood, but if it was only an invitation to a conference, she is hardly ready to compare his current behavior, about which she may know little, to any prior aggressiveness of her son. Again, she cannot view her relationship with Mr. Kelly as a partnership, working to help Bryan. She feels more like a witness being cross-examined at her son's trial in court. Answer (C) initiates the conference with a negative tone. All of the blame is placed upon Mrs. Underwood. She has now become the criminal being charged. Little hope for a positive solution to the problem is indicated by Mr. Underwood's first words. Certainly, Mr. Underwood's direct assault hints at no mutual involvement of parent and teacher working together for the child's benefit, the major purpose of the conference. All of the wrong answers demonstrate how the lack of communication skills can get a parent conference off to a bad start and possibly doom the session to little positive outcome.

3. Carla Mendoza has signed a contract to teach in the Davistown Independent School District. She has just started teaching social studies and reading to seventh graders at the middle school. She had never visited Davistown until she went there for her initial interview. Now, a new resident as well as a new teacher, she is anxious to learn more about her community and the students she has met in her classes. She has driven around the school neighborhood and also shopped in the nearby mall. She has visited three churches but has not decided which one she will join.

    Which of the following activities will be most useful in helping Carla Mendoza learn more about her students, school, and community?

    (A) Attending a local gathering, such as a church meeting

    (B) Visiting the model homes in a new residential area opening soon near the school

    (C) Taking walks around the community to visit with community members, such as business owners, the librarian, residents, and policemen

    (D) Attending a get-acquainted meeting of new residents in her apartment complex

    The correct response is choice **(C)**. By walking through the community, Carla Mendoza observes first hand the characteristics of the community. She sees the influences which are brought into the classroom. She will also see the resources which can be used in the classroom. By speaking to a wide variety of people, she is better able to create an accurate picture of the community. Answer choice (A) will give Ms. Mendoza a good idea of the church member characteristics but it will not be representative of the entire population. Choice (B) may give Ms. Mendoza an image of the new members of the community but, once again, not a representative image of the entire community. Choice (D), attending a get-acquainted meeting may be of some personal benefit, but will acquaint her with only a minute portion of the community at large. As with choice (C), no other answer covers business, religious, educational, and recreational influences on her students.

4. Kate Tillerson is an art teacher at McGregor High School where she has taught for several years successfully. She is respected by her students as well as her fellow teachers. This year, the new Director of Instruction for the McGregor Independent School District has introduced several curriculum ideas, one of which is the concept of authentic assessment. All curriculum areas have had one or more staff development sessions on this concept. The idea will be incorporated into the curriculum as one of the strategies for assessment in each discipline and at each grade level.

Kate has just received a request from the Fine Arts Department chairperson to submit an example of a lesson involving authentic assessment. A central office form to complete the example accompanies the request along with a review of the authentic assessment concept, a model of a completed example, and a deadline for submitting teachers' samples.

Kate's general response to the entire focus on authentic assessment has been that all she does in her classroom is based upon authentic assessment philosophy. She really sees no need for making any changes in the curriculum guide or for preparing the assignment sent to her. On the other hand, Kate is an excellent teacher and generally cooperates in the various curriculum tasks requested of her. She has been a leader of staff development sessions within the district and has shared her innovative ideas with fellow professionals at both regional and state meetings of art educators.

Which of the following responses should Kate make to her departmental chairperson's request?

(A) Kate files the request under things to do and forgets about it.

(B) Kate writes a passionate letter in response to the Fine Arts Department chairperson's request, explaining how she feels about the proposed example of an authentic assessment in art. She sends a copy of this letter to her chairperson and also to the Director of Curriculum and takes no further action.

(C) Kate writes a passionate letter in response to the Fine Arts Department chairperson's request, explaining how she feels about the proposed example of an authentic assessment in art. Attached to the letter is a model unit of study Kate has used in her classes, including an authentic assessment project described in detail but not submitted on the form provided by the Director of Curriculum. Kate sends copies of these items to both her chairperson and the Director of Instruction.

(D) Kate completes an authentic assessment project idea on the form provided by her chairperson. She submits this idea with supplementary examples of students' projects photographed and a copy of the grading rubric returned to the students for each project photographed. She also sends a videotape of a student discussing the project he has submitted for the unit of study.

The correct response is **(D)**. Kate, as an effective teacher and respected professional in her school as well as beyond her district, realizes the intent of central office curriculum efforts is to raise the standards of instruction throughout the district. While Kate, as a team player in the educational process, may be performing at the highest level, other teachers need boosting. The work that Kate submits will probably be used as a model for other teachers throughout the district. The thoroughness of her response indicates that she will be invited to make other presentations at area and state professional meetings, perhaps on the topic of authentic assessment!

Choice (A) is an unprofessional action by Kate. Perhaps she is forgetful or lazy; she is certainly expressing rudeness and lack of cooperation by ignoring the request made of her and all teachers in the district. None of these characteristics represent a teacher who is effective in the classroom and highly respected by her students and peers. Choice (B) indicates that Kate, not forgetful or lazy, is unaware of or resentful of the role she plays as a curriculum developer within her teaching assignment. Her decision to write a "passionate letter in response" to the request is somewhat immature. The professional teacher who seriously questions a curricular approach from central office would discuss the situation reasonably, calmly, and privately with the new Director of Instruction.

Of course, the very fact that Kate feels she has been incorporating authentic assessment ideas in her teaching for some time indicates her valuing the concept. Should her role not be one of support to get other teachers to value authentic assessment as well? Choice (C) is incorrect because Kate, although showing support for the concept of authentic assessment, is still blocking the central office efforts to get some degree of uniformity in preparation of

NYSTCE – New York State Teacher Certification Exam

curriculum material. Again, her "passionate letter in response" to the request for an authentic assessment sample indicates poor judgment on Kate's part. Does the strong expression of her feelings indicate an independent nature or a rebel in regards to teamwork? Is her refusal to rewrite her model unit of study to conform to the district format laziness, a rejection of authority, or some other indicator of malcontent? The effective professional would find some other way to communicate her concerns if the provided format for the model of authentic assessment could be improved. Skill in communications is an essential quality in the educational process, and Kate has demonstrated a lack of understanding of vital components in effective communicating.

Chapter 10

Assessment of Teaching Skills-Performance (ATS-P)

INTRODUCTION

The New York State Teacher Certification Exam is divided into three separate sections: the Liberal Arts and Sciences Test (LAST), the Assessment of Teaching Skills-Written (ATS-W), and the Assessment of Teaching Skills-Performance (ATS-P). The Assessment of Teaching Skills-Performance (ATS-P) is required of candidates who have received a provisional teaching certificate and need a permanent certificate. Individuals who received a provisional certificate, on or after September 2, 1993, for early childhood/elementary education (PreK-6) or secondary (7-12) academic titles are required to attain a passing score on the ATS-P for permanent certification. The teaching performance is to be submitted on video. Candidates must complete the requirements for application and follow specific procedures for proper credit.

The ATS-P is a test used to assess the knowledge and application of teaching skills by an educator. The test was developed by the New York State Education Department (NYSED) and National Evaluation Systems, Inc. (NES) of Amherst, Massachusetts. A candidate for this test must be employed as a regular teacher in a public or nonpublic school with responsibilities between PreK and 12. The test assumes that a standard level of teaching ability is attained before submission of the video. Experience of at least two or more years is beneficial to the teacher. Candidates are reminded that the tapes should be submitted at least six months prior to the expiration of their provisional certificated to allow proper time for processing.

Candidates who are prepared for the test should register for the ATS-P through the application in the NYSTCE registration bulletin. The registration form can be completed and mailed at any time during the program year. This section of the exam does not adhere to registration or late registration deadlines.

When the registration form is received, NES will forward an ATS- P procedures manual within three weeks. The manual will provide the requirements and instructions for completion of an acceptable videotape. Other documents are also included, such as the Candidate Identification Form and the Content of Instruction Form. These forms must be completed by the candidate and a certified teacher.

REQUIREMENTS OF THE ATS-P

The ATS-P is a tool used to assess the teacher's knowledge and application of teaching skills. Several guidelines or objectives have been established in order to assess these skills. These skills are outlined by the NYSTCE in five objectives provided by the ATS framework listed below:

1. Comprehend principles and processes for creating and delivering lessons and implement this knowledge to achieve intended outcomes.

2. Comprehend various instructional methods and use this knowledge in various classroom situations.

3. Comprehend how motivational principles and practices can foster learner achievement and active involvement in learning.

4. Comprehend how to use a number of communication methods to foster student achievement and to create a feeling of trust and support in the classroom.

5. Comprehend how to structure and manage a classroom to foster a secure and productive learning environment.

These objectives should be obvious in the instructional procedures of the teacher. The candidate should also be aware of the goals of the New York State Education Department's *A New Compact for Learning,* which states that the teacher should encourage:

1. Students who are actively engaged in their learning

2. An environment in which every learner can succeed

3.   Numerous teaching methods that foster student mastery of desired outcomes

When assessing the videotapes, the teacher's ability to effectively incorporate the objectives and goals into a lesson will be expected. The candidates should show instructional strategies which promote learners to achieve. In order to view these situations, the videotape must include a minimum of ten minutes of non-whole-group instruction.

Non-whole-group instruction includes such activities as cooperative learning, small group problem solving and presentations, individual assignments, team-learning activities, and original student ideas. These activities will be used to reinforce the presented material. The environment created will support the active learning of the students. Students must be visible and empower themselves.

VIDEO TAPE REQUIREMENTS

Before a candidate starts the tape, he or she should be familiar with the objectives presented by the NYSTCE which were presented earlier. These objectives are the basis of the scoring of the tape.

The ATS-P requires that its procedures and guidelines be followed exactly as prescribed. If any procedure or guideline is not completed to the satisfaction of the ATS-P, the videotape will be considered "unscorable." If a tape is received "unscorable," the candidate will need to re-register and submit a new tape.

The following directions deal with the tape and camera set-up before actual filming begins. First, according to the ATS-P requirements, the tape must contain at least 20 minutes of recorded teaching, but not exceed 30 minutes in length. A tape shorter than twenty minutes will be rated "unscorable." A tape longer than thirty minutes will only have the first thirty minutes scored. All teaching which occurs after the thirty minute period will not be rated. Be sure that when the recording is being made that all teaching begins when the tape begins.

Second, the candidate must choose a class which is representative of his or her certification area. The teaching assignment should be public or nonpublic school PreK through 12 and must be the teacher's regular assignment. It must be a class in which the candidate has applied for permanent certification.

Third, of the thirty minutes which are videotaped, at least 10 minutes must represent non-whole group instruction. This includes instructional activities which are for the individual student, team learning, cooperative learning, student presentations and problem solving.

Fourth, the tape must be a standard, half-inch VHS videotape. The tape must be provided by the candidate and it is recommended that a new tape be used for clarity and accuracy of recording. The scoring will begin at the start of the recorded video.

Fifth, equipment used to make the recording must be provided by the candidate. This can be obtained through the school at which the candidate teaches or the candidate must make necessary arrangements. The recording may only be taken by one VHS recording camera. No extra or additional recording microphones or cameras may be used. The camera should be set on the Standard Play (SP) setting for recording and an AC power source should be used to ensure the quality of the recording.

Sixth, the camera should be set on a camera tripod to ensure the stability of the camera. This will help to ensure the visibility of the recording.

Seventh, at no time should the recording stop. The recording can not be edited. Any breaks or stops in the recording will render the tape "unscorable."

CAMERA SETUP

Before setting up the camera, the candidate should decide if the tape will be self-recorded or camera-operator recorded. A self-recorded video will be set up in a fixed location of the classroom on the tripod. It is recommended that the camera lens be positioned away from windows to ensure proper exposure. The fixed location of the camera will record only the teaching which occurs in the view of the lens. Also, only student activities which are in the field of view will be recorded. However, the microphone will record activities and students' verbal responses in the entire classroom.

With camera-operator recorded videotape, the candidate must have another teacher, teaching intern, a paraprofessional, a student, or member of the staff operate the camera. As in self-recording, the camera must be positioned on a tripod in a fixed location in the classroom. The operator may move the camera lens horizontally and vertically as the lesson evolves. The operator may also use the camera lens to zoom in or out to best record the instructional activities. A camera operator enables the teacher to move about the classroom and record student reaction to the teaching activity. Be aware that at no time may the camera operator stop the recording, not even by accident. All recording must be continual for thirty minutes. If not, the tape will be considered "unscorable."

When setting up the video camera for the recording session the best results will be obtained if the lens is directed away from the windows or any other sources of light. The following paragraphs deal with various positions in which the camera can be positioned. Please consider these possibilities prior to recording the intended lesson.

If the candidate is using a self-recorded videotape, the camera will be set up in a fixed position. The setup should be positioned for the best possible recording of the planned instruction. It may be necessary to make several practice recordings before an accurate recording is produced. The practice recordings will enable the candidate to record the field of view that enhances the instruction and the reaction of the students. The candidate may wish to consider the suggestions below for a fixed camera arrangement.

For a self recording camera arrangement, the candidate may choose to set up the camera in the rear of the classroom with the lens positioned away from the windows. The teacher in front of the classroom should be the center of focus with several students visible. (Fig. 1)

Video Camera Arrangements: Self-recording setup for whole-group instruction

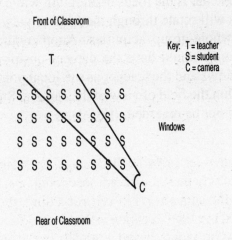

Figure 1. Rear View

A recording may also be set up with the camera arranged for a front view. The camera is set up in the front of the classroom with the lens facing away from the windows. The teacher and several students will be viewed with facial shots. If the classroom seating is arranged in group settings or clusters, a camera's field of view will focus on the teacher and one or more groups of students. These recording arrangements will be beneficial for whole-group instruction. (Fig. 2)

Video Camera Arrangements: Self-recording set up for whole-group instruction

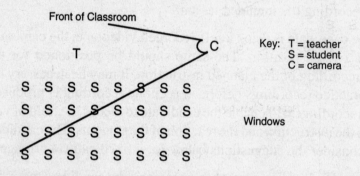

Figure 2. Front View

If the candidate chooses a self-recorded submission, the following positions may be useful for non-whole-group instruction. Position the camera so that the teacher is the focus of attention while the students are in groups. The groups will rotate through the field of view while the teacher monitors the non-whole-group activities. Another alternative for non-whole-group recording would have the camera positioned with the lens away from the windows and the teacher as the focal point. Student groups would be set up within the field of view of the camera. Students outside the field of view would not be recorded. (Fig. 3)

Self-recording setup for non-whole-group instruction

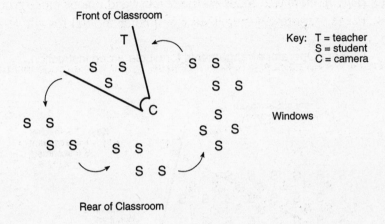

Figure 3a

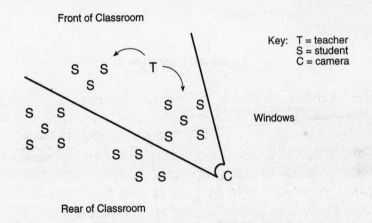

Figure 3b. Groups move through field of view

Candidates who choose to use the camera-operator recording may consider one of the following suggestions. The position of recording will be from a fixed position but the camera-operator may move horizontally or vertically around the classroom. The position of the camera should best represent the instruction of the classroom.

The position of the camera for whole-group instruction with a camera operator may be a rear-view camera position in which the operator can pan the field of view and record the teacher and students. Be sure that the lens is positioned away from the windows for the best recording. The candidate may choose to have a front-view camera position, which will enable the camera operator to record from a fixed location and pan the instruction from side to side. This position would record facial shots of the teacher and students. (Fig. 4)

Camera Operator arrangements for whole-group instruction.

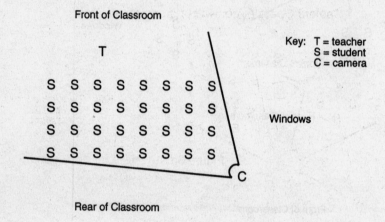

Figure 4a. Rear View

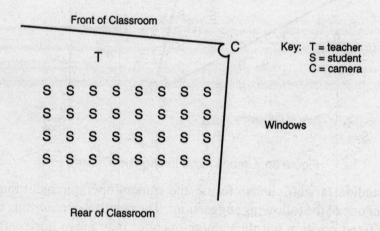

Figure 4b. Front View

When the candidate is recording non-whole-group instruction the camera operator arrangement may be located in the center of the classroom. The students would be set up in small groups around the classroom. The camera operator would pan around the groups as the teacher moves among groups monitoring the students' progress. The camera may also be positioned in the corner of the classroom. The students would be organized in small groups and the camera operator would pan to each group. Groups closer to the lens would appear clearer than other groups. With this setup the teacher would be viewed at all times monitoring the progress of the lesson. (Fig. 5)

Camera Operator non-whole-group arrangement.

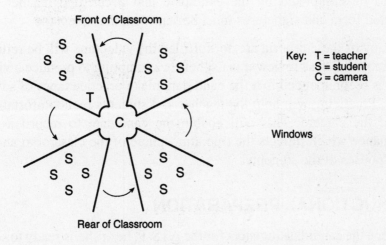

Figure 5a. Central Camera Position

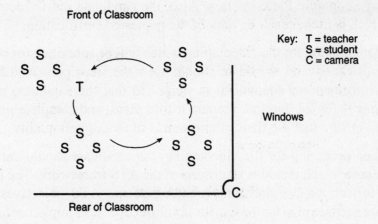

Figure 5b. Corner Camera Position

When positioning the camera it is recommended that the candidate choose the field of view which best records the instruction of the students. Practice tapes are encouraged so that the candidate may present the best recording for a rating.

In addition to the submission of the videotape, the candidate is reminded to submit the documents sent with the manual. The candidate must complete the Context of Instruction Form. This form will assist the scorers in rating the video. If the form is not completed or if information is incorrect the video will be "unscorable." The Candidate Identification Form needs to be completed by the candidate and a certified teacher. The completed form and signatures must be sent with the videotape.

If any of these criteria are not fulfilled the videotape will be returned "unscorable." Please review this list before attempting to produce a videotape. It is recommended that the candidate make practice tapes of several lessons. Practicing will help the teacher and students feel comfortable in front of the camera. This will enable the candidate to record a final performance which reflects the true atmosphere of the classroom and the true responses of the students.

INSTRUCTIONAL PREPARATION

Once the candidate registers for the ATS-P, he or she is ready to select which class and lesson will be appropriate to submit for review. The subject, date, and time of the video is left to the discretion of the candidate. However, the class selected must be from the teachers regular assignment within a public or nonpublic PreK-12 class. Also, the candidate must videotape a class which is in the teaching area of the requested certification.

In preparation for the videotaping which will be submitted for permanent certification, the candidate should view the steps presented by the ATS-P Informational Manual. It is suggested that the candidate review requirements for submission, prepare lesson plans, and complete practice videos to ensure that the final submission is of the highest quality.

When preparing for the videotaping, the candidate should carefully plan a lesson which includes all criteria of the ATS framework. The lesson should reflect the use and understanding of the ATS objectives. The candidate needs to plan for these criteria and be capable of implementing the requirement into a lesson.

The lesson should reveal the teacher's ability to apply principles and procedures for an organized classroom. The procedures used by the teacher should help the learners utilize the presented material and achieve the desired outcome. In order to accommodate all students' learning levels and abilities, the teacher should incorporate a variety of learning techniques. Some of these learning techniques could require visual aides, audio aides, hands-on learning or learning from other students. The teachers must show flexibility and knowledge of various teaching strategies.

The lesson prepared should be enjoyable to the learner. The teacher should present the material in a manner to which the students can relate. The instructional techniques should be motivational and encouraging so that the students are eager to absorb more knowledge. The techniques of motivating students may take practice. It is recommended that a candidate have experience in using motivational techniques in the classroom before submitting a video.

Also, before submitting a video, the candidate should have an atmosphere established in the classroom. The atmosphere desired would be one in which the students are encouraged and comfortable to ask questions, offer suggestions, and communicate ideas. This is acquired only by a teacher who offers support and trust to the students. When videotaping a classroom, the atmosphere of the class will be obvious by the reactions of the students. This is not only through verbal answers or questions, but is also through body language and facial responses to the teacher's instructional style and demeanor. It is essential to the success of a classroom that the students are supported, encouraged and not afraid to succeed.

The climate of the classroom takes time to evolve. The structure of the learning and the quality of the material needs to be maintained. Successful management of a classroom will be the foundation of this structure. Students must be shown that responsibility and respect are needed in a classroom. Students should be nurtured. A solid discipline guide or contract should be established. Rules should be discussed and explained, students should be involved in the process of deciding the goals of the classroom discipline. If the students are given this responsibility, they will value the classroom as their own. The establishment of a discipline contract will help foster an understanding and a safe, productive learning environment. If this is established, the video will show the respect the students have for learning and each other. A solid foundation of trust will enable the progression of successful lessons.

A candidate will be successful when the lesson plan can clearly provide the observation of the appropriate level for assessment. A successful teacher will incorporate both whole group and non-whole-group learning. This needs to be accomplished within the time provided. Remember that the ATS-P requires thirty minutes of taped instruction, ten minutes of which must be non-whole group.

Non-whole-group instructions would be those outlined by the teacher which the students would follow in small-group activities, individual projects, cooperative learning, peer learning, group discussions, group teaching, presentations, or problem solving activities. It is recommended that these activities be presented in previous lessons so that the students are comfortable with responsibilities such situations require. The students are given the material and framework in which to learn, and it is their responsibility to actively achieve. The teacher remains essential to the lesson by observing groups, offering suggestions, rotating through groups and monitoring activities. The activities of non-whole group learning need to be at least ten minutes of the lesson.

Whole group instruction will involve the other twenty minutes required by the ATS-P outline. This instruction involves the activities and objectives of the teacher being presented to a large group or the entire class. The teacher provides the instructional material and monitors the intended outcome of the activities. The teacher must continually monitor the entire class in order to assess the lesson. An effective teacher will provide a lesson which actively involves the entire class.

When preparing the lesson for submission the candidate is reminded that the ATS-P is an evaluation of the his or her ability to teach successfully. Therefore, the candidate should be the primary instructor shown on the video. If you are team teaching, make sure the lesson involves the candidate because recording with others may not meet ATS-P requirements. Limit the use of instructional media such as slides or films. This may not meet the instructional level of the ATS-P. When using instructional media, video, tape recording, or overheads, ensure that the material is being recorded on the videotape. Do not let the use of such devises take away from learning time. Such materials should be set-up prior to recording. Time not spent on instruction may not be acceptable by the ATS-P. Remember, only the first thirty minutes of the tape will be reviewed and scored. If most of this time is wasted setting up equipment, it will lower the candidates rating. Prepare all lessons and materials before videotaping.

MAKING THE RECORDING

When the candidate is ready to conduct the actual taping of the lesson, be sure that all procedures have been considered. The equipment should be checked to ensure that it is functioning properly. The tape should satisfy the requirements of the ATS-P. The field of view of the camera should encompass the teaching area which will be valuable to the assessment of the candidates teaching technique.

Once the video camera is positioned the taping may begin. The candidate should start taping and immediately begin the lesson. Remember that only the first thirty minutes of the tape will be scored. It would be advisable to have another person set the timer or have the video operator record the time being recorded. This will ensure that a minimum of twenty minutes and a maximum of thirty minutes is recorded.

The quality of the recording will be enhanced if the candidate speaks clearly and conveys instructions and objectives to the class in an organized manner. It is recommended that practice lessons be videotaped. This will help the class and teacher remain comfortable with the notion of being recorded. Actions and responses will appear more natural and the atmosphere will be beneficial to the learning process.

When the focus of instruction goes from whole group to non-whole group or from non-whole group to whole group it is important that the transition is smooth. When working with small groups it may be necessary to position the camera in order to record the lesson or activities. If this is required, the candidate should do so in a manner that is as smooth as possible. Remember, at no time during taping can the video camera be stopped. If the recording is stopped or edited the submission will be considered "unscorable." The candidate will then need to reapply and submit another videotape.

When the lesson has included at least twenty minutes of teaching with the required ten minutes of non-whole group instruction, the videotaping should stop. Only the first thirty minutes of the tape will be viewed. Any material or instruction which occurs after the first thirty minutes will not be scored, If the tape contains less than twenty minutes of instruction, the videotape will be considered "unscorable."

REVIEW OF THE RECORDING

Upon completion of the videotaping session, the candidate should view the entire recording using the proper equipment to verify that the submission is accurate. Check for clarity of picture, field of view, audio clarity, and accurate timing of the instructional period. Be certain that the first twenty minutes of the tape include the required instructional material. The tape will be ready for submission if no technical problems have occurred.

The tape should also be reviewed for the accuracy of the lesson presented. Will the scorer be able to view the intentions of the lesson? Are there obstructions from the classroom or camera which will negatively affect the results of the candidates submission? Remember, the scorer is instructed to view the first thirty minutes of the tape. At the end of a timed thirty minutes the scorer will stop the video.

After the candidate reviews the recorded lesson it is suggested that the recording be shown to another certified teacher. This will enable the candidate to receive professional feedback and an assessment of the instruction presented. The feedback will assist the candidate in preparation of another video, highlight the positive aspects of the candidate's teaching, and provide a source of instruction or criticism. In addition to the video, show the Context of Instruction Form to a certified teacher. The feedback received on this information will also be beneficial.

After one or more certified teachers have reviewed the videotape, the candidate can decide if the prepared tape is acceptable for submission. If necessary, now is the time to start planning for a new recording. Use the information provided by your associates and your own reaction to the recording. Plan the intended lesson according to the ATS-P requirements, be sure that the instruction allows for the inclusion of whole group instruction and non-whole-group instruction, and include the objectives provided by the ATS-P manual.

When you decide that the recorded lesson is acceptable for submission, remove the record-prevention tab located on the spine of the video. The removal of these tabs will prevent the tape from being recorded over. If the you desire, a copy of the tape may be made for your own use. The submitted tape will not be returned to you.

Before mailing the tape, rewind it completely. The Context of Instruction Form must be completed accurately. This form will assist the scorer of the video. The card will not be scored but is essential to submission of the video. Do not include any addition forms or information when submitting the videotape.

The Candidate Identification Form must also include accurate information. This form certifies that the candidate presented on the video is indeed the candidate requesting permanent certification. This also verifies that the class which is being instructed is part of your regular assignment. The form contains a Witness Confirmation of Candidate Identity section, which must be completed by a certified teacher in your school district. The witness's signature confirms that he or she is a certified teacher in New York

State, has viewed a segment of the videotaped instruction and that the video and form identify the candidate accurately.

Instructions are provided by the ATS-P test administrators for proper mailing of the video. If all materials are accurate and completed properly once received, the candidate will receive a receipt for the materials. A date will be included for the approximate time of scoring. A score report is usually received within four months of submission of the appropriate materials.

If the video is submitted after June 30 of the program year, the candidate will receive additional procedures to complete. These procedures will not include any additional fees. The video will need to fulfill requirement and policies for the new program year.

SCORING THE RECORDING

This section will provide an overview of how the submitted videotape will be scored by the ATS-P. Once the candidate submits the video, the ATS-P will have the video independently evaluated. The tape will be viewed by at least two teachers with permanent certification in New York State. The scoring will be based on the five Instructional Delivery objectives of the Assessment of Teaching Skills. The score will be an overall judgement of teaching skills. The score will not reflect the quality of the recording. It will be based on the quality of the teaching performance and instructional integrity. The ATS-P has provided a description of the ratings; however, each candidate may not reflect the total description provided. Candidates may receive a "pass," "not pass," "U," or a "B."

To receive a "Pass," the candidate must demonstrate teaching skills which achieve the required level of the ATS Instructional Delivery objectives. The candidate will demonstrate, with a visual performance, a learning environment and atmosphere in which all students are encouraged to succeed. The lesson will be organized and managed in a manner which shows the candidates understanding and implementation of principles and procedures. The candidate will lead learners to develop meaning and produce intended outcomes from the material presented. Communication and teaching techniques will be clear and explained in a variety of strategies. The lesson will be presented in a motivational style which will encourage students to question and become active learners. The lesson will be effective if the learners are provided adequate opportunity to succeed. Positive reinforcement and stimulation should be varied to reach all students. A standard of behavior should be established and maintained during the lesson.

If a candidate should receive a score of "Not Pass," the candidate has not reached a level acceptable to the ATS Instructional Delivery objectives. The submitted lesson reveals that the candidate does not understand and has not implemented the principles and procedures which enable students to achieve, The atmosphere and established behaviors of the classroom do not stimulate the students. A climate of trust and learning has not be maintained or established. The candidate does not utilize motivational techniques and does not provide positive reinforcement for the students. This is reflected by the students not questioning or becoming active learners in the lesson. Communication techniques and teaching strategies are not varied and the teacher does not encourage student involvement. As a result the environment of the classroom is not conducive to learning.

A rating of "U" means the candidate submitted a video which is "unscorable." An "unscorable" submission is one which does not meet the proper requirements of the procedures of the ATS. This would include providing a videotaping which does not exceed twenty minutes of instructional information. The candidate may have submitted a tape which can not be rated because of poor recording quality. The candidate failed to follow proper ATS procedures in the ATS Procedure Manual provided. If a candidate receives a score of "unscorable," the candidate must obtain another registration bulletin and reapply for the ATS-P. Upon receipt of a new registration application, the candidate should follow the procedures as described in the Procedure Manual provided by the New York State Education Department.

If the candidate receives a rating of "B," the ATS has received a blank videotape. A blank videotape contains no visual image or audio track. The candidate will need to reregister for the ATS-P and submit a new registration fee and video. Once the candidate reapplies and receives a new Procedure Manual, the candidate should follow all procedures as described by the NYSED.

The candidate who prepares properly for the ATS-P will complete a successful video. Follow proper procedures and meet the required criteria of the ATS Manual and a passing rating will be achieved. In order to accomplish this goal, incorporate teaching techniques, discipline techniques, motivational strategies, and a variety of learning activities into everyday instructional procedures. Good luck, and have a successful video performance.

NYSTCE
New York State Teacher Certification Examinations

LAST Practice Test One
and
ATS - W Elementary
Practice Test One

LAST
PRACTICE TEST 1

TIME: 4 Hours
80 Multiple Choice Questions, 1 Essay

SECTION 1

> **DIRECTIONS:** Each of the following questions and incomplete statements is followed by four answer choices. Select the choice which best answers each question.

1. A department store is having an inventory reduction sale. Everything in the store is to be discounted by 20%. If Mary purchases a couch and pays $420 for it, which of the following equations, when solved for x, will give the original cost of the couch?

    (A) $0.80x = \$420$

    (B) $0.20x = \$420$

    (C) $1.20x = \$420 + 0.20x$

    (D) $0.80x = \$420 + 0.20x$

2. John is a salesman for a shoe company. He receives a weekly salary plus a commission of 15% of all sales. If his weekly salary is $400 and he sells $500 worth of shoes during the week, which expression would represent his take home pay for the week?

    (A) $0.15 (\$400) + \$500$

    (B) $\$400 + 0.15 (\$500)$

    (C) $0.15 (\$400 + \$500)$

    (D) $\$400 + 0.85 (\$500)$

3. The town of Snowville collected $850,000 in taxes one year. The townspeople voted to set aside 20% for school funding. How much money was set aside?

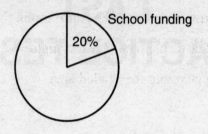

(A) $280,500

(B) $425,000

(C) $170,000

(D) $127,500

4. Read the problem below and then answer the question that follows.

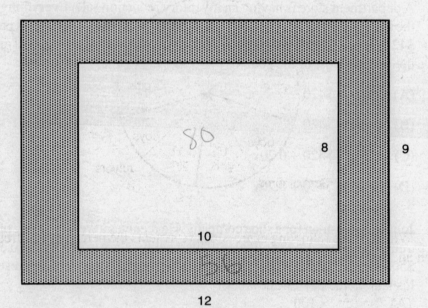

The floor of a rectangular room is to be covered in two different types of material. The total cost of covering the entire room is $136.00. The cost of covering the inner rectangle is $80.00. The cost of covering the shaded area is $56.00.

We wish to determine the cost of material per square foot used to cover the shaded area. What information given below is unnecessary for this computation?

I.   The total cost of covering the entire room.

II. The cost of covering the inner rectangle

III. The cost of covering the shaded area.

(A) I only.

(B) II only.

(C) I and II only.

(D) I and III only.

5.   The distribution of a high school chorus is depicted in the graph below. There is a total of 132 students in the chorus.

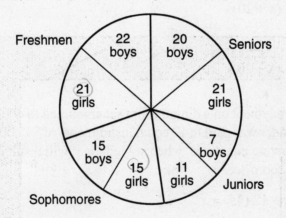

Which of the following expressions represents the percentage of freshman and sophomore girls in the chorus?

(A) $\dfrac{21+15}{132} \times 100$

(B) $\dfrac{21+15}{132} \div 100$

(C) $\dfrac{21+15}{100}$

(D) $\dfrac{21+15}{100} \times 132$

6. The hot water pipe can fill the bathtub twice as fast as the cold water pipe. Together the two pipes require 20 minutes to fill the bathtub. Which of the following equations, when solved for x, will give the number of minutes required for the hot water pipe alone to fill the tub?

(A) $\dfrac{20}{x} + \dfrac{20}{2x} = 1$

(B) $\dfrac{40}{x+2x} = 1$

(C) $\dfrac{20}{x} + \dfrac{20}{(x+20)} = 1$

(D) $\dfrac{20}{2x} + \dfrac{20}{(x+20)} = 1$

7. The down payment on a dining room set amounted to 40% of the price. The remainder was paid in 12 equal installments of $45.00 each. Which of the following equations, when solved for x, will result in the price of the dining room set?

I. $0.40x + 12\,(45) = x$

II. $0.40x + 12\,(45) = 0.60x$

III. $0.40x + 0.60x = 12\,(45)$

IV. $0.60x = 12\,(45)$

(A) I and IV only.

(B) I and II only.

(C) II and III only.

(D) None of the above.

8. Given that the circle is inscribed in a square, what expression below would represent the area of the shaded region?

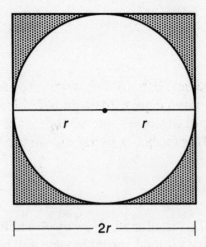

(A) $\pi r^2 - (2r)^2 = \pi r^2 - 4r^2 = r^2(\pi - 4)$

(B) $(2r)^2 - 2\pi r^2 = 4r^2 - 2\pi r^2 = 2r^2(2 - \pi)$

(C) $\pi r^2 - 2r^2 = r^2(\pi - 2)$

(D) $(2r)^2 - \pi r^2 = 4r^2 - \pi r^2 = r^2(4 - \pi^2)$

9. In the diagram below a square is located in the corner of a rectangle. The side of the square is represented by s. The length of the rectangle is represented by y and the width by x.

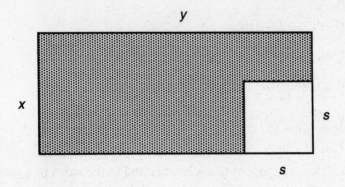

Which of the following terms represents the ratio of the area of the square to the area of the shaded region?

(A) $\dfrac{xy - s^2}{s^2}$

(B) $\dfrac{s^2}{xy - s^2}$

(C) $\dfrac{s^2}{s^2 - xy}$

(D) $\dfrac{xy}{xy - s^2}$

10. A man has \$3,200 invested at 5%. How much additional money must he invest at 2% so that his total annual income will be equal to 3% of his entire investment?

(A) $0.05\,(\$3{,}200) + 0.02x = 0.03\,(x + \$3{,}200)$

(B) $0.05\,(\$3{,}200) + 0.02\,(\$3{,}200) = 0.03(x)$

(C) $0.03\,(3x + \$3{,}200) + 0.02\,(\$3{,}200) = 0.03x$

(D) $0.03\,(\$3{,}200) \times 0.02\,(\$3{,}200) = 0.05(x)$

11. A man drove his son from home to college in 5 hrs. Taking the same route home took 6 hours because he was forced to drive 7 mph slower due to heavy traffic. Which equation below would find his average rate driving to college?

(A) $5r = 6(r - 7)$

(B) $5r + 7 = 6(r - 7)$

(C) $5r + 1 = 6r - 7$

(D) $5r = 6(r + 1)$

12. Two circles are tangent to each other and to the sides of a rectangle as shown in the diagram. The circles both have a radius of r.

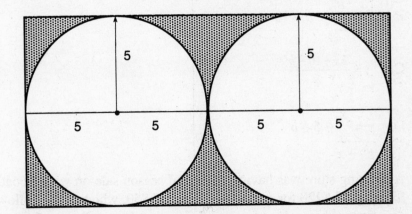

What term below represents the area of the shaded portion?

(A) $200 - 25\pi$

(B) $200 - 50\pi$

(C) $100 - 50\pi$

(D) $200 - 20\pi$

13. Find four consecutive even integers such that the sum of the first three integers is 8 more than the last integer. Which of the following equations below, when solved for n, would give us the value of the first integer?

(A) $3n + 3 = (n + 4) + 8$

(B) $3n = (n + 4) + 8$

(C) $3n + 3 = (n + 5) + 8$

(D) $3n + 6 = n + 14$

14. Solve the following equation for y.

$$x + 5 = \frac{1}{2}(ay + b)$$

Which of the following equations represents this mathematical manipulation?

(A) $y = \dfrac{2x + 5 + b}{a}$

B. $y = \dfrac{1}{2}x + b + 10$

C. $y = \dfrac{2x + 10 - b}{a}$

D. $y = \dfrac{x}{a} + 5 - b$

15. A clothing store was having an end of season sale on winter coats. If Simon paid $220 for a coat and he saved $50, which of the following equations, when solved for x, will give the percent discount?

A. $\dfrac{\$50}{\$220 + \$50} \times 100 = x$

B. $\dfrac{\$220}{\$220 + \$50} \times 100 = x$

C. $\dfrac{\$50}{\$220} \times 100 = x$

D. $\dfrac{\$220}{\$220 + \$50} = x$

16. A biotic community is a naturally occurring group of animals and plants that live together in the same environment. Abiotic factors are physical factors that are important to the biotic community. Examples of abiotic factors include temperature, the availability of minerals and sunlight.

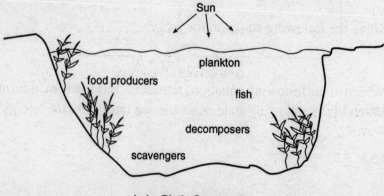

Lake Biotic Community

Given the information and diagrammatic representation of a lake biotic community above, which of the following statements would we expect to occur if one year there was an uncharacteristic amount of ice and snow covering the lake?

I. Photosynthesis would decrease because light would not be able to penetrate as deeply into the lake water.

II. Water temperature would have an effect on the plants and animals living in the lake.

III. There would not be change in the biotic community due to the adaptation of plants and animals.

IV. The remains of dead plants and animals would accumulate faster than organisms of decay could decompose them.

(A) I, II, and IV only.

(B) I only.

(C) II only.

(D) I and II only.

17. Activation energy is defined as the amount of energy required in a collision between reactant molecules to produce a chemical reaction resulting in product molecules.

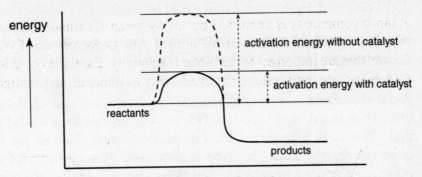

time course of reaction

Which of the following statements can we infer from the energy graph above?

I.   The products of the reaction are at a lower energy level than the original reactants.

II. Addition of a catalyst lowers activation energy.

III. The reaction without the catalyst requires more energy to occur than the catalyzed reaction.

(A) I, II, and III.

(B) I and II only.

(C) II and III only.

(D) None of the above.

18. Osmosis is the diffusion of water through a selectively permeable membrane from an area of greater concentration of water to an area where water is less concentrated. Applying this knowledge to a plant cell, which of the following statement(s) are true?

(A) If the solution outside the cell has a lower concentration of particles and a higher concentration of water than the inside of the cell, there should be a net movement of water into the cell.

(B) If the solution outside the cell has a lower concentration of particles and a higher concentration of water than inside the cell, then there will be a net movement of water from the cell to outside the cell.

(C) We would expect no net movement of water.

(D) We cannot determine whether water will move into the cell or whether water will move outside the cell.

19. A cross between a pure homozygous red snapdragon and a pure homozygous white snapdragon will result in heterozygous snapdragons that are pink. This is an example of Incomplete Dominance. Neither the red genotype nor the white genotype is dominant. Characteristics of the offspring produced are a blend. The physical manifestation of a genotype is referred to as a phenotype. When the pink snapdragons are crossed among themselves, they yield red, pink and white offspring in the ratio of 1:2:1.

Which of the following statement(s) is true?

(A) In Incomplete Dominance we can tell the genotype by looking at the phenotype.

(B) In Incomplete Dominance the offspring of a cross between parents, each of which is homozygous for a trait, will have a phenotype different from both parents.

(C) Both A and B and true.

(D) Both A and B are not true.

20. The diagram shows the distillation curve for the separation of a mixture of two miscible liquids. The distillation temperature is gradually increased from room temperature to 120°C over a period of two hours. Lines *AB* and *CD* represent distillations of the pure liquids, one having a boiling point of 50°C, the other having a boiling point of 120°C.

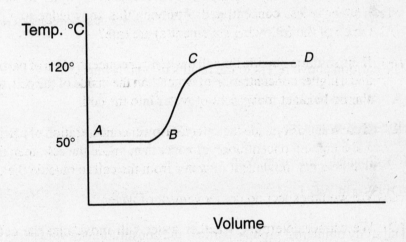

What would we expect to happen if the temperature is increased rapidly from room temperature to 120°C over a time interval of 15 minutes?

(A) We would expect to distill less volume of pure liquids only.

(B) We would expect only to distill more mixture of liquids (line *BC* of the diagram).

(C) Both A and B above.

(D) We would expect no change.

President McKinley (the tailor) measures Uncle Sam for a new suit to fit the fattening results of his imperial appetite.

Puck, XLVIII, September 5, 1900, pp. 7-8.

21. The cartoon above refers to the results of which war?

(A) War of 1812

(B) Civil War

(C) Spanish-American War

(D) World War I

22. The study of interest groups, parties, and constitutions would generally be included under the subject matter of

(A) political science.

(B) economics.

(C) sociology.

(D) geography.

Reprinted by permission of Tribune Media Services.

23. What is the most likely conclusion the artist wants us to derive from the cartoon above?

    (A) The antique store is open for business.

    (B) Americans love their old furniture.

    (C) Antique shops are often found in rural areas.

    (D) At some time ago, gasoline prices were low.

24. The primary objective of social scientists is to

    (A) make humans happier.

    (B) alter society.

    (C) understand society and suggest alternatives to reach social goals.

    (D) determine what social goals should be.

25. The study of how the goods and services we want get produced, and how they are distributed among us is called

    (A) history.

(B) economics.

(C) political science.

(D) geography.

26. Which of the following terms includes all of the others?

(A) Capital goods

(B) Natural resources

(C) Factors of production

(D) Workers

THE UNITED STATES MUST NOT BECOME A "PITIFUL HELPLESS GIANT." – PRES. NIXON

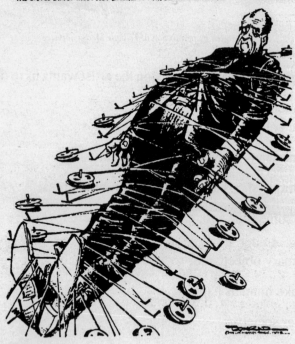

"Pitiful Helpless Giant" by Paul Conrad.
Copyright, 1973, Los Angeles Times.
Reprinted by permission.

27. In the cartoon above, what analogy does the artist draw upon?

(A) *Giants of the Earth*

(B) *Gulliver's Travels*

(C) *Jack and the Beanstalk*

(D) *Animal Farm*

28. Reproduction of the human species, physical care of the offspring, and providing affection and companionship are functions of which social institution?

(A) Economy

(B) Government

(C) Religion

(D) Family

29. Which one of the following rarely adds much toward bringing about social change?

(A) New ideas and ideologies

(B) Climatic changes

(C) Collective group action

(D) Established religious bodies

30. The five pillars of Islam do not include

(A) giving alms to the needy.

(B) performing set rituals of prayer five times daily.

(C) giving to the Mosque each year the value of a goat.

(D) a pilgrimage to the Kaaba stone at Mecca.

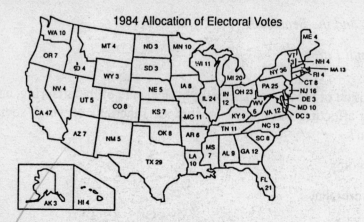

1984 Allocation of Electoral Votes

31. The map above shows the 1984 allocation of electoral votes. What is the basis for the electoral vote?

(A) Number of representatives and senators

(B) Date of state's admission to the union

(C) Location of the state

(D) Tax contributions to the federal treasury

32. Which of the following was not one of the actions of the British government that the American colonies resented in the time preceding the Revolutionary War?

(A) The ban against trade with the French and Spanish West Indies

(B) Drafting troops for fighting in Europe

(C) Enlisting the colonists to support British troops in the colonies

(D) The Stamp Act

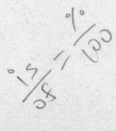

33. Which statement best fits the illustration above, taken from the title page of *Leviathan*, by Thomas Hobbes, published in 1651?

    (A) People form a social contract with a ruler

    (B) People have no rights under this contract

    (C) Symbols of power are relatively unimportant

    (D) Anarchy results when the ruler is powerful

34. Which invention predated the others?

    (A) Edison develops the electric light bulb

    (B) Bell introduces the telephone

    (C) Barbed wire for fences is first manufactured

    (D) Whitney invents the cotton gin

35. A company planning to invest in a foreign country would be deterred most by

    (A) a large population.

    (B) low national income.

    (C) unstable government.

    (D) low life expectancy.

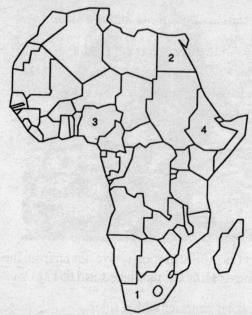

36. Locate the country in which apartheid was once the official government policy.

(A) 1

(B) 2

(C) 3

(D) 4

37. Select the most appropriate time period for the occurrence of the American Civil War.

(A) 1700-1750

(B) 1750-1800

(C) 1800-1850

(D) 1850-1900

38. Which one of the following statements is most correct about people who live in similar habitats, but who are separated by a great distance?

(A) Their cultures are likely to be almost identical.

(B) They are always similar in their social characteristics.

(C) They may have some culture traits that are alike.

(D) They usually speak languages that are similar.

39. The tools, means and methods through which we interact with our environment is a definition of

(A)   technology.

(B)   television sets.

(C)   computer software.

(D)   mass production.

40. Which of the following fostered industrialization in the United States?

(A) Slow growth of the domestic market

(B) Distant foreign markets

(C) Few raw materials

(D) Surplus of labor

41. Which of the following is true about the above music?

(A) It is written in three flats.

(B) The time signature is obvious.

(C) There is a repetitive bass pattern.

(D) The bass clef rests for three measures in this segment.

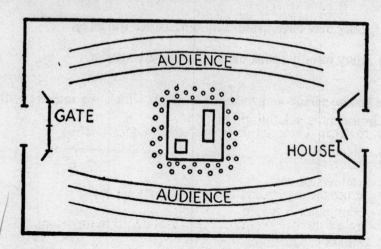

42. The picture above is an example of which of the following types of staging?

(A) Thrust

(B) Proscenium

(C) Theatre-in-the-Round

(D) Centra

Questions 43–45 refer to the following poem.

> My mistress' eyes are nothing like the sun;
> Coral is far more red than her lips' red;
> If snow be white, why then her breasts are dun;
> If hairs be wires, black wires grow on her head.
> I have seen roses damasked, red and white,
> But no such roses see I in her cheeks;
> And in some perfumes is there more delight
> Than in the breath that from my mistress reeks.
> I love to hear her speak, yet well I know
> That music hath a far more pleasing sound;
> I grant I never saw a goddess go;
> My mistress, when she walks treads on the ground.
> And yet, by heaven, I think my love as rare
> As any she belied with false compare.

43. This poem is different from other sonnets in that

(A) it is Shakespearean.

(B) it is Italian.

(C) it describes the appearance of a beloved woman.

(D) it does not describe the woman as beautiful.

44. The last two lines of the poem

(A) reaffirm the argument held throughout the poem.

(B) start a new topic.

(C) refute the argument held throughout the poem.

(D) are a continuation of the ideas introduced in the poem.

45. The poem can best be described as

(A) witty and satirical.

(B) intense.

(C) sarcastic.

(D) brooding.

46. From which of the following structures is the above picture taken?

(A) Notre Dame Cathedral

(B) The Parthenon

(C)   The Sistine Chapel

(D)   Versailles Palace

Galleria degli Ufizi, Florena.

47.   The figure pictured above was most likely which of the following?

(A)   A slave or menial servant

(B)   A knight's page

(C)   A religious novice

(D)   A farmer

Whilom ther was dwellynge at Oxenford
A riche gnof, that gestes heeld to bord,
And of his craft he was a carpenter.
With hym ther was dwellynge a povre scoler.

48.   What can we assume about this passage?

(A) It is probably a translation of some other language into English.

(B) It is written in Middle English.

(C) It is romantic in style.

(D) It is written in Elizabethan English.

Tomb of Nakht, Thebes.

49. All of the following can be construed from the print above EXCEPT

(A) The three figures portrayed are musicians.

(B) The art work conveys a strong sense of depth.

(C) The drawing is representative of Egyptian tomb paintings .

(D) The artist was not concerned with modeling the figures in three dimensions.

50. Which of the following best describes the statue pictured above?

    (A)   Comic

    (B)   Tragic

    (C)   Ornate

    (D)   Imposing

Questions 51-53 refer to the following passages.

    (A)   That's my last duchess painted on the wall,
             Looking as if she were alive. I call
             That piece a wonder, now: Fra Pandolf's hands
             Worked busily a day, and there she stands.

    (B)   <u>Nov. 24</u>. A rainy morning. We were all well except that my head ached a little and I took my breakfast in bed. I read a little of Chaucer, prepared the goose for dinner, and then we all walked out. I was obliged to return for my fur tippet and Spenser it was so cold.

(C)   There were times in early autumn--in September--when the greater circuses would come to town--the Ringling Brothers, Robinson's, and Barnum & Baily shows, and when I was a route-boy on the morning paper, on those mornings when the circus would be coming in, I would rush madly through my route in the cool and thrilling darkness that comes before the break of day, and then I would go back home and get my brother out of bed.

(D)   This American government--what is it but a tradition, though a recent one, endeavoring to transmit itself unimpaired to posterity, but each instant losing some of its integrity? It has not the vitality and force of a single living man; for a single man can bend it to his will. It is a sort of wooden gun to the people themselves; and, if ever they should use it in earnest as a real one against each other, it will surely split.

51. Which of the above passages creates a mood of strange excitement?

52. Which of the above passages is most likely taken from a dramatic monologue?

53. Which of the above passages uses a metaphor to make a point?

Rijk Museum, Amsterdam.

54. From this picture, one can assume that the music being played and sung is

(A) an opera.

(B) a sad, serious melody.

(C) a dirge.

(D) a light, boisterous tune.

L'Unite d'habitation, Marseilles.

55. The designer of the building pictured above seems to have been concerned with which of the following?

    (A) The amount of light available to the building's inhabitants

    (B) Building a modern skyscraper

    (C) Cylindrical shapes

    (D) Hidden staircases

56. King: Take thy fair hour, Laertes; time be thine,
             And thy best graces spend it at thy will!
             But now, my cousin Hamlet, and my son,—
    Hamlet: (*Aside*) A little more than kin, and less than kind.

    In the above lines, what does the stage direction "(*Aside*)" mean?

    (A) The actor steps aside to make room for other action on stage.

    (B) The actor directly addresses only one particular actor on stage.

    (C) The actor directly addresses the audience, while out of hearing of the other actors.

    (D) The previous speaker steps aside to make room for this actor.

57. The building pictured above suggests which of the following?

  (A) Undulating waves of water

  (B) A congested city street

  (C) A chambered nautilus

  (D) A massive mountain

Questions 58-60 refer to the following passage.

  (A) Fair is foul and foul is fair.
  Hover through the fog and filthy air.

  (B) Weary of myself, and sick of asking
  What I am, and what I ought to be,
  At this vessel's prow I stand, which bears me
  Forward, forward o'er the starlit sea.

  And a look of passionate desire
  O'er the sea and to the stars I send:
  "Ye who from my childhood up have calmed me,
  Calm me, ah, compose me to the end!

  (C) There were a king with a large jaw and a queen with a plain face, on the throne
  of England; there were a king with a large jaw and a queen with a fair face on the
  throne of France. In both countries it was clearer than crystal to the lords of the
  state preserves of loaves and fishes, that things were in general settled for ever.

  (D) no thats no way for him he has no manners nor no refinement nor no nothing in
  his nature slapping us behind like that on my bottom because I didnt call him

Hugh the ignoramus doesnt know poetry from a cabbage thats what you get for not keeping them in their proper place

58. Which passage describes a person seeking personal insight and solace?

59. Which passage uses the "stream of consciousness" technique to mimic the workings of the human mind?

60. Which passage contains examples of alliteration?

Questions 61-63 are based on the following passage.

The high school drop out rate remains high in many southern states. An average of 18% of the students who finish sixth grade in Texas, Mississippi, Louisiana and Alabama do not stay in school long enough to graduate from high school. Maintaining a precise count of the number of drop outs is difficult. Some students may still be listed as enrolled when in fact they have stopped attending school and do not plan to return. A slightly larger percentage of male students drop out of school than females. More students tend to leave school during the eleventh grade. Other times most frequently cited reasons for dropping out include failing grades, suspensions and expulsions, conflict with the school, pregnancy, marriage and economic hardship. Generally, students who are incarcerated are not counted in the total number of dropouts. Some school districts have implemented special programs to encourage teens to stay in school. These retention programs usually include tutoring, counseling and opportunities for part time employment at the school or in the neighborhood.

61. What is the main idea of the passage?

    (A) Everyone should graduate from high school.

    (B) More males drop out of school than females.

    (C) There are many reasons why students drop out of school.

    (D) Some southern states have large numbers of students who do not graduate from high school.

62. Which of the following is not stated in the passage?

    (A) Students in jail are not included in the total number of dropouts.

    (B) Some states have dropout rates of 18%.

(C) Some students are labeled drop outs when they have moved out of the district.

(D) Tutoring programs before and after school may be successful in encouraging some teens to stay in school.

63. Which statement best summarizes the author's attitude?

(A) The drop out problem is of little importance to the author.

(B) The author believes that teachers should spend more time encouraging students to stay in school.

(C) The author feels that the drop out problem is complex.

(D) Drop out prevention programs are a simple solution.

Questions 64–65 are based on the following passage.

Petrified trees are unusual artifacts of the Pliocene-Pleistocene Age. The petrification process began about 1.5 million years ago when a tree, often some type of hardwood, fell into a river and was washed into the sand or gravel bank. Water percolating through the sand or gravel deposited silica in the porous cells of the tree. Over time, the cells became a solid mass and the tree was petrified. Animal and plant fossils are often embedded in the tree.

64. According to the passage, what conditions are necessary for trees to petrify?

(A) Water and sand or gravel

(B) Thick mud banks along a river

(C) Heat and time

(D) Heat, pressure, and water

65. Which of the following statements can be inferred from the passage?

(A) Petrified trees are very heavy.

(B) Petrified trees are interesting museum specimens.

(C) Petrified trees may have fossil evidence of other life forms.

(D) Scientists have difficulty dating petrified trees.

Questions 66–70 are based on the following passage.

In medieval times, an almanac was a chart showing the movements of the stars over a period of several years. Eventually, almanacs were printed in book form and included information which was especially useful to farmers. In the sixteenth century, almanacs began to be issued every year and included predictions of the weather based on previous weather patterns. At about the same time, almanacs included elaborate calendars that listed church feast days. In the seventeenth century, almanacs included jokes and short accounts of humorous incidents. Benjamin Franklin continued this tradition with *Poor Richard's Almanac*, which was published from 1732-1758. In Germany, almanacs of the eighteenth century included sophisticated, contemporary poetry by serious authors. The almanacs printed in the United States from 1835-1856 were called "Davy Crockett" almanacs because they included many frontier tall tales based mainly on oral tradition.

66. When did almanacs begin predicting the weather?

(A) Almanacs have always predicted the weather.

(B) In medieval times

(C) In the sixteenth century

(D) In the seventeenth century

67. What was unique about the "Davy Crockett" almanacs?

(A) They were printed in Germany but sold in the United States.

(B) They included tall tales.

(C) They included stories about Davy Crockett.

(D) They were printed during the U.S. Civil War.

68. What was the purpose of the first almanacs?

(A) To list church holidays

(B) To predict the weather

(C) To print poetry and humorous stories

(D) To chart the movement of the stars

69. Which of the following statements best describes the author's attitude toward almanacs?

    (A) Almanacs are an example of popular thinking in the sixteenth century.

    (B) Almanacs are archaic.

    (C) Almanacs made Franklin famous.

    (D) The purpose and content of almanacs has changed over time.

70. Which of the following is NOT included in the passage?

    (A) Some almanacs included serious poetry.

    (B) Jokes were included in some almanacs.

    (C) Davy Crockett wrote almanacs in the 1800s.

    (D) Almanacs include calendars and make weather predictions.

Questions 71–76 are based on the following passage.

Six members of the local university basketball team walked off the court during practice last week. They later said they were protesting unfair treatment by the head coach. The day after walking off the court the players held a meeting with the university president to discuss their complaints. They met with the Director of Athletics two days later and expressed their concerns. They also met with the assistant coach. After refusing to practice for four days, the team apologized to the fans, returned to practice, and promised to play the next scheduled game that season. The players also stated that their opinion of the head coach had not changed, but that they thought the assistant coach was fair.

71. What was the basketball players' complaint?

    (A) Unfair treatment by the coach

    (B) Too many practices

    (C) Practice was too long

    (D) No support from fans

72. Which of the following did the players not do?

    (A) Walk away from practice

(B) Apologize to the fans

(C) Meet with the Director of Athletics

(D) Agree to play for the team next year

73. Which of the following best describes the author's attitude?

(A) The author believes the players' actions were humorous.

(B) The author writes objectively about the players' actions.

(C) The author condemns the players' actions.

(D) The author believes the players are behaving childishly.

74. How long did the players protest?

(A) One day

(B) Two days

(C) Three days

(D) Four days

Questions 75–77 are based on the following passage.

My daughter, Marie, has two cats. The older cat is named Annie. She is white with large black spots. Annie has long hair and sheds constantly in warm weather. Cinnamon is a two-year-old male tabby. He loves to chase squirrels in the backyard, but he probably would be very surprised to catch one. Cinnamon prefers to stay outside all night unless it is extremely cold. In the morning, Cinnamon wants to come into the house and sleep. Annie seldom goes outside. She prefers to sit on the table or a chair where she can look outside through the windows. Marie has cared for both cats since they were kittens. She is very fond of both of them.

75. How old is Annie?

(A) Two years

(B) Five years

(C) Not stated

(D) One year

76. According to the passage, which of the following is NOT true?

    (A) Annie chases squirrels.

    (B) Cinnamon stays outside at night.

    (C) Cinnamon is a male tabby.

    (D) Annie has long hair.

77. According to the passage, which of the following statements is true?

    (A) Marie likes Annie more than Cinnamon.

    (B) Marie has cared for both cats since they were kittens.

    (C) Annie and Cinnamon often fight with each other.

    (D) Annie spends most nights outside.

Questions 78-79 are based on the following passage.

Many people are becoming more conscious of protecting their health by eating correctly and exercising regularly. Jane Fonda has made a fortune selling exercise videos. Richard Simmons gives advice to dieters and suggests aerobic exercises on a series of video tapes. Every major city in the United States has at least one health club and at least one weight reduction program. Membership fees in health clubs range from $50.00 a year to $100.00 or more a month. Participation in weight reduction programs costs as much as $75.00 a week. Clearly, exercise and diet programs are growing businesses. Only time will tell how much more the market can expand.

78. The author of this passage is most interested in which of the following?

    (A) The business side of exercise and diet programs

    (B) The value of exercise and diet for good health

    (C) The average cost of memberships in health clubs

    (D) The number of diet programs available

79. With which of the following would the author agree?

    (A) Jane Fonda has made too much money from her videos.

    (B) Richard Simmons should only give advice on dieting and leave exercise alone.

(C) The future of health clubs and diet programs cannot be predicted.

(D) Health clubs cost $75.00 a month on the average.

Question 80 is based on the following passage.

The domestic oil industry continues to cut back its production, and the percentage of oil imported into the United States continues to increase. Increased dependence on foreign oil will have two results: first, foreign producers will raise prices, and we can be confident that U.S. importers will pay the higher price because of increased demand; second, more huge oil tankers will be needed to move the oil to the U.S. This increases the risk of oil spills and environmental damage to the U.S. shoreline. Domestic producers will be reluctant to increase production because they will benefit more from foreign oil price increases than from expanding their own capacities. Further, after the disastrous oil spill in Alaska, many domestic oil producers feel the need to "lay low" and let foreign oil producers take the blame for future price increases.

80. According to the passage, what is the main reason domestic producers will not increase production?

(A) They have more to gain by not increasing production.

(B) Huge oil tankers are too expensive.

(C) They are afraid of oil spills.

(D) Foreign oil is falling in price.

Section 2: Written Assignment

> **DIRECTIONS:** Plan and write an essay on the topic given below. DO NOT WRITE ON ANY TOPIC OTHER THAN THE ONE SPECIFIED. AN ESSAY ON ANY OTHER TOPIC IS UNACCEPTABLE.

Essay Topic:

In the twentieth century, the concept of heroism is dead.

Assignment:

Do you agree or disagree with the statement? Support your opinion with specific examples from history, current events, literature, or personal experience.

ATS-W ELEMENTARY PRACTICE TEST 1

TIME: 4 Hours
80 Multiple-Choice Questions, 1 Essay

SECTION 1

> **DIRECTIONS:** Read each stimulus carefully, and answer the questions that follow. Mark your responses on the answer sheet provided.

Mr. Drake is a first-grade teacher who is using the whole language method while teaching about animals.

1. Before reading a story to the students, Mr. Drake tells the students what he is expecting to learn from reading the story. What is his reason for doing this?

   (A) The students should know why the instructor chose this text over any other.

   (B) It is important for teachers to share personal ideas with their students in order to foster an environment of confidence and understanding.

   (C) Mr. Drake wants to verify that all students are on-task before he begins the story.

   (D) Mr. Drake is modeling a vital pre-reading skill in order to teach it to the young readers.

2. Mr. Drake wants to ensure that the class will have a quality discussion on the needs of house pets. In response to a student who said that her family abandoned their cat in a field because it ate too much, Mr. Drake

asks: "What is one way to save pets that are no longer wanted." This exercise involves what level of questioning?

(A) Evaluation   (B) Analysis

(C) Comprehension   (D) Synthesis

3.   Mr. Drake has a heterogeneously grouped reading class. He has the students in groups of two—one skilled reader and one remedial reader—reading selected stories to one another. The students read the story and question each other until they feel that they both understand the story. By planning the lesson this way, Mr. Drake has

    (A) set a goal for his students.

    (B) condensed the number of observations necessary, thereby creating more time for class instruction.

    (C) made it possible for another teacher to utilize the limited materials.

    (D) utilized the student's strength and weaknesses to maximize time, materials, and the learning environment.

4.   Mr. Drake is continuing his lesson on the animal kingdom. He wants to ensure that the students learn as much as they can about animals, so he incorporates information they are familiar with into the new information. Knowing that these are first-grade learners, what should Mr. Drake consider when contemplating their learning experience?

    (A) The students will know how much information they can retrieve from memory.

    (B) The students will overestimate how much information they can retrieve from memory.

    (C) The students will be able to pick out the information they need to study and the information which they do not need to study due to prior mastery.

    (D) The students will estimate how much they can learn in one time period.

5.   Before reading a story about a veterinary hospital, Mr. Drake constructs a semantic map of related words and terms using the students' input. What is his main intention for doing this?

(A) To demonstrate a meaningful relationship between the concepts of the story and the prior knowledge of the students

(B) To serve as a visual means of learning

(C) To determine the level of understanding the students will have at the conclusion of the topic being covered

(D) To model proper writing using whole words

Mika Felder's sixth-grade class is studying the world of work. She discusses a new idea related to this study with a more experienced teacher. Ms. Felder is planning to invite all parents to visit the class, talk about their own work, and respond to student's questions. She hopes to have three or four parents a day for this activity over a period of two weeks or so. The fellow teacher encourages Ms. Felder to go ahead and make plans for this activity, after receiving approval of the project from the principal.

6. Which of the following reasons is the major benefit pointed out by the experienced teacher?

(A) Ms. Felder will have the opportunity to further her career awareness goals of the curriculum and the relationship she is trying to establish with the families of her students.

(B) The project will be a free way to have guest speakers for the class.

(C) The project will introduce students to a variety of careers and help students select the careers they want to follow some day.

(D) Ms. Felder will be able to see which parents will cooperate with her when she has a need for their help.

Paula Kresmeier teaches sixth-grade language arts classes. One of her curriculum goals is to help students improve their spelling. As one of her techniques, she has developed a number of special mnemonic devices that she uses with the students, getting the idea from the old teaching rhymes like "I before E except after C or when sounding like A as in neighbor or weigh." Her own memory tricks—"The moose can't get loose from the noose" or "Spell rhyme? Why me?" have caught the interest of her students. Now, besides Mrs. Kresmeier's memory tricks for better spelling, her students are developing and sharing their own creative ways to memorize more effectively.

7.   To improve her student's spelling, Mrs. Kresmeier's method has been successful primarily because of which of the following factors related to student achievement?

   (A)   The students are not relying on phonics or sight words to spell difficult words.

   (B)   Mrs. Kresmeier has impressed her students with the need to learn to spell.

   (C)   The ideas are effective with many students and help to create a learning environment that is open to student interaction.

   (D)   Mrs. Kresmeier teaches spelling using words that can be adapted to mnemonic clues.

Miss Sharp's fourth-grade class is studying a unit entitled "Discoveries" in social studies and science. Miss Sharp has prepared four learning centers for the class. In Learning Center #1 students use information from their science and social studies textbooks to prepare a time line of discoveries that occurred between 1800 and 1997. In Learning Center #2 students use a variety of resource materials to research one particular discovery or discoverer they have selected from a prepared list. Each student then records what they learned about this discovery or discoverer on an individual chart that will later be shared with the whole class. In Learning Center #3 students add small amounts of five different substances to jars of water and record the results over a period of five minutes. In Learning Center #4 students write a description of the need for a new discovery to solve a problem or answer a question. Then students suggest several possible areas of research that may contribute to this new discovery.

8.   Miss Sharp introduces the learning centers by explaining the purpose of each center and giving directions for each activity. Next she divides the class of 22 into four groups and assigns each group to a different center. After 20 minutes, some students are completely finished with one center and want to move on, but other students have only just begun working. What would be the best solution to this situation?

   (A)   Each learning center should be revised so that the activities will require approximately the same amount of time to complete.

(B) Students who finish one center early should be given additional work to complete before moving to the next center.

(C) Students should be permitted to move from center to center as they complete each activity so long as no more than six students are working at each center.

(D) Students should be permitted to work through the activities in each center as quickly as possible so that the class can move on to the next unit.

9. As the students work in the learning centers, Miss Sharp moves from group to group asking questions and commenting on each student's progress. This procedure indicates that Miss Sharp most likely views her role as a (an)

(A) facilitator.

(B) supervisor.

(C) disciplinarian.

(D) evaluator.

10. Which of the following would be the most appropriate concluding activity for the Discoveries Unit?

(A) Students should have a class party celebrating the birthday of Marie Curie, Jonas Salk, and Thomas Edison.

(B) Each student should be required to prepare a verbal report detailing what they learned about an important medical discovery.

(C) Each student should take a multiple-choice test containing questions related to each learning center.

(D) Each student should design a concluding activity, or select one from a prepared list, that reflects what they learned about a discovery they studied.

11. In selecting resource materials for Learning Center #2, Miss Sharp carefully chooses materials that present information about a variety of discoveries made by both men and women from several different

countries. Her purpose in making these selections is most probably to ensure that materials

(A) are challenging but written at the appropriate reading level.

(B) demonstrate the diversity of individuals who have made discoveries.

(C) contain information about discoveries included in the textbook.

(D) will be of interest to the majority of the students.

Mr. Freeman is preparing a year-long unit on process writing for his fifth-grade class. He plans for each student to write about a series of topics over each six-week grading period. At the end of each grading period, students will select three completed writing assignments that reflect their best work. Mr. Freeman will review the assignments and conference with each student. During the conference, Mr. Freeman will assist the students with preparing a list of writing goals for the next grading term.

12. Which of the following best describes Mr. Freeman's plan for reviewing student writing assignments, conferencing with each student, and helping each student set specific goals for writing to be accomplished during the next grading period?

(A) Summative evaluation

(B) Summative assessment

(C) Formative assessment

(D) Peer assessment

13. Mr. Freeman's goal in planning to conference with each student about his/her writing could be described as

(A) creating a climate of trust and encouraging a positive attitude toward writing.

(B) an efficient process for grading student writing assignments.

(C) an opportunity to stress the importance of careful editing of completed writing assignments.

(D) an opportunity to stress the value of prewriting in producing a final product.

14. Philip is a student in Mr. Freeman's class who receives services from a resource teacher for a learning disability which affects his reading and writing. Which of the following is the most appropriate request that Mr. Freeman should make of the resource teacher to help Philip complete the writing unit?

(A) Mr. Freeman should ask the resource teacher to provide writing instruction for Philip.

(B) Mr. Freeman should excuse Philip from all writing assignments.

(C) Mr. Freeman should ask the resource teacher for help in modifying the writing unit to match Philip's needs.

(D) Mr. Freeman should ask the resource teacher to schedule extra tutoring sessions to help Philip with the writing assignments.

Miss Treen is a kindergarten teacher at Green Valley Elementary. Her students are primarily Hispanic. English is a second language for about one-third of the class.

15. Miss Treen wants to encourage her students to view themselves as successful readers and writers. Which of the following instructional strategies would be least effective in accomplishing this goal?

(A) Providing a reading area in the classroom where students can select books to read in a relaxed and comfortable atmosphere.

(B) Reading at least two books aloud each day and discussing the story with the students.

(C) Accepting invented spellings as the students write letters, grocery lists, telephone messages, and describe classroom events.

(D) Requiring students to copy the alphabet using upper- and lowercase letters at least once each day.

16. During the first parent conference of the year, Miss Treen should

(A) keep the conversation light and unemotional, saving any negative comments for the next conference.

(B) include positive comments about each child and make suggestions for how parents can help the child at home.

(C) discuss the importance of speaking only English at home at all times and insisting that the child communicate with all family members in English.

(D) discuss the results of diagnostic testing using technical terms so that parents will understand her desire to help the children.

17. Miss Treen has just finished teaching a unit on community helpers. She is disappointed because the children did not seem interested in the topic and did not want to discuss the community helpers she had listed on the bulletin board. The best course of action for Miss Treen would be to

(A) borrow another kindergarten teacher's unit on community helpers for use next year.

(B) evaluate each lesson in the unit and revise the lessons to make them more meaningful to the students.

(C) save discussions of community helpers for older children because the topic is too difficult for kindergarten students.

(D) show a filmstrip about community helpers and invite a policeman to visit the class.

The fourth-grade students in Mrs. Alvarez's class are studying Native Americans. Mrs. Alvarez wants to strengthen her student's ability to work independently. She also wants to provide opportunities for the students to use a variety of print and media resources during this unit of study. Mrs. Alvarez plans to begin the unit by leading the class in a brainstorming session to formulate questions to guide their research about Native Americans.

18. Which of the following criteria should guide Mrs. Alvarez as she leads the brainstorming session?

(A) The questions should emphasize the factual content presented in the available print materials.

(B) The questions should emphasize higher order thinking skills, such as comparison, analysis, and evaluation.

(C) The questions should reflect the interest of the students.

(D) The questions should include all of the fourth-grade objectives for this unit.

19. Mrs. Alvarez has collected a variety of print and media resources for the students to use in their research. Which of the following will probably be the best way to motivate students to research the questions they have prepared?

   (A) The teacher should assign two to three questions to each student so that all the questions are covered.

   (B) The teacher should allow individual students to select the questions they would like to research.

   (C) The teacher should select three key questions and assign them to all the students.

   (D) The teacher should assign one topic to each student, then provide the students with additional information.

20. Mrs. Alvarez is using which of the following instructional delivery systems?

   (A) Direct instruction

   (B) Role playing and simulation

   (C) Exposition and discussion

   (D) Inquiry and problem solving

21. Mrs. Alvarez plans to use contemporary assessment techniques at the conclusion of the unit. She is also concerned about providing sufficient feedback to the students. Which of the following is most likely to meet these assessment goals?

   (A) A teacher-made objective test should be used because questions can be prepared to match the unit's content and the final grades can be computed quickly.

   (B) A variety of formal and informal assessment tests should be used.

   (C) A standardized test with established reliability and validity should be used.

(D) Individual tests for each student should be used to allow for individual differences.

22. At the conclusion of the unit, Mrs. Alvarez plans to ask her students to present the projects and activities that were prepared for the unit to the other fourth-grade classes in the building. Planning this time for presentation indicates that Mrs. Alvarez

(A) is concerned about bringing appropriate closure to the unit.

(B) wants to work collaboratively with other teachers.

(C) hopes to be appointed grade-level chairperson.

(D) is concerned about promoting a feeling of student ownership and membership in the class.

23. As part of the presentation of projects and activities, Mrs. Alvarez asks her students to write a narrative explanation of their projects. Then she arranges for the class presentations to be videotaped as the students read their prepared explanations. A student is appointed "filming director" for each project, and another student is appointed "reporter." All of the students who participated are "writers" and contribute to the written script. This activity is an example of

(A) using a variety of instructional resources to support individual and group learning.

(B) inappropriate use of school video equipment.

(C) providing "directors," "reporters," and "writers" with information about those careers.

(D) a homogeneously grouped cooperative learning exercise.

24. A museum of Native American culture is located about 45 minutes from school. Mrs. Alvarez is considering a field trip to the museum. Which of the following elements should most influence her decision?

(A) The relevance of the current exhibits to the topics her students researched

(B) The cost of admission, the distance from the school, and the availability of transportation

(C) The difficulty in obtaining permission forms from each student

(D) The loss of class time in other subject areas

Mrs. Gettler teaches 26 third graders in a large inner city school. About one-third of her students participate in the ESL program at the school. Mrs. Gettler suspects that some of the students parents are unable to read or write in English. Four of the students receive services from the learning resource teacher. At the beginning of the year, none of the students read above 2.0 grade level, and some of the students did not know all the letters of the alphabet.

25. Which of the following describes the instructional strategy that is most likely to improve the reading levels of Mrs. Gettler's students?

(A) An intensive phonics program that includes drill and practice work on basic sight words.

(B) An emergent literacy program emphasizing pattern books and journal writing using invented spelling.

(C) An instructional program that closely follows the third-grade basal reader

(D) All the students should participate in the school's ESL program and receive services from the learning resource center.

26. Mrs. Gettler is selecting books for the classroom library. In addition to student interest, which of the following would be the most important considerations?

(A) The books should have a reading level that matches the students' independent reading ability.

(B) The books should only have a reading level that is challenging to the students.

(C) The books should include separate word lists for student practice.

(D) A classroom library is not appropriate for students at such a low reading level.

27. Which of the following individual and small group learning centers is suitable for Mrs. Gettler's class?

I. A post office center where students can write letters to friends and family

II. A restaurant center where students read menus, write food orders, and pay the bill with play money

III. A weather center where students record current conditions, including temperature, cloud cover and wind direction, and prepare graphs of weather patterns

IV. A science center where students record the results of experiments with combining liquids such as bleach, vinegar, cooking oil, food coloring, and rubbing alcohol

(A) I only.   (B) I and II only.

(C) I, II, and III only.   (D) II, III, and IV only.

28. Mrs. Gettler realizes that an individual's preferred learning style contributes to that individual's success as a student. Mrs. Gettler wants to accommodate as many of her student's individual learning styles as possible. Which of the following best describes the way to identify the student's learning styles?

(A) Mrs. Gettler should record her observations of individual student's behaviors over a period of several weeks.

(B) Each of the student's should be tested by the school psychologist.

(C) Mrs. Gettler should administer a group screening test for identifying learning styles.

(D) Mrs. Gettler should review the permanent file of each student and compare the individual's previous test scores with classroom performance.

29. During the first parent-teacher conference of the year, Mrs. Gettler should

(A) stress that it is unlikely that each student in her class will be promoted to the fourth grade.

(B) determine the educational background of each parent and recommend the district GED program as needed.

(C) emphasize her willingness to work with each student to enable each student to be successful.

(D) recommend that parents secure an individual tutor for each student who is reading below grade level.

30. As the school year progresses, Mrs. Gettler includes discussions of holidays of many cultures. She introduces the holiday prior to the actual day of celebration. The children prepare decorations, learn songs, and read stories about children in the countries where the holiday is celebrated. Which of the following best describes the most likely purpose of this activity?

(A) Celebrating holidays of many cultures is one way to teach appreciation of human diversity.

(B) Celebrating holidays of many cultures is one way to satisfy the demands of political action groups.

(C) Celebrating holidays is one way to encourage students to read aloud to one another.

(D) Celebrating holidays is one way to encourage students to participate in class activities.

Mr. Dobson teaches fifth-grade mathematics at Valverde Elementary. He encourages students to work in groups of two or three as they begin homework assignments so they can answer questions for each other. Mr. Dobson notices immediately that some of his students chose to work alone even though they had been asked to work in groups. He also notices that some students are easily distracted even though the other members of their group are working on the assignment as directed.

31. Which of the following is the most likely explanation for the students' behavior?

(A) Fifth-grade students are not physically or mentally capable of working in small groups; small groups are more suitable for older students.

(B) Fifth-grade students vary greatly in their physical development and maturity; this variance influences the students' interests and attitudes.

(C) Fifth-grade students lack the ability for internal control, and therefore learn best in structured settings. It is usually best to seat fifth graders in single rows.

(D) Mr. Dobson needs to be more specific in his expectations for student behavior.

32. Mr. Dobson wants to encourage all of his students to participate in discussions related to the use of math in the real world. Five students in one class are very shy and introverted. Which of the following would most likely be the best way to encourage these students to participate in the discussion?

(A) Mr. Dobson should call on these students by name at least once each day and give participation grades.

(B) Mr. Dobson should not be concerned about these students because they will become less shy and introverted as they mature during the year.

(C) Mr. Dobson should divide the class into small groups for discussion so these students will not be overwhelmed by speaking in front of the whole class.

(D) Mr. Dobson should speak with these students individually and encourage them to participate more in class discussions.

33. In the same class, Mr. Dobson has two students who are overly talkative. These two students volunteer to answer every question. Which of the following is the best way to deal with these students?

(A) Mr. Dobson should call on the overly talkative students only once during each class.

(B) Mr. Dobson should ask these students to be the observers in small group discussions, and take notes about participation and topics discussed.

(C) Mr. Dobson should place these students in a group by themselves so they can discuss all they want and not disturb the other students.

(D) Mr. Dobson should recognize that overly talkative students need lots of attention and should be called on to participate throughout the class period.

34. Mr. Dobson wants his fifth-grade students to serve as tutors for the first graders who are learning addition and subtraction. The main advantage for the fifth graders who participate is

(A) they will develop proficiency and self-esteem.

(B) they will be encouraged to view teaching as a possible career.

(C) they will learn specific tutoring techniques.

(D) they will have an opportunity to become friends with younger children.

35. Mr. Dobson plans mathematics lessons so that all students will experience at least 70 percent success during independent practice. Considering student success during independent practice reflects Mr. Dobson's understanding that

(A) a student's academic success influences overall achievements and contributes to positive self-esteem.

(B) students who are academically successful have happy parents.

(C) if students are successful when working alone they can finish their homework independently.

(D) if the students are successful they will ask fewer questions, giving Mr. Dobson more time to plan future lessons.

36. Mr. Dobson has just explained a new procedure for solving a particular kind of mathematics problem. He has solved several demonstration problems on the board. Several students raise their hands to ask questions. If a student's question requires more than two or three minutes to answer, then Mr. Dobson knows that

(A) the original explanation was faulty.

(B) the students were not paying attention.

(C) the students are below average in listening skills.

(D) the students have a very poor background in mathematics.

37. Mr. Dobson and Mr. Lowery, a science teacher, are planning a celebration of Galileo's birthday. The students will research Galileo's discov-

eries, draw posters of those discoveries, and prepare short plays depicting important events in his life. They will present the plays and display the posters for grades 1–4. This is an example of

(A) an end-of-the-year project.

(B) problem solving and inquiry teaching.

(C) working with other teachers to plan instructions.

(D) teachers preparing to ask the PTA for science lab equipment.

38. Mr. Dobson wants to use a variety of grouping strategies during the year. Sometimes he groups students with others of similar ability; sometimes he groups students with varying ability. Sometimes he permits students to choose their own groupings. Sometimes he suggests that students work with a particular partner; sometimes he assigns a partner. Sometimes he allows students to elect to work individually. This flexibility in grouping strategies indicates Mr. Dobson recognizes that

(A) fifth graders like surprises and unpredictable teacher behavior.

(B) grouping patterns affect students' perceptions of self-esteem and competence.

(C) frequent changes in the classroom keep students alert and interested.

(D) it is not fair to place the worst students in the same group consistently.

39. The principal asks Mr. Dobson and Ms. Gonzalez, another fifth-grade math teacher in the school, to visit the math classes and the computer lab in the middle school that most of the students at Valverde will attend. By asking Mr. Dobson and Ms. Gonzalez to visit the middle school, the principal is most likely encouraging

(A) collaboration among the math teachers at Valverde and the middle school.

(B) Mr. Dobson and Ms. Gonzalez to consider applying for a job at the middle school.

(C) the use of computers in math classes at Valverde.

(D) the use of the middle school math curriculum in the fifth-grade classes.

Mrs. Doe began planning a two-week unit of study of the Native Americans for her fifth-grade class. To begin the unit, she chose a movie on the twenty-first century Native American. As Mrs. Doe reflectively listened, key questions were asked.

The following day Mrs. Doe reviewed the use of encyclopedias, indexes, and atlases. The students were divided into groups and taken to the library. Each group was responsible for locating information on their topic. The topics were maps showing the topography of the land, charts illustrating the climate, plants and animals, a map showing migration routes, and a map showing the general areas where the Native Americans settled.

40. The students' involvement in the unit of study is a result of

   I.   the teacher's reflective listening during the discussion.

   II. the available resources and materials.

   III. careful planning and its relationship to success in the classroom.

   IV. the students' personal acquaintance with Native Americans.

   (A) I only.   (B) I and II only.

   (C) II and III only.   (D) I and IV only.

Days 3 and 4 were spent with each group being involved in library research. Information was written on index cards. Each group prepared a presentation which included a written explanation of an assigned topic, a shadowbox, a sawdust map or models of Native American clothing. A pictograph was to be used in the telling of a legend or folk story. The presentation was concluded with a collage depicting the Native American way of life.

41. Multiple strategies and techniques were used for

    I.   motivation of the group and its effects on individual behavior and learning.

    II.   allowing each student regardless of ability to participate in the project.

    III. integrating the project with other subjects.

    IV. developing a foundation for teaching American history.

    (A) I, II, and III only.   (B) I and II only.

    (C) III only.   (D) IV only.

On day 8, Mrs. Doe arranged a display of Native American artifacts and crafts in the hallway. Having collaborated with the music teacher at the onset of her planning and arranging for a general assembly of the entire student body, she took her students to the auditorium. The general assembly consisted of Native American poetry read by Fawn Lonewolf with Native American music and dance by the school chorus. At the conclusion of the assembly, the class was invited to view the video *The Trail of Tears*. Native American refreshments, including fried bread were served to the students. As the students ate, *Knots on a Counting Rope* was read orally by the reading teacher. Following the reading, the physical education teacher taught the students several games which had been played by Native American children.

42. The planning of the assembly and the following activities required

    I.   the taking of risks by both the teacher and the students.

    II.   stimulating the curiosity of the student body.

    III. recognizing individual talents among the students.

    IV. using the collaborative process of working with other teachers.

    (A) I only.   (B) II only.

    (C) II and III only.   (D) II, III, and IV only.

Day 10 of the unit was Field Trip Day. The students were given a choice of visiting museums. Whatever the student's choice, he or she was to take notes of what was seen, heard, and experienced. These would be shared with the remainder of the class on the following day.

43. Field Trip Day and its experiences

    I.   allowed the student to make connections between their current skills and those that were new to them.

    II. allowed external factors to create a learning environment which would take advantage of positive factors.

    III. allowed a sense of community to be nurtured.

    IV. allowed the students to take responsibility for their own learning.

(A) I and II only.   (B) III only.

(C) IV only.   (D) III and IV only.

44. The choice of field trip locations

    I.   was to enhance the students' self-concept.

    II. was to respect differences and enhance the students' understanding of the society in which they live.

    III. was to foster the view of learning as a purposeful pursuit.

    IV. was an example of using an array of instructional strategies.

(A) II only.   (B) II and IV only.

(C) I and II only.   (D) III only.

Several average classes of fifth graders were found to be inadequately prepared for fifth-grade work. It was important that their problem-solving skills and motivation improve in order to meet the pre-entry criteria for a new middle-school. Most of the students could not comprehend fifth-grade textual material. They lacked enthusiasm for projects and problems. Many of the students had become frightened by their academic failure and were withdrawing in confusion.

Mrs. Sivart is retained to help the classes improve their problem-solving skills and to facilitate motivation and enthusiasm. After reviewing test scores and evaluating daily work, she called for a conference with the concerned teachers. "Mrs. Dunn, what do you perceive to be the problem?" "Those students just did not learn the appropriate skills in the lower grades. What can I do when they come to me with deficient skills? After all, I teach social studies, I do not teach basic reading skills." "Mr. Ellis, what is your perception?" "I believe, as does Mrs. Dunn, that these students were not taught these skills in the lower grades. They were just promoted along." "Do you feel a responsibility toward the students to correct this deficiency?" asked Mrs. Sivart. "Yes, I really do, but my first responsibility is for each student to meet the objectives required by the state each year. I just don't have time to remediate the students."

Mrs. Sivart was reflective for a moment, then gently asked "What would you say if I told you that at least part of the problem does not lie with the students? What text do you currently use?" "We use the standard fifth-grade social studies text from Blank Publishing Company." "May we meet again tomorrow at this same time?" asked Mrs. Sivart. "I have something to show you."

The following day Mrs. Sivart appeared in the meeting with readability charts, texts, paper, and pencils. Each teacher agreed to do a readability on the text. As they completed the readability, a stunned silence followed. "I certainly did not know I was expecting these students to read materials which are three years above their grade level. No wonder, they don't comprehend. Mrs. Sivart, what can we do to remedy this situation?"

45. At this point in the solving of the problem, Mrs. Sivart had

   (A) caused each teacher to focus upon reflection and self-evaluation and to recognize their bias.

   (B) allowed the teachers to shift part of the blame to the publisher from the elementary teachers.

   (C) allowed the teachers to seek out opportunities to grow professionally by using different sources of support and guidance to enhance his/her own professional skills.

   (D) used informal assessment to understand the learners.

46. Mr. Ellis' statement that he was expected to meet the state objectives each year revealed that he

   (A) was refusing to reflect upon his responsibility to the students and was unwilling to change teaching strategies.

(B) understood the requirements and expectations of teaching.

(C) was inflexible in his strategies and the use of collaborative processes.

(D) probably had a deficiency in using a variety of instructional materials.

At the following planning meeting, Mrs. Sivart agreed to demonstrate a strategy which could be used in each class to make the adopted text appropriate for that class. Following her demonstration, she asked the teachers to develop an exam which would cover the material they had just modified. Each teacher was then to do a readability on the exam. As Mrs. Sivart circulated among the teachers, she saw puzzled expressions and overheard "I have just written a ninth-grade exam for fifth-grade students. I can't believe I did that. What do I do now?" With a smile, Mrs. Sivart responded, "You rewrite the exam until it is on the fifth-grade level. Using your readability chart, check each item on the exam, keep modifying the item until it is written on the correct level." She continued, "What you have done is very common among teachers, but with practice you will soon be writing exams on grade level. By combining modification of the text with writing your exams on grade level and using a few techniques for increasing comprehension, you should see a great change in your students. Nothing breeds success like success."

47. Through the demonstration, the in-service training of writing exams, and the extra techniques for improving comprehension, Mrs. Sivart had demonstrated that

(A) the teacher is to constantly monitor and adjust strategies in response to student feedback.

(B) the teacher could promote student learning by designing instruction for different situations.

(C) the teacher should be able to recognize factors and situations that will either promote or diminish motivation.

(D) external factors may affect students' performance in school.

48. The concept that Mrs. Sivart had caused the teachers to focus upon was that

(A) most of the time when a student fails, it is not his/her fault.

(B) individualizing instruction does not have to be tedious and time consuming.

(C) external factors may affect students' performance in class.

(D) diversity in the classroom may affect learning.

A traditional elementary school reading program for grades K-6 has been evaluated. The results show that a majority of students are not reading at grade level. Library records reveal the students' lack of interest in reading. The reading coordinator, Mrs. Sivart, has been charged with coordinating efforts to improve the reading skills for all grades. The improvement of reading skills on or near grade level is the school objective.

Mrs. Sivart's first action was to form a committee of the school psychometrist, the media specialist, and one teacher from each of the seven grades. The psychometrist was to study the test results and determine which of the reading skills were lacking in the students. She reported that only 30 percent of the students were deficient in specific reading skills. The remainder of the students were deficient in no particular area but had an overall deficiency. She explained that there were developmental progressions and ranges of individual variation in each domain which would account for about 10 percent of the students.

Mrs. Sivart asks the teachers to design a plan of study for those students who fell within the 10 percent.

49. The rationale for her request was based upon

   (A) lessening the work load for the teachers.

   (B) obtaining a framework for remediating the other 20 percent of the students.

   (C) facilitating the development of a project plan best suited to address the academic needs of individual students.

   (D) recognizing the benefits of working cooperatively to achieve goals.

Mrs. Sivart began to design a plan of study for those students who were deficient in one or more areas of reading skills. She chose a plan which would allow the student to rotate from one teacher to another, remediating one reading skill with each teacher. When the student had mastered all deficient skills, they no longer attended the sessions.

50. Mrs. Sivart planned her strategy based upon the knowledge that

   (A) students learn faster when they perceive they are learning less.

   (B) teachers would be more receptive to teaching one skill instead of all reading skills.

   (C) parents would be less likely to perceive the remediation as a negative activity.

   (D) assimilation occurs more rapidly for the student when new information is linked to old information.

The media specialist suggested a library reading program which would correlate highly with the teaching program and reward the students as they read. The rewards would be provided by the business community. A pencil carrier would be the reward for having read 25 books, a baseball cap the reward for having read 30 books, a tee shirt for 50 books, and a backpack for having read 100 books.

51. The media specialist's suggestion was based on her knowledge that

   (A) students enjoy doing those things they do well.

   (B) students would read to receive the reward.

   (C) instruction which is planned to enhance students' self-esteem will create an environment where the student feels accepted, competent, and productive.

   (D) library materials which correlate with teaching strategies are more meaningful and help to create an atmosphere which motivates students to continue to read additional books.

Mrs. Sivart requested that computers be made available in the small group area of the library. Software would be provided which contained comprehension questions for 500 books. As each student completed reading the book, they were free to come to the library and take the comprehension quiz. The computer kept a record of those books read and comprehended. If comprehension fell below 80 percent, the student alone knew if he/she needed to reread the book and retake the exam.

52. Mrs. Sivart felt that student privacy was important because

    (A) students' self-esteem is easily lowered if others are aware of their failures.

    (B) this strategy would remove the teacher from the role of informing the student if he/she needed to reread and retake the test.

    (C) the use of the computers would prevent the media specialist from having an increased workload.

    (D) the combination of appropriate instructional materials and resources helps students to understand the role of technology as a learning tool.

After yet another brainstorming session with all members of the action committee, the group decided to post then repost the title of each book each time it was read and comprehended.

53. Publicly displaying the titles of the books was based upon

    (A) understanding the uses of formal and informal assessment to monitor instructional effectiveness.

    (B) facilitating motivation of all the students.

    (C) helping the students to become independent thinkers and problem-solvers.

    (D) varying the role of the teachers in the instructional process.

54. As the action committee reviewed the design of the curriculum, they recognized that

    (A) the amount of classroom time would be maximized.

    (B) a positive atmosphere in the classroom would be preserved.

    (C) routines and transitions would be managed.

(D) they had structured a learning environment which not only maintained a positive classroom environment but would promote the lifelong pursuit of learning.

The home economics teacher, Mrs. Green, was planning a unit on nutrition. Her first task was to identify the performance objectives. She concluded that she wanted the students to master the content of her lecture, but she also wanted them to be able to do independent research in the library on the topic of nutrition. Her second task was to prepare an evaluation tool to be used at the completion of the unit. She decided to have a paper and pencil test as well as a performance exam. Step 3 consisted of choosing resources for the class presentation. She chose a beginning text on foods, the nutrition unit from the curriculum materials, two *Measure Up* games from the media center, teacher-made worksheets covering the appropriate content, a computer program for enhancing the classroom presentation, and the required tools and ingredients for the performance aspect of the unit. The unit would be concluded with a field trip.

55. The presentation of the unit was designed to

(A) communicate through verbal, nonverbal, and media thus imparting the expectations and ideas to create a climate of inquiry.

(B) present the material in a variety of media using several techniques.

(C) give the students a choice of what they were to learn.

(D) integrate with other subjects in the school.

56. The strength of requiring a cognitive objective and a performance objective is that

(A) some students are not test takers and do poorly on paper and pencil tests.

(B) the score for one objective could offset the score for the other objective.

(C) the developmental level in one domain may affect performance in another domain.

(D) the teacher is matching the students' learning styles to her teaching style.

57. The multiple resources planned for by Mrs. Green provided for

(A) enhancing student achievement.

(B) engaging the students in meaningful inquiry.

(C) eliciting different levels of thinking from the students.

(D) promoting problem solving.

To begin the unit, Mrs. Green presented the information through the lecture technique. The students were instructed to add notes to the outline of the lecture which had been provided to them. After the information was presented, the students completed the supplementary activities and planned the activities which would be carried out in the labs. The labs contained the ingredients. Some of the students were instructed to deliberately mismeasure one of the key ingredients in the recipe. Later the recipe was analyzed to determine why the result was a failure. A discussion followed with various students reporting that while watching their parents cook, many times they had used a "dab," a "dash," or a "pinch" of ingredients, not actually measuring.

58. The demonstration of not accurately measuring the ingredients in a recipe was used to

I. show the students what happens when directions are not followed.

II. to evaluate the observation techniques used by the students.

III. to stimulate curiosity in the students.

IV. to illustrate how waste can occur in the kitchen.

(A) I only.   (B) II only.

(C) III and IV only.   (D) I, III, and IV only.

The culminating field trip was to the cafeteria where the students were familiarized with special measuring tools, e.g., scales, gallons, and pounds. As the students observed the use of these special tools and amounts, they were asked to try to imagine the quantity that a particular recipe would produce and how many servings it would provide.

59. The field trip was planned as a culminating experience

   (A) to bring closure to the unit.

   (B) to promote responsibility for one's own learning.

   (C) to confine the students' learning to the classroom, keeping it in an academic setting.

   (D) to allow the students to make the connection between their current skills and those that are new to them.

Bill Drayton is a first-year teacher whose teaching field is reading. Bill is an exemplary teacher and is already assuming a leadership role in both the community and within the school district. He has started taking classes at a university in order to earn a Master of Teaching credential.

Late in the fall semester, Bill arrived home right as a rental moving truck pulled up in front of the house across the street. The "for sale" sign on the house had recently been taken down, and Bill was eager to meet his new neighbors. He trotted across the street and introduced himself to the man who crawled out of the truck.

As the introductions were taking place, a van pulled up into the driveway and a woman came around the side of the van in order to help a young girl in a wheelchair exit the van. "Come and meet my wife, Rachel, and our daughter, Myra," said the new neighbor, who had introduced himself as Harry Jacobsen.

"Myra is in fourth grade," said her mother.

"Then you'll be in one of my classes," said Bill. "We have two fourth-grade classes. Each one spends half the day in Ms. Wade's room, and the other half of the day in mine. I teach language arts and math, while she teaches social studies, science, and art. We have a lot of fun, because we teach around themes. For example, Ms. Wade's social studies classes are learning about how New York history was influenced by geography, so in my language arts class, we're reading stories about New York history and discussing how the geography contributed to the things that happened in those stories. We also pretend that we are early New Yorkers and write journals and newspapers about the events that shaped our history as those events relate to geography. In my math classes, we're using math to better understand New York geography. Things like lengths of rivers, miles between cities located on the waterways, and so forth."

Myra's eyes lit up. "Can I be in his room, Mama?" she asked.

Rachel shook her head. "No, honey, I'm sorry." Then she explained to Bill that Myra had to go to a private school because the local schools were not wheelchair accessible. "Myra can't get through the outer doors, the inner doors, up the stairs to the classroom, the cafeteria, the gym, or anywhere else. In fact, she can't even get into the toilet stalls," she explained. "These changes would take many thousands of dollars, and the district can't spend that kind of money on Myra."

60.   What should Bill say?

(A)   "I'm sorry. But maybe I can bring home some fun materials from school to share with Myra."

(B)   "It is illegal for the school not to make itself accessible to all people with handicaps, regardless of the cost. Let me talk to the principal."

(C)   "I'm sorry. If the costs were reasonable, perhaps the district could make changes. But you're right. We can't make changes that expensive for only one student."

(D)   "You should sue the school district and make them do the changes"

That evening, Bill and his wife went out to eat to celebrate her birthday. They went to a movie, and then finding that there was a full moon, decided to go for a drive before they went home. As they rounded a corner not far from their home, Bill saw one of his students, Cade Evans, running down the street. Cade was with a group of other boys, one of whom threw something down as they ran. Although Bill did not see the faces of any of the boys except for Cade, judging from their size, he thought that they were probably also fourth graders. Bill stopped his car and looked around. He discovered newly painted graffiti on the side of the building by the corner.

61.   What is Bill's best course of action?

I.   Chase down the boys with his car and make a citizen's arrest.

II.   Call the police and report what he saw.

III. Call the superintendent immediately and report what he saw.

IV. Refer Cade to Big Brothers' as a child in need of a special friend.

(A) I and II only.   (B) II and IV only.

(C) II and III only.   (D) III and IV only.

Troubled by what seems to be an increase in gang-type activity among younger and younger children, Bill wants to find out what his students think about and know about gangs. He wants to learn the most he can about the students' thinking about this topic in the least amount of time. He wants all students to have the chance to share what they think/know, yet he also wants to maximize interaction among students as well. The students will spend the entire morning reading, talking, and writing a group report about this subject.

62. Which of the following seating arrangements would best help Bill meet his objectives?

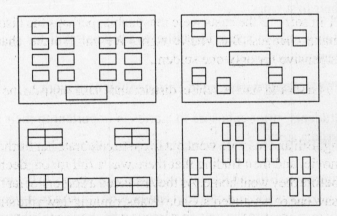

(A) The upper left-hand diagram

(B) The lower left-hand diagram

(C) The upper right-hand diagram

(D) The lower right-hand diagram

63. One of the activities that Bill decides to employ in his language arts class during the thematic study of the impact of geographic features on the history of New York is storytelling. Bill has studied the art of storytelling

and one day aspires to be a master storyteller. What would be the most important reason that Bill learn to be a master storyteller?

(A) Everyone loves a good story.

(B) Storytelling is a highly cost-effective method of teaching.

(C) Storytelling is one of the most effective ways of teaching field dependent students.

(D) Storytelling is one of the most effective ways of teaching field independent students.

64. Following two days of activities which include Bill's storytelling sessions, Bill tells the children that they are to each write a story to tell to the class. What is most likely the instructional reason that Bill is having the children write a story with the intent of telling it to the class as opposed to merely writing a story?

(A) Publication is a highly effective tool in motivating people to do their best work.

(B) Being able to speak in public is a crucial skill for success in a democratic society.

(C) The students will learn to critique their own work.

(D) Students' prior exposure to stories is important to their ability to write a story.

65. That afternoon, Bill and Kayla Wade meet after school to begin planning for the next thematic unit of study. Kayla, who is also a first-year teacher, is ready to move into the unit on persons who made contributions to the development of New York . Which strategy for planning for outcome-oriented learning experiences would be the best one with which to start?

(A) Select desired learning activities.

(B) Determine time and space constraints.

(C) Determine desired learner outcomes.

(D) Solicit input from students.

Bill comes to the planning session with a notecard on which he has listed the essential elements that he plans to address during the new unit of study:

> *LISTENING*
> Distinguish between fact and opinion.
>
> *SPEAKING*
> Adapt content and formality of oral language to fit the purpose and audience.
>
> *READING*
> 1. Identify multiple causes of character's actions.
> 2. Understand the feelings of characters.
>
> *WRITING*
> Use ideas/sources other than personal opinion/experiences.

66. Which of the following resources are most likely to be of use to Bill?

    I.   Computer with word-processing program

    II.   Laser disk player with laser disk of influential New Yorkers

    III. Primary sources

    IV. Local expert on ecology

(A) I only.   (B) I and IV only.

(C) II only.   (D) II and III only.

Gerene Thompson is a first-year teacher who has accepted a position as a first-grade teacher in an inner city school. In college, Gerene's elementary teaching field was science. She is eager to begin working with her first graders so that in addition to teaching them literacy skills, she can teach them to enjoy science and mathematics.

67. In the last week before school starts, Gerene has much to do in order to get ready for the first day of school. Of the many tasks that she must perform, which is likely to have the biggest impact on her students' success in first grade?

    (A) Having a wide variety of teaching material ready and available

    (B) Making the room look inviting by creating bulletin boards depicting students of many nations

    (C) Personally contacting the parents of each child

    (D) Coordinating her science activities with her reading activities

68. Of all of her students who do not have documented handicaps, which of her students are most likely to be poor readers?

    (A) Those whose parents seldom read aloud to them

    (B) Those whose parents place them in daycare for more than three hours per day

    (C) Those whose parents allow them to watch more than two hours of television daily

    (D) Those who are being raised by a grandparent

69. In planning her first week's activities, what factors should Gerene consider?

    I.   The interests of first graders

    II. Her students' prior knowledge

    III. The affective needs of her students

    IV. The nutritional needs of her students

    (A) I and II only.   (B) II and IV only.

    (C) I, II, and III only.   (D) All of the above.

70. On the first day, Gerene plans to introduce her students to the phoneme/ grapheme relationship of the letter M. Which of the following would be the best set of strategies for this objective?

   (A) Gerene should tell her students what sound the letter M makes. She should then provide them with a wide variety of fun paper/pencil and coloring activities as independent work to help them internalize the letter name with its sound. She should schedule the students throughout the day to take turns on the class computer's phonics program.

   (B) Gerene should engage the students in a repetitive, rhythmic oral activity using the letter M phoneme/grapheme relationship. She should use a picture as a cue card and display the cue card where the students can see it at all times. She should not place students at the computer without direct supervision for the first several times.

   (C) Gerene should not engage the students in repetitive activity, as repetition will quickly bore them and act as an aversive reinforcer to the reading activity. She should employ paper/pencil activities supplemented with coloring and making M's out of clay, papier-mache, and other manipulative materials. She should also use large-muscle movement activities to reinforce the letter-sound relationship. She should use the interactive laser disk with the entire group to show the students many objects that start with the M sound, but she should not allow students to use the equipment individually.

   (D) Gerene should engage the students in repetitive, rhythmic activities using the letter M in its phoneme/grapheme relationship. She should read at least one picture book aloud to the students in a story-circle, and discuss it at length with them as she reads it. She should display a picture cue card for the letter M in a prominent place. She should use a wide variety of paper/pencil and art activities employing the letter M.

71. Gerene wants to teach her students about ways of collecting data in science. This is a skill required by the New York state curriculum for first graders. First graders are also required to learn about living things. Which of the following describes the most appropriate method of teaching Gerene's students about collecting data in science.

   (A) Gerene should group the students into groups of four. She should then have each group observe while she gently touches the class's pet mouse with a feather. The students should record how many out of ten times the pet mouse moves away from the feather. Then Gerene should gently touch the class's philodendron ten times with a feather. The students should record how many out of ten times the philodendron moves away from the feather.

(B) Gerene should group the students into groups of four. She should give each group five solid balls made of materials that will float and five solid balls made of materials that will not float. She should have the students drop the balls into a bowl of water and record how many float and how many do not.

(C) Gerene should show the students a video about scientific methods of gathering data.

(D) Gerene should have a scientist come and talk to the class about methods of collecting data. If she cannot get a scientist, she should have a science teacher from the high school come and tell about scientific methods of data collection.

72. Gerene wants to reinforce the notion of data collection by assigning a homework project which will involve the students' families. Which of the following would be the most appropriate assignment?

(A) Have the students and their families watch a program on data collection on the Discovery channel

(B) Have the parents take their students to the exhibit on data collection at the local museum

(C) Have the students ask their parents to help them count the number of times that their heart beats per minute at rest and after five minutes of exercise

(D) Have the students ask their parents to read to them about a famous scientist

73. How can Gerene best teach her students to be lifelong learners and lovers of science?

I. Give them examples of famous people who were/are lifelong learners.

II. In an enthusiastic manner, frequently say "Isn't this exciting? Isn't it fun to learn new things!" during science activities.

III. Employ many hands-on activities that are difficult enough to challenge the students, yet simple enough that the students will succeed.

IV. Reward students who work hard and punish students who do not perform.

(A) I and II only.   (B) II and III only.

(C) III and IV only.   (D) III only.

74. In general, how can Gerene best address the learning styles of her female students in science activities?

(A) Employ cooperative, noncompetitive teaching strategies that utilize many experiences with hands-on activities.

(B) Employ competitive teaching strategies that utilize many experiences with hands-on activities.

(C) Employ teaching strategies that require students to work independently on hands-on activities.

(D) Employ teaching strategies utilizing computer-assisted programmed instruction.

75. In general, when Molly Carter, a student of African-American heritage, makes statements such as "My mama, she works at the store down the block." How should Gerene respond?

(A) Gerene should tell Molly that it is important that she learn to speak standard English.

(B) Gerene should not reinforce Molly's speech patterns by interacting with her when she does not speak standard English.

(C) Gerene should say, "Molly dear, it is not correct to say 'my mama, she works' you should say, 'my mama works' if you want people to understand you."

(D) Gerene should say, "Tell me what kinds of things that your mama does at work."

Although Ms. Axtel has two years of experience teaching sixth grade, she has been asked to teach a group of 25 second graders for the new school year. She wants to prepare several units before school begins.

76. Which of the following principles is the most important to consider as she prepares her units?

(A) The major difference between sixth-grade students and second-grade students is their physical size.

(B) Second grade students are very different developmentally from sixth-grade students.

(C) Some second-grade students read as well as sixth-grade students.

(D) Sixth-grade students like to read books on topics that are very different from the topics that second grade students prefer.

77. In January a new student, Jerry Rodriguez, joins Ms. Axtel's class. Neither Jerry nor his parents speak much English. It is most important that Ms. Axtel

(A) give Jerry a non-verbal intelligence test.

(B) be certain that Jerry receives the services of the school's ESL instructor.

(C) keep Jerry isolated from the other students until he feels more comfortable.

(D) be certain that Jerry's parents are learning English.

78. Ms. Axtel's knowledge of Spanish is limited. She is concerned about communicating with Jerry during class activities. Which of the following is the best approach?

(A) Appoint another student to be Jerry's buddy.

(B) Ask Jerry to do math worksheets until he learns basic English.

(C) Give Jerry picture books, paper, and markers.

(D) Allow Jerry to look and listen for as long as he likes.

79. At the end of each week, Ms. Axtel takes a few minutes to write in her journal. She makes written comments about the lessons she taught that week, as well as the student's response to those lessons. She also includes comments about how to change or revise the lessons in the future. This practice indicates that Ms. Axtel is

   (A) concerned about process writing.

   (B) a reflective practitioner.

   (C) keeping notes for her formal evaluation.

   (D) is a habitual journal writer.

80. Ms. Axtel is concerned that Jerry is not making much progress in learning English. She borrows a series of Spanish language computer programs in a variety of content areas from the local Education Service Center. She uses the programs to set up a special learning center with several computers in the classroom. A computer is available to Jerry at any time during the day, and any of the students can use the center if they choose. This indicates that Ms. Axtel is

   (A) concerned that Jerry can learn material best only when it is presented in a visual manner.

   (B) concerned that Jerry will not meet state mandated requirements.

   (C) concerned that Jerry has special needs which can only be met by using a wide variety of learning materials.

   (D) concerned that Jerry may need the assistance of a resource teacher.

Section 2: Written Assignment

> **DIRECTIONS:** Plan and write an essay on the topic given below. DO NOT WRITE ON ANY TOPIC OTHER THAN THE ONE SPECIFIED. AN ESSAY ON ANY OTHER TOPIC IS UNACCEPTABLE.

Essay Topic:

Many schools group students by ability, feeling that this provides the best environment for bright students to excel and remedial students to gain the skills they need to succeed. Many feel, however, that ability grouping prevents some students from reaching their full potential.

Assignment:

Are you in favor of ability grouping? Explain your position by discussing the positive or negative consequences of ability grouping for students and teachers.

LAST
PRACTICE TEST 1

ANSWER KEY

1.	(A)	21.	(C)	41.	(C)	61.	(D)
2.	(B)	22.	(A)	42.	(D)	62.	(C)
3.	(C)	23.	(D)	43.	(D)	63.	(C)
4.	(C)	24.	(C)	44.	(C)	64.	(A)
5.	(A)	25.	(B)	45.	(A)	65.	(C)
6.	(A)	26.	(C)	46.	(B)	66.	(C)
7.	(A)	27.	(B)	47.	(A)	67.	(B)
8.	(D)	28.	(D)	48.	(B)	68.	(D)
9.	(B)	29.	(D)	49.	(B)	69.	(D)
10.	(A)	30.	(C)	50.	(D)	70.	(C)
11.	(A)	31.	(A)	51.	(C)	71.	(A)
12.	(B)	32.	(B)	52.	(A)	72.	(D)
13.	(D)	33.	(A)	53.	(D)	73.	(B)
14.	(C)	34.	(D)	54.	(D)	74.	(D)
15.	(A)	35.	(C)	55.	(A)	75.	(C)
16.	(A)	36.	(A)	56.	(C)	76.	(A)
17.	(A)	37.	(D)	57.	(D)	77.	(B)
18.	(A)	38.	(C)	58.	(B)	78.	(A)
19.	(C)	39.	(A)	59.	(D)	79.	(C)
20.	(C)	40.	(B)	60.	(A)	80.	(A)

ATS-W ELEMENTARY PRACTICE TEST 1

ANSWER KEY

1.	(D)	21.	(B)	41.	(A)	61.	(B)
2.	(D)	22.	(D)	42.	(D)	62.	(B)
3.	(D)	23.	(A)	43.	(A)	63.	(C)
4.	(B)	24.	(A)	44.	(B)	64.	(A)
5.	(A)	25.	(B)	45.	(C)	65.	(C)
6.	(A)	26.	(A)	46.	(B)	66.	(D)
7.	(C)	27.	(C)	47.	(A)	67.	(C)
8.	(C)	28.	(A)	48.	(C)	68.	(A)
9.	(A)	29.	(C)	49.	(C)	69.	(D)
10.	(D)	30.	(A)	50.	(D)	70.	(D)
11.	(B)	31.	(B)	51.	(C)	71.	(B)
12.	(C)	32.	(C)	52.	(D)	72.	(C)
13.	(A)	33.	(B)	53.	(A)	73.	(B)
14.	(C)	34.	(A)	54.	(D)	74.	(A)
15.	(D)	35.	(A)	55.	(D)	75.	(D)
16.	(B)	36.	(A)	56.	(C)	76.	(B)
17.	(B)	37.	(C)	57.	(A)	77.	(B)
18.	(C)	38.	(B)	58.	(D)	78.	(A)
19.	(B)	39.	(A)	59.	(B)	79.	(B)
20.	(D)	40.	(C)	60.	(B)	80.	(C)

LAST PRACTICE TEST 1

DETAILED EXPLANATIONS
OF ANSWERS

1. **(A)** The correct answer is (A). Since the discount is equal to 20%, Mary must pay 80% of the original cost. We are given that 80% is equal to $420. Solving for x in choice (A) gives us the following:

$$0.80x = \$420$$

$$\frac{0.80x}{0.80} = \frac{\$420}{0.80}$$

$$x = \$525$$

The original cost of the couch is $525. Answer choice (B) is incorrect because it is saying that 20% of the original cost of the couch is equal to $420. Choice (B) is incorrect because it is adding 20% to the original cost of the couch on the left side of the equation and adding 20% of the original cost to the discounted price on the right side of equation. Choice (D) is incorrect because 80% of the original cost of the couch is being set equal to the discounted price plus an additional 20% of the original cost.

2. **(B)** The correct answer is (B). His take-home pay would equal his weekly salary, $400, plus his sales commission which is equal to 15% of $500. In order to express this in algebraic terms we must change the 15% to the decimal 0.15. Answer (A) is incorrect because it represents 15% of his weekly take-home pay plus $500. Answer (C) is incorrect because it represents 15% of the sum of his take-home pay plus his sales for the week. Answer (D) is incorrect. It represents his weekly take-home pay of $400 plus 85% of his weekly sales of $500.

3. **(C)** The correct answer is (C). We need to determine 20% of $850,000. 20% must be converted to a decimal, 0.20. We then multiply this by $850,000 to obtain the amount of money set aside for the funding, $170,000. Choice (A) is incorrect because it represents $\frac{\$280,000}{\$850,000}$ or 33% funding. Choice (B) is incorrect because it represents $\frac{\$425,000}{\$850,000}$ or 50% funding. Choice (D) is incorrect because it represents $\frac{\$127,500}{\$850,000}$ or 15% funding.

4. **(C)** The correct answer is (C). I and II are not necessary to ascertain the cost of material per square foot used to cover the shaded area. The total area of the larger rectangle is

$$\text{base} \times \text{height} = 12 \times 9 = 108 \text{ sq. ft.}$$

Therefore, the area of the shaded portion surrounding the inner rectangle is

$$108 \text{ sq. ft.} - 80 \text{ sq. ft.} = 28 \text{ sq. ft.}$$

If the total cost of material used to cover the shaded area is $56 and we have 28 sq. ft., the cost per square foot is $\frac{\$56}{28 \text{ sq. ft.}} = \$2.00$ per square foot.

Choices (A), (B), and (D) are incorrect. Both I and II are not necessary to determine the cost per square foot of the shaded area. (D) is incorrect because III is needed to determine the cost per square foot.

5. **(A)** The correct answer is (A). In order to solve this problem we must first add the number of freshman girls to the number of sophomore girls, (21 + 15). In order to find the percentage we divide this sum by the total number of students in the chorus and multiply by 100.

$$\frac{21+15}{132} \times 100 = \% \text{ of freshman and sophomore girls in chorus}$$

Choice (B) is incorrect. In order to find the percentage we need to multiply the fraction by 100 not divide by 100. Choice (C) is incorrect because the number of freshman and sophomore girls must be divided by the total number of students in the chorus and then multiplied by 100. Choice (D) is incorrect. Here the sum is being divided by 100 and multiplied by total number of students in the chorus.

6.   **(A)** The correct answer is (A). The solution is as follows.

let x = the number of minutes required for the hot water pipe operating alone to fill the tub.

   $2x$ = the number of minutes required for the cold water pipe operating alone to fill the tub.

$\dfrac{1}{x}$ is then the part of the tub filled by the hot water pipe in 1 minute. $\dfrac{1}{2x}$ is the part of the tub filled by the cold water pipe in one minute. Then $\dfrac{20}{x}$ equals the part of the tub filled by the hot water pipe in 20 minutes and $\dfrac{20}{2x}$ equals the part of the tub filled by the cold water pipe in 20 minutes.

   When the bathtub is filled, the sum of the fractional part of the tub filled by the hot water pipe and the fractional part filled by the cold water pipe must equal 1. Therefore,

$$\frac{20}{x}+\frac{20}{2x}=1$$
$$\frac{2(20)}{2x}+\frac{20}{2x}=1$$
$$\frac{40+20}{2x}=1$$
$$\frac{60}{2x}=1$$
$$30=x$$

It would take the hot water pipe operating alone 30 minutes to fill the tub. Choice (B) is incorrect because a common denominator must be found in order to combine the terms. Choice (C) is incorrect because incorrect terms are used to denote fractional parts of the tub filled by the cold water pipe. Choice (D) is not correct because an incorrect term is used to denote the fractional part of the tub filled by the hot water pipe.

7.　**(A)** The correct answer is (A), I and IV. In equation I we are taking 40% of the total x and adding 12 installments of $45 each. This equals the total cost x of the dining room set. Therefore, $0.40x + 12 (45) = x$.

In equation IV an alternative approach is used. Since we know that 40% of the total cost was used as a down payment, we know that 60% of the total still had to be paid. 60% of the total, x, is equivalent to the 12 installments of $45 each. Therefore $0.60x = 12 (45)$.

Solving for x in either of these two equations will give us a value of $900 for x.

equation I

$$0.40x + 12 (\$45) = x$$

$$0.40x + \$540 = x$$

$$\$540 = 0.60x$$

$$\$900 = x$$

equation IV

$$0.60x = 12 (\$45)$$

$$x = \frac{\$540}{0.60}$$

$$x = \$900$$

Choice II is incorrect because the term on the right is 60% of the total cost. Choice III is incorrect because it sets the down payment, $0.40x$, and the remainder of the balance, $0.60x$, equal to the cash value of the balance.

8.　**(D)** The correct answer is (D). The shaded area is represented by $r^2(4 - \pi)$. The area of the shaded portion is obtained by subtracting the area of the circle from the area of the square. The area of the circle is πr^2. The area of a square is found by squaring the side. The side of this square is $2r$. The square of the side $2r$ is $4r^2$. Therefore, the area of the shaded portion of the square is $4r^2 - \pi r^2$. If we simplify by factoring out r^2, we obtain $r^2(4 - \pi)$.

Choice (A) is incorrect because here the area of the square is being subtracted from the area of the circle. Choice (B) is incorrect because the second term in the equation should be πr^2, not $2\pi r^2$. Choice (C) is incorrect.

9. **(B)** The correct answer is (B). We know that the area of a square is equal to the side squared, s^2. The area of the shaded region is equal to the area of the rectangle minus the area of the enclosed square. The area of a rectangle is found by multiplying the length by the width, xy. Therefore the area of the shaded region is represented by $xy = s^2$.

The ratio of the area of the square to the area of the shaded region is therefore $\dfrac{s^2}{xy - s^2}$.

Choice (A) is incorrect because it represents the ratio of the area of the shaded region to the area of the square. Choice (C) is incorrect because the area of the rectangle is being subtracted from the area of the square. Choice (D) is incorrect because it represents the ratio of the area of the rectangle to the area of the shaded region.

10. **(A)** The correct answer is (A). The rate of interest multiplied by the principal is equal to the annual interest. The man initially invested $3,200 at 5%. His annual interest on this is represented by 0.05 ($3,200). His second investment can likewise be represented by 0.02x. The total annual income equals 3% of the entire investment. The entire investment can be represented by 0.03 (x + $3,200).

Choice (B) is incorrect because it does not contain correct terms for the annual interest for the 2% investment or for 3% of the investment. Choices (C) and (D) are incorrect because they do not contain correct terms for the first investment, the 2% investment or 3% of the entire investment.

11. **(A)** The correct answer is (A). The following diagram may help to visualize this problem.

We know that the distance travelled to and from the college is the same. Since distance is equal to rate × time we know that the distance to the college can be written as 5r, where r represents the rate. The distance coming home can be represented as 6(r − 7).We can now set these two values equal to each other to solve for the rate r.

$$5r = 6(r - 7)$$

$$5r = 6r - 42$$

$$0 = r - 42$$

$$42 \text{ mph} = r$$

Choices (B), (C), and (D) are incorrect because they do not properly represent either the rate going or the rate coming home.

12. **(B)** The correct answer is (B). In order to solve this problem we must subtract the total area of the two circles from the area of the rectangle. The area of the rectangle is base × height. The base can be computed by adding the lengths of the radii across, 20. The width is the equivalent of two radii, 10. Therefore the area of the rectangle is $20 \times 10 = 200$.

The area of a circle is found by substituting 5 for the radius in the term πr^2. πr^2 is the term for the area of a circle. Since there are two circles, the total area of the circles is $2\pi(s)^2 = 50\pi$. The area of the shaded region is therefore $200 - 50\pi$.

Choice (A) is incorrect because it subtracts the area of only one circle from the area of the rectangle. Choice (C) is incorrect because the area of the triangle is incorrect. Choice (D) is incorrect because the term for the area of the circles is incorrect.

13. **(D)** The correct answer is (D). If we let n represent the first even integer then n equals $(n + 2)$. $(n + 4)$ and $(n + 6)$ represent the next three even consecutive integers. If we add n plus $(n + 2)$ plus $(n + 4)$ we have the sum of the first three consecutive even integers. The fourth consecutive even integer $(n + 6)$ plus 8 is equal to the sum of the first three consecutive even integers. Answer choice (D) represents this statement. Choices (A), (B) and (C) are incorrect. They do not properly designate the consecutive integers.

14. **(C)** The correct answer is (C).

Given $x + 5 = \dfrac{1}{2}(ay + b)$:

$$2(x + 5) = ay + b$$

$$2x + 10 = ay + b$$

$$2x + 10 - b = ay$$

$$\frac{2x + 10 - b}{a} = y$$

We must follow the proper order for operations. Since the last operation performed on y was division by 2 we must reverse this by multiplying both sides by 2. Our next step is to subtract b from both sides. The last step is to isolate y by dividing both sides by a.

(A), (B), and (D) are incorrect.

15. **(A)** The correct answer is (A). The discount is $50. Simon paid $220. The original cost of the coat is therefore $220 + $50 = $270. To find out what percent $50 is of $270 we divide 50 by 270 and multiply by 100.

Choice (B) is incorrect because it represents the percentage paid by Simon. Choice (C) is incorrect because we need to divide by the original cost of the coat. Choice (D) is incorrect because we need to multiply by 100 to obtain a percent.

16. **(A)** The correct answer is (A). Statements I, II, and IV would be expected to occur if there was an uncharacteristic amount of snow and ice covering the lake. Photosynthesis would decrease because light would not be able to penetrate as deeply into the lake. Water temperature would affect plant life which in turn would have an effect on animal life. Dead plants and animals would accumulate.

Choice (B) is incorrect because it states that only statement I would be expected. Choice (C) is incorrect because it states that no change would occur to adaptation. Choice (D) is incorrect because it states that only statements I and II would be expected.

17. **(A)** The correct answer is (A). The products of the reaction are at a lower energy level than the original reactants. The addition of the catalyst lowers the activation energy necessary for the reaction. The activation energy of the reaction without the catalyst requires more energy to occur than the reaction that is catalyzed.

Answer (B) is incorrect because it omits statement III. Answer (C) is incorrect because it omits statement I. Answer (D) is incorrect because the information is given in the diagram.

18. **(A)** The correct answer is (A). This is the definition of osmosis. Answer (B) is incorrect because we would expect there to be a net movement of water from the cell to outside the cell. Answer (C) is incorrect. We would expect the movement of water. Answer (D) is incorrect.

19. **(C)** The correct answer is (C). Both (A) and (B) are true. The genotype can be determined by looking at the phenotype. The offspring of a cross between parents each of which is homozygous for a trait, will have a phenotype different from both parents in Incomplete Dominance.

20. **(C)** The correct answer is (C). We would expect to distill less volume of pure liquids. We would obtain more volume of a mixture of the two liquids. If the distillation temperature is increased rapidly over a shorter time interval there is less time for the lower boiling liquid to separate from the mixture and distill. This is why a greater mixture of the two liquids is obtained. Answers (A) and (B) would not be the only consequence of rapidly increasing temperature. Answer (D) is incorrect because a change would result.

21. **(C)** The question deals with the growth of the United States during President McKinley's tenure. President Madison was in office during the War of 1812. President Lincoln headed the government during the Civil War. President Wilson led the country in World War I. Thus, the correct answer is (C).

22. **(A)** This question calls for you to understand the subject matter included in several social sciences. The correct answer is (A). Choice (B) deals with the productive and distributive use of resources. Choice (C) deals with behavioral sciences. Choice (D) deals with humans' relations with the earth.

23. **(D)** While answers (A), (B), and (C) have some measure of truth and may seem plausible, they are not the cartoonist's concern. This cartoon was created in the late 1970's and reflects the steep increase in gasoline prices which occurred when the OPEC oil cartel met and demanded higher prices for their product. The correct response is (D).

24. **(C)** This question helps you to understand the function social scien-

tists play in our society. Though a by-product of their work may be choices (A) and (B), those are not primary objectives. Choice (D) is the responsibility of all citizens in a democratic society. Therefore, choice (C) is the correct one.

25. **(B)** What are the definitions of the social sciences and history is the subject of this question. Choice (A) deals with the past. Choice (C) is the study of power and its allocation in the society. The study of humans' relations with the earth is choice (D). So, choice (B), the "dismal science," economics, is the correct response.

26. **(C)** This question requires you to find the broadest term, or most inclusive term. Choice (A) refers to those goods which produce more goods. Choice (B) refers to such things as raw materials, trees, coal, gold, and the like. Choice (D) refers to the people who make something using choices (A) and (B). Thus, the term which includes all the others is choice (C).

27. **(B)** This question deals with political and literary history. A sophisticated knowledge is required to reject choices (A), (C), and (D) as incorrect. The artist shows President Nixon, during the Watergate crisis, as a giant tied down by puny bits of tape. The President would not release the tapes, claiming executive privilege (the Watergate Scandal). The analogy is to Jonathan Swift's satire, *Gulliver's Travels* (B), in which Gulliver gets tied down during his voyage to Lilliput.

28. **(D)** Here, the respondent is required to know the functions of several social institutions. Choice (A) deals with the production and distribution of goods and services. Choice (B) is about the structure and allocation of power in the society. Choice (C) deals with philosophical questions about the origins of life and death. The best response is choice (D), family.

29. **(D)** Choices (A), (B), and (C) all possess the potential for bringing about social change. Choice (D) is correct because it wants to preserve the status quo and does not seek to alter society.

30. **(C)** The religion of Islam was founded by Mohammed, who claimed no divinity. The sacred book of Islam is the Koran, which contains the revelations of the prophet Mohammed. This religion was influenced by Judaism and Christianity. The five pillars of Islam state the religious duties of a believer. Choice (C) is not one of those duties and thus, the correct answer.

31. **(A)** Since 1790, the United States has counted the people living in the country at the time of the decade year. This census forms the basis for the allotment of representatives to each state. The electoral vote is derived from the total number of representatives and senators in each state; therefore, choice (A) is the correct answer.

32. **(B)** The Navigation Act listed goods that could be shipped only to England from the colonies. The Quartering Act required local civil authorities to provide quarters and supplies for British troops. The Stamp Act, which called for a tax in the form of stamps affixed to newspapers and other papers, was much hated. The correct response, (B), was not contemplated by the British.

33. **(A)** Responses (B), (C), and (D) are incorrect. Hobbes wrote about the social contract between the people and the ruler, thus choice (A) is correct.

34. **(D)** This question in the history of technology tests the respondent's knowledge of chronology. Choice (A) is the most recent development. Choices (B) and (C) were introduced in 1876. The correct response (D) was invented relatively early in the Industrial Revolution, 1814.

35. **(C)** Governmental stability is the greatest factor for a firm intending to invest abroad. If the government is unstable it may topple, causing disruption in business and possible nationalization of foreign-owned companies. Therefore, the best choice is (C).

36. **(A)** Choice (B) represents Egypt. Choice (C) refers to Nigeria. Choice (D) stands for Ethiopia. The correct choice is (A), which stands for South Africa.

37. **(D)** This question requires you to place the Civil War in the correct half century. Choices (A), (B), and (C) are too early. Thus, the correct response is choice (D), the second half of the nineteenth century.

38. **(C)** Since culture is a human construct, people who live in similar habitats do not necessarily have similar cultures. Thus, choices (A), (B), and (D) are all incorrect. The most tentative response, (C), is the best answer.

39. **(A)** While aspects of choices (B), (C), and (D) might be considered as tools, the best choice is (A) since it includes and encompasses the other choices.

40. **(B)** At the time of the growth of industrialization in the United States, the domestic market was growing rapidly (A). America had plentiful raw materials (C) and labor was scarce (D). Since foreign markets were at some distance, choice (B) is correct.

41. **(C)** After studying the musical piece, you are asked to choose which statement is the best description. The music is in two flats, indicated by the key signature at the beginning of each line, so (A) is not the correct choice. The only time signature shown is at the end of the segment and follows a double bar, which indicates a change in the time. Thus, the time signature for the segment shown is not obvious (B). The bass pattern, when studied, does reveal itself to be repetitive (C). There is no rest in the bass clef (D), thus making (C) the only correct choice.

42. **(D)** Thrust staging has the stage projecting into the audience and the audience surrounding the stage on three sides. The audience in the picture is on only two sides of the stage, which is known as central staging (D). Proscenium (B) is traditional staging in a theatre with a proscenium arch. Theatre-in-the-round has the audience completely surrounding the playing area. Choice (D) is the correct answer.

43. **(D)** While the sonnet "My mistress' eyes are nothing like the sun" is Shakespearean, this does not make it different from other sonnets. A majority of sonnets are written in this form, so (A) is incorrect. The poem does describe the appearance of a beloved woman; this choice is incorrect, however; because many other sonnets do the same. Beautiful women were traditional subject matter for Elizabethan sonneteers. (D) is the correct choice because Shakespeare undermines the traditional beauty of the women who are normally written about and states that his mistress is far more beautiful than the other "goddesses," even though she is realistically ordinary.

44. **(C)** The last two lines of a Shakespearean sonnet generally provide an ironic twist to the rest of the poem. In this sonnet, the lines refute the argument of the rest of the poem because the speaker states that even though his mistress is ordinary he still finds her beautiful. Thus, choice (C) is the correct choice.

45. **(A)** Choice (A) is correct because the poem is witty in the way it takes standard sonnet conventions (a woman's eyes, lips, hair, etc.) and twists them to make a point. By doing this, Shakespeare is also satirizing standard sonnet conventions of his time (which he himself never hesitated

to employ). The poem is not intense (B), sarcastic (C), or brooding (D).

46. **(B)** You are asked to determine which of the buildings named is pictured. Each edifice listed is built in a different style, which should be easily recognizable. Notre Dame Cathedral is French, characterized by its flying buttresses. This is a picture of the frieze of the west cella of the Parthenon, which is characterized by Doric columns (as pictured) and the high-relief metopes of the Doric frieze. The Sistine Chapel (C), Michelangelo's masterpiece, is known for its frescoes and barrel-vaulted ceilings. Versailles (D), is the palace of Louis XIV, outside of Paris, and is an example of the ornate style of baroque grandeur. One distinguishing factor is that all the choices other than the Parthenon are structures which are in much better repair, since they are more recent than the pictured ruins of the Parthenon.

47. **(A)** The squatting position of the figure is indicative of a low position, like that of a slave (A). Since he is wearing only a cloak thrown back over one shoulder, this, too, indicates the clothing of a commoner or a person of low status. The action, that of sharpening a knife, is a job which would be designated to a slave. The muscle structure of the figure would not really indicate social level, making (B), (C), and (D) unlikely choices.

48. **(B)** This question tests your knowledge of the development of the English language. This passage is taken from one of Chaucer's *Canterbury Tales*, written in the late fourteenth century. This is evident from the highly "irregular" spelling of words such as "dwellynge" ("dwelling") and "povre" ("poor"). (A) is incorrect because a translation would be translated into standard, modern English. Choice (C) is wrong, because while the poem may be romantic, it is impossible to tell from this passage. Elizabethan English is completely different from Middle English, so (D) is incorrect. (B) is the correct choice.

49. **(B)** This question asks you to look at the print and come to some conclusions. Since each figure is holding or playing a musical instrument (double aulos, lute and harp), it can be surmised that they are musicians (A). Choice (B) states that the artwork creates the illusion of depth. Since there is not a strong sense of depth and you are looking for the exceptional choice, this is the correct choice. The lack of a three-dimensional aspect (D) and the absence of a background against which the figures are placed, all point to the deduction that this is an Egyptian tomb painting (C).

50. **(D)** The pictured statue is a portrait of Augustus that was found near

Rome. The effect of this figure, with the serious expression and gesture, is not comic (A). There is nothing in the stance, expression or dress to suggest levity. Conversely, although the face is not smiling, it is also not a tragic figure (B). Although the breastplate or cuirass has scenes in low relief carved on it, the figure itself is not ornate or excessively decorated (C). Finally, the large gesture and stance of an imperator, or commander-in-chief, makes for an imposing figure (D). The carved armor, careful draping of the cloak and the rod the figure holds, all add to this impression. Thus, (D) is the correct choice.

51. **(C)** This question asks you to read and determine the mood created by an author in a short selection. Passage (C), taken from Thomas Wolfe's "Circuses at Dawn," uses such words and phrases as "thrilling darkness"and "rush madly" to let the reader share the narrator's strange excitement as he anticipates the circus. Therefore, (C) is the correct choice.

52. **(A)** A dramatic monologue is a poem in the form of an extended speech by an identifiable character. Passage (A), the beginning of Robert Browning's "My Last Duchess," is unquestionably spoken by one character to another; therefore, (A) is the correct choice.

53. **(D)** A metaphor is a literary device whereby an author compares two seemingly unlike things to achieve an effect. Passage (D), taken from Henry David Thoreau's essay "Civil Disobedience" compares two seemingly unlike things—the American government and a wooden gun—to make a point; therefore, (D) is the correct choice.

54. **(D)** This question requires that you study the mood of the people in the picture and make a connection between the instruments pictured, the actions of those pictured, and the type of music being played. Since an opera (A) is usually a formal, upper-class form of music and the picture is of a coarse tavern scene, the music would not be operatic. The individuals appear festive and seem to be enjoying taking part in the merry-making, not singing a sad, serious melody (B), or a funeral hymn (C) dirge. Therefore, the correct choice is (D). The music is a light, boisterous tune.

55. **(A)** Le Corbusier's L'Unite d'Habitation (Union for Living) is an apartment house in Marseilles. Corbusier set out to build apartments vibrating with light. This is obvious from the many windows almost covering the side of the building. Thus, choice (A) is correct. The building is obviously not a skyscraper (B), since there are no more than eight floors. The building is structured around rectangular and linear shapes, rather

than cylindrical (C). And, the staircase at left is not hidden, but in full view (D).

56. **(C)** This question tests your knowledge of the use of the dramatic term "aside." An aside is a comment spoken directly to the audience that the other actors on stage are supposedly unable to hear. Thus, the correct answer is choice (C).

57. **(D)** You are asked to look at the structure of a building and relate to it in terms of natural forms. Since this contemporary building stacks and masses cubes or facets from a broad base to an increasingly narrow peak, much like a mountain, the correct answer is (D). It does not have wave-like lines which would connote undulating water. Likewise, it does not reveal the concentric spirals of a snail or nautilus shell, while choice (B), a city street, offers an example of a man-made, not a natural object, and is therefore not relevant to the question.

58. **(B)** The correct choice is (B). The first two lines tell us that the speaker has been doing some inner questioning and searching. The last two lines are almost a prayer to the sea, a prayer that asks the sea to calm the speaker and "compose (him) to the end." The line which reads, "Ye who from my childhood up have calmed me" suggests that the sea has been able to calm the speaker before; it is this same calming which the speaker now "passionately desire(s)."

59. **(D)** The correct choice is (D). The "stream of consciousness" technique is a modern invention used by writers to mimic, and if possible, duplicate, the quick workings of the human mind. This passage from James Joyce's *Ulysses* describes Molly Bloom's thoughts of the character Hugh as she thinks of him: how he slapped her "on my bottom," and how he is an "ignoramus" that "doesn't know poetry from a cabbage." The passage lacks punctuation because (as the technique ascribes) people do not think in properly punctuated sentences. The passage is meant to display how thoughts lead to other thoughts by association.

60. **(A)** The correct choice is (A). Alliteration is a poetic device where writers repeat consonant sounds at the beginning of successive (or almost successive) words. "Fair is foul and foul is fair" is an example of alliteration because of the repeated "f" sound; the same is true for "fog and filthy."

61. **(D)** Although the author of the passage might agree with choice (A),

this belief is not expressed in the paragraph. Choices (B) and (C) are both included in the paragraph but neither statement summarizes the content of the whole passage. The correct choice is (D) because it paraphrases the topic of the entire passage which is stated in the first and second sentences.

62. **(C)** Choice (A) is specifically stated in the eighth sentence of the passage. Choice (B) is stated in the second sentence. Choice (D) is stated in the last two sentences. Choice (C) is correct because the paragraph does not discuss students moving out of the district.

63. **(C)** This question requires you to determine the author's attitude although it is not specifically stated in the passage. Choice (A) is not appropriate because the entire passage discusses the drop out problem, and the topic must be of concern to the author. Choice (B) is incorrect because there is no mention of teachers in the passage. Choice (D) is possible because the author does discuss drop out prevention programs; however, the author does not state or imply that such programs are simple solutions to the problem. Choice (C) is the best answer because it refers to the main idea, and it can be inferred from the discussion that the author feels the drop out problem is complex and has many contributing factors.

64. **(A)** Choice (A) is correct because sand, gravel, and water are specifically mentioned. Choice (B) specifies "mud" which is not in the passage. Choices (C) and (D) both include "heat," which is not mentioned.

65. **(C)** Question 65 asks you to infer information from the passage. Choice (A) is incorrect because the passage does not imply any information concerning the weight of petrified trees. Choice (B) specifies museums which are not mentioned. Choice (C) is correct because fossils are mentioned in the passage, and it can be inferred that these fossils provide evidence of other life forms. Choice (D) is not discussed.

66. **(C)** Choice (C) is correct. The time period when weather predictions were included in almanacs is specifically stated in the passage. Choice (A) is incorrect because early almanacs were charts of the stars and did not include other information.

67. **(B)** Choice (B) is correct. The only description of features of the Davy Crockett almanacs is in the last sentence of the passage. Choices (B) and (C) are incorrect because there is no mention in the passage of these almanacs being printed in Germany or being written about Davy Crockett.

Since the U.S. Civil War was between 1861-1865 and the almanacs were printed between 1835-1856, choice (D) is incorrect.

68. **(D)** According to this passage the purpose of almanacs has changed over time. However, early almanacs were charts of the movements of stars. Therefore, choice (D) is correct. Choices (A), (B), and (C) state items that were included in later almanacs.

69. **(D)** The entire passage discusses the changing content of almanacs over time, therefore, choice (D) is the best statement of the author's attitude. Choice (A) is incorrect because it ignores more recent almanacs. Choice (B) is incorrect because "archaic" means out of date, and this does not agree with the author's position. While the author may agree with choice (C), it does not summarize the author's attitude toward almanacs.

70. **(C)** This question must be answered using the process of elimination. The information stated in choices (A), (B), and (D) is specifically included in the passage. The passage does not specify who wrote the Davy Crockett almanacs. Therefore, choice (C) is correct.

71. **(A)** The second sentence of the passage states that the players were protesting unfair treatment, so choice (A) is correct. There is no information in the passage to support any of the other answers.

72. **(D)** This is another question that requires the process of elimination. Choices (A), (B), and (C) are included in the passage. The players' plans for next year are not discussed, therefore choice (D) is correct.

73. **(B)** This question requires you to make a judgment concerning the author's attitude based on the information in the passage. There is no evidence to suggest that the author has a humorous attitude, or that the author condemns the players, or believes that they are behaving childishly. The author may agree that the team has damaged the university's reputation, but this is not evident in the passage. Overall, the author writes objectively about the incident, so choice (B) is correct.

74. **(D)** This question requires you to do some careful reading because several time periods are included in the passage. However, the passage specifically states that the players returned after four days, so choice (D) is correct.

75. **(C)** The correct choice is (C) because Annie's age is not included.

76. **(A)** This question requires the process of elimination. The passage states that Cinnamon stays outside at night and that Cinnamon is a male tabby. The passage also states that Annie has long hair and is a female cat. Cinnamon chases squirrels, but the passage does not state that Annie also chases squirrels. Choice (A) is correct.

77. **(B)** Choice (B) is correct. This information is stated in the next to the last sentence. There is no mention of Marie preferring one cat to the other, so choice (A) is incorrect. Cinnamon, not Annie, spends most nights outside, so choice (C) is incorrect. The passage does not discuss the cats fighting with each other, so choice (D) is incorrect.

78. **(A)** The correct choice is (A). The last two sentences of the passage indicate that the author's interest is clearly the business aspect of exercise and diet programs. The author probably agrees that these programs are valuable, but that is not the main idea of the passage, so choice (B) is incorrect. Although the author does mention the cost of memberships and the large number of diet programs, neither topic is emphasized. Therefore, choices (C) and (D) are incorrect.

79. **(C)** Choice (C) is correct because this is a re-wording of the last sentence of the passage. The author acknowledges that Jane Fonda has made a lot of money from her exercise videos. However, it is not stated that this is "too much" money, therefore choice (A) is incorrect. The author states that Richard Simmons gives diet advice in his exercise video but does not discuss whether this is appropriate, so choice (B) is incorrect. Choice (D) is incorrect because the average cost of health clubs is never discussed.

80. **(A)** This question asks you to determine why domestic oil producers will not increase production. The correct choice is (A) because this is specifically stated in the sixth sentence. Choice (D) states information that is opposite to what is stated in the paragraph. Although oil tankers are expensive and producers are afraid of spills, these are only contributing reasons to the problem. Therefore, choices (B) and (C) are incorrect.

Section 2: Essay

The following essay received scores at the highest end of the scale used in LAST essay scoring.

Essay A

A poll was recently conducted to determine American heroes. Sadly, most of the heroes listed in the top ten are cartoon characters or actors who portray heroic roles. What does this say about American ideals? Perhaps we do not know enough, or perhaps we know too much in order to have heroes. Having access to instant information about a variety of military, political and religious figures, citizens of modern society have outgrown the innocence of previous centuries.

The ancient hero possessed many idealized virtues, such as physical strength, honesty, courage, and intelligence. Oedipus saved his people from pestilence by solving the riddle of the Sphinx. As leader, he was sworn to find the murderer of the previous king; Oedipus' brave pursuit of justice was conducted with honesty and integrity. Beowolf, another famous ancient hero, existed at a time when life was wild, dangerous, unpredictable.

Modern society is missing several of the ingredients necessary to produce a hero of this calibre. For one thing, there are no mythical monsters such as the Sphinx or Grendel. War is left as the stuff of heroic confrontation, but modern wars only add to our confusion. Men have been decorated for killing their brothers and friends in the Civil War; America fought the Germans in World War I and the Germans and Japanese in World War II, but our former enemies are our current allies. As for honesty, modern role models too often let us down. The media exposes politicians who are involved in scandal, sports figures who do drugs, and religious leaders who make multi-million dollar incomes.

No wonder Americans name Superman and actors John Wayne and Clint Eastwood to the list of modern heroes. These heroes are larger than life on the theatre screen, and their vices are at least predictable and reasonably innocuous. Wisely, we have chosen those who will not surprise us with ugly or mundane reality.

Analysis

Essay A is the strongest of the three essays. Although it is not perfect, it shows a good command of the English language and depth of thought. The writer employs a traditional essay structure: the first paragraph is the introduction and ends with the thesis statement; the second and third paragraphs discuss traditional and contemporary heroes, as stated in the last sentence of the thesis paragraph; the fourth paragraph concludes. Each of the two body paragraphs has a clear topic sentence. The writer gives several distinct examples to support his ideas. Vocabulary is effective, and sentence structure is varied.

The following essay received scores in the middle of the LAST essay scoring scale.

Essay B

I would say that there are some heroes still left in modern society. Although we don't have heroes like we used to, our heroes are different now.

When I was a child, I thought that Superman was a real person. He was my hero. He was strong and always vanquished his foes. Villains didn't stand a chance with him. My parents thought I should watch *Sesame Street,* but I wanted to go to the moves to see Luke Skywalker. Even though I later knew it was not real, I still enjoy going to the movies. I want to see a good conflict between the forces of good and the forces of evil, especially when justice prevails.

Now I am more realistic. My heroes are good, honest, successful people. My uncle, for example. He owns his own business andI work there part time to earn extra money. This is the type of person I want to be, someone who is successful and independent but is still willing to help people less fortunate than himself. When a person is brave, that's heroism too. My friend's brother has a medal for being a hero in Viet Nam. You have different ways to be brave now. The innocent days of childhood are gone, but there are still people to be admired.

Analysis

Essay B contains a thesis in the opening paragraph, and the remaining two paragraphs are organized so as to support that thesis. However, this paper is not as strong as the previous one. The conclusion is not well defined. Also, the writer uses mixed voice, slang, and contractions. His use of the first person pronoun becomes intrusive, and all examples are drawn from his personal experience. The sentence structure could be better, and the sentence fragment should be corrected. Finally, the essay is marred by numerous spelling errors.

The following essay received scores at the lowest end of the LAST essay scoring scale.

ESSAY C

It is not true that there are no heroes nowadays. Everywhere you look, a person sees heroes to believe in.

When you go to the movie theatre, many movies are about good versus evil. Not just Westerns. Sometimes the good cop gets killed. But he usually kills a few criminals for himself before he dies. In many movies, justice wins when the villain is defeated. No matter who wins, people in the audience know what is right and what is wrong because the heroes kill because he needs to defend themselves or because the villian ghave him no other choice. These movies express the vaules of society. They teach good values about heroes and their motives since people like to go to the movies, they see alot of heroes.

When there are not enough heroes in real-life, people are forced to turn to the movies for someone to believe in. These stories teach valuable lessons, although they suggest that to be a hero, you have to be violent, and this is not always the case.

Analysis

Essay C is the weakest of the three essays. The ideas are inexact and the sentences are ill-formed. This essay uses mixed voice and slang. There is a pronoun-antecedent agreement error and a fragment. The most serious faults of this essay are the lack of specific examples and the use of sweeping generalizations. The conclusion fails to affirm the original thesis, then introduces a new argument without thoroughly explaining it.

ATS-W ELEMENTARY PRACTICE TEST 1

DETAILED EXPLANATIONS
OF ANSWERS

1. **(D)** The correct response is (D). Comprehension is shown when the reader questions his or her intent for reading. For example, one may be reading a story to find out what terrible things may befall the main character. The rationale for choosing a book may be an interesting bit of information (A), but it is not a major topic of discussion with the students. Sharing personal information (B) creates a certain bond, but this is not directly relevant to the question. It is also important that all students are on-task before the beginning of a lesson (C), but this is a smaller part of the skill modeled in response (D).

2. **(D)** The correct response is (D). A question testing whether or not a student can synthesize information will include the need to make predictions or solve problems. An evaluation question (A) will require a judgment of the quality of an idea or solution. In order to be real analysis (B), the question would have to ask to analyze given information to draw a conclusion or find support for a given idea. Comprehension questions, (C) require the rephrasing of an idea in his or her own words then use this for comparison.

3. **(D)** The correct response is (D). By having a mixed level pair read together, the remedial student receives instruction and the skilled student receives reinforcement. It uses alternate teaching resources, the students themselves, to enhance the learning environment. A certain goal, comprehension, has been set (A), but this is not the most important outcome. The teacher will need to observe less groups (B), but it is unlikely that this will change the time needed to work with all groups as long as quality is to be maintained. Although reading in pairs, each student should have a book, and it would be impractical to permit another teacher to utilize the books

while one teacher is using them.

4.   **(B)** The correct response is (B). Students at this age do not have the cognitive skills to realize how much they have actually learned, or how much they will actually be able to retain. For this reason, (A) must be incorrect. Students cannot differentiate material that is completely understood and that which they have not completely comprehended at this stage in their intellectual development (C). Students will generally feel that they are capable of learning much more than they will actually retain.

5.   **(A)** The correct response is (A). By mapping out previous knowledge, information already known can be transferred to support new information. Although words on the board are visual (B), this is not the underlying motive. Semantic mapping done at the beginning of a story tests how much prior knowledge the students have about the topic at the outset (C). This does model proper use of words (D), but this is not the main intent of the exercise.

6.   **(A)** The correct response is (A). At this grade level, awareness of job roles and developing good attitudes about work ethics related to all forms of employment are major goals of the curriculum. To help accomplish these goals, Ms. Felder's invitation to the parents of children in her class to visit and talk about their careers continues her effort to build a close working relationship with the parents. With three or four parents visiting on a given day, she will have the opportunity to talk with each and strengthen her own communication with each child's family. Even if a parent cannot participate in the project, Ms. Felder will have the opportunity to talk with the parent and perhaps encourage the parent to send some information about his or her career to the class. Certainly, some parents will be unable to leave work for the project, others may be apprehensive about talking to the students in the class. Having only a few parents a day will enable Ms. Felder to plan her lesson well so that she can focus upon the role each worker plays in benefiting the students in her class. (B) is incorrect because it focuses on an unimportant aspect of the career awareness unit. (C) is incorrect since it is not based upon the goals of career awareness at this stage of schooling. The teacher is not trying to get 11 year olds to choose a career; she is just trying to make them aware of the career choices available to them. (D) is incorrect because it places an invalid inference on the parent's being able to speak to the class.

7.   **(C)** The correct response is (C). Mrs. Kresmeier uses effective communication strategies to teach the students and encourages them to interact

for the same purposes. Mnemonic devices are apparently a new technique for most of the students; at least the teacher's own creative spelling clues are often new ones matching the age level interests and patterns of humor enjoyed by her students. The most success is probably derived from her encouragement to examine the words to find a feature that can be turned into a mnemonic device. (A) is incorrect since there has been no attempt to rule out other techniques of learning to spell. (B) is incorrect because certainly other teachers have impressed upon the students that spelling is important. The creative methodology is the major difference between Mrs. Kresmeier's method and those that students have encountered in the past. (D) is incorrect since no evidence exists to show that Mrs. Kresmeier is especially selective in choosing her spelling lessons.

8.   **(C)** The correct response is (C). This response recognizes that children learn at different rates and suggests a structured method to limit the number of children per center. It is impossible for all students to work at the same rate (A). Children who finish early should not be given extra work merely to keep them busy (B). Speed is not the primary goal of this activity.

9.   **(A)** The correct response is (A). When a teacher provides instruction as a facilitator, he or she adjusts the amount and type of help provided to each student based on their individual needs and abilities. This creates independent learners. A supervisor oversees activities but does not necessarily offer assistance or support independent activities (B). Although a teacher often has to be a disciplinarian, this is not the primary goal of moving from group to group (C). A teacher moving from group to group may also be informally assessing student work, but it is not the main goal of the activity.

10. **(D)** The correct response is (D). A concluding activity should encourage students to summarize what they have learned and share this information with other students. A class party celebrating scientists is a valuable experience but does not allow students to share what they have learned (A). A topic for cumulative reviews should not be limited to only medical discoveries when the unit's topic was much broader (B). A test is considered an evaluation technique and should not be confused with a concluding activity (C).

11. **(B)** The correct response is (B). Materials should represent a wide range of topics and people, thereby fostering an appreciation for diversity in the students. An appropriate reading level (A), related information (C),

and a majority of interest (D) are all important, but cannot be called the main reason for selecting a book.

12. **(C)** The correct response is (C). Formative assessment is continuous and intended to serve as a guide to future learning and instruction. Summative evaluation (A) and summative assessment (B) are both used to put a final critique or grade on an activity or assignment with no real link to the future. Peer assessment would require students to critique each other (D).

13. **(A)** The correct response is (A). By meeting one-to-one to discuss a student's strengths and weaknesses creates a feeling of trust and confidence between the students and the teacher. Grading papers solely on the content of a conference is not an efficient means of grading (B). The student/teacher conference should not focus on only one part of the writing process, such as careful editing (C) or prewriting (D).

14. **(C)** The correct response is (C). The role of the resource teacher is to provide individual instruction for students who qualify for services and through collaborative consultation, work with the classroom teacher to adapt instruction to match student needs. A resourceful teacher should not be entirely responsible for teaching a learning disabled student (A). A learning disabled student should not be totally excused from assignments (B). A resource teacher is not responsible for tutoring outside of the scheduled class meetings (D).

15. **(D)** The correct response is (D). Writing the alphabet simply to write it is an isolated act which will do little to create fluency and self-confidence in reading and writing. Reading in a comfortable atmosphere (A), modeling fluent reading for students (B), and using real-life skills to practice spelling and writing (C) present skills to enhance reading and writing in a manner that is neither threatening nor boring.

16. **(B)** The correct response is (B). All parent conferences should begin and end on a positive note and should avoid technical terms and educational jargon. Any problems should be discussed at once and not left for the second conference (A). Bilingual students should be encouraged to develop fluency in both languages, not exclusively English (C). A teacher is best liked and appreciated if he or she speaks in a way that parents readily understand (D).

17. **(B)** The correct response is (B). By reviewing the lessons, the teacher

is reflectively self-evaluating his or her teaching, and reviewing ways he or she can improve to better fit the needs of the students. Although good ideas can be shared, all plans must be modified to fit the class and teacher style (A). "Community helpers" is a topic appropriate for kindergarten (C). Although a class visitor and filmstrip may increase motivation and enthusiasm, (D) does not address the need to evaluate the entire unit.

18. **(C)** The correct response is (C). The use of instructional strategies that make learning relevant to individual student interests is a powerful motivating force that facilitates learning and independent thinking. (A) and (B) are both important factors to consider during a brainstorming session of this type, but both of these factors should influence the teacher only after the student interests have been included. (D) indicates a misunderstanding of the situation described. The students are setting the objectives for the unit as they brainstorm questions.

19. **(B)** The correct response is (B). Choice is an important element in motivating students to learn. (A) is contradictory with the stated purpose of the activity. The students proposed the questions, so covering all the questions should not be a problem. (C) is incorrect because the students have chosen what they consider to be key questions; the teacher should select different or additional key questions. (D) is a possibility, but only if there is a specific reason why all the students should not research all the questions.

20. **(D)** The correct response is (D). The instructional strategy described is one technique used in inquiry and problem solving. (A) is incorrect because direct instruction requires the teacher to present the content to be learned, asking students frequent questions to monitor comprehension. (B) is incorrect because role playing and simulation are not part of a brainstorming session. (C) is incorrect because exposition and discussion are teacher led activities using previously established objectives and content.

21. **(B)** The correct response is (B). Ongoing assessment and evaluation using a variety of formal and informal assessment techniques is essential to quality instruction. (A) is incorrect because although the teacher may want to use an objective test as part of the overall assessment and evaluation of the unit, an objective test is insufficient assessment without additional instruments. (C) is incorrect because a standardized test is rarely an appropriate tool for an individual unit of instruction. Standardized tests are best used as an end-of-the-year evaluation. (D) is incorrect because every assessment should provide for individual differences. Individual assess-

ments might be part of a total assessment program, but would be inappropriate when used in isolation.

22. **(D)** The correct response is (D). Providing an opportunity to share class projects and activities with other classes will promote a feeling of student ownership and reinforce a feeling of membership in the class as a group. (A) is incorrect because closure refers to that part of a lesson plan that reminds the teacher to conclude the lesson by restating the purpose of the lesson or by summarizing the content of the lesson. (B) is incorrect because although teachers are expected to work collaboratively with other teachers, sharing a class project involves little actual collaboration. (C) is incorrect because although a teacher may be interested in being appointed grade-level chairperson, sharing class projects is a valuable instructional strategy that is not related to a promotion in a school.

23. **(A)** The correct response is (A). Asking students to videotape their project explanations could be highly motivating to the entire class and is an additional way to focus attention and reinforce the significance of the content. (B) is incorrect because this is an appropriate use of video equipment. The value of the equipment and that it is school property is not an issue. (C) is incorrect because the purpose of the activity is to motivate students and does not necessarily accurately represent these careers. (D) is incorrect because nothing is explicitly stated regarding student grouping.

24. **(A)** The correct response is (A). The relevance of the current exhibits to the unit the students are studying is the most important factor in determining if a field trip should be planned. (B) is incorrect because the school should be able to afford the cost of admission for each student or at least for those students who are not able to pay for their own admission. The distance from the school is simply an element that must be considered when planning the field trip, not a deciding factor in whether or not the trip should be planned. School buses are generally available for field trips, but must be reserved in advance. (C) is incorrect because although obtaining permission slips for each student can be difficult it should not prevent a teacher from planning a field trip. (D) is incorrect because adjusting the scheduled time for each subject in the following weeks can compensate for any time lost for a particular subject during the field trip.

25. **(B)** The correct response is (B). The best way to teach children to read, regardless of grade level, is to use a program of emergent literacy which includes pattern books and journal writing with invented spelling.

(A) is incorrect because although an intensive phonics program that includes drill and practice seat work on basic sight words may be effective with some students, it is not the most effective way to teach all students to read. (D) is incorrect because an ESL program is intended to provide assistance to only those students who are learning English as a second language. Additionally, the learning resource teacher should provide assistance to only those students who have been identified as having a learning disability that qualifies them to receive services.

26. **(A)** The correct response is (A). By selecting books for the classroom library that match students' independent reading abilities, the teacher is recognizing that students must improve their reading ability by beginning at their own level and progressing to more difficult materials. (B) is incorrect because books that are so difficult that they are challenging will most likely be frustrating to many students. (C) is incorrect because the presence or absence of separate word lists should not be a determining factor in selecting books for a classroom library. (D) is incorrect because all children need access to a classroom library regardless of their reading abilities.

27. **(C)** The correct response is (C). A post office center, restaurant center, and a weather center all encourage a variety of reading and writing activities which is what these students need most. (A) and (B) are incorrect because they are incomplete. (D) is incorrect because the science center is included and combining the chemicals in that center poses an obvious danger to young children.

28. **(A)** The correct response is (A). One of the most reliable ways to identify individual learning styles is to observe the students over a period of time and make informal notes about their work habits and the choices they make within the classroom. (B) is incorrect because although a school psychologist could provide information about each student's learning style, the teacher can identify this information on his or her own. (C) is incorrect because although administering a group screening test will identify learning styles, such a test may be difficult to obtain, and the teacher could gain the same knowledge through simple observation. (D) is incorrect because each student's permanent file may or may not contain this information, and an individual student's learning style may have changed over the years, and there is no guarantee that this change will be noted in the permanent record.

29. **(C)** The correct response is (C). The teacher must make clear that he

or she is willing to work with each child and that he or she believes that each child can be successful. (A) is incorrect because emphasizing failure early in the year is not appropriate in establishing a feeling of trust with parents. (B) is incorrect because the teacher should emphasize the child during a parent/teacher conference and not discuss the parent's education unless he or she is asked specifically for advice. (D) is incorrect because asking parents to secure an individual tutor may be an unrealistic financial burden. In addition, all children reading below grade level do not necessarily need a tutor.

30. **(A)** The correct response is (A). Celebrating holidays of different cultures teaches appreciation for human diversity. (B) is incorrect because while celebrating different cultures has become a political issue, this should not force or prevent a teacher from planning such a lesson. (C) is incorrect because although celebrating holidays is one way to encourage students to read, this may or may not be related to encouraging students to read aloud. (D) is incorrect because celebrating holidays may encourage all students to participate in class activities, but teaching an appreciation for human diversity is a more accurate statement of the most significant reason for the activity.

31. **(B)** The correct response is (B). The variance in fifth graders' physical size and development has a direct influence on their interests and attitudes, including their willingness to work with others and a possible preference for working alone. Working in small groups enhances student achievement. It is a learned skill that must be practiced. (A) is incorrect because fifth graders do have the physical and mental maturity to work in small groups. (C) is incorrect because not all fifth-grade students lack the ability for internal control. (D) is incorrect because although Mr. Dobson might need to be more specific in his directions to the students, this is not the main reason for the behavior.

32. **(C)** The correct response is (C). Students who are naturally shy are usually more willing to participate in small groups than in discussions involving the entire class. (A) is incorrect because calling on each student once per day will not necessarily assist shy students to participate in class discussions even if participation grades are assigned. (B) is incorrect because although students may become less shy as the year progresses, the teacher still has a responsibility to encourage students to participate. Choice (D) is incorrect because although speaking to each student individually may help some students participate, it is likely more students will participate if the procedure outlined in choice (C) is implemented.

33. **(B)** The correct response is (B). Student's who are overly talkative are usually flattered to be asked to take a leadership role. Asking these students to take notes also assigns them a task that allows the other students to voice their opinions uninterrupted. Choice (A) is incorrect because calling on these students only once during the class period will most likely frustrate them and create problems. (C) is incorrect because placing overly talkative students in a group by themselves does not teach them to listen to other student's opinions. (D) is incorrect because although overly talkative students usually need attention, they must be helped to recognize that other students also have opinions, even though they may not be assertive in voicing them.

34. **(A)** The correct response is (A). Students who tutor peers or younger students develop their own proficiency as a result of assisting other students. Response (B) is incorrect because although some students may view teaching as a possible career, this is not the intended purpose of the tutoring. Choice (C) is incorrect because helping first graders learn addition and subtraction facts is the goal, not necessarily learning specific tutoring techniques. Choice (D) is incorrect because becoming friends with younger children may occur as a result of tutoring; however, it is not the main goal of the activity.

35. **(A)** The correct response is (A). Planning lessons that will enable students to experience a high rate of success during the majority of their practice attempts is directly related to enhanced student achievement and heightened self-esteem. Choice (B) is incorrect because although parents are often happy as a result of a student's academic success, this is the result of structuring lessons so students will be successful. Response (C) is incorrect because although students are more likely to complete homework if they are successful in early practice attempts, this is only part of answer (A). Choice (D) is incorrect because students who are successful in independent practice may or may not ask more questions.

36. **(A)** The correct response is (A). As a general rule, if student questions require lengthy responses then the initial explanation was probably faulty. Choices (B) and (C) are incorrect because there is insufficient information to suggest that the students were not paying attention, or that they have below average listening skills. (D) is incorrect because a teacher should direct all explanations of new information to the level of the students. Even if students did have poor backgrounds in mathematics, the teacher should take that into account when explaining new information.

37. **(C)** The correct response is (C). This is an example of working with other teachers to plan instruction. Response (A) is incorrect because it is incomplete. This activity may complete the school year, but this activity is not necessarily an end-of-the-year project. (B) is incorrect because problem solving and inquiry teaching are only small components of the activity. Choice (D) is incorrect because asking students to research Galileo and asking the PTA to buy science equipment are not necessarily related.

38. **(B)** The correct response is (B). Grouping patterns affect a student's perceptions of self-esteem and competence. Maintaining the same groups throughout the year encourages students in the average group to view themselves as average, students in the above average group to view themselves as above average, and students in the below average to view themselves as below average. Choice (A) is incorrect because most students do not like unpredictable teacher behavior. Response (C) is incorrect because changes in the classroom often create an atmosphere of mistrust and uneasiness, and do not cause students to be more alert. Choice (D) is incorrect because although the explanation is correct, it is incomplete when compared to the answer (B).

39. **(A)** The correct response is (A). Visiting other teachers in other schools will promote collaboration and cooperation. Choice (B) is incorrect because there is no reason to believe that the principal is encouraging these teachers to apply for a job in the middle school. Response (C) is incorrect because although using computers in math classes may be a topic on which teachers choose to collaborate, choice (A) is more complete. (D) is incorrect because the middle school math curriculum is not intended for use in the fifth grade.

40. **(C)** The correct response is (C). Careful planning includes checking on the availability of resources and materials. (A) Mrs. Doe did reflective thinking during the discussion. However, reflective thinking is only a component of communication and is included in careful planning and its correlation to success in the classroom. (B) Resources and materials were available. This is a result of careful planning. (D) Personal acquaintance with a Native American would have helped shape the student's attitude. Either positive or negative attitudes could provide intrinsic or extrinsic motivation which again is a part of careful planning.

41. **(A)** The correct response is (A). Multiple strategies were planned for the motivation of the students, but a result of the strategies was that each student participated in some way regardless of ability and the unit was

integrated into other subjects through library assignments, reading, writing, music, and dance. (B) Using multiple techniques in the classroom does allow for each student to participate; however, it is only when all students participate that the entire group will be motivated. (C) Ultimately, the unit will be integrated with other subjects; although at this point, integration of the project into other subjects is not the goal. (D) Developing a foundation for teaching American history is not even a long-range goal, but the attitudes and beliefs developed in the project may become the foundation upon which the students will build their philosophy of American history.

42. **(D)** The correct response is (D). Working collaboratively with other teachers was the avenue through which the talents of the students were identified. Choice (A) is a false statement. No risks were taken. (B) Curiosity of the student body was stimulated, however, the assembly had other goals. (C) individual talents were utilized in the assembly, but the goal of the assembly was to familiarize the students with cultural aspects of the Native American.

43. **(A)** The correct response is (A). The external factors of the field trip could create a positive motivation and would allow the students to make the connection between their old skills and the new skills they were just learning. The external factors involved in a field trip are positive; however, Mrs. Doe gave instructions that each student was to take notes on what he/she saw, heard, and experienced. The skill of note taking was founded upon the library assignment which had preceded the field trip. The students were to make the connection. (B) No mention is made of community involvement in the field trip; the statement is not relevant. (D) The students did not take responsibility for their own learning. They were given instructions concerning what they were to do before they left for the field trip.

44. **(B)** The correct response is (B). By allowing the students a choice of field trips, respect was shown to the students. Each student could visit the area to which he/she could relate, helping him/her to better understand the society in which he/she lives. It was but one of an array of strategies used throughout the unit. (A) Enhancing self-concept is encompassed in respecting differences and understanding the society in which we live. (C) Fostering learning as a purposeful pursuit is the result of respecting differences and understanding the society in which we live. (D) An array of instructional strategies has been used throughout this unit; however, the field trips were similar except for location. All instructions given to the

students were the same.

45. **(C)** The correct response is (C). The teacher was allowed to seek opportunities to grow professionally by using different sources of support and guidance to enhance his/her own professional skills. (A) Within the framework of enhancing his/her own professional skills is the ability to reflect and self evaluate. This statement is implied within the correct response (C). (B) This statement is not true. (D) The issue is not assessing the learners, but cooperative reflection and self-evaluation.

46. **(B)** The correct response is (B). The teacher is familiar with the various expectations, laws, and guidelines relevant to education. (A) This is a subjective statement and is not the issue. The statement made by the teacher was that he knew of the expectations of the state for his class each year. (C) Again, this is a subjective statement and is not germane to the question. (D) This may or may not be a true statement. It is not relevant to the question.

47. **(A)** The correct response is (A). The teacher is to constantly monitor and adjust strategies in response to learner feedback. (B) is an untrue statement. A teacher does not design instruction for different situations but monitors and adjusts instruction as situations change. (C) is a true statement; a teacher should be able to recognize factors that promote or diminish motivation. This skill comes from monitoring and adjusting instructional strategies. (D) is true; the teacher becomes aware of external factors or internal factors through monitoring and adjusting instructional strategies; however, it is included in the correct response (A).

48. **(C)** The correct response is (C). The teacher recognizes signs of stress in students (e.g., drop in grades) and knows how to respond appropriately to help the student. The teacher understands factors outside the classroom may influence students' perceptions of their own self-worth and potential. (A) The statement is generic and cannot be substantiated in support of nor against. (B) Although the statement is true, and individualizing may have occurred, the demonstration by Mrs. Sivart was for modifying the text and tests. (D) Although the statement is true, diversity in the classroom did not cause the text to be written three years above grade level. The statement is not germane to the question.

49. **(C)** The correct response is (C). The teacher uses an understanding of human developmental processes to nurture student growth through developmentally appropriate instruction. (A) The statement is not relevant to

the scenario. (B) The framework used in the plan of study designed for the 10 percent could be used for the other 20 percent; however, the framework is a result of the plan of study, not the criteria for a plan. (D) There are benefits derived from cooperatively working to achieve goals. The benefits are intrinsic. The cooperative work called for was not to achieve teacher benefits, but to develop a plan of study.

50. **(D)** The correct response is (D). The teacher understands how learning occurs and can apply this understanding to design and implement effective instruction. (A) The statement is false. (B) This statement may or may not be false, but is an attitude distinctive to each teacher. (C) This statement is subjective; it is an opinion and dependent upon individual parents.

51. **(C)** The correct response is (C). The teacher understands factors inside and outside the classroom that influence students' perceptions of their own potential and worth. (A) This is a true statement; however, it is encompassed within response (C). (B) Some students are extrinsically motivated but some are intrinsically motivated, yet the basic foundation of motivation lies in self-esteem. (D) This is a true statement. Library materials which are highly correlated to instruction are more meaningful, yet this statement is implied in the correct response (C).

52. **(D)** The correct response is (D). The combination of appropriate instructional materials helps students to understand the role of technology as a learning tool. (A) Students' motivation might or might not be lowered if others knew of their need to reread a book and retake an exam. The statement is subjective. (B) This strategy would remove the teacher from the role of informing the student; however, teachers fill many roles each day. Filling the role is not the key; the teacher's attitude and communication with the student will be the critical element. (C) This is a true statement, but the work load of the media specialist is not the issue. The issue is student privacy.

53. **(A)** The correct response is (A). The instructor understands the uses of informal and formal assessment to monitor instructional effectiveness. The number of books read by each student would be in direct proportion to his/her level of reading skills and interest in reading. (B) This statement is true, but is incorporated in the correct response (A). (C) Becoming independent thinkers and problem-solvers would be a result of higher level reading skills and an interest/curiosity in books. (D) The teacher's role would be varied and would not be emphasized as much at this phase of the

instructional strategy. The issue is not the teacher's role but the effectiveness of instruction and techniques for monitoring it.

54. **(D)** The correct response is (D). The goal of the instructional design was to structure a positive classroom environment which would promote lifelong learning. (A) This is a true statement. Classroom time is maximized and is a component of a positive classroom environment which is encompassed in choice (D). (B) This is a true statement but is encompassed within the correct response (D). (C) This is a true statement; however, it is encompassed within the correct response (D).

55. **(A)** The correct response is (A). Choices (B), (C), and (D) are all a part of communicating expectations and ideas, thereby creating a climate of inquiry. (B) Although a variety of materials were presented using several techniques, the goal for the class was to impart teacher expectations to the students and to create a climate of inquiry. (C) The students were not given a choice of what they were to learn. (D) The unit could be integrated across campus into other curricula, but this was not the goal for which many strategies were used.

56. **(C)** The correct response is (C). By requiring both a cognitive and a performance objective, the student was required to show that he or she had not only the knowledge but could apply that knowledge to a life situation. (A) Although this statement is true, it is not the foundation for developing specific objectives. (B) Again, this is an assumption and not relevant to the setting of certain objectives. (D) Teaching style and learning styles are not relevant to the behavioral objectives.

57. **(A)** The correct response is (A). Choices (B), (C), and (D) are components of (A). (B) Enhancing student achievement encompasses active inquiry. (C) Eliciting different levels of thinking from the students is included in student achievement. (D) Problem solving is a component of student achievement.

58. **(D)** The correct response is (D). The demonstration was to show what happens when directions are not followed. The result of such actions could be waste in the kitchen. An expected behavioral outcome was curiosity. (A) This is a true statement and is incorporated in the correct answer (D). (B) The terminal goal for the activity was not assessment, but to gain the knowledge of the importance of correct measurement. (C) The statement is true, and is included in the correct response (D).

59. **(D)** The correct response is (D). The field trip was to extend an academic environment into the community. The students were to see the relationship between what they were taught in the classroom and its practical application in the community. (A) The final activity for the unit will be an evaluation. (B) The field trip did not promote responsibility for one's own learning, because the students were given no instructions prior to arriving in the cafeteria. (C) The field trip was to extend the students' learning beyond the classroom and into the community.

60. **(B)** The correct response is (B). Both federal and state law require that schools be accessible to persons who use wheelchairs. Bill should make the principal aware that Myra resides in the district and that the building is not accessible to her. Disregarding the school's noncompliance with the law by simply offering to share materials with Myra is in no way sufficient (A). The expense to the school posed by making the necessary accommodations does not excuse the school from compliance with the law (C). There is no reason to believe, however, that the school has intentionally failed to comply with the law; proposing a lawsuit (D) is not called for. The school may be eager to comply once the noncompliance is called to their attention.

61. **(B)** The correct response is (B). As a responsible member of the community, Bill should notify the police of the vandalism. He should also make use of community resources by referring Cade to Big Brothers as a child in need of a positive role model. While Bill should call the police and report the vandalism, chasing the boys down himself may place him in great danger, and is therefore not a good solution (A). Calling the superintendent is not an appropriate response. This is a legal issue that does not involve the school in any way (C) and (D).

62. **(B)** The correct response is (B). Placing the students in small groups in which they meet face to face will allow Bill to maximize the students' interaction while giving each student the maximum opportunity to speak. Placing students in the traditional rows facing the front discourages student interaction and minimizes each student's opportunities to speak. While placing students in pairs maximizes each student's opportunity to speak, it limits the sources of interaction; each student may share thoughts with only one other student. In contrast, a group of four allows the student to interact as part of three dyads, two triads, and a quadrat (C). When placing the students in cooperative groups, it is wise to arrange the desks within the physical space of the classroom in such a way that each group's talking does not distract the members of other groups (D).

63. **(C)** The correct response is (C). Storytelling and other narrative approaches are highly effective ways of teaching field sensitive students. While most people do enjoy a good story, this is not the most important reason why teachers should be good storytellers (A). While storytelling is also a highly cost-effective teaching technique, its cost-effectiveness is only a secondary advantage to its utility in teaching field dependent students (B). Storytelling is not one of the most effective ways of teaching field independent students (D).

64. **(A)** The correct response is (A). People seldom perform to the best of their ability. Knowing that their work will receive public attention, however, is an important way to motivate people to do their best. While being able to speak in public is undoubtedly a crucial skill for success in a democratic society, this choice is not worded in such a way that it would be an instructional reason for having students tell their stories (B). Having students tell their stories to the class does focus on having students learn to critique their own work (C), however, this is encompassed by choice (A). Prior exposure has nothing to do with Bill's instructional reason to have students tell the stories that they write (D).

65. **(C)** The correct response is (C). The first task in developing a unit of study is to determine learner outcomes. Activities are contingent on desired learner outcomes (A). While time and space constraints affect activities, Bill and Kayla must determine desired learner outcomes before they proceed to consider other planning factors (B). Soliciting input from students helps assure student ownership; however, this step in planning a unit comes after determining learner outcomes (D).

66. **(D)** The correct response is (D). The laser disk and player comprise a superb supplement to primary sources written by the influential New Yorkers themselves. While a computer and word processing program are valuable tools, they are not the most valuable tools for this activity (A), because students must know something about content before they can write. A local expert on ecology is not relevant to a study of persons who make contributions to the development of New York (B). A laser disk player with a laser disk about influential New Yorkers is an important tool for this thematic unit; however, this is not the best answer, since primary sources provide much insight into the causes of one's actions and to the feelings and emotions which one experiences.

67. **(C)** The correct response is (C). Making a personal contact with each child's parents is the most crucial task that Gerene can perform in

order to assure the success of her students. Having a variety of teaching materials ready and available is helpful, but would not have the most important impact on the students' success (A). Using bulletin boards to make the room look inviting and using materials representing the students of many nations will assist in making the new students feel at home; however, the effects of this task are secondary to that of establishing a strong home-school relationship (B). Coordinating science activities with reading activities would not have a significant impact on insuring the success of first graders (D).

68. **(A)** The correct response is (A). The most important predictor variable of reading success is whether or not a child's parents immerse her in print (read to her) before she starts school. An enriched daycare environment can be beneficial to a child's development (B), especially if shared reading and story activities are stressed. While research suggests that excessive television watching by young students may have deleterious effects, the amount of time spent watching television is not the important predictor of reading success that being read to by a parent is (C). Being raised by a grandparent is not a predictor of poor reading ability (D).

69. **(D)** The correct response is (D). Gerene should consider all of the factors listed. Students' basic nutritional needs must be met before they can be efficient learners (A and C). Students with unmet affective needs will not be able to learn effectively (A and B). Teaching builds on prior knowledge; experiential deficits must be considered if students are to construct new meaning in their worlds. Employing student interests increases student motivation to learn new material (B).

70. **(D)** The correct response is (D). Gerene should employ a wide variety of instructional strategies and materials in order to teach to the phoneme/grapheme relationship. This is a bottom-up approach to teaching reading. Gerene should also use a top-down approach by reading a story to the students and discussing it at length. The first choice (A) does not include a wide variety of learning activities. In addition, the choice omits the important book reading activity. Like the first choice, the second choice (B) fails to employ a wide variety of learning activities and fails to employ the book reading activity. Whether or not to place students at the computer without direct supervision depends on the students involved and the software employed. Choice (C) employs a wide variety of learning activities; however, it includes the false statement that students dislike repetitive activities and that repetition serves as an aversive reinforcer to reading. Although adults become bored with repetition, young students enjoy re-

petitive activity, as it gives them a sense of mastery.

71. **(B)** The correct response is (B). The hands-on activity will best help the students learn about data collection. Since choice (B) is the only one that employs a hand-on activity, this is the best answer. The students would learn about direct observation by watching Gerene tickle the mouse and the philodendron; however, this method would not be as effective as allowing the students to conduct their own data collection (A). Research suggests that viewing a video is an inefficient method of learning (C). Having a guest speaker tell the students about data collection is not a good choice for first graders (D).

72. **(C)** The correct response is (C). As in the previous question, the hands-on activity is the best choice; however, another issue should be considered in this question: the child's econiche. Many families cannot afford cable television's premium channels, and therefore do not have access to the Discovery channel (A). Parents may lack transportation, time, or money to take their child to a museum (B). Parents may not have access to books, or they may work schedules which prevent them from reading to their students. In addition, some parents may be unable to read themselves (D).

73. **(B)** The correct response is (B). By modeling enthusiasm for learning, Gerene will help her students become lifelong learners (D). In addition, by employing developmentally-appropriate hands-on activities, Gerene will help her students to become enthusiastic learners. Giving students examples of famous people who were lifelong learners is not a strong instructional technique for helping the students become lifelong learners (A). Punishing students who do not perform will not help students to become lifelong learners (C).

74. **(A)** The correct response is (A). Recent research suggests that girls learn science best in cooperative groups that employ many hands-on experiences. In contrast, competitive teaching strategies are contraindicated in helping girls learn science (B). Independent activities are also not good choices in helping girls learn science (C). Although computer-assisted instruction may be helpful, the key ingredients in developing a successful science program for girls are cooperative and frequent hands-on experiences (D).

75. **(D)** The correct response is (D). Research suggests that the best teachers of African-American students are those who themselves are com-

petent speakers of Ebonics (Black English). However, even teachers who do not speak Ebonics should respect Ebonics as a legitimate language, rather than considering it a substandard form of English. By respecting Molly's mother tongue, Gerene will encourage her to engage in literacy activities and will promote her self-esteem. By criticizing Molly's use of Ebonics, Gerene will negatively impact Molly's self-esteem and will discourage her from engaging in literacy activities (A). By refusing to speak to Molly, Gerene will also negatively affect both her self-esteem and her desire to engage in speaking, reading, and writing activities (B). Since Molly knows that people understand her when she says, "My mama, she works," the statement that people won't understand her will be confusing to Molly (C). It is appropriate to encourage Molly to use standard English when engaging in formal language and literacy instruction; however, it is inappropriate to discourage her from using her mother tongue in casual interaction.

76. **(B)** The correct response is (B). There are many significant developmental differences between second and sixth graders. These differences must be considered when planning instruction. Choice (A) is incorrect because physical size is only one of the ways in which the students differ. Choice (C) is incorrect because reading ability is an issue to consider, but developmental differences include more than just reading ability. Response (D) is incorrect because preferred topics for reading reflect overall development.

77. **(B)** The correct response is (B). All non-native speakers of English are eligible for the services of an ESL teacher. It is the responsibility of the classroom teacher to be certain that the ESL teacher is aware of the student's needs. Response (A) is incorrect because if Jerry speaks little English such a test would be useless. Additionally, Jerry's intelligence is not the issue. The teacher's attention should be focused on helping Jerry learn English rather than determining his IQ. Choice (C) is incorrect because isolation from other students would only slow Jerry's progress. Choice (D) is incorrect because while it might help Jerry to learn English along with his parents, this is certainly not the most important thing for Ms. Axtel to do.

78. **(A)** The correct response is (A). One of the best ways to assists students who are learning English is to appoint a classroom "buddy" who is willing to explain directions using nonverbal examples and sign language. Choice (B) is incorrect because asking Jerry to concentrate on math will only extend the time it takes for him to learn English. Choice (C) is

incorrect because although picture books might help him learn English, he must have the opportunity to discuss these books with English speakers. (D) is incorrect because Jerry must be actively encouraged to participate in class activities so he can learn English quickly.

79. **(B)** The correct response is (B). Maintaining a written journal about events in the classroom and student responses is a technique used by reflective practitioners to review and evaluate their personal growth as professionals. Choice (A) is incorrect because journal writing may or may not indicate a concern about process writing. Additionally, journal writing alone is not the same as process writing. Choice (C) is incorrect because although the instructor may use some of her journal entries in her formal evaluation, the purpose of the journal is much broader. Choice (D) is incorrect because it is too simplistic. If the teacher was a habitual journal writer, she would be writing about a variety of topics, not just emphasizing those related to teaching.

80. **(C)** The correct response is (C). The instructor has made special provisions for Jerry to learn content material using the Spanish language computer programs as he develops fluency in English. Choice (A) is incorrect because it is too early to determine Jerry's learning style, and even if this is the case, visual learning is no better or worse than any other learning style. Choice (B) is incorrect because the instructor's main concern should be that Jerry learn English and content material. In addition, testing requirements make special provisions for students not fluent in English. Response (D) is incorrect because there is no evidence to suggest that Jerry needs the services of a resource teacher.

Section 2: ESSAY

The following essay received scores at the highest end of the scale used in ATS-W essay scoring.

Essay A

The practice of grouping students by ability in the elementary school has negative social and academic consequences for students. The negative effects of ability grouping overshadow the few positive benefits that may be derived from this practice. Grouping by ability may be appropriate for certain subjects, such as reading, within a particular classroom as long as the group membership changes for instruction in other subjects. However, I feel that grouping by ability is an inappropriate practice at the elementary school level if all students remain in that group throughout the day.

One of the negative effects of ability grouping is that it contributes to the development of a poor self-image for many students. Children of all ages are very adept at recognizing and correctly identifying high-, middle- and low-ability groups. Assigning non-threatening names to the groups has no effect on children's ability to identify these groups. This is apparent when observing or talking with students in schools that use ability grouping. It does not matter whether the teacher calls the top group "Red Birds," "Group 3," "Triangles," or "Mrs. Smith's class" — students are keenly aware of their membership in the group and the perceived ability of that group.

Students make comparisons between the ways teachers interact with different groups, the types of assignments groups receive and privileges different groups enjoy. Students in the high-ability group may look down on other students and may refer to students in other groups as "stupid" or "dumb." Name-calling may result. Students in the low-ability group may resent their placement in that group. Students in the middle-ability group may feel ignored or may even resent being labeled "average." The naturally occurring friction between groups creates a climate in which teachers will have difficulty building positive self-images for all students.

Ability grouping also necessarily limits peer interaction, both in and out of the classroom. Elementary students need to interact with many students to develop mature social and intellectual skills.

An additional negative effect of ability grouping is the stilted instructional environment that is created within the classroom. Teachers of high-ability students are encouraged to feel privileged to teach this group and usually prepare creative, challenging lessons. Teachers of the low-ability group usually provide many drill and practice worksheets and seldom assign text materials. Middle-ability students may receive assignments based on the text, but these assignments are often accompanied by drill and practice worksheets. The result of these practices is that only the high-ability students are challenged to work to their capacity.

The negative consequences of ability grouping are experienced by students of all ability levels. For these reasons, the practice of ability grouping in the elementary school should be abandoned.

Analysis of Essay A

This essay addresses the topic directly. The topic of ability grouping is narrowed in the first sentence to the use of this practice in elementary school. The author's point of view and the focus of the essay (the negative social and academic consequences) are also established in the first sentence. Specific negative effects are named and briefly discussed. The last paragraph restates the author's point of view.

Several sentences in the essay are wordy and seem to ramble. Some of the issues raised (peer interaction) are not fully discussed. The author mentions the "positive benefits" of ability grouping but does not specifically name or discuss the benefits. There are a few errors in punctuation and spelling. However, the author demonstrates the ability to clearly state a topic and present a specific point of view.

The following essay received scores in the middle of the ATS-W scoring scale.

Essay B

Most teachers prefer ability grouping. I know I would. Ability grouping allows teachers to plan asignments for specific groups of students. In this way, teachers can make assignments fit the needs of specific groups of students, instead of just making one assignment for everybody. Teachers can spend additional time helping slower students because the advanced group will be able to complete their assignments independantly. Teachers can also give the advanced students extra work or projects to keep them busy. This gave the teachers more time to work with students who really need help.

Schools that group by ability can plan smaller classes for slow students and larger classes for average and advanced students. This is better for the students because those who really need extra help have a better chance of receiving it. Smaller classes for slow students also helps the teachers give more attention to slow students.

Ability grouping is especially important in math and reading because these subjects give many students difficulty.

Analysis of Essay B

Although the essay is satisfactory given the time limit, it is flawed for several reasons. The major error is the lack of a controlling central idea or theme. The topic stated in the first sentence, that most teachers prefer ability grouping, is never fully developed. Instead of developing this topic, the writer discusses the advantages of small classes for slower students. The last two paragraphs seem tacked on and are not smoothly connected to the first paragraph. In addition, there are several spelling errors and verb tense is inconsistently used.

The following essay received scores at the lowest end of the ATS-W scoring scale.

Essay C

Ability grouping is terrible. Its awful to be in the slow group because everybody in the whole school knows it. Average students don't like ability grouping either because teachers don't pay any attention to them. Only the smart kids recieve any attention. Even then it only shows how differant they are. Some kids in the slow class like it because they never have homework and the teachers don't expect them to finish asignments so they get lots of time in class to do everything.

I observed in a school that ability grouping and I would not want to teach there. They would probably assign a new teacher to the slow class.

Analysis of Essay C

This essay does discuss the topic, but the opinions stated are never developed. Although the writer gives several specific examples to support his point of view (that ability grouping is terrible) he does not develop any of these examples so that the reader can understand the reasons behind his conclusions. There are several punctuation errors. Several words are mis-spelled, and the writer has left out a word in the second paragraph.

NYSTCE
New York State Teacher Certification Examinations

LAST Practice Test Two
and
ATS - W Secondary
Practice Test Two

LAST PRACTICE TEST 2

TIME: 4 Hours
80 Multiple Choice Questions, 1 Essay

SECTION 1

> **DIRECTIONS:** Each of the following questions and incomplete statements is followed by four answer choices. Select the choice which best answers each question.

1. Which of these is NOT a correct way to find 66% of 30?

   (A) $(66 \times 30) \div 100$

   (B) 66.0×30

   (C) $2/3 \times 30$

   (D) 0.66×30

2. A shopper bought $4.83 of groceries. There were three foods purchased: potatoes, tomatoes, and green beans. The shopper purchased 2 lbs. of potatoes and 3 lbs. of tomatoes. What data do you need to determine cost per lb. of the green beans?

   (A) Potatoes are 49¢/lb. and 2 lbs. green beans purchased

   (B) Tomatoes are 79¢/lb. and 2 lbs. green beans purchased

   (C) Tomatoes cost/lb, potatoes cost/lb, number of lbs. of green beans, and grocery bill total

   (D) $4.83; potatoes cost/lb; tomatoes cost/lb.

789

3. Evaluate this expression:

   $2X^2 - 9/Y$ When X is 6 and Y is 3.

   (A) 9

   (B) 69

   (C) 141

   (D) 63

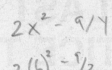

4. In the figure below, what is the area of the shaded region?

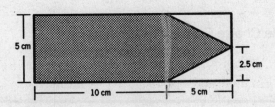

   (A) 75 cm^2

   (B) 62.5 cm^2

   (C) 40 cm

   (D) 35 cm

5. Examine the elementary student's work below. Analyze what the error pattern is that the student is making. If the student worked the problem 88 plus 39, what incorrect answer would the student give (assuming the use of the error pattern exhibited below)?

74	35	67	56
+ 56	+ 92	+ 18	+ 97
1,210	127	715	1,413

   (A) 127

   (B) 131

   (C) 51

   (D) 1,117

6. The needle on the dial points most nearly to which reading?

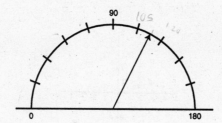

(A) 108

(B) 128

(C) 114

(D) 117

 7. How many ten thousands are there in one million?

(A) 100

(B) 10

(C) 1,000

(D) 10,000

8. An owner of 2 twin Siamese cats knows the following data:

I. Cost of a can of cat food

II. Volume of a can of cat food

III. Number of cans of cat food eaten each day by one cat

IV. The weight of the cat food in one can

Which of the above data can be used to determine the cost of seven days' worth of cat food for the 2 cats?

(A) I and II only.

(B) I and III only.

(C) I and IV only.

(D) III and IV only.

9. What are the coordinates of point *W*?

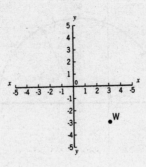

(A) (3, –3)

(B) (0, 3)

(C) (3, 0)

(D) (–3, 3)

× first

10. All angles in the figure are right angles. Find the total area of the enclosed region.

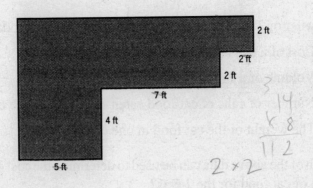

(A) 72 ft²

(B) 112 ft²

(C) 158 ft²

(D) 38 ft²

14 × 8

11. The diagram below shows a path for electric flow. As the electrically

15. What causes day and night?

    (A) The tilt of Earth on its axis.

    (B) The rotation of Earth on its axis.

    (C) The revolution of Earth about the Sun.

    (D) The rotation of the Sun about Earth.

16. Scurvy is the result of which of the following?

    (A) Insufficient sunshine

    (B) Insufficient calcium

    (C) Insufficient Vitamin C

    (D) Insufficient Vitamin B

17. Which statement about cells, the basic building blocks of everything that is living, is true?

    (A) Animals, unlike plants, have cells.

    (B) Plant cells, unlike animal cells, have a nonliving cell wall.

    (C) Chlorophyll is found only in the cells of plants.

    (D) Animal cells, unlike plant cells, contain the DNA molecule used to carry genetic information.

18. Which of the following facts about elements is true?

    (A) Elements are found in nature; nonelements are made by scientists.

    (B) Elements are made by scientists; nonelements are found in nature.

    (C) Some elements are found in nature, but others are made by scientists.

    (D) There are 107 presently-known atoms, so there are 214 identified elements.

19. Biologists use a classification scheme to classify living things; which of the following schemes is correctly ordered?

    (A) Kingdom, class, order, phylum, family, species, genus

    (B) Kingdom, order, class, family, phylum, species, genus

    (C) Genus, species, family, order, class, phylum, kingdom

    (D) Kingdom, phylum, class, order, family, genus, species

charged particle flow moves through one complete circuit, it would NOT have to go through

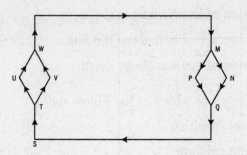

(A) V to get to W.

(B) W to get to M.

(C) Q to get to T.

(D) T to get to S.

12. A litmus test conducted on HCl would have which of the following results?

(A) There is no effect on the color of the litmus paper.

(B) The litmus paper disintegrates.

(C) The litmus paper turns blue.

(D) The litmus paper turns pink.

13. Water is which of the following?

(A) A base

(B) An acid

(C) A compound

(D) All of the above.

14. When is Earth closest to the Sun (for residents of New York)?

(A) During the summer

(B) During the fall

(C) During the winter

(D) During the spring

20. Which of the following resources are renewable?

    (A) Coal, oil, gas

    (B) Metals, minerals, coal

    (C) Soil, vegetation, animals

    (D) Freshwater, coal, vegetation

21. Which one of the following was published earliest?

    (A) Harriet Beecher Stowe's *Uncle Tom's Cabin*

    (B) Mark Twain's *The Adventures of Huckleberry Finn*

    (C) Ralph Waldo Emerson's *Nature*

    (D) Ernest Hemingway's *The Sun Also Rises*

22. In the *Plessy v. Ferguson* case, the Supreme Court decided that

    (A) separate but equal facilities are constitutional.

    (B) due process of law applies only to the federal government.

    (C) government efforts to regulate business are permissible.

    (D) workers cannot be forbidden to join labor unions.

23. Which of the following is the correct chronological order for the events in history listed below?

    I.   Puritans arrive in New England

    II. Protestant Reformation begins

    III. Columbus sets sail across the Atlantic

    IV. Magna Carta is signed in England

    (A) IV, III, II, I

    (B) IV, III, I, II

    (C) III, IV, II, I

    (D) III, II, I, IV

24. The intellectual movement which encouraged the use of reason and science and anticipated human progress was called the

    (A) American System.

    (B) mercantilism.

    (C) Enlightenment.

(D) age of belief.

25. The Bill of Rights (the first ten Amendments to the U.S. Constitution) deal with

    (A) limits on individual rights.

    (B) federalism.

    (C) expanded government.

    (D) basic rights and liberties.

26. The idea that the advance of American settlement in the west promoted democracy and individualism as part of the way of life is called

    (A) boom towns.

    (B) frontier thesis.

    (C) assimilation.

    (D) vertical integration.

27. Which of the following groups did not play a role in the settlement of the English colonies in America?

    (A) Roman Catholics

    (B) Puritans

    (C) Mormons

    (D) Quakers

28. The Morrill Act of 1862

    (A) abolished segregation in state supported colleges.

    (B) established the land grant system of universities.

    (C) provided for state control of education.

    (D) had no lasting effect on American education.

29. The effect of the 1921 Immigration Quota Act was to

    (A) sharply reduce immigration from the south and east of Europe.

    (B) greatly increase immigration from the south and east of Europe.

    (C) greatly reduce immigration from the countries of northern Europe.

    (D) reduce Mexican immigration.

30. Aside from the native Americans who were already inhabitants, the first settlers of the southwestern part of what became the United States were

    (A) cowboys from Texas and Kansas.

    (B) French missionaries.

    (C) Spaniards and Mexicans.

    (D) gold rush miners from the east.

31. In a free enterprise economy, production and consumption are allocated mainly through

    (A) trade associations.

    (B) price changes in the markets.

    (C) central planning.

    (D) taxes and subsidies.

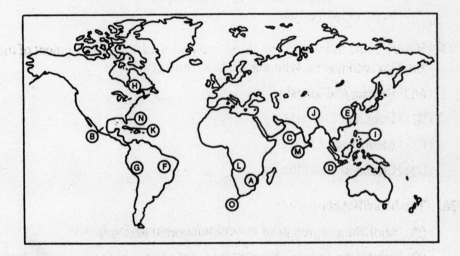

32. On the map above, which letter represents the Philippines?

    (A) K

    (B) D

    (C) I

    (D) M

WONDER HOW LONG THE HONEYMOON WILL LAST?

33. In the cartoon above, who are the bride and groom?

   (A) Goering and Trotsky

   (B) Hitler and Stalin

   (C) Goebbels and Marx

   (D) Hitler and Mussolini

34. The Bill of Rights

   (A) listed the grievances of the colonists against the British.

   (B) forbade the federal government from encroaching on the rights of citizens.

   (C) gave white males the right to vote.

   (D) specified the rights of slaves.

35. The government of the United States is

   (A) unitary, presidential, and parliamentary.

   (B) democratic, republican, and federal.

   (C) democratic, unitary, and federal.

   (D) presidential, parliamentary, and federal.

36. The amount of a product that people are willing to sell at a given price and time is the

(A) market supply.

(B) supply curve.

(C) demand curve.

(D) equilibrium price.

37. The principal legal forms of business organization are

(A) single proprietorship, partnership, corporation.

(B) single proprietorship, partnership, charter.

(C) corporation, charter, stock company.

(D) closed shop, open shop, union shop.

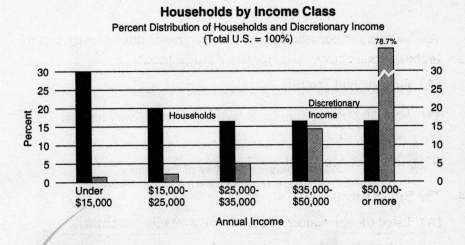

Households by Income Class
Percent Distribution of Households and Discretionary Income
(Total U.S. = 100%)

38. According to the graph "Households by Income Class" above, which one of the following statements is true?

(A) About 50% of households had under $15,000

(B) Almost 75% of households had at least $50,000 or more

(C) About 78% of households had $50,000 or more

(D) About 20% of households had between $15,000 and $25,000 annual income

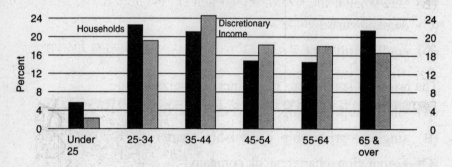

Age of Household Head
Percent Distribution of Households and Discretionary Income
(Total U.S. = 100%)

39. According to the graph, "Age of Household Head," which one of the following statements is true?

(A) Middle age households tend to have greater discretionary income

(B) The youngest have the most discretionary income

(C) The oldest have the most discretionary income

(D) The older one gets, one has the least discretionary income

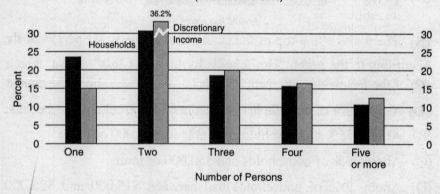

Households by Number of Persons
Percent Distribution of Households and Discretionary Income
(Total U.S. = 100%)

40. According to the graph, "Households by Number of Persons" which one

of the following is true?

(A) The larger the number of persons, the greater the percent of discretionary income available

(B) The smaller the size of the household, the greater the amount of discretionary income available

(C) Two-person households have the least discretionary income

(D) None of the above.

41. Who is the central focus in the picture above and why?

(A) The two men lower right, because they are separate and thus draw attention

(B) The guard at the top of the stairs, because he is the person at the highest elevation

(C) The man to the left of the flag, because he rises above the crowd

(D) The man on the middle of the stairs in the long, belted robe, because he is the focus of the other players

1   2   3   4   5

42. Which of the figures pictured above would be most appropriate for a medieval cycle play?

(A) 1

(B) 2

(C) 3

(D) 4

Questions 43 through 54 are based on the following passage.

It was the best of times, it was the worst of times, it was the age of wisdom, it was the age of foolishness, it was the epoch of belief, it was the epoch of incredulity, it was the season of Light, it was the season of Darkness, it was the spring of hope, it was the winter of despair, we had everything before us, we had nothing before us, we were all going direct to Heaven, we were all going direct the other way—in short, the period was so far like the present period, that some of its noisiest authorities insisted on its being received, for good or for evil, in the superlative degree of comparison only.

There were a king with a large jaw, and a queen with a plain face, on the throne of England; there were a king with a large jaw, and a queen with a fair face, on the throne of France. In both countries it was clearer than crystal to the lords of the State preserves of loaves and fishes, that things in general were settled for ever.

43. The vast comparisons in the above passage indicate that the speaker is describing

(A) a placid historical time period.

(B) a time of extreme political upheaval.

(C) a public event.

(D) a time when anything was possible.

44. The last sentence of the passage

(A) mocks the self-assuredness of the governments of England and France.

(B) comments on the horrible poverty of the two nations.

(C) most likely foreshadows an upcoming famine or drought.

(D) attacks the two governments for neglecting the poor, hungry masses.

45. The phrase, "some of its noisiest authorities insisted on its being received, for good or for evil, in the superlative degree of comparison only"

(A) mocks the arrogance of the governments.

(B) mocks the arrogance of the people.

(C) compares the attitude of the people to the attitude of the governments.

(D) Both (A) and (B).

Pylon Temple of Horus, Edfu

46. In the example pictured above, which of the following contributes most to an effect of stability and changeless grandeur?

(A) The strong horizontal thrust of the architecture

(B) The wealth of elaborate ornamental detail

(C) The vast open courtyard with its surrounding columns

(D) The simplified geometry of the massive forms and the sloping diagonal walls

Galleria Borghese, Rome

47. Which of the following seems most true of the sculpture pictured above?

(A) The statue is conceived as a decorative work without a narrative function.

(B) The figure seems to be static, passive, and introverted.

(C) The figure is depicted as though frozen in a moment of action.

(D) The figure's garments indicate that he is a soldier or warrior.

Merry days were these at Thornfield Hall; and busy days too: how different from the first three months of stillness, monotony and solitude I had passed beneath its roof! All sad feelings seemed now driven from the house... there was life everywhere, movement all day long.

48. In the above passage, what is the significance of the three consecutive periods?

(A) They indicate a lapse in thought on the author's part.

(B) They indicate that the speaker is unable or unwilling to finish his/ her sentence.

(C) They indicate that part of the quote has been omitted.

(D) They indicate that part of the original manuscript has been lost.

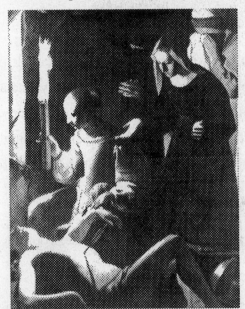

Gemäldegalerie, Staatliche Museen, Berlin-Dahlem

49. In this painting, light is used to do all of the following EXCEPT

(A) model and define the forms.

(B) create an atmosphere of stillness and calm.

(C) convey a sense of intimacy.

(D) establish a recession into space.

Palazzo Torlonia, Rome

50. Which of the following best describes the example pictured above?

   (A) The subject appears to be poetic, dreamy, and aristocratic.

   (B) The sculptor was not concerned with descriptive detail.

   (C) The hard material counteracts the effect desired by the sculptor.

   (D) The subject appears to be hard-bitten, pragmatic, and realistic.

51. (A)

   Once upon a time and a very good time it was there was a moocow coming down along the road and this moocow that was coming down along the met a nicens little boy named baby tuckoo…

   (B)

   And thus have these naked Nantucketers, these sea hermits, issuing from their ant-hill in the sea, overrun and conquered the watery world like so many Alexanders…

   (C)

   A large rose tree stood near the entrance of the garden: the roses growing on it were white, but there were three gardeners at it, busily painting them red. Alice thought this a very curious thing, and she went nearer to watch them, and, just as she came up to them, she heard one of them say "Look out now, Five!"

   (D)

   Emma was not required, by any subsequent discovery to retract her ill opinion of Mrs. Elton. Her observation had been pretty correct. Such as Mrs. Elton appeared to her on the second interview, such she appeared whenever they met again—self-important, presuming, familiar, ignorant, and ill-bred. She had a little beauty and a little accomplishment, but so little judgement that she thought herself coming with superior knowledge of the world, to enliven and improve a country neighborhood...

51. Which passage makes use of allusion?

52. Which passage employs a discreet voice to imitate the speech of a character?

53. Which passage is most likely taken from a nineteenth century novel of manners?

The Art Institute of Chicago

54. Which of the following best characterizes the artist's approach in this picture?

    (A) Spontaneous and impulsive

    (B) Emotionally tormented

    (C) Detached and systematic

    (D) Passionate and romantic

Arch of Constantine, Rome

55. In the example pictured above, the four slender columns at the front of the arch do all of the following EXCEPT

(A) lead the eye from ground level to the upper story.

(B) establish a horizontal rhythm across the facade of the arch.

(C) provide structural support for the upper story of the arch.

(D) help to divide the elaborate facade into regular units.

(The veranda of the Voynitzevs' country house. It looks out onto a sunlit garden, with the tall trees of the forest beyond, bisected by a grassy walk.

The whoosh of a rocket taking off. The lights come up to reveal YAKOV in the garden with a large box of assorted fireworks in his arms. Beside him stands DR. TRILETZKY, a match in his hand. They are gazing up into the sky—DR. TRILETZKY with delight, YAKOV with apprehension. There is a smell of sulfur in the air. The rocket bursts, off.)

56. The above passage is most likely taken from

(A) a Victorian novel.

(B) the stage directions of a play.

(C) the critical notes to a literary work.

(D) the rough draft of a literary work.

Eero Saarinen, interior of Trans World Airlines Terminal, John F. Kennedy International Airport

57. Which of the following is an important feature of the building pictured above?

(A) A dependence on rectilinear lines and angles

(B) An emphasis on the structural framework of the building

(C) An interplay of large and small geometric shapes

(D) The use of curvilinear forms to suggest organic growth or motion

(A)

My life closed twice before its close;
It yet remains to see
If immortality unveil
A third event to me,

(B)

Hark, hark!
Bow-wow,
The watch-dogs bark!
Bow-wow.
Hark, hark! I hear
The strain of strutting chanticleer
Cry, "Cock-a-doodle-doo!"

(C)
A narrow fellow in the grass
Occasionally rides;
You may have met him. Did you not,
His notice sudden is:
The grass divides as with a comb,
A spotted shaft is seen,
And then it closes at your feet
And opens further on.

(D)
Gather ye rosebuds while ye may,
Old Time is still a-flying;
And this same flower that smiles today
Tomorrow will be dying.

58. Which passage espouses the philosophy of *carpe diem*?

59. Which passage employs the technique of onomatopoeia?

60. Which passage employs the technique of alliteration?

Questions 61 through 65 are based on the following passage.

The issue of adult literacy has finally received recognition as a major social problem. Unfortunately, the issue is usually presented in the media as a "women's interest issue." Numerous governors' wives and even Barbara Bush have publicly expressed concern about literacy. As well-meaning as the politicians' wives may be, it is more important that the politicians themselves recognize the seriousness of the problem and support increased funding for literacy programs.

Literacy education programs need to be directed at two different groups of people with very different needs. The first group is composed of people who have very limited reading and writing skills. These people are complete illiterates. A second group is composed of people who can read and write but whose skills are not sufficient to meet their needs. This second group is called functionally illiterate. Successful literacy programs must meet the needs of both groups.

Instructors in literacy programs have three main responsibilities. First, the educational needs of the illiterates and functional illiterates must be met. Second, the instructors must approach the participants in the program with empathy, not sympathy. Third, all participants must experience success in the program and must perceive their efforts as worthwhile.

61. What is the difference between illiteracy and functional illiteracy?

   (A) There is no difference.

   (B) A functional illiterate is enrolled in a literacy education program but an illiterate is not.

(C) An illiterate cannot read or write, a functional illiterate can read and write but not at a very high skill level.

(D) There are more illiterates than functional illiterates in the United States today.

62. What does "women's interest issue" mean in the passage?

(A) The issue is only interesting to women.

(B) Many politicians' wives have expressed concern over the issue.

(C) Women illiterates outnumber male illiterates.

(D) Politicians interested in illiteracy often have their wives give speeches on the topic.

63. What is the purpose of the passage?

(A) To discuss the characteristics of successful literacy programs.

(B) To discuss the manner in which literacy programs are viewed by the media.

(C) To discuss some of the reasons for increased attention to literacy as a social issue.

(D) All of the above.

64. According to the passage, which of the following is NOT a characteristic of successful literacy programs?

(A) Participants should receive free transportation.

(B) Participants should experience success in the program.

(C) Instructors must have empathy, not sympathy.

(D) Programs must meet the educational needs of illiterates.

65. What is the author's opinion of the funding for literacy programs?

(A) Too much

(B) Too little

(C) About right

(D) Too much for illiterates and not enough for functional illiterates

Questions 66 through 70 are based on the following passage.

The price of cleaning up the environment after oil spills is on the increase. After the massive Alaskan spill that created miles of sludge-covered beach, numerous smaller spills have occurred along the Gulf Coast and off the coast of California. Tides and prevailing winds carried much of this oil to shore in a matter of days. Workers tried to contain the oil with weighted, barrel-shaped plastic tubes stretched along the sand near the water. They hoped to minimize the damage. Generally, the barriers were successful, but there remained many miles of oil-covered sand. Cleanup crews shoveled the oil-covered sand into plastic bags for removal.

Coastal states are responding to the problem in several ways. California is considering the formation of a department of oceans to oversee protection programs and future cleanups. Some states have suggested training the National Guard in cleanup procedures. Other states are calling for the creation of an oil spill trust fund large enough to cover the costs of a major spill. Still other states are demanding federal action and funding. Regardless of the specific programs that may be enacted by the various states or the federal government, continued offshore drilling and the shipping of oil in huge tankers creates a constant threat to the nation's shoreline.

66. According to the passage, where have oil spills occurred?

   (A) U. S. Gulf Coast

   (B) Alaskan coast

   (C) California coast

   (D) All of the above.

67. What was the purpose of the barrel-shaped plastic tubes?

   (A) To keep sightseers away from the oil

   (B) To keep oil-soaked animals off the beach

   (C) To force the oil to soak into the sand

   (D) To keep the oil from spreading on the beach

68. Which of the following solutions is NOT discussed in the passage?

   (A) Create an oil cleanup trust fund

   (B) Increase federal funding for cleanups

   (C) Reduce oil production

   (D) Use the National Guard for cleanups

69. According to the passage, which of the following is the largest oil spill?

   (A) Alaskan coastal spill

(B) Spill off the California coast

(C) North Sea oil spill

(D) Spill off the U. S. Gulf Coast

70. What is the author's opinion of the hazards created by oil spills?

(A) Oil spills must be expected if the present methods of production and shipment continue.

(B) Oil spills are the result of untrained crews.

(C) Oil spills would not be a problem if the government was better prepared to cleanup.

(D) Oil spills are the responsibility of foreign oil producers.

Questions 71 through 73 are based on the following passage.

Children, young adults, the middle-aged, and retirees all experience some types of stress. Excessive stress, or the inability to cope with normal levels of stress, can lead to high blood pressure, heart disease, mental disorders, infections, and prolonged or aggravated minor illnesses. Although few people can actually eliminate all stress from their lives, the lack of stress can be just as bad as too much stress. Extremely low levels of stress can cause boredom and depression and can contribute to mental illness. Many adults develop strategies for coping with stress. Some of the common strategies, which may include diet and exercise, focus on goal setting, establishing deadlines and developing contingency plans. Often, adults learn to recognize their own signs of excessive stress. Common symptoms include headaches, stomach upsets, personality changes and chronic tiredness.

71. Boredom, depression, and symptoms of mental illness are the possible result of what condition?

(A) High stress levels

(B) Low stress levels

(C) Inability to cope with stress

(D) Insomnia

72. Which of the following are suggested by the passage?

(A) Adults can seldom eliminate all stress from daily life.

(B) Most adults can learn coping strategies for excessive stress.

(C) A certain amount of stress is desirable.

(D) All of the above.

73. Which of the following is NOT suggested as a method for coping with stress?

   (A) Diet

   (B) Exercise

   (C) Goal setting

   (D) Sleep

Questions 74 through 76 are based on the following passage.

   Reducing the amount of fat in the foods we eat is the goal of an ever increasing number of people. Many restaurants are responding to the demand for low fat foods by adding "Light" or "Good For You" entrees to their menus. These entrees are usually traditional foods prepared without added fat. Cooking methods that require little or no fat include steaming, poaching, broiling and searing. Stir-fried vegetables and chicken dishes are especially popular with diet conscious people. Almost all fried foods should be avoided when eating out, and it is best to avoid foods in cream sauces or gravies. Although salads are very healthful foods, the value of the salad can be ruined by the addition of thick, creamy salad dressings. Desserts based on fresh fruit are usually a better choice than desserts thick with cream, butter or sugar. If you are concerned about the content or preparation of any food on a restaurant menu, it is best to ask lots of questions about ingredients and methods of preparation in order to make intelligent choices.

74. What is the purpose of the author in this passage?

   (A) To warn people of the dangers of fat in the diet

   (B) To suggest ways to avoid excessive fat when eating out

   (C) To discourage eating in restaurants

   (D) To encourage the use of broiling, searing and steaming to cook food

75. Which of the following should be avoided by diet conscious diners?

   (A) Salads

   (B) Creamy sauces or gravies

   (C) Stir-fried vegetables and chicken

   (D) Fresh fruit desserts

76. According to the passage, what does "Light" or "Good For You" mean on a restaurant menu?

   (A) These foods are not deep-fat fried.

   (B) These foods have reduced salt.

(C) These foods are especially good.

(D) These foods are prepared without added fat.

Questions 77 through 80 are based on the following passage.

The pituitary is a very small gland about the size of a marble. Located at the base of the brain, the pituitary produces many different hormones which are released into the blood. Hormones produced by the pituitary control the growth of bones and the function of the kidneys. The pituitary also controls the thyroid, a gland located in the throat, which is essential in regulating metabolism. The parathyroids, four tiny glands at the back of the thyroid, control the amount of calcium and phosphate in the blood. The parathyroids are also controlled by the pituitary. The adrenal glands, also controlled by the pituitary, are located on top of the kidneys. The adrenals have many functions, including controlling the amount of sodium and potassium in the body and producing hormones used in the metabolism of food. Another important function of the adrenal glands is the production of a hormone to help people cope with stress.

77. According to the passage which of the following is NOT controlled by the pituitary?

(A) Growth of bones

(B) Adrenal glands

(C) Parathyroids

(D) Blood circulation

78. What do the parathyroids control?

(A) Metabolism

(B) Calcium and phosphate in the blood

(C) Sodium and potassium in the blood

(D) The kidneys

79. Where are the adrenals located?

(A) Near the pituitary

(B) At the back of the thyroid

(C) Near the liver

(D) On top of the kidneys

80. If a child is not growing at a normal rate, what glands discussed in the passage might be responsible?

(A) Adrenals

(B) Kidneys

(C) Pituitary

(D) Parathyroids

Section 2: Written Assignment

> **DIRECTIONS:** Plan and write an essay on the topic given below. DO NOT WRITE ON ANY TOPIC OTHER THAN THE ONE SPECIFIED. AN ESSAY ON ANY OTHER TOPIC IS UNACCEPTABLE.

Essay Topic:

Many leaders have suggested over the last few years that instead of a military draft, we should require all young people to serve the public in some way for a period of time. The service could be military or any other reasonable form of public service.

Assignment:

Do you agree or disagree with the statement? Support your opinion with specific examples from history, current events, literature, or personal experience.

ATS-W SECONDARY PRACTICE TEST 2

TIME: 4 Hours
80 Multiple-Choice Questions, 1 Essay

SECTION 1

> **DIRECTIONS:** Read each stimulus carefully, and answer the questions that follow. Mark your responses on the answer sheet provided.

1. Patrick O'Brien is a high school communications teacher. At the end of the school year, he reviewed the topics he had taught and the assignments he had given. He then used this review to direct his professional development activities over the summer months by

   (A) identifying areas not covered or new topics to study and research over the summer months.

   (B) updating his files on each of the topics.

   (C) assessing the quality of the assignments received from students over the past school year.

   (D) revising student assignments by re-evaluating educational objectives for each.

2. Mr. O'Brien discovers that he spends virtually no class time discussing the differences in the ways females and males communicate although he notes that several best-selling books by academic scholars have been written on this topic. Furthermore, he has observed some recurring gender differences among the students he has taught over the years and he wonders if he should add this timely topic to the list of those he now teaches. He decides to discuss this possibility with other teachers at his school to

(A) demonstrate for the benefit of his peers his knowledge of current professional and academic topics.

(B) solicit their ideas and input on expanding and/or revising the curriculum in communication classes.

(C) determine if he should do any additional professional reading on this topic.

(D) ascertain any gender differences in communication styles among his colleagues.

3. When Mr. O'Brien brings up the topic of gender differences in styles of communication, he discovers that two of his colleagues have opposite views. Subsequently, he decides that the best course of action to take is to

(A) go immediately to the department chair or curricular supervisor and let that party know about the dissension in the ranks.

(B) drop the topic since it is clearly too controversial to pursue.

(C) invite both colleagues to help him develop lessons on the topic which would include both viewpoints.

(D) argue with both colleagues to clearly state his own view of the topic based on current research findings.

4. Mr. O'Brien reads Deborah Tannen's book *You Just Don't Understand: Women and Men in Conversation* and decides that he would like to use the book as a reference tool for introducing some gender-related ideas to his students. By selecting a current best-seller as a reference, Mr. O'Brien is

(A) attempting to locate contemporary and relevant sources of information for his students.

(B) expecting students to purchase an additional book for his course.

(C) demonstrating to his colleagues that he is aware of current research in his discipline.

(D) requiring students to do more outside reading in the course.

5. The literature Mr. O'Brien surveys reveals that female students are less likely to participate in classroom discussions than are male students. Some researchers cite this behavior as an illustration of females' lower self-esteem. In an effort to boost the self-esteem of female students in his class, Mr. O'Brien

    (A) endeavors to ask the female students easier questions so they will get the answers right.

    (B) develops a question grid to enable him to call on all students in the class, both male and female, an equal number of times.

    (C) does not call on female students if the question is one requiring higher-ordered thinking skills.

    (D) attempts to give no critical feedback to female students who give incorrect answers.

6. As Mr. O'Brien learns about female students' problems with self-esteem, he recalls a former student, Shonda Harris, who was a very shy, quiet student. Shonda never volunteered to answer questions or participate in class discussions although she made the top grades in his class. Mr. O'Brien never called on her in class and now he wonders if he acted appropriately. In retrospect, he concludes that in the future he should

    (A) continue to call only on those students who raise their hands or otherwise indicate their willingness to respond so as not to unduly pressure students.

    (B) gently tease to provoke shy, quiet students to participate in class discussions.

    (C) require students to participate in class discussions with the result of lowered grades if they fail to do so.

    (D) meet with the student privately and discuss why he, as the teacher, wants students to participate in class discussions and then listen to her or his reasons for not volunteering to do so.

7. Mr. O'Brien decides that he will require his students to participate in discussions and that class participation will account for a percentage of students' grades in his communications course. This new requirement will

    (A) be an effective motivational tool for all students in his classes.

(B) motivate only some of the students in the course to participate.

(C) result in improved grades for all students in his classes.

(D) discourage the majority of students from participating in class discussions.

8. Before introducing the topic of gender differences in communication styles to his students, Mr. O'Brien asks the class to brainstorm individually ten situations wherein each student would like to improve his or her communication skills. In each situation, students are then asked to identify the gender of their audience (or the receiver of the communication, the other party in the situation). Students next are asked to tally the number of times there is a sex difference between themselves as the sender of the message and the receiver of the message. In this activity, Mr. O'Brien

(A) avoids a classroom activity that could deteriorate into an argument.

(B) utilizes a strategy to promote student learning.

(C) saves classroom time.

(D) finds a way to assess who's having trouble communicating and who's not.

9. As students tally their responses from the brainstorming activity, they indicate that many of the communication problems they routinely encounter involve members of the opposite sex. This discovery allows Mr. O'Brien to

(A) capitalize on students' self-motivation to learn how to communicate more effectively.

(B) skip over a formal introduction to the topic of gender differences in communication.

(C) pinpoint whether male or female students are having greater difficulty communicating.

(D) dismiss students' concerns about their problems in communicating with others.

10. Mr. O'Brien asks students to form groups of three or four to describe some of the factors which are commonly associated with the "communication conflicts" involving members of the opposite sex. By asking students to work in groups, Mr. O'Brien's instructional strategy is to

   (A) avoid a tedious lecture.

   (B) encourage students to develop better social skills.

   (C) allow students to structure their own time in class.

   (D) promote collaborative learning.

11. Mr. O'Brien ends the class by telling students that over the next few weeks they will be required to keep a communications journal. Every time they have an eventful exchange — either positive or negative, they are to record the details of the exchange in their journal. This assignment is given as

   (A) a way to help students improve their composition and rhetorical skills.

   (B) a way of understanding individual students, monitoring instructional effectiveness, and shaping instruction.

   (C) a way of helping students become more accountable for the way they manage their time.

   (D) the basis for giving daily grades to students.

12. Joan Jaynes is a secondary special education teacher and reading specialist. Her teaching assignment requires her to provide for the special needs of students who are experiencing difficulties in reading. Among her first actions is to

   (A) interview the students' previous teachers to solicit their opinions and advice on meeting the educational needs of the students.

   (B) review school files on each student, including assessment and testing history.

   (C) meet students individually and informally discuss school, reading, and how they feel about each.

(D) administer a standardized reading test to determine their current reading performance.

13. In selecting a test to administer to students, Ms. Jaynes needs to be relatively certain that she has selected a test which is not biased. Test bias refers to whether or not

(A) a test measures what it purports to measure.

(B) a test consistently measures what it purports to measure.

(C) the test discriminates between students who are intelligent or lacking in intelligence.

(D) the test discriminates among students on the basis of ideographic characteristics.

14. Ms. Jaynes gives a standardized reading test to a student in her class on Friday afternoon (Test Time 1). The following Monday morning, Ms. Jaynes is absent and the substitute teacher gives the same form of the test to the student again (Test Time 2). The student's parents are surprised and pleased to learn that their student's grade level score improved significantly from Test Time 1 to Test Time 2. Ms. Jaynes subsequently has to explain the difference in scores to the parents; she explains the difference as a result of test-practice effects. Test-practice effects are the phenomenon of

(A) students' scores improving when they take the same form of a test shortly after the first testing.

(B) students' scores improving as a result of having received adequate instruction and practice time with the skills being tested.

(C) a test not measuring what it claims to measure.

(D) students answering questions the way they think the examiner wants the question answered.

15. Ms. Jaynes wants her students to feel better about themselves and to develop positive attitudes about reading. Therefore, when she gives them a reading assignment she

(A) sends them to the library and lets each student pick whatever he or she would like to read.

(B) tends to guide students in their selection of reading materials, pointing out to them books on topics about which they have expressed an interest.

(C) ensures that students read only worthwhile material, such as literary classics.

(D) makes certain that students do not select books that are written at too high a level so as to result in reading frustration.

16. At the beginning of the semester, Ms. Jaynes has her students read together in class. Initially, she reads a paragraph and then asks the students to find answers to the following questions: "Who... is the paragraph about?," "What... does the paragraph say about the person, event, or action?," "When... did it take place?," "Where... did it occur?," "Why... did it happen?," and "How... did it happen?" For several weeks, she leads the class through this protocol. After weeks of practice, students are expected to follow this protocol on their own. Ms. Jaynes is attempting to teach her students

(A) an elaboration strategy to help them monitor their reading comprehension.

(B) about the importance of topic sentences in paragraphs.

(C) about the importance of topic sentences and supporting details in paragraphs.

(D) important decoding skills.

17. Ms. Jaynes spends much of her instructional time teaching her students different reading strategies and giving them opportunities to practice these strategies in class. By teaching her students reading strategies they can use on their own, she is

(A) creating a quiet classroom environment conducive to the learning of all students.

(B) able to spend more class time on grading students' work.

(C) stressing to her students the importance of reading as a social activity.

(D) promoting students' sense of responsibility for their own learning.

18. Ms. Jaynes determines that she will base students' grades in her class on students' performance on homework, daily work in class, and informally-constructed (teacher-made) tests. However, the deciding factor as to whether or not students have made sufficient progress to exit her special reading class will be students' performance on standardized reading tests. This decision is based on the proposition that

    (A) standardized tests are easier to grade than informally-constructed tests.

    (B) standardized tests are more subjective than informally-constructed tests.

    (C) statistical procedures used in the construction of standardized tests result in greater test validity and reliability as measures of overall reading achievement.

    (D) standardized tests are more economical in terms of both time and money.

19. As a special education teacher, Ms. Jaynes has learned that an essential part of her job is to confer with her colleagues who teach core academic classes. She spends time giving her colleagues weekly reports on students' progress and learning about what the students are doing in their academic classes. Ms. Jaynes believes that this practice is

    (A) an effective way of gaining popularity and respect among her colleagues.

    (B) an effective way to discipline students since they know she has influence among their other teachers.

    (C) an important part of her profession as a member of a community who must work effectively with all members of that community to reach common goals.

    (D) the only way to qualify for merit pay and salary increases.

20. Suli Aljuhbar is an ESL teacher. She works with high school-aged students, typically with groups of six to twelve students who possess varying degrees of ability in understanding English. Her primary objective in working with her students is to help them understand the American English spoken in their classes and to help them communicate more effectively in English with their other teachers and classmates. Her

secondary objective is to create cultural awareness within her students and expose them to customs of the United States. These objectives are examples of

(A) behavioral objectives.

(B) performance objectives.

(C) instructional objectives.

(D) outcome-based education.

21. As Ms. Aljuhbar develops her weekly lesson plans, she identifies specific behavioral objectives for each class session. By doing this, Ms. Aljuhbar

(A) specifies exactly which instructional methods should be used.

(B) lists the materials and equipment that will be needed.

(C) describes what students will be able to do as a result of receiving instruction.

(D) focuses attention on teacher-centered activities.

22. Just as Ms. Aljuhbar hopes that her ESL students will learn about the customs and characteristics of people in the United States, she also wants other students at her school to have the opportunity to learn about the culture and practices in the native lands of her ESL students. Thus, to bring about a reciprocal and active learning dynamic, Ms. Aljuhbar

(A) collaborates with other teachers for ESL students to make presentations in classes.

(B) gives the ESL students a library research assignment to learn about the United States.

(C) arranges field trips for the ESL students to visit local points of interest.

(D) invites a guest speaker to class to talk about how Christmas is celebrated in different countries.

23. One of Ms. Aljuhbar's students, Lee Zhang, had been enthusiastic in class and eagerly participated in class activities until the end of the fall

semester. When the spring semester began, Lee seemed despondent. She no longer participated in class activities and she stopped turning in her homework or even doing assignments in class. The best thing for Ms. Aljuhbar to do to help Lee is to

(A) contact Lee's family to see if they are having family problems.

(B) confer with other teachers at the school to determine if Lee is acting the same way in all of her classes.

(C) ask Lee if something is wrong.

(D) give Lee extra credit work to help her catch-up and improve her grades.

24. One activity that Ms. Aljuhbar uses with her ESL students requires that each student chose a fable or folk tale that he or she learned as a child. The student is then videotaped (privately) telling the story in his or her native language. The student next is given the tape and allowed time to view it, critique it, and then translate it into English. Finally, at a second taping, the student is videotaped telling the story in English. The student is then given the tape with both versions. Ms. Aljuhbar has found that this is an effective instructional strategy because

(A) it is based on the premise that practice makes perfect.

(B) it allows the student to make choices and to move from the familiar to the novel or unfamiliar at his or her own pace.

(C) it permits the student to critique the tape in private.

(D) it is done in a nonthreatening environment.

25. When students are satisfied with their tape, they are encouraged to submit it to Ms. Aljuhbar who compiles the stories for the collection in the elementary school library. ESL students are also invited to partici- pate in story sessions at the public library whereby they tell their folktales to children in the community. These activities

(A) assure that student performance on the tapes is standardized.

(B) are inappropriate for high school-aged students.

(C) restrict student initiative and creativity.

(D) motivate ESL students.

Mr. Reams' science class of ninth graders ranged in abilities from gifted (Joe and Sue) to low-average, (Hank).

The previous day had been recognized as Earth Day. Focusing the students' attention upon the environment, Mr. Reams wanted to extend the text to portray the significant difference one small group could make toward a cleaner environment.

The class reviewed Earth Day and the need for its existence. Mr. Reams followed by asking "What are some of the pollution problems present in our own school?" Class responses included a tobacco polluted environment, the use of non-biodegradable styrofoam containers and the lack of recycling aluminum soft-drink cans. Forming small groups with a cross-section of abilities, each was charged to determine which offenses could be changed, how they could be changed, the resources needed for the change, and the benefits which could be derived from the change.

While monitoring the groups as they brainstormed, Mr. Reams observed that both Hank and Joe were actively involved in making suggestions as another group member took notes. Mr. Reams paused with each group, listening, reiterating, and encouraging students.

26. Which of the following learning environmental factors was Mr. Reams using for this phase of his class?

    (A) Small groups are unstructured, therefore he was without a role.

    (B) By making use of small groups, he had assured the students of success in the classroom.

    (C) He was modeling effective communication strategies of reflective listening, simplifying, and restating.

    (D) He had made the instruction relevant to the students' own needs.

27. When Mr. Reams divided the class into cross-sectioned groups he was attempting to

    (A) select appropriate materials and resources for particular situations and purposes.

    (B) use observation as an informal assessment.

    (C) use an array of instructional strategies to actively engage students in learning.

(D) prevent any social/emotional atmosphere from developing in the classroom.

Ideas generated in small groups were written on the chalkboard. Each entry was discussed according to the four criteria given by Mr. Reams. It was concluded that a smoke free environment required the legislation of a group with more power than the ninth grade class. The use of non-biodegradable styrofoam containers would require research as to why the school chose to use such containers. Research would also be required to answer why there had been no recycling effort by the school.

Three days later, the class presented their research in class. The school's choice to use non-biodegradable containers was based on economics. Biodegradable containers were more expensive and it was felt that most of them were placed in the trash and hauled to the landfill and posed no problem. Therefore, the school would continue its present policy. Research also revealed that the school had no recycling program because there had been no interest by the students, faculty, or staff for such a program. Hank volunteered to question the soft-drink man concerning the volume of drinks delivered weekly to the school. Sue volunteered to contact Ace Manufacturing Company to find out how they collected the cans, where they recycled them and how much they were paid for them. Other students agreed to interview students, custodians, cafeteria workers, and the administration.

28. As the students conducted the research and began the interview process, Mr. Reams felt he had successfully

(A) developed an interdisciplinary activity for the class.

(B) designed the instruction taking into account the learners' backgrounds and abilities.

(C) almost achieved his goals for the class.

(D) helped the students understand the role of technology as a learning tool.

One week later, the students reported that collection of the cans would be accomplished by placing receptacles purchased by the administration in strategic places, the custodians would deliver weekly the cans for recycling, and the school would receive $.023 per pound for them.

29. Mr. Reams was congratulated by the principal for having

    (A) presented a new and unique problem to the students.

    (B) made the instruction relevant to the students' own needs.

    (C) helped the students feel they are members of a community.

    (D) used an on-going assessment as an instructional tool.

The class began to discuss ways the recycling money could be used. It was concluded that the class would purchase trees to be planted on campus. Mr. Reams asked if the class had considered how the trees were to be cared for. No one had thought of the care that must follow the planting. Hank volunteered that his father was a gardener and knew all about trees. Sue asked if Hank's father could speak to the class about tree care. As the trees were being planted on Arbor Day, several parents and community members were present to encourage the class in their endeavor.

30. Mr. Reams had

    (A) gotten the students to work with members of the community.

    (B) conferenced with parents to explain what the students had yet to do.

    (C) taken advantage of community strengths and resources to foster student growth.

    (D) used a variety of strategies to achieve his goal of trees being planted on campus.

The Social Studies department of an inner city high school wanted to change to a more relevant curriculum. The department wanted to have units on economics throughout the world instead of only regions of the U.S. Mrs. Dunn was asked to submit a proposal for the new curriculum, related activities, sequencing, themes, and materials. In consultation with the other teachers in the department, a needs assessment was planned.

31. The group felt that the needs assessment would

    (A) help the students make a connection between their current skills and those that will be new to them.

(B) reveal community problems that may affect the students' lives and their performance in school.

(C) foster a view of learning as a purposeful pursuit, promoting a sense of responsibility for one's own learning.

(D) engage students in learning activities and help them to develop the motivation to achieve.

When the needs assessment was evaluated, it revealed an ethnically diverse community. Student interests and parental expectations varied, different language backgrounds existed, student exceptionalities were common, and academic motivation was low. The question confronting the teachers was how to bridge the gap from where the students are to where they should be.

32. The available choices were

(A) change the text only.

(B) relate the lessons to the students' personal interests.

(C) create a positive environment to minimize the effects of the negative external factors.

(D) help students to learn and to monitor their own performance.

It was decided that the students would be administered an interest inventory at the beginning of the semester. The questions would range from "Are you currently working?" "What is your salary?" to "What salary do you want to earn in ten years?" "What skills will you need for earning that salary?" and "How are salaries determined?"

33. The results of the interest inventory would allow Mrs. Dunn to

(A) nurture their academic growth through developmentally appropriate instruction.

(B) plan instruction which would enhance their self-esteem.

(C) invite community professionals to speak to the class.

(D) plan instruction which would lead students to ask questions and pursue problems that are meaningful to them.

An activity was planned to follow the interest inventory. Mrs. Dunn contacted various members of the business community. Each agreed to send a representative to the class to discuss those jobs which required the minimally skilled, those which required the semi-skilled, and those requiring the highly skilled. A question-and-answer period would be the format.

34. The above planning reveals that Mrs. Dunn is aware of

    (A) problems facing the students and understands how these problems may affect their learning.

    (B) the multiplicity of roles that teachers may be called upon to assume.

    (C) being a member of a learning community and knowing how to work effectively with all members of the community to solve problems and accomplish educational goals.

    (D) the need to establish a relationship of trust with the parents/guardians from diverse backgrounds to develop effective parent-teacher partnerships that foster all students' learning.

It was determined that at the end of the question-and-answer period, the students would have an awareness of the correlation between their skills or lack of skills and their salaries. A parental guardian support group would be established to enhance the students' motivation to master new skills. Strategies for use at home and in the classroom would be developed.

35. Mrs. Dunn felt that with the aid of parents

    (A) she could promote her own professional growth as she worked cooperatively with professionals to create a school culture that would enhance learning and result in positive change.

    (B) she would be meeting the expectations associated with teaching.

    (C) she would be fostering strong home relationships that support student achievement of desired outcomes.

    (D) she would be exhibiting her understanding of the principles of conducting parent-teacher conferences and working cooperatively with parents.

Mrs. Walker is thinking about developing a tenth-grade world history unit. The unit needs to emphasize Virgil's attempt to connect the origins of Rome to the events that followed the destruction of Troy by the Greeks. She wants the unit to be challenging, and yet the students must be able to handle the work. She is aware that this is the semester the students will take their first college entrance exam. The information from a cooperative learning workshop taken during the summer should be included in the unit.

36. What should be Mrs. Walker's first step in planning the unit?

   (A) Combining cooperative learning and the content

   (B) Deciding on an evaluation that will be fair to all students

   (C) Developing objectives for the unit

   (D) Finding available materials and resources

37. Mrs. Walker's understanding of human development is evident because her planning alludes to which statement about cognitive growth?

   (A) Students will learn whatever they need to learn if they are given enough time and proper instruction.

   (B) Students will use higher order thinking skills in real world situations.

   (C) Students will develop a sense of involvement and responsibility in relation to the larger school community.

   (D) Constant difficult schoolwork and demands will cause students to become interested.

38. Which of the following is an indication that Mrs. Walker is aware of the environmental factors that may affect learning?

   (A) She is developing a tenth-grade world history unit.

   (B) She wants to be sure that the students are challenged.

   (C) She is aware that this is the semester the students will take their first college entrance exam.

   (D) She decides to utilize group work for a large portion of the unit.

39. In planning for the unit, what information about students is not needed?

    (A) Individual learning style

    (B) Student's cultural background

    (C) Student's grades in previous history courses

    (D) Student's daily class schedule

40. What might Mrs. Walker include in her planning to keep gifted students challenged?

    (A) An extra report on the history of the Greeks

    (B) Let them tutor the students that are unmotivated.

    (C) Encourage students to plan learning activities of their own.

    (D) Create, for the student, a tightly-organized and well-designed unit.

41. What concepts are always present in cooperative learning?

    I.   Team rewards

    II. Individual accountability

    III. Equal opportunities

    IV. Rules

    V.   Specific tasks

    (A) I, III, and IV only.   (B) I, II, and III only.

    (C) II, IV, and V only.   (D) II, III, and V only.

Mr. Brown feels very uncomfortable when he has to make decisions about the assessment of students. He has had some difficulty with various types of assessment. He decides it is time to talk to Mr. Williams, the principal.

42. Which of the following would be the most effective way for Mr. Brown to document his teaching in an authentic setting and to be aware of student's efforts, progress, and achievements in one or more areas?

    (A) Standardized tests

    (B) Teacher-made tests

    (C) Observation

    (D) Portfolio

43. Which would be the most effective way to evaluate specific objectives and specific content in Mr. Brown's course?

    (A) Self and peer evaluation

    (B) Portfolio

    (C) Teacher-made test

    (D) Observation

44. Mr. Williams asks Mr. Brown what type of test scores are rated against the performance of other students and are reported in terms of percentiles, stanines, and scaled scores. Mr. Brown should give which response?

    (A) Portfolio

    (B) Teacher-made test

    (C) Observation

    (D) Standardized test

45. When the teacher's role is that of facilitator who utilizes students' knowledge and understanding of specific evaluation criteria, what type of assessment is being used?

    (A) Portfolio

    (B) Teacher-made test

    (C) Self and peer assessment

    (D) Observation

Tom Jones was asked to improve the remedial reading curriculum for ninth-grade students. He found that the students were continually tested and evaluated on reading, that the current objectives were unclear, and that the teaching materials were inappropriate. Following a lengthy observation of Mrs. Ratu's teaching strategies, Mr. Jones concluded that she was teaching basic reading skills in the same manner as did the lower elementary teachers.

The teaching materials used a controlled vocabulary and simple sentences. The students were being taught to rely heavily upon pictures and illustrations for the story. Most of the material was fictional in genre. Rote was Mrs. Ratu's preference for learning.

46. Mrs. Ratu's method of teaching remedial reading focused upon

    I. the level at which the students should have learned the basic reading skills.

    II. her own minimal competency in instructional design and evaluation.

    III. her lack of understanding of the learners in her class.

    IV. her desire to make remedial reading easy for the students.

    (A) I only.   (B) I and IV only.

    (C) II and III only.   (D) II only.

Mr. Jones analyzed the test results and found that many of the students in Mrs. Ratu's class had average scores in the areas of art, math, and music. He concluded that with the exception of reading most were normal students and would be successful when their remediation was complete. Mr. Jones made several decisions: (1) the students would be evaluated annually with an achievement test; (2) reading materials of interest to teenagers would be substituted for elementary materials; (3) each student would be encouraged to read about the subject of his or her choice; (4) roundtable discussions would be developed for each "favorite subject."

47. Mr. Jones, having reviewed the students' scores in other classes, knew

    I. that development in one area would lead to development in another area.

II.   how to use a variety of techniques for creating intrinsic and extrinsic motivation.

III. that allowing students to have choices in their learning would create camaraderie.

IV.   that roundtable discussions would lead to questions and the solving of problems.

(A) I only.   (B) II only.

(C) I, II, and III only.   (D) IV only.

An interest inventory was conducted with the students to determine those subjects in which they were interested. New materials were ordered. While students were waiting for the new materials, they were instructed to bring to class materials which dealt with the subject of their choice. If there was a deficiency of materials in the home, the student was to go to the library for magazine articles to bring to class.

After some debate the students decided that the first roundtable discussion should be about gun control, an issue about which many students had very strong feelings. Ray was the first student to speak. "Guns have always been a right in this country. Now people are trying to take them away, just when people need them more than ever to protect themselves." Stan supported Ray's opinion but for different reasons. He added "Yeah, every year around this time my father and I take a hunting trip. If we weren't allowed to have guns, we couldn't go." At this point, Tracy entered the discussion. "It's not hunting guns they want to ban, it's machine guns. Nobody needs a machine gun to go hunting." When Tracy was finished speaking, Brian raised his hand. When he was given permission to speak, he stated "But if you take away those guns, then the only people who would have them would be the gangs and the drug dealers." "And the government," Tracy added. As the discussion drew to a close, Mr. Jones asked each student to continue to read about their favorite subject.

48.   Mr Jones' lively roundtable discussion was a success because

I.   diversity can be used as an advantage by creating an environment that nurtures a sense of community.

II.   the students had been allowed to discuss their feelings about that which interested them.

III. the students had recognized those factors which diminish motivation.

IV. the students had begun to respect their differences.

(A) I only.

(B) II only.

(C) II and IV only.

(D) III only.

49. When Mr. Jones instituted the roundtable discission, he was using a process which would

I. vary his role with the group.

II. serve as one form of assessment.

III. design outcome-oriented learning experiences that fosters understanding.

IV. structure the learning environment to maintain a lifelong pursuit of learning.

(A) I and II only.

(B) II only.

(C) I and III only.

(D) III and IV only.

50. As the facilitator of the roundtable discussion, Mr. Jones was

I. able to manage the classroom environment as he chose.

II. able to model effective communication strategies, thereby shaping the learners into active inquiry.

III. able to determine the socioeconomic level of the home.

IV. able to monitor student input on the subject and encourage all students to participate.

(A) I only.

(B) II and IV only.

(C) I and III only.

(D) I, II, and IV only.

Phyllis Johnson is a junior high school teacher who has chosen human diversity as the topic for a lesson unit. She has decided to approach the topic, initially, by asking students to engage in introspective activities. On the day she introduces the topic to the class, she asks the students to make a list of the things they like about themselves. Then, she asks them to write two paragraphs in class, describing their personal strengths in terms of (a) their classroom behavior, and (b) their behavior (or relationships) with others outside class.

51. By asking her students to make a list of the things they like about themselves, Ms. Johnson is

    (A) giving the class an easy assignment, something that everyone can do.

    (B) making sure that everyone writes something.

    (C) stimulating students' thinking and providing the class with a prewriting activity to help students identify ideas to include in their paragraphs.

    (D) specifically teaching the students the importance of outlining.

52. By asking her students to think about their own characteristics, Ms. Johnson is promoting her students' cognitive development by helping them to

    (A) activate prior knowledge as a basis for understanding new concepts.

    (B) demonstrate their ability to write personal narratives.

    (C) practice their grammar and sentence structure.

    (D) develop positive self-esteem by identifying their assets and skills.

53. In asking her students to think about their behavior both in class and outside class, Ms. Johnson is acknowledging that her students

    (A) are entitled to their own opinions.

    (B) are affected by multiple factors, some which she can control and others she cannot.

    (C) are sure to have some strengths they can write about.

    (D) can consider themselves successful either inside or outside class.

54. When Ms. Johnson asks the students to write about their behavior in class and their behavior (or relationships) outside class, she is taking into consideration aspects of human development by

    (A) stressing that some students are concrete thinkers in adolescence, according to Piaget.

    (B) noting that most adolescents are thinking at the stage of formal operations, according to Piaget.

    (C) observing that students' cognitive functioning is a product of both their innate intellectual characteristics and their environment.

    (D) pinpointing that adolescent students tend to be socially unaware and cognitively insensitive to the thoughts of others.

55. By requiring that students write about themselves, Ms. Johnson is

    (A) fulfilling her responsibilities as an English teacher.

    (B) preparing her class to create autobiographies.

    (C) relying on a language-experience-approach (LEA) for instruction.

    (D) preparing her class to read biographies about great Americans from diverse cultural backgrounds.

56. Ms. Johnson collects the students' papers at the end of class. As she reads the papers, she decides that the best way to give her students positive feedback is to

    (A) not mark errors on the paper so as not to discourage or inhibit their creativity.

    (B) make at least one positive comment about each paragraph.

    (C) begin with one or two positive comments about the paper and then suggest how students could improve their writing.

    (D) give everyone a high grade on the paper for participating in the assignment.

57. After Ms. Johnson finishes reading all the students' papers, she observes that some of the students had difficulty identifying and describing their strengths, whether in class or outside class. She believes that all of her

students have strengths and she wants to help them see the assets they possess. She decides that in the next class, students will

(A) take a learning style assessment to uncover their particular learning strengths and characteristics.

(B) listen to a lecture about how everyone possesses special skills and strengths.

(C) read a chapter from a book about Guilford's Structure of Intellect, as a precursor to a discussion about how intelligence is specialized and diverse.

(D) rewrite their papers, correcting their errors and revising their paragraphs to name at least two additional classroom strengths they possess and at least two additional interpersonal skills they possess.

58. The next lesson in Ms. Johnson's unit on diversity is a library project. In order to determine what kind of project students will undertake, Ms. Johnson leads the class through a brainstorming activity, allowing the students to generate a list of possible topics for the library project. By doing this, Ms. Johnson

(A) can determine the students' interests.

(B) gives everyone a chance to participate in class.

(C) demonstrates an approach for solving problems creatively.

(D) avoids giving everyone in class the same assignment which might not appeal to every student and that might result in some students cheating.

59. Students decide that they would like to read about an American they admire. Asking the members of the class to work together in pairs, Ms. Johnson requests that the students select and find a magazine article about the person they have chosen. In order to form pairs so that students can work together in the library, Ms. Johnson decides that the approach which will allow students to be most productive is to assign students to work together so as to assure that learning preferences and learner characteristics are compatible for the pair of students. In choosing this approach, Ms. Johnson

(A) avoids having students form their own groups so that the students simply end up working with someone she or he likes.

(B) takes advantage of the information she has about students' individual learning styles so as to maximize student learning effectiveness and efficiency.

(C) avoids randomly assigning students to pairs.

(D) risks having incompatible students working together in pairs.

60. Before the class goes to the library, Ms. Johnson asks the students to predict how they will find the information they will need for the assignment. By doing this, Ms. Johnson is

(A) engaging the students in hypothetical thinking and inductive reasoning.

(B) saving time so that the students will be able to go straight to work once they get to the library.

(C) helping her students acquire good self-management skills.

(D) assisting the librarian by covering important information in class.

Mrs. Gomez teaches a seventh grade English class. As she, Mrs. Rodriquez, and Mrs. Smith planned for the semester, they designed a "Writers Workshop." The workshop would be both a reading and writing experience for all the ninth graders. The teachers as well as the students would read the works of published authors, as well as the writing of each other. The goal of the workshop was to better one's own writing and to help one's peers become better writers.

The first element of writing to be introduced would be a metaphor. To introduce the concept of a metaphor, an overhead projector would be needed. The definition and examples of a metaphor would be displayed on the overhead. The display would remain visible to the students as the reading of a poem followed. The students' response was to correctly identify the metaphors in the poem. The class further would practice identifying metaphors through a paper and pencil exercise.

Following the paper and pencil exercise, each student would develop their own metaphors and share them with the class. Initially, the metaphors were to be simple while gradually becoming complex. A filmstrip would be viewed and its metaphors identified and discussed.

To stimulate the students in writing their own poetry containing metaphors, brightly colored transparencies of works of art would be displayed. The students would be instructed to write a poem about the art or an object found in the art transparency.

Students will be evaluated through class participation, completion of the steps of the writers' flowchart, special directions given in class, and a poem containing at least three metaphors.

61. The writing workshop was designed in an effort to

    I.   use a variety of teaching techniques.

    II.   encourage all students to be creative.

    III.   promote a sense of responsibility for one's own learning.

    IV.   develop each student's language and ability.

    (A) I only.   (B) II and III only.

    (C) I and II only.   (D) I, II, III, and IV.

62. Attention to the details of instruction preceding the creative writing of the poem allowed Mrs. Gomez to

    (A) vary her role in the classroom.

    (B) enhance the students' understanding of the society in which they live.

    (C) identify each students' talents.

    (D) engage the students in learning activities which help them to develop the motivation to achieve.

63. The display of brightly colored transparencies of works of art was included to

    I.   stimulate the creativity of the students.

    II.   allow students to have choices in their learning.

   III. create curiosity and a desire to know more about art.

   IV. expose them to art as well as good writing.

   (A) I only.   (B) I and II only.

   (C) III only.   (D) IV only.

64. The multiple evaluation tools used by Mrs. Gomez exhibited her own competency in

   (A) creative thinking.

   (B) communication through the use of various media.

   (C) being a reflective questioner.

   (D) working with other teachers.

65. Class participation and the completion of the poem containing metaphors allowed for

   I. respect for the differences among the students.

   II. individual learning styles.

   III. an informal assessment of the students' performance.

   IV. a variety of opinions to be expressed.

   (A) I only.   (B) II and IV only.

   (C) III only.   (D) I and IV only.

Valley Lake High School is organized as a site-based management campus. The Campus Leadership Council (CLC), after much discussion, has decided to accept the attendance improvement proposal of Lynn Stanford, librarian serving on the CLC for the first time. The librarian's plan is to solicit support of the community businesses to reward students who are not absent during the spring semester. Businesses wishing to join in the effort to combat an increasing absentee problem at Valley Lake may offer an award. All awards sponsored by the community businesses will be distributed by a random drawing from a list of names of students who have not been absent during the spring semester except for official school business. The principal, expressing appreciation of the idea that originated with Miss Stanford, is ready to implement the plan for the campus during the spring semester.

66. Which of the following does the principal give to the CLC as sound educational strategies and therefore his primary reasons for approving the plan?

   I.   The financial advantages for the school

   II. The opportunity to strengthen the working relationship between the school and the community to improve student achievement

   III. The substantial awards some students will receive

   IV. The favorable publicity the plan will create among other school districts

   (A) I only.   (B) III and IV only.

   (C) III only.   (D) I and II only.

Martin Janowsky's Creative Writing class is beginning a study of creative expression and design in advertising. Mr. Janowsky's evaluator has come to visit the class. In his later conference with Mr. Janowsky about the class visit, he discusses the following notations about Mr. Janowsky's lesson:

Mr. Janowsky used slides of various billboards displayed in the community to stimulate class discussion. He also had taped portions of the Clio Awards (an annual international awards program for advertising) and used these to show differences in various cultures' advertising patterns. Among the samples of individual advertisement methods he brought in for student analysis were three-dimensional magazine ads, endorsement ads using well-known people, and product sample packaging.

67. Which of the following comments will the supervisor make in evaluating Mr. Janowsky's teaching of the class?

   (A) Mr. Janowsky's understanding of the importance of using multiple resources is clearly evident.

   (B) Too much clutter used by Mr. Janowsky causes confusion in students' minds about the focus of the lesson.

(C) Mr. Janowsky should let students participate in gathering materials and resources related to the focus of the lesson.

(D) The supervisor discusses the varied materials with Mr. Janowsky since he is interested in advertising techniques himself.

Dominique Woods has two years of teaching experience at a large urban high school. This is her first year teaching at a small, suburban, ethnically-mixed high school.

68. Ms. Woods wants to take advantage of the week of faculty meetings before school opens to become better acquainted with the school grounds, faculty, curriculum, and available materials. How could she best utilize her time?

(A) Tour the school noting the teacher's room, materials room, and other important rooms.

(B) Talk to the principal about what is expected of her.

(C) Talk with a willing English teacher, who has spent several years at the school, about community characteristics and available materials as they apply to the curriculum.

(D) Obtain a copy of the curriculum to take to the materials room where it can be determined what materials are available for classroom use.

69. Ms. Woods is reviewing her class lists and curriculum guide wondering what to plan for the first day of school. Taking into account her first-year status at the school, Ms. Woods would most likely

(A) present the class with a year long outline of the novels they will be reading and when they will be reading them.

(B) have the class fill out a questionnaire to ascertain what types of literature they like best.

(C) have each student introduce himself or herself to the class and suggest a favorite book.

(D) give pairs of students an interview to conduct with one another, asking about their favorite books and their favorite English class activities.

Three months have passed and Ms. Woods is preparing to submit grades and conference request forms. Although students have done well in reading, writing grades seem to be low.

70. Ms. Woods has come to the conclusion that her students are having trouble assessing their own writing strengths and weaknesses. Which of the following would be appropriate ways of monitoring and improving the student's writing?

    I.   Have students submit an original work on the topic of their choice every day to be graded.

    II. Have students identify, with the help of the teacher, one area of writing in which they feel they need improvement, then focus on this area until their goal has been reached and a new area has been identified.

    III. All draft and final copies will be kept in a portfolio from which the student will pick a piece to discuss with the teacher at a teacher-student conference.

    IV. Once a week the teacher will read a quality composition written by a class member.

    (A) II and III only.   (B) I and III only.

    (C) I, III, and IV only.   (D) II, III, and IV only.

71. It is time for parent-teacher conferences. Ms. Woods has prepared a discussion checklist so that she is certain to cover all essential topics during the conference. Which of the following will she need to remember?

    (A) First address the problems then address the positive aspects with whatever time is remaining.

    (B) Begin with a positive note about the student then ease into concerns about the negative aspects.

    (C) Present as many technical facts as possible so the parents sense an aire of confidence and experience in her ability as a teacher.

(D) Present the solutions that she, the teacher, feels are most advantageous and continue to support this issue until the parents have agreed to your recommendations.

72. Ms. Woods attended a seminar on improving the classroom environment. She is looking for more interaction and participation in her classroom. The seminar suggested changing one thing at a time to see what works best. Which of the following would make the fastest change in class participation?

(A) Assigning seats row by row, alternating boys and girls.

(B) Having the industrial arts teacher build new bookshelves for the classroom.

(C) Presenting a new policy where each person must bring one debatable question to class each day.

(D) Arrange the desks into a circle so everyone can see one another.

73. The seminar stressed a multicultural classroom. Every student should be recognized as having important values and ideas. What could Ms. Woods include in her syllabus that would both fit her curriculum and celebrate the cultural diversity in her classroom?

(A) She could have students choose an author to read from their cultural background, or another cultural background that interests them. Then she could have each student present an informal oral report on the cultural aspects found in the book.

(B) Each month she could introduce a new author, focusing on non-American authors.

(C) The students can find their ancestral country on the classroom map during a discussion of a book in which a character takes a journey.

(D) A day will be declared "Cultural Diversity Day" and the teacher will display novels by authors of varied ethnic backgrounds.

74. Ms. Woods uses a seminar suggestion, cooperative grouping, to complete a class project. This project should include chances for the students to do which of the following:

I. Demonstrate leadership ability.

II. Organize and distribute appropriate work for all members of the group.

III. Self-evaluate the role each has played in the learning activity.

IV. Be grouped in a way that allows for a high and low learner to be in each group.

(A) III and IV only.　　　　　(B) II only.

(C) I, II, III, and IV.　　　　　(D) I, II, and III only.

The cooperative learning exercise is based around an historical novel of the group's choice. They will need to present information to the class about the history that took place in the time around the setting of the novel. Ms. Woods has asked a social studies teacher to demonstrate how the students can prepare a timeline of historical facts simply by reading a novel. In addition, the librarian spoke to the class about the many uses the library serves while students are working on a project such as this.

75. What was Ms. Woods main objective for organizing these speakers?

(A) To give herself a free period to prepare other lessons

(B) To acquaint the students with other faculty members whom they may not have met

(C) The students will have to do less work on their own in preparing their projects.

(D) The students will know what material is at their disposal and how they can gain access to it.

76. While working in their groups, Ms. Woods notices a problem continually surfacing. Ms. Woods would best handle this situation by

(A) listening to the class as they suggest what they feel the problem is and ways to solve it while she organizes the discussion.

(B) speaking to the group leaders and telling them to overlook the problem and continue the activity.

(C) letting the groups work out the problem at their own pace and in their own way.

(D) stopping the group work, stating that it is not working out as planned and the class will not be finishing the project.

Mr. Shah teaches middle-school English. His job in the school is both teacher and supervisor.

77. Mr. Shah's goal for the marking period is to increase the students' intrinsic motivation to learn and succeed. To accomplish this he should

(A) reward every good grade with a tangible reward.

(B) permit students to choose from a teacher generated list of interesting topics, about which they want to read and learn.

(C) relate lessons to those topics which he, as a teacher, feels interested in teaching.

(D) provide students with a list of questions on varying topics to answer for each week.

78. After reading a novel in which a character, having hit hard times, makes a decision to commit a crime, Mr. Shah poses this question for homework: "What would you have the character do such that the story ends in a positive manner?" What was Mr. Shah's purpose for doing this?

(A) He wanted to develop moral reasoning and problem solving skills.

(B) He wanted to give the students a creative idea about which to write.

(C) He wanted to prompt the students to evaluate themselves and their reading skills.

(D) He wanted to propose a more suitable ending of the story so as not to set a bad example for future citizens.

79. Mr. Shah has given an assignment where four students will work together to present a reflection on an author and his/her works. Mr. Shah, through a survey, has realized that many students have not worked in such a group before, so he reviews the rules of participation. Which of the following are vital rules to achieve the desired outcome?

I. Take turns talking quietly.

II. Listen to each other's ideas.

III. Help each other when asked.

IV. Base the outcome on how each individual participated.

(A) II and III only.　　　　(B) I and III only.

(C) I, III, and IV only.　　(D) I, II and III only.

80. In order to prepare students for a national writing test, Mr. Shah has created a folder for each student. The folder includes rough drafts, final copies, and a personal check list of criteria for grading of the test samples. Why has Mr. Shah included one check list for every student?

(A) So the students may conduct an informal assessment of their own work.

(B) In case the students forgot the requirements and needed a quick reference to use during grading.

(C) So the teacher will have a means of evaluating their writing samples.

(D) So that the student is aware of the criteria on which the samples are being graded.

Section 2: Written Assignment

DIRECTIONS: Plan and write an essay on the topic given below. DO NOT WRITE ON ANY TOPIC OTHER THAN THE ONE SPECIFIED. AN ESSAY ON ANY OTHER TOPIC IS UNACCEPTABLE.

Essay Topic:

What specific characteristics do you think a person must possess in order to be an effective teacher? Fully explain each characteristic and show how the absence of each will reduce effectiveness in the classroom.

LAST
PRACTICE TEST 2

ANSWER KEY

1.	(B)	21.	(C)	41.	(D)	61.	(C)
2.	(C)	22.	(A)	42.	(B)	62.	(B)
3.	(B)	23.	(A)	43.	(D)	63.	(D)
4.	(B)	24.	(C)	44.	(A)	64.	(A)
5.	(D)	25.	(D)	45.	(A)	65.	(B)
6.	(D)	26.	(B)	46.	(D)	66.	(D)
7.	(A)	27.	(C)	47.	(C)	67.	(D)
8.	(B)	28.	(B)	48.	(C)	68.	(C)
9.	(A)	29.	(A)	49.	(D)	69.	(A)
10.	(A)	30.	(C)	50.	(D)	70.	(A)
11.	(A)	31.	(B)	51.	(B)	71.	(B)
12.	(D)	32.	(C)	52.	(A)	72.	(D)
13.	(D)	33.	(B)	53.	(D)	73.	(D)
14.	(C)	34.	(B)	54.	(C)	74.	(B)
15.	(B)	35.	(B)	55.	(C)	75.	(B)
16.	(C)	36.	(A)	56.	(B)	76.	(D)
17.	(B)	37.	(A)	57.	(D)	77.	(D)
18.	(C)	38.	(D)	58.	(D)	78.	(B)
19.	(D)	39.	(A)	59.	(B)	79.	(D)
20.	(C)	40.	(D)	60.	(C)	80.	(C)

ATS-W SECONDARY PRACTICE TEST 2

ANSWER KEY

1.	(A)	21.	(C)	41.	(B)	61.	(D)
2.	(B)	22.	(A)	42.	(D)	62.	(D)
3.	(C)	23.	(C)	43.	(C)	63.	(B)
4.	(A)	24.	(B)	44.	(D)	64.	(B)
5.	(B)	25.	(D)	45.	(C)	65.	(A)
6.	(D)	26.	(C)	46.	(C)	66.	(D)
7.	(B)	27.	(C)	47.	(C)	67.	(A)
8.	(B)	28.	(A)	48.	(A)	68.	(C)
9.	(A)	29.	(C)	49.	(C)	69.	(D)
10.	(D)	30.	(C)	50.	(B)	70.	(D)
11.	(B)	31.	(A)	51.	(C)	71.	(B)
12.	(C)	32.	(C)	52.	(A)	72.	(D)
13.	(D)	33.	(D)	53.	(B)	73.	(A)
14.	(A)	34.	(C)	54.	(C)	74.	(C)
15.	(B)	35.	(C)	55.	(C)	75.	(D)
16.	(A)	36.	(C)	56.	(C)	76.	(A)
17.	(D)	37.	(A)	57.	(A)	77.	(B)
18.	(C)	38.	(C)	58.	(C)	78.	(A)
19.	(C)	39.	(D)	59.	(B)	79.	(D)
20.	(C)	40.	(C)	60.	(A)	80.	(A)

LAST PRACTICE TEST 2

DETAILED EXPLANATIONS
OF ANSWERS

1.   **(B)** The choices illustrate various ways to express 66%; e.g., 0.66, 66/100, 2/3. Thus choices (C) and (D) are correct. Choice (A) is correct, since percent is based on 100. You multiply the whole numbers and divide by 100 to locate the decimal point in the answer. The answer actually is not equal to 20, unless rounded off. Choice (B) is the wrong expression for 66%. Thus, the best answer is (B). Choice (B) is incorrect because 66% cannot be expressed as 66.0. Also, if you multiply 66 by 30, you obtain a very large number, which makes no sense, since 66% is a fraction of 30. Thus a reasonable answer must be less than 30.

2.   **(C)** You multiply the cost per lb. times the number of lbs. purchased for each of the items: potatoes and tomatoes. Add these products and subtract from the $4.83. This gives the amount of money spent on green beans. Divide by 2, since 2 lbs. were purchased. Thus, all the data listed in choice (C) is what you need:

$$0.49 \times 2 \quad = \quad 0.98 \text{ potatoes}$$
$$0.79 \times 3 \quad = \quad \underline{2.37} \text{ tomatoes}$$
$$3.35$$
$$\$4.83 - 3.35 \quad = \quad \$1.48$$
$$\$1.48 \div 2 \quad = \quad \$0.74/\text{lb. for green beens}$$

3.   **(B)** You must substitute the appropriate values of X and Y into the expression and calculate the value of each term before subtracting the Y term from the X term.
$2X^2$ is $2(6)^2$ or $2(36)$ or 72. $9/Y$ is 9/3 or 3. Thus $72 - 3 = 69$.
Choice (B) is correct. The other choices result from incorrect sequences of performing the term evaluations.

4.   **(B)** First, you should note that you want area, not perimeter. Next, you can imagine the figure divided into a rectangle 10 cm by 5 cm or 50 square centimeters of area. The triangle can be computed in several ways. The easier way is to note that the shaded triangle is one half of the square, which is 5 cm by 5 cm or 25 square centimeters. Thus, the shaded triangle is 12.5 square centimeters. The total shaded area is 50 plus 12.5, or 62.5 square centimeters. Thus, choice (B) is correct. Choice (C) would be discarded immediately, since it is not in square units of area. It is in fact the perimeter of the total rectangle (15 + 15 + 5 + 5 or 40 cm). Choice (A) is the area of the total rectangle (15cm by 5cm or 75 square cm). Choice (D) is not close to the shaded area, but rather, closer to the perimeter of the shaded area. Choice (B) is the correct area for the shaded part of the figure, 62.5 square centimeters.

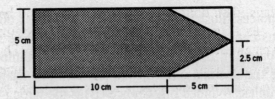

5.   **(D)** You should note that the student is failing to carry in both the ones and tens places. Eg., 56 + 97

    6 + 7 = 13   Record the 3 ones and carry the one ten.

    5 + 9 = 14   plus the one ten is 15, thus, 153, not 1413.

Choice (A) is the standard answer. It is eliminated, since there is no error pattern. Choice (C) exhibits switching from addition to subtraction (9 − 8 = 1) and (8 − 3 = 5). Also, the child subtracts the top number from the bottom one on the first step. In choice (B) the child subtracts 8 from 9, and also 3 from 8, and then adds to the 8 in the tens place. Only choice (D) illustrates the pattern of recording the sum and not carrying. The correct answer is (D).

6.   **(D)** You should first count the number of spaces on the dial. There are 10 spaces. Five spaces equals 90 units. 90 divided by 5 is 18 units. Each space is worth 18 units. The needle points to, most likely, about halfway between the marks numbered 6 and 7. Thus, one half of 18, plus 6 times 18, is 117. Choice (D) is the correct reading.

7.   **(A)** You know that ten thousand contains 4 zeros, or 10^4 in place value. One million contains 10^6, or six zeros. Thus 10^6 divided by 10^4 is 10^2 or 100. You may divide out 10,000 into one million, but that is the laborious way to solve this. Choice (A) is correct.

$$10,000\overline{)1,000,000}^{\,100} \qquad \text{or} \qquad 1\overline{)100}^{\,100}$$

$$10^4 \qquad 10^6$$

$$\frac{1,000,000}{10,000} = \frac{10^6}{10^4}$$

$$10^{6-4} = 10^2$$

In dividing exponents, you subtract them. Thus 10^4 becomes 10^{-4} and is subtracted from 10^6.

8. **(B)** You are challenged to analyze which data you would need to calculate the cost of feeding 2 cats for 7 days. If you calculate the cost for one cat for 7 days, then double the answer, you would have an approximate cost for 2 cats. Total cost is cost of a can of food, times the number of cans of food eaten each day by one cat, times 7 days. Thus choice (A) is incorrect. You do not need to know volume of food, unless you wish to feed the cats according to their weight. Choices (C), and (D) are incorrect because you either have unneeded information (C) IV, or incorrect data for problem solving [(D) IV]. Thus choice (B) is correct.

9. **(A)** You read coordinates of a point in pairs. The X position or horizontal direction is read first. It is always the first number in the pair of numbers representing the point plotted. The Y position is read second. This is the vertical direction, either up or down on the coordinate plane. The Y position is always the second number in the pair of numbers representing any point in the plane.

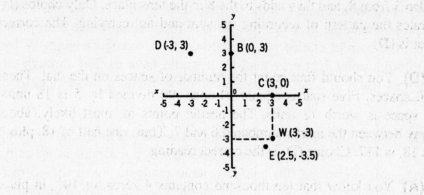

Thus choice (A) is correct. The X position is 3 units to the right along the x-axis. *The* Y position is -3 units downwards along the y-axis. Where the two lines intersect from +3 and –3 is where the point is located (3, –3). Choices (B), (C), and (D) are plotted below for you to compare their locations in the plane with the correct answer, (A).

10. **(A)** You can construct rectangles in numerous ways to cover the total area. One approach is illustrated below for you. You have three rectangles and one square covering the shaded area. Find the areas of each figure and add the areas for the total area. Rectangles 1 and 2 are each 5 ft by 4 ft², yielding 20 ft² plus 20^2 ft, or 40 ft². Rectangle 3 is 7 ft by 4 ft, giving 28 ft². The square is 2 ft by 2 ft, or 4 square feet. The sum is 40 plus 28 plus 4, or 72 square feet. Choice (B) is the area of a rectangle: 14 ft by 8 ft, or 112 square feet. This area is too large, since it ignores the stepwise figure removed, or not shaded, in the original problem. Choice (C) has no numerical connection to the area dimensions. Choice (D) is the area of rectangle 3, plus one half of either rectangle 1 or 2 (28 ft² plus 10 ft²). Thus, choice (A) is the correct answer, 72 ft².

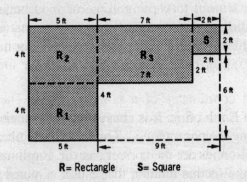

R= Rectangle   S= Square

11. **(A)** You should note that the particle flow divides at 2 points, T and M. At these points the flow has two paths to reach either point W or point Q. Thus, the correct choice is (A). Particle flow can reach point W by going through point U, rather than V. It would have to flow through all other points listed in order to make a complete circuit or total clockwise path.

12. **(D)** You would first have to recognize that HCl is hydrochloric acid. Then you would have to know that litmus paper turns pink in an acid. Following this reasoning, the reader is now ready to make the correct choice. (A) is false; there should be a reaction. The paper should turn pink. (A) is not the correct choice. Since the litmus paper does not disintegrate but instead turns pink, (B) is not the best answer. Litmus paper turns blue in a base. Since HCl is an acid, the paper turns pink, not blue. (C) is an

incorrect answer. The litmus paper does turn pink with an acid; (D) is the correct answer.

13. **(D)** Water has properties of a base; it also has properties of an acid, and is classified as a compound. For these reasons (A), (B), and (C) alone may not be selected. Since (A), (B), and (C) are all correct, (D) allows you to choose all three answers.

14. **(C)** Despite the fact that summer is the season when Earth is warmest, Earth is not closest to the Sun. Earth is warm because of the way that the Sun's rays are concentrated on Earth. (A) is not the correct answer. Earth moves in an elliptical orbit about the Sun. It moves closest to the Sun in the winter (for New York residents). Although it is approaching its closest position, Earth is not closest in the fall. (B) should not be chosen. Even though the winter season (C) is the coldest, Earth is closest to the Sun during this time. The Sun's rays are not concentrated directly on the part of Earth that is experiencing winter; winter is, therefore, colder. (C) is the correct answer. During the spring (D), Earth is beginning to move away from the position in the winter when it was closest to the Sun. It is not, however, closest to the Sun during the spring season. (D) is not the right choice. Earth is not closest to the Sun in either the spring or the summer.

15. **(B)** The tilt of Earth on its axis causes the seasons because it allows the rays of the Sun to be concentrated on one area. The tilt causes seasons, not day and night, so (A) is not the correct answer. Earth rotates on its axis once every 24 hours. It is this rotation that causes day and night, so (B) is the correct answer. The revolution of Earth about the Sun results in our calendar year—not day and night; (C) is an incorrect answer. Earth rotates on its axis; the Sun does not move about Earth. Earth revolves around the Sun. (D) is not the right choice.

16. **(C)** Sunshine (A) is rich in Vitamin D. Since scurvy is caused by insufficient Vitamin C, it could not result from inadequate sunshine alone. (A) is not the correct answer. Calcium (B) is necessary for bones and teeth. Its absence does not cause scurvy. Since scurvy does result from insufficient Vitamin C, answer (C) is correct. Insufficient Vitamin B may cause pellagra, but not scurvy. (D) is not the right choice.

17. **(B)** Both plants and animals are made of cells; (A) is not the correct answer. Plant cells do usually have a nonliving cell wall; (B) is true. The Euglena (C) is a single-celled organism that swims freely like a typical

animal; it can, however, manufacture food with its green chlorophyll like a plant. This is one instance of a "non-plant" with chlorophyll. (C) is incorrect. Both plant and animal cells contain DNA. (D) is, therefore, not the right choice.

18. **(C)** Some elements are found in nature, but others may be made by scientists. (A) is not the correct answer. Elements may or may not be made by scientists; the nonelements are made by scientists. (B) should not be chosen. (C) is the correct answer; some elements are found in nature; others may be made by scientists. There are 214 presently-known elements—hence 214 presently-known atoms; (D) is incorrect.

19. **(D)** The correct answer for the classification scheme is (D). All the other choices are incorrect because the order of items has been switched. If you are not familiar with the entire classification order, chances are you will know that the kingdom (animalia, plantia) comes first, and that the scientific name of a living thing comes from genus and species. The first item (kingdom) and the last two items (genus, species) are two good clues. Only (D) meets these qualifications. (A), (B), and (C) all give the wrong order and should not be selected.

20. **(C)** Neither coal, oil, nor gas are renewable. These fuels would take years to form even if all of the needed conditions and elements are present. (A) is not the correct answer. The items in (B) are nonrenewable; (B) should not be chosen. Soil, vegetation, and animals can be renewed in a relatively short period of time. (C) is the best answer. Although the other two items in item (D) are renewable, coal (a fossil fuel) is not; (D) is not the correct choice.

21. **(C)** The question asks you to place the works by American authors in chronological order. Choice (D), about WWI, was printed in 1926. Choice (B) is a late nineteenth century work. Choice (A) was published shortly before the Civil War (1852). The correct choice (C) was published during the transcendental era, 1836.

22. **(A)** The correct response (A), occurred in 1896, when the Supreme Court gave constitutional backing to segregation, ruling that separate but equal facilities on a Louisiana railroad coach did not deprive the Negro of equal protection under the Fourteenth Amendment. This ruling was overturned in 1954, in *Brown v. Board of Education of Topeka*, which held that segregation in the elementary schools of Topeka violated the Fourteenth Amendment.

23. **(A)** Columbus's voyages began in the fifteenth century. The Protestant Reformation occurred in the sixteenth century. The Puritans came to America in the seventeenth century. The Magna Carta was signed in 1215. Therefore, the best choice is (A).

24. **(C)** Choice (A), as conceived by Henry Clay, referred to the nationalist policy of uniting the three economic sections of the United States in the time following the War of 1812. Choice (B) is an economic theory whose principal doctrine was the belief that the wealth of nations was based on the possession of gold. Choice (D) is tied to tradition and emotion. Choice (C) is the best possible answer.

25. **(D)** Contrary to choice (A), the Bill of Rights is about the expansion of individual rights, such as freedom of speech and religion. Choice (B) is not the major topic of the first ten Amendments. Since the Bill of Rights clearly spelled out a limited role for government, item (C) is wrong. Thus, the correct response is (D).

26. **(B)** Choice (A) was a result of people moving west and quickly setting up communities. Choice (C) refers to the process of becoming like the majority. Item (D) is a monopolistic practice of corporations in the later nineteenth century. The correct answer is choice (B), the idea proposed by the historian, Frederick Jackson Turner, who wrote *The Frontier in American History*.

27. **(C)** Choices (A), (B) and (D) all played a role in the early settlements of the English colonies in America. The correct response is item (C), because Mormonism was founded at Fayette, New York, in 1830, by Joseph Smith. *The Book of Mormon* was published in 1830 and it described the establishment of an American colony from the Tower of Babel.

28. **(B)** The Morrill Act granted each Union state 30,000 acres for each Senator and Representative in Congress in order to endow an agricultural college. This led to the founding of 69 land grant colleges, making (B) the correct response.

29. **(A)** Until 1921 no general limitation of immigration was attempted by Congress. In that year (and again in 1924 and 1929) Congress enacted the first general restrictive legislation in its history. The act of 1921 set the quotas at three percent of the 1910 census, and thereby reduced the quotas from eastern and southern Europe. Thus, item (A) is correct.

30. **(C)** Cowboys (A) were relative latecomers to the southwest. The French explored and settled in the northern part of the continent. Gold seekers came in the mid-nineteenth century. Farmers from New England were not early settlers in the southwest. The correct answer is (C), Spaniards and Mexicans.

31. **(B)** Choices (A), (C), and (D) are incorrect. The right choice is (B), because in a private enterprise economy individuals have significant freedom to own and operate productive enterprises, to produce economic goods, and to develop specialized institutions like banks and insurance companies to meet their needs. Thus, price changes generally tend to indicate what is produced and consumed.

32. **(C)** The letter K represents Cuba. Letter D stands for Java. Letter M stands for Sri Lanka. The correct answer is (C) because letter I represents the Philippine Islands.

33. **(B)** On August 23, 1939, Germany and the Soviet Union signed a nonaggression pact, which meant that the two nations could partition Eastern Europe, each without fear of becoming involved in a second war front with the other. The leaders of the countries at this time were Hitler and Stalin, which makes (B) the correct answer. In mid-1941, Germany invaded Russia, in violation of their treaty.

34. **(B)** A list of grievances is contained in the Declaration of Independence. Choices (C) and (D) are incorrect because the Bill of Rights does not talk about voting rights or slaves. Rather than limiting the rights of citizens, the Bill of Rights extends rights. The correct answer is (B), since the document clearly states that Congress may not make laws abridging citizens' rights and liberties.

35. **(B)** Choices (A), (C), and (D) are wrong. Item (B) is correct, since the people rule by electing their representatives and the powers of the government are divided on national, state, and local levels.

36. **(A)** Choices (B), (C), and (D) are incorrect. The best response is (A), which represents the combined willingness of individuals or firms to supply specific resources (such as labor) or products (such as wheat or cars) at specific prices.

37. **(A)** The correct answer is (A). A single or sole proprietorship is one that is owned and managed by one person. The partnership is a business that is owned by two or more individuals. The corporation (or joint stock

company as it is sometimes called) is owned by stockholders, each owning one or more shares of stock. Choices (B) and (C) are partially correct. Choice (D) is totally wrong.

38. **(D)** Choice (A) is wrong because about 30% of households had under $15,000. Choices (B) and (C) are incorrect, since slightly more than 15% fell into this category. The correct choice is item (D). This question asks the respondent to read the graph carefully.

39. **(A)** Graph reading and interpretation is the primary focus of this question. Choice (B) is obviously wrong, since the youngest have the least income. Items (C) and (D) are incorrect.

40. **(D)** Since choices (A), (B), and (C) are incorrect, the right answer is (D). (A) is incorrect because the statement is not applicable to all household sizes, such as one-person, for example. (B) may seem correct, but the amount of discretionary income fluctuates up and down according to household size. (C) is completely false. Two-person households have the most discretionary income: 36.2%. One-person households have less discretionary income than two-, three-, and four-person households.

41. **(D)** This question tests your ability to determine the central focus in a staged dramatic production and to explain why there is such a focus. The central attraction in this picture is the man at the center of the stairs (D). Almost all eyes are turned to him, as well as the bodies of the other characters. The men in the right foreground (A) have their backs to the audience and are directing their attention to the central character. Since this character is in a full front position, he will draw more attention than those in profile or full back, which are weaker positions. Choice (D) is correct.

42. **(B)** Figure 1 is an Elizabethan nobleman, appropriate for a play set in the 1600s. Figure 2 is a medieval old man and would be appropriate for a medieval cycle play. This is the style appropriate during the medieval period. Figure 3 is a Royalist trooper. Figure 4 is a Chinese Mandarin. Choice (B) is the correct answer.

43. **(D)** The above passage, which opens Charles Dickens's *A Tale of Two Cities*, contains numerous and vast comparisons. By making these comparisons and descriptions of the time period ("we had everything before us, we had nothing before us, we were all going direct to Heaven, we were all going direct the other way," etc.), Dickens is illustrating how

during this period (just before the French Revolution) anything was possible: "wisdom," "foolishness," "Light," or "Darkness." This "anything is possible" tone also foreshadows the French Revolution, which the Aristocracy never expected. Dickens will, later in the novel, describe extreme political upheaval, but does not here, so (B) is wrong. (A) is wrong because "placid" implies settled and calm; if "anything is possible," then the times are the exact opposite. There is no mention of a public event or the attitudes of people at war, so (C) is also incorrect.

44. **(A)** The Bible tells of how Christ was able to feed hundreds of hungry people with only seven loaves of bread and fish until all were satiated. By jokingly suggesting that the two governments contain the positions "lords of the State preserves of loaves and fishes," Dickens mocks their self-assuredness and unflinching certainty that the "preserves" will never be depleted and that "things in general [are] settled for ever." The phrase "clearer than crystal" helps, through its sarcasm, to give this attack more sting. All of the other choices are not alluded to or discussed in the passage, and are thus incorrect.

45. **(A)** The "superlative degree" refers to the utmost degree of something being compared (the *hottest* day, the *fastest* runner, the *most beautiful* object, etc.). The phrase indicates that some of the time periods "noisiest authorities" (a sarcastic euphemism for members of the governments) wanted time to be remembered as the "most" or "best" of something—regardless of whether it was "the most evil" or "the most productive." All that mattered to these "authorities" was to be at the top of every comparison, regardless of its implications. Thus, (A) is correct. The people are not mentioned here, so (B) and (C) are both incorrect, as is (D).

46. **(D)** The Egyptian Temple of Horus, c. 212 B.C., pictured in the example displays elements typical of the monumental architecture which developed during Egypt's Old Kingdom period (c. 2600-2100 B.C.) and continued until Egypt became a province of the Roman Empire (c. 31 B.C.). This architecture achieved an effect of imposing grandeur and durability through the use of simple, solid geometric forms, constructed on an overwhelming scale and laid out with exacting symmetry. The Temple of Horus avoids any emphasis on horizontal lines, and relies instead on the sloping outer walls to visually "pull" the massive building to the ground and make it seem immovable and eternal. Additionally, although the temple carries minor ornamental detail, displays huge reliefs of figures, and is set within a large open courtyard, all of these elements are secondary to the massive character of the building itself.

47. **(C)** Gianlorenzo Bernini's *David* of 1623 is a perfect example of the Baroque sculptor's wish to express movement and action and to capture a fleeting moment of time. Here, the figure's twisting posture and intense facial expression create a dynamic, not a static, character, as David begins the violent twisting motion with which he will hurl the stone from his sling. His gaze is directed outward at an unseen adversary, implying inter-action with another character and denying any purely ornamental concep-tion behind this work. The figure's meager garments, far from identifying him as a warrior, emphasize both his physical vulnerability and his ideal-ized, heroic beauty.

48. **(C)** This question asks you to demonstrate knowledge and awareness of a widely used symbol, the ellipsis. Within a sentence, three periods with a space after each period indicate that material has been purposefully omitted while quoting from the original. Thus, choice (C) is the correct answer.

49. **(D)** In *The Lamentation Over St. Sebastian* of 1630, the French Ba-roque painter Georges de la Tour used the candle held by the kneeling woman as the single light source for his picture. De la Tour specialized in this type of intimate night scene, in which the light gently but dramatically illuminates the human figures. The simplified, almost abstract forms of the figures bathed in this quiet light create a sense of Classical calm which, in this case, heightens the poignancy of the episode. All of the figures, how-ever, occupy a shallow space toward the front of the picture plane, almost "falling" into the viewer's space. Therefore, de la Tour's light, though it models and defines the forms in space, does not create a convincing reces-sion into depth.

50. **(D)** This marble portrait bust of the first century B.C. is typical of a style which flourished during the late Roman Republic, and which aimed for a literal, super-realistic depiction of a certain type of individual. The sculptor here avoided any tendency to idealize his subject, and pursued instead an expressive, realistic depiction, in which each particular feature of his subject's face and expression was painstakingly recorded. The choice of hard, chiselled marble, rather than modelled clay or incised relief, helped to accentuate the craggy details of his subject's face. The sitter here repre-sents not the jaded, effete aristocracy of the later Roman Empire, but rather the simple, unsophisticated citizen-farmer of the earlier Republic, whose labor and determination helped to build the Roman state.

51. **(B)** This passage from Melville's *Moby Dick* contains an allusion in the phrase, "like so many Alexanders." Melville is illustrating the strength and power of whalers ("naked Nantucketers") by alluding and comparing them to Alexander the Great, the famous conqueror who died in 323 B.C.

52. **(A)** This passage, which opens James Joyce's *A Portrait of the Artist as a Young Man* is written in "baby talk" ("moocow," "nicens," "baby tukoo") to convey to readers the age, speech, and mental set of the narrator.

53. **(D)** Nineteenth century novels of manners employed such themes as the importance (or unimportance) of "good breeding," the elation (and suffocation) caused by society, and the interaction of individuals within the confines of a closed country community (to name just a few). This passage, taken from Jane Austen's *Emma*, mentions "opinions" of other characters, the importance of "beauty" and "accomplishment" (note how Emma sees them as almost saving graces for Mrs. Elton), and the "improvement" of a "country neighborhood."

54. **(C)** In the example, *Sunday Afternoon on the Island of La Grand Jatte*, 1884-86, the French Post-Impressionist painter Georges Seurat developed a systematic, intellectual art in which color values were carefully calculated, composition was rigidly structured, and an overall effect of static, well-ordered design replaced the vibrant spontaneity of the earlier Impressionists' work. In *La Grand Jatte* the motionless vertical forms of the human figures are carefully positioned and repeated, and are deftly coordinated with both the diagonal shadows on the ground and with the distant horizon line. The approach overall is detached and scientific, and avoids both spontaneous emotional impulse and any poetic, personal content.

55. **(C)** The arch pictured in the example is characteristic of much later Roman imperial architecture, in which elaborate combinations of Classical architectural elements were employed in a purely non-structural manner. Although the four columns at the front of the arch appear to lend support to the heavy upper story, they are in fact merely applied to the facade of the arch and serve no functional purpose. They do, however, create a strong vertical thrust which leads the viewer's eye to the sculpted figures above, while simultaneously setting off and accenting the three small arches which serve as the monument's basic structural units.

56. **(B)** You can tell that this passage is taken from the stage directions

of a play because of the visual and auditory descriptions you are given. Also, you are told that "lights come up" and a "rocket bursts, off," here meaning "offstage." (B) is the correct answer.

57. **(D)** The architect of the building illustrated was intent on avoiding traditional building forms in the search for a new, expressive use of space. The design pictured, therefore, carefully avoids all reminders of the symmetrical, balanced floor plans of Classical and Renaissance architecture. It also dispenses with a conventional structural framework and with the geometric forms and angles of traditional buildings. Instead, it exploits fully the potential of a new material—in this case, poured concrete—to create dynamic, curving forms whose arcs and spirals echo both the shape of growing organisms and the motion of wind and water.

58. **(D)** The theme of *carpe diem*, Latin for "seize the day," urges people to enjoy their present pleasures and lives, because the future is so uncertain. Passage (D), taken from Robert Herrick's, "To the Virgins to Make Much of Time," urges its readers to act now ("Gather ye rosebuds while ye may") because time will never stop and all things must come to an end ("... Tomorrow will be dying").

59. **(B)** Onomatopoeia refers to the formation of words imitating the sound of the object or action expressed, such as "Buzz," "clang," "boom," and "meow." Passage (B) contains two examples of onomatopoeia: "Bow-wow," to imitate the barking of a dog, and "Cock-a-doodle-doo" to imitate the sound of the rooster.

60. **(C)** Alliteration refers to the repetition of consonant sounds at the beginning of successive (or nearly successive) words in a line (or lines) of poetry. Passage (C) contains the line, "A spotted shaft is seen," which alliterates the "s" sound for poetic effect. Thus, choice (C) is correct.

61. **(C)** Choice (C) is correct because this is the definition of illiterate and functional illiterate stated in paragraph two. Choice (A) cannot be correct because the passage clearly distinguishes a difference between illiterates and functional illiterates. Choice (B) is not correct because the definition stated is not related to participation in a program. The relative number of illiterates and functional illiterates is not discussed, so choice (D) is incorrect.

62. **(B)** Choice (B) is correct because the passage begins by stating that many politicians' wives have expressed interest in literacy. Choice (A) is incorrect because the author of the passage does not suggest that only

women are interested. Choice (C) is incorrect because the passage does not discuss the number of male or female illiterates. Choice (D) is incorrect because there is no discussion in the passage of politicians' wives giving speeches.

63. **(D)** This passage has several purposes. First, the author presents some complaints concerning the way literacy issues are presented in the media. The author also discusses the attention given literacy issues by politicians' wives. Third, the author discusses many aspects of successful literacy programs. Therefore, choice (D), which includes all of these purposes, is correct.

64. **(A)** This question must be answered using the process of elimination. You are asked to select a statement that names a possible program component which is not characteristic of successful literacy programs. Choice (A) is correct because choices (B), (C), and (D) are specifically mentioned in the passage.

65. **(B)** Choice (B) is correct because the author specifically states that politicians should support increased funding for literacy programs. Choices (A) and (C) are incorrect because the author states that funding should be increased. There is no discussion of funding for different programs so choice (D) is incorrect.

66. **(D)** Choice (D) is correct because the passage specifically mentions the California coast, the Alaskan coast, and the U. S. Gulf Coast as sites of oil spills.

67. **(D)** Choice (D) is correct because workers were trying to keep the oil in the water and away from the beach. Choice (A) is incorrect because sightseers are not discussed in the passage. The problem of oil-soaked animals is not mentioned in the passage so choice (B) is incorrect. Choice (C) is incorrect because the cleanup crews wanted to remove the oil, not let it soak into the sand.

68. **(C)** Choice (C) is correct. This question must be answered using the process of elimination. Cleanup trust funds, increased federal spending, using the National Guard, and creating a department of oceans are all discussed in the passage. Therefore, choices (A), (B), and (D) are incorrect. Only choice (C) names a solution not mentioned in the passage.

69. **(A)** Choice (A) is correct. The passage describes the Alaskan spill as "massive." The spill off the coast of California and the spill off the U.S.

Gulf Coast are described as "smaller." Therefore, choices (B) and (D) are incorrect. Spills in the North Sea are not discussed in the passage, so choice (C) is incorrect.

70. **(A)** Choice (A) is correct. The last sentence of the passage specifically states that spills are a constant threat if offshore drilling and the shipment of oil in tankers continues. Choice (B) is incorrect because the passage does not discuss crews or training programs. While the passage does imply that the government should be better prepared to clean up, the author does not state that oil spills would cease to be a problem if the government was better prepared. Therefore, choice (C) is incorrect. Choice (D) is incorrect because foreign oil producers are not mentioned.

71. **(B)** Choice (B) is correct. These symptoms are listed in the fourth sentence as the possible results of low stress levels, so choices (A) and (C) are incorrect. Neither insomnia nor heart disease is discussed in relationship to low stress, so choice (D) is incorrect.

72. **(D)** Choice (D) is correct. The passage states that few people can eliminate stress and that people can learn coping strategies so choices (A) and (B) are correct. Although the passage does not state that stress is desirable, the author does state that the lack of stress is harmful, so logically a certain amount of stress must be beneficial. Therefore, choice (C) is correct.

73. **(D)** Choice (D) is correct because sleep is not mentioned as a technique for coping with stress. This question requires the use of elimination to determine the correct answer. Diet, exercise, goal setting, and establishing deadlines are all included in the sixth sentence as strategies for eliminating stress.

74. **(B)** Choice (B) is correct because the passage suggests several ways to reduce the total fat in what we eat. Choice (A) is incorrect because the author of the passage does not try to convince readers that too much fat in the diet is bad. The author is assuming that this is the goal of many people, as stated in the first sentence. Choice (C) is incorrect because the author states that you can reduce fat in your diet and still eat in restaurants. Choice (D) is incorrect because although these cooking methods are recommended, that is not the main purpose of the passage.

75. **(B)** Choice (B) is correct. The suggestion to avoid creamy sauces and gravies is in the seventh sentence. Choice (A) is incorrect because the

author states that salads are healthful. Choice (C) is incorrect because stir-frying is listed as a preferred cooking method. Choice (D) is incorrect because the author suggests fresh fruit desserts.

76. **(D)** Choice (D) is correct. The author states this information in the third sentence. Choice (A) is probably a true statement, but the meaning is too narrow. It does not specify what cooking method is used, only that the food is not deep-fat fried.

77. **(D)** This question requires you to use the process of elimination. The passage specifically mentions the growth of bones, the adrenal glands, and parathyroids as being controlled by the pituitary. Blood circulation is not mentioned so choice (D) is correct.

78. **(B)** Choice (B) is correct because the fifth sentence specifically states that the parathyroids control the amount of calcium and phosphate in the blood. Choice (A) is incorrect because the thyroid and adrenals control metabolism. Choice (C) is incorrect because the adrenals control sodium and potassium. Choice (D) is incorrect because the pituitary controls the kidneys.

79. **(D)** The correct answer is (D); the adrenal glands are located on top of the kidneys. Choice (A) is incorrect because the passage does not discuss anything that is located near the pituitary. Choice (B) is incorrect because the parathyroids are located at the back of the thyroids. Choice (C) is incorrect because the liver is not mentioned in the passage.

80. **(C)** Choice (C) is correct because the pituitary controls the growth of bones. Choice (A) is incorrect because the adrenals control responses to stress and metabolism. Choice (B) is incorrect because the kidneys function to clean the body of waste products. Choice (D) is incorrect because the parathyroids control the amount of calcium and phosphate in the blood.

Section 2: Written Assignment

The following essay received scores at the highest end of the scale used in LAST essay scoring.

Essay A

The cynic in me wants to react to the idea of universal public service for the young with a reminder about previous complaints aimed at the military draft. These complaints suggest that wars might never be fought if the first people drafted were the adult leaders and lawmakers. Still, the idea of universal public service sounds good to this concerned citizen who sees everywhere—not just in youth—the effects of a selfish and self-indulgent culture.

One reads and hears constantly about young people who do not care about the problems of our society. These youngsters seem interested in money and the luxuries money can buy. They do not want to work from the minimum wage up, but want instead to land a high paying job without "paying their dues." An informal television news survey of high school students a few years ago suggested that students had the well-entrenched fantasy that with no skills or higher education they would not accept a job paying less than $20 an hour. Perhaps universal service helping out in an urban soup kitchen for six months would instill a sense of selflessness rather than selfishness, and provide the perspective necessary to demonstrate the flaw in this perception.

The shiny gleam of a new expensive sports sedan bought on credit by a recent accounting student reflects self indulgence that might be toned down by universal service. That self indulgence may reflect merely a lack of discipline, but it also may reflect a lack of purpose in life. Philosophers, theologians and leaders of all types suggest throughout the ages that money and objects do not ultimately satisfy. Helping others—service to our fellow human beings often does. Universal public service for that accounting student might require a year helping low income or senior citizens prepare income tax forms. This type of service would dim that self indulgence, give the person some experience in the real world, and also give satisfaction that one's life is not lived only to acquire material things.

Universal service might also help young people restore faith in their nation and what it means to them. Yes, this is the land of opportunity, but it is also a land of forgotten people, and it is a land that faces outside threats. Part of the requisite public service should remind young people of their past and of their responsibility to the future.

Analysis

Essay A uses a traditional structure: the first paragraph states the topic, the second and third present development with specific examples from personal observation. The fourth ends the essay, but it is not as strong a conclusion as it could be. The writer probably ran out of time. The essay as a whole is unified and uses pertinent examples to support the opinion stated. The sentence structure varies, and the vocabulary is effective. Generally, it is well done within the time limit.

The following essay received scores in the middle of the LAST essay scoring scale.

Essay B

In the U.S. today, when a boy turns 18 he is obligated, by law, to register for the military draft. This is done so that in case of a war or other catastrophic event, these boys and men can be called upon for active duty in the military. It is good to know that we will have the manpower we need in case of a war, but my opinion on the military draft is negative. I don't like the idea of forcing someone to sign up at a certain age for something that they don't want to happen. Of course, I know that we need some sort of military manpower on hand just in case, but it would be so much better if it was left to the individual to decide what area to serve in and at what time.

When a boy turns 18, he's a rebel of sorts. He doesn't want someone telling him what to do and when to do it; he's just beginning to live. In Switzerland, when a boy turns 18, he joins some branch of the military for a time of training. He is given his gun, uniform and badge number. Then, once a year for about two weeks he suits up for retraining. He does this until he is about 65 years old. In a way this is like a draft, but the men love it and feel that it is honorable. I think that they like it because it does not discriminate and their jobs pay them for the time away. Switzerland seems to give the 18 year old some choice regarding what division to join, and whether or not to join at all. They're not as strict on joining as we are so it's more of an honorable thing to do.

Of course, I'd love to see this decision be strictly up to the individual, but it can't be that way. We have too many enemies that we might go to war with and we would need a strong military. Switzerland's neutrality provides more options than we in the United States have.

Analysis

Essay B displays competence in overall thought. It does not state its topic quite as well as Essay A. The extended example of Swiss military conscription is the main strength of the essay. The writer hedges a bit but manages to convey an opinion. Sentences have some variety, and the vocabulary is competent. Some spelling and grammatical errors interfere with the communication.

The following essay received scores at the lowest end of the LAST essay scoring scale.

Essay C

I agree with the many leaders who suggest we require young people to serve the public in some way, rather than the military draft.

There are several reasons this could benefit our country. The first being giving the young people, perhaps just out of high school, with no job experience, an opportunity to give something to his community. In return for this, he gains self-respect, pride, and some valuable experience.

Whether it be taking flowers to shut-ins or just stopping for a chat in a rest home, a young person would have gained something and certainly given, perhaps hope, to that elderly person. I can tell from my own experience how enriched I feel when visiting the elderly. They find joy in the simplest things, which in turn, teaches me I should do the same. This type of universal service would also strengthen the bonds between the younger generation and the older generation.

Another thing gained by doing voluntary type work, is a sense of caring about doing the job right-quality! If you can't do it for your country, what else matters? Maybe, if a young person learned these lessons early, our country would be more productive in the global economy.

Analysis

Essay C has major faults, not the least of them the lack of a clear sense of overall organization. The thoughts do have some coherence, but they don't seem to have a plan, except to express agreement with the statement. Examples from personal observation do help, but the paragraphs are not well developed. Several severe grammatical problems interfere with the communication.

DETAILED EXPLANATIONS
OF ANSWERS

1. **(A)** The correct response is (A). Since his goal is his own professional development, the answer is (A). Mr. O'Brien would not assess the quality of students' assignments (C) or revise students' assignments (D) to enhance his own growth and development. Choices (B), (C), and (D) refer to instructional activities, not professional development activities.

2. **(B)** The correct response is (B). Mr. O'Brien is demonstrating that he is a reflective practitioner who can work cooperatively with others in his school. (A) describes a form of intellectual snobbery that does not lead to collegiality. (C) is a given—independent of others' views, Mr. O'Brien has a professional responsibility to keep pace with developments and issues in his teaching field. Finally, (D) is poor because it would not necessarily help him reach his goal of improving instruction.

3. **(C)** The correct response is (C). Including both colleagues' viewpoints is an effort to bring students a balanced and fair presentation on the topic and to work effectively with other professionals at his school. Choices (A) and (D) would not promote collegiality or demonstrate Mr. O'Brien's ability to work with other members of the teaching community; choice (B) would mean that Mr. O'Brien refused to consider the issue carefully simply because it was not an issue with a singular point of view; many topics discussed at the secondary level are subject to multiple points of view.

4. **(A)** The correct response is (A). Mr. O'Brien is designing a supportive classroom for all students, both males and females. Using a particular book as a reference work for a course would not result in (B)—students having to buy the book—or (D)—students having to read the reference book—nor would colleagues necessarily be aware of the practice (C). In

sum, Mr. O'Brien would simply have access to Professor Tannen's findings and her interpretation of her data.

5. **(B)** The correct response is (B). An effective and equitable practice is to give all students an opportunity to participate in class discussions. (A) and (C) are different ways of stating the same practice, in both cases, treating the female students differently. (D) is incorrect; research does show that male students tend to receive more feedback when they answer questions—supporting their self-esteem, whereas female students are seldom given feedback, positive or negative.

6. **(D)** The correct response is (D). Sensitivity to students' self-esteem means that teachers take an interest in their students, visiting with them privately and trying to understand the reasons for their behavior in class. Taking an interest in the student may provide the encouragement the student needs to start participating in class activities. (B) is a harassing behavior to be avoided. (A) and (C), although reasonable educational practices, would probably have little direct effect on changing the behavior of the students the teacher is concerned about helping.

7. **(B)** The correct response is (B). Some students, especially those who respond well to external validators, will be motivated to participate in class when their grades are affected by their participation. (A) is incorrect because this practice will not motivate all students. (C) is incorrect because there is nothing inherent to this practice that would result in all students earning higher grades—only those who participate would improve their grades. This practice of rewarding students for their participation would not be expected to discourage student participation (D).

8. **(B)** The correct response is (B). Mr. O'Brien's strategy involves everyone in class and encourages each student to discover the practical applications for the information to be learned in class. (A) is incorrect because in a communications class, discourse and discussions are encouraged, not avoided; in communications classes, students learn to argue and disagree in a civil manner. (C) is incorrect because this strategy takes quite a bit of classroom time since it allows all students to be actively involved; thus, it is not a timesaving device. (D) is incorrect because brainstorming is a creative activity, not an activity aimed at assessing skills or knowledge.

9. **(A)** The correct response is (A). Mr. O'Brien has employed a brainstorming activity to allow students to uncover their own, personal communication problems and needs. Therefore, they will have more motivation

and interest in learning about communication differences between men and women. (B) is incorrect; in fact, Mr. O'Brien may choose to introduce the topic formally at the next class meeting. (C) is incorrect in that at no point has Mr. O'Brien presented information to pit men and women against each other nor is that the purpose of presenting this topic. (D) is incorrect as Mr. O'Brien's choice of activities will have the opposite effect of dismissing students' concerns as he recognizes and helps them to identify their problems.

10. **(D)** The correct response is (D). Activities (or group work) allow students to learn cooperatively. (A) is incorrect because it does not specify an instructional goal for the group work. Choice (B) is incorrect because the goal is problem-solving not merely improving social skills. (C) is incorrect because students are not structuring their own time in this example.

11. **(B)** The correct response is (B). Students often disclose more personal information in journals than when speaking in class. The teacher can also check for comprehension of content and the success or failure of class objectives. Journals typically are not graded with consideration to standard usage or grammatical constructions; therefore, (A) is incorrect. The assignment has no direct bearing on time-management skills; therefore, (C) is incorrect. Choice (D) is irrelevant: No mention is made of giving daily grades on the journal writing.

12. **(C)** The correct response is (C). Meeting each student and determining needs individually and informally is the best first step to establish rapport with each student. Subsequently, Ms. Jaynes will want to review school files (B), and administer tests (D). Ms. Jaynes will want to be careful in discussing students with other teachers so as not to be influenced by biased opinions or stereotypes against students with learning disabilities or other special needs.

13. **(D)** The correct response is (D). This choice is a definition of test bias. (A) refers to test validity; choice (B) refers to test reliability. Choice (C) is the objective of intelligence tests.

14. **(A)** The correct response is (A). Practice effects are seen when students are retested with the same instrument shortly after the first testing. It is assumed that students' scores will improve with subsequent exposure to the same material. (B) is not a practice effect, but the desired effect of improved skills or enhanced performance; it, indeed, is the purpose of

instruction. Choice (C) pertains to the issue of test validity and choice (D) refers to the issue of social desirability (that is, when students answer the way they believe is desired). Social desirability is an issue with opinion or attitude tests, not achievement or skills tests.

15. **(B)** The correct response is (B). As a reading specialist, Ms. Jaynes understands the important role that motivation plays in reading comprehension. Students are more likely to both read and understand things that they enjoy and are interested in not just literary classics (C). Readability studies reveal that students can comprehend material written at very high levels when they are interested in the material (D). The teacher, certainly, has a responsibility to guide students' choices and not to simply *send* them to the library, choice (A).

16. **(A)** The correct response is (A). Ms. Jaynes has attempted to increase students' metacognitive awareness and fluency by directly teaching them an elaboration strategy to aid and monitor their reading comprehension. This is a holistic approach to teaching reading versus a specific skill or component approach as referred to in choices (B), (C), and (D).

17. **(D)** The correct response is (D). When students are taught effective strategies to use as tools, they can become independent learners. Choice (A), a quiet classroom, is not conducive to the learning of all students; research on learning styles indicates that only some students prefer quiet when reading or studying. Ms. Jaynes must be actively involved in each class, monitoring students' performance, so she does not have any extra time for paperwork in class, choice (B). Although reading can be a social activity, most important reading done by students (in and out of school) is a solitary activity (C).

18. **(C)** The correct response is (C). Statistical procedures used to standardize tests usually result in high validity and reliability; reading tests, in particular, usually are good measures of overall reading achievement as compared to the more specific and narrow purview of most informally-constructed tests. Standardized tests are not always easier to grade (A), nor are they more subjective (B), nor are they usually more economical (D) than informally-constructed tests.

19. **(C)** The correct response is (C). Although choices (A), (B) and (D) are possible products of Ms. Jaynes' actions, they are not the certain reason she engages in this practice. Popularity, higher salaries, and better-disciplined students do not always accompany involved and caring in-

struction. However, many intangible rewards are products of being a team member of the learning community.

20. **(C)** The correct response is (C). These broadly-stated goals for instruction are examples of instructional or educational objectives. Behavioral objectives (A) must describe specific skills or knowledge to be acquired and demonstrated by students. Performance objectives (B) include performance standards and other specific performance criteria. The question has nothing to do with outcome-based education (D).

21. **(C)** The correct response is (C). Behavioral objectives describe what students will be able to do as a result of having received appropriate instruction. A variety of teaching methods may be used to reach these objectives, (A) and teacher-centered or student-centered (better to use both) activities may be used, (D). Materials and equipment lists may or may not be given on lesson plans; if so, they are separate from behavioral objectives (B).

22. **(A)** The correct response is (A). Ms. Aljuhbar makes use of collaborative processes in planning instruction and designing activities. Choices (B) and (C) would not create reciprocal learning situations; ESL students would only be learning about life in the United States. Choice (D) is poor because it does not include an active role for ESL students nor does it recognize that some ESL students from non-Christian countries might feel excluded by an activity focusing on a Christian holiday.

23. **(C)** The correct response is (C). This action shows concern for the student and opens the door for dialogue with the student. For high school-aged students, a direct approach which recognizes the student's own responsibility for his or her own learning and behavior is usually the best approach. Choices (A) and (B) are indirect and could exacerbate the student's present problems. (D) fails to get at the cause of Lee's difficulties.

24. **(B)** The correct response is (B). The instructional principle illustrated here is that students can more easily learn new information (English) when linked with the familiar (their native language). Moreover, learning becomes more effective when students are allowed to make choices about the learning activities in which they engage. Choices (A) and (C) are plausible, however, poor choices in comparison with (B). Choice (D) is incorrect in as much as filming one's performance involves some level of risk.

25. **(D)** The correct response is (D). Sharing stories with youngsters allows the older students to instruct younger students, assuming an authority role as teacher; these activities can motivate and reward ESL students. These activities have nothing to do with standardizing student performance (A) nor are they inappropriate for high school-aged students since adults routinely engage in such behaviors (B). Moreover, these activities do not restrict but rather encourage student initiative and creativity (C).

26. **(C)** The correct response is (C). Mr. Reams was modeling effective communication techniques. Choice (A) is incorrect because the teacher's role changes from structured to unstructured situations, but it is never minimized. (B) is false because no teaching strategy can assure success. (D) is incorrect because at this point, students are not aware of environmental needs. They are still in the brainstorming section of the instruction.

27. **(C)** The correct response is (C). The instructor is attempting to vary his instructional strategies to keep students involved. (A) is incorrect because no selection of materials and resources has occurred at this point. Small heterogeneous ability groupings allow for input from all students. (B) is wrong because in a brainstorming situation, assessment is not used and creativity is encouraged. (D) stifles, rather than encourages the positive social and emotional climate in the classroom that the instructor wishes to create at all times.

28. **(A)** The correct response is (A). Mr. Reams had developed a successful interdisciplinary activity for his class. (B) is incorrect because maintaining class control is not inherently part of brainstorming. (C) is incorrect because promoting problem solving does not allow for a preconceived agenda. (D) is wrong because technology as a learning tool has not been introduced at this point.

29. **(C)** The correct response is (C). The instructor has made the students feel that they are members of a smoothly functioning community. Choice (A) is a false statement. Environmental pollution is not a new or unique problem. (B) expresses only part of the complete answer (C). (D) is incorrect because there has been no assessment thus far.

30. **(C)** The correct response is (C). The instructor has taken advantage of community strengths to foster student growth. (A) is incorrect because the teacher is a role model and has worked cooperatively with the community himself. (B) is incorrect because parent-teacher conferences should begin and end on a positive note. (D) is incorrect because achieving teacher

determined personal goals indicates student manipulation rather than student problem solving.

31. **(A)** The correct response is (A). A needs assessment will help students make the connection between their current skills and those that will be new to them. (B) is wrong because a needs assessment focuses on the skills a student currently possesses. (C) is incorrect because the needs assessment is designed to determine what needs to be taught that is not currently in the curriculum. (D) is a false statement. A needs assessment is not designed to motivate students.

32. **(C)** The correct response is (C). A positive environment must be created to minimize the effects of negative external factors. (A) is inappropriate because changing the text but allowing the environment to remain the same only results in maintaining the status quo. (B) is incorrect because relating the student's personal interest to the new material is a part of creating a positive environment. (D) is wrong because again it is only a small part of maximizing the effects of a positive learning environment.

33. **(D)** The correct response is (D). The instructor should plan instruction that will lead students to ask questions and pursue problems that are meaningful to them. (A) is a part of (D). Meaningful instruction will nurture student growth and the instruction will be developmentally appropriate. (B) is incorrect because it is incomplete. The type of instruction indicated in (D) would enhance students' self-esteem. (C) is incorrect because it may or it may not include an invitation to community professionals to speak in class.

34. **(C)** The correct response is (C). The instructor knows how to work effectively with all members of the community to solve problems and accomplish educational goals. (A) is encompassed in (C). Working with community leaders, identifying community problems and, if possible, solving those problems with the students will motivate students and affect their learning. (B) A teacher's role does change from situation to situation. His or her work within the community would not be one of teacher/instructor, but rather one of facilitator/helper. (D) is incorrect because before any community change can occur, there must be a bond of trust between the parent and the teacher.

35. **(C)** The correct response is (C). The teacher would be fostering strong home relationships which support student achievement of desired outcomes. Choice (A) is the result of (C). As the teacher interacts with

professionals in the community, her own professional growth would be promoted. (B) is also the result of (C). All teachers are expected to interact with the community and work to develop strong home relationships which will support student achievement of desired outcomes. (D) is incomplete since strong home relationships are developed through the principles of conferences, trust, and cooperation.

36. **(C)** The correct response is (C). This question relates to planning processes to design outcome-oriented learning experiences. Developing objectives is the first step in planning. Cooperative learning and the content are used to reach the objectives (A). Evaluation is the last step in the planning process, (B). (D) Finding materials and resources is an important step in planning, but the incorrect choice for this situation.

37. **(A)** The correct response is (A). This question relates to an understanding of human developmental processes. This understanding nurtures student growth through developmentally appropriate instruction. Higher order thinking skills are important instructional strategies (B) is not the best answer. Promoting the lifelong pursuit of learning is achieved through structuring and managing the learning environment, (C). Understanding how learning occurs would show that constant difficult schoolwork causes students to become disinterested, which renders (D) an incorrect choice.

38. **(C)** The correct response is (C). This question relates to environmental factors. Being aware of external forces will help in the planning and designing of the unit to promote students' learning and self-esteem. (A) relates to the development of the unit which requires choosing lessons and activities that reflect the principles of effective instruction and renders (A) incorrect. Challenging students requires the teacher to be aware of the learners' interests while designing the instruction, (B) is part of the planning process and incorrect for this situation. (D), the grouping of students, is an instructional strategy and is incorrect.

39. **(D)** The correct response is (D). This question relates to how learning occurs and applying this understanding to the design and implementation of effective instruction. A student's daily class schedule is an external factor. Learning styles affect how a student learns, therefore, (A) is incorrect for this question. Although cultural background affects how students may develop knowledge and skills and is an important consideration of how learning occurs, (B) is incorrect for this question. Previous grades would indicate the ability of a student to learn through linking new information to old, and would make (C) incorrect for this question.

40. **(C)** The correct response is (C). This question relates to human diversity and the knowledge that each student brings to the classroom a constellation of personal and social characteristics related to a variety of factors such as exceptionality. (A) is simply more of the same kind of schoolwork and not an acceptable answer. Being intrinsically motivated, exceptional students often find unmotivated students difficult to tutor, choice (B) is incorrect. Teacher made, tightly-organized units do not allow the exceptional student the opportunity to experience the learning situation; (D) is incorrect.

41. **(B)** The correct response is (B). Team rewards, individual accountability, and equal opportunities for success are always present in cooperative learning. Rules and specific tasks may be part of the instructions given for cooperative learning groups, but are not required in cooperative learning situations, therefore, choices (A), (C), and (D) are incorrect.

42. **(D)** The correct response is (D). This question relates to enabling teachers to document their teaching and to be aware of student's efforts, progress, and achievements. A portfolio is a purposeful collection of work that exhibits efforts, progress, and achievement of students and enables teachers to document teaching in an authentic setting. Standardized tests are commercially developed and are used for specific events (A). A teacher-made test is used to evaluate specific objectives of the course (B) is not the best choice. Observation is used to explain what students do in classrooms and to indicate some of their capabilities, therefore, (C) is not correct.

43. **(C)** The correct response is (C). This question relates to evaluating specific objectives and content. Teacher-made tests are designed to evaluate the specific objectives and specific content of a course. (A) is incorrect because self and peer evaluation utilizes student's knowledge according to evaluation criteria that is understood by the student. A portfolio (B) is a purposeful collection of work that exhibits effort, progress, and achievement of students and enables teachers to document teaching in an authentic setting. Observation (D) is used to explain what students do in classrooms and to indicate to some degree their capabilities.

44. **(D)** The correct response is (D). This question refers to student performance in terms of percentiles, stanines, and scaled scores. Standardized tests rate student performance against the performance of other students and report the scores in terms of percentile, stanines, and scaled scores. A portfolio is a collection of student effort, progress, and achievement. Teacher-made tests (A) evaluate specific objectives and content, therefore

(B) is incorrect. What students do in classrooms and their capabilities are evaluated through observation making (C) incorrect.

45. **(C)** The correct response is (C). This question relates to a form of assessment that utilizes student's knowledge and understanding of specific criteria and the teacher's role is that of facilitator. Self and peer assessment requires that the student be aware of the evaluation criteria and the student understands that criteria. A collection of work that exhibits students success and enables teachers to document teaching is a portfolio. A teacher-made test (A) evaluates specific objectives and content, therefore, (B) is not correct. Observation is used to indicate capabilities and actions of students (D).

46. **(C)** The correct response is (C). Mrs. Ratu's lack of competency is exhibited in her lack of understanding of her students. (A) The effect of Mrs. Ratu's minimal competency resulted in her teaching on the elementary level. (B) Mrs. Ratu's minimal competency resulted from her lack of understanding of the learners in her class. Had she understood the learners, she would have recognized her lack of competency in both the teaching and evaluating of the students. (D) Mrs. Ratu's desire to make remedial reading easy for the students by teaching them on a lower elementary level again exhibits lack of competency. When appropriate techniques are used, teaching ninth-graders to read is no more difficult for the ninth-grade student than it is for the third-grade student.

47. **(C)** The correct response is (C). Mr. Jones knew that development in one area leads to development in another area. He also knew that using a variety of instructional techniques could lead to inquiry, motivation, and even further development in certain areas. Allowing students to have choices in their learning leads to a positive self-concept and can lead to camaraderie. (A) Statement I is a possibility, not an absolute. Therefore it is a false answer. (B) Allowing students to have choices in their learning should create camaraderie, however, camaraderie is only one component of intrinsic motivation. (D) Round table discussions do lead to questions and often to the solving of problems. For this scenario round table discussions were but one of the variety of techniques which he was using.

48. **(A)** The correct response is (A). Diversity of students can be an advantage. Similarities and differences need to be discussed in order to create a respect for those differences. Discussions are but one avenue for creating an open, secure environment. Forbidden discussion diminishes motivation. (B) The students had been allowed to discuss their feelings

about subjects of interest, however, their feelings were but one element of their diversity. (C) This statement is false. (D) The students may have begun to respect their differences, but respect of diversity is a part of advantage.

49. **(C)** The correct response is (C). Mr. Jones' role was varied. In the discussions he was the facilitator not the teacher. He had planned the discussion as an outcome-oriented learning experience. (A) Mr. Jones' role did vary, but the activity did not function as an assessment tool. (B) Mr. Jones had already made the decision to evaluate the students yearly by an achievement test. The round table was not a form of assessment. (D) Maintaining a lifelong pursuit of learning is the ultimate goal for all education, however, the immediate and more pressing goal was to improve the reading skills of the concerned students.

50. **(B)** The correct response is (B). As a facilitator, Mr. Jones listened and monitored the discussion. His duty as facilitator was to model effective communication strategies, to monitor the students' input and to encourage all students to participate. (A) Mr. Jones would be able to manage the classroom environment which is a part of shaping the learners through effective communication strategies. (C) The amount of information each student had collected could be indicative of the homes' socioeconomic level, but this statement is not an absolute. The student could have just forgotten to look for material at home. The statement is false. (D) Mr. Jones was able to monitor student input and encourage all students to participate. He was also modeling effective communication through reflective listening, simplifying and restating, and being sensitive to nonverbal cues given and received.

51. **(C)** The correct response is (C). A prewriting activity stimulates students' thinking and helps them with the writing process. Choices (A) and (B) are too general and superficial. Choice (D) refers specifically to outlining, something not mentioned in the context of the problem set.

52. **(A)** The correct response is (A). Introspective activities help students to connect new information to previously learned information, an important cognitive process. Choice (B) refers to personal narrative whereas the writing assignment is a personal description. Choice (C) is inappropriate at this point in the learning process. Choice (D) is an affective goal for instruction, but the question specifically asks about cognitive development.

53. **(B)** The correct response is (B). Students are affected by multiple factors, including environmental factors both inside and outside class. Choices (A), (C), and (D) are too general and broad. Choice (A) is a broad generalization that has no direct application to Ms. Johnson's request that students think about their own behavior inside and outside class. Choice (C) is superficial and assumes that students can easily identify their own strengths when research shows that students (and adults) often have difficulty identifying their specific strengths and assets. Choice (D) is incorrect because of the same rationale.

54. **(C)** The correct response is (C). One of the central tenets of human development is the constant interaction and precarious balance of nurture and nature. Choices (A) and (B) specifically refer to Piaget's theory of cognitive development, a specific subset of human development theories. Choice (D) is a false statement; theories of human development support the notion that adolescence is a time of increased social cognition and the awareness of the thoughts of others. (Hence, the adolescent phenomena of "personal fable" and "imaginary audience" as identified by Elkind.)

55. **(C)** The correct response is (C). The Language-Experience-Approach (LEA) is a proven method of increasing students' reading and writing proficiency, their overall language competency. It requires that students write about what they know. Choices (A), (B), and (D) are irrelevant. Choice (A) superficially addresses that Ms. Johnson is an English teacher; choice (B) refers to autobiographies, something that is not mentioned in the preceding information; and choice (D) foreshadows the library project, but it has not yet been introduced into the context of these questions.

56. **(C)** The correct response is (C). A basic principle in providing students with appropriate feedback is to first note the student's strengths (or positive aspects of the student's work and/or performance) and then to note specific ways the student can improve her/his work and/or performance. Therefore, the best approach for a teacher to take in providing students with feedback on written work is to first note the good things about students' writing and then to suggest ways to improve. Choices (A) and (B) are in essence the same; both choices indicate that only students' strengths would be acknowledged, omitting the important aspect of addressing ways students can improve. Neither action would enhance students' cognitive skills or their metacognitive skills (or self-awareness). Choice (D) is unacceptable because it denigrates the teacher's responsibility to evaluate students' performance on the basis of individual merit against the standards established by particular disciplines.

57. **(A)** The correct response is (A). This is the best answer of the four options for the following reasons: First, learning style information acknowledges that although learners acquire knowledge in different ways, those differences can lead to effective learning when students are taught cognitive strategies which complement their natural learning tendencies; basically, teaching students about learning styles (and especially about their own learning style) is a recognition of human diversity. Second, beyond mere recognition of human diversity is the legitimacy of different approaches to learning: Every student can perform at a level of proficiency although not every student will attain that level in the same manner; in other words, learning styles validate students as learners and promote high standards for academic achievement. Third, when students are taught not only about learning styles in general, but specifically about their own learning style, they are empowered to take responsibility for their own learning. Fourth, of the four options, only choices (A) and (D) are tasks actively engaging the student. Both choices (B) and (C) are passive activities, thus, both (B) and (C) are poor choices. Choice (D) requires that students perform a task without any help (direct instruction) for accomplishing the task; simply asking students to name additional strengths without giving them an opportunity to self-examine, to self-assess, and to explore their strengths will not produce the desired outcome. Only choice (A) gives students the information they need in order to accomplish the task the teacher has identified as being important.

58. **(C)** The correct response is (C). Although brainstorming activities benefit learning by determining students' interests choice (A) and giving everyone a chance to participate (B), choices (A) and (B) are merely benefits, not the real purpose of the activity. (D) is incorrect because it is irrelevant to the situation described; brainstorming, as an activity, has no direct relationship to honesty or cheating.

59. **(B)** The correct response is (B). Although (A), (C), and (D) are possible choices, the best answer to the question is (B). (A), (C), and (D) are basically restatements of the same idea: that the teacher forms the groups instead of the students; this was specified in the context of the question. The only option which gives a rationale for the teacher choosing her action is answer (B).

60. **(A)** The correct response is (A). Only choice (A) recognizes the cognitive principle underlying the teacher's assignment. Choices (B) and (D) are essentially the same; although the assignment may result in these timesaving features, they are not the instructional principle guiding the

teacher's practice. Choice (C) is irrelevant. Asking students to hypothesize is not directly related to inculcating self-management skills in learners.

61. **(D)** The correct response is (D). (A), (B), (C), and (D) were included in the planning. (A) is a true statement but is only one element of the correct response of (D). (B) Both statements are true but again are only one element of the correct response. (C) The statements are true, but are only one element of the correct response of (D). (D) contains all the elements.

62. **(D)** The correct response is (D). All preceding activities were for the purpose of engaging the students in order to motivate them to achieve. (A) Mrs. Gomez' role is not the issue, it is the students and their learning. (B) The purpose of the workshop was to better each students' writing, not understand the society in which one lived. (C) Again, the purpose of the workshop was not to identify the talents of the students, but to teach them how to creatively write using metaphors.

63. **(B)** The correct response is (B). Bright colors have a stimulating effect. By displaying multiple transparencies of works of art the students could choose the one they wanted to write about. (A) Stimulation of the creativity of the students was not the only goal for using the bright transparencies. The goal was to stimulate creativity and to allow students to have a choice in their learning. (C) The issue is writing not art, however, exposure to the art could create a desire to know much more about it. (D) The purpose of the assignment was not just to expose them to art but to stimulate good writing.

64. **(B)** The correct response is (B). In the assessment Mrs. Gomez had to communicate effectively with the students. To accomplish this she used various media. She was connecting the media to the different learning styles. (A) Evaluation generates divergent thinking but never creative thinking. The statement is false. (C) The evaluation tools were not to evaluate Mrs. Gomez' competency but were designed to evaluate the students' competency in identifying and creating metaphors. (D) Working with other colleagues is not the issue, but using a variety of communication techniques in the evaluation.

65. **(A)** The correct response is (A). The poem was a creative expression, allowing the freedom for each learner to express his/her differences. (B) Statement two is correct but statement four is incorrect. (C) Both class participation and the completion of the poem were included in the formal

assessment designed by Mrs. Gomez. (D) Class participation and completion of the poem allow respect for the differences among students, however, it did not allow for a variety of opinions to be expressed. "Opinion" is defined as a belief stronger than an impression but less strong than positive knowledge.

66. **(D)** The correct response is (D). Although there may be some value in all of the responses offered, the two that are educationally sound are those that will strengthen the relationship between the community and the school. The savings of money, since school funding is tied into the Average Daily Attendance for a school district, is one way to win favor with members of the community, especially since recent school funding problems in New York have tended to increase taxation supporting the public schools in many communities. Since research also indicates that the better the attendance record, the more likely a student is to achieve success in school, parents and other concerned members of the community will react favorably to the plan. The incentives for the students to attend, derived from the community businesses, may well make the youth more appreciative of their community support structure. Choices (A), (B), and (C) are incorrect. Choice (A) considers only the financial advantage and does not take into account the positive interaction of school and community promoted by the attendance plan. Choice (B) is not the best answer. Some students will be excited about their awards; however, their greatest reward will be the increased opportunity for learning. All schools like positive publicity, but the value of the proposal goes well beyond mere publicity with other school districts. Choice (C) is incorrect since the students' receiving of awards or prizes may be exciting and motivating to some, the major advantage, as previously stated, is to the students' improved chance to learn.

67. **(A)** The correct response is (A). Mr. Janowsky has enhanced the introductory lesson to the unit of study on advertising by using a variety of materials and resources that pique students' interests and response. The ideas spark the students' own future gathering of advertising ideas for a project during this unit of study. The several primary examples of advertisements and the varied techniques clearly contrasted serve to demonstrate the creativity associated with this area of study. Even cultural differences and preferences are shown by his use of the Clio Awards videotape clippings. (B), (C), and (D) are incorrect. (B)'s negative assessment of the use of varied resources is completely unacceptable in a class of creative thinking and production. Even if Mr. Janowsky has overdone the display of examples, the negative connotation of the word clutter makes the

supervisor's comment inappropriate. (C) is not the best answer for this introductory lesson. The examples of materials and resources displayed by Mr. Janowsky serve as a model to stimulate the students' gathering of samples as the unit of study progresses. (D) is incorrect for a supervisor, no matter how interested in this subject, who is having a conference to evaluate Mr. Janowsky as a professional educator. This focus of evaluation should be the clear purpose of the supervisor's comments. Of course, as an advertising buff, the supervisor may want to meet with Mr. Janowsky again after the formal evaluation conference to discuss their joint interest.

68. **(C)** The correct response is (C). The most efficient way to gain information about a new setting is to speak with someone who is familiar with the circumstances. Orienting oneself with the physical layout (A) would be helpful but cannot tell you about the student population or materials. Although communication with the principal (B) is always a good idea, the principal usually will have little time to have an in depth discussion and will not be able to tell specifically which books are available for your use. Eventually Ms. Woods will need to match curriculum guidelines to the material available (D), but sitting in a closet will not introduce her to staff and student characteristics.

69. **(D)** The correct response is (D). By having students interact with each other on the first day, the nervousness is broken and Ms. Woods will have quality student profiles to use when preparing suitable lessons. Handing out a syllabus (A), which will change greatly by year's end, does nothing to introduce the students to each other or the teacher to the class. A questionnaire of favorite literature (B) will help the teacher prepare topics around student interests, but the individual questionnaire does nothing to involve students in familiarizing themselves with one another. Individually introducing oneself by name and favorite book (C) puts the students on the spot, which may make a new high school student nervous, and one book will not help the teacher develop a good student profile.

70. **(D)** The correct response is (D). This includes all of the techniques that would be useful in improving and monitoring writing. The students have set goals toward which they will strive (II) bit by bit until they reach them. The teacher and student have an opportunity to discuss good and bad points of the student's writing in a non-threatening atmosphere (III). It is always helpful to have a model of good writing (IV) and by choosing student's papers, self-esteem is enhanced. Forcing a student to write every night will do little to create quality work. Therefore choices (A), (B), and (C) are incorrect.

71. **(B)** The correct response is (B). Parent-teacher communication should always begin and end on a positive note, so as not to offend parents and turn them off to future suggestions. Never leave problems for the end (A), because parents may be put on the offensive if they sense a negative attitude from the teacher. Parents do not want to feel as if they are being put down, which will often occur if the teacher uses too much technical jargon (C). Teachers must gain the parent's cooperation (D) so that both parent and teacher feel comfortable with the plan of improvement at home and at school.

72. **(D)** The correct response is (D). The classroom arrangement can control how the students respond in class. Students tend to respond more openly if they are communicating face to face with each other, which makes a circle the optimal desk arrangement. Putting students in rows by sex does little to stimulate discussion (A). The physical aesthetics of the classroom are important (B), but nice looking book cases will not encourage participation. A new topic each day may spur limited conversation at the time but does little to encourage continual class participation.

73. **(A)** The correct response is (A). Many authors include cultural aspects in their books. By reading an author from an appealing culture, a student not only learns about the character, but also the character's culture. By presenting their findings to the class, classmates are exposed to this information as well. Exposure to new authors is important but highlighting a new author once a month is not enough exposure to be significant (B). Although knowing geographical locations of countries is important (C), cultural diversity encompasses much more. Mere exposure to varied authors is necessary, but multicultural awareness is meant to be integrated into the entire curriculum, rather than relegated to one day (D).

74. **(C)** The correct response is (C). Cooperative grouping should give the students a chance to display leadership abilities (I), organize and distribute materials so that all members play a vital part in the final product (II), and evaluate for themselves how the group functioned and whether or not they did the best job they could (III). The teacher should have a way to group the students so they are balanced for optimal learning by everyone (IV). All of the aspects should be included, therefore (A), (B), and (D) are incorrect.

75. **(D)** The correct response is (D). The social studies teacher demonstrates how curricula can cross and how students can use prior knowledge and non-novel resources to aide them in their project. Students new to a

school need to know how to gain access to information, which is best done with the help of the librarian. Ms. Woods has used her faculty resources to enhance her teaching and build a good working environment among faculty members. Although Ms. Woods will not be teaching class at the time, it is not necessarily free time, and this was not her main objective (A). The students will become more familiar with these faculty members (B), but they will gain more than just this. If the students listen carefully they will learn time-cutting information-gathering techniques, but the discussion will not serve as a way to get out of doing work.

76. **(A)** The correct response is (A). Ms. Woods will best serve as a facilitator in this situation. She knows how to let the students solve the problem by discussing options while she guides and directs the students. She does this without overtly telling them how to solve the problem. By overlooking the problem (B), the teacher is setting an example that says working problems out is not necessary. By not presenting a model to follow (C) the teacher may be letting the group flounder and waste precious time, even though they may solve the problem in the end. An activity should never be stopped with the only explanation being that it is not working (D).

77. **(B)** The correct response is (B). Intrinsic motivation and the desire to learn is shown to increase when students are given a role to play by choosing their own learning processes and materials. Continuous tangible rewards (A) increase extrinsic motivation but decrease intrinsic motivation. A lesson is usually of high quality if the teacher is interested in the topic (C) but this is not relevant to increasing student's intrinsic motivation. Rote question answering (D) provides little stimulation, therefore has no positive effect on motivation.

78. **(A)** The correct response is (A). Literature often mimics real life situations which can be used to discuss how and why people choose what they do. By this age students can and should further their moral reasoning skills. This assignment serves as a prompt to classroom discussion about acceptable and unacceptable conclusions in problem solving. This exercise serves as a way to write creatively (B) but creativity is not the main thrust of this assignment. Improvement in reading skills is always an underlying purpose, but not the most important for this exercise (C). It is not the teacher's place to rewrite the novel's ending, but to use it as a catalyst for thought and contemplation.

79. **(D)** The correct response is (D). When working in cooperative groups it is important that members take turns talking quietly (I), listening to each other (II) and helping each other when asked (III). To truly assess the outcome it is necessary to look at each student's performance within the group and individually (IV). Choice (D) is the only answer to contain all three points.

80. **(A)** The correct response is (A). Students can use the checklist to monitor the content and quality of their writing as they go along, thereby making it self-assessment. Although the list may serve as a quick reference during grading (B) this was not the main purpose for it. This list will give a means of evaluating but this does not address why each student is given one (C). A fair grading system may ensue but this is not the most important reason for using this list individually (D).

Section 2: Written Assignment

The following essay received scores at the highest end of the scale used in ATS-W essay scoring.

Essay A

When I think of what specific characteristics a person must possess in order to be an effective teacher I think of these characteristics: upstanding values, compassion, and a thorough knowledge of their subject matter.

First, a person who becomes a teacher must keep in mind that they are a role model to the children in their midst. Their private and professional life must be beyond reproach. A teacher is responsible for setting values as well as teaching values. A teacher has a big influence on a child's life; therefore, a teacher must be careful about the kinds of signals he sends out to the children in his environment. Today, it is hard to tell teachers from students because they dress alike, wear their hair alike, associate together, and act the same. A teacher should set himself apart if he is to be a positive influence on the students he comes in contact with. Once a teacher loses his credibility and/or self-respect, he is no longer effective in the classroom.

Compassion is a quality that allows a teacher to have a sense of humor, get to know students' qualities, and be supportive of students' efforts. A teacher must be able to laugh with his students. This creates a relationship between learner and teacher, and shows the students that the teacher has a human side, and tells the students that the teacher is approachable. A good teacher will get to know each of his student's learning abilities and styles. This will allow the teacher to get the most from each student. Compassion allows the teacher to empathize with the students who are having problems in school or at home by being supportive and by providing a positive direction. Students can be turned off if they perceive that a teacher does not care.

Finally, if a person is going to be an effective teacher, he must have a thorough knowledge of his discipline. This gives the teacher a sense of confidence and allows the teacher to be well organized. An effective teacher knows and likes what he teaches, and the enthusiasm will show and will become a part of the students. Without a good mastery of the subject matter, a teacher is unable to make well-informed decisions about objectives to be covered.

In conclusion, by possessing and demonstrating upstanding values, showing compassion, and exhibiting a thorough knowledge of his subject area, the right person can make a good teacher. If students are to learn, they must be influenced by persons who have all three of these characteristics.

Analysis

This essay, even though it contains minor errors in punctuation and pronoun-antecedent agreement, is well written, as evidenced by the clarity, organization, and mature language.

The opening sentence is a complex sentence. Therefore, a comma should have been used to separate the dependent clause ("When I think of what specific characteristics a person must possess in order to be an effective teacher,") from the rest of the sentence (the independent clause). Also, in the first sentence, the pronoun *their* (plural) is used to refer to a *person* (singular). This a pronoun-antecedent disagreement. The pronoun *his* or *her* should have been used. This problem disappears later, suggesting that the writer may have been careless. Always save enough time to proof your essay. When writing hurriedly, it's very easy to make careless mistakes: their for there, a for an, no for know.

The writer adequately introduces the topic "Characteristics of an Effective Teacher" by outlining the three characteristics to be discussed. Each of the three paragraphs of the body contains a characteristic as the main idea and details to explain and/or support it. The conclusion is a summary of the essay and an explanation of why these characteristics are important. The reader should have no difficulty understanding the message the writer is conveying.

The following essay received scores in the middle of the ATS-W scoring scale.

Essay B

A teacher must have the following characteristics in order to be effective: dedication, knowledge of the subject matter, and versatility. A dedicated teacher is one who is always willing to go that extra mile to help a student to learn. A dedicated teacher is not one who is just looking for a paycheck every other week. This type of teacher will find the students' weaknesses and start building on those points day-by-day. A dedicated teacher is also a caring person who will help build confidence in students' ability to learn. Without this type of dedication, there will be a decrease in effective teaching because if the teacher does not show his dedication and concern for the students to learn the material, then the students will not reflect that initiative to learn.

Teachers must be knowledgeable in the subject areas that they are teaching. Teachers with more formal education, teaching experience, and hours of training are more successful in helping students achieve educational goals. Now, without this knowledge and education, you will have a reduction in the effective teaching method. Teachers who do not know the academic subject that they are teaching cannot make clear presentations or use effective teaching strategies. They cannot answer questions fully and must be very evasive in their answers.

Another characteristic that a teacher must possess is the versatility to teach slower and advanced learners in a manner that both will be able to receive and retain the given information. A teacher must be able to make the subject matter come alive, demanding quality work meeting personal as well as academic needs of students and adding humor to the classroom. With the absence of this versatility, a teacher will only reach a small number of students in the classroom.

All of the above characteristics are important. Teachers who do not possess them will have difficulty reaching their students, and the drop-out rate will continue to climb.

Analysis

The writer of this essay addresses the topic well, and the essay is without major errors in mechanics of grammar. Nevertheless, the essay lacks clarity in organization and presentation of ideas. No introductory paragraph exists. This is very important because the introductory paragraph sets parameters for the remaining parts of the essay. The writer, in this case, combined the introduction and the first paragraph of the body. The introduction should have read: *A teacher must have the following characteristics in order to be effective: dedication, knowledge of subject matter, and versatility.* In earlier years, a one-sentence paragraph was not allowed. That, however, is no longer true; "A dedicated teacher..." should have been the beginning of the next paragraph.

The remaining paragraphs are well organized. Each is introduced by a characteristic (the main idea), and that characteristic is explained and supported by adequate details. However, a bit of ambiguity exists in paragraph three: *A teacher must be able to make the subject matter come alive, demanding quality work meeting personal as well as academic needs of students and adding humor to the classroom.* For clarity purposes, there should have been a comma after work and a comma after students.

Some awkward expressions exist throughout the essay, but considering the time factor, this essay is considered adequate.

The following essay received scores at the lowest end of the ATS-W scoring scale.

Essay C

If you pick up a newspaper, turn on your radio, you will hear, see, and read about the declining of education. Discipline is a problem, test scores are down, and the teacher is being slained. Society has asked the perplexing question: What makes an effective classroom teacher?

First, to become an effective classroom teacher, there has to be an internal love within self, along with external love of the art of teaching. Secondly, devotion, dedication, and discipline among self and the environment in which you are entering will demonstrate the first procedure of effectiveness in the classroom and set up the essential elements involved in teaching. Thirdly, carrying the three "P's" in your heart will produce an effective classroom teacher, being "Proud" of what you are, being "Patient" with whom you are teaching, and being "Persistent" in what you are teaching. Finally, living beyond the classroom, I think, is the most effective in an effective classroom teacher, staying beyond your paid time, getting emotionally involved with your students after your paid time and setting up the ability to cope with the stress of the educational process before your paid time. In order to endure effectiveness, there is long-suffering, perservance, and understanding any situation at any given moment to entitle all children to a worthwhile education of an effective classroom teacher.

Analysis

The writer of this essay partially addresses the topic, but the essay itself is totally unacceptable. The initial paragraph, which should have outlined the characteristics to be discussed, leads one to believe that the essay will address "declining of education," "test scores," and "slained teachers." To identify problems that demand effective teachers is an acceptable way to introduce the topic, but the writer of this essay does it very poorly. Additionally, the past participle of *slay is slain,* not *slained.*

The writer does present the characteristics of an effective teacher, but these characteristics are all contained in one paragraph, and they are very unclear due to poor word choice, ambiguous expressions (awkward), and poor sentence structure. Three paragraphs should have been used, one for each characteristic; and each should have contained details to explain and support the characteristic.

This essay is filled with awkward expressions that suggest an inability to effectively use the language: "declining of education, internal love within self," "external love of the art of teaching," "demonstrate the first procedure of effectiveness in the classroom," "set up the essential elements," "Finally, living beyond the classroom, I think, is the most effective in an effective classroom teacher," "staying beyond your paid time," and others.

The writer excessively uses "you" and "your"—second person. Essays should be written in the third person—he, she, or they. For example, the noun *teacher* or *teachers* should have been used as well.

NYSTCE

New York State Teacher Certification Examinations

LAST
Practice Test Three
and
ATS - W
Elementary / Secondary
Practice Test Three

LAST
PRACTICE TEST 3

TIME: 4 Hours
80 Multiple Choice Questions, 1 Essay

SECTION 1

DIRECTIONS: Each of the following questions and incomplete statements is followed by four answer choices. Select the choice which best answers each question.

---

1. The area of a triangle is always

   (A) equal to half the area of a rectangle.

   (B) cannot be found without the dimensions.

   (C) $A = a + b + c$ where a, b, and c are the lengths of the three sides of a triangle.

   (D) $A = 1/2\ abc$, where a, b, c are the lengths of the three sides of a triangle.

2. A scalene triangle has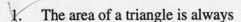

   (A) three equal sides.

   (B) two equal sides.

   (C) an obtuse angle in it.

   (D) three sides unequal in length.

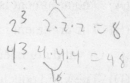

3. In the formula for the volume of a cube, s units on a side is $V = s^3 = sss$. If the length of the sides is doubled, what happens to the volume?

   (A) Volume is doubled

(B) Volume is tripled

(C) Volume is quadrupled (increased by a factor of 4)

(D) Volume is increased by a factor of 8

4. Consider the following argument:

> My coat is in the hall or in the bedroom.
> My coat is not in the bedroom.
> Therefore, my coat is in the hall.

(A) The argument is invalid.

(B) The argument is valid.

(C) A valid argument is not available.

(D) The valid conclusion is my coat is not in the hall.

5. Consider the following argument:

> If I work, then I make money.
> I do not work.
> Therefore, I do not make money.

(A) The argument is invalid.

(B) The argument is valid.

(C) A valid argument is not available.

(D) The valid conclusion is I make money.

6. Consider the following argument:

> If a felony was involved, then the extradition papers were
>   signed.
> The extradition papers were not signed.
> Therefore, a felony was not involved.

(A) The argument is invalid.

(B) The argument is valid.

(C) A valid argument is not available.

(D) The valid conclusion is a felony was involved.

7. Consider the following argument:

> If Barry saw the sunset, then it was snowing.
> Barry saw the sunset.
> Therefore, it was snowing.

(A) The argument is invalid.

(B) The argument is valid.

(C) A valid argument is not possible.

(D) The valid conclusion is it was not snowing.

8. Mrs. Garcia was looking at her windows. One in her living room resembled the picture below. She said to her son Pedro, "All I can see is that pane of glass." What kind of perception is Mrs. Garcia using?

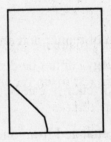

(A) Geometric

(B) Euclidean

(C) Projective

(D) Topologic

9. Aaron lived on one side of the river and Samuel on the other. The river is wide, very wide. Aaron knows that the river _____ Samuel and himself.

(A) connects

(B) is inside

(C) is outside

(D) is between

10. Why is 1/2 called a unit fraction?

(A) People frequently use the expressions half a unit, meaning half an inch or half cup, thus it is a unit fraction.

(B) The number two is in the denominator.

(C) It is between 0 and 1, the basic unit.

(D) Unit fractions have one in the numerator.

11. Which of the following does **not** have potential energy?

    I.   A moving automobile   IV. Gunpowder

    II. Expanding gas   V.   Stretched rubber band

    III. Water at the top of a dam

(A) I and II only.

(B) III and II only.

(C) III, IV, and V only.

(D) III only.

12. The law of conservation of matter and energy states

(A) that matter and energy cannot be destroyed.

(B) that either matter or energy can be changed into other forms of matter or energy.

(C) that energy can be changed from one form to another.

(D) All of the above.

13. Which of the following is true of Einstein's deduction(s) on the relationship between energy and mass?

(A) $e = mc^2$

(B) The total amount of matter and energy in the universe always stays the same.

(C) Matter cannot be changed into energy nor energy into matter.

(D) (A) and (B) only.

14. The result of a deficiency of calcium in the body is that

(A) the body converts carbon into calcium if the situation becomes critical.

(B) the vertebrate body "robs" calcium from the skeleton.

(C) the body fails to replace, atom for atom, the normal withdrawal.

(D) All the above.

15. Sound energy is a type of which of the following?

(A) Mechanical energy

(B) Electrical energy

(C) Wave energy

(D) Nuclear energy

16. All of the following statements about plants are true EXCEPT which one?

(A) The plant kingdom is divided into two major phyla called the tracheophytes and the bryophytes.

(B) The plant kingdom is divided into two broad groups: plants that produce seeds and plants that do not produce seeds.

(C) Plants are living things that can make their own food.

(D) Chlorosynthesis is the process by which plants utilize light energy to create their own food.

17. Which of the metric terms is most appropriate for measuring the height of a doorknob from the floor?

(A) Meter

(B) Liter

(C) Gram

(D) Decimeter

18. Which of the following is true of the roots of plants?

(A) Roots generally can do little to hold plants in the ground since most soils are so shallow.

(B) In a diffuse root system, there is a primary root that grows until it is the largest root in the root system.

(C) In a taproot system the primary taproot grows until it is the major root in the system.

(D) Only plants with a diffuse root system store food in the roots since the taproots live for such a short time.

19. Which of the following is the symbol on the periodic table for hydrogen?

   (A) H

   (B) Hy

   (C) He

   (D) Hi

20. Which of the following is **not** a mammal?

   (A) A shark

   (B) A whale

   (C) A gibbon

   (D) An elephant

21. Which of the following does **not** fall within the authority of most state governors?

   (A) Name a person to fill the unexpired term of one of the state's U.S. Senators

   (B) Call out the national guard to quell civil unrest

   (C) Veto laws passed by the legislature

   (D) Make foreign policy

22. In American government, "checks and balances" were developed to

   (A) regulate the amount of control each branch of government would have.

   (B) make each branch of government independent from one another.

   (C) give the president control.

   (D) give the Supreme Court control.

23. Indicate the correct chronological order of the Presidents.

   (A) Abraham Lincoln, Woodrow Wilson, Theodore Roosevelt, Franklin D. Roosevelt

   (B) Abraham Lincoln, Theodore Roosevelt, Woodrow Wilson, Franklin D. Roosevelt

   (C) Abraham Lincoln, Franklin D. Roosevelt, Woodrow Wilson, Theodore Roosevelt

(D) Abraham Lincoln, Woodrow Wilson, Franklin D. Roosevelt, Theodore Roosevelt

24. The practice of viewing other societies and cultures in terms of one's own cultural standards best describes

(A) Ethnocentrism.

(B) Institutionalization.

(C) Social Placement.

(D) Social Control.

25. The capacity of a person or social unit to exercise authority or influence on others, regardless of active resistance best describes

(A) wealth.

(B) prestige.

(C) power.

(D) status.

26. The Populists and Progressives are examples of political parties that developed

(A) as third party organizations outside the Democrat and Republican parties.

(B) to enlist support for the Democratic and Republican parties.

(C) to protest the current political parties.

(D) Both (A) and (C).

27. Which of the following states was not part of the original 13 colonies?

(A) Delaware

(B) Virginia

(C) Vermont

(D) Maryland

28. Which of the following was **not** a cause of the American Revolution?

(A) Alien and Sedition Acts

(B) Quebec Act

(C) Stamp Act

(D) Writs of Assistance

29. Directions: RELEVANT information will help us solve a problem or aid us in answering a question. IRRELEVANT information does not aid us in solving a problem or in answering a question. You are trying to answer the question "WHAT DO RECENT TRENDS IN TERRORIST ACTIVITY TELL US ABOUT THE TWO MAIN TYPES OF TERRORISM—LOCAL AND INTERNATIONAL?" To answer the question, you skim through a book containing different kinds of statistical information. Below are a list of the titles of the tables, graphs, and charts. Read each title and select the one that is irrelevant to the above question.

(A) "Terrorist Acts Involving Citizens or Territories or More Than One Nation (1985)"

(B) "International Terrorism Around the World (1984)"

(C) "U.S. Casualties (Wounded and Killed) of International Terrorism (1984)"

(D) "Local Terrorism Activities During the 1896 Haymarket Square Riot"

30. Directions: Read each of the following statements and select the one that NEITHER supports nor opposes the idea of assimilating immigrants into the United States.

(A) By being a haven for those being politically and religiously oppressed, the U.S. became rich in a variety of thoughts, ideas, and philosophies.

(B) If these immigrants are going to live in the U.S. they must learn our language. We don't have the time or the money to make signs that are written in more than one language.

(C) Between 1868 and 1882, more than 200,000 Chinese came to the U.S.

(D) Immigrants take jobs away from native Americans, causing higher unemployment. The foreigners come here looking for work. Each job they get is one less job for an American to fill.

31. Read the following statements and determine the one that supports the idea of government sponsored child care.

   (A) "Most parents choose not to send their children to licensed child care facilities."

   (B) "Experts predict that a two-year freeze in social spending could save $860 billion by 2015—a significant start on reducing the debt."

   (C) "Government-licensed child care centers would provide my kids a secure atmosphere and valuable early learning experiences."

   (D) "This is just another expensive government program that the taxpayers can't afford."

32. Medicare and Medicaid were two programs that were part of a government financed health system introduced during the administration of

   (A) Lyndon Johnson (1963-1969).

   (B) Richard Nixon (1969-1974).

   (C) Gerald Ford (1974-1977).

   (D) Jimmy Carter (1977-1981).

33. The Arab oil embargo of 1973 had a great impact on life in the United States. One of the root causes of this embargo was

   (A) the cheap prices that OPEC (the Organization of Petroleum Exporting Countries) was charging for a barrel of oil.

   (B) Jimmy Carter's energy policies.

   (C) the United States' support of Israel in the Middle East.

   (D) the 1980 oil glut.

34. The writings of John Locke and Montesquieu, European philosophers who believed in democracy, influenced our structure of government. They advocated

   (A) parliamentary democracy.

   (B) a system of checks and balances.

   (C) strong local governments, followed by weak state and national governments.

   (D) direct election to the Supreme Court.

35. Women got the right to vote

    (A) with the Emancipation Proclamation.

    (B) with the Bill of Rights.

    (C) after WWI.

    (D) after WWII.

36. Tension between two different economies also contributed to the Civil War. The agrarian South was in conflict with the _____ North.

    (A) industrial

    (B) farming

    (C) seafaring

    (D) slave-owning

37. Which of the following is correctly matched with the following map of Southeast Asia?

    (A) Sri Lanka

    (B) Burma

    (C) Thailand

    (D) India

38. Where is Central America located on the following map?

(A) A

(B) B

(C) C

(D) D

39. Capitalism describes the American economic system. It got its name because

(A) it was first described by Alfred Benson Capital.

(B) it was first used in Washington, D.C.

(C) it is a different type of communism.

(D) money, also called capital, is invested for personal profit.

40. Countries with very little rainfall have a problem growing food. They usually have to

(A) use salt water from the closest ocean to grow crops.

(B) change to a more centralized economy.

(C) plant fruit orchards instead of crops.

(D) install irrigation systems to grow crops.

41. Which of the following best describes the example pictured above?

    (A) Monumental architecture dominates the scene.

    (B) The scene is viewed from the window of a passing train.

    (C) Human drama is the artist's main concern.

    (D) The scene is viewed as though from a second-story window.

David Smith, Cube Series, 1964

42. Which of the following is probably true of the sculpture pictured on the previous page?

   (A) The artist modelled it with his hands.

   (B) The artist poured it into a mold.

   (C) The artist shaped his materials with a blowtorch and welding tools.

   (D) The artist shaped natural materials with a chisel.

Questions 43–45 refer to the following excerpts.

(A)   Where the Bee Sucks, There Suck I
       Where the bee sucks, there suck I:
       In a cowslip's bell I lie;
       There I couch when owls do cry.
       On the bat's back I do fly
       After summer merrily.
       Merrily, merrily shall I live now
       Under the blossom that hangs on the bough.

               William Shakespeare

(B)   George had turned at the sound of her arrival. For a moment he
       contemplated her, as one who had fallen out of heaven. He saw radiant
       joy in her face, he saw the flowers beat against her dress in blue waves.
       The bushes above them closed. He stepped quickly forward and kissed
       her.

       From *A Room with a View*

(C)   Life, how and what is it? As here I lie
       In this state chamber, dying by degrees,
       Hours and long hours in the dead night, I ask
       "Do I live, am I dead?" Peace, peace seems all.
       Saint Praxed's ever was the church for peace;
       And so, about this tomb of mine.

       From *St. Praxed's*

(D)   Generous tears filled Gabriel's eyes. He had never felt like that
       himself towards any woman but he knew that such a feeling must be love.
       The tears gathered more thickly in his eyes and in the partial darkness
       he imagined he saw the form of a young man standing under a dripping

tree. Other forms were near. His soul had approached that region where dwell the vast hosts of the dead. He was conscious of, but could not apprehend their wayward and flickering existence. His own identity was fading out into a grey impalpable world: the solid world itself which these dead had one time reared and lived in was dissolving and dwindling.

From *The Dubliners*

43. Which speaker considers himself a part of nature?

44. Which passage is most likely taken from a dramatic monologue?

45. Which speaker has just experienced a personal revelation?

Tawaraya Sotatsu and Hon-Ami Roetsu, *Deer and Calligraphy*

46. Which of the following is the most important artistic device in the example shown above?

(A) Line

(B) Tone

(C) Color

(D) Volume

Banqueting House at Whitehall, Inigo Jones, London, 1619.

47. Which of the following **does not** contribute to order and regularity in the example pictured above?

(A) The repeated second-story window design

(B) A facade which lacks deep recesses and voids

(C) The use of columns at the center and corners of the building

(D) A subtle use of the arch

Jacques Louis David, *Oath of the Horatii*, 1784.

48. In the painting illustrated on the previous page, all of the following are important compositional devices EXCEPT

    (A) the perspective grid of the checkerboard floor.

    (B) the strong highlighting of the foreground figures.

    (C) the arcade of arches in the background.

    (D) the vigorous movement of the main figure group.

49. The building pictured above was produced in which of the following countries?

    (A) Japan

    (B) Indonesia

    (C) Easter Island

    (D) Greece

Questions 50–52 refer to the following excerpts.

(A) For shade to shade will come too drowsily,

   And drown the wakeful anguish of the soul.

(B) Rocks, caves, lakes, fens, bogs, dens, and shades of death.

(C) ... yet from these flames

No light, but rather darkness visible

(D) Because I could not stop for Death—

He kindly stopped for me—

50. Which passage contains an oxymoron?   C

51. Which passage uses assonance?   B

52. Which passage is written in iambic pentameter? D A

Questions 53–54 refer to the following passage.

Come, now, there may as well be an end of this! Every time I meet your eyes squarely I detect the question just slipping out of them. If you had spoken it, or even boldly looked it; if you had shown in your motions the least sign of a fussy or fidgety concern on my account; if this were not the evening of my birthday and you the only friend who remembered it; if confession were not good for the soul, though harder than sin to some people, of whom I am one,—well, if all reasons were not at this instant converged into a focus, and burning me rather violently in that region where the seat of emotion is supposed to lie, I should keep my trouble to myself.

Bayaro Taylor, Beauty and the Beast, Tales from Home (1872)

53. The speaker of the above passage feels

(A) guilty.

(B) anxious.

(C) ashamed.

(D) sorrowful.

54. The speaker feels that confession is

(A) unnecessary.

(B) nonsensical.

(C) healthy.

(D) impossible.

Questions 55–57 refer to the following examples.

(A) Subjects Bringing Gifts to the King (detail) from the stairway to the royal audience hall, Persepolis c. 500 B.C. Limestone

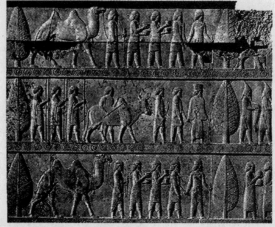

(B) King Smenkhkare and Meritaten Tel-el-Amanra, c. 1360 B.C.

(C) The Warrior Vase, Mycenae, c. 1200 B.C.

(D) Psalm 150, from the Utrecht Psaltar c. 830

55. Which example seeks to give a schematic representation of a ceremonial event?

56. In which example is the human figure most stylized and repeated in order to fit its container?

57. In which example do the figures show the greatest tendency toward rhythmic calligraphy?

Questions 58–59 refer to the following poem.

The Sick Rose

O Rose, thou art sick.
The invisible worm
That flies in the night
In the howling storm

Has found out thy bed
Of crimson joy,
And his dárk sécret love
Does thy life destroy.

William Blake

58. The imagery in this poem is mainly

    (A) religious.

    (B) sexual.

    (C) animal.

    (D) light.

59. The word "life" in line 8 means

    (A) passion.

    (B) spirit.

    (C) love.

    (D) beauty.

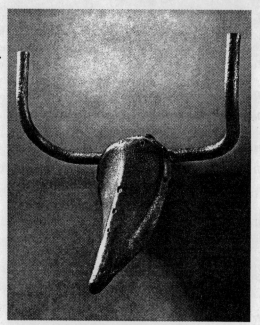

Pablo Picasso, Bull's Head, 1943.

60. In combining found objects to make the sculpture shown above, the artist sought to create

    (A) a contrast of line and tone.

    (B) a religious symbol.

    (C) a visual analogy to a living creature.

    (D) a metaphor for human experience.

Questions 61–65 refer to the following passage.

Spa water quality is maintained through a filter to ensure cleanliness and clarity. Wastes such as perspiration, hairspray, and lotions which cannot be removed by the spa filter can be controlled by shock treatment or super chlorination every other week. Although the filter traps most of the solid material, to control bacteria and algae and to oxidize any organic material, the addition of disinfectants such as bromine or chlorine is necessary.

As all water solutions have a pH which controls corrosion, proper pH balance is also necessary. A pH measurement determines if the water is acid or alkaline. Based on a 14-point scale, a pH reading of 7.0 is considered neutral while a lower reading is considered acidic, and a higher reading indicates alkalinity or basic. High pH (above 7.6) reduces sanitizer efficiency, clouds water, promotes scale formation on surfaces and equipment, and interferes with filter operation. When pH is high, add a pH decrease such as sodium bisulphate (e.g., Spa Down). Because the spa water is hot, scale is deposited more rapidly. A weekly dose of a stain and scale fighter also will help to control this problem. Low pH (below 7.2) is equally damaging, causing equipment corrosion, water which is irritating, and rapid sanitizer dissipation. To increase pH add sodium bicarbonate (e.g., Spa Up).

The recommended operating temperature of a spa (98° – 104°) is a fertile environment for the growth of bacteria and virus. This growth is prevented when appropriate sanitizer levels are continuously monitored. Bacteria can also be controlled by maintaining a proper bromine level of 3.0 to 5.0 parts per million (ppm) or a chlorine level of 1.0 – 2.0 ppm. As bromine tablets should not be added directly to the water, a bromine floater will properly dispense the tablets. Should chlorine be the chosen sanitizer, a granular form is recommended, as liquid chlorine or tablets are too harsh for the spa.

61. Although proper chemical and temperature maintenance of spa water is necessary, the most important condition to monitor is

    (A) preventing growth of bacteria and virus.

    (B) preventing equipment corrosion.

    (C) preventing soap build up.

    (D) preventing scale formation.

62. Of the chemical and temperature conditions in a spa, the condition most dangerous to one's health is

    (A) spa water temperature above 104°.

    (B) bromine level between 3.0 and 5.0.

    (C) pH level below 7.2.

    (D) spa water temperature between 90° and 104°.

63. The primary purpose of the passage is to

    (A) relate that maintenance of a spa can negate the full enjoyment of the spa experience.

    (B) provide evidence that spas are not a viable alternative to swimming pools.

    (C) convey that the maintenance of a spa is expensive and time consuming.

    (D) explain the importance of proper spa maintenance.

64. The spa filter can be relied upon to

    (A) control algae and bacteria.

    (B) trap most solid material.

    (C) oxidize organic material.

    (D) assure an adequate level of sanitation.

65. Which chemical should one avoid when maintaining a spa?

    (A) Liquid chlorine

    (B) Bromine

    (C) Sodium bisulfate

    (D) Baking soda

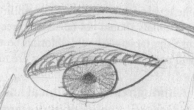

Questions 66–70 refer to the following passage.

The relationship of story elements found in children's generated stories to reading achievement was analyzed. Correlations ranged from .61101 (p = .64) at the beginning of first grade to .83546 (p = .24) at the end of first grade, to .85126 (p = .21) at the end of second grade, and to .82588 (p = .26) for fifth/sixth grades. Overall, the correlation of the story elements to reading achievement appeared to indicate a high positive correlation trend even though it was not statistically significant.

Multiple regression equation analyses dealt with the relative contribution of the story elements to reading achievement. The contribution of certain story elements was substantial. At the beginning of first grade, story conventions added 40 percent to the total variance while the other increments were not significant. At the end of first grade, story plot contributed 44 percent to the total variance, story conventions contributed 20 percent, and story sources contributed 17 percent. At the end of second grade, the story elements contributed more equal percentages to the total partial correlation of .8513. Although none of the percentages were substantial, story plot (.2200), clausal connectors (.1858), and T-units (.1590) contributed the most to the total partial correlation. By the fifth and sixth grades three other story elements—T-units (.2241), story characters (.3214), and clausal connectors (.1212)—contributed most to the total partial correlation. None of these percentages were substantial.

66. Which of the following is the most complete and accurate definition of the term "statistically significant" as used in the passage?

    (A) Consists of important numerical data

(B) Is educationally significant

(C) Departs greatly from chance expectations

(D) Permits prediction of reading achievement by knowing the story elements

67. The passage suggests which of the following conclusions about the correlation of story elements to reading achievement?

(A) That there are other more important story elements that should also be included in the analyses

(B) That children's inclusion of story elements in their stories causes them to achieve higher levels in reading

(C) That these story elements are important variables to consider in reading achievement

(D) That correlations of more than 1.0 are needed for this study to be statistically significant

68. The relative contribution of story conventions and story plot in first grade suggests that

(A) children may have spontaneously picked up these story elements as a result of their exposure to stories.

(B) children have been explicitly taught these story elements.

(C) these story elements were not important because in fifth/sixth grades other story elements contributed more to the total partial correlation.

(D) other story elements were more substantial.

69. The content of the passage suggests that the passage would most likely appear in which of the following?

(A) *Psychology Today*

(B) *The Creative Writer*

(C) *Educational Leadership*

(D) *Reading Research Quarterly*

70. "None of these percentages were substantial" is the last statement in the passage. It refers to

(A) the story elements for fifth/sixth grades.

(B) the story elements for second grade.

(C) the story elements at the end of first grade.

(D) the story elements at the beginning of first grade.

Questions 71–73 refer to the following passage.

There is an importance of learning communication and meaning in language. Yet the use of notions such as communication and meaning as the basic criteria for instruction, experiences, and materials in classrooms may misguide a child in several respects. Communication in the classroom is vital. The teacher should use communication to help students develop the capacity to make their private responses become public responses. Otherwise, one's use of language would be in danger of being what the younger generation refers to as mere words, mere thoughts, and mere feelings.

Learning theorists emphasize specific components of learning: behaviorists stress behavior in learning; humanists stress the affective in learning; and cognitivists stress cognition in learning. All three of these components occur simultaneously and cannot be separated from each other in the learning process. In 1957, Festinger referred to dissonance as the lack of harmony between what one does (behavior) and what one believes (attitude). Attempts to separate the components of learning either knowingly or unknowingly create dissonances wherein language, thought, feeling, and behavior become diminished of authenticity. As a result, ideas and concepts lose their content and vitality, and the manipulation and politics of communication assume prominence.

71. Which of the following best describes the author's attitude toward the subject discussed?

(A) An informed concern

(B) A mild frustration

(C) A moral indignation

(D) A passive resignation

72. The primary purpose of the passage is to

(A) explain the criteria for providing authentic communication in classroom learning.

(B) discuss the relationships between learning and communication.

(C) assure teachers that communication and meaning are the basic criteria for learning in classrooms.

(D) stress the importance of providing authentic communication in classroom learning.

73. Which of the following is the most complete and accurate definition of the term "mere" as used in the passage?

(A) Small

(B) Minor

(C) Little

(D) Poor

Questions 74–76 refer to the following passage.

In 1975, Sinclair observed that it had often been supposed that the main factor in learning to talk is being able to imitate. Schlesinger (1975) noted that at certain stages of learning to speak, a child tends to imitate everything an adult says to him or her, and it therefore seems reasonable to accord to such imitation an important role in the acquisition of language.

Moreover, various investigators have attempted to explain the role of imitation in language. In his discussion of the development of imitation and cognition of adult speech sounds, Nakazema (1975) stated that although the parent's talking stimulates and accelerates the infant's articulatory activity, the parent's phoneme system does not influence the child's articulatory mechanisms. Slobin and Welsh (1973) suggested that imitation is the reconstruction of the adult's utterance and that the child does so by employing the grammatical rules that he has developed at a specific time. Schlesinger proposed that by imitating the adult the child practices new grammatical constructions. Brown and Bellugi (1964) noted that a child's imitations resemble spontaneous speech in that they drop inflections, most function words, and sometimes other words. However, the word order of imitated sentences usually was preserved. Brown and Bellugi assumed that imitation is a function of what the child attended to or remembered. Shipley et al. (1969) suggested that repeating an adult's utterance assists the child's comprehension. Ervin (1964) and Braine (1971) found that a child's imitations do not contain more advanced structures than his or her spontaneous utterances; thus, imitation can no longer be regarded as the simple behavioristic act that earlier scholars assumed it to be.

74. The author of the passage would tend to agree with which of the following statements?

(A) Apparently, children are physiologically unable to imitate a parent's phoneme system.

(B) Apparently, children require practice with more advanced structures before they are able to imitate.

(C) Apparently, children only imitate what they already do, using whatever is in their repertoire.

(D) Apparently, the main factor in learning to talk remains being able to imitate.

75. The primary purpose of the passage is to

(A) explain language acquisition.

(B) explain the role of imitation in language acquisition.

(C) assure parents of their role in assisting imitation in language acquisition.

(D) relate the history of imitation in language acquisition.

76. An inference that parents may make from the passage is that they should

(A) be concerned when a child imitates their language.

(B) focus on developing imitation in their child's language.

(C) realize that their child's imitations may reflect several aspects of language acquisition.

(D) realize that their talking may over-stimulate their child's articulatory activity.

Questions 77-78 refer to the following passage.

A major problem with reading/language arts instruction is that practice assignments from workbooks often provide short, segmented activities that do not really resemble the true act of reading. Perhaps more than any computer application, word processing is capable of addressing these issues.

77. The author would tend to agree that a major benefit of computers in reading/language arts instruction is

(A) that the reading act may be more closely resembled.

(B) that short segmented assignments will be eliminated.

(C) that the issues in reading/language arts instruction will be addressed.

(D) that computer application will be limited to word processing.

78. The appropriate use of a word processor to assist in making practice resemble a reading act is

 (A) detailed.

 (B) desirable.

 (C) unstated.

 (D) alluded.

Questions 79–80 refer to the following passage.

In view of the current emphasis on literature-based reading instruction, a greater understanding by teachers of variance in cultural, language, and story components should assist in narrowing the gap between reader and text and improve reading comprehension. Classroom teachers should begin with students' meaning and intentions about stories before moving students to the commonalities of story meaning based on common background and culture. With teacher guidance, students should develop a fuller understanding of how complex narratives are when they are generating stories as well as when they are reading stories.

79. Which of the following is the intended audience for the passage?

 (A) Students in a reading class

 (B) Teachers using literature-based curriculum

 (C) Professors teaching a literature course

 (D) Parents concerned about their child's comprehension of books

80. Which of the following is the most complete and accurate definition of the term "variance" as used in the passage?

 (A) Change

 (B) Fluctuations

 (C) Diversity

 (D) Deviation

Section 2: Written Assignment

DIRECTIONS: Plan and write an essay on the topic given below. DO NOT WRITE ON ANY TOPIC OTHER THAN THE ONE SPECIFIED. AN ESSAY ON ANY OTHER TOPIC IS UNACCEPTABLE.

Essay Topic:

"There is a wonderful, mystical law of nature that the three things we crave most in life — happiness, freedom, and peace of mind — are always attained by giving them to someone else."

Assignment:

Do you agree or disagree with the statement? Support your opinion with specific examples from history, current events, literature, or personal experience.

ATS-W ELEMENTARY/ SECONDARY PRACTICE TEST 3

TIME: 4 Hours
80 Multiple-Choice Questions, 1 Essay

SECTION 1

> **DIRECTIONS:** Read each stimulus carefully, and answer the questions that follow. Mark your responses on the answer sheet provided.

1. One Monday morning, Ms. Axtel arrives early for school. She notices that Angela, a second-grade student in her class, is waiting outside the front door even though it is at least an hour before the earliest bus should arrive. When Ms. Axtel stops to ask Angela if she is all right, Angela begins to cry. Ms. Axtel notices several large bruises on her legs and arms. It is Ms. Axtel's responsibility to

    (A) notify the principal as soon as possible that she suspects that Angela may have been beaten or abused.

    (B) comfort Angela and call her mother later in the day to learn what happened.

    (C) recognize that Angela must have misbehaved and was punished by her parents.

    (D) learn more about Angela's family before making any other decisions.

2. Ms. Axtel realizes that she has much to learn about the second-grade curriculum. Which of the following would probably be the best way to quickly acquaint herself with the curriculum and materials used in her school?

   (A) She should ask the other second grade teachers in her school for assistance.

   (B) She should call the local textbook representative and arrange a time to meet.

   (C) She should study the scope and sequence provided by each publisher for the text used in second grade.

   (D) She realizes that the best way to become acquainted with a curriculum is over time, and not to be in a hurry to learn it.

3. Ms. Axtel's school district requires teachers to attend one in-service session per month. The in-service workshop this month is about the special needs of emotionally disturbed children. None of the children in Ms. Axtel's class have been identified as emotionally disturbed. There are no other in-service workshops offered this month. What should Ms. Axtel do?

   (A) Skip the in-service, stay home, and prepare for future lessons

   (B) Complain to the principal about the lack of choices and stay home in protest

   (C) Attend the in-service because she might have an emotionally disturbed student in the future.

   (D) Attend the in-service but plan to leave early

Buzz Huerta is a first-year teacher in a town of 30,000 in New York State. Buzz was one of the top students in the teacher education department of his university. He is highly dedicated to both his students and to the school district where he is employed. Buzz makes his instructional decisions based upon sound educational theory and research.

Buzz is teaching sixth grade. He has organized his classroom into a self-governing body which is conceptualized as "The Family." Each student has a "twin" of the same gender who serves as his/her thinking/working partner. Each pair of twins has a second pair of twins (either the same or opposite gender) with whom they make up a sib-group. Dividing The Family into sib-groups allows Buzz to have stable heterogeneous cooperative groups of four, yet maintain the sense of class unity that the family metaphor provides.

While the class is largely self-governing, Buzz retains final authority over all classroom life. He seldom feels the need to exert his authority, but when he feels the need to do so, he does not hesitate, and the students take appropriate note.

Elena Monteverde ran up to Buzz Huerta as he was finishing grading a math assignment before school.

"Mr. H.," said Elena. "Look at this."

Elena handed Buzz a news clipping about a pen pal program which matches a North American class with a South American class. "Can we do this?"

Buzz read the clipping and struggled to keep from smiling.

"Sounds interesting," he said. "What do you think?"

"I think it would be neat. We could learn a lot."

"You might be right. What should you do first?"

Elena furrowed her brow for a moment. "I know. Maybe we should ask the class to vote on it."

"Good idea," said Buzz. "Tomorrow is class meeting day. Ask Freeman to put it on the agenda for new business."

4. Buzz had planned to begin a unit on South America the following week. Why didn't he tell Elena that when she approached him with the idea of South American pen pals?

    (A) Buzz wanted to give Elena and the class a delightful surprise when he announced the study unit on South America following the class's vote on the pen pal project; he knew that the surprise would provide a strong motivational basis for the unit.

    (B) Buzz wanted Elena and the class to feel ownership of the pen pal activity and subsequently of the South American unit of study. He knew that it would appear to the students that the South American unit had grown out of the pen pal project. Buzz knew that this sense of ownership of the South American unit would provide a strong motivational base.

    (C) Buzz didn't want Elena and the class to start thinking about the South American unit before they finished with the current unit; he knew that the quality of the present unit would suffer if Elena and the class became excited thinking about the next unit of study.

(D) Buzz wanted Elena to assess her own understanding of the pen pal activity; he did not want to complicate the issue by introducing new information related to the unit of study.

5. Instead of praising Elena for her suggestion, Buzz told her that her idea "sounded interesting," and he asked her what she thought about the idea. Evaluate this strategy.

(A) This was a poor strategy. Buzz should have reinforced Elena for bringing her idea to him, therefore assuring that she would continue to share her ideas with him.

(B) This was a good strategy. Buzz's response probed Elena to evaluate her own thinking, thus promoting a climate of active inquiry.

(C) This was a good strategy. Buzz understands cognitive child development and used this opportunity to assess Elena's cognitive development.

(D) This was a poor strategy. Buzz understands the outside factors that affect a child's learning. Since the clipping about the pen pals resulted from an outside factor, he was assessing the impact of this outside influence. However, that was not an appropriate strategy, since he should have reinforced her instead.

6. Buzz then asks Elena, "What should you do first?" What was his purpose in asking this particular question in this way?

(A) He wanted to scaffold her in problem solving.

(B) He wanted to encourage her to make her own decision about the project.

(C) He wanted her to consider all of the alternatives available to her.

(D) He wanted to reinforce her initiative by prolonging the conversation.

7. Near the end of their encounter, Buzz says, "Good idea." Why?

(A) Buzz is trying to increase Elena's self-esteem.

(B) Buzz is signalling Elena that the conversational transaction has been completed.

(C) Buzz is attempting to reinforce Elena for her self-evaluative behavior.

(D) Buzz is attempting to reinforce Elena for suggesting that the idea be put to a vote of the class.

At noon, Buzz goes to the cafeteria for lunch. Buzz knows that the cafeteria is serving Sloppy Joes today, which Buzz does not like very well. He would prefer to spend the break in his room reading and drinking a diet soda, but he nevertheless takes a tray and joins his colleagues at the faculty table.

"How's the Family Man?" asks Tom Reynolds as he motions to the empty seat beside him.

Buzz grins. He is growing used to the teasing of the older teachers who do not understand his use of the family metaphor as a classroom organizational framework. "The Family Man is rolling along," he says.

As they eat, Buzz tells Melody Wilson, the choir teacher, that he is beginning a unit on South America soon. He asks her whether she might be able to incorporate some South American music into her curriculum during the next month. She tells him that she has several Latin American songs that she usually teaches later in the year, but that she can move them up and accommodate him. Although music is not an interest of his, Buzz asks her to tell him what makes Hispanic music sound so different from the traditional American forms of music. Melody enters into a rather complicated discussion of Latin melodic structures. Buzz nods and listens carefully.

When he leaves, Tom Reynolds says, "So long, Family Man" and Buzz salutes him.

"I think this family thing you do is interesting," says Melody. "I'd like to know more about it."

8. Why does Buzz choose to eat lunch in the cafeteria?

(A) Buzz knows that first-year teachers are at increased risk of illness and understands the importance of maintaining good nutrition during this crucial year.

(B) Buzz wants to set a good example for his students by eating in the cafeteria.

(C) Buzz wants to know more about South American music and hopes to find Ms. Wilson in the cafeteria so that he can ask her to explain its elements to him.

(D) Buzz is trying to promote collegiality, thereby creating a school culture that enhances learning and encourages positive change.

9. Buzz is pleased that Melody has asked about his classroom organization. What does he tell her?

(A) Since he does not have a family of his own, Buzz feels like the children belong to him.

(B) Buzz has found the family metaphor to be the best organizational framework to help him cover the most amount of material in the least amount of time.

(C) Since his class is heavily Hispanic and African-American, Buzz employs the family metaphor because this appears to be a culturally appropriate structure for teaching field-dependent students.

(D) Since his class is heavily Hispanic and African-American, Buzz employs the family metaphor because this appears to be a culturally appropriate structure for teaching field-independent students.

On Class Meeting Day, Freeman Morgan asks Elena to present her pen pal idea to The Family. Elena's classroom twin moves that The Family write for pen pals; another sib in her sib-group seconds the motion. The motion carries 14-2.

The two votes against the motion are cast by Dave Botts and Norman Rogers. Both boys are students who are diagnosed as having special needs and who attend the resource room for literacy help and social skills instruction for one hour each day. Before this year, the boys attended a self-contained class for five hours daily. This year, however, the district has implemented an inclusion program, and the boys' ARD committees wrote IEP's that placed them in Buzz's class. Both boys' IEP's require that they participate in all classroom activities for the time that they are in their inclusion classes, and that individual support be provided as necessary in order to assure them an appropriate education.

10. What are the likely reasons that Dave and Norman rejected the motion?

    I.   They don't like Elena.

    II. They don't know what a pen pal is.

    III. They don't want to have to do something that requires them to write.

    IV. They are prejudiced against people from South America.

    (A) I and IV only.   (B) II and III only.

    (C) II and IV only.   (D) IV only.

11. Since Dave and Norman both have disabilities and don't want to participate, what should Buzz do?

    (A) Exempt them from participating in the activity and have them spend pen pal time in the resource room.

    (B) Exempt them from participating in the activity but let them stay in the classroom with the rest of The Family during pen pal time.

    (C) Require them to participate, but encourage them and tell them just to do the best that they can.

    (D) Require them to participate, but provide them with individual assistance if needed.

After the vote, Buzz assumed leadership of the class. "We are going to be studying South America this semester," he said. "Would you like to go ahead and start our South America unit next week so that we can all learn more about South America before we write?" Buzz then tells each sib-group to discuss this idea and report back. All of the groups respond positively.

"Fine," he said. "Each sib-group will choose one country in South America. Your group will study your chosen country and become our resident experts on it. You may approach this in any way you like. For example, you may want to tell about folkways of the country. You may want to wear clothing or bring food from the country. Perhaps you'd like to make a papier-mache map of the country or show a short video about it. Or see if you can find a laser disk. However your group chooses to approach the project is the right way for you. There is no right or wrong way to do this. Each person in your group might do a different part, or you might choose to do all work on each part together. Your group will then teach a lesson to the rest of the class about your country."

12. Why does Buzz choose to approach the unit in this way when he could present the material more quickly and complete the unit faster than the students can working in teams?

(A) He employs a constructivist perspective of learning.

(B) He knows that the children will enjoy the project more if they work in teams.

(C) He is constrained by state curriculum which mandates that students work in groups on social studies assignments.

(D) He is required by the IEP's of Dave and Norman to organize his class into cooperative groups since this is the way in which Dave and Norman learn best.

13. What term best describes the type of cooperative grouping activity that Buzz is using for this unit?

(A) STAD

(B) TGT

(C) Jigsaw

(D) Group Investigation

On the first Wednesday of the South America unit, Buzz loads all the students into a school minivan and drives them to the local library. Buzz asks Betty Kelly, the librarian, to take eight of the students to the periodical section to teach them how to use the *Readers' Guide to Periodical Literature*. Buzz takes the other eight students and teaches them how to use a computer based book search. Buzz and Betty then exchange students.

14. Why does Buzz take the class to the local library?

(A) Buzz understands the relationship of the school to the larger community in general and to the library in particular. He wants to develop a mutually supportive relationship between his students and the community.

(B) Buzz cannot provide his students with the variety of materials that they need in order to complete their four units of study. Only by taking them to the library to secure resources can he provide them with a sufficient variety of learning materials.

(C) Buzz wants to make use of the library in order to forge strong home-school relationships.

(D) Buzz appreciates student and family diversity and wants to promote it through the use of the local library.

15. Why does Buzz ask Betty Kelly to take half of the students while he takes the other half?

(A) He does not know how to use the periodical section of the library as well as the librarian does.

(B) He needs to keep closer track of his special needs students than he can do if he has all 16 children at once.

(C) He knows how to use a variety of resources to support student learning.

(D) He wants to promote outcome-oriented behavior in his students.

At the library, Buzz shows the students how to find books and nonprint materials on their South American countries. He helps his students select 14 books, two laser video discs, one software game that teaches Spanish, and the computer game "Where in the World is Carmen Sandiego?" Betty Kelly helps the students select 17 magazine articles about their South American countries.

At the front desk, a well-dressed woman bystander criticizes Buzz's decision to allow the students to check out nonprint materials. She introduces herself as a retired English professor from a respected university. "You know, young man, it's no wonder that kids these days can't read. They ought to be checking out books and magazine articles exclusively. Checking out computer games and videos doesn't teach children to read. If we don't get back to the basics of reading and writing, we're going to become a third world country. Teach the children to read. They have enough time to play at home, when our tax dollars aren't paying for it."

16. Which of the following statements are true?

    I.   The bystander was right. Instructional time should be spent on printed material rather than on computer games and video material. Children spend many hours engaged in these activities on their own time. School time must be reserved for books and traditional printed matter.

    II. The bystander was wrong. It is important to use a variety of instructional materials to support student learning.

    III. Computers and laser disks are important technologies for students to master. They are best mastered within the context of learning academic content, rather than in decontextualized settings.

    IV. Computers and laser disks are important technologies for students to master. They are best mastered in computer literacy classes which should be offered to all students. Only in decontextualizing technology will students be able to master it and generalize skills.

    (A) I only.   (B) II and III only.

    (C) II and IV only.   (D) IV only.

"I have an idea," said Buzz to the class on the morning after the library visit. "What do you think about each sib-group inviting their parents to come to school the day that group gives their presentation?"

The class discussed this idea at length. Although Marianne Griego is a developmentally-advanced, mature child who comes from a supportive, well-educated family, she leads the resistance to inviting the parents. Four other girls of varying degrees of maturity join Marianne's camp, but the majority vote to invite the parents.

17. What is the most likely reason that Marianne does not want to invite her parents?

    (A) Marianne is embarrassed because her parents are more educated and more well-dressed than the parents of many of the other children.

    (B) Marianne's parents want to move her to a private school. She is afraid that when they find that she is working in a group with students who are less able than she that they will pull her out of public school.

(C) Marianne has moved into the developmental level in which she is beginning to separate from her family and emotionally move toward her peers. She feels embarrassed when her parents treat her like a child in front of her peers and teachers.

(D) Marianne has a crush on Mr. Huerta. She is afraid that her parents will tell him and thereby embarrass her in front of him and her friends.

18. Why does Buzz suggest that the students invite their parents to watch them present their projects?

(A) Buzz wants to curry strong home-school relationships.

(B) Buzz knows that the students will be nervous since this is their first class presentation. He wants to make them feel less anxious by having their parents present.

(C) Buzz understands the interrelationship between the school and the larger community. He wants to create strong school-community bonds.

(D) Buzz knows that having their parents present will provide a strong motivator for excellence on the part of his students.

On the day of the first class presentation, Buzz developed the following form to complete on each group:

> Did sib-group demonstrate:
>
> 1. Higher level thinking skills? How?
> 2. Ability to use technology? How?
> 3. Involvement of all sibs? How?
> 4. Use of in-school resources? Which?
> 5. Use of community resources? Which?
> 6. Evidence of problem-solving skills? How?
> 7. Which of these should I target next time?

19. Buzz developed this form in order to conduct what type of assessment?

    (A) Informal assessment to shape instruction

    (B) Informal assessment to understand individual learners

    (C) Formal assessment to monitor instructional effectiveness

    (D) Formal assessment to understand individual learners

Buzz asked the school counselor, the resource teacher, the principal and her staff, and the fifth-grade teacher whose children were in music class at that time to also attend his children's presentations. Unknown to his students, Buzz gave each confederate a question to ask, and requested that they each preface the question with a statement somewhat similar to the following: "I would like to know more about what you said regarding _____ in your presentation. This is a topic of interest to me and about which I would like to learn more."

20. What was Buzz's purpose in using his colleagues in this way?

    (A) Buzz wants to use a variety of instructional strategies in order to make his students become self-directed problem solvers.

    (B) Buzz wants to use the questions as a form of formal assessment.

    (C) Buzz wants his colleagues to become reflective professionals who know how to promote their own intellectual growth.

    (D) Buzz wants his students to see adults model the behavior of being lifelong learners.

The day following the last of the group presentations, Buzz gave direct instruction to the class in order to fill in any gaps which he thought were important to the students' understanding of the unit on their South American countries. Then, on the following day, he allowed the students to work in their cooperative groups on a review for a test to be given the following day. The test was an objective multiple-choice test covering all four countries. Here is the first page showing the first five of the 25 multiple-choice items on the test.

---

1. Which country has Bogota as its capital?
   a. Colombia
   b. Argentina
   c. Chile

2. Which country is the most likely to directly affect the climate of the United States?
   a. Brazil
   b. Chile
   c. Paraguay

3. Where would the people be most likely to wear little clothing year round?
   a. Southern Colombia
   b. Central Chile
   c. Southern Argentina

4. Which country is the largest?
   a. Colombia
   b. Argentina
   c. Brazil

5. Which of these things most closely ties together Brazil and Argentina?
   a. Religion
   b. Language
   c. Vegetation

---

21. Based upon these sample questions, what type of knowledge does the multiple-choice section of the test assess?

    (A) Lower level thinking only

    (B) Higher level thinking only

    (C) Both higher and lower level thinking

    (D) Informational knowledge only

22. Which one of the following best describes the purpose of this assessment?

    (A) A summative assessment of individual learners

    (B) A summative assessment of group performance

(C) A formative assessment to shape future instruction

(D) A formative assessment to understand individual learners

23. In planning his next social studies unit, what factors should Buzz take into consideration in planning instruction for the group?

I. State curriculum guidelines

II. The results of the assessment conducted in sample test

III. His proposed learner outcomes

IV. The IEP's of his students with disabilities

(A) I and III only. (B) I, II, and III only.

(C) II and IV only. (D) I only.

Mr. Treskoski is a first-year teacher who has recently moved from another state to a small town in New York State. In his sixth-grade social studies class, Mr. Treskoski has his students read the local newspaper each Monday in order to increase their understanding of and involvement in civic issues at the local and national levels. In addition, the students are assigned to watch the local and national news at home on either Tuesday nights or Wednesday mornings in order to use this information to supplement their understanding of the issues.

For several weeks, the class has been following the upcoming mayoral election. The incumbent mayor, The Honorable Mayor Lucinda Griego, is running for reelection against a political newcomer, Tambra Crumpler. While Mayor Griego has a strong record of advocating for better living conditions for all the citizens of the town, Candidate Crumpler is an attorney whose platform is based upon taking a strong stand in combatting the illicit gangs which she says are creeping into the community.

When the class is discussing the candidates' platforms, Molly Winters says, "My dad says that there isn't a gang problem here. He told me that it's just news media hype to sell papers and to get Ms. Crumpler elected. What do you think, Mr. T?"

As one, the students turn their eyes to Mr. Treskoski.

"That's an interesting thought," says Mr. Treskoski. "Let me think about that and get back to you tomorrow. I'll need to do some research before I decide what I think. But right now, let's talk about what you think."

24. Mr. Treskoski's statement about doing research before making a decision reflects

   (A) using planning processes to design outcome-oriented learning.

   (B) being a reflective practitioner who knows how to promote his own growth.

   (C) promoting diversity by allowing the students to express their opinions rather than expressing his own.

   (D) maximizing the amount of time that students spend on their own group discussions.

During his planning time, Mr. Treskoski goes to Mr. Hinohosa, the school librarian, and asks him to recommend sources for learning about gangs, and whether the district has the technological capabilities to link with the nearest university in order to conduct a computer search for information related to gangs.

25. What is the key advantage to Mr. Treskoski's asking Mr. Hinohosa for help, rather than seeking out the answers to these questions himself?

   (A) Mr. Treskoski can save a great deal of valuable planning time by having Mr. Hinohosa help him as opposed to finding the material himself, thus making better use of his limited time resource.

   (B) Mr. Treskoski can begin to develop a collegial relationship with Mr. Hinohosa in which each will view the other as a member of a mutually supportive learning community.

   (C) Mr. Treskoski can better understand factors outside the classroom that contribute to his individual students' growth.

   (D) Mr. Treskoski can make certain that his actions are in compliance with the school library regulations.

After Mr. Hinohosa helps Mr. Treskoski select a variety of materials on gangs from the school library, he explains to Mr. Treskoski that the school does not have the technological capability to link with a university for a computer search. He suggests that instead Mr. Treskoski conduct a computer search of Infotrak at the local community college. Mr. Hinohosa calls Dr.

Harvill, the librarian at the community college, and she gives Mr. Treskoski a set of instructions for selecting terms and setting limitations for an Infotrak search.

The next day, Mr. Treskoski explains to his class about the computer search and asks the students to keep the computer search in mind as they examine the school's library materials on gangs. On Friday, after all students are thoroughly acquainted with the library materials, Mr. Treskoski has a "Town Meeting" of the class in order to decide how to structure the computer search. The class selects three terms for which to search, and limits the search to the most current 30 magazine and newspaper articles which contain a combination of these terms. Then after school, Mr. Treskoski meets with Dr. Harvill at the college to conduct the search.

26. Mr. Treskoski's activities demonstrate

   (A) selecting appropriate materials to address individual students' needs.

   (B) knowing how to foster growth in each domain.

   (C) taking advantage of community resources to foster student growth.

   (D) understanding the relationship between planning and student growth.

During the following week, the students eagerly wait for all the articles to arrive through Interlibrary Loan at the community college. During this time, Mr. Treskoski's class begins to explore the idea of yellow journalism. Casey Bradford raises her hand. "I live with my Aunt Tommie and Uncle Bob," she says. "Aunt Tommie works for the paper as editorial director." Mr. Treskoski asks Casey whether she thinks Ms. Bradford would like to come talk to the class. Casey suggests that she go to the office and call her aunt. She returns to the classroom with an affirmative answer, and tells Mr. Treskoski that he is to call her aunt with a proposed date and time.

27. Mr. Treskoski's behavior demonstrates

   (A) using a variety of instructional strategies.

   (B) developing strong family-teacher partnerships.

   (C) an understanding of individual talents and abilities.

   (D) employing the use of preferred modalities in student instruction.

Molly Winters says that since her dad was the one who originally said that the notion of gangs in the town was hype by the media, that he should come talk to the class, too. She asks if she may call him at work to see if he will come. Mr. Treskoski asks if that will be a problem for him at work. "No," says Molly. "He's the personnel manager at the electronics parts factory, and he lets me call any time." Mr. Treskoski gives Molly permission to call, and Mr. Winters agrees to come.

28. In agreeing to allow Molly to invite her father, Mr. Treskoski demonstrates

    (A) an appreciation of a diversity of ideas.

    (B) an understanding of the importance of prior learning.

    (C) taking advantage of community resources.

    (D) stimulating curiosity in students.

When the Interlibrary Loan photocopies arrive from the community college, Mr. Treskoski assigns each student to one of six groups of four children each. He gives each group five of the 30 articles to examine for evidence of gangs in New York and for signs of yellow journalism. Each group will then present a report to the entire class. To each group he assigns one high, two medium, and one low-achieving student. The low-achieving student in one group is Lynn Stovall, a student who is involved in the district's full inclusion program for students with developmental disabilities.

After three days, Mr. Treskoski receives a phone call from the mother of Carlita Rivas, the high-achieving student in Lynn's group. Ms. Rivas is upset because her daughter has been assigned to work in the same group as Lynn. "This boy can do nothing to help with the project," complains Ms. Rivas. "I'm sure that he is a nice boy, but I don't want my daughter to have to work with such a poor student. What is wrong with him, anyway? Is he retarded, or what?"

29. What should Mr. Treskoski do?

    (A) Tell Ms. Rivas that he understands her concern, and patiently explain to her that Lynn has fetal alcohol syndrome and is mentally retarded. Offer to send her a variety of materials about fetal alcohol syndrome in order that she may better understand Lynn's problems and perhaps identify ways that Carlita may work with him in the group.

(B) Explain that he understands her concern, and that he will move Lynn out of the group immediately.

(C) Firmly explain that he has to make the instructional decisions about the class, and that since Lynn is mentally retarded, Carlita has the social obligation to help him. Explain to Ms. Rivas that unless students work together to build community, they will not learn the value of civic virtue, which is a main goal of social studies education.

(D) Explain that throughout the year, students will be grouped in a variety of ways, and that a major goal of the class is for students to learn to work with others who are both very like and very unlike themselves in a number of ways. Explain that he is sorry, but he will not to be able to answer her questions about Lynn, since it would be unethical and illegal to do so.

After Casey Bradford's aunt and Molly Winter's dad have each come and talked to the class, Mr. Treskoski has the students work in groups in order to determine what the basic disagreements between the two positions are. The groups report to him, and he writes the issues on the board.

Just because kids get in trouble, it doesn't constitute gang activity.	The police department classifies current crime as gang activity.
The Newspaper writes to sell, not represent the truth.	The paper writes to sell, but does represent the truth.
The paper supports Ms. Crumpler.	Yes, but restricts partisan views to editorials.

30. Mr. Treskoski could best foster developmental growth of his students by which of the following?

(A) Having each child work individually on writing an essay about the first issue

(B) Having the children work in cooperative groups in order to decide whether it is Casey's mom or Molly's dad who is telling the truth on the second issue

(C) Within groups, having each child list what s/he considers the three best-tasting foods and then compare lists; asking the children how that activity relates to the second issue

(D) Having each child give a talk on the third issue

Next, Mr. Treskoski says to the class, "Concerning the first issue, in order to determine whether or not the paper does print what the police department tells them, what might we do?"

31. Mr. Treskoski's question is designed to

I. develop problem-solving skills.

II. encourage divergent thinking.

III. act as an informal assessment in order to determine whether the students are actually understanding the material.

IV. help students learn to monitor their own performance.

(A) I and II only. (B) I and III only.

(C) II and III only. (D) II and IV only.

A number of students offer suggestions, which Mr. Treskoski writes on the board. Maria Velasquez suggests that the group examine public police documents. Levar Freeman suggests that the class invite Chief of Police Gene Capps to come and speak to the class. The latter suggestion meets with overwhelming approval from the group. Mr. Treskoski suggests writing a letter to Chief Capps inviting him to come.

32. The method of writing the letter which would best facilitate student learning would be

(A) to have each group write a letter, and then have the class vote for the best one.

(B) to have Mr. Treskoski write the letter for the class in order to expedite matters.

(C) to link the computer to the overhead projector, have Mr. Treskoski sit at the computer, and have the students tell him what to write.

(D) to have students nominate the best writers in the class, and then vote on which one would write the letter.

After hearing from Chief Capps that the paper did accurately reflect the police reports, the students decided that they would like to hear a debate between Mayor Griego and Candidate Crumpler on the issues of 1) gangs in their community and 2) Mayor Griego's proposed new youth community center. Mr. Treskoski asked the students what they thought about having a dinner meeting at a local restaurant and asking the candidates to come and debate. The students were excited at the prospect and voted unanimously to do so.

Foreseeing that money might be a problem for some students, Mr. Treskoski immediately called his neighbor, the president of the local Optimist's Club, and asked if the club could donate money to cover the dinners of any children who would not be able to come because of money problems. The neighbor said that the Optimists would be delighted.

The next morning, as Mr. Treskoski had predicted, three students each came privately to him and said that they could not attend the meeting because they did not have the money to spend. Mr. Treskoski told each student not to worry, and wrote a note for each student to take home explaining that the Optimist Club had given money to assure that all students could participate. The three students returned to school happy the next day, and announced that they could participate.

33. Mr. Treskoski's behavior demonstrated

(A) an understanding of human developmental processes.

(B) an understanding of environmental factors that affect learning.

(C) an understanding of the importance of motivation to learning.

(D) the creation of an environment that respects cultural differences.

Lacie Parks teaches fifth grade in a community of 100,000 which includes the residents of a military base. Whenever a new student enrolls in her class, Lacie encourages the student's parents to complete a paper listing: 1) places they have lived about which they would be willing to participate in helping their child to present a program to the class; and 2) other topics or hobbies about which they would be willing to present a program to the class. Then, when a new student arrives, Lacie quickly makes a point to incorporate whatever topics that new student's parents may present to her curriculum.

When Renee Bonaly transfers into Lacie's class in January, her mother, Captain Bonaly lists Turkey as a country in which the family has lived. She agrees to come February 10 and, along with her daughter, present a program on Turkey.

"Be sure to talk about the Islamic religion," Lacie tells Captain Bonaly. "And it would be wonderful if you could help Renee prepare a Turkish dish that the students could taste!"

34. What is likely to be the most important consequence of this activity for Renee?

   (A) Having her mother become more involved with her school

   (B) Learning more about Turkey

   (C) Appreciating the strength of her own diversity

   (D) Promoting her own growth

35. Why does Lacie tell Captain Bonaly to make certain to tell the students about the Islamic religion?

   (A) Lacie knows that a study of comparative religions is a requirement of the fifth-grade curriculum.

   (B) Lacie wants her students to understand that not all peoples have the same religious beliefs.

   (C) Lacie knows that students are highly motivated to learn about religions.

   (D) Lacie uses good planning in order to create students who are self-directed learners.

On the following Tuesday, Summer Rawlings comes to see Lacie before school. "Ms. Parks, I saw Renee at the skating rink over the weekend. She told me that her mom is going to come to school in a couple of weeks. She said her mom is going to tell us about the Islamic religion. Is that right?

Lacie nods. "Yes, Summer. Isn't that exciting?"

"I guess so," says Summer. "Ms. Parks, since Renee's mom is going to tell us about the Islamic religion, can my minister come and have a little prayer service with our class afterwards?

36. How should Lacie respond?

   (A) Lacie should contact Captain Bonaly immediately. She should apologize for having offered the invitation to speak to the class and withdraw the invitation.

   (B) Lacie should contact Captain Bonaly immediately. She should apologize for having asked Captain Bonaly to speak about the Islamic religion. She should ask Captain Bonaly to present the program about Turkey, but omit information related to the Islamic religion.

   (C) Lacie should say that since Captain Bonaly is going to tell about the Islamic religion, it is only fair that Summer's minister should come to have the prayer service as long as it is a nondenominational service.

   (D) Lacie should explain that while teaching about different religions is appropriate at school, having a minister come to conduct a prayer service is not allowed.

In Lacie's science class, the students are studying sound. Lacie is using level four interactive laser disk technology to teach the science unit. Using computers, appropriate software, and the laser disk player, each cooperative group is to create a lesson on a particular facet of sound, such as volume or pitch. Each group will then teach their lesson to the rest of the class.

37. What is the major benefit of having the students teach a lesson about sound to the rest of the class?

   (A) When a student prepares a lesson to teach peers, the student learns about learning theories and subsequently becomes a better student.

(B) When a student prepares a lesson to teach peers, the student learns to better appreciate the efforts of the classroom teacher.

(C) When a student prepares a lesson to teach to peers, the student is highly motivated to learn the subject matter involved.

(D) When a student prepares a lesson to teach peers, the student learns organizational skills which generalize to improve academic performance in other areas.

38. One advantage of using the interactive videodisc technology is that students have the opportunity to actually observe demonstrations of how such phenomenon as sound waves work. Teaching students by allowing them to see the natural phenomenon of sound waves taking place instead of merely offering complex theoretical descriptions of sound waves is most important for students at what stage of development?

(A) Piaget's sensorimotor stage

(B) Piaget's concrete operational stage

(C) Piaget's formal operational stage

(D) Piaget's interpersonal concordance stage

39. Following the successful completion of the sound unit, Lacie wants to learn other ways to use the technology in her school to increase her students' learning and technological literacy. Lacie can best do his by

(A) asking her mentor teacher to help her find out about technologies available in her district.

(B) enrolling in a computer-technology course at her local university or community college.

(C) reading the computer and technology books and periodicals available in her school library.

(D) asking the media center specialist to teach her to use the available technologies.

40. As Lacie and her fifth-grade students become more and more technologically literate through their science-technology classes, she asks her students how their class can use the technological skills that they have

developed in order to be of service to the school. Several of the students suggest that the class adopt a class of second graders to introduce the use of interactive video disk technology within the context of language literacy. The class enthusiastically votes to undertake this project. What is the most likely outcome of the project?

(A) The students will gain an appreciation of their ability to communicate effectively with peers, younger students, and teachers.

(B) The students will develop a sense of responsibility toward their school community and a sense of the interrelatedness of the school community.

(C) The students will develop an appreciation for the potential of technology as a teaching tool.

(D) The students will make a personal commitment to learn more about technology and to increase their technological skill.

Lacie is interested in teaching in an interdisciplinary way. For example, she wants her students to understand how science impacts the community in which they live. The state curriculum guide for her grade focuses on scientific methods, such as data collection, organization, and reporting. Lacie wants her program to stress real-life examples of scientific methods used in local businesses.

She decides to contact businesses in the community and arrange for field experiences for her students. First, she wants each business that she selects to have a person come and talk to her students about science's role in their field. Then she wants to spend several days helping the students do library and computer database research on the topics introduced by the speaker. Next, she wants to use the school science lab to practice using the data collection and other scientific procedures employed by the business. Finally, thus prepared, she wants to take her students to see science in action at the work site.

Lacie lists the community businesses that she selects on a sheet of butcher paper which she posts on a bulletin board.

Local Businesses That Use Science		
Chemistry	**Biology**	**Physics**
Soda pop bottling factory	Hospital Medical Lab	Geotech Architecture, Inc.
ABC Concrete Contractors	Ms. Grant's truck farm	Maria's Auto Shop

41. What is most likely to be a benefit of making community businesses a part of Lacie's students' science program?

   (A) The community would become aware of the importance of their involvement in the education of the students.

   (B) The community would increase their understanding of the problems facing today's students.

   (C) The community would increase their understanding of the problems facing today's teachers.

   (D) The students would be more likely to stay in the community upon graduation rather than leaving for more lucrative employment in metropolitan areas.

During the period of community-involvement field experiences, Lacie continually directs her students' attention to the fact that science is a way of solving problems. Following the period of field experiences, Lacie asks her students to identify a problem in their school and to devise a scientific way of studying that problem and solving it.

Lacie's students work in groups for two class periods and select the following problem for investigation: It is late spring, and the classroom gets so hot during the afternoon that the majority of the students are uncomfortable. Their research question becomes, "Why is it hotter in our classroom than in the music room, art room, or library? How can we make our classroom cooler?

42. Of the following choices, what is the most important benefit of allowing the students to select their own problem to investigate, rather than having Lacie assign them a problem?

   (A) Students become self-directed problem-solvers who can structure their own learning experiences.

   (B) Lacie can best assess individual students' academic and affective needs in a naturalistic setting.

   (C) Students will have the opportunity to work with a wide variety of instructional materials.

   (D) Students will learn to appreciate opposing viewpoints.

43. Which of the following is the most important force at work when students are allowed to select their own problem for investigation?

    (A) Increased student motivation

    (B) Increased student diversity

    (C) Increased structure of student groups

    (D) Increased use of self-assessment

Ms. Dominguez is teaching a lesson on finding the area of irregular polygons. In her lesson she uses illustrations and equations from the chalkboard as well as large, moveable, cardboard polygons.

44. What was Ms. Dominguez's intention in using the cardboard polygons?

    (A) To incorporate visual and tactile learning styles into the lesson presentation

    (B) To assess eye-hand coordination of the students when using the manipulatives

    (C) To spice up her lesson

    (D) To stress self-directed learning

45. Ms. Fields, a computers teacher, is passing by Ms. Dominguez's classroom while she is teaching her lesson. Later that day Ms. Fields asks Ms. Dominguez if she would like to teach her class a lesson using the computers in the lab. Ms. Dominguez politely responds that she thinks she will pass on the offer. Which best evaluates Ms. Dominguez's response?

    (A) It was correct, because classes should always be taught in the same environment since retention occurs best when in a familiar setting.

    (B) It was correct because using the room once would provide little knowledge to the students and important instructional time would be lost.

    (C) It was incorrect because utilizing the computers, Ms. Dominguez's lesson planning would be eased since one lesson would not have to be planned.

(D) It was incorrect because Ms. Fields can serve as an excellent resource since computer programs can be conducive to understanding and retention of mathematical concepts.

Ms. Dominguez has just returned an exam. One student, Shane, received a failing grade and a note to have signed by his parents. He is afraid of the repercussions he might receive from his father who expects perfection. Shane is not a straight A student but usually earns B's.

46. What should Ms. Dominguez do about this situation?

(A) Exempt him from having to return a signed exam, figuring he is certain to improve in the future.

(B) Call his parents personally.

(C) Write a note explaining the failing grade, but detail as many of the student's positive qualities as are applicable, as well as the confidence the teacher has in his future success in the class.

(D) Counsel Shane on how to better cope with a demanding household.

47. Upon further review, Ms. Dominguez has realized that Shane has trouble using theorems and rules necessary to complete the mathematical questions on the exam. Ms. Dominguez wants to help Shane learn material by developing a learning strategy for him. To do this properly, she should

I.   increase his awareness of metacognition.

II. help him analyze the information.

III. aid him in devising a suitable plan for better learning.

IV. monitor and modify any learning plan put into use.

(A) I only.   (B) II and III only.

(C) II, III, and IV only.   (D) I, II, III, and IV.

48. Ms. Dominguez wants to help her students remember the value of π. She wrote this poem on the board:

Pie
I wish I could reproduce pi.
Eureka cried the inventor,
Christmas pudding, Christmas pie
Is the problem's very center.

The number of letters in each word produces a string of numbers equal to π: 3.14159265358979323846. When Ms. Dominguez taught her students this, she was using

(A) an acronym.

(B) an acrostic.

(C) rhyme.

(D) peg-word.

As a teacher, Ms. Dominguez must deal with problems other than whether or not her students are learning math.

49. While on after-school hall duty, Ms. Dominguez notices a boy showing another student a shiny object. On further inspection, she notices that it is a hunting knife. The best plan of action would be for her to

(A) tell the boys that they must get on the bus immediately or leave school grounds, ignoring the knife.

(B) take the knife from the boy and escort him to the principal's office.

(C) take the knife from the boy with the stipulation that his parents must contact her if he wants it back.

(D) lecture to the boy the dangers of bringing a knife of any sort to school and warn him not to bring it again on penalty of losing the knife permanently.

50. One of Ms. Dominguez's students has been repeatedly playing practical jokes during class. She has arranged for a parent-teacher conference. During the conference, Ms. Dominguez should

I. list the practical jokes the student has played.

II. express concern for the class and the student's safety.

III. convey to the parents that the student is disruptive and disrespectful.

IV. set up a discipline plan for the home and school to which the parents must agree before they leave.

(A) II and IV only. (B) I and III only.

(C) II, III, and IV only. (D) I and II only.

Miss Eagleton is a first-year U.S. History teacher in a high school. Her first period class has 30 students, all of whom are in tenth or eleventh grade. She plans to begin a unit on immigration to the United States by presenting several charts indicating the population of selected cities in Northern Europe and the Eastern U.S. before 1850 and after 1890. She plans to ask students to suggest possible explanations for the trends.

51. Which of the following best describes this instructional technique?

(A) Cooperative learning

(B) Problem solving

(C) Teaching higher order thinking skills

(D) Inquiry teaching

52. Miss Eagleton divides her class into several groups. She asks each group to select a specific European country and to research the reasons people chose to leave that country and immigrate to the U.S. She plans to ask each group to report their findings to the whole class. At the conclusion of the group reports, Miss Eagleton should plan

(A) an essay test covering the major reasons for immigration.

(B) a group discussion comparing and contrasting reasons for immigration.

(C) requiring a written paragraph summary of the reasons people immigrated to the U.S.

(D) assigning another topic for research to reinforce this learning technique.

53. Miss Eagleton plans to include cooperative learning activities that incorporate group goals and require individual accountability. Which of the following results would be expected?

I. Increased competition for grades

II. Increase in students' self-esteem

III. Increase in amount of time students spend on academic tasks

IV. Increase in positive attitudes toward other class members

(A) I and II only.
(B) I and IV only.

(C) II, III, and IV only.
(D) IV only.

54. Soon after beginning the cooperative learning activity, Miss Eagleton receives a call from a parent who is concerned that the students will not be prepared for the college entrance exams which must be taken individually. Which of the following would be the best response for Miss Eagleton to this concern?

(A) Explain that students can take a review course for the college entrance exams during their junior year.

(B) Explain that colleges are more concerned about high school grades than college entrance exam scores.

(C) Explain that each student is individually responsible for the course content even though the students work cooperatively to learn the information, developing skills needed for the exam.

(D) Explain that learning U.S. History and taking college entrance exams are two very different tasks.

55. Miss Eagleton wants all of her students to participate in independent research about a topic related to U.S. History. She checks the school library for resources and prepares a list of 50 suggested topics. She also prepares a list of 20 different types of projects, ranging from constructing a model, to preparing a poster, to writing and performing a one-act play, to preparing a written report. The number of choices Miss Eagleton suggests is likely to

(A) confuse, frustrate, or overwhelm the students.

(B) cause concern about the grading format for the projects.

(C) cause angry phone calls from parents who do not understand her purpose.

(D) motivate students.

56. Miss Eagleton has noticed that during class discussions, many students answer her questions with one or two words or a short phrase. She makes certain that she provides enough time for students to consider the question and prepare an answer before calling in a student to respond. Which of the following reasons is probably the cause of the students' short answers?

(A) The students are too intimidated to provide lengthy answers.

(B) The questions usually require factual recall.

(C) The students are uncertain about the answer, so they keep their comments short.

(D) The questions are probably too difficult for these students.

57. Miss Eagleton can reserve the use of the computer lab during the first period. As the students complete their research about immigration, she has assigned a 500-word essay summarizing their findings. Miss Eagleton has asked the students to prepare a handwritten rough draft and make the final copy using the computer. She has encouraged students to read each other's essays, and make as many changes on their own rough copies as necessary. Which of the following terms best describes this activity?

(A) Revising and editing

(B) Peer group work

(C) Process writing

(D) Cooperative learning

58. The students in first period U.S. History have become interested in the local election for mayor. The two candidates for mayor have both proposed a curfew of 10:00 p.m. for anyone under eighteen for Sunday through Thursday and 1:00 a.m. on Friday and Saturday. The students complain to Miss Eagleton for several days. She decides to have the

students write individual letters expressing their point of view to the mayor. What would most likely be the effect of this activity?

(A) Promoting a sense of civic responsibility

(B) Causing individual students to reflect on the specific reasons that they oppose the curfew

(C) Encouraging student to plan a sidewalk protest of the curfew

(D) Causing parents to express concern over a youngster's involvement in politics

Joe Thacker has joined the staff of Edgemont High School. He will be teaching sophomore English, a course taught by four teachers who follow the same curriculum but use their own ideas for instructional strategies. The first unit of study is a novel with which Mr. Thacker is not familiar—*Laughing Boy*. Since he has just completed his student teaching at the tenth-grade level, he is very familiar with *The Red Badge of Courage*, a novel often taught at the tenth-grade level in New York, and would like to begin the school year with it rather than the novel the other teachers are using. As a football coach, his first weeks of school will be very busy. He also feels that the purpose of the unit—to study the structure of the novel—could be accomplished with either book equally well. When he mentions his idea and the reasons for it to his fellow sophomore English teachers, however, they are not in favor of his varying from the set curriculum.

59. What steps should Joe Thacker take next regarding the first unit of study?

(A) Mr. Thacker should go ahead and teach the book he wants to teach.

(B) He should talk to the departmental chairperson and explain his position. If she approves of this change in titles, he will make the substitution. If she does not, he will teach *Laughing Boy*.

(C) He should talk to the principal, who had the greatest influence in hiring him, and follow his advice.

(D) He should send a note to his students' parents on the first day of school and see if they mind the substitution of one novel for the other. He will abide by their majority opinion.

The Biology I textbooks are up for adoption in New York. The science teachers at Lenere High School have met and discussed the type of book that would best serve their goals and the needs of the students. A list of their preferences has been prepared so that when the textbook samples are delivered, they will be able to match the available books to the ideal books they have discussed.

Janelle Kent, a Biology I teacher at Lenere High School, has been asked to serve on the Central Textbook Committee for Lenere, a town with a population of 42,000. She has never served in this capacity before and is excited about the opportunity.

60. When recommendations for the textbooks to select for the Lenere School District arrive from local campus committees, the Central Textbook Committee members discover that two high schools agree on all textbook selections except in the area of Biology I. Since Ms. Kent is the teacher with a science background, the other members ask her what their next step should be. Which answer best demonstrates her decision-making skills?

   (A) She recommends the textbook requested by the Lenere science teachers, since her own school's teachers would be disappointed in her if she made any other vote.

   (B) She recommends an immediate meeting of the Biology teachers from both high schools. Each group should prepare a list of advantages of the textbook they favor. A vote at this meeting, after the lists have been presented, will determine Ms. Kent's vote. If a tie occurs she will make the decision based upon her own preference.

   (C) She recommends drawing the name of one of the two textbooks to break the tie out of a hat. Since both books have been chosen for consideration by the state, either could be used with great benefit in the classroom.

   (D) Ms. Kent recommends that neither of the high schools' first choices for a textbook be selected. Instead, a second place book selected by each campus—the same textbook in both cases—should be submitted for adoption.

61. As part of the follow-up work for the selection and adoption of a new Biology I textbook, the teachers are making preliminary suggestions for

revising the curriculum guide to make better use of the new textbook. Ms. Kent's assignment is to make a list of resources in the community that will supplement instructional units of study throughout the year. Which of the following should she include?

I.   A visit to the water treatment plant

II. A trip to the nearby beach to collect shells

III. A speaker from the medical research unit at the Lenere Hospital to discuss the latest in organ transplants

IV. A fingerprint session by the police department, with accompanying analysis of work with the science of fingerprint analysis

(A) I and III only.   (B) II, III, and IV only.

(C) I, II, and IV only.   (D) I, II, III, and IV.

62. After the new textbooks are being used in the Biology I classrooms, Ms. Kent is planning a unit of study in which the students will visit the nearby beach areas. After introducing the unit to the class, she encourages them to suggest ways a visit to the nearby beaches will enhance and direct their study. During the discussion, she serves as recorder, jotting down their ideas on the board. What is the major benefit of Ms. Kent's technique to introduce the new unit of study to her students?

(A) Students become co-designers of the unit of study and develop both excitement and curiosity about the proposed field trip.

(B) All students have the opportunity to express their own ideas during class discussion.

(C) Ms. Kent can compare her students' ideas about the visit to the beach with those listed in the teacher's guide to the new textbook to evaluate the effectiveness of the new book.

(D) Ms. Kent can assess which students have little experience or knowledge relating to the beaches.

After the study of *The Diary of Anne Frank* and *Flowers for Algernon*, Elaine Mitchell, a teacher of ninth-grade English, requires her students to keep an informal journal during a six week period. The students are required to write in their journals for at least ten minutes every day. The students may write in diary form as Anne Frank and Charlie did in the respective novels or on any topic they wish, including several ideas Ms. Mitchell places on the board each day. Students may write in prose or poetry. She has told her students that she will be the only reader of whatever the students write and will evaluate the journals based upon daily effort, not upon accuracy of mechanics and sentence structure.

After the journal has been completed, Ms. Mitchell finds one of the students, a very quiet girl named Alicia has repeatedly expressed morbid thoughts. Statements regarding "going to sleep and never waking up...watching blood swirling in the water...life down the drain" and wishes that she had never been born abound in the intensely personal writing.

63. What should be Ms. Mitchell's next action?

(A) She should watch Alicia's writing carefully in the future to see if other depressing thoughts occur with regularity.

(B) She should show the journal to another teacher to see what he or she thinks about the writing.

(C) She should not worry about the writing since many girls at Alicia's age are overly temperamental and like to dramatize their feelings. After grading the journal, she should return it with a written inquiry about the depressing ideas in it.

(D) She should make an appointment with Alicia's counselor and discuss the writing she has read and Alicia's withdrawn behavior in class.

Eric Svensen is a computer science teacher in Belford High School. One of the campus regulations is that each teacher sends progress reports to students who are in danger of failing a six-week period. Although the school has a form that most teachers use for the progress report, teachers may develop their own in order to reflect specific grading requirements in various subjects. These progress reports generally are sent by the end of the third week of each six-week marking period so that the student will have time to bring up any lagging grade before report card time.

Because of his computer skills, Mr. Svenson has created an extremely detailed report of his student's grade standing that he plans to send to all of his students' parents at the end of the third week. The report provides detailed positive comments, accounts of low grades, missing homework, and discipline problems. A few teachers have questioned the necessity and indeed the wisdom in sending out such a detailed three week's report.

64. What is Mr. Svenson's primary justification for using such a detailed progress report form?

    (A) He will be showing parents how skilled he is in using the computer.

    (B) He will be able to improve his communication with parents in this more detailed form.

    (C) He will be able to show his principal how much better his form is than the school-adopted one.

    (D) He will need less time to complete his forms since the school form required pen and ink.

Jenny Walker is teaching in an area of Brooklyn known for its gang activity. Ms. Walker has grown up in a small town environment. Her only contact with information about gangs and their activities has been through the media or short units of study during sociology and education courses in college. She is very concerned about her ignorance in this area of contemporary life.

65. Which of the following should Ms. Walker first try in order to gain confidence in working with students whose lives are often centered around gang loyalties?

    (A) She should call in a few of the well-known gang members on the campus and ask them to tell her about their groups since she is new to the community.

    (B) She should read the latest bestseller about gang activity throughout the nation.

    (C) She should attend an informal course offered at the local recreation center co-taught by the police department, youth workers, and a psychologist.

    (D) She should ask students during class discussion to tell her about the gangs in the community, their characteristics, requirements, membership, and influence on the community.

Hiro Asaki's eighth grade reading class has been applying their reading skills to a variety of real-life reading situations — comic strips, sports pages and ads in newspapers, a driver's ed manual, employment applications, and other areas of interest for students with remedial reading needs. Most of the students in Mr. Asaki's class are one to three years older than the typical eighth grader. One area that has created unexpected interest among the students has been the area of greeting cards.

Building upon the students' interests, Mr. Asaki has arranged for an art teacher from the high school to talk with the students about the basic elements of design in greeting cards. The students will then design a card of their own in the computer lab for any holiday they wish. The computer lab technician will teach the students how to use the graphics applications in the word processing program.

66. By planning this unit of study, Mr. Asaki is demonstrating which of the following attitudes?

   I. A willingness to have other teachers assist with his instructional plans

   II. A degree of laziness by asking other instructors to do part of his work

   III. A total disregard of the intent of the course he is teaching—to help students improve their reading skills

   IV. The ability to enhance his students' learning experiences by using the computer facilities within the school

   (A) I only.   (B) III only.

   (C) II and III only.   (D) I and IV only.

67. Following the production of the greeting cards, Mr. Asaki arranges for a display of the students' greeting cards at the local shopping mall. What is a major gain for the school through this activity?

   (A) Visitors in the mall can see what good work the students have completed.

   (B) The display helps foster stronger ties between the school and the community.

(C) The students are even more excited about having their work displayed in a public place.

(D) Other schools can see the result of Mr. Asaki's project and use a similar project with their own students.

Since the students showed only a positive response throughout the greeting card project, a month later Mr. Asaki asks the class if they would like to complete a project for Mother's Day. The original card may be for a student's mother or any other significant person to whom the student wishes to express appreciation for understanding and nurturing shown to him or her throughout their growing years. The students again express an interest in the project. Most students choose their mothers as the recipients for their cards, some others chose a grandparent, an aunt, a neighbor, or a single father.

68. Mr. Asaki's Mother's Day card project demonstrates what special professional awareness of the teacher?

(A) Mr. Asaki knows the importance of including the home and family relationship in the educational process.

(B) Mr. Asaki knows that not all the students have mothers.

(C) Mr. Asaki knows that not all the students have mothers with whom they have a positive relationship.

(D) Mr. Asaki knows that students who are often unsuccessful like to repeat successful learning activities.

Several of the individuals and groups visiting the shopping malls and viewing Mr. Asaki's students' greeting cards have written notes of appreciation to the students about sharing the work. One letter especially elicited an action response from the class. Several elderly residents of a community nursing home had seen the exhibit and wrote a letter to Mr. Asaki. In the letter they expressed the wish that their bedridden co-residents could see some of the original designs and humorous messages. Spirited class discussion resulted in the decision by the students that they would reproduce some of the cards, make a portable display of them, and present them to the nursing home, particularly for the bedridden residents.

69. What is the major benefit to the school of this additional activity?

(A) People who could not see the cards otherwise could get to see them.

(B) The school-community relationship is positively enriched again through the efforts of Mr. Asaki's students.

(C) Mr. Asaki's students realize that visitors to the shopping mall actually did view their work.

(D) The nursing home will have a visit from some of the youth from Mr. Asaki's class.

Ms. Allen is a first year English teacher. She is teaching two sections of ninth-grade English and three sections of tenth-grade English. She has implemented a process writing model of instruction. Her students have just completed their first essay of the year. As she is reading the student's papers she realizes that one ninth-grade student and one tenth-grade student have turned in exactly the same essay.

70. What should she do first?

(A) Report the students to the principal

(B) Call their parents

(C) Talk with each student individually

(D) Assign an "F" to each paper

71. Later, both students admit to Ms. Allen that they wrote the paper together. Which of the following would most likely be the best response for Ms. Allen?

(A) Assign each student seven days detention and schedule a conference with their parents.

(B) Require each student to write an essay on why cheating is negative.

(C) Require each student to write another paper, but assign each student a zero.

(D) Require each student to write another paper, but assess a penalty of one letter grade.

72. Ms. Allen and Mr. Ramirez, a history teacher, plan to teach an integrated unit on the American Revolution. All of Ms. Allen's second period class is with Mr. Ramirez for sixth period World History. They plan to coordinate their lessons so that the topics the students study in World History are the topics that the students read and write about in English. What will be the most likely consequence of the integrated unit?

    (A) The students will be totally confused and frustrated by so much emphasis on the same topics.

    (B) The students will remember more about this topic for a longer period of time.

    (C) The students will believe that they are doing one assignment for two teachers.

    (D) Ms. Allen and Mr. Ramirez will appear to be over-teaching the topic because they are both discussing the same topics although they teach in different subject areas.

73. Mr. Stephens, a science teacher, has the students in Ms. Allen's second period class during first period physical science. He tells Ms. Allen and Mr. Ramirez that he would like to collaborate with them by integrating some science topics into their unit on the American Revolution. This will most likely

    (A) frustrate Ms. Allen and Mr. Ramirez because they will now have to discuss science.

    (B) cause the students to develop a broader view of the Revolutionary time period.

    (C) irritate the school librarian who must put all the books related to the revolution on reserve.

    (D) cause the students to do English homework in science class and science homework in history class.

In Manhattan, an exhibit of Mayan artifacts is on display in the month of November. Pete Mendez, a new eighth grade Spanish teacher, has mentioned the exhibit to students in his two Spanish classes. The students have responded with many questions about Mayan people and culture, expressing more interest in this topic than any other concept studied as of yet.

Although Mr. Mendez has encouraged his students to attend the free exhibit, many lack transportation to the museum. Although warned by the other Spanish teacher about the trouble involved in setting up a field trip, his students' enthusiasm urges him to seek approval from the principal to make the necessary arrangements. With his principal's approval and warning to follow the guidelines for a field trip in the teacher's handbook, Mr. Mendez is ready to make plans for his students to view the Mayan exhibit in two weeks.

74. Which of the following steps in planning for the trip is faulty?

(A) Pete Mendez has prepared a notice to let other teachers know the date the students will be missing afternoon classes when they attend the exhibit. He has alerted the students to prepare, prior to the field trip, any work due for classes missed.

(B) Mr. Mendez has sent a note to each parent with information about the field trip plans, including learning objectives.

(C) Mr. Mendez has received his principal's approval for the field trip.

(D) Mr. Mendez has arranged for six parents with vans to help him transport the students to and from the exhibit. He has sent each a schedule for the field trip and the names of the students who will be riding in each vehicle.

The Foreign Language Department at Northside High School is planning a multi-faceted celebration during the week of April 15-22. Activities from the various language areas taught at Northside will be presented—dances, games, costumes, foods, and other cultural features. Ms. Longacre, a chairperson of the department, has discussed with the other language teachers a new idea—asking parents to contribute their favorite recipes for ethnic dishes. Before the weeklong celebration, the students will type up the recipes, giving credit to each contributing parent and collating the recipes in the form of a cookbook. The cookbooks will be sold for two dollars each; the proceeds will go toward helping fund a student to attend one of the state meetings for each language taught.

The other teachers liked the idea very much. The principal approves the idea. In speaking to the foreign language teachers he states, "You know, your idea has an even greater value for our school than helping a student attend one of the foreign language student conferences."

75. What is the benefit perceived by the principal?

(A) Students will get to have the experience of preparing a finished product and selling it—an activity promoting free-enterprise.

(B) The project is an interdisciplinary activity for students.

(C) Teachers, students, and parents will cooperate to carry out an idea.

(D) Many students will get to see their parents' names in print in the cookbook.

76. Tina Salinger, a speech teacher at Mayville High School, is organizing a speech tournament for students at her school for the first time. She is preparing a list of people to serve as judges. Which of the following should she use as her primary targets?

I. Business people and community leaders from Mayville

II. Other teachers of different subjects from her high school

III. Speech teachers from other school districts throughout the state

IV. Recent graduates of Mayville High School

(A) I only.   (B) I and IV only.

(C) II only.   (D) III only.

77. The new sociology teacher is setting up a service requirement for her students to meet during the semester of study. Each student must complete 20 hours of community service along with other requirements of the course in order to pass. Which of the following ideas would be acceptable as part of a classroom discussion about this component?

I. light yardwork or shopping for elderly residents in the neighborhood.

II. writing letters for sick people in the hospital.

III. baby-sitting with siblings.

IV. reading to the blind at a nearby residential home for the elderly.

(A) I, II, and IV only.   (B) II, III, and IV only.

(C) I and IV only.   (D) II and III only.

James Kanfield, a high school math teacher, eats lunch every day with several other teachers. The four or five teachers from different teaching disciplines routinely sit at the same table and enjoy a lively discussion as they eat. As Mr. Kanfield joins the group several minutes late today, they inquire about his late arrival.

"I had to keep Pearl White after class again today. First, she rushed into class just as the tardy bell was ringing. She had done less than half of her homework as usual. When I started to review the assignment, she began to freshen her make-up. I just don't know what I can do to make that girl get with the program in my class. Even though her records show a high math aptitude—her non-verbal IQ is 123, I think—this is the second time she's taken Algebra 2 and she's certainly going to fail again at this rate," the frustrated teacher told the group.

78. Which of the following statements best analyzes Mr. Kanfield's behavior?

   (A) As a professional with a group of professionals, Mr. Kanfield can share his experiences and feelings freely, reducing the stress he is feeling.

   (B) Mr. Kanfield is seeking advice from the other teachers to help him with a difficult student.

   (C) Mr. Kanfield is not being ethical in revealing information from a student's records.

   (D) Mr. Kanfield is indicating his sexual bias by not allowing Pearl to fix her make-up at the start of class.

Mona Stewart is a seventh grade teacher in middle school. She is a hardworking, highly organized teacher who plans for her classes very carefully. She is considered a very strict teacher in matters of discipline. Enrolled in her class recently is a student named Billy who has previously been taught in a self-contained special education class in another state. Ms. Stewart has received several modifications and accommodations of instruction to use with this student to help him perform adequately in class.

79. Which of the following is the recommended procedure for Ms. Stewart to follow in working with Billy?

(A) Ms. Stewart modifies Billy's work to conform to the modifications given for working with him. She allows more time on written assignments than she gives other students in the class. She also lets him take some assessment activities orally instead of in written form.

(B) Ms. Stewart, after watching Billy for several weeks in class, uses her own experienced judgments and has Billy perform exactly as she expects all of her students to perform.

(C) Ms. Stewart is willing to let Billy have more time on written work since he writes very slowly and tediously, however, she refuses to substitute oral assessments as the modifications indicate.

(D) Ms. Stewart requires Billy to do all that the other students do; however, she also lets him do the same activity according to the modification or accommodation. Sometimes this approach means that Billy must take a test or do an activity twice, coming in before school or staying late after other students have left. She maintains careful records of how he does on a task in the initial attempt and then compares that to the second attempt.

80. Mr. Deavers, a high school physical education teacher, usually has from 50 to 60 students in each class. He often has difficulty in checking roll and sometimes doesn't know who is present and who is absent from class. He realizes that he needs to institute a new plan. What would be the best procedure for him to institute?

(A) Have students gather on the bleachers, call each student's name and have each student respond, then put a check on the roll sheet.

(B) Divide students into ten groups of five or six, appoint a leader, and have the leader report absences.

(C) Design a chart with ten rows, assign each student a specific place to stand or sit at the beginning of class, then check roll visually using the chart.

(D) Have students start an activity, then visually identify each student and put checks on the roll sheet.

Section 2: Written Assignment

DIRECTIONS: Plan and write an essay on the topic given below. DO NOT WRITE ON ANY TOPIC OTHER THAN THE ONE SPECIFIED. AN ESSAY ON ANY OTHER TOPIC IS UNACCEPTABLE.

Essay Topic:

Explain your philosophy of homework.

LAST
PRACTICE TEST 3

ANSWER KEY

1.	(A)	21.	(D)	41.	(D)	61.	(A)
2.	(D)	22.	(A)	42.	(C)	62.	(A)
3.	(D)	23.	(B)	43.	(A)	63.	(D)
4.	(B)	24.	(A)	44.	(C)	64.	(B)
5.	(A)	25.	(C)	45.	(D)	65.	(A)
6.	(B)	26.	(D)	46.	(A)	66.	(D)
7.	(B)	27.	(C)	47.	(D)	67.	(C)
8.	(D)	28.	(A)	48.	(D)	68.	(A)
9.	(D)	29.	(D)	49.	(A)	69.	(D)
10.	(D)	30.	(C)	50.	(C)	70.	(A)
11.	(A)	31.	(C)	51.	(B)	71.	(A)
12.	(D)	32.	(A)	52.	(A)	72.	(D)
13.	(D)	33.	(C)	53.	(B)	73.	(C)
14.	(C)	34.	(B)	54.	(C)	74.	(C)
15.	(C)	35.	(C)	55.	(A)	75.	(B)
16.	(D)	36.	(A)	56.	(C)	76.	(C)
17.	(A)	37.	(B)	57.	(D)	77.	(A)
18.	(C)	38.	(C)	58.	(B)	78.	(C)
19.	(A)	39.	(D)	59.	(D)	79.	(B)
20.	(A)	40.	(D)	60.	(C)	80.	(C)

ATS-W ELEMENTARY/SECONDARY PRACTICE TEST 3

ANSWER KEY

1.	(A)	21.	(C)	41.	(A)	61.	(D)
2.	(A)	22.	(A)	42.	(A)	62.	(A)
3.	(C)	23.	(B)	43.	(A)	63.	(D)
4.	(B)	24.	(B)	44.	(A)	64.	(B)
5.	(B)	25.	(B)	45.	(D)	65.	(C)
6.	(A)	26.	(C)	46.	(C)	66.	(D)
7.	(D)	27.	(B)	47.	(D)	67.	(B)
8.	(D)	28.	(A)	48.	(C)	68.	(A)
9.	(C)	29.	(D)	49.	(B)	69.	(B)
10.	(B)	30.	(C)	50.	(D)	70.	(C)
11.	(D)	31.	(A)	51.	(D)	71.	(D)
12.	(A)	32.	(C)	52.	(B)	72.	(B)
13.	(D)	33.	(B)	53.	(C)	73.	(B)
14.	(A)	34.	(A)	54.	(C)	74.	(B)
15.	(C)	35.	(B)	55.	(D)	75.	(C)
16.	(B)	36.	(D)	56.	(B)	76.	(A)
17.	(C)	37.	(C)	57.	(C)	77.	(A)
18.	(A)	38.	(B)	58.	(A)	78.	(C)
19.	(A)	39.	(D)	59.	(B)	79.	(A)
20.	(D)	40.	(B)	60.	(B)	80.	(C)

DETAILED EXPLANATIONS
OF ANSWERS

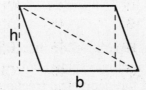

1. **(A)** Given any triangle, a rectangle may be formed that is equal in area to two triangles. This is why the area of a triangle is given by $A = \frac{1}{2} bh$. This parallelogram can be made into two triangles. Formulas do not need dimensions. Thus (B) is incorrect. (C) represents perimeter not area. (D) is an incorrect recall of the area formula and is nonsense here.

2. **(D)** (A) defines an equilateral triangle. (B) defines an isosceles triangle. (C) Some scalene triangles have obtuse angles but many more do not, they have only acute angles or acute angles and one right angle. This is an incomplete choice, hence inappropriate.

3. **(D)** For problems of this type it helps to substitute dimensions for the letters, follow the directions and compare the original volume and the volume of the changed figure. Original cube is 1 unit on a side, volume is 1 cubic unit. Changed cube is 2 units on a side, volume is $2 \times 2 \times 2 = 8$ cubic units. Volume is increased by a factor of 8 when each dimension is doubled.

4. **(B)** The inference pattern represented by this argument is a valid argument form (called disjunctive syllogism) $p \vee q$ and $\sim q$ therefore p. It is a common form used in daily conversation; i.e., if one part of an or statement does not occur, the other part does.

NYSTCE – New York State Teacher Certification Exam

5. **(A)** The inference pattern represented by this argument is an invalid inference pattern, $p \rightarrow q$ and $\sim p$, therefore $\sim q$. It is a commonly used, but invalid argument form. It uses an incorrect assumption that an inverse statement is equivalent to the original statement. Some authors consider this a misapplication due to incorrect or incomplete understanding of the contrapositive. It is an invalid inference pattern; no conclusion will result from the two premises.

6. **(B)** The inference pattern represented by this argument is valid, $p \rightarrow q$ and $\sim q$, therefore $\sim p$. It is an example of the indirect method of proof. Some authors consider it the application of the contrapositive. It is valid and the conclusion follows from the two premises.

7. **(B)** This is a valid inference pattern, $p \rightarrow q$ and p therefore q. It is the most frequently used direct method of proof. The conclusion follows from the two premises.

8. **(D)** The concept of separation or discontinuous (not a continuous, solid pane of glass) is a topologic spatial concept. When it supersedes the mention or recognition of the geometric (rectangular) shape, we conclude the topologic concepts dominate or even supersede the Euclidean concept of shape. Separation is more elemental than shape (Piaget).

9. **(D)** The river is between Aaron and Samuel, since Aaron must cross (intersect) the river to reach Samuel. The river does not connect the two, a bridge would do that, so (A) is not a choice. There is no closed curves here so inside (interior) and outside (exterior) is inappropriate, thus so is (B) and (C).

10. **(D)** Part of (A) may be a true statement, but this is not the reason fractions with a one in the numerator are called unit fractions. By definition a unit fraction is a number of the form 1/2, 1/3, 1/4, ..., 1/a, ... and so on, where the denominators are non-zero natural numbers and the numerator is always 1. Although it is true that the unit fractions are between 0 and 1, this is not the reason why fractions of the form 1/a are called unit fractions; furthermore there are numerous fractions between 0 and 1 that *are not* unit fractions (consider 2/3, 3/5, 3/4, 7/9, 11/16), so it is a true statement but not the correct choice for the question. (B) is not an appropriate solution to the problem.

11. **(A)** Neither a moving automobile (I), nor expanding gas (II), have potential or stored up energy; rather, the two have kinetic (moving) energy. The other items have potential or stored up energy. When the poten-

tial energy is set free, they too will then have kinetic energy. (A) is the correct answer since it enables the reader to choose both the moving automobile and the expanding gas. Since the other items are examples of potential energy, they cannot be chosen; notice that the reader is looking for the ones which do NOT have potential energy.

12. **(D)** Choice (D) is the correct answer. This answer enables the reader to choose all the phrases for the best answer. Matter and energy cannot be destroyed; (A) is therefore true. Matter or energy can be changed into other forms of matter or energy. (B) is also a correct answer. Energy can be changed from one form to another (C). For example, electrical energy may be converted to light energy in the case of an electric light bulb. Again, (D) enables the reader to choose all three correct answers.

13. **(D)** Choice (D) enables the reader to choose both (A) and (B) which are correct answers. In answer (A), e (energy) equals m (mass, the amount of matter in a body) times c^2 (the speed of light squared). (B) is also a true statement for it states that the total amount of matter and energy in the universe remains the same. Choice (D), again, enables the reader to choose both. Choice (C) is incorrect because matter can be changed into energy and energy can be changed into matter. (C) should not be selected since it is false.

14. **(C)** The body does not "rob" materials from the skeleton when calcium is in short supply (B). Neither does it convert carbon to calcium (A). Rather, the body fails to replace atom for atom the normal withdrawal of calcium (C). A simple exchange has become a one-sided situation; as a result the skeleton (the support mechanism) may be seriously weakened. All of the above (D) is also incorrect. Only (C) is the correct answer.

15. **(C)** Sound energy is a type of wave energy so (C) is correct. Mechanical energy (A) is the most common form of energy about us. All moving bodies produce mechanical energy. The energy produced from machines is also mechanical energy. It is apparent that sound energy does not fit in this category. (A) is not the correct answer. Electrical energy (B) is the energy produced by the moving of electrons through a substance; electrical energy runs motors, lights homes, and makes telephones work. Sound energy is not a type of electrical energy. Choice (B) is incorrect. Nuclear energy (D) comes from the nucleus of an atom when it splits into two parts or when nuclei of atoms are fused together. Clearly sound waves do not fit into this classification. (D) is incorrect. Sound energy would not fit under the category of radiant energy since radiant energy (another form of wave energy) includes light rays, infrared rays, radio waves, cosmic

rays, radiant heat, X-rays and ultraviolet rays. (C) is the correct answer.

16. **(D)** Since the reader is looking for the one answer that is incorrect, (D) must be chosen. Photosynthesis is the process by which plants create their own food. The other choices (A), (B), and (C) are correct statements and should not be chosen.

17. **(A)** Since a meter is 39.37 inches or about the height of a five-year-old child, (A) is the best choice. A liter (B) is a measure of volume; it is slightly more than a quart. It is not the best unit to use to measure the height of a doorknob. A gram (C) is about the weight of a paper clip; since a gram is a measure of weight (mass) and not length, gram is not the best unit to use. A decimeter (D) is one tenth of a meter; a personal reference for a decimeter is about the distance between the end of the thumb and the end of the middle finger. This distance is a little more than 3" in an adult—about the length of a new piece of chalk. A decimeter could be used to measure the height of a doorknob from the floor but is not the measurement closest to the height. (D) is not the right answer.

18. **(C)** In a taproot system there is a primary taproot that grows until it is the major root in the system. An example of a plant that has a taproot system would be a carrot. (A) is a false statement; roots generally help to hold the plant in the ground. In a diffuse root system there is a network of roots. The primary root lives only for a short time so (B) is false. Both diffuse and taproot systems may be used to store food in the roots; (D), therefore, is false.

19. **(A)** The symbol for hydrogen is H. The other items are not symbols for hydrogen. No element on the periodic table of the elements is represented by Hy (B). He (C) is the symbol for helium, not hydrogen. Hi is not a symbol on the periodic table; (D) should not be chosen.

20. **(A)** A shark (A) is not a mammal; rather it is classified as a fish. Since it is NOT a mammal, a shark (A) is the correct answer for the question asking for the item which is not a mammal. All the other items (a bat, a whale, a gibbon [ape], and an elephant) are mammals; (B), (C), and (D) may not be chosen.

21. **(D)** Part of the power of the governor is the ability to name people to fill empty seats in the Senate for that state (A). As head of a state's executive branch, the governor can use the national guard in times of civil unrest, natural disasters, or for any emergency situation identified by the

governor (B). As part of the checks and balances of one branch of government on another, the governor has the authority to veto laws passed by the legislature (C). The area of trade agreements, however, is within the jurisdiction of the federal government (more specifically, the Congress and the President) because the implications of such treaties go far beyond individual state boundaries. Therefore, the correct response is choice (D).

22. **(A)** Because of the interdependence as explained above, (B) is not correct. Branches of the Federal government do not achieve independence from each other due to checks and balances. Choices (C), and (D) are also not correct because they deal with only one branch, and checks and balances involves the manner in which the branches interrelate. Choice (A) is correct, because checks and balances control and regulate the power and actions of the three branches of the Federal government.

23. **(B)** (B) is the correct answer. Abraham Lincoln was in office between 1860 and 1864. Theodore Roosevelt was in office between 1901 and 1909. Woodrow Wilson was in office between 1912 and 1916. Franklin D. Roosevelt was in office between 1932 and 1944.

24. **(A)** This is the definition of ethnocentrism (A). (B) Institutionalization is the patterning of social interaction in ways that reduce the possibility for tension, conflict, and deviance. (C) Social Placement is the allocation of positions in a society. (D) Social Control are processes which attempt to maintain conformity to existing norms; maintenance of the status quo.

25. **(C)** Wealth describes goods and material possessions which have social value. Prestige is defined as the amount of esteem and deference an individual receives from others. Power is the ability to attain individual goals or socially determine the lives of others. Status is the position or rank of an individual in relation to others; it is based on prestige or social honor. Therefore, (C) is the correct answer.

26. **(D)** The Populists of the late 1800s and the Progressives of the early 1900s arose due to dismay with the current Democratic and Republican political platforms. Therefore (B) is incorrect. These two groups organized themselves and campaigned outside of the structure of the Democratic and Republican parties. Therefore, the answer to the question is (D).

27. **(C)** The answer is (C). The original colonies included Delaware (A), Virginia (B), and Maryland (D), which were then part of the original thirteen states. Vermont was originally owned by Massachusetts, but claimed

independence later and subsequently joined the United States as the four-teenth state in 1791.

28. **(A)** The answer is (A). The Quebec Act (B) occurred in 1774; and because it seemed to give greater advantage to French Canadians, it aroused the ire of the American colonists. The Stamp Act (C) of 1765 was seen as unfair taxation by the colonists. The Writs of Assistance (D) in 1766 made unfair demands on the colonists. Thus, all were causes of the Revolution. The Alien and Sedition Acts occurred in 1798 during the administration of John Adams, almost twenty years after the Revolution began.

29. **(D)** Choice (D) fits this question—1896 should not be considered a recent trend.

30. **(C)** The correct answer is (C). The statement, "Between 1868 and 1882, more than 200,000 Chinese came to the U.S.," neither supports nor opposes the idea of assimilating immigrants into the United States. To demonstrate this, compare selection (A) with the question. Selection (A) provides a positive consequence of immigration (a variety of thoughts, ideas, and philosophies). Selection (C) gives no reason, for or against, the immigration of the Chinese between 1868 and 1882.

31. **(C)** Choice (A) does *not* support child care; rather, it provides a reason against child care. Choice (B) provides an economic reason against government-sponsored child care. Choice (D) reflects the opinion that the Federal government should not be involved in expensive programs at the taxpayers' expense and that child care would be one of these programs. Choice (C) is correct because the response supports child care as a viable program for children.

32. **(A)** Choice (A) is correct. As a part of LBJ's Great Society pro-grams, health care programs financed by Federal and state governments were instituted during his terms in office. (B) is not correct as Nixon's administration did not initially enact these programs. (C) is not correct as Ford's administration did not initially enact these programs. (D) is not correct as Carter's administration did not enact these programs.

33. **(C)** Choices (B) and (D) occurred after 1973. Choice (A), cheap prices for a barrel of oil, is the reverse of what actually happened. Oil prices saw a steady increase that particular year. Therefore, (C) is the correct response.

34. **(B)** The correct answer is (B). The key to answering this question is

in the question itself. The question asks about "our structure of govern-ment." The United States does not have a parliament, but has a representa-tive democracy. Those who govern the nation acquire their position through competition and elections. Therefore, (A) is incorrect. (C) is wrong be-cause the national government takes precedence over the state and local governments. The local governments must work within the legal, eco-nomic, and other various frameworks set forth by the state and national governments. Of the three levels of government, the local government is the weakest and most dependent. (D) is incorrect because Supreme Court judges are not elected to the Supreme Court but are appointed by the President of the United States when a vacancy in the Supreme Court occurs and when the Senate approves the nomination.

35. **(C)** Choice (C) is the correct answer. Women got the right to vote with the passage of the nineteenth Amendment in 1920. World War I ended in 1918. Choice (A) is not correct as the Emancipation Proclama-tion enacted by President Lincoln in 1863 during the American Civil War, freed black slaves in the militarily occupied South. The Bill of Rights, choice (B), or the first 10 Amendments to the Constitution, were approved in 1789 and did *not* give women the right to vote. Choice (D) is not correct as World War II was over in 1945 and the nineteenth Amendment was passed in 1920.

36. **(A)** (A) is the correct answer. The North's economy was more diver-sified than the South's. The North possessed a greater manufacturing ca-pacity than did the South. The South, with its economy being dominated by its reliance on agriculture, (cotton, tobacco, etc.) was not nearly as well industrially equipped to sustain a war with the far more industrially diver-sified Northern states. (B) is not correct because, while the North did have farming, farming would not have caused a conflict with the agrarian-based economy of the Southern states. (C) is not correct because the North did not rely on international trade via the seas for its economic livelihood. (D) is not correct, as in the vast majority of Northern states slavery was either illegal or economically impractical.

37. **(B)** (B) is correct. Burma's distinctive location and elongated shape makes it noticeably different from the other available countries. (A) is not correct as Sri Lanka is an island nation south of India. (C) is not correct as Thailand is to be found in a more eastern location than Burma. (D) is not correct as India, being west of Burma, is far larger than Burma.

38. **(C)** The correct answer is (C). (A) marks the Bahamas, (B) is Mexico, and (D) is Brazil.

39. **(D)** The correct answer is (D). Capitalism may be defined as the private ownership of land, the means of production, and exchange. Money, as (D) states, is invested for personal profit. This is the basis of the American economic system. Therefore, (D) is the correct answer. (C) is incorrect. Capitalism is not a different type of communism. According to Karl Marx, who conceptualized the historical development of communism, the conflicts arising out of capitalism would ultimately lead to communism. But, capitalism is not a form of communism. Alfred Benson Capital may have conceptualized capitalism, but, that fact alone does not substantiate the reason why "Capitalism describes the American economic system." (A) is incorrect. Similarly, the fact that Washington, D.C. is the place of origin, also does not substantiate capitalism as describing the American economic system. (B) is incorrect.

40. **(D)** The correct answer is (D). (A) is incorrect because salt water cannot be used for irrigation; it changes the pH balance in the soil, making the soil incapable of sustaining plant life. (B) might occur, but not necessarily in response to lack of rainfall. (C) is incorrect because fruit orchards typically require much more water, and the source of water must be both predictable and readily available.

41. **(D)** This city view by the French Impressionist Camille Pissarro is one of many in which the artist painted the scenes he saw beneath his second- or third-story Paris hotel windows—the correct answer is (D). The tilted perspective, with diagonal street axes and no horizon line, may owe a debt to photography, to Japanese prints, or to the example of his Impressionist peers. The resulting composition lacks not only a central focal point, but any single focal point at all; likewise, the only architecture visible does not dominate the scene, but, rather, acts as incidental local detail. The anonymous figures in the crowds below the artist's window share this lack of focus: they are busy in normal daily activity, without the least suggestion of drama. Finally, the idea that this scene was recorded from the window of a train lacks evidence: the scene is distinctly urban, not rural, and it is unlikely that a train would either pass through the crowded centers of a city or that it would be elevated to this height.

42. **(C)** In the work pictured, the American sculptor David Smith used power tools to cut, weld, and polish industrial-strength steel to create an ensemble in which the heavy, cubic forms balance in arrested motion. The sculptor obviously neither modelled the materials with his hands nor poured them into a mold: these forms have a rigid, machine-like, technological perfection to them and lack any such irregularities as those resulting from

the molding action of human fingers. This same cubic perfection, and the gleaming, reflective surfaces, refute the idea of chisel work as well.

43. **(A)** In this passage, the speaker tells of how he is everywhere and a part of everything in the natural world. This is done by example: "Where the bee sucks, there suck I," "In a cowslip's bell I lie," and, "Merrily, merrily shall I live now/Under the blossom that hangs on the bough" are all examples of how the speaker makes himself a part of nature.

44. **(C)** A dramatic monologue is a speech or narrative spoken by a single character, designed to sound more like everyday speech than lyrical poetry. (A) and (C) are all lines of poetry, but (C) is considered an example of dramatic monologue because of the way in which it sounds more like words spoken by a specific character as opposed to simply "the poet" or "the speaker" of (A).

45. **(D)** The passage begins with a character crying, so we know that it is most likely a moment of high emotion. Next we are told that the character, "had never felt like that himself towards any woman, but he knew that such a feeling must be love." The character, Gabriel, has just discerned, through what he has heard about "that" (as in "he had never felt like that himself"), the meaning of love. Once this happens, his own identity begins "fading out into a grey impalpable world"; his state of consciousness, and even existence, is being altered because of his recent discovery.

46. **(A)** The seventeenth century Japanese ink-on-paper scroll painting shown in the example relies almost exclusively on the qualities of line to convey the graceful forms of two leaping deer. In this painting, called *Deer and Calligraphy*, both the animals and the scripted characters share the same quality of fluid, rhythmic, spontaneous "writing." Gradations of tone are unimportant here, since the images are defined by black line on white, and volume, too, is absent, since these forms show no shading or modulation of tone.

47. **(D)** The arch, whether rounded or pointed, is completely absent from the building pictured in the example, even though the alternating use of windows with rounded pediments in the lower story seems to suggest the presence of arches. Otherwise, all of the other features listed in the answer choices do help regularize the design of this seventeenth century English Renaissance structure. The uniform second-story windows assert a regularity over the alternating window designs below them; they also emphasize a strong horizontal thrust across the building's facade, which is re-

peated in the balustrade at roof-level. The nearly-flush front surface of the building is broken only by the window openings and by the engaged columns at the building's center and the pilasters at the outer corners. Both of these features project just enough to establish a vertical contrast to the horizontal facade, but not enough to create a system of alternating solids and voids.

48. **(D)** The late eighteenth century Neoclassical painting shown in the example illustrates an episode from ancient Roman legend and attempts to simulate the static, balanced, monumental character of much Classical relief sculpture. The men in the main figure group, therefore, are represented in statuesque, absolutely motionless poses, and the correct answer choice here is (D). The compositional devices listed in all of the other answer choices are important to the painting. The figures stand within a shallow pictorial space, which is marked off by the arches in the background; these arches also serve to focus the man in the center. This shallow space, however, is modified somewhat by the checkerboard floor, which creates a slight perspective recession into the background and makes the figures' space seem logical and convincing. The strong highlighting on the foreground figures accentuates their static, sculptural quality, even as it pulls them to the absolute front of the picture.

49. **(A)** This question asks you to consider both geographical proximity and some general characteristics of Eastern architecture in order to logically determine who would have the most direct influence on Japanese style. Of the answer choices, Greece falls well outside the Asian sphere both in distance and in building styles, while Easter Island, a Pacific site, is not known for a distinctive native architecture. Indonesian temple buildings may share something of the exotic, heavily-ornamented character of the structure pictured but the most representative Indonesian buildings are both much larger and are constructed of stone. The seventh century building pictured, in fact illustrates the strong dependence of Japan on the arts of China. The Chinese character of the structure is visible in the distinctive silhouette of the roof, with its long sweeping pitch and upturned corners in the heavy tiled roof, and in the wealth of elaborate brackets which support the dramatically projecting eaves.

50. **(C)** An oxymoron is an apparent contradiction in terms, such as "jumbo shrimp," "cruel kindness," or (as some would say), "military intelligence." Passage (C) contains an oxymoron because it mentions flames which give "No light, but rather darkness." Choice (C) is the correct answer.

51. **(B)** Assonance is the repetition of vowel sounds in a single line of poetry. Passage (B) contains three examples of assonance: the words "Rocks" and "bogs," the words "caves," "lakes," and "shades," and the words "fens" and "dens." Thus, passage (B) is the correct answer.

52. **(A)** Iambic pentameter refers to the meter, or rhythm, of a line of poetry composed of five feet, each of which is an iamb, having one unstressed syllable followed by a stressed syllable. A line of poetry written in iambic pentameter is ten syllables long. Passage (A) contains two lines of poetry written in iambic pentameter. When read aloud, the unstressed-stressed pattern emerges: "For SHADE to SHADE will COME too DROWsiLY, / And DROWN the WAKEful ANGuish OF the SOUL." Thus, choice (A) is the correct answer.

53. **(B)** The passage serves to introduce an upcoming story to be told by the narrator. He begins by exclaiming, "there may as well be an end of this!" and then gives a list of reasons why he has finally decided not to "keep my trouble to myself." He is about to relate an event, or series of events, to his friend, because keeping silent has been "burning [him] rather violently." He is very excited about what he has to say; choice (B) is correct. There is no evidence that the speaker feels guilty, ashamed, or sorrowful, so (A), (C), and (D) are all incorrect.

54. **(C)** The speaker gives, as one of the reasons for telling his story, "if confession were not good for the soul, though harder than sin to some people, of which I am one," showing that he regards confession as a healthy, although difficult activity. (C) is the correct answer. He never speaks of confession as being unnecessary, nonsensical, or impossible, so (A), (B), and (D) are all incorrect.

55. **(A)** Three of the answer choices—(A), (C) and (D)—show groups of figures engaged in activities which might be interpreted as ceremonial. Choice (C) illustrated a column of soldiers marching across the midsection of a ceramic vessel: while they may be marching in a ceremonial function such as a parade or assembly, they are most likely intended to be shown advancing into battle, and, in any case, their primary function on this vase is decorative. Choice (D) shows figures engaged in music-making activities in formally arranged groups, but here, too, the illustrations serve the secondary purpose of amplifying the accompanying text. Only answer choice (A), an ancient Persian relief sculpture, uses a rigidly schematized, formal composition and style to record an actual ceremonial event. Here, the clear-cut, well-defined figures are strictly arranged in three horizontal

tiers, and each carries an accessory or attribute which identifies his role within this state occasion.

56. **(C)** Only answer choices (A) and (C) repeat the simplified forms of the human figure within a sculptural or ceramic context. Choice (A) appears to continually repeat a series of nearly-identical figures arranged on three horizontal levels, but close inspection reveals several types of figures here, each marked by a variety of detail in posture, costume, accessories, etc. Further, the figures are sculpted in a softly-rounded, convincing style. The figures in choice (C), in contrast, are grouped in a horizontal sequence which appears to show variety and movement; close examination, however, shows that the artist here has simply repeated figures whose clothing, weapons, postures, positions, and facial features are identical. While this serves to illustrate an anonymous mass of marching soldiers, it is even more important in helping the group of figures fit neatly, conveniently, and decoratively into its allotted space on the round "belly" of the vase.

57. **(D)** Calligraphy, or "fine writing," implies a two-dimensional or graphic format. Two of the possible answer choices, (A) and (B), are forms of sculpture or sculptural relief, and therefore contain no drawn, calligraphic elements. Choice (C) presents a flat, two-dimensional illustration painted in black and white and minimal color. However, the images here are rigidly formalized and static, and display none of the rhythmic curves or flourishes of artistic penmanship. Only choice (D), a ninth-century manuscript illustration, links calligraphy with figure drawing in the same rhythmic, linear style. In this illustration of the Bible's Psalm 150, the text written in ink above accompanies the figures below. Each is drawn in the same bold, agitated black and white line, with a sketchy spontaneity that creates an animated, nervous tension.

58. **(B)** The rose has, for centuries, been a symbol of virginal love and beauty. By calling the rose "sick," the poet is implying that somehow this virginal beauty has been lost. This is due to, as the poet states, an "invisible worm," that has found the rose's "bed/Of crimson joy." The loss of virginity has been equated with "sickness," and the sex act causing the loss is alluded to in terms of "worms" and "beds of crimson joy."

59. **(D)** Because of the "worm," the "rose" is "sick"; choice (D) is the best answer because it addresses the archetypical symbol of the rose as virginal love and beauty. Since the rose is "sick," this beauty is gone. Some of the other choices may adequately answer the question, but not as well as (D).

60. **(C)** In the example shown, the *Bull's Head* of 1943, the Spanish artist Pablo Picasso joined a bicycle seat and a set of handlebars in a clever, unexpected combination to produce a sculptural analogy to an actual bull. Thus, the artist was concerned here with form and substance, not with a contrast of line and tone. Likewise, even though the bull has mythological connotations and figures prominently in many ancient religions, the artist was intent not on creating a religious symbol, but in exploring the visual unity of common objects brought together in new ways. The result is a strictly visual, sculptural effect, and in no way provides a metaphor for human experience.

61. **(A)** Choices (B) and (D) present minor problems in spa maintenance, whereas choice (C) cannot be prevented. As bacteria and virus are controlled by both temperature and chemicals, it becomes a possible source of health problems if ignored.

62. **(A)** Choices (B), (C), and (D) are correct levels or degrees. Temperatures in excess of 104° can cause dizziness, nausea, fainting, drowsiness, and reduced awareness.

63. **(D)** Choices (A), (B), and (C) represent an inference that goes beyond the scope of the passage and would indicate biases of the reader.

64. **(B)** The other choices (A), (C), and (D) refer to chemical or temperature maintenance.

65. **(A)** Choices (B), (C), and (D) are appropriate chemicals.

66. **(D)** Choices (A) and (B) appear to be acceptable. Although choice (C) is a definition of statistical significance, choice (D) is correct as the passage is about correlational statistical significance which permits prediction.

67. **(C)** Choice (A) goes beyond the information provided in the passage. Choice (B) is incorrect as correlation cannot indicate causality. Choice (D) is not statistically possible. The high positive correlation trend indicates that these variables are important to consider for future research, thus choice (C).

68. **(A)** Choices (B), (C), and (D) represent inferences that are based on inadequate information which go beyond the scope of the passage. As these story elements are not taught explicitly in the first grade or prior to entering school, children apparently have picked up these elements from

their exposures to stories as indicated by choice (A).

69. **(D)** Although the content might be appropriate for each of the journals, choices (A), (B), and (C), the style of writing suggests that it would be most appropriate for choice (D), *Reading Research Quarterly,* as this passage reports research results.

70. **(A)** The passage provides information for the grade level and mentions if it was significant or substantial. As this statement follows information provided for fifth/sixth grades, it refers to that level, thus choice (A).

71. **(A)** Choices (B), (C), and (D) all connote extreme or inappropriate attitudes not expressed in the passage. The author presents an informed concern—choice (A).

72. **(D)** For the other choices, (A), (B), and (C), the criteria, the role, the discussion, and the assurance for communication or learning are not provided in the passage. The passage stresses the importance of authenticity in communication—choice (D)

73. **(C)** Each of the choices is a possible definition, but the passage overall suggests that communication needs to be developed so that students' responses may become more significant and authentic—choice (C).

74. **(C)** Choices (A) and (B) are not supported by the passage. Choice (D) represents an incorrect conclusion. Choice (C) is supported by the various investigators' explanations.

75. **(B)** As stated explicitly in the passage, the various investigators have attempted to explain the role of imitation in language—choice (B). The other choices go beyond the scope of the passage.

76. **(C)** As the investigators studied different aspects of language while attempting to explain the role of imitation in language, choice (C) is correct. The other choices go beyond the scope of the passage.

77. **(A)** The passage explicitly states that computers are capable of addressing the issues of practice and the true act of reading, choice (A). The other choices represent inferences that are not supported by the passage.

78. **(C)** Although the reader might make inferences to select choices (A), (B), and (D) ways to use a word processor to make practice resemble the true reading act are not stated in the passage, thus choice (C).

79. **(B)** Although audiences in choices (A), (C), and (D) may benefit from the information provided in the passage, the passage explicitly states that a greater understanding of the information in the passage should assist teachers—choice (B).

80. **(C)** Each of the choices is a definition of variance. However, for this passage, choice (C) is the most appropriate.

Section 2: Written Assignment

The following essay received scores at the highest end of the scale used in LAST essay scoring.

Essay A

Happiness, freedom, and peace of mind are goals that everyone wants in life. Yet they are very abstract and difficult to measure. Happiness is a frame of mind that means we enjoy what we do. Freedom is the ability to do what we want, although it is limited to not doing anything that takes away freedom from other people. Peace of mind is a feeling that we are all right and that the world is a good place. How does one achieve these important goals? They can best be acquired when we try to give them to other people rather than when we try to get them ourselves.

The people who feel happiest, experience freedom, and enjoy peace of mind are most often people who are concentrating on helping others. Mother Theresa of Calcutta is an example. Because she takes care of homeless people and is so busy, she probably doesn't have time to worry about whether she is happy, free, and peaceful. Her cheerful, high-spirited demeanor suggests that she has attained these common goals.

There are other people in history who seem to have attained the goals we all want by helping others. Jane Addams established Hull House in the slums of Chicago to help other people, and her life must have brought her great joy and peace of mind. She gave to the mothers in the neighborhood freedom to work and know that their children were being taken care of; and Jane Addams apparently had the freedom to do what she wanted to help them.

On the other hand, there are people in literature who directly tried to find happiness, freedom, and peace of mind, and they were often miserable. The two people who come to mind are Scrooge and Silas Marner. Scrooge had been selfish in the past, and he wouldn't give anything for the poor. He wasn't a bit happy, even at Christmas. Later, when he began helping others, he became happy. Silas Marner was very selfish, hoarding his money and thinking it would make him happy. Only when he tried to make little Eppie happy was he able to be happy, too, even without his stolen money.

If we want to achieve happiness, freedom, and peace of mind, we should get involved in helping others so much that we forget ourselves and find joy from the people we are helping. When we try to give away the qualities we want, we find them ourselves.

Analysis

Essay A is well organized, with the opening paragraph serving as the introduction and stating the thesis of the paper in its last sentence. Defining the terms serves as an effective way to introduce the paper. The last paragraph concludes the essay, restating the thesis. The three middle paragraphs support the thesis with specific examples that are adequately explained and have a single focus. Transitions effectively relate the ideas. The sentence structure varies, and the vocabulary is effective. There are no major errors in sentence construction, usage, or mechanics. Although the essay would benefit from some minor revisions, it is well done considering the time limit imposed upon the writer.

The following essay received scores in the middle of the LAST essay scoring scale.

Essay B

I agree with the idea that you don't get happiness without trying to make other people happy. But I'm not sure that you *always* get happiness when you give it to someone else. You may try to make someone else happy, but they have a role in process as well. They must be receptive to your efforts.

For instance, I've tried many times to make my grandmother happy. No matter what I do, she complains, and laments about her life. Yet she does nothing to change her situation. Its just the opposite when you let someone else be free he takes away from your freedom and you don't feel free at all.

So, all in all, I think maybe sometimes you get happiness and freedom when you give it to others but sometimes things just get worse. The people you are trying to help have to first help themselves.

Analysis

In Essay B, the writer attempts to introduce his topic in the first paragraph, but the thesis is not stated precisely. Although the last paragraph serves as a conclusion, it, too, lacks clarity and singleness of purpose. Paragraph 2 gives a specific illustration to develop the theme, but paragraph 3 lacks specific detail. Although there are some transitional words, the essay rambles with words and ideas repeated. In addition, the essay contains errors in usage, sentence construction, and mechanics.

The following essay received scores at the lowest end of the LAST essay scoring scale.

Essay C

I don't think you can give happiness or piece of mind to anyone, because these are things that a person has to find for themselves, however, you may be able to give freedom. I remember when I was a child, and my parents tried to give me more freedom than I used to have. So you can give that to someone else. But nobody knows what makes me happy so I can be happy only if I decide what it is I want and go out and get it for myself. And then I'll have piece of mind, too.

If I can be free, then I can find out what will make me happy and go out and get it. When I get it, then I will have peace of mind. So freedom is the most important aspect of the question, because with it you can obtain the other two. Our country gives us a lot of freedom, but some people think that it's not enough. These people think that taxes are too high and that the government has to much control over their daily lives.

There are other people who think that the government is not controlling enough, and that's why people commit crimes and use drugs. With freedom comes responsibility, and if you uphold that responsibility, you will obtain happiness and peace of mind.

Analysis

Essay C contains major errors. The writer states the thesis in the first sentence, but fails to have an introductory paragraph; and there is no conclusion at all. The writer does give some specific details but rambles, failing to use the details effectively to support his thesis. The writer never establishes a clear thesis; in fact, the writer appears to change his argument in mid-sentence. In addition, there are serious errors in sentence construction, like the run-on sentence in the beginning of the paper. There are also major problems with spelling, usage, and mechanics.

DETAILED EXPLANATIONS OF ANSWERS

1. **(A)** The correct response is (A). Teachers are responsible to report any suspected cases of child abuse to school officials. Response (B) is incorrect because regardless of the parent's explanations, if the instructor feels that the child may have been abused, it must be reported. (C) is incorrect because the bruises described would not be consistent with an ordinary spanking for misbehavior. (D) is incorrect because while further information might be helpful, the instructor must still report the incident.

2. **(A)** The correct response is (A). The best source of information about a school's curriculum is the teachers themselves. (B) is incorrect because a textbook company representative could provide information about the publisher's intended curriculum, but not that of the school. (C) is incorrect for the same reason as response (B). (D) is incorrect because an instructor cannot wait for time to fix a problem, but should seek out solutions on his or her own.

3. **(C)** The correct response is (C). It is a teacher's responsibility to be prepared to work with a child with learning or emotional problems. Even though a teacher may not have a child with these problems this year, she should still attend the workshop. (A) is incorrect because the teacher is required to attend the in-service provided by the district. (B) is incorrect because to stay home in protest would be childish and serve no purpose. (D) is incorrect because all teachers are expected to attend the entire in-service session.

4. **(B)** The correct response is (B). By allowing Elena and the class to feel that the pen pal activity which they initiate results in the class's study of South America, the students will feel ownership of the activity, and will therefore be more highly motivated to learn the material. There is no research which suggests that surprise provides strong motivation for students (A). It is unlikely that the class would become so excited about the South American unit that their attention to the current unit of study would suffer (C). In addition, Buzz plans to allow the class to vote on the pen pal project the next day, and this information would probably be more stimulating to the students than thinking about a social studies unit. If Buzz feared that the students would be sidetracked by the pen pal information, he would have likely asked Elena to wait until the current unit was completed to ask them to vote on it. While teaching students to self-assess is important, self-assessment is not germane to the question of why Buzz did not tell Elena about the South American unit (D).

5. **(B)** The correct response is (B). Buzz's response called for Elena to self-assess, which in turn promotes active inquiry. This was not a poor strategy. By encouraging her to think about her idea and subsequently suggesting that she take the idea to the group meeting, Buzz was reinforcing her for bringing the idea to him (A). While asking Elena what she thought about her idea may have helped Buzz assess her cognitive development in a small way, the important factor involved was in teaching her to evaluate her own thinking (C). Assessing the outside influences that affect a child's learning is not relevant to this question (D).

6. **(A)** The correct response is (A). Gagne's concept of scaffolding subsumes choices (B) and (C). By scaffolding her, Buzz helped Elena to consider all of the alternatives available to her and to make her own decision about the project (B) and (C). Therefore, choice (A) is the preferred answer. While pleasant interaction with an adult is considered to be reinforcing to a child, Buzz's purpose in asking Elena what she should do first would not have been to reinforce her by prolonging a pleasant interaction, but to scaffold her as she planned a course of action (D).

7. **(D)** The correct response is (D). Telling a student that she has expressed a good idea reinforces the idea which was positively evaluated. The expression of approval will reinforce the antecedent to the comment. In this case, the antecedent was Elena's suggestion to ask the class to vote on the pen pal idea. Therefore, this was the behavior which was reinforced. While such reinforcement enhances student self-esteem, such enhancement is only a by-product of the reinforcement, and not the purpose of it in this scenario (A). While the conversational transaction was coming

to an end, Buzz's purpose in saying "Good idea" would not have been to signal the end of the transaction, but rather to reinforce a behavior (B). Although Elena did self-evaluate in this transaction, this was not the behavior reinforced, since it was not the antecedent to the reinforcing remark (C).

8. **(D)** The correct response is (D). Eating together is an important way of developing social bonds. By eating with his colleagues, Buzz is promoting collegiality which in turn creates a positive school culture. It is true that first-year teachers are at increased risk of illness; however, there are a variety of ways of maintaining good nutrition that do not include eating in the cafeteria with one's colleagues (A). Nothing in the scenario suggests that Buzz is trying to encourage students to eat in the cafeteria (B). The scenario explains that Buzz is not interested in music; therefore, he would not have eaten lunch in the cafeteria in order to learn about the elements of Latin music (C).

9. **(C)** The correct response is (C). Students who share the African-American or the Hispanic culture tend to be field dependent learners. The family metaphor is a culturally appropriate structure for teaching field dependent students. Nothing in the scenario suggests that Buzz does not have a family of his own. Were it to be the case that Buzz did not have a family of his own, he would be irresponsible to organize his classroom for the express purpose of meeting his own affective needs (A). Although organizing the classroom by the family metaphor is the most culturally appropriate structure for teaching field dependent students, it is not necessarily the best organizational framework to cover the most amount of material in the least amount of time (B).

10. **(B)** The correct response is (B). Students who were previously enrolled in a special class for the majority of the day are likely to want to avoid activities that require them to engage in difficult activities such as writing. In addition, it is unlikely that Dave and Norman know what a pen pal is. Many teachers assume that special students have knowledge of common words that they in fact do not understand. There is no reason to assume that Dave and Norman dislike either Elena or persons from South America (A).

11. **(D)** The correct response is (D). Dave and Norman have IEP's which require that they participate in all classroom activities and that individual assistance be provided as necessary. It is required that Buzz comply with

the boys' IEP's. The IEP's do not state that the boys may be exempted from activities in which they do not want to participate (A) and (B). In addition, sending them to the resource room when the IEP states that they should be in the regular classroom is segregation on the basis of their disabilities (A). While they are to engage in the activity, the IEP's also require that Dave and Norman be given whatever individual support is needed in order to assure that they receive an appropriate education. It is not enough to tell them to do the best that they can and then not provide individual support (D).

12. **(A)** The correct response is (A). People construct knowledge from their experiences. Buzz knows that people construct their own knowledge, and therefore he employs a constructivist perspective of learning. Having the children develop their own units to teach to the class employs such a perspective. While children typically do enjoy work more when they work in teams, their enjoyment would not be Buzz's primary motivator for using this particular instructional approach. Their enjoyment should be a result of good instructional strategy, rather than a reason for employing a particular instructional strategy (B). The state curriculum guide does not mandate instructional strategies (C). The IEP's of special students are not mandates governing the organization of mainstream classrooms. The needs of the special students are to be met within the framework of the main-stream classroom (D).

13. **(D)** The correct response is (D). Buzz's unit of study employs the cooperative learning activity Group Investigation, because each group of students work on one project in any way in which they choose. STAD, or Student Teams Achievement Division, does not describe this activity; STAD places heterogeneously grouped students in teams in which they study material together. Each member then competes for her/his team against members of other teams who resemble her/him in ability (A). TGT, or Teams Games Tournaments, describes a cooperative group activity in which groups compete with other groups on mastery of the same material (B). In Buzz's activity, teams become resident experts on their country, and are not competing with other groups. Jigsaw is an organizational arrangement in which students are arranged in cooperative groups (C), and then each person in the group is assigned to become an expert on one facet of a unit of study. This person meets with students from other groups who are to become experts on the same facet. Once s/he has mastered the material, s/he reports back to the group. The facets of study then fit together like a jigsaw puzzle.

14. **(A)** The correct response is (A). Students should view their school as an integral part of their community, rather than as an isolated entity unto itself. As such, students should view the entire community as both a source of knowledge and a source of problems to investigate and solve. By taking his students to the library, Buzz is affirming the relationship between the community and the school in general, and the library and the school in particular. Buzz could have gone to the library himself and borrowed the necessary resources if the school was unable to supply sufficient resources; this would have been faster and less complicated than taking the entire class, so this is not a good answer (B). Taking the students to the library is not likely to forge strong home-school relationships except for the child whose parent is the librarian (C). Using the library does not promote student and family diversity (D).

15. **(C)** The correct response is (C). The librarian is a human resource for helping Buzz's students learn. As a graduate of a teacher education program, Buzz should know how to use the periodical section of the library (A). While Buzz needs to keep track of his special students, his primary reason for asking the librarian to help half of the students would be to maximize the learning of all students by using her as a learning resource, rather than to more closely supervise two students (B). While using the librarian as a resource may well promote the children in learning to problem solve, Buzz's immediate concern would be in using her as an immediate resource for student learning (D).

16. **(B)** The correct response is (B). The bystander was wrong. By using a variety of instructional materials, Buzz offers students with diverse learning styles and interests more opportunities to learn content matter than by using only one type of instructional material. In addition, students must master new technologies in order to be prepared for adult living, and such technologies are best mastered within the context of academic subjects. While books and traditional printed matter are important learning resources, technologies and appropriate software are also important learning resources which a good teacher will not overlook (A). New teachers may find that many conservative members of the community will fail to appreciate the role that new technologies play in classroom instruction. Computer literacy classes should be offered to all students; however, technologies are best mastered when contextualized (C) and (D).

17. **(C)** The correct response is (C). As a student developmentally enters the adolescent years, she begins to separate from family and move toward

peers. The student who was close to her parents suddenly finds herself embarrassed to be seen with them, because she wants to be seen by her peers as an adult, rather than a child. A student whose parents are less well-educated and less well-dressed than the parents of her peers would be far more likely to be embarrassed to have her parents come to school than would a student whose parents were more well-educated and well-dressed than the parents of her peers (A). Nothing in the scenario suggests that Marianne's parents want to move her to a private school, and nothing suggests that her parents object to her working in a group with children who are less able than she (B). While students frequently have crushes on teachers, nothing in this scenario suggests that this issue is germane (D).

18. **(A)** The correct response is (A). Asking parents to come to school for positive reasons does curry strong home-school relationships. Many parents are asked to come to school only when problems arise; this weakens the home-school relationship. Parents need to see the school showcasing their children and valuing their strengths. Having a parent present at a classroom presentation is more likely to increase a student's anxiety rather than to allay it (B). While improving home-school bonds also improves school-community bonds, school-community bonds are secondary to the home-school bonds in this scenario (C). While having their parents present should be a strong motivator for students to do good work (D), other motivational techniques would be equally as effective. The primary benefit of inviting parents is to curry home-school bonds (A).

19. **(A)** The correct response is (A). The assessment is informal since it is not standardized and normed. It is designed to shape instruction since Buzz's last question specifically asks how future instruction should be shaped. The performance of individual learners is not addressed. Only the performance of the group as a whole is assessed (B) and (D). Formal assessments must be standardized and normed (C) and (D).

20. **(D)** The correct response is (D). By seeing adults model the behavior of being active inquirers, the students will learn to value lifelong learning. Having adults ask students questions at their presentation does not facilitate the students in becoming self-directed problem-solvers (A). The questions do not constitute formal assessment of the student's learning outcomes for this project (B). Buzz is not helping his colleagues to become reflective professionals by having them ask his students questions (C).

21. **(C)** The correct response is (C). The test assesses both lower and higher level thinking. Items 2, 3, and 5 require analytical thinking, a higher level thinking skill (A) and (D). Items 1 and 4 assess factual knowledge, the lowest level of thinking (B). Therefore, Buzz's test assesses both higher and lower level thinking skills.

22. **(A)** The correct response is (A). Summative assessments occur after learning has taken place. Summative assessments are employed to measure the end result of instruction. They are typically used to grade students. This assessment has taken place after the South American unit of study has been completed. The students will be given grades based upon this assessment. Therefore, it is a summative assessment. The students take the test individually. Therefore, this is a summative assessment of individual learners. Since the group did not complete the assessment, it is not a group assessment (B). In contrast to summative assessments, formative assessments take place during the teaching/learning process while skills are being formed. Formative assessments, such as the one that Buzz conducted during the group presentations, are designed to help a teacher monitor the teaching process and make changes. Since Buzz will continue to work on the complex skills assessed in the group presentation, he used a formative assessment. However, since the class has completed the informational unit on South America, this individual test is a summative assessment of the content matter (C) and (D).

23. **(B)** The correct response is (B). Buzz must consider state curriculum guidelines and proposed learner outcomes in developing his next unit of study (I) and (III). He should also take into consideration the findings from the assessment of his previous unit of study (II). He does not have to take into consideration the IEP's of Dave and Norman in developing his next unit of study (IV).

24. **(B)** The correct response is (B). Mr. Treskoski's behavior demonstrates that he wants to study the gang issue further and reflect upon that research before he gives an answer to the class. This indicates that he knows how to promote his own growth. It also demonstrates that he is modeling behavior which creates a school culture that enhances learning. Mr. Treskoski's statement does not indicate that he will be planning for a lesson (A), but rather studying in order to develop a reasoned opinion of his own. (C) Mr. Treskoski clearly intends to share his opinion with the class after he has formulated one; sharing his opinion will promote diversity, rather than inhibit it. (D) Mr. Treskoski indicates that deferring to

answer is not due to time constraints, but to his need to explore the issue further.

25. **(B)** The correct response is (B). Mr. Treskoski demonstrates to Mr. Hinohosa that he considers Mr. Hinohosa an important source of advice by asking his recommendations; he also demonstrates that he considers Mr. Hinohosa an important source of information. This is a step toward developing a collegial relationship and toward creating a mutually supportive learning environment. It would not take a great deal of time to find the information in the school's library, nor would it be difficult to ascertain the computer capability of the library (A). The question does not concern individual student development (C). Nothing suggests that Mr. Treskoski's actions could be out of compliance with customary library regulations (D).

26. **(C)** The correct response is (C). Rather than aborting the project because of the school's lack of computer capability, Mr. Treskoski seeks assistance from a community resource, the local community college. This will foster student growth in at least three ways: first, the students will receive materials that would not otherwise be available to them; second, the students will become aware of a source of local computer access which they may use later in their own endeavors; third, students will become the beneficiaries of a close community tie between the school and the community college. Nothing in the question suggests that individual needs are being addressed (A). Indeed, until the material arrives, Mr. Treskoski has no way of knowing the difficulty or exact content of the articles; therefore, he has no way of knowing whether any of the articles will meet the needs of any particular student. The question does not address the various domains of student growth (B). While gathering materials can be considered part of the planning activity (D), the focus in this scenario is not on planning, but on the use of community resources.

27. **(B)** The correct response is (B). Mr. Treskoski is developing a strong partnership with Casey's aunt when he demonstrates his interest in having her share a role in classroom instruction. Although having a guest speaker is an instructional strategy (A), the important issue is having Casey's aunt be the speaker. Since her aunt is editorial director, she may not be as well qualified to address the issue of the newspaper's partisanship as some other member of the newspaper staff, such as the managing editor, would be. Therefore, Mr. Treskoski's interest would be in fostering a strong parent-teacher relationship rather than in instructional strategy. The emphasis is not on an individual talent and ability (C), although Casey and

her aunt would have talents and abilities. The emphasis is on Casey's inviting her aunt and Mr. Treskoski's encouragement of the aunt's taking part in the classroom life. Nothing in the question addresses the issue of modalities (D).

28. **(A)** The correct response is (A). By allowing Molly's father to come and express a dissenting opinion, Mr. Treskoski demonstrates that he appreciates diversity of ideas. This in turn creates an environment that celebrates the diversity of groups and the uniqueness of individuals. While Molly's prior learning is demonstrated by her telling Mr. Treskoski what her father has said (B), the emphasis is not on her prior learning, but on inviting Mr. Winters to share his unique perspective. Since Mr. Winters is the personnel manager at the electronics factory instead of an authority on either crime or the newspaper, he could not be considered a community resource on this issue (C). If the issue had to do with electronics or personnel matters, he would have been considered a community resource. While the students may be curious as to what Mr. Winters has to say, the emphasis is not on stimulating student curiosity (D), but on inviting Mr. Winters to come and share his perspective.

29. **(D)** The correct response is (D). It is a violation of both legal and ethical guidelines to discuss a special education student's handicapping condition with another student's parent. The Family Right to Privacy Act (FRPA) assures the confidentiality of student records. Mr. Treskoski would be committing ethical and legal violations (A) to discuss Lynn's disability with Ms. Rivas. Moving Lynn out of the group simply because Mrs. Rivas did not want her daughter to be grouped with him (B) would violate the spirit of the Fourteenth Amendment, as it would segregate Lynn from his assigned group because he has a disability. While it is a major goal of social studies to instill civic virtue in students (C), Mr. Treskoski cannot violate the legal and ethical guidelines that protect Lynn's confidentiality regarding his disability.

30. **(C)** The correct response is (C). By having children define their realities concerning food and then compare lists, Mr. Treskoski is promoting their cognitive development by assisting them in understanding that there may be many perspectives on what is true; the students are then given the opportunity to generalize that information to the issue of whether or not what the newspaper prints is true. Since the students are in the sixth grade, they are beginning to develop the ability to think abstractly, or in what Piaget called formal operational thought. Activities designed to chal-

lenge sixth-grade students to think abstractly best foster developmental growth of students this age. While writing can be an excellent educational tool (A), in this case, the students would not be pressed to move from concrete to abstract thought by engaging in an individual writing assignment. Until the children are engaged in an activity structured to assist them in understanding the constructive nature of truth in this incident, it is unlikely that they will be able to move beyond the stage of unreasoned argument (B). Indeed, it is likely that having students debate whose parent was telling the truth would result in creating unbreachable ill feelings between the school and the families involved, and an insurmountable loss of esteem for Casey and Molly. The children do not have access to all the articles which might be construed as pertinent in this issue (D). In addition, they will not have the cognitive ability to address this issue until they are given more experience in thinking abstractly.

31. **(A)** The correct response is (A). Mr. Treskoski explicitly states a problem and asks the students what possible solutions might be. He is using communication skills to stimulate the students to develop problem-solving skills and to think divergently. Mr. Treskoski is not assessing understanding of material (B) and (C) which he has presented. He is explicitly seeking to have children problem-solve. While students may make informal assessments of how good their suggestions are, Mr. Treskoski's question is not designed to help students monitor their performance (D).

32. **(C)** The correct response is (C). By allowing all students to participate in the construction of the letter, Mr. Treskoski is allowing them to compare, analyze, and evaluate ideas in order to select the best ways of formulating their letter. This method also assures that all students receive the affective benefits of student ownership of the letter. While all students would have the opportunity to compare, analyze, and evaluate ideas in their groups if each group wrote a letter and the class voted on the best one (A), only one group would have ownership of the letter. While it would expedite matters for Mr. Treskoski to write the letter himself (B), it would neither facilitate student learning nor student ownership of the process. If the class voted on the best writer and s/he wrote the letter (D), only one student would be involved in comparing, analyzing, and evaluating ideas, and only one student would have ownership.

33. **(B)** The correct response is (B). Mr. Treskoski demonstrated an understanding of environmental factors that affect learning by making ar-

rangements for students from impoverished families to participate in the event. An understanding of human developmental processes (A) is not an issue here. An understanding of the importance of motivation (C) is not an issue here. While socioeconomic class does represent an important cultural difference (D), the scenario does not address the respect of cultural differences, but an understanding of an environmental problem that could prevent children from participating in a learning activity.

34. **(A)** The correct response is (A). When Captain Bonaly becomes involved in her child's schooling, Renee derives important benefits. Communication between home and school is enhanced; Renee will have increased pride in her academic achievements. Her self-esteem will grow. Captain Bonaly will have increased interest in Renee's school activities. Although Renee will probably learn more about Turkey, this limited benefit pales in comparison to the benefit of having her mother become involved with her school (B). Although Renee has lived in Turkey, it is more likely that the activity will help her learn to better appreciate the diversity of the Turkish people than to appreciate her own diversity (C). Completing the project will promote Renee's growth, but this benefit is secondary to the benefit of having her mother become involved in her new school (D).

35. **(B)** The correct response is (B). Fifth graders are beginning to move from concrete thinking to abstract thinking. Learning that not all peoples have the same religious beliefs is an important diversity notion for new abstract thinkers to understand. A study of comparative religions is not a curricular requirement for fifth graders (A). While some students may be highly motivated to learn about religions, this interest is not necessarily widespread (C). Using good planning to create self-directed learners is not a reason to ask Captain Bonaly to be sure to tell students about the Islamic religion (D).

36. **(D)** The correct response is (D). Having Summer's minister come conduct a prayer service is a violation of the separation of church and state (C). In contrast, teaching about different religions does not violate the separation of church and state. Lacie should explain the difference in the two activities to Summer. There is no reason to withdraw the invitation to Captain Bonaly to come speak to the class (A), nor is there a reason to ask Captain Bonaly to omit information about the Islamic religion (B).

37. **(C)** The correct response is (C). Publication of work is a strong

motivator to produce good work. Teaching a unit to classmates is a form of publication. Although students may teach a unit to their peers, it is highly unlikely that the young teachers will learn about learning theories in the process (A). Although learning to appreciate their teacher's efforts might be a pleasant benefit of teaching a lesson to the class, it is not a major benefit of the activity (B). Students should learn organizational skills when they prepare a lesson for the class; however, the extent to which this learning would generalize to improve academic performance in other areas is questionable (D).

38. **(B)** The correct response is (B). Children operating at the concrete operational stage greatly benefit from direct observation. Infants operate at the sensorimotor stage; observing a demonstration of how sound waves work would be of no use to infants (A). While students operating at the formal operational level would greatly benefit from direct observation of sound waves in addition to complex theoretical descriptions, the direct observation is absolutely essential to the understanding of the concrete thinker (C). There is no Piagetial interpersonal concordance stage. Interpersonal concordance is a stage of moral development described by Lawrence Kohlberg.

39. **(D)** The correct response is (D). The media specialist would be Lacie's best resource for learning about the technologies available in her school. Lacie's mentor teacher may not know the capabilities of available technologies; in addition, teaching new teachers how to use school technologies is the responsibility of the media specialist, not mentor teachers (A). While Lacie would benefit from enrolling in a computer/technology course at her local university or community college, the courses would not necessarily teach her how to use the technologies available in her school (C).

40. **(B)** The correct response is (B). By taking responsibility for teaching younger students, Lacie's students will develop a sense of responsibility for their school community. While they may communicate effectively with other members of the school community in the course of this project, it is unlikely that the students will learn to appreciate their communication skill (A). The students may develop an appreciation of the potential of technology as a teaching tool, but this outcome is less likely than their development of a sense of responsibility toward their school community (C). Although a few students may make a personal commitment to developing technological skills as a result of teaching younger peers, making a personal commitment as a result of this activity is a morally advanced action

that few fifth graders would be capable of making (D).

41. **(A)** The correct response is (A). By participating in the students' education, the community members will learn that their involvement in the students' education is important. The businesses' involvement is unlikely to help the community to better understand the problems of students (B). Although the community may come to understand something about discipline problems facing teachers as they interact with Lacie's students, this is not the most likely benefit of their involvement (C). Having the businesses involved in the students' education in fifth grade is unlikely to persuade them seven years later to remain in the community in lieu of seeking lucrative employment in the cities (D).

42. **(A)** The correct response is (A). When students are allowed to select their own problems for study, they become self-directed problem-solvers. As such, they have the opportunity to structure their own learning experiences. Assessing students' needs in a naturalistic setting is highly time consuming and not an important benefit of having students select their own problem to investigate (B). There may or may not be a wide variety of instructional materials available to the students as they engage in studying the temperature problem (C); this is not likely to be a major benefit. Learning to appreciate opposing viewpoints is a competency that would be better addressed in social studies and language arts than in an activity which deals with a natural empirical science (D).

43. **(A)** The correct response is (A). People are more highly motivated to solve problems which they choose than problems which are chosen for them. Choosing a problem for investigation does not increase student diversity (B). Problem selection has nothing to do with the structure of student groups (C). Although students may engage in more self-assessment, this is not the most important force at work (D).

44. **(A)** The correct response is (A). A good lesson contains opportunities for all types of learners. Assessing hand-eye coordination (B) is not an objective of this lesson. Manipulatives often spice up a lesson, but this is not the main objective of using the manipulative (C). The activity may become self directed (D) but this is not specified in the question.

45. **(D)** The correct response is (D). For a computers teacher, hardware and software can serve as an excellent resource even if it is utilized only occasionally. Although test taking is usually more beneficial in a familiar

place, classes do not always have to be in the same place (A) and minimal exposure (B) to new technology is still beneficial. A lesson utilizing computers requires planning, and this would not be a free period for the teacher (C).

46. **(C)** The correct response is (C). A teacher needs to know the best type of tone to take when conversing with parents. Knowing how the parents feel about education and the fears the child has about failure, the teacher should do his or her best to show the student in a favorable light. Letting the student off the hook (A) would not solve the problem. In this case calling the parents personally with news of a failing grade (B) would do more harm than good. Except in unusual circumstances, it is not the teacher's place to counsel a student on a family problem (D). The teacher can lend an ear, give support when it comes to raising self-esteem in the classroom, or suggest a talk with the school counselor.

47. **(D)** The correct response is (D). The steps in developing a learning strategy include becoming aware of metacognition, analyzing information to be learned, devising a plan to learn the information, implementing the plan, and monitoring and modifying it as needed. Therefore all the choices are included.

48. **(C)** The correct response is (C). The teacher used a rhyme to help the students remember the number. An acronym (A) is a word made from the first letters to be learned. An acrostic (B) is a sentence made up from words derived from the first letters of the items to be learned. The pegword method (D) involves matching up information needed to be learned with a previously memorized set of words for easier recall.

49. **(B)** The correct response is (B). It is against school policy to bring any sort of weapon to school. The only choice the teacher has if he or she wants to follow school rules is to turn the knife and the student over to the principal. Ignoring the incident (A), taking the weapon away but not reporting it (C), and letting the weapon remain in the boy's possession would be a violation of school policy (D).

50. **(D)** The correct response is (D). A teacher, when discussing with parents a behavior problem, should always present documentation of the incidents so that it is presented in a fair and accurate manner (I). The best way to keep parents on your side is to convey concern (II) rather than aggravation (III). A teacher should work with parents' suggestions (IV).

51. **(D)** The correct response is (D). Searching for reasons and suggesting possible explanations for factual information is inquiry teaching. (A) is incorrect because although cooperative learning could be used in the activity described, the situation described does not mention it. (B) is incorrect because although the activity described contains elements of problem solving, it is more accurately described as inquiry teaching. (C) is incorrect because inquiry teaching includes the use of higher order thinking skills, however, the overall teaching strategy described here is inquiry teaching.

52. **(B)** The correct response is (B). Since the planning activity involves group research, the concluding activity should also include groups. (A) and (C) are incorrect for similar reasons. An essay test or a paragraph summarizing the reasons for immigration might be used at a later time, but it should not be used as the concluding activity to group reports of research findings. The concluding activity should match the strategy used to learn the materials. (D) is incorrect because the teacher needs to plan a conclusion to this topic before proceeding to another topic.

53. **(C)** The correct response is (C). Increased student self-esteem, increased time spent on academic tasks and increased positive attitudes toward other students are all expected results of properly structured cooperative learning activities. (D) is incomplete. (A) and (B) include increased competition for student grades which is not expected as a result of cooperative learning.

54. **(C)** The correct response is (C). When cooperative learning activities are correctly implemented, individual students are responsible for content, even though the information was learned in a cooperative manner. (A) is incorrect because whether or not students can take a review course for the college entrance exam is irrelevant. (B) is incorrect because individual colleges have different admissions standards. Some colleges emphasize grades; some emphasize entrance exams. (D) is incorrect because it avoids the issue and does not respond to the parent's concern.

55. **(D)** The correct response is (D). Permitting student choice is a major factor in creating a learning environment that will be self-motivating. (A) is incorrect because numerous choices may overwhelm learning disabled students, but there is no indication that in the situation described that these students are learning disabled. Even learning disabled students can be provided with one-to-one assistance to make individual selections from a lengthy list of choices. (B) is incorrect because choosing topics is the

primary concern here, not grades. It is reasonable to assume that the teacher will consider the nature of the project when assigning grades. (C) is incorrect because there is no reason to believe that parents would be angry because the teacher provided many choices for the students as they selected topics.

56. **(B)** The correct response is (B). Questions that demand recall of factual information can be answered in one or two words or a short phrase. If lengthy answers are desired, then the question format must change. There is no information to indicate that students are intimidated, therefore (A) is incorrect. Uncertainty about answers usually causes students to provide long, rambling responses, so (C) is incorrect. (D) is incorrect because the students are providing answers so it does not seem reasonable that the questions are too difficult.

57. **(C)** The correct response is (C). The writing process is the term used for the steps described in preparing a written paper. The steps in the writing process include: prewriting, drafting, revising, editing, and writing the final copy, or publishing. (A) is incorrect because writing and editing are only parts of the writing process. The situation described does not include peer group work, so (B) is incorrect. This is not a description of cooperative learning, so (D) is also incorrect.

58. **(A)** The correct response is (A). A sense of civic responsibility is promoted by a classroom discussion of civic events, like local elections. (B) is incorrect because the situation described indicates that students have already determined their reasons for opposing the curfew. There is no reason to believe that students will stage a sidewalk protest as a result of the classroom activity, so (C) is incorrect. (D) is incorrect because the response the teacher suggests, the writing of letters, should cause no concern from parents.

59. **(B)** The correct response is (B). Although for a yearlong cooperative working relationship Joe Thacker should probably go ahead and teach the novel specified in the curriculum guide, Joe's sincere desire to get off to a strong start with his teaching by using *The Red Badge of Courage* may convince the chairperson to discuss the matter again with the other sophomore teachers and allow Joe to teach the novel. If the curriculum is inviolate the chairperson will know which of the other three sophomore English teachers will be the most helpful to Joe and share teaching resources and strategies with him for the novel all are teaching. (A) is incorrect since Joe

is dooming himself to being the outcast on the sophomore English team by going against the usual team commitment regarding curriculum. (C) is incorrect since Joe is showing he does not understand the hierarchy of authority on the school campus. By not following the advice of the other teachers and by overlooking the departmental chairperson, Joe is politically unwise in his decision-making. (D) is incorrect since he is ignoring the total input from school professionals and co-workers about his teaching and instead asking the parents to make a curriculum decision. Actually, his letting the parents vote about the book to use with their sons and daughters may well be an unfavorable action in the parents' perspective. He will have difficulty regaining their confidence in his effectiveness as a teacher.

60. **(B)** The correct response is (B). Ms. Kent is demonstrating the best way to work with the teachers from the two high schools and to determine an equitable solution to the problem. By refraining from voting herself, unless a tie occurs, and by requesting individual teachers' votes be counted, she is removing the possibility of a stalemate that could create rivalry between the two high school science departments. She also is not showing favoritism for her own campus with the procedure she is recommending. (A) is incorrect since it shows poor decision-making skills for a teacher placed in a position of leadership. By placing her loyalty to her own school's teachers above the responsibility she has to represent the entire district in her work on the Central Textbook Committee, Ms. Kent shows immaturity. (B) is incorrect since it shows a somewhat flippant attitude about the importance of selecting the textbook that most teachers will find most useful in teaching Biology I in a high school in Lenere. Leaving the choice to luck of the draw, although perhaps occasionally the only solution, is far down the list of recommended ways to solve the problem. (D) is incorrect since the second-ranked book may actually be the third-ranked, behind both of the other textbooks selected in first place by the Lenere teachers. As the teachers re-study their choices and share their information and rationale for selection, indeed the second-ranked book may become the final choice of all teachers; however, one of the first-ranked textbooks should have consideration.

61. **(D)** The correct response is (D). Each of the listings (I) through (IV) has a relationship to the units of study in Biology I; therefore, each could be an appropriate activity making use of resources within the community of Lenere. Although the curriculum guide will list many resources that teachers may not select, all listings should be potential activities a teacher

may pursue with her classes. (A), (B), and (C) are incorrect since each lists only some of the resources that are available within the community. The curriculum guide should provide as many ideas as possible.

62. **(A)** The correct response is (A). Ms. Kent is using excellent communication techniques to prepare the students for the unit of study. The students, by suggesting their ideas and hearing elaboration of their ideas from other students and Ms. Kent, indeed feel a sense of proprietorship in the forthcoming unit of study. The excitement created by the discussion will promote inquiry and active participation as the study unfolds. Ms. Kent's communication techniques of encouraging feed-in from other students about each idea and recording all ideas submitted demonstrates her communication skills. (B) is not the best answer since in all activities that occur in the classroom, all students should have the opportunity to express their ideas. Open communication within the classroom, among students and between teacher and students, is an essential to an effective teaching environment and not a benefit limited to this one project. (C) is incorrect since little can be gained by further evaluation of the adopted Biology I textbook. Perhaps Ms. Kent will be interested to see how many of the suggested activities in the teacher's guide are also mentioned by her students, but the information will not result in a better unit of study. (D) is incorrect since the activity could only slightly provide information about each students' knowledge of the beach. It would not be a good pre-unit assessment in itself, since some students are never as active in class discussion as their ability or information level would suggest they could be.

63. **(D)** The correct response is (D). Alicia's veiled threats of suicide may be merely creative expression, but a teacher cannot risk postponing investigation to see if the girl needs psychological help, especially since Alicia's behavior in class is another indication of deep emotional disturbance. Ms. Mitchell is ethically and legally responsible for reporting to an appropriate school authority any suspicious behavior of a student. Ms. Mitchell is not herself trained to investigate the situation and provide assistance if Alicia is a victim of child abuse or has a history of emotional instability. On most campuses, the person to whom the teacher should first talk is the student's counselor. All counselors are thoroughly trained in the procedures to follow once such a case is reported. Ms. Mitchell should certainly continue to observe Alicia carefully in class, perhaps keeping notes of any unusual actions or continued depression exhibited in writing. A personal conference with Alicia about her journal may be helpful in building a closer communication link with the girl. Hereafter, Ms. Mitchell

should modify her statement about the confidentiality of the journal written by students to include the need to share some content with trained personnel to get help for students in need. Since the law is clear on this point, the students cannot expect their teacher to behave in any other way.

(A) is incorrect since a delay in getting help for the girl could be disastrous. (B) is incorrect since another teacher has no greater potential to aid Alicia than does Ms. Mitchell. The sharing of the journal's contents with the teacher would violate Ms. Mitchell's agreement with the students, as well. (C) is incorrect since the teacher needs to take more action to prevent a possible tragedy. The idea of writing a few carefully phrased comments on the journal as part of the assessment response is good and should be done as Ms. Mitchell consults with the counselor. Perhaps the counselor can even help the inexperienced teacher with the message that should be written.

64. **(B)** The correct response is (B). The form that Mr. Svensen has developed will give details of each student's performance in the computer lab—both strengths and areas of weakness. This information becomes a working focus for the parents and the teacher as they try to help the student improve. Since the computer has excellent memory, maintaining a record of signs of improvement in deficient skills can be easily achieved. The continuing analysis of student performance becomes an excellent basis for a parent conference. (A) is incorrect because teachers are expected to have skills in their area of instruction; therefore, Mr. Svensen's students' parents do not need to be impressed with his use of the computer. (C) is incorrect because the form developed is specifically for reporting on the classes taught in computer science by Mr. Svensen. His form would not be useful for other courses of study. Often, a general form adapts poorly for performance or skill classes. (D) is incorrect since actually Mr. Svensen may be spending more time in preparing progress reports for all students. Certainly, however, the legibility of Mr. Svensen's communication to the parents will be greatly improved through the use of the computer-generated form.

65. **(C)** The correct response is (C). Since Ms. Walker admits to little knowledge of gangs in general and absolutely nothing about the gangs in the school and community where she is teaching, she should first talk to those in the community who have the greatest knowledge of local gang activity. The information she will receive as well as possible future contacts if she needs help in dealing with a gang-related problem will be

invaluable as she continues to teach in the community. The realistic perspective of those presenting the course will be most pertinent for her needs. By making a personal connection with community leaders in the constant war against gangs, she is making a statement about the sincerity of her interest and intent to be an effective teacher for the youth she will meet. (A) is a naive approach that could create more problems than solutions. Only biased views would be given by a gang leader anyway; therefore, she should look elsewhere to start gathering information about the gangs in her new community. (B) is not the best answer. Although she might find out more about gangs, as a bestseller, the book may be one based upon only the sensational aspects of gang life. Ms. Walker's greatest need is to find out about her specific community and the youth therein. Her college course information presumably included the general knowledge about gangs across the nation. Now, facing the prospect of working with gang members in her classes, she finds national attitudes only minimally helpful. (D) is not the best answer for Ms. Walker since she seems to have slight background of information. Before she organizes a class discussion about gangs in the community, she needs to be better informed herself. A class discussion if held, should grow out of a reasonable relationship to a concept studied in class.

66. **(D)** The correct response is (D). Mr. Asaki is using a variety of instructional methods and materials to work with his remedial reading students. His use of other instructors as well as the computer lab indicates his awareness of effective teaching techniques. By noting the interests of his students and extending a lesson based upon these interests, Mr. Asaki demonstrates superior adaptation of time and resources to achieve the goals of the class. By creating their own cards for a real holiday their initial interest in reading card messages will probably be rekindled, and they will have fun while reading one another's cards. (A) is incorrect because it mentions only half of the correct answer (D). (B) is incorrect because the use of resource instructors in a class is an excellent way to plan some lessons. Using guest instructors can actually create more work for a teacher, who must prepare the students for the guest's lessons, be ready to assist at any point, and continue the lesson after the guest leaves. (C) is incorrect because no degree of laziness is implied by the teacher who uses such strategies for the appropriate learning activities.

67. **(B)** The correct response is (B). The project displayed at a local shopping mall becomes another positive tie between the school and the community. The students feel good about having their work displayed and

will probably visit the exhibit several times during the course of the display. (A) is incorrect because the important value of the project is not the individual recognition, but the worth of the project in building community esteem for the work accomplished by a remedial class—or any class—at the school. (C) is incorrect because the major benefit of the project comes from the positive response of the community. (D) is incorrect because although sharing the project with other schools is a good idea, just seeing the end product at a shopping mall is not very useful for other teachers. Perhaps through staff development in the district, other teachers can hear about the setting up of the project and the suggestions for designing a similar one.

68. **(A)** The correct response is (A). Mr. Asaki realizes that by the age of most of his students, their messages from home have been mainly of a negative nature since most of them have failed several subjects and had other problems in school. The assignment is based on valid instructional wisdom and also promotes the positive aspects of school and home. The teacher's role in this activity cannot be ignored by the parents, thus Mr. Asaki's cooperative working relationship with the parents of his students has been reinforced. Both (B) and (C) are demonstrated by the project planned, however neither answer reflects the best professional awareness shown by Mr. Asaki. (D) is also a valid response, but cannot be considered the best. Repeating a lesson for the sake of fun or excitement does not deserve merit for the teacher's decision making ability. The activity planned goes well beyond mere repetition especially since the final result should create a positive note between school and home.

69. **(B)** The correct response is (B). The variety of interaction with the community Mr. Asaki has fostered will benefit the school in good will as well as foster student growth in several ways. Mutual support among the students of Mr. Asaki's class and a community group that normally would have little or no contact with the school offers many positive rewards for everyone. (A) is incorrect because it focuses only upon the greeting cards. Seeing the cards is not nearly as important as the interaction between the older residents and the youth of the community. (C) is incorrect since the questions asks for a benefit to the school. Certainly, the students will become even more aware of the impact of their work on people in the community through the mail responses and indirectly the school will also be noted, but it is not the *best* answer. (D) is not the best answer either, because while having the young people visit the nursing home will be a welcomed event, that will be of primarily personal benefit. The school's

primary benefit comes from the positive relationship with the community through the additional project undertaken by Mr. Asaki's class.

70. **(C)** The correct response is (C). If two students turn in the same essay for credit, the first thing the teacher should do is talk individually with each student. The teacher's next action should depend on what was learned from speaking with the students involved. (A) is incorrect because at this point it is unclear what the students have done and reporting their behavior would be premature. (B) is incorrect because until the teacher has spoken to each student individually there is not enough information to determine whether or not the parents should be notified. (D) is incorrect because assigning an "F" to the paper without first discussing the situation with the students would be unfair, and would only serve to anger the students. After learning the reasons for the students behavior, then the teacher may determine that both students deserve a failing grade.

71. **(D)** The correct response is (D). If both students admitted that they wrote the paper together, the best response would be for the teacher to ask each student to write another paper and assess a grade penalty. (A) is incorrect because while the punishment may be appropriate, the issue of the duplicate paper for one assignment has not been resolved. (B) is incorrect because this is a mindless punishment and serves a very limited purpose. (C) is incorrect because there is no incentive to prepare another paper if the student knows in advance that they will receive a zero.

72. **(B)** The correct response is (B). Teaching integrated lessons causes students to remember information for a longer period of time and in greater detail. (A) is incorrect because integrated lessons do not cause students to become frustrated or confused. Instead, integrated lessons have the opposite effect. (C) is incorrect because while lessons will be related, the classes will require individual assignments. (D) is incorrect because teachers who prepare integrated lessons must be very knowledgeable about the subject for which they are responsible.

73. **(B)** The correct response is (B). Integrating another content area into the students' study of the American Revolution will develop a broader view of that period in history. (A) is incorrect because although the teachers are integrating their lessons, they are each responsible for their own subject area. (C) is incorrect because librarians are usually pleased when books are used by teachers and students. (D) is incorrect because teaching integrated units does not mean that students will be doing homework for

one subject during another's class period.

74. **(B)** The correct response is (B). Mr. Mendez has made an attempt to notify all parents, but he has not verified that all parents received his notification. He must also have a signed statement from the parent of every child. This statement gives permission for the child to ride with Mr. Mendez or one of the parents driving a van. Such a release form is required in Manhattan public schools. Some school districts have even more rigid rules, not allowing students to attend a field trip unless a school employee is driving each vehicle used in transport. The handbook referred to by the principal will specify the regulations required by the Ft. Worth district. Incorrect responses to the question are (A), (C), and (D) since all contain steps that Mr. Mendez should take in arranging for the field trip. After obtaining the school administrator's approval for the field trip, he has considered the needs of other teachers of his students as well as of the parents who will assist him in transporting the students.

75. **(C)** The correct response is (C). The major benefit the principal sees is probably based upon the school and parents working together to promote student learning. The activity will potentially strengthen the relationship between school and home, especially for the students with diverse backgrounds whose parents may sometimes feel left out of activities that are planned for their participation. (A) will provide an excellent chance for students to practice a free-enterprise activity and evaluate the result of their effort. They will learn the organizational perspective on the work as well as the economics involved. (B) is a practical approach to teaching across disciplines. Perhaps the homemaking, computer lab, and the business education instructors will assist in the Foreign Language Department project. (D) provides the opportunity for the community as a whole to gain appreciation for those parents who contribute recipes. Certainly most students will be proud of their parents contributing to the project.

76. **(A)** The correct response is (A). Business people and other community leaders will have good communications skills and recognize these same traits in others. They are also influential in expressing the qualities they want their high school's graduates to demonstrate. Also, using community judges would be an asset to school/community relations. Ms. Salinger will be demonstrating her confidence in the adults of her school community and building contacts that may serve the school well in the future. (B) is incorrect since using recent graduates may present a problem. The graduates will still be very close in age to the contestants, and

therefore could still be close friends. This type of loyalty could cloud their judgment. (C) is not the best choice, however it is very likely that any last minute cancellations, or lack of interest could be remedied by faculty members willing to assist. (D) is unrealistic. The expense of bringing in speech teachers from other schools would be beyond the budget of most schools.

77. **(A)** The correct response is (A). All of the activities listed in I, II, and IV are services provided to members of the community. The remaining activity, babysitting for one's siblings, would be helpful to the student's parents but could not be considered community service. Perhaps volunteering to help with a community nursery project could substitute as an acceptable activity.

78. **(C)** The correct response is (C). Although unwise to reveal the problems he is having with a specific student as a topic for lunchroom conversation, Mr. Kanfield is being unethical when he brings in specific information about a student's records. Legally, these records are not to be revealed to others. Even though the information about a high nonverbal IQ may be considered positive, it is not information he is permitted to share with other teachers. Leaving out the student's name as her behaviors are listed would still allow his peers to offer advice if that is what he is seeking. If it is just his frustration with her behavior spilling over, better that he wait until he can talk with Pearl's parent or counselor to try to find the cause of her behavior. (A) ignores the legal and ethical concerns of talking to others about a student's private records. (B) changes the attitude of Mr. Kanfield when he spoke but not the lack of wisdom shown. Certainly, talking with Pearl is the first step to begin solving the problem, then perhaps her parent or counselor. (D) is incorrect because fixing make-up in class is poor judgement on Pearl's part, not Mr. Kanfield's. There is no evidence to suggest that a sexist bias exists.

79. **(A)** The correct response is (A). Regardless of her experience with students, Ms. Stewart is not free to alter the modification plans given to her for teaching Billy. In fact, she must keep records to show when and how she provided the modifications required to help Billy. By allowing more time than the other students have had by permitting oral work for some testing situations, Ms. Stewart is continuing to demonstrate her understanding of the art as well as the legal requirements of teaching students who have special needs. (B) is incorrect since the classroom teacher does not have the right to disregard modification recommendations pre-

scribed for a student with special needs. Monitoring of special needs students will check on the type and frequency of Ms. Stewart's modifications for Billy so that his educational performance is acceptable. If Ms. Stewart has a question about the need for such modifications, her questions should be directed to Admission, Review and Dismissal (ARD) meetings that establish modification recommendations for students. (C) is incorrect because again Ms. Stewart is ignoring part of the modification prescribed for Billy's instructional leader, the teacher. (D) is incorrect because Ms. Stewart is not carrying out the modifications as intended by the ARD committee. By requiring Billy to do twice as much work, she is punishing him for his difficulties regardless of her detailed record keeping.

80. **(C)** The correct response is (C). The question asks for an effective method of taking roll that doesn't detract from class. (C) is the best option. By assigning each student a specific place to stand, Mr. Deavers can quickly check attendance, in a method similar to the one he would use in assigning seats in a classroom. If teachers use seating charts in the classroom, this method would be familiar to the students. By requiring students to take this position immediately, he can also assign students to lead warm-up exercises while he checks roll, thus making good use of time. (A) is a poor choice. Although it might increase his awareness of who is absent and who is present, this method wastes instructional time. Also, without organization, one student may answer for another. (B) may be effective, but it assumes that all student leaders will be present each day and that they will all be responsible. A teacher who wants to teach responsibility may use a similar system, but would need to teach responsibility to the student leaders and to have assistant leaders as a backup. (D) is almost impossible if the students are engaged in an activity that requires movement. It would be very time-consuming as well, distracting the teacher's attention from the activity itself.

Section 2: Written Assignment

The following essay received scores at the highest end of the scale used in ATS-W essay scoring.

Essay A

Homework assignments can be an important part of the instructional program, or they can be meaningless, busy-work activities. Quality, meaningful homework assignments have several characteristics. First, they are appropriate for the age and grade level of the student. No more than 20 minutes of homework should be assigned to students in grades 1 to 4. As a student matures, longer and more complex homework assignments are appropriate. For students in grades 5 to 8 assignments that require 30 or 40 minutes to complete are appropriate. High school students are able to concentrate for longer periods of time, consequently, longer homework assignments are appropriate for them.

Second, homework assignments should be directly related to classwork. Homework quickly becomes busy-work if the teacher simply hands out another worksheet to complete. However, homework becomes a valuable learning experience if the assignment is designed to provide an additional opportunity for students to practice a new concept introduced in class.

Third, students should be able to the complete the assignment independently. An exception to this characteristic of quality homework is that teachers may occasionally ask students to complete a project or poster as homework. Students may need to consult reference books, parents, or friends in order to complete some projects. This can as so be a valuable learning experience.

A fourth characteristic of quality homework assignments is that the teacher must evaluate the homework in some manner. The teacher may want to grade the assignment, have the students put answers on the chalkboard, display the papers on the bulletin board, or discuss answers as a form of evaluation. The key issue is that the teacher must acknowledge the work the student has done and give credit and recognition for a completed assignment.

The fifth characteristic of quality homework is that the teacher needs to inform parents early in the school year that homework will be assigned regularly. Parents need to be supportive of the educational plan.

Too often, teachers assign meaningless, repetitious, drill and practice activities for homework that are not specifically related to classwork. Students quickly identify these assignments as busy-work and may become resentful of future homework assignments.

Carefully planned homework assignments not only reinforce classwork, but also teach responsibility and independent work habits. Each school needs to develop a clearly defined homework policy that recognizes the necessity of making homework assignments meaningful, appropriate to the student's age and grade level, directly related to classwork, and evaluated by the teacher upon completion.

Analysis

This essay is well planned and organized. The main idea is clearly stated in the first sentence. The author lists five characteristics of quality homework assignments and explains each. The last paragraph summarizes the writer's main points. Nevertheless, there are some problems with the essay. Several sentences in the essay are long and seem to ramble. The author does not clearly explain how parents can "be supportive of the educational plan" in relationship to homework. There are a few errors in punctuation, but the writer has demonstrated the ability to focus on a specific topic and write an organized essay with a definite introduction, body and conclusion.

The following essay received scores in the middle of the ATS-W scoring scale.

Essay B

All students need homework—it is an important part of the educational process. The school day is to short to allow teachers to provide time to complete all the activities students need to do. Some of these assignments must be taken home for completion.

There are to major problems with homework assignments. The first is that teachers often assign too much work to completed at home. Homework assignments should not require anymore than thirty minutes to compete. If the assignment will require more time, then it should be split into two parts. The second problem is that teachers often make an assignment at the end of class. This does not give students a change to begin the assignment during class so they can ask questions if they need to. It also does not give teachers a chance to see if students have stated the assignment correctly.

Homework is important! All teachers should assign homework regularly! Students need to become accustom to working on their own! Parents expect homework! It keeps students busy after school and helps develop self-responsibility!

Analysis

The length of the essay is satisfactory for the time period. However, the essay does not have a clearly stated main idea. Many topics are discussed (students need homework, the school day is too short, problems with homework) but the writer's position on these topics is never fully explained. The last paragraph introduces three new ideas (homework should be assigned regularly, parents expect homework, and homework develops responsibility). None of these topics is completely discussed. The essay lacks a definite introduction and conclusion. There are several spelling and punctuation errors. A word has been omitted ("be") in the second sentence of the second paragraph. The exclamation point is overused in the last paragraph.

The following essay received scores at the lowest end of the ATS-W scoring scale.

Essay C

Students need homework, but generally teachers give too much. Assignments are usually too long and don't allow any time for students to participate in outside activities. School need to develop a system so that students would not have homework in more than one subject every day. That way students could consentrate on one subject and not have to worry about remembering assignments in other areas.

Teachers needs to plan homework assignments that are easy to grade. Everyone know that teachers have to many papers to grade already. Homework assignments should be short and easy to grade.

Teachers should also remember to look at the football and basketball game schedules to avoid giving homework on game nights. Not fair to teem members and cheerleaders to have homework on game nights. Besides, teachers can always give class time to do homework.

Analysis

This writer has focused on the problems related to homework. The issues raised are important (assignments should not be too long, be easy to grade, and not interfere with team sports). However, the writer discusses these issues from only one point of view—that of the students. He fails to consider or even acknowledge the goals of teachers in assigning homework. The essay seems to take the opinion that "teachers don't understand." If this is true, the writer does not explain why he has this opinion. Additionally, there are numerous spelling and punctuation errors. One sentence is an incomplete thought. There are several errors in subject-verb agreement.

NYSTCE

New York State Teacher Certification Examinations

Answer Sheets

LAST Test 1

1. Ⓐ Ⓑ Ⓒ Ⓓ
2. Ⓐ Ⓑ Ⓒ Ⓓ
3. Ⓐ Ⓑ Ⓒ Ⓓ
4. Ⓐ Ⓑ Ⓒ Ⓓ
5. Ⓐ Ⓑ Ⓒ Ⓓ
6. Ⓐ Ⓑ Ⓒ Ⓓ
7. Ⓐ Ⓑ Ⓒ Ⓓ
8. Ⓐ Ⓑ Ⓒ Ⓓ
9. Ⓐ Ⓑ Ⓒ Ⓓ
10. Ⓐ Ⓑ Ⓒ Ⓓ
11. Ⓐ Ⓑ Ⓒ Ⓓ
12. Ⓐ Ⓑ Ⓒ Ⓓ
13. Ⓐ Ⓑ Ⓒ Ⓓ
14. Ⓐ Ⓑ Ⓒ Ⓓ
15. Ⓐ Ⓑ Ⓒ Ⓓ
16. Ⓐ Ⓑ Ⓒ Ⓓ
17. Ⓐ Ⓑ Ⓒ Ⓓ
18. Ⓐ Ⓑ Ⓒ Ⓓ
19. Ⓐ Ⓑ Ⓒ Ⓓ
20. Ⓐ Ⓑ Ⓒ Ⓓ
21. Ⓐ Ⓑ Ⓒ Ⓓ
22. Ⓐ Ⓑ Ⓒ Ⓓ
23. Ⓐ Ⓑ Ⓒ Ⓓ
24. Ⓐ Ⓑ Ⓒ Ⓓ
25. Ⓐ Ⓑ Ⓒ Ⓓ
26. Ⓐ Ⓑ Ⓒ Ⓓ
27. Ⓐ Ⓑ Ⓒ Ⓓ

28. Ⓐ Ⓑ Ⓒ Ⓓ
29. Ⓐ Ⓑ Ⓒ Ⓓ
30. Ⓐ Ⓑ Ⓒ Ⓓ
31. Ⓐ Ⓑ Ⓒ Ⓓ
32. Ⓐ Ⓑ Ⓒ Ⓓ
33. Ⓐ Ⓑ Ⓒ Ⓓ
34. Ⓐ Ⓑ Ⓒ Ⓓ
35. Ⓐ Ⓑ Ⓒ Ⓓ
36. Ⓐ Ⓑ Ⓒ Ⓓ
37. Ⓐ Ⓑ Ⓒ Ⓓ
38. Ⓐ Ⓑ Ⓒ Ⓓ
39. Ⓐ Ⓑ Ⓒ Ⓓ
40. Ⓐ Ⓑ Ⓒ Ⓓ
41. Ⓐ Ⓑ Ⓒ Ⓓ
42. Ⓐ Ⓑ Ⓒ Ⓓ
43. Ⓐ Ⓑ Ⓒ Ⓓ
44. Ⓐ Ⓑ Ⓒ Ⓓ
45. Ⓐ Ⓑ Ⓒ Ⓓ
46. Ⓐ Ⓑ Ⓒ Ⓓ
47. Ⓐ Ⓑ Ⓒ Ⓓ
48. Ⓐ Ⓑ Ⓒ Ⓓ
49. Ⓐ Ⓑ Ⓒ Ⓓ
50. Ⓐ Ⓑ Ⓒ Ⓓ
51. Ⓐ Ⓑ Ⓒ Ⓓ
52. Ⓐ Ⓑ Ⓒ Ⓓ
53. Ⓐ Ⓑ Ⓒ Ⓓ
54. Ⓐ Ⓑ Ⓒ Ⓓ

55. Ⓐ Ⓑ Ⓒ Ⓓ
56. Ⓐ Ⓑ Ⓒ Ⓓ
57. Ⓐ Ⓑ Ⓒ Ⓓ
58. Ⓐ Ⓑ Ⓒ Ⓓ
59. Ⓐ Ⓑ Ⓒ Ⓓ
60. Ⓐ Ⓑ Ⓒ Ⓓ
61. Ⓐ Ⓑ Ⓒ Ⓓ
62. Ⓐ Ⓑ Ⓒ Ⓓ
63. Ⓐ Ⓑ Ⓒ Ⓓ
64. Ⓐ Ⓑ Ⓒ Ⓓ
65. Ⓐ Ⓑ Ⓒ Ⓓ
66. Ⓐ Ⓑ Ⓒ Ⓓ
67. Ⓐ Ⓑ Ⓒ Ⓓ
68. Ⓐ Ⓑ Ⓒ Ⓓ
69. Ⓐ Ⓑ Ⓒ Ⓓ
70. Ⓐ Ⓑ Ⓒ Ⓓ
71. Ⓐ Ⓑ Ⓒ Ⓓ
72. Ⓐ Ⓑ Ⓒ Ⓓ
73. Ⓐ Ⓑ Ⓒ Ⓓ
74. Ⓐ Ⓑ Ⓒ Ⓓ
75. Ⓐ Ⓑ Ⓒ Ⓓ
76. Ⓐ Ⓑ Ⓒ Ⓓ
77. Ⓐ Ⓑ Ⓒ Ⓓ
78. Ⓐ Ⓑ Ⓒ Ⓓ
79. Ⓐ Ⓑ Ⓒ Ⓓ
80. Ⓐ Ⓑ Ⓒ Ⓓ

ATS-W Elementary Test 1

1. Ⓐ Ⓑ Ⓒ Ⓓ
2. Ⓐ Ⓑ Ⓒ Ⓓ
3. Ⓐ Ⓑ Ⓒ Ⓓ
4. Ⓐ Ⓑ Ⓒ Ⓓ
5. Ⓐ Ⓑ Ⓒ Ⓓ
6. Ⓐ Ⓑ Ⓒ Ⓓ
7. Ⓐ Ⓑ Ⓒ Ⓓ
8. Ⓐ Ⓑ Ⓒ Ⓓ
9. Ⓐ Ⓑ Ⓒ Ⓓ
10. Ⓐ Ⓑ Ⓒ Ⓓ
11. Ⓐ Ⓑ Ⓒ Ⓓ
12. Ⓐ Ⓑ Ⓒ Ⓓ
13. Ⓐ Ⓑ Ⓒ Ⓓ
14. Ⓐ Ⓑ Ⓒ Ⓓ
15. Ⓐ Ⓑ Ⓒ Ⓓ
16. Ⓐ Ⓑ Ⓒ Ⓓ
17. Ⓐ Ⓑ Ⓒ Ⓓ
18. Ⓐ Ⓑ Ⓒ Ⓓ
19. Ⓐ Ⓑ Ⓒ Ⓓ
20. Ⓐ Ⓑ Ⓒ Ⓓ
21. Ⓐ Ⓑ Ⓒ Ⓓ
22. Ⓐ Ⓑ Ⓒ Ⓓ
23. Ⓐ Ⓑ Ⓒ Ⓓ
24. Ⓐ Ⓑ Ⓒ Ⓓ
25. Ⓐ Ⓑ Ⓒ Ⓓ
26. Ⓐ Ⓑ Ⓒ Ⓓ
27. Ⓐ Ⓑ Ⓒ Ⓓ

28. Ⓐ Ⓑ Ⓒ Ⓓ
29. Ⓐ Ⓑ Ⓒ Ⓓ
30. Ⓐ Ⓑ Ⓒ Ⓓ
31. Ⓐ Ⓑ Ⓒ Ⓓ
32. Ⓐ Ⓑ Ⓒ Ⓓ
33. Ⓐ Ⓑ Ⓒ Ⓓ
34. Ⓐ Ⓑ Ⓒ Ⓓ
35. Ⓐ Ⓑ Ⓒ Ⓓ
36. Ⓐ Ⓑ Ⓒ Ⓓ
37. Ⓐ Ⓑ Ⓒ Ⓓ
38. Ⓐ Ⓑ Ⓒ Ⓓ
39. Ⓐ Ⓑ Ⓒ Ⓓ
40. Ⓐ Ⓑ Ⓒ Ⓓ
41. Ⓐ Ⓑ Ⓒ Ⓓ
42. Ⓐ Ⓑ Ⓒ Ⓓ
43. Ⓐ Ⓑ Ⓒ Ⓓ
44. Ⓐ Ⓑ Ⓒ Ⓓ
45. Ⓐ Ⓑ Ⓒ Ⓓ
46. Ⓐ Ⓑ Ⓒ Ⓓ
47. Ⓐ Ⓑ Ⓒ Ⓓ
48. Ⓐ Ⓑ Ⓒ Ⓓ
49. Ⓐ Ⓑ Ⓒ Ⓓ
50. Ⓐ Ⓑ Ⓒ Ⓓ
51. Ⓐ Ⓑ Ⓒ Ⓓ
52. Ⓐ Ⓑ Ⓒ Ⓓ
53. Ⓐ Ⓑ Ⓒ Ⓓ
54. Ⓐ Ⓑ Ⓒ Ⓓ

55. Ⓐ Ⓑ Ⓒ Ⓓ
56. Ⓐ Ⓑ Ⓒ Ⓓ
57. Ⓐ Ⓑ Ⓒ Ⓓ
58. Ⓐ Ⓑ Ⓒ Ⓓ
59. Ⓐ Ⓑ Ⓒ Ⓓ
60. Ⓐ Ⓑ Ⓒ Ⓓ
61. Ⓐ Ⓑ Ⓒ Ⓓ
62. Ⓐ Ⓑ Ⓒ Ⓓ
63. Ⓐ Ⓑ Ⓒ Ⓓ
64. Ⓐ Ⓑ Ⓒ Ⓓ
65. Ⓐ Ⓑ Ⓒ Ⓓ
66. Ⓐ Ⓑ Ⓒ Ⓓ
67. Ⓐ Ⓑ Ⓒ Ⓓ
68. Ⓐ Ⓑ Ⓒ Ⓓ
69. Ⓐ Ⓑ Ⓒ Ⓓ
70. Ⓐ Ⓑ Ⓒ Ⓓ
71. Ⓐ Ⓑ Ⓒ Ⓓ
72. Ⓐ Ⓑ Ⓒ Ⓓ
73. Ⓐ Ⓑ Ⓒ Ⓓ
74. Ⓐ Ⓑ Ⓒ Ⓓ
75. Ⓐ Ⓑ Ⓒ Ⓓ
76. Ⓐ Ⓑ Ⓒ Ⓓ
77. Ⓐ Ⓑ Ⓒ Ⓓ
78. Ⓐ Ⓑ Ⓒ Ⓓ
79. Ⓐ Ⓑ Ⓒ Ⓓ
80. Ⓐ Ⓑ Ⓒ Ⓓ

LAST Test 2

1. Ⓐ Ⓑ Ⓒ Ⓓ	28. Ⓐ Ⓑ Ⓒ Ⓓ	55. Ⓐ Ⓑ Ⓒ Ⓓ
2. Ⓐ Ⓑ Ⓒ Ⓓ	29. Ⓐ Ⓑ Ⓒ Ⓓ	56. Ⓐ Ⓑ Ⓒ Ⓓ
3. Ⓐ Ⓑ Ⓒ Ⓓ	30. Ⓐ Ⓑ Ⓒ Ⓓ	57. Ⓐ Ⓑ Ⓒ Ⓓ
4. Ⓐ Ⓑ Ⓒ Ⓓ	31. Ⓐ Ⓑ Ⓒ Ⓓ	58. Ⓐ Ⓑ Ⓒ Ⓓ
5. Ⓐ Ⓑ Ⓒ Ⓓ	32. Ⓐ Ⓑ Ⓒ Ⓓ	59. Ⓐ Ⓑ Ⓒ Ⓓ
6. Ⓐ Ⓑ Ⓒ Ⓓ	33. Ⓐ Ⓑ Ⓒ Ⓓ	60. Ⓐ Ⓑ Ⓒ Ⓓ
7. Ⓐ Ⓑ Ⓒ Ⓓ	34. Ⓐ Ⓑ Ⓒ Ⓓ	61. Ⓐ Ⓑ Ⓒ Ⓓ
8. Ⓐ Ⓑ Ⓒ Ⓓ	35. Ⓐ Ⓑ Ⓒ Ⓓ	62. Ⓐ Ⓑ Ⓒ Ⓓ
9. Ⓐ Ⓑ Ⓒ Ⓓ	36. Ⓐ Ⓑ Ⓒ Ⓓ	63. Ⓐ Ⓑ Ⓒ Ⓓ
10. Ⓐ Ⓑ Ⓒ Ⓓ	37. Ⓐ Ⓑ Ⓒ Ⓓ	64. Ⓐ Ⓑ Ⓒ Ⓓ
11. Ⓐ Ⓑ Ⓒ Ⓓ	38. Ⓐ Ⓑ Ⓒ Ⓓ	65. Ⓐ Ⓑ Ⓒ Ⓓ
12. Ⓐ Ⓑ Ⓒ Ⓓ	39. Ⓐ Ⓑ Ⓒ Ⓓ	66. Ⓐ Ⓑ Ⓒ Ⓓ
13. Ⓐ Ⓑ Ⓒ Ⓓ	40. Ⓐ Ⓑ Ⓒ Ⓓ	67. Ⓐ Ⓑ Ⓒ Ⓓ
14. Ⓐ Ⓑ Ⓒ Ⓓ	41. Ⓐ Ⓑ Ⓒ Ⓓ	68. Ⓐ Ⓑ Ⓒ Ⓓ
15. Ⓐ Ⓑ Ⓒ Ⓓ	42. Ⓐ Ⓑ Ⓒ Ⓓ	69. Ⓐ Ⓑ Ⓒ Ⓓ
16. Ⓐ Ⓑ Ⓒ Ⓓ	43. Ⓐ Ⓑ Ⓒ Ⓓ	70. Ⓐ Ⓑ Ⓒ Ⓓ
17. Ⓐ Ⓑ Ⓒ Ⓓ	44. Ⓐ Ⓑ Ⓒ Ⓓ	71. Ⓐ Ⓑ Ⓒ Ⓓ
18. Ⓐ Ⓑ Ⓒ Ⓓ	45. Ⓐ Ⓑ Ⓒ Ⓓ	72. Ⓐ Ⓑ Ⓒ Ⓓ
19. Ⓐ Ⓑ Ⓒ Ⓓ	46. Ⓐ Ⓑ Ⓒ Ⓓ	73. Ⓐ Ⓑ Ⓒ Ⓓ
20. Ⓐ Ⓑ Ⓒ Ⓓ	47. Ⓐ Ⓑ Ⓒ Ⓓ	74. Ⓐ Ⓑ Ⓒ Ⓓ
21. Ⓐ Ⓑ Ⓒ Ⓓ	48. Ⓐ Ⓑ Ⓒ Ⓓ	75. Ⓐ Ⓑ Ⓒ Ⓓ
22. Ⓐ Ⓑ Ⓒ Ⓓ	49. Ⓐ Ⓑ Ⓒ Ⓓ	76. Ⓐ Ⓑ Ⓒ Ⓓ
23. Ⓐ Ⓑ Ⓒ Ⓓ	50. Ⓐ Ⓑ Ⓒ Ⓓ	77. Ⓐ Ⓑ Ⓒ Ⓓ
24. Ⓐ Ⓑ Ⓒ Ⓓ	51. Ⓐ Ⓑ Ⓒ Ⓓ	78. Ⓐ Ⓑ Ⓒ Ⓓ
25. Ⓐ Ⓑ Ⓒ Ⓓ	52. Ⓐ Ⓑ Ⓒ Ⓓ	79. Ⓐ Ⓑ Ⓒ Ⓓ
26. Ⓐ Ⓑ Ⓒ Ⓓ	53. Ⓐ Ⓑ Ⓒ Ⓓ	80. Ⓐ Ⓑ Ⓒ Ⓓ
27. Ⓐ Ⓑ Ⓒ Ⓓ	54. Ⓐ Ⓑ Ⓒ Ⓓ	

ATS-W Secondary Test 2

1. Ⓐ Ⓑ Ⓒ Ⓓ
2. Ⓐ Ⓑ Ⓒ Ⓓ
3. Ⓐ Ⓑ Ⓒ Ⓓ
4. Ⓐ Ⓑ Ⓒ Ⓓ
5. Ⓐ Ⓑ Ⓒ Ⓓ
6. Ⓐ Ⓑ Ⓒ Ⓓ
7. Ⓐ Ⓑ Ⓒ Ⓓ
8. Ⓐ Ⓑ Ⓒ Ⓓ
9. Ⓐ Ⓑ Ⓒ Ⓓ
10. Ⓐ Ⓑ Ⓒ Ⓓ
11. Ⓐ Ⓑ Ⓒ Ⓓ
12. Ⓐ Ⓑ Ⓒ Ⓓ
13. Ⓐ Ⓑ Ⓒ Ⓓ
14. Ⓐ Ⓑ Ⓒ Ⓓ
15. Ⓐ Ⓑ Ⓒ Ⓓ
16. Ⓐ Ⓑ Ⓒ Ⓓ
17. Ⓐ Ⓑ Ⓒ Ⓓ
18. Ⓐ Ⓑ Ⓒ Ⓓ
19. Ⓐ Ⓑ Ⓒ Ⓓ
20. Ⓐ Ⓑ Ⓒ Ⓓ
21. Ⓐ Ⓑ Ⓒ Ⓓ
22. Ⓐ Ⓑ Ⓒ Ⓓ
23. Ⓐ Ⓑ Ⓒ Ⓓ
24. Ⓐ Ⓑ Ⓒ Ⓓ
25. Ⓐ Ⓑ Ⓒ Ⓓ
26. Ⓐ Ⓑ Ⓒ Ⓓ
27. Ⓐ Ⓑ Ⓒ Ⓓ

28. Ⓐ Ⓑ Ⓒ Ⓓ
29. Ⓐ Ⓑ Ⓒ Ⓓ
30. Ⓐ Ⓑ Ⓒ Ⓓ
31. Ⓐ Ⓑ Ⓒ Ⓓ
32. Ⓐ Ⓑ Ⓒ Ⓓ
33. Ⓐ Ⓑ Ⓒ Ⓓ
34. Ⓐ Ⓑ Ⓒ Ⓓ
35. Ⓐ Ⓑ Ⓒ Ⓓ
36. Ⓐ Ⓑ Ⓒ Ⓓ
37. Ⓐ Ⓑ Ⓒ Ⓓ
38. Ⓐ Ⓑ Ⓒ Ⓓ
39. Ⓐ Ⓑ Ⓒ Ⓓ
40. Ⓐ Ⓑ Ⓒ Ⓓ
41. Ⓐ Ⓑ Ⓒ Ⓓ
42. Ⓐ Ⓑ Ⓒ Ⓓ
43. Ⓐ Ⓑ Ⓒ Ⓓ
44. Ⓐ Ⓑ Ⓒ Ⓓ
45. Ⓐ Ⓑ Ⓒ Ⓓ
46. Ⓐ Ⓑ Ⓒ Ⓓ
47. Ⓐ Ⓑ Ⓒ Ⓓ
48. Ⓐ Ⓑ Ⓒ Ⓓ
49. Ⓐ Ⓑ Ⓒ Ⓓ
50. Ⓐ Ⓑ Ⓒ Ⓓ
51. Ⓐ Ⓑ Ⓒ Ⓓ
52. Ⓐ Ⓑ Ⓒ Ⓓ
53. Ⓐ Ⓑ Ⓒ Ⓓ
54. Ⓐ Ⓑ Ⓒ Ⓓ

55. Ⓐ Ⓑ Ⓒ Ⓓ
56. Ⓐ Ⓑ Ⓒ Ⓓ
57. Ⓐ Ⓑ Ⓒ Ⓓ
58. Ⓐ Ⓑ Ⓒ Ⓓ
59. Ⓐ Ⓑ Ⓒ Ⓓ
60. Ⓐ Ⓑ Ⓒ Ⓓ
61. Ⓐ Ⓑ Ⓒ Ⓓ
62. Ⓐ Ⓑ Ⓒ Ⓓ
63. Ⓐ Ⓑ Ⓒ Ⓓ
64. Ⓐ Ⓑ Ⓒ Ⓓ
65. Ⓐ Ⓑ Ⓒ Ⓓ
66. Ⓐ Ⓑ Ⓒ Ⓓ
67. Ⓐ Ⓑ Ⓒ Ⓓ
68. Ⓐ Ⓑ Ⓒ Ⓓ
69. Ⓐ Ⓑ Ⓒ Ⓓ
70. Ⓐ Ⓑ Ⓒ Ⓓ
71. Ⓐ Ⓑ Ⓒ Ⓓ
72. Ⓐ Ⓑ Ⓒ Ⓓ
73. Ⓐ Ⓑ Ⓒ Ⓓ
74. Ⓐ Ⓑ Ⓒ Ⓓ
75. Ⓐ Ⓑ Ⓒ Ⓓ
76. Ⓐ Ⓑ Ⓒ Ⓓ
77. Ⓐ Ⓑ Ⓒ Ⓓ
78. Ⓐ Ⓑ Ⓒ Ⓓ
79. Ⓐ Ⓑ Ⓒ Ⓓ
80. Ⓐ Ⓑ Ⓒ Ⓓ

LAST Test 3

1. (A) (B) (C) (D)	28. (A) (B) (C) (D)	55. (A) (B) (C) (D)
2. (A) (B) (C) (D)	29. (A) (B) (C) (D)	56. (A) (B) (C) (D)
3. (A) (B) (C) (D)	30. (A) (B) (C) (D)	57. (A) (B) (C) (D)
4. (A) (B) (C) (D)	31. (A) (B) (C) (D)	58. (A) (B) (C) (D)
5. (A) (B) (C) (D)	32. (A) (B) (C) (D)	59. (A) (B) (C) (D)
6. (A) (B) (C) (D)	33. (A) (B) (C) (D)	60. (A) (B) (C) (D)
7. (A) (B) (C) (D)	34. (A) (B) (C) (D)	61. (A) (B) (C) (D)
8. (A) (B) (C) (D)	35. (A) (B) (C) (D)	62. (A) (B) (C) (D)
9. (A) (B) (C) (D)	36. (A) (B) (C) (D)	63. (A) (B) (C) (D)
10. (A) (B) (C) (D)	37. (A) (B) (C) (D)	64. (A) (B) (C) (D)
11. (A) (B) (C) (D)	38. (A) (B) (C) (D)	65. (A) (B) (C) (D)
12. (A) (B) (C) (D)	39. (A) (B) (C) (D)	66. (A) (B) (C) (D)
13. (A) (B) (C) (D)	40. (A) (B) (C) (D)	67. (A) (B) (C) (D)
14. (A) (B) (C) (D)	41. (A) (B) (C) (D)	68. (A) (B) (C) (D)
15. (A) (B) (C) (D)	42. (A) (B) (C) (D)	69. (A) (B) (C) (D)
16. (A) (B) (C) (D)	43. (A) (B) (C) (D)	70. (A) (B) (C) (D)
17. (A) (B) (C) (D)	44. (A) (B) (C) (D)	71. (A) (B) (C) (D)
18. (A) (B) (C) (D)	45. (A) (B) (C) (D)	72. (A) (B) (C) (D)
19. (A) (B) (C) (D)	46. (A) (B) (C) (D)	73. (A) (B) (C) (D)
20. (A) (B) (C) (D)	47. (A) (B) (C) (D)	74. (A) (B) (C) (D)
21. (A) (B) (C) (D)	48. (A) (B) (C) (D)	75. (A) (B) (C) (D)
22. (A) (B) (C) (D)	49. (A) (B) (C) (D)	76. (A) (B) (C) (D)
23. (A) (B) (C) (D)	50. (A) (B) (C) (D)	77. (A) (B) (C) (D)
24. (A) (B) (C) (D)	51. (A) (B) (C) (D)	78. (A) (B) (C) (D)
25. (A) (B) (C) (D)	52. (A) (B) (C) (D)	79. (A) (B) (C) (D)
26. (A) (B) (C) (D)	53. (A) (B) (C) (D)	80. (A) (B) (C) (D)
27. (A) (B) (C) (D)	54. (A) (B) (C) (D)	

ATS-W Elementary / Secondary Test 3

1. Ⓐ Ⓑ Ⓒ Ⓓ	28. Ⓐ Ⓑ Ⓒ Ⓓ	55. Ⓐ Ⓑ Ⓒ Ⓓ
2. Ⓐ Ⓑ Ⓒ Ⓓ	29. Ⓐ Ⓑ Ⓒ Ⓓ	56. Ⓐ Ⓑ Ⓒ Ⓓ
3. Ⓐ Ⓑ Ⓒ Ⓓ	30. Ⓐ Ⓑ Ⓒ Ⓓ	57. Ⓐ Ⓑ Ⓒ Ⓓ
4. Ⓐ Ⓑ Ⓒ Ⓓ	31. Ⓐ Ⓑ Ⓒ Ⓓ	58. Ⓐ Ⓑ Ⓒ Ⓓ
5. Ⓐ Ⓑ Ⓒ Ⓓ	32. Ⓐ Ⓑ Ⓒ Ⓓ	59. Ⓐ Ⓑ Ⓒ Ⓓ
6. Ⓐ Ⓑ Ⓒ Ⓓ	33. Ⓐ Ⓑ Ⓒ Ⓓ	60. Ⓐ Ⓑ Ⓒ Ⓓ
7. Ⓐ Ⓑ Ⓒ Ⓓ	34. Ⓐ Ⓑ Ⓒ Ⓓ	61. Ⓐ Ⓑ Ⓒ Ⓓ
8. Ⓐ Ⓑ Ⓒ Ⓓ	35. Ⓐ Ⓑ Ⓒ Ⓓ	62. Ⓐ Ⓑ Ⓒ Ⓓ
9. Ⓐ Ⓑ Ⓒ Ⓓ	36. Ⓐ Ⓑ Ⓒ Ⓓ	63. Ⓐ Ⓑ Ⓒ Ⓓ
10. Ⓐ Ⓑ Ⓒ Ⓓ	37. Ⓐ Ⓑ Ⓒ Ⓓ	64. Ⓐ Ⓑ Ⓒ Ⓓ
11. Ⓐ Ⓑ Ⓒ Ⓓ	38. Ⓐ Ⓑ Ⓒ Ⓓ	65. Ⓐ Ⓑ Ⓒ Ⓓ
12. Ⓐ Ⓑ Ⓒ Ⓓ	39. Ⓐ Ⓑ Ⓒ Ⓓ	66. Ⓐ Ⓑ Ⓒ Ⓓ
13. Ⓐ Ⓑ Ⓒ Ⓓ	40. Ⓐ Ⓑ Ⓒ Ⓓ	67. Ⓐ Ⓑ Ⓒ Ⓓ
14. Ⓐ Ⓑ Ⓒ Ⓓ	41. Ⓐ Ⓑ Ⓒ Ⓓ	68. Ⓐ Ⓑ Ⓒ Ⓓ
15. Ⓐ Ⓑ Ⓒ Ⓓ	42. Ⓐ Ⓑ Ⓒ Ⓓ	69. Ⓐ Ⓑ Ⓒ Ⓓ
16. Ⓐ Ⓑ Ⓒ Ⓓ	43. Ⓐ Ⓑ Ⓒ Ⓓ	70. Ⓐ Ⓑ Ⓒ Ⓓ
17. Ⓐ Ⓑ Ⓒ Ⓓ	44. Ⓐ Ⓑ Ⓒ Ⓓ	71. Ⓐ Ⓑ Ⓒ Ⓓ
18. Ⓐ Ⓑ Ⓒ Ⓓ	45. Ⓐ Ⓑ Ⓒ Ⓓ	72. Ⓐ Ⓑ Ⓒ Ⓓ
19. Ⓐ Ⓑ Ⓒ Ⓓ	46. Ⓐ Ⓑ Ⓒ Ⓓ	73. Ⓐ Ⓑ Ⓒ Ⓓ
20. Ⓐ Ⓑ Ⓒ Ⓓ	47. Ⓐ Ⓑ Ⓒ Ⓓ	74. Ⓐ Ⓑ Ⓒ Ⓓ
21. Ⓐ Ⓑ Ⓒ Ⓓ	48. Ⓐ Ⓑ Ⓒ Ⓓ	75. Ⓐ Ⓑ Ⓒ Ⓓ
22. Ⓐ Ⓑ Ⓒ Ⓓ	49. Ⓐ Ⓑ Ⓒ Ⓓ	76. Ⓐ Ⓑ Ⓒ Ⓓ
23. Ⓐ Ⓑ Ⓒ Ⓓ	50. Ⓐ Ⓑ Ⓒ Ⓓ	77. Ⓐ Ⓑ Ⓒ Ⓓ
24. Ⓐ Ⓑ Ⓒ Ⓓ	51. Ⓐ Ⓑ Ⓒ Ⓓ	78. Ⓐ Ⓑ Ⓒ Ⓓ
25. Ⓐ Ⓑ Ⓒ Ⓓ	52. Ⓐ Ⓑ Ⓒ Ⓓ	79. Ⓐ Ⓑ Ⓒ Ⓓ
26. Ⓐ Ⓑ Ⓒ Ⓓ	53. Ⓐ Ⓑ Ⓒ Ⓓ	80. Ⓐ Ⓑ Ⓒ Ⓓ
27. Ⓐ Ⓑ Ⓒ Ⓓ	54. Ⓐ Ⓑ Ⓒ Ⓓ	

REA's Test Prep Books Are The Best!

(a sample of the <u>hundreds of letters</u> REA receives each year)

" I am writing to congratulate you on preparing an exceptional study guide. In five years of teaching this course I have never encountered a more thorough, comprehensive, concise and realistic preparation for this examination. "
Teacher, Davie, FL

" I have found your publications, *The Best Test Preparation...*, to be exactly that. "
Teacher, Aptos, CA

" I used your *CLEP Introductory Sociology* book and rank it 99% – thank you! "
Student, Jerusalem, Israel

" Your GMAT book greatly helped me on the test. Thank you. "
Student, Oxford, OH

" I recently got the French SAT II Exam book from REA. I congratulate you on first-rate French practice tests."
Instructor, Los Angeles, CA

" Your AP English Literature and Composition book is most impressive."
Student, Montgomery, AL

" The REA LSAT Test Preparation guide is a winner! "
Instructor, Spartanburg, SC

(more on front page)